BRITTON

THE FRENCH TEXT CAREFULLY REVISED
WITH AN ENGLISH TRANSLATION
INTRODUCTION AND NOTES

BY

FRANCIS MORGAN NICHOLS M. A.

OF LINCOLN'S INN BARRISTER AT LAW
FORMERLY FELLOW OF WADHAM COLLEGE

VOLUME II.

THE LAWBOOK EXCHANGE, LTD.
Clark, New Jersey
2003

ISBN 1-58477-258-1

Printed in the United States of America
on acid-free paper

The Lawbook Exchange, Ltd.
33 Terminal Avenue
Clark, New Jersey 07066

Please see catalogue at rear of this volume
or our website
www.lawbookexchange.com
for a selection of our other publications and fine
facsimile reprints of classic works of legal history.

Library of Congress Cataloging-in-Publication Data

Britton / the French text carefully revised with an English translation, introduction, and notes by Francis Morgan Nichols.

p. cm.

Originally published: Oxford: Clarendon Press, 1865.

Includes bibliographical references and index.

ISBN 1-58477-258-1 (cloth: acid-free paper)

1. Law—England. I. Nichols, Francis Morgan, 1826-

KD600 .B74 2002

349.42—dc21 2002024326

BRITTON

THE FRENCH TEXT CAREFULLY REVISED
WITH AN ENGLISH TRANSLATION
INTRODUCTION AND NOTES

BY

FRANCIS MORGAN NICHOLS M.A.

OF LINCOLN'S INN BARRISTER AT LAW
FORMERLY FELLOW OF WADHAM COLLEGE

VOLUME II.

Oxford
AT THE CLARENDON PRESS
M DCCC LXV.

BRITTON.

LIVRE III.

CHAPITRE I. [LXV.]

[1]De Intrusions[1]. [161.]

I.

FINIE[2] la manere de pleder, coment chescun pleyntif deit repurchacer sa seisine de fraunc tenement, pur fere redrescer tort fet a sa persone demeyne, ore fet a dire la fourme, coment hom deit repurchacer par plee la seisine de soen auncestre. Car si acun moerge, soen heir deit aver la successioun de quant qe il morust seisi en Brac. 252; Fle. 277.

1—1. *so NS. sim. DGMA.* De Mort de Auncestre *L. om. H.* 2. Dist auoms en partie *N.*

BOOK III.

OF INTRUSIONS AND THEIR REMEDIES.

CHAPTER I.

Of Intrusions.

I.

HAVING concluded the process whereby a plaintiff may recover his seisin of freehold, in redress of a wrong done to his own person, we shall now speak of the method of recovering by plea the seisin of his ancestor. For when any one dies, his heir ought to succeed to whatsoever he died seised of in his demesne as of fee, although another may have had more Remedy for recovering seisin of ancestor. Seisin distinct from property.

soen demeyne cum de fee, tut i eust autre plus de proprelé de ly, s'il ne eit esté mort cum feloun par jugement. Et si il eit esté mort sauntz heir, le chief seignur en lu de heir serra.

Brac. 160; Fle. 273, 274. 2. Mes pur ceo qe acun, qi nul dreit [1]ne ad, purra sei enbatre[1] freschement apres acuni mort en le heritage le dreit heir, et tener hors le heir et le chief seignur del fee, et[2] nuli dreit ne suffreit, qe la seisine demorast en tele manere, voet ley en teu cas qe ceux entrusours pusent estre engettez freschement apres la intrusioun par les verreis heyrs ou par les chiefs seignurs del fee sauntz tort fere; issi qe [3]cest mot[3] freschement soit entendu solom ceo qe le dreit heir le poet saver, et solom ceo qe il estoit pres ou loinz, sicum dit est en le livre de Disseisines[4]. Et si fere ne[5] le pusent, ou si il eynt eu si lounge et si pesible seisine qe il ne deivent point estre engettez sauntz jugement, adounc covent qe il soint eydez par remedie de nostre court. Mes pur ceo qe il i ad plusours maneres de intrusions, si covendra varier les fourmes des brefs solom lour divers cas.

Ante, l. ii. c 13. s. 3.

[161 *b*.]

1—1. ne ad enbatre *L.* ne ad purra sei abatre *N.* *sim. G.* nen ad se purra abatre *M.* ni ad se purra enbatre *S.* *sim. CH.* 2. ou *M.* 3—3. *so verb. AH.* ceste mort *LSGMC.* si cel tort *N.* 4. *so GAM.* disseisours *LNDCH.* *sim. S.* 5. *om.* *LNDSARMWCHF.* ne *interl. G.*

right of property therein, unless he died as a felon convict. And if he died without any heir, the chief lord shall stand in the place of heir.

Abatement. 2. But because a person that has no right may immediately after the death of any one abate himself into the inheritance of the right heir, and keep out the heir and the chief lord of the fee, and no law would permit the seisin to remain in that fashion, the law allows such intruders to be ejected while the intrusion is fresh by the right heirs or the chief lord of the fee without any wrong being done; and the word 'fresh' shall be so understood, according as the right heir has means of knowing the fact, and according as he was near or far, as has been said in the Book of Disseisins. If they cannot so eject, or if the abators have had so long and so peaceable a seisin, that they ought not to be ejected without judgment, then they must be aided by remedy of our court. But because there are several kinds of intrusions, the form of the writ must be varied according to the different cases.

Remedy by fresh ejectment.

Remedy by writ.

3. Intrusioun est torcenous abatement vacaunt le soil, taunt cum nul ne est en seisine par presence de cors ne par continuaunce de volunté; sicum apres la mort acun qi en morust seisi del fee et del fraunc tenement, eynz ceo qe le heir al mort i eit pris [1]nule manere de[1] seisine; ou sicum apres le desces acun qi en morut seisi del fee et del fraunc tenement en mesme la manere sauntz heir, ou cum feloun, eynz ceo qe le seignur, a qi le eschete deit estre, eit aprosché la seisine; ou sicum apres la mort acun qi ne morut pas seisi for qe de fraunc tenement soulement par fin fete et par cirographe, ou par fourme de doun, ou par autre manere de tenure a terme de vie, eynz ceo qe celi, a qi la terre dust reverter, en eit aprosché la seisine. Brac. 160; Fle. 273, 274.

4. Et sicum en touz ces cas sount intrusiouns, si covendra diversier les fourmes des brefs solom les diversetez des cas. Et acune foiz est la accioun et la pleynte a les dreitz heirs, et acune foiz as chiefs seignurs par la resoun de eschete, et acune foiz par la resoun de garde. Et pur ceo qe hom deit plus haster pletz qe delayer, bon est qe teus brefs i soint ordinez, qe plus chacent les intrusours a respouns par le [162.] Brac. 160 b; Fle. 274; Reg. Brev. Orig. 233 b, 234.

1—1. acune manere de *N.* acune *M.*

3. Intrusion is a wrongful abatement during the vacancy of the soil, when no one is in seisin either by corporeal presence or by continuance of will; as after the death of a person who died seised of the fee and freehold, before the heir of the deceased has taken any sort of seisin; or after the decease of one who in like manner died seised of the fee and freehold without heir or as a felon, before the lord to whom the escheat belongs has attained to seisin thereof; or after the death of any one who died seised only of the freehold by fine levied and chirograph, or by form of gift, or by other kind of tenure for term of life, before he to whom the land ought to revert has attained to seisin. Abatement and intrusion.

4. As all these cases are intrusions, the forms of the writs must be varied according to the diversity of the cases. Sometimes the action and the plaint belong to the right heirs, and sometimes to the chief lords by reason of escheat, and sometimes by reason of wardship. And because pleas ought rather to be hastened than delayed, it is proper that such writs be provided as drive the intruders to answer by the great and Forms of writs of intrusion. Process by *Cape.*

Brac. 161 (§ 8); Fle. 275 (§ 11).

graunt *Cape* et par le petit, qe autres maneres de brefs pledables par personeles destresces. En cest bref ne gist point de vewe ne voucher, pur ceo qe le plee savoure[1] en[2] partie de [3]la nature de[3] novele disseisine et de trespas pur[4] l'embatement.

Stat. Marl. (52 Hen. III) c. 16; Glan. li. 7, c. 9; li. 9. c. 6; Brac. 252; Fle. 277 (§ 2).

5. Et si acun soit de plener age en le tens de la mort soen auncestre, qi heir il est, et se tiegne en seisine de soen heritage oveqe le mort, et apres la mort soit trové en seisine, ou si apres la mort soen auncestre troeve soen heritage vacaunt, et entre [5]einz ceo[5] qe le chief seignur le eit seisi, bien lit a tiel heir de plener age tener hors le chief seignur, si fere le puse, si ne deyve tener de nous en chief tel heritage; mes qe il soit touz jours prest a fere al seignur homage ou relef ou autre service solom ceo qe ley et [6]dreit condoune[6].

6. Mes pur ceo qe touz heirs ne sount mie tenuz a fere homage[7] a lour[8] seignurs, en[9] primes fet a saver des natures des tenementz, queus sount enservez vers les seignurs des feez en homages et queus noun; et queus tenementz et queus heirs deyvent estre en garde des seignurs, et queus noun; et

1. en sauoure *S.* ensauore *G.* 2. so *NGAM.* en *om. LS.* 3—3. so *NSGAM.* nature de la *L.* 4. so *NGAMCH.* par *LS.* 5—5. so *NSGMH.* en ceo *LA.* 6—6. dreiture le condoune *N.* *sim. M.* 7. so *NSGAMCH.* homages *L.* 8. chiefs *add. N.* 9. so *NGAM.* Et *L.* *sim. CH.*

little *Cape*, rather than other kind of writs pleadable by personal distresses. In this writ neither view nor voucher lies, because the plea savours in part of the nature of novel disseisin and of trespass by reason of the abatement.

No view or voucher in writ of intrusion.

Heirs of full age may hold possession against the lords;

5. If the heir be of full age at the time of the death of his ancestor, and holds himself in seisin of his inheritance with the deceased, and after the decease is found in seisin, or if after the death of his ancestor he finds the inheritance vacant, and enters before the chief lord has seised it, it is lawful for such heir being of full age to keep out the chief lord if he can, unless he ought to hold the inheritance of us in chief, so as he be always ready to perform to the lord homage or relief or other service according as law and right require.

except tenants *in capite.*

Homage, wardship, &c. incident to some tenements.

6. But because all heirs are not bound to perform homage to their lords, we must first understand the nature of tenements,—which are subject, in relation to the lords of the fees, to homage, and which not; and what tenements and what heirs ought to be in ward of the lords, and what not; and in

par resoun [1]de quele manere[1] des tenementz seignur deit aver gardes et mariages homages et relefs, et des queus noun.

CHAPITRE II. [LXVI.]

[2]*Des Gardes*[2]. [162 *b.*]

1. Plusours maneres des feez sount et de tenures, dount touz [3]les plus[3] sount [4]de chevalerie[4] et de graunt serjaunties, les queus feez furent purveuz a la defense de noster reaume, dount les heirs ne sount mie ables a defenses ne de armes porter jekes autaunt qe il eynt acompli le age de xxi. an. Et Glan. li. 7. c. 9; Brac. 86; Fle. 4, 5.

1—1. *so NM. sim. AG.* des queus maners *L.* 2—2. De diuerse des tenures *A. sim. R.* 3—3. *so NDAMCF.* le plus *LWH. sim. SGR.* 4—4. feez de Cheualers *N. sim. D.*

respect of what kind of tenements lords ought to have wardship, marriage, homage, and relief, and of what not.

CHAPTER II.

Of Wardship; of the various tenures of land; and of the remedy against supposititious children.

1. There are several kinds of fees and tenures, the chief whereof are those of knight service and grand serjeanty [a], which fees were provided for the defence of our realm, and of which the heirs are not capable of defence or of bearing arms until they have accomplished the age of twenty-one years; and it is therefore ordained that the lords of the fees Wardship incident to knight service and grand serjeanty.

[a] 'Note, that knight's fee is dependent on the shield (del escu); and signifieth that one ought to do knight's duty (fere chivalerie) for such tenements, i. e. exercise arms (hantier les armes) in time of war. So Grand Serjeanty is a diminutive of the shield (un deminutif del escu); and signifieth that one should do esquire's duty (esquierie) for such tenure, i. e. be armed, as belongeth to an esquire, to combat in time of war, or otherwise serve, as the king or his lord hath need. And he shall do homage, for he will do honourable service (honesté fra) in battle, and fight armed with his target hanging from his neck, which is to him in stead of shield. And this you may understand by the name, for *esquier* is, as it were, *escuer*. But there is a difference between the arms (armures) of knights and esquires. So Petty Serjeanty is a diminutive of Grand Serjeanty. For knights and serjeants cannot endure in war without being served with provisions (vitaille) and other things. Wherefore for footmen (home a pié) were such tenures provided, to do such various duties as belong to their service; because a footman (poun) cannot do noble acts (honesté fere); and gentlemen (gentiz gentz) hold no feat honourable except prowess of arms. All the other tenures, save ancient demesnes, are dependent upon the fees aforesaid. For frank farms, fee farms, and frank almoigne, were changed (translateez) from knights' fees into socages discharged of such foreign service for a certain sum by the year. Ancient demeynes were and are the king's villenages; whereof burgages and sokemanries are changed for such villenages into free tenure (franchise) at a certain service done to their lord. And as ancient demesnes are the king's villenages, to be cultivated and dealt with as may please him (pur gayner e pur fere quantque lui plest), so are other kinds of villenages the demesnes of other lordships.' Note in MS. *N.*

pur ceo est ordeiné, qe les seignurs des fez eyent les gardes de lour feez, et touz les profitz des issues, et les avowesouns des eglises, et les gardes des gardes, en tut le meen tens, sauntz fere wast des boys, destruccioun des tenementz, exil des vileyns, ou vente de terres.

Glan. l. 7. c. 10; Brac. 87; Fle. 10 (§ 7).

2. Dount[1] acun pora estre heir de plusours feez, des queus feez acun est plus auncien feffement de autre. Et pur ceo qe le premer feffour, ou le seignur de plus auncien fee, ad major dreit en la garde del cors et par consequent del mariage, [2]pur la ligeaunce, qe autre plus tardif feffour, ou le dreyn quidera estre le premer feffour[3] et aver plus graunt dreit, avient acune foiz, qe cil qi nul dreit ad[4] deforce[2] la garde a celi qi major dreit ad[5]; sur quel tort est purveu remedie par noster bref de dreit de garde, qe veut estre terminé par simple juree de la priorité del feffement sauntz bataile ou graunt assise. Et ausi brefs de dreit de mariages ne sount mie fraunc tenement, eynz sount chateus moebles devisables en testament; dount la nature del proces de cel bref apres la graunt distresce agardé est contenu en nos estatuz de Westmouster.

Reg. Brev. 161 *b*. Fle. 6 (§ 3).

[163.]

Stat. West. 1. (3 Ed. I) c. 22, 45; Stat. West. 2 (13 Ed. I.) c. 35.

1. *so LSGM.* Ou *N.* 2—2. dount si le pluis tardif feffour deforce *A.* 3. feffe *M.* 4. ne ad *N.* nen ad *MSGH.* 5. en ad *NSGAM.*

Rights of guardians.

shall have for all the intermediate time the wardship of their fees, and all the profits of the issues, and the advowsons of churches, and the wardship of wards, without making waste of woods, destruction of tenements, exile of villains, or sale of lands.

Of several lords, wardship belongs to first feoffor.

2. The same tenant may be heir to several fees, of which one is of more ancient feoffment than another. And whereas the first feoffor or the lord of the most ancient fee has a better right to the wardship of the body, and consequently to the marriage, by reason of the allegiance, than another later feoffor, it sometimes happens, where the last feoffor thinks that he is the first and has a greater right, that he who has no right deforces the wardship from him who has a better right. For which wrong a remedy is provided by our writ of right of ward, which is intended to be determined by a simple jury upon the priority of feoffment without battle or great assise. So writs of right of marriage are not frank tenement, but movable chattels devisable by testament; the manner of proceeding in which writ, after the great distress awarded, is contained in our Statutes of Westminster.

Remedy of first feoffor, by writ of right of ward.

Right of marriage is a chattel devisable by testament.

Process in writ of right of marriage.

3. Des queus heirs neqedent si il i eit acun qi auncestre morust seisi de acune terre tenue de nous en chief des aunciens feez de nostre Coroune, voloms aver les gardes [1]de totes les terres dount garde apent[1], qe deyvent descendre a tiels heirs cum lour heritage oveke touz les blez en celes terres trovez, meyntefoiz[2] de qi fee qe les terres soint. Et si les auncestres de ceux heirs eint tenu acune terre de nous en chief cum de nos eschetes ou de nos purchaz, ou de nos petites serjaunties, ou de nos socages, ou de nos fee[3] fermes, en teus cas voloms qe la garde des cors des heirs en lour tendre age remeigne a nous, et qe lour mariages soint nostres; et qe chescun seignur eit la garde de soen fee et de terre tenu de ly jekes ataunt qe tels heirs eint prové lour age en nostre court, et [4]eint recoveré[4] lour heritage hors de nostre meyn.

Prærog. Reg. (Stat. incert. temp.) c. 2; Glan. l. 7. s. 10; Brac. 87 (§ 5); Fle. 5 (c 11. § 2).

Mag. Cart. c. 27; Brac. 87 *b*; Fle. 6 (§ 2).

4. Et taunt cum les terres de tels heirs demorunt en nostre meyn, voloms qe les heirs soint quites vers totes gentz de

1—1. *so verb. NDSGAMCH.* dount garde apent de totes les terres. *L.* 2. *so N. sim. MGSCHF.* meytefoiz *L. om. A.* 3. *so S.* feez *LGAM.* 4—4. adounc eint recoverir de *N. sim. D*

3. Nevertheless if there be any such heirs whose ancestors died seised of any land held of us in chief of the ancient fees of our Crown[b], we will that we have the wardship of all the lands which ought to descend to those heirs as their inheritance, with all the corn found on such lands, to whose fee soever the lands belong. And if the ancestors of such heirs held any land of us in chief as of our escheats, or of our purchases, or of our petty serjeanties, or of our socages, or of our fee farms, in that case the custody of the bodies of such heirs during their tender age shall remain with us, and their marriages shall be ours[c]; but each lord shall have the wardship of his own fee and of the land held of him, until such heirs have proved their age in our court, and have recovered their inheritance out of our hand.

If any land be held *in capite*, king is guardian.

Distinction where land not held of the Crown.

King's ward free during minority from services and from ancestor's obligations.

4. As long as the lands of such heirs remain in our hand, we will that they be quit as against all people of suits of courts

[b] The annotator in MS. *N.* applies the term 'homage ancestrel' to the case here supposed, and says that it was then to be presumed (dunc deyt hom entendre) that the tenant or his ancestors were enfeoffed by the king before any of his other feoffors.

[c] There is some confusion in this statement; the rule that the custody of the body and the marriage belonged to the king applied only where the land was held of the king, though not *de corona*, by military service, and not to the other cases mentioned in the text of tenants in socage or by petty serjeanty. Compare Magna Carta, c. 27; and the parallel passage in Bracton.

sutes des courtz et de touz autres services qe hom lour porra demaunder par la resoun de lour tenementz, et qe il soint quites, taunt cum eus serrount [1]en nostre[1] garde, de tote
[163 *b*.] manere de obligacioun et demaunde qe hom lour porra fere
Ante, l. ii. c 33. s. 4. par la resoun de lour auncestres. Et si acunes terres eynt esté lessez a ferme a terme des aunz ou autrement meyns qe a terme de vie ou en fee, les queles terres sount heritages a teus enfauntz, en teus cas voloms nous, qe les fermers soint engettez de celes terres, sauve a eus lour chateus en les terres trovez, issi qe chescun seignur eit la garde de soen fee. Et quaunt les heirs averount acompli lour age, adounc eient les fermers accioun de recoverer le tens qe arere lour serra de lour fermes par noster bref de covenaunt, si sauntz bref ne les porrount recoverir.

Mag. Cart. c. 27; Glan. l. 7. c. 11; Brac. 87 *b*; Fle. 5, 6.

5. Et sount autres maneres de tenures, sicum petites serjaunties, sokemaneries, fraunches[2] fermes, fee[3] fermes, burgages, auncienes demeynes, fraunche aumoyne, fraunc mariage, et villenages; des queus feez nule garde ne apent, mes norriture soulement de celi qi [4]proscheyn ly serra en parenté devers la mere de heritage descendaunt de par le pere, ou de

1—1. oue nous en *N*. 2. *so DAG*. *so corr*. *N*. fraunchises *LMCH*. *sim*. *S*. 3. *so LNS*. feez *AH*. fees *M*. 4. plus *add*. *M*.

and of all other services which may be demanded of them by reason of their tenements, and be quit also, so long as they are in our wardship, of all manner of obligations and demands which may be made upon them on account of their ancestors.

Rights of termors suspended during minority.

And if any lands have been let to farm for term of years, or otherwise for a less term than term of life or in fee, such lands being part of the inheritance of the infants, we will that the farmers be ejected from the lands, saving to them their chattels found thereon, so that each lord may have the wardship of his fee. And when the heirs shall have accomplished their age, then the farmers shall have their action by our writ of covenant to recover the remainder of their terms, if they cannot recover it without writ.

Tenures not subject to wardship.

5. There are other kind of tenures, as petty serjeanties, sokemanries, free farms, fee farms, burgages, ancient demesnes, free alms, free marriages, and villenages; to which fees no

Guardians in socage

wardship appertains, but only nurture by him who shall be nearest of kin to the heir on the mother's side when the inheritance descends on the part of the father, or by the

plus proscheyn de saunc devers[1] le piere de heritage descendaunt de[2] la mere. Et les queus gardeyns sount plus serjauntz qe gardeyns; car si il ne rendent leal acounte des issues de teus heritages, quel houre qe les heirs voderount acounte oyer, si sount teus gardeyns enprisounables et punisables par la peyne purveue en noster estatut, cum autres serjauntz. Et dount nul certeyn tens est limité del age de teus heirs; mes sitoust cum il sachent descrescioun de terres gayner, de dras auner, de deners counter, et sagement[3] marchaunder, si voloms qe il seint de age, et les femeles sitoust cum eles severount descrecioun et les ordinaunces qe appendent a fere en hostel.

Stat. Marl. (52 Hen. III.) c. 23; Stat. West. 2 (13 Ed. I.) c. 11.

[164.]

Glan. l. 7. c. 9; Brac. 86 b; Fle. 6 (§ 6, 7).

1. so *SGAM.* ver *L.* 2. de par *NG.* 3. so *SGARMCH.* sachent *LNDW.*

nearest of blood on the father's side when the inheritance descends from the mother. Such guardians are rather bailiffs than guardians; for if they do not render a lawful account of the issues of such inheritances, at such time as the heirs choose to require the same, such guardians may be imprisoned and punished like other bailiffs, according to the penalty provided in our statute. And in the case of such heirs no certain time is limited for their full age; but as soon as they have discretion to till land, measure cloth, count money, and to manage their trade, they shall be deemed of age; and the females as soon as they have attained discretion and have learned the management of household affairs[d].

must account to heirs.

Minority, when terminated.

[d] The older authorities fix fifteen years as the age of majority for socage tenants, and apply the shifting test of 'discretion' only to the children of burgesses or tenants in burgage. The following note may serve in some measure to show how the old rule in this respect was gradually set aside, and the age of twenty-one established as the period of majority for all classes. 'Of heirs in socage, the common age for males is sixteen years, and for females fourteen. This is so (Oyl), for having and administering their inheritance; but not for aliening it conclusively (finalment) *secundum quosdam:* for they say that the writ of entry *dum fuit infra ætatem* supposes the age of twenty-one years. Others say that this age is given for knights' fees only, and that they are so long in ward in regard to the administration for fear of the aliening and dismemberment of their inheritance. Whence it follows, he who by law can and ought to administer, can by law alien; but in socage the tenant at sixteen years of age can and ought to administer,—*eadem ratione,* to alien.' Note in MS. *N.*

Shortly after the time of this note, the question as to the power of alienation by socage tenants under twenty-one appears to have been settled in the negative; and in the following case, decided 13 Edw. III., the power of aliening a burgage tenement before that age is treated as resting upon special custom. 'In *dum fuit infra ætatem* in Gloucester, the tenant pleaded that the usage of the town is such, that when a man knows how to count 12*d.* and to measure an ell of cloth, he is of age to alien his land, and of such age was the demandant when he leased. And because the tenant did not state the age in certain, so that the demandant might answer it, it was awarded that the demandant should recover.' T. 13 Ed. III. cited Vet. Nat. Br. 128; Bro. Abr. *Dum fuit.* 3; Fitzh. Nat. Brev. 192 H. (note by Hale).

Stat. de Wardis et Releviis (inc. temp.) Brac. 356, 87 b; Fle. 5, 198, 207.

6. Graunt serjauntie est service de tenement, le quel service touche defense a la terre, [1]cum est la Marchauscie ou de mettre host en guerre, et[1] cum trover un homme au cheval covert en host; ou de garder nos ostours[2], et autres grauntz services semblables. Petite serjauntie est service issaunt de tenement a fere a nous acun petit service, quant nous deyvoms chevacher en host, mountaunt a demi marc et a meins,

1—1. *so verb. ND. sim. AR.* de nostre guerre *L.* en nostre guerre *S.* com est a la Marchaucie en houst de nostre guerre e *M.* *sim. GCHW.* 2. *so LNS.* hostours *DM.* estours *G.* estouers *CH.* estors *ARWF.*

Grand serjeanty.

6. Grand serjeanty is a service due from a tenement, which service concerns the defence of the country; as to be Marshal or to set our host in battle, or to find a man mounted and armed for the field[e]; so, to be the keeper of our goshawks[f], or other like great services.

Petty serjeanty.

Petty serjeanty is a service issuing from a tenement by performing to us[g] some little service, when we are about to take the field, amounting to half a mark or less, as are the services of bring-

[e] As to the question whether this is great or little serjeanty, see Lit. Ten. s. 157; Co. Lit. 107 a.; and Butler's Note, ib.

[f] This example does not agree with the description of grand serjeanty, as connected with the defence of the country. Some of the manuscripts remedy this inconsistency by reading *estours*, or *estovers*, so as to make the service that of guarding the king's stores or provisions. Abundant examples of tenure by the service of keeping hawks and falcons may be found in Blount's Tenures by Beckwith, pp. 263–280. In one case at least (p. 275) the service was connected with homage, which affords some presumption that it was considered a grand serjeanty. (See Bracton 79 (§ 6); Fleta 204 (c. 16. § 2); 207 (§ 19); Co. Lit. 86 a). And the estates held by such services were frequently of importance. The lords Grey of Wilton are stated by Camden to have held their manor of Acton by the service of keeping a gerfalcon for the king. Camden's Britannia by Gough, vol. i. p. 315. In later times such tenures were classed as petty serjeanties.

[g] This passage of Britton appears to be the first authority for confining the term Serjeanty to tenures *in capite*. (See Lit. Ten. s. 161.) In Bracton, serjeanty is a tenure by a special or extraordinary service either to the king or any other lord. And Britton in a subsequent chapter speaks of a grand serjeanty not held of the king in chief. (Post, c. iv. s. 3.) The words of Britton may also have given occasion to the distinction afterwards adopted, by which the term 'petty serjeanty' was confined to 'small things *belonging to war*.' (Lit. Ten. s. 159.) The principal examples of minor serjeanties in Bracton are connected with the occupations of peace, as the serjeanty of riding with the lord from one manor to another, of holding the lord's court, or of carrying his precepts (portandi brevia). We may also see in Britton's examples the germ of Littleton's distinction of great and little serjeanty, that the one ought to be done in the tenant's proper person, while the other obliges him to nothing but a mere rendering or payment, as of a rent. (Lit. Ten. 153, 160.) In Bracton, serjeanties are called great and little, either with reference to their value (Brac. 87 *b*), or to the nature of the duty, as concerning the king's army or the defence of the realm on the one hand, and peaceable services or duties to inferior lords on the other. (Brac. 35 *b*.) And it would seem to have been Bracton's opinion, that all serjeanties *in capite*, whether great or small, brought to the king the right of wardship. (Brac. 87 *b*; 35 *b*, 36.) The account given of great and little serjeanty and their incidents in the fragment of law, printed under the title of *Statutum de Wardis et Releviis* (Stat. temp. incer.), is similar to that of Britton.

cum sount les services de nous porter en host un sak ou une broche ou un bozoun ou un arc saunt corde [1]ou uns esporouns ou uns gauntz[1], ou acun service semblable.

7. Sokemaneries sount terres et tenementz, qe ne sount mie tenuz par fee de chevaler, ne par graunt serjaunties, ne par petites, mes par simples services, sicum terres enfraunchies par nous et par nos predecessours de nos auncienes demeynes. Brac. 37, 77 b, 209; Fle. 3, 4, 204.

8. Fraunches fermes sount terres et tenementz dount la nature del fee est chaungé par feffement hors de chevalerie par certeins services par an, dount homage, garde, mariage, ne relef ne poent estre demaundez ne autre service nient contenu en lour feffementz. [164 b.] Fee[2] fermes sount terres tenuz en fee a[3] rendre pur eux par an la verreye value, ou plus ou meyns; de la quele rente si les feffez cessent a rendre par deus aunz ensemble, par taunt acrest accioun as feffours ou a Brac. 35, 35 b, 86. Stat. Glouc. (6 Ed. I.) c. 4; Stat. West. 2. (13 Ed. I.) c. 21.

1—1. so *L.* sim. *SG.* ou une esperouns ou une gayne gauns *N.* ou une peyre des esporouns ou vne gayne gauns *D.* ou un esporon ou une Gaunt *AR.* ou esporouns ou gaunz *M.* 2. so *NDSG.* Feez *L.* sim. *M.* 3. so *NGAMCH.* pur *LS.*

ing to us in the field a bag, or a brooch[h], or an arrow, or a bow without a string, or a pair of spurs or gloves, or some like service.

7. Sokemanries are lands and tenements which are not held by knight service or by grand or petty serjeanties, but by simple services, as lands enfranchised by us or by our predecessors of our ancient demesnes. Sokemanry.

8. Free farms are lands and tenements, whereof the nature of the fee is changed by feoffment out of chivalry, to be held by fixed yearly services, and in respect whereof neither homage, wardship, marriage, nor relief can be demanded, nor any other service not specified in the feoffment. Fee farms are lands held in fee by rendering for them yearly the true value, or more or less; which rent if the feoffees cease to pay for two years together, an action thereby accrues to the feoffors, or Free farm and fee farm,

h 'Thomas Carnifex tenet de domino Rege in capite manerium de R. in com. Ebor. per serjantiam inveniendi domino Regi in exercitu in Wallia unum equum, unum falcem, unam brochiam, et unum saccum, &c.; et prædictus Thomas in misericordia pro injusta detentione.' Plac. Cor. 7 Ed. I. Ebor. cited in Blount's Tenures, p. 49; Blount's Tenures by Beckwith, p. 137. See also Bracton, f. 36. The word *brochia*, which in several services reserved in tenures is connected with *saccus*, is conjectured to mean the instrument, either a pin, or a brooch or buckle, with which the bag of leather or canvas was fastened. See Blount's Tenures by Beckwith, p. 110, 133; Ducange Gloss. s. v. *broca, brochia.*

lour heirs a demaunder les tenementz en demeyne; des queus tenementz ne pount estre demaundez homages ne gardes ne mariages ne relefs sauntz especiauté de escritz.

Brac. 78 b, 286 b; Fle. 205 (§ 12, 13). 9. Fraunche aumoyne est [1]terre doné a Deu et a[1] acune gent Deu servauntz en pure et perpetuele aumoyne; dount les feffours nule manere de terrien[2] service ne porrount demaunder, taunt cum tieles terres demorrount en meyns les feffez, et la quele aumoyne establie soit duement fete. Terre [3]en aumoyne[3] est terre ou tenement qe est doné en aumoyne, Glan. l. 7. c. 1, 18. l. 9. c. 2; Brac. 78; Fle. 204 (§ 4). dount acun service est retenu al feffour. Et sicum est de fraunche aumoyne et de terre [4]en aumoyne[4], ausi est de terre doné en fraunc[5] mariage.

Brac. 272. 10. Bourgage est tenement de cité ou de bourg, ou de autre lu privilegié par nous ou par nos predecessours, les queus tenementz sount devisables solom ceo qe eus sount de purchaz ou de heritage solom le usage del leu.

Brac. 7, 209; Fle. 4. 11. Auncienes demeynes sount terres de nos veuz maners [165.] annex a nostre Coroune, en les queles demeynes demurent acunes gentz fraunchement par chartre feffez, et ceux sount

1—1. quant acune terre est donee a dieu oue *N.* *sim. D.* quant asqune tere est donee a *AR.* 2. so *NDMH.* *sim. corr. R.* certeyn *LW.* *sim. AC.* 3—3. en aumoynee *N.* enaumosnee *M.* en asmonee *G.* en aumosnee *S.* 4—4. en almoynee *N.* en amosnee *M.* enaumonee *G.* en aumosnee *S.* 5. fraunc *om. AMH.*

not subject to wardship, &c. without specialty. their heirs, to demand the tenements in demesne; for which tenements neither homage, wardship, marriage, nor relief can be demanded without specialty in writing.

Frank-almoign. 9. Free alms is where land is given to God, and to some persons serving God, in pure and perpetual alms, for which the feoffors can demand no kind of earthly service, so long as the lands remain in the hands of the feoffees; the constitution of Tenure in alms. which alms is to be duly observed. Land held in alms is when land or tenement is given in alms, some service being reserved thereout to the feoffor. And as it is of free alms and of land given in alms, so is it of land given in free marriage.

Tenure in burgage. 10. Burgage is a tenement in a city or borough or other place privileged by us or our predecessors; and such tenements are devisable according as they are derived by purchase or inheritance, agreeably to the custom of the place.

Ancient demesne. 11. Ancient demesnes are lands which were part of the ancient manors annexed to our Crown, in which demesnes dwell some who have been freely enfeoffed by charter,—and

nos fauncs tenauntz, et acunes gentz qe[1] sount [2]de faunc saunc[2], et tienent de nous terre en villenage, et ceux sount proprement nos sokemans et privelegez en ceste manere, qe nul ne les deit ouster de teus tenementz taunt cum il fount les services qe a lour tenementz appendent, ne nul ne put lour services accrestre, ne chaunger a fere autres services ou plus ou autrement qe [3]il soleint[3]. Et pur ceo qe teus sokemans sount nos gaynours de nos terres, ne voloms mie qe teles gentz seint a nule part somouns de travailler en jurez ne en enquestes, for qe en maners a queus il appendent. Et pur ceo qe nous voloms qe il eyent tele quiete, est ordeyné le bref de dreit clos pledable par baillif del maner de tort fet del un sokeman al autre, qe il tiegne les pleyntifs a dreit solom les usages del maner par simples enquestes. En pletz neqedent de trespas et de autres personeles acciouns voloms nous, qe il soint somounables et responables ausi cum autres. Brac. 7; Fle. 4 (§ 4); Reg. Brev. 9.

12. Villenage est tenement de demeynes de[4] chescun seignur[5], baillé a tenir a sa volunté par vileins services de Brac. 26, 26b.

1. qe *om. MH.* qi *A.* 2—2. faunch de saung *N.* *sim. H.* fraunks du saunc *A.* *sim. C.* 3—3. fere ne soleynt *N.* *sim. A.* i ne solerent *M.* 4. *so MCH.* et *L.* e *SG.* qe *N.* 5. eit *add. N.*

these are our free tenants,—and others who are free of blood and hold land of us in villenage,—and these are properly our sokemen, and are privileged in this manner, that they are not to be ousted from such tenements so long as they perform the services which appertain to their tenements, nor can their services be increased or altered, so that they shall do any other or greater services, or in any other way than as they have been used to do. And because such sokemen are the tillers of our lands, we will that they be not summoned anywhere to toil in juries or inquests, except in the manors to which they belong. And because we will that they enjoy such immunity, the writ of right close is provided, which is pleadable before the bailiff of the manor for a wrong done by one sokeman to another, that the bailiff may do the plaintiff right according to the custom of the manor by means of simple inquests. Nevertheless we will that in pleas of trespass and other personal actions, sokemen be summonable and answerable as well as others.

Sokemen, tenants in ancient demesne. *Immunities of sokemen.* *Writ of right close.*

12. Villenage is a tenement of the demesne of any lord, delivered to be held at his will by villain services, to be culti- *Villenage.*

enprouwer[1] al oes le seignur, et liveré par verge et nient par title de escrit ne par successioun de heritage; dount gardes ne mariages ne autres services reals, cum homages et relef, ne poent des auncienes demeynes ne de villenages estre demaundez. Et en mesmes les maners de nos auncienes demeynes sount purs vileyns de saunc et de tenementz, les queus porrount estre oustez de lour tenementz et de lour chateus a la volunté de lour seignurs.

Glan. l. 9. c. 2; Brac. 77 *b*, 78; Fle. 204.

Brac. 7; Fle. 4 (§ 5).

[165 *b*.]

13. [2]Acune foiz avent qe les femmes [3]el tens de[3] la mort lour barouns sei feignent [4]estre enceyntes de lour barouns quaunt eles[4] ne sount mie, en grefs damages des heirs; en quel cas nous volums qe tiel remedie soit ordiné, qe cum acun [5]de tele desceite[5] se pleyndra, voloms qe il eit de nous bref al viscounte del lu qe il sauntz delay face vener devaunt luy et devaunt les Corouners en pleyn Counté la femme de qi la pleynte serra fete; et soit enquis de ly si ele soit enceynte et de qi, et si ele die de soen baroun qi morust, tauntost face le viscounte venir[6] sages femmes et leales jekes a vi.[7] [8]al meyns[8]

Brac. 69; Fle. 13.

Reg. Brev. 227; Brac. 69 *b*.

1. apprower *N.* 2. *In AR. a new chapter begins here, entitled in rubric* Des verreis heirs. 3—3. *conj.* el tenauntz de *L.* *sim. S.* as tenauntz *G.* tenauntz de *CH.* *sim. F.* apres *NDAMW.* 4—4. e dient qe de lour barouns sount enceyntes e *N.* *sim. A.* 5—5. *so G.* *sim. NAMCHF.* *om. LS.* de la deceyte *N.* 6. *so NDAMCF.* *om. L.* 7. *so NDGACHW.* vij. *L.* siz *S.* sis *M.* v. *F.* 8—8. *om. N.*

Livery by the rod.

vated for the use of the lord, and whereof livery is given by the rod and not by title of deed or by succession of inheritance. Neither wardship nor marriage nor other real services, as homage and relief, can be demanded from ancient demesnes or villenages. In the same manors of our ancient demesnes there are also pure villains both by blood and by tenure, who may be ousted from their tenements and deprived of their chattels at the will of their lords.

Villain tenants in manors of ancient demesne.

Supposititious children.

13. It sometimes happens that women at the time of the death of their husbands feign themselves with child by their husbands when in fact they are not, to the great damage of the heirs; in which case we will that the following remedy be ordained. When any one complains of such deceit, he shall have our writ to the sheriff of the district, commanding him without delay to cause to come before him and before the coroners in full county court the woman against whom the complaint is made; and it shall be inquired of her, whether she be with child, and by whom; and if she says, by her husband who is dead, the sheriff shall forthwith cause to come

Writ *de ventre inspiciendo.*

Proceedings in *ventre inspiciendo.*

et les face jurer sour saintz de leaument fere et verrément presenter en les articles dount eles serrount chargez de par nous. Et puis soynt chargez qe eles sur lour serment enquergent de la femme qe se fet enceynte par tast de soen ventre et de ses mameles et en totes autres maneres dount eles porrount estre certefiez, lequel ele est enceynte, ou noun. Et puis la prengent en une mesoun privément et enquergent la verité.

14. Et si les femmes dient qe ele est enceynte, ou soint de Brac. 69 *b*; Fle. 13.
ceo en dotaunce lequel ele soit ou noun, adounc voloms nous [166.]
qe le viscounte face cele femme mettre en noster chastel ou aylours en sauve garde, issi qe nule femme ne autre, de qi acune suspecioun porra estre de fausine [1]fere, ne la puisse adessier, et[1] illucs demoerge a ses propres custages jekes al houre qe ele deit enfauntet, issi qe nule femme ne veinge a luy el meen tens, for qe del linage le pleyntif. Et si ele ne eit enfaunt de eynz les xl. simeynes apres la mort soen baroun, ou si ele ne soit trové enceynte, si soit ele punie par

1—1. *so ND.* fete et *L.* *sim. S G C H.* fere ne aproche e *M.* fere i seit e *A.*

discreet and lawful women to the number of six at least, who are to be sworn upon the holy Evangelists, that they will lawfully act and true presentment make of the articles wherewith they shall be charged on our behalf. Then let them be charged that they upon their oath search the woman who pretends to be with child by handling her belly and her breasts, and using all other means whereby they may be certified whether she is with child or not. Then they shall take her privately into a house, and inquire into the truth.

14. If the women declare that she is with child, or they are in doubt whether she be or not, then the sheriff shall cause the woman to be placed in our castle or elsewhere in safe custody, so that no woman or other person who may be suspected of any fraud have access to her; and there she shall remain at her own charge till the time when she should be delivered, and no woman in the meantime shall go near her, unless she be of the lineage of the plaintiff. Woman, if pregnant, to be kept in custody till delivery.

And if she have not a child within forty weeks after the death of her husband, or if she is not found to be with child, let her be punished by imprisonment and fine; and the chief lords of the fees If no child be born within forty weeks, the heir to be admitted.

Brac. 71 (§ 10); Fle. 14 (§ 6). prisoun et par fin; et les chiefs seignurs des feez tauntost prengent les homages des heirs, sauntz plus[1] delay fere.

15. Et si ele [2]eit enfaunt[2] de eynz les xl. simeines, adounc Brac. 63 b, 70; Fle. 14 (§ 4). soit cel enfaunt resceu al heritage, si autre heir ne puse averrer tiel enfaunt estre engendré de autre homme qe de le baroun, cum s'il puse averrer qe le baroun fu [3]escoillé ou[3] en prisoun ou en autre reaume par deus aunz ou par treis avaunt qe cel enfaunt fu neez [4]et apres[4], sauntz aproscher la femme, ou par autre apparaunte[5] presumpcioun communement testmonié de totes gentz. Et en teus cas, ne voloms nous mie qe les dreitz heirs soint desheritez par le putage des femmes.

Brac. 63 (§ 4); Fle. 13 (§ 3). [166 *b.*] 16. Et si deus freres ou autres[6] se profrent a fere homage a lour seignur pur un heritage, et le un soit nee de eynz esposailes et le autre avaunt les esposailes, en teu cas voloms nous qe les seignurs receyvent al heritage celi qi fu nee de Decret. Greg. l. iv. tit. 17. c. 2; Brac. 63 (§ 3); Fle. 12, 13. eynz esposailes, tut soit il pusnee del autre. Et si acun heir se profre a fere homage a soen seignur pur le heritage soen auncestre, qi piere et qi mere furent departiz par Saincte

1. lung *add.* *H.* 2—2. enfaunte *A.* seit enfaunte *H.* 3—3. descoyllee ou *N.* *sim.* *MGHC.* *om.* *A.* 4—4. *so* *LNDSGAMCHF.* 5. aperte *NA.* 6. *so* *LMGS.* iij. *ND.* treys *W.*

shall forthwith take the homage of the heir without further delay.

Presumption of paternity, how rebutted. 15. If she is delivered of a child within the forty weeks, the child shall be admitted to the inheritance, unless the next heir can prove that such child was begotten by another man than her husband, as if he show that the husband was impotent, or that he was in prison or in another kingdom for two or three years before the child was born, and remained so until after the birth, without coming near his wife, or aver some other apparent presumption notorious to everybody. For in such cases we will not that the right heirs shall be disinherited by the wife's adultery.

Child born in marriage preferred to one born before. 16. If two brothers, or other persons, offer themselves to do homage to their lord for the same inheritance, and one of them was born in marriage and the other before marriage, we will that in such case the lord shall admit to the inheritance him who was born within marriage, although he be younger Child born in marriage inherits, although his parents be divorced. than the other. And if any heir offer himself to do homage to his lord for the inheritance of his ancestor, whose father and

Eglise, pur ceo[1] qe le matrimonie entre eux fet fut trové desleal, pur ceo ne lessent mie les seignurs a prendre les homages de teus enfantz engendrez en matrimonie, lequel qe le matrimonie soit leal ou desleal.

17. Et si acun heir soit engendré de autre qe del baroun sa mere, [2]en tens[2] noméement qe presumpcioun put fere pur le baroun qe il le put aver engendré en matrimonie, en teus cas ne volom mie qe putage de la mere [3]soit bare del[3] heritage al enfaunt. Et ausi de enfaunt engendré de autre et supposé pur la engendrure le baroun, [4]le quel[4] le baroun avera norri et avowé pur soen heir, voloms qe teus enfauntz soint receyvables al heritage, si presumpcioun face qe le baroun la mere les put aver engendré. Mes si les barouns de teles femmes, qe norisent enfauntz pur heirs, qi ount esté engendrez [5]des autres qe des barouns, eint[5] esté destourbez par aperte maladie ou par distaunce del lu et del tens, si qe aperte presumpcioun et commune fame, cum avaunt est dit, face encountre teus barouns, qe il ne poeynt mie teus enfauntz aver engendré, tut

Glan. l. 7. c. 12, *ad fin.*; Brac. 63, 70, 88; Fle. 13 (§ 4).

1. so *NAMCH.* tut *L.* 2—2. so *MCH.* *sim. G.* teus *LS.* e ce ly *N.* e teus *A.* 3—3. forbarre le *M.* 4—4. le quel enfaunt *NGMH.* *sim. SA.* 5—5. des queus de les baruns eient *A.* des autres eient *G.* des barons qe unt *M.* des barouns qe ount *C.* iesques les Barouns eient *H.*

mother were divorced by holy church by reason of the marriage between them being found unlawful, the lord shall not upon that account fail to take the homage of such children begotten in marriage, whether the marriage was lawful or unlawful.

17. If any heir is begotten by another than the husband of his mother, that is to say, at a time when it may be presumed that the husband might have begotten the child in matrimony, we will not that the adultery of the mother be a bar to the inheritance of the child. So, where a child begotten by another and imposed upon the husband as his issue, is brought up by the husband and owned by him as his heir, we will that such children be admissible to the inheritance, if it may be presumed that the husband of the mother may have begotten them. But if the husbands of such wives, who bring up as their lawful heirs children that were begotten by others than the husbands, were hindered by manifest infirmity or distance of place and time, so that evident presumption and common fame, as before mentioned, operates against the husbands having been capable

Child born in marriage presumed legitimate.

Presumption of legitimacy, how rebutted.

[167.] voillent teus barouns teus enfauntz nurryr en lour mesouns et avower pur lour, pur ceo neqedent ne soint mie teus enfauntz receivables as heritages. Ne les enfauntz ausi qe les barouns troverount en lour hosteus engendrez de autres qe de eus, les queus les barouns averount tauntost remuez de lour hosteus et desavowez pur lour engendrure. Et pur ceo voloms nous qe chescun en tiel cas apertement desavowe et tauntost face remuer tele engendrure, supposé estre sue[1], si tost cum il le[2] savera. Car puis qe il[3] avera une foiz avowé pur sue[4], et ceo soit testmoigné par visnee, il ne le porra james disavower.

Brac. 70 *b*; Fle. 14.

18. Et si pleinte nous veigne de acun dreit heir, de tel enfaunt supposé nurri et avowé pur heir par acun baroun et sa femme en disheritaunce[5] del dreit heir, tauntost maunderoms al viscounte del leu a la seute le pleyntif, qe il eit le cors de tel baroun et de tele sa femme et de tel enfaunt, qe il nurrisent, par devant nos Justices a certeyn jour et leu a respoundre a tel pleyntif, qi se dit estre heir mesmes celi baroun, pur quei il nurrissent en desheritesoun de ly le

1. soen *LGSHC.* le soen *NDAR.* le soen *MW.* 2. *so NDGMCW.* le *om. LS.* 3. le *add. N.* 4. *so LS.* le soen *ND.* soen *GAR.* la suwe *M.* souwe *W.* 5. *so LS.* disheritesoun *N.* *sim. MGAH.*

Husband cannot legitimate a bastard by acknowledging him.

of begetting those children, although they choose to bring them up in their houses and to acknowledge them as their own, yet such children shall not be admissible to the inheritances. Neither shall those, whom husbands shall find in their houses begotten by others, and whom they shall straightway remove out of their houses and disown as their issue. Therefore we will that every one in such case do openly disown and straightway cause to be removed such supposititious issue, as soon as he shall know of it. For after he has once owned the child to be his, and this fact is testified by the neighbourhood, he may never after disown it.

Proceeding by heir presumptive to remove a supposititious child.

18. And if a complaint come before us from any right heir concerning a supposititious child so brought up and acknowledged as heir by any husband and his wife to the disherison of the right heir, we will straightway command the sheriff of the county, at the suit of the plaintiff, that he have the bodies of such husband, and of such a one his wife, and of such child whom they are bringing up, before our Justices at a certain day and place to answer to such plaintiff, who alleges himself to be heir to the same husband, why they do in disherison

avauntdit enfaunt et avowent[1] pur lour engendrure, qe il ne est mie. Au quel jour il covendra al pleyntif a moustrer certeynes presumpciouns [2]pur ly, a prover[2] sa entente, et si noun, soit jugé encountre le pleyntif. Et si par proces de play entre parties se face jugement encountre l'enfaunt et pur le pleyntif, soit la malice del baroun et de sa femme punie par prisoun et par fin.

19. Et si acun enfaunt qi serra moustre, cum cil qi ad trop graunt superfluité des menbres, ausi cum treis meyns[3] ou treis peez, ou trop graunt defaute, ausi cum [4]nule meyn ou nul pié[4], demaunde le heritage soen auncestre, en teus cas voloms nous qe teus enfauntz ne soint a nul heritage receyvables ne countez pur enfauntz mes pur bestes ou[5] moustres; par [6]quei qe nul[6] qi les avera engendrez[7] puse par tele engendrure clamer title de fraunc tenement en le heritage de sa femme par la resoun de la ley de Engleterre. [167 *b.*] Brac. 5 (§ 7), 70, 438 (§ 10); Fle. 2.

1. *so NGAW.* auower *LSMCH.* 2—2. pur auerrer *A.* 3. nees *AR.* 4—4. nule meyn ou nul pie ou cum vne meyn ou vn pie *N. sim. D.* la vne meyne ou lun pee *C.* 5. bastardz e *N. sim. A.* ne pur *H.* 6—6. *so L. sim. G.* quei nul *M. sim. SH.* quei qe il *N. sim. C.* 7. ne *add. N.*

of the plaintiff bring up the aforesaid child and own him for their issue, which he is not. At which day it will be necessary for the plaintiff to show some presumptions in his favour to make good his charge; which if he cannot do, it shall be adjudged against him. And if by the proceedings in the plea between the parties judgment be given against the infant and for the plaintiff, the malice of the husband and of his wife shall be punished by imprisonment and fine.

19. And if any child which is born a monster,—as one that has more than the proper number of members[i], as three hands or three feet, or a deficiency in the same, as no hands or no feet,—demands the inheritance of his ancestor, such children shall not be admissible to any inheritance, or accounted as children, but as beasts and monsters. Wherefore no one who has begotten them can by such issue claim title of freehold in the inheritance of his wife by virtue of the law of England. Monster cannot inherit. Birth of monster no ground for title by curtesy.

[i] Bracton repeats in all the passages above cited, that an increase or decrease in the number of members not affecting the human form of the offspring, as where a child is born with six fingers on one hand, or only four, does not affect its rights. See Digest, li. i. tit. 6. l. 14.

Prærog. Reg (Stat. temp. incert.) c. 11; Brac. 420 *b*; Fle. 6 (§ 10), 434; Reg. brev. orig. 266.

20. Et pur ceo qe acune foiz avent qe acun heir [1]est sot nastre[1], par quei il ne est mie able a heritage garder, voloms nous qe teus heirs, de qi qe il unques tienent, madles ou femeles, demurgent en nostre garde oveke touz lour heritages, sauve a chescun seignur touz autres services qe ly appendent de terre tenue de ly, et issi remaignent[2] en nostre garde, taunt cum il durent[3] en lour sotie. Et ceo ne voloms nous mie de ceux qi deveignent fous par acune maladie.

Glan l. 7. c. 9; Reg. brev. orig. 294.

21. Et cum acun qi avera esté en garde, qi deit tenir de nous en chief, eit acumpli le age de xxi. an, et ly ou autre demaunde heritage hors de nostre meyn, de quel age qe le autre soit, enprimes voloms nous qe teus par solempnes enquestes fetes par nos brefs proevent lour age par lour parentz
[168.] et par autres leales gentz de visneez ou il furent neez, si il soint pleynement de xxi. an ou noun, et s'il soint proscheins heirs.

22. Et si acun proeve soen age par bone enqueste, enselé de suth les seaus des jurours, retourné en nostre Chauncelerie

1—1. so *GSMH*. soit nastre *L*. est fol nastre *NC*. sot de Nature *A*. 2. demorgent *M*. 3. serrount *NA*. durront *G*. *sim*. *H*. demorent *M*. *sim*. *C*.

Idiots *a nativitate* in custody of the king.

20. And whereas it sometimes happens that the heir is an idiot from his birth, whereby he is incapable of taking care of his inheritance, we will that such heirs, of whomsoever they hold, and whether they be male or female, remain in our custody, with all their inheritances, saving to every lord all other services belonging to him for lands held of him, and that they so remain in our wardship as long as they continue in their idiotcy. But this rule shall not hold with regard to those who become insane by any sickness.

Inheritance of tenant *in capite*, how obtained out of king's hand.

21. When any one who has been in ward, and who ought to hold of us in chief, has reached the age of twenty-one years, if he demand the inheritance out of our hands, or if any other heir of whatever age he be do the like, such persons must first, by solemn inquests taken by virtue of our writs, prove their age by their kindred and by other lawful people of the neighbourhood where they were born,—to wit, whether they are of the full age of twenty-one years or not, and whether they are next heirs.

Writ *de ætate probanda*.

Inquest of age

22. And if any one proves his age by good inquest sealed under the seals of the jurors and returned into our Chancery

a[1] sauvement garder[2], adounc voloms nous qe il nous face homage et serment de feutee et prenge de nous bref a noster eschetour ou a noster viscounte, qe il li face aver la seisine des terres qe furent en nostre meyn par la mort le auncestre tiel heir en sa baillie; qe si noster eschetour ou le viscounte aperceyve fraude estre fete a nous en la proeve avauntdite, qe il cesse de fere la seisine, jekes a taunt qe nous eyoms prise atteynte sur les xii. premers jurours. Et si il soint atteyntz de faus serment, soint puniz cum dit serra el chapitre de atteyntes. Et si le encusour eit fausement encusé, soit puni par prisoun et par fin solom la malice graunde ou petite.

Reg. brev. orig. 293 *b.*

23. Et cum il avera la seisine des terres tenues de nous, tauntost eit la seisine des terres de autri feez sauntz fin fere as seignurs et sauntz rien doner del soen for qe ses relefs. Et cum il recovera la seisine de soen heritage hors de autri meyns, voloms nous qe lour terres lour soint liverez estorez de charues et ove le autre estor, au meyns solom ceo qe les seignurs les troverent estorez. Et si les seignurs facent wast,

Mag. Cart. c. 3, 4, 5; Fle. 7.

Mag. Cart. c. 5; Glan. l. 7. c. 9; Brac. 87.

Mag. Cart. c. 4; Stat. Marl. (52 Hen. III.) c. 17; Stat. West. 1. (3 Ed. I.) c. 21; Stat. Glouc. (6 Ed. I.) c. 5;

1. so *H.* et *L.* e *NGSM.* 2. so *LMSGH.* garde *N.*

to be safely kept, then we will that he perform homage and swear fealty to us, and obtain our writ to our escheator or to our sheriff, that he cause him to have seisin of the lands which were in our hand, by the death of the ancestor of such heir, in his bailiwick. But if our escheator or sheriff perceives that fraud has been practised upon us in the aforesaid proof, he shall defer the delivery of seisin until we have taken an attaint against the twelve first jurors. And if they are attainted of a false oath, let them be punished as shall be mentioned in the chapter concerning attaints. And if they have been falsely accused, let the accuser be punished by imprisonment and fine, which may be great or small in proportion to the malice of the offender.

Homage and fealty. Writ to escheator *de terris liberandis.* Attaint of jurors on inquest of age.

23. When the heir has obtained the seisin of the lands held of us, let him straightway have seisin of his lands held of the fees of others, without making fine to the lords, and without giving anything of his goods except his reliefs. And when he shall recover the seisin of his inheritance out of the hands of others, we will that his lands shall be delivered up to him stocked with ploughs and other stock at least as well as the

Seisin of lands held of other lords to be delivered at the same time.

Waste by guardians.

Stat. West. 2. (13 Ed. I.) [168 *b*.] c. 14; Brac. 316 *b*, 317; Fle. 7, 8. vente, destruccioun, ou exil de teus heritages, avaunt ceo qe les heirs eynt lour ages proevez, adounc porrount les heirs estre eydez par nos brefs de trespas, de wast, ou par assise de novele disseisine par eus mesmes ou[1] par lour amis, solom ceo qe contenu est en nos estatuz, ou [2]les peynes sount[2] ordeinez. Brac. 317; Fle. 9 (§ 20). De aventure neqedent de fu, ou de ewe, ou de autre wast semblable, dount les gardeins serrount de nule malice coupables, soint touz[3] gardeyns excusetz.

CHAPITRE III. [LXVII.]

[4]*De Mariage*[4].

Glan. l. 7. c. 12; Brac. 88 *b*; Fle. 9, 10. 1. Cum acun qi avera tenu de nous en chief se lesse morir, et lesse soen heir apres ly, et le heir madle soit de plener age, si voloms nous qe tiel heir se puse marier par la ou il vodera sauntz fin fere pur soen mariage a nous ou a autre. Et si tiel heir soit de eynz age, adounc voloms nous qe le mariage de ly soit noster et qe il ne puse marier sauntz coungé de nous sur nostre greve forfeture.

1. so *ANSGM.* et *L.* 2—2. la peine est *M.* 3. tiels *N.* teus *SGAH.* teuz *M.* ceus *C.* 4—4. Des gardes e des mariages *AR.* *sim. W.*

Remedy for waste, lords found them. And if the lords make waste, sale, destruction, or exile in such inheritances, before the heirs have proved by writs of trespass or waste or by assise. their age, then the heirs may be aided either by our writs of trespass or of waste, or by assise of novel disseisin, to be brought by themselves or their friends according as is contained in our statutes, in which the penalties are ordained. Accidental destruction excused. All guardians shall however be excused from liability in respect of accident by fire or water, or other like waste, where they shall not be guilty of any malice.

CHAPTER III.

Of Marriage.

Heir, of age, may marry where he pleases. 1. When any one holding of us in chief shall die, leaving a male heir of full age, we will that such heir may marry where he pleases without paying a fine to us or to any other. Marriage of heir, minor, tenant in chief, belongs to the king. But if such heir be under age, then the marriage of him shall belong to us, and he may not marry without our leave under pain of heavy forfeiture.

Brac. 78; Fle. 205 (§ 6, 7).

2. Et de heirs femeles, ou heritage en tut ou en partie tenu de nous en chef descent a plusours filles, ou lour issue cum a un heir, voloms qe la eynzneesce nous face homage pur totes ses parceners, et qe les autres achevent a la eynznesce. Les mariages neqedent de totes voloms nous aver, de quel age qe eles soint, a totes les foiz qe eles serrount a marier, issi qe eles ne se pusent marier sauntz noster coungé. Et ceo fut primes defendu, pur ceo qe les heirs femelles de nostre terre ne se mariasent a nos enemys, et dounc il nous covendreit [169.]
lour homage prendre, si eles se pusent marier a lour voluntez.

Prerog. Reg. (Stat. incert. temp.) c. 5, 6; Glan. l. 7, c. 12; Brac. 88, 88 *b*; Fle. 11 (§ 10).

3. En dreit des mariages purteynauntz as autres qe a nous, voloms qe les seignurs dounent ou profrent mariages às heirs madles, avaunt ceo qe il eynt plenerement lour ages, et s'il ne lour eynt mariage tendu de eynz lour age, adounc soint les seignurs forclos de chescune accioun a rien demaunder pur lour mariages. Et si les seignurs lour eynt tendu mariage sauntz [1]disparagacioun, ou les heirs ne[1] voillent[2] assenter, si courge la peyne purvewe en noster estatut. Et as heirs femeles soint les mariages profertz[3] avaunt ceo qe il soint de

Brac. 89. Stat. Mert. (20 Hen. III.) c. 6, 7; Brac. 89; Fle. 9, 10, 11, 12. Stat. West 2. (13 Edw. I.) c. 22.

1—1. disparager les heirs et il ne se *N.* tenduz *A.* fetes *H.* 2. voleyent *M.* 3. profrez *SGM.*

Of parceners, the eldest does homage to the king, the others to her.

2. With respect to female heirs, where an inheritance wholly or partly held of us in chief descends to several daughters or their issue, as one heir, the eldest shall do homage to us for all her parceners, and the others shall do homage to the eldest. We will nevertheless have the marriages of them all of whatever age they may be, as often as they are to be married, so that they cannot be married without our leave. This prohibition was first made, lest the female heirs of our land should marry with our enemies, whose homage we should then be obliged to take, if the heirs might marry at their will.

The king has the marriage of all, every time they are married.

Marriages to be tendered to males under age.

3. With respect to marriages belonging to others than us, we will that the lords give or offer marriages to the heirs male before they have completed their age. And if they have not tendered them marriage while under age, then the lords shall be barred of any action to demand anything for their marriage. But if the lords have tendered them marriage without disparagement, and the heirs will not consent thereto, the penalty provided in our statute shall take effect. Marriages

Penalty for refusing.

xiiii. aunz pleynement, ou, si noun, qe les seignurs soint forclos de lour dreit.

Mag. Cart. c. 6; Stat. Mert. (20 Hen. III.) c. 7; Brac. 91 b; Fle. 9.

4. Et si acune de juvene age soit marié a tiel ou ele est desparagé, adounc volom nous qe, si ele fust de xiiii. aunz [1]et plus[1], issi qe ele pout consentir a mariage, adounc courge nule peyne, et si ele fust de meyndre age, si courge tele peyne, qe le seignur perde la garde a cele foiz, et face satisfaccioun[2] as amys la femme issi marié, et tut le profit [3]qe il prist[3] pur le mariage [4]soit restoré[4] as amis et as parentz la femme pur emprover al oes la femme. Et si ele soit marié
[169 b.] a acun de ses vileyns, soit le seignur, qi la dona, puni par prisoun jekes autaunt qe dues amendes soint fetes par la ordinaunce des parentz la femme, et puis [5]soint reyntz[5] pur la malice.

Stat. Mert. c. 7; Brac. 91 b; Fle. 10 (§ 8).

5. Et defendoms qe nul seignur ne aforce enfaunt en sa garde, madle ne femele, a femme prendre ou baroun. Et cum

1—1. ou plus *NSC.* *sim. GA.* ou de plus *MH.* 2. assez *A.* 3—3. qe pout auenir *A.* *om. M.* 4—4. so *AMCH.* *sim. NSG.* *om. L.* 5—5. so *L.* *sim. MHS.* soit reyntz *ND.* seit reint *A.* reintz *G.*

Marriage to be tendered to females under fourteen years.

shall be tendered to female heirs before they be fourteen years old, otherwise the lords shall be debarred of their right[k].

Disparagement.

4. If any female heir of tender years be married where she is disparaged, then we will that, if she was of fourteen years or upwards, so that she was able to consent to marriage, no penalty shall be incurred; but if she was under that age, the

Penalty.

penalty shall be this, that the lord shall lose the wardship for that time, and make satisfaction to the friends of the person so married, and that all the profit received for the marriage shall be restored to the friends and kindred of the woman, to be

Marriage to lord's villain.

improved for her use. And if she be married to any of his villains, the lord who gave her away shall be punished by imprisonment, until due amends be made by appointment of the kindred of the wife; and such persons shall afterwards be put to ransom for the malice.

Marriages not to be forced.

5. We forbid any lord to force an infant in his ward, male or female, to take wife or husband. And when any heirs,

[k] Our author omits to state the modification of the law introduced by the Statute of Westminster I (3 Ed. I. c. 22), by which the right was granted, or confirmed, to lords to retain the wardship of female heirs for two years after they had reached the age of fourteen years, and to offer them a suitable marriage within that time. If the heiress refused the marriage, the lord might hold the lands till she attained twenty-one, and for a further time until he had received the value of the marriage. Cf. Littleton, Tenures, s. 103; Coke Lit. 79 a; 2 Inst. 202; Lord Darcie's Case, 6 Co. Rep. 71.

acun ou acune eit une foiz pris femme ou baroun par soen seignur en qi garde il eit esté, ou une foiz fet gree de soen mariage, tut soit il ou ele autre foiz a marier, a touz jours mes soint en lour mariages demeyne, taunt cum il tendrount rien de nous. Et ausi en cas ou il ou eles eyent esté mariez en les vies lour peres. Cf. Mag. Cart. c. 7; Glan. l. 7. c. 12; Brac. 88 *b*; Fle. 9 (§ 4), 10 (§ 5, 6), 11 (§ 16).

6. Et cum deus seignurs ou plusurs chalengent mariage de un enfaunt, touz neqedent [1]ne le[1] purrount mie aver[2], tut eit le auncestre de cel enfaunt tenu de touz par service de chevalerie; en queus cas nous voloms qe solom la priorité des feffementz soit jugé, issi qe cil de qi auncestre serra trové eynzné feffement, a cely soit agardé le mariage, et le deforceour soit puni, solom ceo qe est contenu en nos estatuz. Et voloms qe la ou nule priorité de feffement ne est trové par enqueste, cum si le auncestre del enfaunt se purchacea de touz les Stat. West. 2. (13 Edw. I.) c. 16; Glan. l. 7. c. 10; Brac. 90; Fle. 10 (§ 7). Stat. Mert. c. 6.

1—1. *so ND.* ne *LAR.* nel *M.* ne les *SG.* 2. le mariage *add. AR.*

male or female, have once been married by their lords in whose wardship they were, or have once made satisfaction for their marriage, if they be to marry again, they shall for ever after be at their own disposal, provided they hold nothing of us. So also, where they have been married in the lifetime of their fathers[1]. Lords paravail have the first marriage only.

6. When two or more lords claim the marriage of one infant, it is impossible for all of them to have it, although the ancestors of such infant may have held of all by knight service; in which case let it be adjudged according to the priority of the feoffments, so that the marriage shall be awarded to that lord by whose ancestor the earliest feoffment shall be found to have been made; and let the deforceor be punished according to the tenor of our statutes. If no priority of feoffment is found by inquest, as where the ancestor of the infant Of several lords, marriage belongs to the earliest feoffor. If feoffments are coeval, question settled by possession.

1 'An infant under age, married in the life of his ancestor, comes into ward of his lord. His wife dies. His lord tenders him another wife, whom he refuses. *Qu.* Whether forfeiture of marriage lies or not. Surely not; for no force of law can compel the heir to be bigamous.' (Note in MS. *N.*) This question is resolved in the same way by Babington, the king's attorney, in the seventh year of Henry VI, the same reason being given.—'Par le prise del seconde feme *efficitur bigamus*, a qe la Ley ne luy coherte.' So Vet. Nat. Brev. 93. b. But if the heir was married by his ancestor, *infra annos nubiles*, and the wife died before the age of consent, the lord, it is said, should have the marriage. (Y. B. 7 Hen. VI. f. 11 b.) This latter statement is adopted by Fitzherbert (Nat. Brev. 143 M.), and Coke (Co. Lit. 79. b.) It will be remembered that bigamy (in the ancient and proper sense of the word) involved the loss of the benefit of clergy. (See Ante, l. 1. c. 5. s. 5, p. 28.) On this account it was, according to Lord Coke, a disparagement for a lord to marry an heir to a widow, 'whereby he should by reason of the bigamie have lost the benefit of his cleargie, whereby he might save his life.' (Co. Lit. 80. b.)

seignurs a une foiz en le tens del Conquest, ou en cas semblables, qe en teu cas soit jugé pur celi qi serra en seisine del enfaunt.

[170.] Brac. 91, 91 b; Fle. 11 (§ 17).

7. Et cum acun qe point de dreit ne avera eit seisi le cors de acun heir de eynz age et le mariage de cel enfaunt vendu a acun autre, et celi soit enpledé, en teu cas voloms qe les enpledez pusent voucher a garaunt, issi qe chescun trespassour porte sa peyne de soen propre trespas.

CHAPITRE IV. [LXVIII.]

De Homage.

Glan. l. 9. c. 4; Brac. 78 b; Fle. 205 (§ 8).

1. Homage est un lyen de dreit, dount homme est lié et tenu de garraunter acquiter et defendre soen tenaunt en sa seisine vers totes gentz pur les services dues del tenement qe il tendra de ly, et ausi la reverse, dount le tenaunt est reobligé et relié a fere a soen seignur les services dues del tenement qe il tient de ly, en service ou en demeyne, et sa fey garder vers luy desblemie. Dount autretaunt est le seignur tenu a soen homme, cum le homme a soen seignur, for qe soulement en reverence.

purchased of all the lords at once at the time of the Conquest, or in like cases, the judgment shall be in favour of him who shall be in seisin of the infant.

In plea of marriage, voucher is allowed.

7. Where any one who has no right has seised the body of the heir within age, and sold the marriage of such infant to another, and he is impleaded, in such case the person impleaded may vouch to warrant, so that each offender may bear the penalty of his own trespass.

CHAPTER IV.

Of Homage.

Homage, defined.

1. Homage is a legal bond, whereby a person is bound and obliged to warrant, acquit, and defend his tenant in his seisin against all persons for the services due from the tenements which he holds of him, and whereby, on the other hand, the tenant is obliged and bound in return to perform to his lord the services due from the tenement, which he holds of him, in service or in demesne, and to keep his faith towards him inviolate. And the lord is thereby as much bound to his man as the man is to his lord, reverence only excepted.

The lord is bound to warranty, the tenant to service.

Lord and man equally bound.

2. Et cum acun neqedent soit vouché par homage, et le seignur tende de averrer, qe le tenement, dount il est vouché, fut translaté hors del saunc del premer purchaceour par feffement ou par acune autre translacioun, en teu cas soit le tenaunt chargé de voucher soen feffour ou ses auncestres[1]. Stat. de big. (4 Edw. I.) c. 6. Hengham M. c. 13. p. 72, 76.

3. Homage lie deus hommes par lour commun assent, et par commun assent [2]purra homage[2] estre delié et defet, et ne mie par le assent de un de eus soulement. Brac. 78 b (§ 2); Fle. 205 (§ 9).

4. Et cum acun heir vodera estre resceu al heritage soen auncestre, de qi nule dotaunce ne est qe il ne soit le proscheyn heir mesme celi auncestre, en primes voloms nous qe il face homage a soen seignur, ou tende a fere, des terres noméement tenues [3]par fee de chevalerie, et qe[3] le seignur prenge soen [170 b.] Glan. l. 9. c. 1, 6; Brac. 80; Fle. 207.

1. heirs *ND*. 2—2. *so NDSG*. put un homme *L*. purra homme *M*. *sim. A*. 3—3. *so verb. G*. *sim. M*. par de cheualerie qe *L*. par fee de cheualer. E qe *N*. *sim. A*. par feez de cheualeries qe *S*.

2. Nevertheless if any one be vouched by reason of homage, and the lord offers to prove that the tenement for which he is vouched was transferred from the blood of the first purchaser by feoffment or some other conveyance, in such case the tenant shall be charged to vouch his feoffor or the feoffor of his ancestors[m]. Warranty by homage does not extend beyond the heirs of feoffee.

3. Homage binds two persons by their mutual consent; and by their mutual consent it may be released and undone, but not by the assent of one of them only. Homage released by mutual consent.

4. When any heir is desirous of being admitted to the inheritance of his ancestor, and there is no doubt of his being the nearest heir, we will that he in the first place do homage to his lord, or offer to do it,—in respect, that is to say, of his lands held by knight's service,—and that the lord receive his Heir of tenant by knights' service upon admission to inheritance should tender homage.

m 'Note, that homage ancestral, and homage purchased by attornment made in the king's court, give warranty and none other, without an especial clause of warranty, or what is equivalent thereto, as the word *dedi*; as, where B held of A by homage before the statute [Stat. Quia Emptores, 18 Ed. I.], and afterwards has given the land to another, doing the services to the chief lord. For all purchases are now made by *dedi*, and with an especial clause of warranty; and the purchaser may thus vouch the feoffor or his heirs, who are bound to warranty by deed. Therefore he who holds by specialty ought to vouch by specialty, and he who holds by homage ancestral, ought to vouch by the same. And note, that homage is ancestral from the time of the Conquest, or before the limitation of the writ of right, or from the great grandfather of the lord, of whom the great grandfather of the tenant held, and so from heir to heir on each side. When there are fewer degrees, the tenant cannot vouch by homage without specialty.' (Note in MS. *N*.) Cf. ante, liv. ii. cap. 3. s. 8. See the later doctrine as to homage ancestral in Littleton, Ten. Sect. 143–152, with Coke's Commentary, Co. Lit. 100. b. See also 2 Inst. 275.

homage, si resounable destourbaunce ne soit, sicum avent de homage tendu de autre fee qe de chevalerie ou de graunt serjauntie, si le usage del leu ne[1] soit a ceo contrarie, et acune foiz par la resoun des tenauntz, sicum est de ceux qi tienent en villenage.

Glan. l. 9. c. 2; Brac. 77 b, 78; Fle. 204.

5. De part le tenaunt est acune foiz le homage dedit et a dreit, sicum des terres donez en fraunche aumoyne, ou des terres qe sount tenuz par petites serjaunties ou par [2]fraunc socage[2]. Et acune foiz par la resoun des persones les seignurs, sicum est de ceux qi espousent les heirs femelles, et demaundent homage en lour noun demeyne la ou lour femmes [3]dussent demaunder; et ausi de ceux qi demaundent homage eynz ceo qe lour tenauntz soint seisiz, ou eynz ceo qe eus mesmes soint seisiz de lour heritage; et de autres qi point de dreit n'en ount a homage demaunder, sicum termers et autres.

Brac. 79 b, 87 (§ 5); Fle. 206 (§ 16).

6. Et cum acun heritage soit descendu a acun heir qi deyve tener de nous et de plusours autres, en teu cas voloms nous, qe la leggeaunce[4] de sa seignurie soit nostre, sauntz estre barré par acune resoun de priorité de autre feffour. Et

1. *so NAGSMH.* ne *om. L.* 2—2. *so NMG.* fraunce socages *L.* *sim. AH.* 3. les *add. NA.* le *M.* 4. ligiaunce *N.* liaunce *M.* alleggaunce *A.* alliaunce *H.*

Homage may be refused by lord, where.

homage, unless there is a reasonable impediment. This may arise in the case of homage tendered for a fee not held by knight's service or grand serjeanty, except where the custom of the place is contrary; and sometimes on account of the condition of the tenants, as where they hold in villenage.

Homage may be refused by tenant, where.

5. On the part of the tenant again, homage is sometimes refused, and that rightly, as where the lands are given in free alms, or are held by petty serjeanties or by free socage; and sometimes on account of the persons of the lords, as where they have married female heirs, and demand the homage in their own names, whereas their wives ought to demand it; so likewise where the lords demand homage before their tenants are in seisin, or before they are themselves seised of their inheritance; and when it is demanded by those who have no right to demand homage, as termors and others.

Allegiance prerogative of the king.

6. When an inheritance descends to any heir who holds of us and of several others, in such case the allegiance of the seigniory shall belong to us, and we shall not be barred by reason of the priority of any other feoffor. But if such heir

si tiel heir ne deyve tenir de nous, adounc soit la aleggeaunce[1] de la seignurie a celi qi major dreit avera en soen mariage. Ante, c. 2. s. 2, c. 3. s. 6. [171.]

7. Et pur ceo qe damage purroit avener a nous et as autres seignurs des feez par cours de tens, si plusours, a qi heritage descend cum a un heir, faisent lour services as seignurs solom lour porciouns, voloms nous qe chescun seignur prenge homage de trestouz les parceners madles et femeles, s'il voillent, ausi cum de un heir, et cel homage ne soit tenu for qe un soul homage pur la unité de dreit, issi qe nul seignur ne perde garde ne mariage de nul tenaunt par chevalerie de soen fee, sauve qe un des parceners jurge la feuté, a fere al seignur les services de tut le heritage entier, si le seignur le voille, issi qe nous, ne autres ne pregnoums les services de nos feez par parceles ne par deverses meyns; et les autres parceners facent feuté et les services de lour porciouns a lour chiefs parceners.

Stat. Hib. de cohœr. (14 Hen. III.); Glan. l. 7. c. 3; Brac. 78; Fle. 205.

Post, s. 23.

8. Et tut soit qe enfaunt de eynz age face homage, pur ceo ne voloms mie qe il face serment de feuté jekes autaunt qe il

Mag Car. c. 3; Glan. l. 9. c. 1; Brac. 78 *b*; Fle. 205 (§ 10).

1. ligeaunce *N.* *sim. G.* legeance *S.* liaunce *M.* alliaunce *AH.*

does not hold of us, the allegiance of the seigniory shall belong to that lord who has the best right to his marriage.

7. Whereas damage might accrue to us and other lords of fees in course of time, if several persons, to whom an inheritance descends as to one heir, should perform their services to the lords according to their portions, we will that every lord, if he pleases, may take the homage of all the parceners, male and female, as of one heir, such homage being considered as only one homage by reason of the unity of right, so that no lord may lose the wardship or marriage of any tenant in chivalry of his fee; but that one of the parceners may, if the lord choose, swear the fealty to perform to him the services of the whole inheritance, so that neither we nor any other may receive the services of our fees by parcels nor by different hands[n]; and in such case the other parceners shall do fealty and the services of their portions to their chief parceners.

In the case of parceners the homage of all may be taken, but the entire services received from one.

8. Although an infant under age do homage, yet we will not have him take the oath of fealty until he be of full age.

Infants are capable of doing homage.

n It appears from a subsequent section, that it was not considered altogether safe for a lord to avail himself of the right of taking the entire service by the hands of the eldest parcener, inasmuch as his title to the wardship of the descendants of the junior parcener might be thereby endangered. See below, s. 23.

soit de plener age. Et tut soit ceo commun dit del poeple, qe fet de enfaunt fet de eynz age ne fet mie a tener estable, voloms neqedent qe chescun homme et chescune femme receivable a heritage, de quel age qe il soit, face homage a soen seignur, solom le estatut de la Graunt Chartre, issint [171 *b.*] qe les seignurs ne eint mie les profitz des gardes, ne des mariages de une part, qe il ne seint tenuz as perils des garraunties de autre part.

Glan. l. 9. c 1, ad fin.; Brac. 78 *b*; Fle. 205.

9. Et touz pount[1] fere homage, qi tienent par fee de chevaler en lour noun[2] demeyne. Mes gentz de religion, et clers, et autres qi tienent en autri noun ne deyvent nul homage fere pur teus tenementz, [3]sicum des tenementz[3] qe il tienent en noun de lour eglises, et dount il sount derreyn nomez es feffementz, sicum piert par les chartres, qe comencent issi: Jeo doune a Deu et al eglise de tiel lu et as gentz leynz Deu servauntz: [4]en le queus douns est [5]Deu premerement feffé et sa eglise[5], et puis les gentz la eynz Deu servauntz[4]. Les queus gentz ne pount fere nul homage, mes soulement serement de feuté. Et teus gentz fount acune foiz

Brac 79; Fle. 205 (§ 13).

1. ceux purrount *N.* teus poent *S.* ceus poent *M.* *sim. G.* 2. so *N.* *om. LGSMF.* 3—3. so *N.* *sim. SGAMF.* *om. L.* 4—4. *om. NDH.* 5—5. so *verb. MW.* *sim. GAR.* doun premerement feffe a sa eglise *LS.*

And although it is commonly said, that the act of an infant, done under age, ought not to be held binding, yet we will that every man and woman admissible to an inheritance, of what age soever they be, do homage to their lords according to the statute of the Great Charter; so that the lords shall not have the profits of wardships or marriages on the one hand without being bound to the risk of warranties on the other.

No homage done by parsons or monks; but fealty.

9. All those who hold by knight's service in their own names may do homage; but persons in religion, and clerks, and others holding in others' names, ought not to do homage for the tenements so held, as in the case of tenements which they hold in the names of their churches, where the persons are named last in the feoffments, as appears by the charters, which begin thus: I give to God and the church of such a place, and to the persons therein serving God. In these gifts therefore the feoffment is made first to God and his church, and afterwards to the persons therein serving God. Which persons cannot do any homage, but only take the oath of fealty. And such persons do sometimes make a payment to

a lour seignurs une paye al double de la value de lour service de un an en remembraunce de relef a chef de chescun xxx. aunz, sicum en Normaundie le[1] fet hom de commun usage.

10. Celi qi homage deit fere, il deit [2]quere soen seignur[2] pur reverence de ly; et cum il ly trovera, si ly tende soen homage a joyntes meyns devaunt bones gentz, qi de ceo purrount porter testmoynage, si mester soit. Et s'il refuse de prendre soen homage, autre foiz le querge apres les xv. jours passez et le ly tende ausi cum devaunt, et issi jekes a treis foiz. Et si il eit refusé treis foiz a tort par testmoynage des bones gentz, adounc voloms nous qe teus seignurs soint forclos de teus homages[3], et [4]qe les tenauntz[4] pusent fere lour homages as sovereyns seignurs des feez. Et cum autre avera soen homage resceu, voloms qe a ly soint fetz les services, et jalemeyns soit le premer seignur tenu a la garauntie, si le tenaunt soit enpledé de soen tenement. Et si le sovereyn seignur refuse le homage, soit tendu de seignur en seignur jekes a nous mesmes; les queus homages nous porroums prendre sauntz peril.

Glan. l. 9. c. 1; Brac. 80; Fle. 207.

Glan. l. 9. c. 4, 5; Brac. 82 b; Fle. 210.

[172.]

Brac. 82 b; Fle. 210.

1. le *om. M.* 2—2. *so NM.* quere soen gre *L. sim. GSA.* quere a fere sun gree *H.* 3. *so NG. sim AMH.* heritages *LS.* 4—4. *so N. sim. A.* qe tenauntz *L. sim. SH.* qe teus *M.* qe teus tenantz *G.*

their lords of double the yearly value of their services at the end of every thirty years, in remembrance of relief, as is the common custom in Normandy.

10. He who is to do homage ought to seek out his lord from reverence to him; and when he has found him, let him tender his homage, with his hands clasped, before good people, who, if there be occasion, may bear witness thereof. If the lord refuses to take his homage, let him seek him again fifteen days after, and tender it to him as before, and so for three times. And if he wrongfully refuses it three times by the testimony of good people, then we will that the lords be foreclosed of such homage, and that the tenants may perform their homage to the superior lords of the fees. And when another lord has thus received his homage, we will that the services be performed to him; and yet, if the tenant be impleaded concerning his tenement, the first lord shall be bound to warranty. And if the next superior lord refuse his homage, let it be tendered from lord to lord until it comes to us; which homage we may safely take.

Homage to be tendered by tenant.

Tender, if refused, to be thrice repeated.

If thrice refused, to be tendered to superior lord.

Lord cannot, by refusal of homage, evade warranty.

Mag. Cart. c. 3; Glan. l. 9. c. 4; Fle. 210 (§ 38).

11. Et si acun seignur refuse ou delaye a prendre le homage soen tenaunt en fraude, par aventure qe il ne ly soit tenu a la garrauntie, en teu cas voloms nous qe le tenaunt puse retenir relef et totes maneres des services par ly dues al seignur jekes autaunt qe il eit pris soen homage, issi qe le seignur ne eit en ly nule seignurie enceys qe le seignur ly eit resceu pur tenaunt; ne qe nul tenaunt en teu cas soit rien tenu a satisfaccioun des arrerages des services[1] avaunt le homage resceu.

Glan. l. 9. c. 5; Brac. 83, 83 b; Fle. 210.

[172 b.]

12. Et si teus tenauntz ne voillent a autre seignur achever[2], adounc soint il eydez par noster bref al viscounte del lu; qe [3]il die a tel seignur, qe[3] a dreit et sauntz delay prenge le homage un tiel qi tient de ly et de ly cleyme a tener par service de chevaler, et si il ne face, qe il soit a certeyn jour et lu devaunt nos Justices a moustrer pur quei il ne ad fet. A quel jour ambideus porrount estre essoniez. Et si le seignur face defaute, si curgent sur ly les grauntz destresces, ausi cum en personels pletz, jekes autaunt qe il [4]aperge.

Glan. l. 9. c. 6.

1. *so NH.* fermes *LASGMC.* 2. escheuir *M.* cheuer *A.* eschure *H.* 3—3. il a tel iour qe *L.* il comaunde a vn tiel seignur qe *N.* *sim. S.* die a teu seignur qe *M.* *sim. GH.* tel seignour *A.* 4—4. *so verb. S.* aperge en Court et covendra. *L.* apierge. E cum il apparra en Court si couendra *NG.* *sim. DH.* apierge. E com il apara en Court i couendra *M.* *sim. A.*

Tenant may refuse services until homage is received.

11. If any lord fraudulently refuses or delays to take the homage of his tenant, in order, perchance, that he may not be held to warranty, the tenant in such case may keep back relief and all kinds of services due from him to the lord until he has taken his homage, so that the lord shall have no seigniory over him until he has received him as his tenant; and no tenant in such case shall be obliged to make satisfaction for arrears of services before the homage has been received.

Remedy of tenant against lord, refusing his homage. Form of writ.

12. And if such tenants are not willing to transfer their homage to another lord, let them be aided by our writ to the sheriff of the county, to command the lord that he justly and without delay take the homage of such a one who holds or claims to hold of him by knight's service; and that, if he omits doing it, he be at a certain day and place before our Justices to show cause why he has not done it. At which day both may be essoined; and if the lord make default, the process against him shall be by great distresses, as in personal pleas, until he shall appear.

Process by distress, to compel appearance.

13. Et cum il aparra en court et covendra[4] qe il respoigne al accioun del pleintif, si[1] porra il dire qe il ne prist mie soen homage, pur ceo qe il ne est mie proschein heir le auncestre qi heir il cleyme estre, car il ad un frere eynznée en pleyne vie par de la mer ou aylours, qi est plus proscheyn heyr [2]mesme cel auncestre[2]; ou pur ceo qe il est bastard; ou pur ceo qe il est feffé de acun qi avera fet felonie, ou qi est appelé de felonie dount jugement de mort ou de utlagerie ou de abjuracioun deit sourdre, et le quel feffour est uncore en pleyne vie; ou pur ceo qe ly ou acun de ses auncestres sount entrez en les tenementz qe il cleyme a tener de ly par viciouse entré, sicum par intrusioun, ou par disseisine, ou par defaute apres defaute fete en nostre court, ou par acun qi tint[3] les tenementz a terme de vie ou en villenage ou a volunté ou a terme des aunz ou en gage ou par fee taillé ou en garde, ou par baillif, ou en cas semblables; ou pur ceo qe le tenement, dount il tendi le homage, fu doné en mariage, et dounc il espeire reversioun jekes a la apparaunce de tiels heirs; ou pur ceo qe il ne ad point de heir de sei, par quei il

Glan. l. 9. c. 6; Brac. 83 *b*; Fle. 210, 211.

Brac. 83 *b*; Fle. 210 (§ 40).

Stat. de ten. per leg. Angl. (inc. temp.); Glan. l. 9. c. 2; Brac. 21 *b*, 24; Fle. 190.

1. so *L.* sim. *S.* e si *MA.* 2—2. le auncestre mesme cely par qi mort il cleyme estre heir *N.* sim. *D.* le auncestre mesmes par qi mort il cleime estre heir *M.* sim. *A.* le auncestre *G.* 3. tient *LNGM.* tent *S.*

13. When the lord appears and has to answer to the action of the plaintiff, he may say that he refused to take his homage, because he is not next heir to the ancestor whose heir he claims to be, inasmuch as he has an elder brother alive beyond sea or elsewhere, who is nearer heir to the same ancestor; or because he is a bastard; or because he is the feoffee of one who has committed felony, or who is appealed of a felony from which judgment of death, outlawry, or abjuration may ensue, and which feoffor is still living; or by reason that he or some of his ancestors entered into the tenements which he claims to hold of him by a defective entry, as by intrusion, disseisin, or by default after default made in our court, or by means of one who held the tenements for term of life, or in villenage, or at will, or for term of years, or in mortgage, or in fee tail, or in ward, or by means of a bailiff, or in like cases; or because the tenement for which he tendered homage, was given in marriage, and therefore he expects the reversion until the appearance of heirs; or because the tenant has no heir of his body,

Exceptions to the action.

Plaintiff not next heir,

or bastard,

or feoffee of felon.

Plea of defective entry of plaintiff.

Plea that defendant expects reversion,

[173.] entent qe cele purpartie ly deit uncore accrestre si le tenaunt moerge sauntz heir de sei; ou pur ceo qe mesme cely tenaunt ad acune chose fet pur quei il ne deit soen homage receyver; les queles excepciouns voloms qe soient allouwables, si eles soint vereyes.

Brac. 80; Fle. 207 (§ 23, 24). 14. Et pur ceo affiert, qe chescun seignur face[1] examinacioun, eynz ceo qe il prenge homage de soen tenaunt, si il soit dreit heir, et de totes les circumstaunces nomez avaunt en les excepciouns, et qe il sache de quel tenement et de cum bien il deit homage prendre, et de cum bien le tenaunt est seisi en demeyne et de cum bien en service, issi qe nul ne soit deceu quant a peril qe apent en[2] la garrauntie.

Brac. 83 *b*; Fle. 210 (§ 39). 15. Ou, quant le seignur vendra en court, a ceo qe le [3]pleyntif dit[3], qe soen piere tint[4] de ly et homage ly fist, ou a soen piere, ou a autre auncestre, par teus certeyns services,

1. bone *add. NAGSM.* bon *H.* 2. a *M.* 3—3. tenaunt dit *M.* 4. so *G.* tient *LMA.* tynt *N.* tent *S.*

or accruer. wherefore the defendant contends that the tenant's portion ought still to accrue to him if the tenant should die without any heir of his own[o]; or because this same tenant has done some act by which the lord is discharged from receiving his homage; and such exceptions, if true, shall be allowed.

Plea of discharge by act of plaintiff.

Precautions to be taken by lord. 14. Therefore it behoves every lord, before he takes the homage of his tenant, to examine whether he is the right heir, and concerning all the circumstances named in the above exceptions, and that he know for what tenement and for how much he ought to take homage, and of how much the tenant is seised in demesne, and of how much in service, so that no one may be deceived as to the risk which he runs in respect of warranty.

Plea, that plaintiff holds nothing of defendant. 15. Again, the lord, when he comes into court, in answer to the allegation of the plaintiff, that his father held of him and did homage to him, or to his father or other ancestor, by such

o These two justifications of refusal of homage refer to the two cases of tenants in frank-marriage, and co-parceners; the feoffor in the one case and the elder parcener in the other being justified in refusing the homage until the third generation. See Glan. li. 7. c. 3; li. 9. c. 2; Brac. 21, 21 *b*; Fle. 190, 191. The reason of this was, that the acceptance of homage might prejudice his right of succession to the inheritance, upon the principle laid down in Glanville: 'Nemo potest simul esse hæres et dominus.' See Glan. li. 7. c. 1. Compare Littleton's Tenures, s. 19, 20, where it appears that in later times the tenant in frank-marriage was quit of all service, except fealty, until the succession of the issue in the fifth degree.

porra le seignur dire, qe il tint[1] riens de ly ne nul homage ne ly fist ne rien de ly deit tener. Et si il ceo profre a defendre par champioun, soit a ceo receu, si le tenaunt le voille entendre[2]; et s'il de ceo se[3] voille mettre en la graunt assise, dounc soit ele chargé a dire qi ad major dreit a tener le tenement en demeyne, le seignur de qi le tenaunt se est pleynt, ou le tenaunt a tener de ly. Car bien porra estre, qe le pleintif ou[4] ses auncestres firent homage as auncestres mesmes celi de qi il se est pleint, et qe unques ne avoint seisine del tenement ne del fee, dount il firent le homage, ou, s'il avoient seisine, ceo avoient il de lour intrusioun et ne mie par inducciouns[5] de acun feffour en tens de vacacioun; et en teu cas bien list refuser homage, par la accioun qe il ad a demaunder le tenement en demeyne pur la viciouse entré del tenaunt ou de ses auncestres.

Brac. 83 *b*; Fle. 210 (§ 39).

Glan. l. 9. c. 6, 7; Brac. 83 *b*; Fle. 210, 211.

[173 *b*.]

16. Et cum acun countrelute a fere homage a soen seignur, adounc destreigne le seignur pur arrerages des services si point i eynt. Et si le tenaunt face replever la destresce, eit

Brac 83 *b*; Fle. 211.

1. *so G.* tient *L.* ne tient *M.* tent *SC.* 2. attendre *NH.* tendre *A.* 3. *so NAM.* se *om. LSGH.* 4. e *M.* 5. *so G.* *so on eras. N.* condicioun *LDMCH.* *sim. SAWF.*

certain services, may say that he held nothing of him, nor did any homage to him, nor ought to hold anything of him. And if he offers to make this good by his champion, he shall be admitted thereto if the tenant chooses to accept it; but if he chooses to put himself upon the great assise, it shall be charged to say, whether the lord, of whom the tenant complains, has the better right to hold the tenement in demesne, or the tenant to hold it of him. For it may well be, that the plaintiff or his ancestors did homage to the ancestors of the same person of whom he complains, and yet never had seisin of the tenement or of the fee for which they performed the homage; or if they had seisin, yet they had it by their own intrusion, and not by induction of any feoffor at a time when the tenement was vacant; in which case homage may lawfully be refused, on account of the right of action which the lord has to demand the tenement in demesne by reason of the defective entry of the tenant or his ancestors.

Trial by battle,

or great assise.

Form of issue, upon the right, not upon the fact of homage.

16. When any tenant resists doing homage to his lord, the lord should distrain for the arrears of the services if any are due. And if the tenant causes the distress to be replevied,

Remedy of lord for homage refused, by distress,

le seignur adounc remedie, ou [1]il ne porra mie counter[1] de sa seisine demeyne[2], par bref de custumes et de services. Et si celi tenaunt eit juree feuté a soen seignur, tut ne ly eit il fet autre service, mes ne porra il disavower a tenir de soen seignur en court qe porte record, qe accioun ne acrest tauntost al seignur a demaunder soen fee en demeyne. Et si le seignur eit esté seisi de acun service de cel fee par mi la meyn de acun verrei tenaunt, tut ne fust il seisi par celi qi replevist ses avers, jalemeyns ne recovera le seignur par assise de novele disseisine.

Reg. brev. orig. 159.

Ante, l. ii. c. 11. s. 7.

Glan. l. 9. c. 1; Brac. 80; Fle. 207 (§ 21); Mod. fac. homag. (Stat. inc. temp.)

17. [3]De homage[3] qe hom deit fere[4],—deit hom fere en ceste manere. Le tenaunt deit tendre soen homage a soen

1—1. il purra meuz counter *C*. 2. ou des ses ancestres denz le temps limite *interl. N.* 3—3. *so LSGM.* Des homages *NA*. 4. si les *add. N.*

the lord, where he cannot count of his own seisin, shall have his remedy by writ of customs and services [p]. And if the tenant has sworn fealty to his lord, although he has done no other service to him, he cannot disclaim holding of his lord in any court of record, without an action immediately accruing to the lord to demand his fee in demesne. And if the lord has been seised of any service of that fee by the hand of any actual tenant, although he was not seised by means of him who replevied the cattle, the lord shall nevertheless recover by assise of novel disseisin.

by writ of customs and services.

Forfeiture for disclaimer of tenure.

Lord, if seised of service, may recover by assise.

Ceremony of homage.

17. When homage is to be done, it should be done in this manner. The tenant should tender his homage to his lord

p 'If the tenant refuses homage, the lord may distrain his fee for the services which are in arrear. But he should make avowry in the first place for custom, as well as for service; as for homage and fealty, which are not properly services, but customs depending upon service. For homage is appurtenant to escuage, and is a security for whatever belongs to knight's service; and fealty is appurtenant to rent, and is a security for what belongs to socage. Wherefore the security should first be demanded between lord and tenant, as between others who make contracts. And the lord may make avowry of his own seisin, or that of his father or grandfather, against the tenant by whose hand, or that of his father or grandfather, he was seised; so, in more distant degrees, provided he can assign seisin of his ancestors within the time limited in writs of novel disseisin. But where he can only say that his ancestors, or himself, were seised of the homage or fealty, without seisin of escuage or rent, he cannot say that he is disseised; for rent gives seisin, and not fealty, nor homage. But the lord ought not to distrain but for arrears of rent or service, of which he can allege seisin as aforesaid; which seisin of rent gives him continuance of possession, and authority to distrain for the arrears, and for the fealty by reason of the service which is in arrear. And if he cannot allege seisin as aforesaid, he cannot make avowry for homage or fealty, although he have received them within the time limited, nor consequently recover by assise of novel disseisin for the replevin of him who should be his tenant, but shall be driven to his writ of customs and services.' (Note in MS. *N.*) Compare Brac. 83 *b*, 84; Fle. 211.

seignur as meyns joyntes en signe de subjeccioun et de reverence, et le seignur en signe de garrauntie de acquitaunce et de defense deit enclore entre ses meyns les meyns al tenaunt. Et si acun deit fere homage a nous, si le deit fere par cestes paroles. Jeo deveing voster homme de feez et de tenementz qe jeo de vous tieing et tener dei, et fey vous porteray de vie et de membre de cors et de chateus et de chescun terrien honour encountre[1] touz ceux qi porrount vivre ou morir. Et puis deit le seignur beyser soen tenaunt, quelqe unqe soit le seignur, nous ou autre, malle ou femelle, clerc ou lay, viel ou juvene, en signe de perpetuele [2]affiaunce et aliaunce[2] de graunt amité, qi qe unque soit le tenaunt, povre ou riche, led ou beal. Et cum acun avera fet homage a nous, voloms qe chescun autre seignur soit forclos de la ligeaunce de la seignurie. [174.] Ante, c. 4. s. 6.

18. Et si acun deive fere homage a autre seignur lige qe a nous, si le face par cestes paroles. Jeo devieng voster homme de feez et de tenementz qe jeo de vous tieng et tener dei, et noméement pur tel tenement nomé[3] par certeyne quantité et Brac. 80.

1. *so LDG. sim. S.* outre *MRW.* 2—2. *so verb. AC.* affiaunce aliaunce *LG. sim. S.* affinitee e alliaunce *N. sim. H.* alliaunce *M.* 3. *om. N.*

with his hands joined in token of subjection and reverence; and the lord, in token of warranty acquittance and defence, ought to hold the tenant's hands between his own. And where homage is to be done to us, it ought to be done with these words: 'I become your man for the fees and tenements which I hold and ought to hold of you, and will bear you faith of life and limb of body and chattels and of every earthly honour against all who can live or die.' Then the lord, whosoever he may be, whether ourself or another, and whether male or female, clerk or lay, old or young, ought to kiss his tenant, whether he be poor or rich, ugly or handsome, in token of perpetual affiance, and obligation of strict friendship. And when any one has done homage to us, every other lord shall be foreclosed of the allegiance of seigniory.

Formula of homage to the king.

Of several lords, king alone entitled to allegiance.

18. Where homage is to be done to any other liege lord than us, let it be done in these words: 'I become your man for the fees and tenements which I hold and ought to hold of you, and particularly for such a tenement named by certain

Form of homage to a subject.

par certeynes boundes, et pur[1] tels feez, et fey vous porterai de vie et de membre outre[2] totes gentz, sauve la fey qe jeo doi au Roi et as ses heirs; issi qe le seignur sache de cum bien il serra tenu de garraunter soen tenaunt.

Fle. 207 (§ 20). 19. Et si homage deit estre fet a autre seignur qe a soen lige seignur, adounc le tenaunt die issi. Jeo deveing voster homme de feez et de tenementz qe jeo de vous tieng et tener [174 *b*.] dei, et nomément pur [3]cele certeine terre ou[3] tenement en tiele ville, ausi cum desu est dit, et fey vous porteray outre[4] totes gentz sauve la fey qe jeo doi au Roi, et a mes autres seignurages.

20. Et cum acun deive fere homage pur pensioun de chaumbre, sicum serjaunt fet au seignur, cum serjaunt et nient cum homme, adounc soint les paroles tieles sauntz plus. Jeo deveing voster homme et fey vous porteray outre[5]

1. so *NA*. par *LMH*. 2. so *LNDSGAMCHW*. 3—3. certeyn *N*. teu certeyn *M*. *sim*. *ACH*. 4. so *LNDSGAMCHFW*. 5. so *LNDSGAMCHFW*.

quantity and certain bounds, and for such fees, and will bear you faith of life and limb above[q] all people, saving the faith which I owe to the king and his heirs.' The lord may thus know for how much he will be bound to warrant his tenant.

Form of homage to a lord, not liege. **19. If homage is to be performed to any other than to a liege lord, the tenant shall say thus: 'I become your man for the fees and tenements which I hold and ought to hold of you, and in particular for certain land or a certain tenement in such a vill,' as is above-said, 'and will bear you faith above all people, saving the faith which I owe to the king and to my other lords.'**

Homage of pensioner or servant. **20. When any one is to do homage for a pension *ex camerâ*[r], as a servant may do to his lord, as his servant and not as his man, the words shall be simply these: 'I become your man, and will bear you faith above all people as long as the homage**

q In Bracton and Fleta the word is *contra*, and a misreading may be suspected. Compare the form in s. 17. But *outre* is found in all the MSS. which have been consulted, both here and in the corresponding places of ss. 19, 20.

r Compare Bracton, 79 *b* (§ 6); Fle. 20 (§ 18, 19); and see post, s. 31. Bracton says, that no homage was done for a rent *ex camerâ*, where no land was bound: Fleta, that it ought not to be done, and if it be done, no right of wardship or marriage arises. The general rule is laid down by Glanville, and repeated by Bracton: 'Pro solo dominio fieri non debent homagia alicui excepto Principe.' (Glan. li. 9. c. 2; Brac. 79 *b*, § 6). But it is mentioned by Bracton and Fleta, that it was the common practice for champions to do homage to their principals, which could only be *ratione dominii:* and see post, s. 31. This probably arose from the form in which the wager of battle was tendered: 'et hoc promptus sum probare per hunc liberum meum hominem.' (Glan. li. 2. c. 3.)

totes gentz taunt cum le homage dure, sauve la fey qe jeo doi au Roi et a touz mes autres seignurs[1]. Et tels homages pur-rount estre renduz par le weyver des pensiouns et[2] par le rendre des obligaciouns. Et par novele constitucioun est taunt fet, qe les homages pris des feffours en prejudice des chiefs seignurs ne lient nient, ne de nule force ne sount.

Brac. 80; Fle. 209 (§ 35); post. 5. 25.

Stat West. 3. (18 Ed. I.) c. 1.

21. Et quaunt le homage serra fet, tauntost soit pris ser-ment de feauté de ceux qi serrount tenuz a fere acuns services as seignurs pur les tenementz. A nous issi, paumez[3] les saintz Ewangellies[4]. Ceo oyez, vous bones gentz, qe jeo, tiel par noun, fey a noster Seignur le Roi Edward porteray de ceo jour avaunt, de vie et de membre, de cors et de chateus et de terrien honour, et les services, qe a ly appendent des feez et des tenementz qe jeo tieng de ly, leaument le fray as[5] termes dues a moen poer, si mei ayde Deu et les Saintz.

Mod. fac hom. et fidelit. (Stat. temp. incert.); Brac 80; Fle. 207 (§ 22).

22. Et si feuté deit estre fete a autre seignur lige qe a nous, adounc le face par cestes paroles. Ceo oyez vous moen

Fle. 207 (§ 21).

1. seigneurages *NCH.* 2. et *om. LSGA.* e *NMCH.* 3. so *S.* *sim. NA.* paume *LS.* par *M.* 4. dieu *add. N.* 5. so *GMA.* a *LSCH.*

shall endure, saving the faith which I owe to the king and to all my other lords.' And such homages may be released by waiver of the pensions and by release of the obligations. And a recent change in the law has had this effect, that homages taken by feoffors to the prejudice of the chief lord are not binding or of any force[s].

Effect of the statute *Quia emptores terrarum.*

21. As soon as homage is performed, those who are bound to do any services to the lords for the tenements shall straight-way take the oath of fealty,—if to us, in the following form, laying their hands upon the Holy Gospels: 'Hear this, ye good people, that I, such a one by name, faith will bear to our lord king Edward from this day forward, of life and limb, of body and chattels, and of earthly honour, and the services which belong to him for the fees and tenements which I hold of him, will lawfully perform to him as they become due to the best of my power, so help me God and the Saints.'

Fealty.

Form of fealty to the king.

22. If fealty is to be done to any other liege lord than to us, then let it be done in these words: 'Hear you this, my

Form of fealty to a liege lord.

[s] This passage is important, as shewing the age of Britton. The statute referred to as a 'new constitution' can be no other than the statute of Westminster the third, *Quia emptores terrarum,* passed in the 18th year of Edward I, A. D. 1290. See Introduction by the Editor.

Seignur Johan, qe jeo Piers de ceo jour en avaunt fei vous porteray de vie et de membre, sauve ma fey vers le Roy et ses heirs, et les services qe a vous appendent des feez et des tenementz qe jeo tieng de vous leaument vous fray as[1] termes dues a moen poer, si moi ayde Deu et ses Sainctz.

23. Et si acun countredie de jureer feauté a soen seignur,
[175.] adounc list au seignur destreindre soen tenaunt jekes autaunt
Ante, s. 7. qe il eit fet. Mes nul parcener [2]ne sa issue[2] ne jurge feauté a autre si noun a soen eynznee parcener, ne a ly si le seignur ne le voille; eynz [3]soit en sa eleccioun al[3] seignur, a prendre ses services par mi une meyn, ou par les meyns de touz les parceners. Car autrement perdereit il les gardes et les mariages des autres pur les paroles en le bref de garde, ou le pleyntif dit qe le auncestre l'enfaunt par qi il demaunde garde fust soen tenaunt et ly fist service de chevaler; et ceo serroit faus, si le service fust aylours fet qe a ly.

24. Et de parcener a parcener issi. Ceo oyez vous Johan, qe jeo Piers fey vous porteray de ceo jour en avaunt, et les

1. so *NGAMC*. a *LF*. 2—2. so *GSAMCHF*. se affie *L*. ne soen issue *N*. 3—3. so *verb. SCH*. soit fet en sa eleccioun al *L*. soit en la eleccioun le *N*. *sim. G*. soit a la eleccion le *M*. *sim. AF*.

lord John, that I, Peter, from this day, from this day forward, will bear you faith of life and limb, saving my faith to the king and his heirs, and the services, which belong to you for the fees and tenements which I hold of you, lawfully will perform to you as they become due to the best of my power, so help me God and the Saints.'

Fealty enforced by distress.

23. If any one refuses to do fealty to his lord, the lord may distrain his tenant until he does it. But no parcener or his issue shall swear fealty except to the eldest parcener, nor to him, unless the lord consents; but it shall be in the election of the lord to take his services by the hands of one or of all the parceners. For otherwise he might lose the wardships and marriages of the other parceners, by reason of the words in the writ of ward, where the plaintiff says that the ancestor of the infant, in respect of whom he demands wardship, was his tenant, and performed to him knight's service; which would be false, if the service was done to any other than to him.

Lord may take service from one parcener or from all.

Risk of taking it from one.

Form of fealty from parcener to parcener

24. From parcener to parcener fealty is sworn thus: 'Hear you this, John, that I, Peter, will bear you faith from this day

services dues de ma porcioun del heritage, qe fust a Teobaud noster commun auncestre, leaument vous fray as termes dues a moen poer, si me ayde Deu et les Saintz. Et a autre seignur issi. Ceo oyez vous moen seignur Johan, qe jeo Piers fey vous porteray de ceo jur en avaunt, et les services qe a vous appendent de feez et de tenementz—et le surplus ausi cum devaunt, issi qe feauté de vie et de membre ne soit james juree for qe a nous et as seignurs liges.

25. Car[1] ligeaunce est de si haute nature qe, si deus seignurs soint en destaunce, si covendra al tenaunt fere soen service a soen [2]seignur lige encountre soen autre[2] seignur [3]en sa propre persone et de fere soen service a soen autre seignur[3] par attourné. Car homage est si fort lien entre seignur et tenaunt, qe nul ne put sauntz jugement ou sauntz commune volunté des parties departer del homage, nomément taunt cum le tenaunt tendra en sa meyn les tenementz ou les feez dount il est obligé a tiel service fere; ne le seignur ne porra fere rien qe touche la desheritesoun soen tenaunt, ou autre graunt tort a[4] damage de ly de vie ou[5] de membre,

Glan. l. 9. c. 1; Brac. 79 *b*; Fle. 207 (§ 16).

Brac. 80 *b*, 81 *b*; Fle. 207, 208.

[175 *b*.]

Ante, s. 20.

1. quele *N*. 2—2. *om. ND*. 3—3. *so verb. AMW*. *sim. GR*. *om. LSFCHB*. 4. ou grant *A*. 5. *so NSACHB*. et *L*. o *M*. au *G*.

forward, and the services due for my portion of the inheritance which was Theobald's, our common ancestor's, lawfully will perform to you as they become due to the best of my power: so help me God and the Saints.' And to the other lords thus: 'Hear you this, my lord John, that I, Peter, will bear you faith from this day forward, and the services which belong to you for the fees and tenements',—and so on, as before, fealty of life and limb being never sworn except to us and to liege lords.

Fealty to a lord, not liege.

25. For allegiance is of so high a nature, that if two lords are at difference, the tenant must perform his service to his liege lord against his other lord in his own person, and must perform his service to his other lord by attorney. And homage is so strong a bond between lord and tenant, that none may without judgment or the mutual consent of the parties recede from the homage, so long as the tenant shall keep in his hands the tenements or fees, for which he is bound to perform such service; neither may the lord do anything which touches the disherison of the tenant or other great wrong to his damage

Obligation of allegiance.

Obligation of homage.

Homage how infringed by lord, and by tenant.

ne le tenaunt al seignur, puis soen homage fet, [1]qe el fet mesme[1] ne soit rumpu la confederacioun entre eus et le homage esteint.

Brac. 80 *b*; Fle. 208 (§ 25). 26. Et si cel graunt tort soit atteynt par jugement vers le seignur, soit agardé qe le seignur soit forjugé de la seignurie a touz jours et autrement puni solom le trespas, et qe le Glan. l. 9. c. 1; Brac. 80 *b*, 81 *b*; Fle. 208, 209. tenaunt face soen homage au seignur sovereyn. Et si le tort soit atteint en la persone le tenaunt, soit agardé qe il perde le tenement ou le fee, dount il fist homage[2].

Brac. 81, 81 *b*, 83 *b*; Fle. 208 (§ 29, 30). 27. Et voloms qe, si acuns tenauntz desavowent lour seignur ou a tener de ly en nostre[3] court qe porte record, qe le seignur eit accioun a recoverir [4]le tenement de tiel tenaunt[4] de soen fee en demeyne, pur le homage et pur le serment del Brac. 81 *b*; Fle. 208 (§ 31). feauté qe il ad enfreint, par tiel bref. Comaundez a un tiel, qe a dreit et sauntz delay rende a tiel taunt de terre, ou tauntz des feez, ove les apurtenaunces en tiel lu qe li avauntdit [175 *c*.] tiel ly detient, et de ceo homage ly fist et service[5], et qe deit estre eschete pur ceo qe le avauntdit tiel encountre soen

1—1. qe il fet mesme *L*. *sim. NSA*. qe le fait *G*. qe en le fet memes *M*. quel mesmes fet *C*. *sim. H*. 2. le homage *NMCH*. 3. so *LNACHFW*. nostre *om. MB*. 4—4. tiel tenaunt *L*. les tenementz *N*. *sim. H*. les terres de cel tenant *GS*. les tenemenz celi tenant *M*. *sim. AF*. le tenement *C*. 5. feaute *B*.

in life or limb, nor the tenant to the lord after performance of homage, without by the very act breaking the league between them and extinguishing the homage.

Forfeiture of lord for breach of homage. 26. If the lord be convicted by judgment of this great wrong, it shall be awarded that he be forejudged of his seigniory for ever, and be otherwise punished according to the offence, and that the tenant perform his homage to his Forfeiture of tenant. superior lord. And if the wrong be convicted in the person of the tenant, let it be awarded that he lose the tenement or fee for which he did homage.

Disclaimer of tenure, cause of forfeiture. 27. And we will that if any tenants disavow their lord, or disclaim holding of him in a court bearing record, the lord, on account of the homage and the oath of fealty which the tenant has broken, shall have an action to recover the tenement of such tenant of his fee in demesne, by the following writ: Writ for recovery upon disclaimer. 'Command such an one that justly and without delay he surrender to such an one so much land, or so many fees, with the appurtenances in such a place, which the aforesaid such an one detains from him, and for which he did homage and service to him, and which ought to be his escheat, inasmuch as the

homage et le serment de feauté qe il de ceo ly avoit fet, maliciousement a sa desheritesoun ly disavowa pur seignur ou de rien tener de ly, et si il ne face, qe il soit a certeyn jour et lu devaunt nos Justices[1] a moustrer[2] pur quei il ne ad fet.

28. Le quel bref ne serra mie mester qe soit pledé par descente; eynz porra estre terminé par juree, et par enqueste del fee et de la quantité. Car par descente ne porra mie le seignur proprement counter pur les auncestres le tenaunt, qi ount esté touz jours en possessioun. Et lequel qe il plede par descente ou noun, ne voloms mie qe la parole soit terminé par batayle ou par graunt assise, eynz [3]grauntoms bien pur mestier[3], qe le tenaunt se puse mettre en juree a la semblaunce de graunt assise par cestes paroles, a saver moun, lequel il ad major dreit a tener cel fee, ou le tenement demaundé, en demeyne, ou celi qi demaunde, et a qi mesme celi tenaunt ou acun de ses auncestres qi heir il est de ceo fist homage et service[4], et puis encountre soen homage et sa feuté

Brac. 81 *b*; Fle. 209 (§ 31, 32).

1. a Euerwik *add. NC.* a Westm. *HB.* 2. respoundre *C.* 3—3. *om. N.* bien est mestier pur ceo *A.* grantoms bien *H.* 4. feaute *B.*

aforesaid such an one, contrary to his homage and the oath of fealty which he had taken to him for the same, maliciously to his disherison disclaimed him for his lord and the holding of anything of him, and that, if he omits doing it, he be at a certain day and place before our Justices to shew why he has not done it.'

28. This writ need not be pleaded by descent, but may be determined by a jury and inquest as to the fee and the quantity thereof. For the lord cannot properly count by descent by reason of the ancestors of the tenant, who have been always in possession. And whether he plead by descent or not, we will not have the action determined by battle or great assise; but we allow, if there be occasion, that the tenant may put himself on a jury after the manner of a great assise by these words, to wit, whether he has most right to hold this fee, or the tenement demanded, in demesne, or he who demands it, and to whom this same tenant, or some of his ancestors whose heir he is, did homage and service for the same, and afterwards, contrary to his homage and fealty,

Pleadings in this writ.

Trial, not by battle or great assise, but by jury.

Form of the issue.

maliciousement le desavowa. Et solom le verdit se face le
Brac. 79, 79 *b*, 82 *b*, 83; Fle. 206 (§ 15), 211 (§ 41). jugement.

29. Et mesme la accioun eit le seignur vers le tenaunt, [175 *d*.] [1]qi avera[1] fet homage a autre qe a ly, [2]le quel il dust aver fet a ly[2], si fraude ou malice i soit atteinte; et ausi si il eit fet homage a autre qe a ly a tort, puis qe il avera fet soen homage a ly a dreit. Mes si il le tenaunt le eyt fet par destresce de autre ou par folie, et nient par malice, en tel cas voloms qe hom face venir les seignurs et le tenaunt en nostre court, et la soit discus[3] qi avera majour dreit en le homage. Et cil qi dreit avera recovere, et qi tort avera seit puni.

Brac. 81 *b*; Fle. 209 (§ 35). 30. Et pur ceo qe bataille ne se put joyndre par jugement entre seignur et tenaunt duraunt le homage, voloms nous qe si acun tenaunt voille soen seignur appeler de felonie, ou autrement coumbatre ove ly, qe il rende a soen seignur le fee ou le tenement qe il avera tenu de ly, issi qe le homage soit issi rendu. Car autrement ne voloms nous mie qe homage puse estre rendu.

1—1. qe ly auera *L.* qe auera *G.* *sim. S.* cum soen tenaunt auera *N.* *sim. AMCH.*
2—2. so *N.* *sim. AGSMHFBC.* *om. L.* 3. descous *N.* dischus *M.*

maliciously disclaimed him. And let judgment be given according to the verdict.

Subtraction of homage, cause of forfeiture.

29. The lord has likewise the same action against his tenant, where the tenant has performed to another that homage which he ought to have done to him, if it be found that there was fraud or malice in the act; or if he has done homage wrongfully to another after he had rightfully performed homage to him. But if the tenant has done it by the distress of another, or by folly and not by malice, in such case we will that the lords and the tenant be made to appear in our court, and it shall be there discussed which has the better right to the homage. And he who is in the right shall recover, and he who is in the wrong shall be punished.

Where homage is enforced by another lord, the claimant is to be summoned.

Homage to be released before battle between lord and tenant.

30. Whereas battle may not be joined between lord and tenant during the homage, we will that if any tenant would appeal his lord of felony or otherwise fight with him, that he surrender to the lord the fee or tenement which he holds of him, so that the homage may thus be released. For homage cannot in any other way be released.

31. Et si homage soit fet sauntz seisine de fee ou de tenement, tel homage ne soit de nule force. Ne ausi ne soit homage fet des feez ou des tenementz dount nule garde ne eschet[1] ne mariage[2]. Ne ausi ne soit homage de nule force pur graunt serjauntie, tut soit il fet, si la serjauntie ne soit tenue de nous en chief, nent plus qe homage fet pur rente de chaumbre, ne nient plus qe homage de chaumpioun ou de autre serjaunt.

Glan. l. 9. c. 2; Brac. 79, 79 *b*; Fle. 206 (§ 14). Ante, c. 2. § 5.

Ante, s. 20.

[176.]

32. Car homage, une foiz duement fet entre tenaunt et seignur, dure taunt cum ambideus viverount. Et si homage defaut[3] par la mort le seignur, uncore remeint il entier en la persone le tenaunt. Car tut face le tenaunt homage al heir soen seignur, et issi de heir en heir, pur ceo ne fet il mie plusours homages mes sovent renouvele un homage. Et pur ceo suffit de un tenaunt de une foiz relever sa terre, tut face il sovent homage. Mes si plusours homages viegnent de par

Brac. 79, 80 *b*, 81 *b*; Fle. 206.

1. eschete *NAH.* chiet *M.* 2. ne est *add. N.* 3. deface *NA.* defaile *M.*

31. If homage be done without the possession of any fee or tenement, that homage shall be of no force. Neither let homage be done for those fees or tenements from which no wardship or marriage arises[t]. Neither let homage for grand serjeanty, although it be performed, be of any force, unless the serjeanty be held of us in chief,—no more than homage done for a rent *ex camerâ*, or by a champion or other servant.

No valid homage without a tenement; nor for serjeanties other than in chief; nor for rent *ex camerâ*.

32. For homage once properly performed between tenant and lord endures as long as they both live. And although homage fail by the death of the lord, yet it remains entire in the person of the tenant. For although the tenant does homage to the heir of his lord, and so from heir to heir, yet he does not thereby perform several homages, but renews several times the same homage. Therefore it is sufficient for a tenant to take up his land by relief once, although he does homage several times. But if several homages become due on

Renewal of homage on death of lord.

Tenant liable to one relief only.

[t] This rule was not of universal application, since homage was sometimes due from socage tenements, where neither wardship nor marriage could be claimed. Brac. 77 *b*; Fle. 207 (§ 17, 18). The rights of wardship and marriage were inseparably connected, as appears in the argument used in the following note: 'An infant under age marries a wife, to whom after marriage a knight's fee descends. *Qu.* Shall the lord have relief, or wardship until the husband's age? Some say wardship, because he must take his homage, and he ought to have the wardship of his tenant holding of him by homage. But wardship belongs where marriage belongs; and the marriage of the infant, even if he were unmarried, could not belong to the lord. Therefore the wardship does not belong to him.' (Note in MS. *N.*)

le tenaunt, sicum de heir en heir, en tel cas voloms nous qe a chescun homage sue garde ou relief. Un tenaunt neqedent porra fere plusours homages de divers tenementz, a une foiz ou a plusurs, a un seignur. Et cum homage serra fet une foiz entre seignur et tenaunt, il ne deit mes estre fet entre mesmes les persones de un tenement.

Brac. 81 *b*, 82; Fle. 209 (§ 36). 33. Ne encountre la volunté le tenaunt ne voloms nous mie qe seignur puse attourner le homage et le service de soen tenaunt a qi qe ly plera, et nomément au mortel enemi le tenaunt, ne a celi qi rien ad dount il ly put garaunter, si mester fust. Mes en autres cas voloms bien, qe ceo soit soeffert issi, qe si acun tenaunt de soen gré ne se voille attourner a tener de autre seignur solom la volunté le seignur, adounc voloms nous qe le feffement soit fet par fin [176 *b*.] levé en nostre court par entre le seignur et le feffé del service Brac. 82. 82 *b*; Fle. 209 (§ 35). al tenaunt. Par mi qele fin nous maunderoms par noster bref de jugement al viscounte del lu, qe il face venir le tenaunt en nostre court a moustrer quels tenementz et quels feez il avera tenuz de cel seignur et par quels services. Et cum il vendra en court, et die qe il tient rien de ly ne ne

New homage due on death of tenant, with relief or wardship. the part of the tenant, as from heir to heir, we will that wardship or relief follow every homage. One tenant nevertheless may perform several homages for different tenements at one time, or at several times, to the same lord; but when homage has been once performed between lord and tenant, it ought not to be done again between the same persons for the same tenement.

Rule, that tenant shall not be attorned against his will, 33. Neither will we that the lord attorn the homage and service of his tenant against the will of the tenant to whomsoever he pleases, and particularly to the mortal enemy of the tenant, or to one who has nothing whereby he can warrant **modified by operation of fine.** him if need be. But in other cases we are willing it should be so far permitted, that if a tenant will not of his own consent attorn to hold of another lord according to the wish of the lord, the feoffment shall be made by fine levied in our court between the lord and his feoffee, of the service of the tenant. **Fine enforced against tenant by writ of judgment.** By virtue of which fine, we will command the sheriff of the county by our writ of judgment to cause the tenant to come into our court to shew what tenements and what fees he holds of the lord and by what services. When he appears, if he says that he holds nothing, and does not claim to hold

cleyme a tener, si serra agardé qe il s'en voist quites, et le seignur en la merci; et le seignur se purchace sicum de sus est dit. Et si le tenaunt die, qe il tient de tiel seignur certeyns tenementz ou feez, et par certeynes services, soit agardé qe il soit assouz del premer seignur et achevé a la terce persone, a qi soen seignur le avera attourné. Ante, s. 27.

34. Et si il die qe il ad fet homage pur le tenement, le quel homage ne est uncore esteint, et demaunde jugement, si il a deus hommes de un tenement deyve fere deus homages vivaunt soen premer seignur, de qi il ne voit departer, en teu cas ne voloms nous mie, qe hom agarde qe nul face homage, si il ne voille, a autre qe a celi a qi [1]il fist primes[1], vivaunt soen premer seignur. Et si il ne sache rien dire, pur quei il ne deit fere feauté a celi a qi il est attourné, soit agardé qe il ly face serment de feauté, et si de soen gré ne le voille fere, soit agardé qe le purchaceour destreyne les tenementz ou les feez dount les services deyvent issir jekes autaunt [177.] qe il ly face la feuté. Car qi graunte service, il graunte

Brac. 82, 82 *b*; Fle. 209 (§ 35).

1—1. *so LSF.* il fust primes attournee ou a ses heirs *ND.* il fit primes [ou *ins.*] as heirs *A.* il le fit primes *G.* il est primes ahers *M.* il est primes acheuie e a ses heirs *C.* *sim.* *HB.* il est primes aers *W.*

anything of him, it shall be awarded that he go quit, and that the lord be in mercy; and the lord may then obtain his remedy as above mentioned. If the tenant say that he holds of the lord certain tenements or fees, and by certain services, let it be awarded that he be released from the first lord and his homage transferred to the third party, to whom his lord has attorned him.

Tenant not obliged to do homage twice during life of first lord.

34. If the tenant say that he has done homage for the tenement, which homage is not yet extinct, and demand judgment whether he ought to perform two homages to two persons for one tenement in the lifetime of his first lord, from whom he does not wish to separate; in such case we will not have it awarded that any do homage against his will to another than him to whom he first did it in the lifetime of his first lord. But if he can give no reason why he ought not to do fealty to him to whom he is attorned, let it be awarded that he take the oath of fealty to him; and if he will not do it of his own accord, let it be awarded that the purchaser distrain the tenements or the fees whereout the services should issue, until he shall do fealty to him. For

Fealty to be done to purchaser.

Services may be enforded by distress.

destresce. Et cum le feffour se lerra[1] morir, tauntost voloms nous qe le homage soit esteynt en les persones des heirs le feffour, et recomence ove le purchaceour solom la vertue de la fin levé en nostre court.

Brac. 82 *b*; Fle. 209, 210 (§ 37).

35. Et si celi purchaceour destreyne cel tenaunt pur homage ou pur autre service, et cel tenaunt face replevir sa destresce, et en plee pledaunt die, qe a tort prist ses avers, de sicum il ne cleyme nient tenir de ly, ja par tiele replicacioun ne voloms nous en tel cas qe il cesse a destreyndre. Car en teu cas purrount bien ester ensemble destresce et disavowerie.

Brac. 82; Fle. 210 (§ 37).

36. Acun cas est neqedent qe valer put as tels tenauntz pur excepcioun, qe il ne deyvent estre attournez encountre lour voluntez, sicum en cas ou acun seignur vodera attourner soen tenaunt [2]a tiel, qi rien ne ad dount il ly put[2] garraunter, ou fere a la vaillaunce si mester fust, pur soen tenaunt encombrer et li mesmes descharger; quele excepcioun voloms qe soit allouwable a chescun tenaunt, issi qe nul seignur pur

1. lesse *A.* 2—2. a tiel dount il ne put rien *L.* *sim. GS.* a cely qe ne ad riens dount il puit *ND.* a celi qi nad rien dount il li puit *AR.* *sim. FW.* a tel qe rien nad dont il le poet *M.* e tel qe rien nad dount il luy purra *C.*

whosoever grants service, grants a right to distrain. And when the feoffor dies, we will that the homage be immediately extinct in the persons of the heirs of the feoffor, and take place anew in that of the purchaser according to the force of the fine levied in our court.

Purchaser may distrain, though tenant disclaim tenure.

35. And if such purchaser distrain the tenant for homage or for other service, and the tenant cause his distress to be replevied, and in his pleading says that he wrongfully took his cattle, inasmuch he does not claim to hold anything of him, yet notwithstanding such replication, we will not that he cease to distrain; for in this case distress and disclaimer may well stand together.

Tenant may object to be attorned where a feoffment is made to evade warranty.

36. Nevertheless there are cases, in which such tenants may avail themselves of the exception, that they ought not to be attorned against their consent, as where a lord, for the purpose of burdening his tenant and discharging himself, wishes to attorn his tenant to one who has nothing whereby he can warrant him, or satisfy him for the value, if need be. In this case the exception shall be allowable to every tenant, so that it shall not be in the power of any lord, on account of the

nule petitesce de service puisse weyver soen fee, pur issi estre deschargé del peril de la garrauntie.

CHAPITRE V. [LXIX.]

De Reliefs. [177 *b.*]

1. Si acun tenaunt soit de plener age en le tens de la mort soen auncestre qi heir il est, tauntost voist quere soen seignur, et ly face homage et reliefve[1] soen heritage, qe fust [2]endormi et desconselé[2] par la mort soen auncestre. Le quel relef est limité en certeyn entre les pointz de la Graunt Chartre. Glan. l. 9. c. 4; Brac. 84; Fle. 211. Mag. Chart. c. 2.

2. Mes si acun eit esté taunt en la garde soen seignur apres la mort soen auncestre, qe le seignur eit pris acune manere des espletz de soen heritage en noun de garde, tut soint les espletz de povre[3] quantité, voloms nous qe les heirs soint quites de reliefs. Et tut soit un homage sovent renovelé par mort de divers seignurages[4], pur ceo ne voloms nous mie Mag. Chart. c. 3; Glan. l. 9. c. 4; Fle. 212 (§ 8). Brac. 84 *b*; Fle. 212 (§ 2, 9).

1. releue *NG*. relieue *M*. Releef pur *A*. *sim*. *CHB*. 2—2. endormie desconsele *L*. *sim*. *S*. endormi e descounseillee *N*. *sim*. *GM*. endormie de counseil *H*. *sim*. *CB*. 3. pure *LSC*. poure *GM*. pouere *H*. petite *NA*. 4. *so LSGAMC*. seignurs *N*. *sim*. *HB*.

smallness of the service, to waive his fee, in order to be discharged from the risk of warranty.

CHAPTER V.

Of Reliefs.

1. If any tenant is of full age at the time of the death of his ancestor whose heir he is, let him immediately go and find his lord, and do him homage and relieve his inheritance which lies dormant and unsupported upon the death of his ancestor. Which relief is reduced to a certainty among the articles of the Great Charter. Relief due by heir of full age. Relief fixed by *Magna Charta*.

2. But if anyone has been so long in ward of his lord after the death of his ancestor, that the lord has taken any sort of profits of his inheritance in however small a quantity on account of wardship, the heir shall be quit of relief. And although homage be often renewed on the death of several lords, yet no tenant shall be obliged to relieve his No relief where the heir has been in ward. One relief only due by each successive tenant.

qe acun tenaunt soit tenu a releiver sa terre plus qe une foiz en sa vie, et soen heir un autre foiz, et issi de heir en heir, sicum de sus est dit entre les homages.

Brac. 84 *b*; Fle. 212 (§ 5, 6, 7, 8). 3. Et tut soit qe acun aliene ses tenementz, pur ceo ne voloms nous mie qe le seignur del fee puse demaunder del fee nul relef. Car nous voloms qe touz purchaceours soint quites de relief a lour vies des tenementz purchacez; et ausi a touz ceux, a qi seignurs sount chaungez[1]; et ceux ausi qi tienent a terme de vie soulement; et ceux ausi qi ount esposé femmes, qe par acun tens furent en la garde lour seignurs, Brac. 85, 85 *b*; Fle. 212 (§ 3, 10). et noméement des heritages lour femmes. Et sicum nous ne voloms mie, qe acun de eynz le age de xxi. an doigne relief, [178.] ausi ne voloms nous qe a nul ne soit relief doné, qi serra de eynz mesme le age, ne avaunt ceo qe soen seignur soit seisi de soen heritage, ne avaunt ceo qe soen seignur ly eit rendu les chartres de soen heritage, si il les eit.

Brac. 85 *b*; Fle. 212 (§ 11, 12, 13). 4. Et tut ne voille dreiture qe autre tenement soit relevié, qe fee de chevalerie ou de graunt serjauntie, des tenementz neqedent qe ne sount mie de ceux feez, dount le service est mis en certeyn, voloms qe chescun tenaunt doigne a soen

1. *so AMC. sim. GHB.* chargeez *LNS.*

land more than once in his lifetime, and his heir another time, and so from heir to heir, as above is mentioned in treating of homage.

No relief paid upon a purchase; 3. And although any one alien his tenements, yet the lord of the fee may not demand of the feoffee any relief. For we will that all purchasers shall be quit of relief for their nor upon attornment of tenant; lives in respect of the tenements purchased. So likewise, all those whose lords are changed. And those who hold for nor by tenant for life; term of life only. And those, who marry women, who were some time in ward of their lords, that is to say, for the nor to lord under age, or not seised of lordship; inheritances of their wives. And as we will not that any under the age of twenty-one years shall give relief, so neither will we that relief be paid to any under that age, nor before nor until charters are restored to the heir. the lord is seised of his inheritance, nor before the lord has restored to the tenant the charters of his inheritance, if in his hands.

Quasi-relief from tenants in socage, one year's rent. 4. Although the law does not require relief in the case of any tenement other than a fee of chivalry or grand serjeanty, yet for tenements which are not of such fees, where the service is fixed, we will that every tenant give to his lord in acknow-

seignur en reconisaunce de seignurie taunt cum sa rente de un an amounte, issi qe le seignur eit en cel an ausi cum la rente de soen tenaunt doublé. Et mesme le ordre soit agardé en teles reconisaunces cum dit est de reliefs, issi qe nul ne face tele reconisaunce avant le age qe il put fere serment de feuté; ne for qe une foiz; ne jekes a taunt qe soen seignur soit de plener age et en seisine de soen heritage. Et des tenementz tenuz a fee ferme ou en fraunche aumoygne ne soit rien doné for qe solum ceo qe contenu est par especiauté de escrit.

5. En dreit de heriet ne voloms nous qe nul tenement soit obligé, ne nul heir; desicum doun de heriet est un reward fet par la mort del tenaunt de acun seignur de la[1] meillure beste trové en la possessioun le mort, ou de autre qe de la meillure solom le ordeynement le moriaunt, al oes le seignur; le quel reward de rien ne touche le heir ne soen heritage; ne nule comparisoun ne ad a relief; car il vient plus de grace qe de dreit, et plus de vileins qe des frauncs. Glan. l. 7. c. 5; Brac. 86; Fle. 212 (c. 18).

1. so *GAMC.* la *om. LSH. interl. N.*

ledgment of his seigniory the amount of one year's rent, so that the lord in that year shall have as much as double his tenant's rent. And in such acknowledgments the same rule shall be observed as has been mentioned concerning reliefs, that none make the acknowledgment before he is of age to take the oath of fealty,—nor more than once,—nor until his lord be of full age and in seisin of his inheritance. And for tenements held in fee-farm or in free alms, let nothing be given, except what is specially expressed in the deed. **Acknowledgment for fee-farm and frank-almoign according to grant.**

5. With respect to heriots, we will that no tenement, nor any heir, be bound. **Heriot not due from heir.** For the gift of an heriot is a payment made, on account of the death of the tenant of some lord, of the best beast found in the possession of the deceased, or of one not the best, according to the appointment of the dying person, to the use of the lord; which payment does not at all concern the heir or his inheritance. Neither is it to be compared with relief; for it arises more out of favour than of right, and is more paid by villains than by freemen. **Distinction between relief and heriot.**

CHAPITRE VI. [LXX.]

[178 *b.*]

De Mort de auncestre.

Stat. Marl. (52 Hen. III.) c. 16; Glan. l. 7. c. 9; Brac. 71 *b*, 252 *b*; Fle. 277 (§ 4).

Glan. l. 9. c. 1; Brac. 71 *b*, 252; Fle. 277 (§ 3).

1. Touz jours affiert, qe les heirs, quant il se pernent a lour heritages par successioun, soeffrent lour seignurs fere une simple seisine sauntz fere nule manere de damage par quei il soint [1]conuz as seignurs[1]. Et si tels heirs soint de eynz age, et deivent tenir de[2] fee de chevaler[3], primes prengent les seignurs lour homages, et puis eynt la garde de lour feez. Et si les seignurs troevent lour feez vacauntz, bien list a eus de les seiser simplement en noun de seignurie, et plenerement el noun del[4] dreit heir, ou qe il unques soit. Et ceste dreyne resoun soit garraunt a [5]teus seignurs[5] a delayer a prendre le homage ou rendre[6] le heritage a autre qe a dreit heir.

1—1. *so LSG.* conuz cum seignurs *ND.* conuz as heirs *M.* conuz au seigneur *C.* conuz au seignur *H.* tenuz as seignurs *A.* 2. par *CH.* 3. cheualerie *M.* 4. *so M.* de *LNDSGA.* le *CH.* 5—5. *so GAH. sim. NDS.* touz seignurs teus *L.* 6. a delaer a rendre *M.* a rendre *ND.*

CHAPTER VI.

Of Mortdancester.

On death of tenant, the lord entitled to 'simple seisin.'

1. It is always the duty of heirs, when they come to their inheritances by succession, to permit their lords to make a simple seisin[u], without doing any sort of damage, whereby they may be recognised as lords. And if such heirs are under age, and ought to hold by knights' service, let the lords first take their homages, and afterwards have the wardship of their fees.

If the fee be vacant, the lord may enter, in right of the heir.

If the lords find their fees vacant, they may seize them simply in right of seigniory, and fully in right of the lawful heir, whosoever he may be. And this last clause shall be a justification for all such lords delaying to take the homage or to yield up the inheritance to any other than the lawful heir.

[u] This is the rule laid down by Bracton (f. 252 *b*), and confirmed by the Statute of Marlborough, c. 16. Lord Coke, in commenting upon this statute, interprets 'simple seisin' to mean relief. But although in all probability it soon became the practice to be contented with this recognition of seigniory, the words of the statute, as well as those of Bracton, appear rather to contemplate a formal possession of the tenement, it being expressly provided that the lord was not to take or remove anything from the land, or to eject the heir. It will be seen that in the next sentence of the text, the simple, or formal, seisin of the lord, is contrasted with the full, or beneficial, possession of the heir.

2. Et si acun seignur par malice ou par negligence prenge le homage de acun qi ne serra mie dreit heir, ou le seignur set bien qe il i ad autre heir plus proschein, ou de ceo soit en dotaunce par acun qi se profre pur dreit heir, ou par commun dit del visné, et apres soen homage resceu ly eit liveré la seisine del heritage demaundé, et le dreit heir eit puis purchacé sour le tenaunt assise de mort de auncestre, et le tenaunt vouche[1] le seignur a garraunt par soen homage qe [179.] le seignur resceust, en tel cas voloms nous qe le seignur soit tenu a la garauntie et as chaunges, tut die le seignur pur excepcioun qe il prist soen homage sauve chescuni dreit, quaunt il comencea a desheriter le dreit heir. Mes si nul autre ne eust chalengé le heritage, ne[2] nule dotaunce [3]ne eust le seignur eu[3] de autre heir, en tel cas [4]serreit resoun[4] qe la condicioun el prendre de homage ly fust[5] allouwable[6]; et en tel cas voloms nous qe tieles condicioneles prises del homage soint allouwables, et en nul autre cas.

Brac. 252 b; Fle. 277, 278.

3. Mes[7] volums qe si acun seignur soit en seisine de soen

Glan. l. 9. c. 6; Brac. 252 b,

1. de ceo *add. M.* 2. de *LS.* dount *G.* *sim. M.* e *NDHC.* de [ne] *A.* 3—3. ne est al seignur *ND.* ne ust en le seignur *M.* eust le seigneur *HC.* 4—4. soit resceu *ND.* 5. soit *N.* *sim. D.* 6. resceiuable *CH.* 7. so *ND.* ne *LAGSEM.*

2. If any lord through malice or negligence shall take the homage of one who is not the right heir, where the lord well knows that there is a nearer heir, or has reason to suspect it by another offering himself as right heir, or by common report of the neighbourhood, and after receiving such homage, shall deliver to him seisin of the inheritance in demand, and the right heir shall then bring an assise of Mortdancester against the tenant, and the tenant shall vouch the lord to warranty by reason of the homage which the lord received of him; we will that in such case the lord shall be bound to warranty and to exchange, although he alleges by exception that he took his homage saving every person's right, since he took the first step to disinherit the right heir. But if no other had claimed the inheritance, and the lord had had no suspicion that another was heir, it would have been reasonable that such a condition in the taking of homage should have been allowable; and in such a case we will that such conditional receptions of homages shall be allowed, but in no other cases.

Lord knowingly investing one not heir, bound to warranty.

Homage taken, with saving of rights, where allowable.

3. If any lord be in seisin of his fee, and be doubtful of

Lord, being in seisin may

253; Fle. 277 (§ 6), 278 (§ 8). fee, et il soit en dotaunce de plusours qi demaundent le heritage, et qi se profrent pur heirs, qi homage il deit prendre, qe il se puse tener en le heritage sauntz rien clamer for qe la seignurie jekes a taunt qe il sache certeynement qi de ceux est plus proschein heir le auncestre qi mort est.

Brac. 252 b; Fle. 278 (§ 8). 4. Et si par cas aveigne qe le frere eynznee et le dreit heir soit hors de pays el tens de la mort le auncestre, et le puisnee frere eit trové le heritage[1] voide, et [2]se seit boté en[2] clamaunt le heritage cum dreit heir, en tel cas porra le seignur prendre le homage cel frere puisnee par tele condicioun, qe la seisine del heritage soit liveré al frere eynznee ou a sa
[179 b.] issue, quant il vendra soen heritage demaunder, qi qe unques en[3] soit tenaunt. Car si le seignur engette le frere puisnee, puis qe il avera esté seisi, il recovera par assise de novele disseisine, a tener neqedent solom la condicioun avauntdite. Et si le seignur soit en seisine, et tiegne hors le frere puisnee, et il se purchace devers le seignur par assise de mort de auncestre, et trové soit par la assise, qe il ad un frere eynznee, soit agardé a ly la seisine par la premere con-

1. vacaunt ou *add. ND.* 2—2. soit seisi en *NDH.* *sim. C.* se seit botee *A.*
3. en *om. NDMC.*

retain it until heir is ascertained. several persons who demand the inheritance and offer themselves as heirs, whose homage he ought to take, such lord may keep himself in the inheritance, without claiming anything but the seigniory, until he be certainly informed which is the nearest heir to the deceased ancestor.

If an elder brother is abroad, the younger is entitled to seisin till his return. 4. If it happens that the elder brother and right heir is out of the country at the time of the death of his ancestor, and the younger brother finds the inheritance vacant, and thrusts himself in, claiming the inheritance as right heir; in such case the lord may take the homage of the younger brother, under condition that seisin of the inheritance be delivered to the elder brother or his issue whenever he shall appear to demand his inheritance, whoever be then tenant. For if the lord eject the younger brother after he has been seised, he shall recover by assise of Novel Disseisin, to hold nevertheless according to the condition aforesaid. And if the lord is in seisin, and keeps out the younger brother, who proceeds against the lord by assise of Mortdancester, and it is found by the assise that he has an elder brother, seisin shall be awarded to him under the before-

dicioun avauntdite. Mes si acun bastard se tiegne en tele seisine, ou nul heir ne se profre al heritage, en tel cas list bien al seignur del engetter fors qe en cas ou sa lounge seisine ly vaut pur title de fraunc tenement pur la negligence ou pur la noun-pusaunce del seignur. Brac. 253; Fle. 278 (§ 8).

5. Et pur ceo voloms nous qe chescun seignur seisise soen fee freschement apres la mort de soen tenaunt, si il le troeve vacaunt. Et si le heir soit de plener age et soit eynz, et ne [1]veut soeffrer[1] le seignur aver la seisine ne ly reconustre[2] pur seignur, en teu cas list bien al seignur de tener [3]sei seisi de[3] soen fee oveke le heir et oveke celi qi se fet heir sauve, qe le seignur nel engette. Et si plus ne puse fere, bien list a ly a destourber tiel heir de user sa seisine, jekes autaunt qe il ly reconuse pur seignur. Et cum il ly reconustra, tauntost [180.] prenge le seignur soen homage et suerté de soen relief, et serment de feuté et de les services a ly leaument fere qe de soen heritage apendent; et sauntz delay ly soit rendu soen heritage et de ceo fraunche administracioun. Brac. 252 b. Brac. 253 b; Fle. 279 (§ 10).

1—1. soeffre mie *ND.* 2. conustre *MAH.* reconusse *ND.* 3—3. seisine de *NDCH.* sey de *S.* sei en *G.*

mentioned condition. But if a bastard keeps himself in seisin, where no heir offers himself for the inheritance, in such case it is lawful for the lord to eject such bastard, except where his long possession through the negligence or weakness of the lord constitutes a valid title to the freehold. **But a bastard may be ejected by the lord.**

5. Therefore it behoves every lord to seize his fee without delay upon the death of his tenant, if he finds it vacant. And if the heir is of full age, and in seisin, and will not suffer the lord to have seisin nor acknowledge him as lord; in such case the lord may lawfully keep himself in seisin, together with the heir or the person who pretends to be heir, but he must not eject him; and if he can do nothing more, he may disturb such heir in the enjoyment of his seisin until he acknowledges him as his lord. When he shall acknowledge him, let the lord forthwith take his homage and security for his relief, and his oath of fealty, and that he will lawfully perform to him the services which belong to his inheritance; and let his inheritance and the free management thereof be then restored to him without delay. **Remedy of lord, where the heir is in seisin and will not acknowledge him.**

Glan. l. 13. c. 2, 3; Brac. 253 *b*; Fle. 279 (§ 10).

6. Et si le seignur [1]eit la premere[1] seisine, et le heir soit de plener age, et le seignur ne [2]voille le conustre a[2] heir, adounc [3]a primes avera leu[3] assise de mort de auncestre. Et cum acun vodra purchacer de nos Justices sur un heritage issi detenu, en primes troeffe surté par pleges conuz de sure sa pleinte, si il les eit prest; et si noun, si maunderoms al viscounte del leu qe il prenge la seurté; et si le pleintif soit si povere qe il ne puse suerté trover, suffit [4]la plevine[4] par sa fey. Et tauntost voloms qe il eit de nous [5]ses brefs qe[5] appendent a sa querele. Et si le pleintif soit de eynz age adounc ne voloms nous mie, qe il troeffe surté de sure sa pleynte, ne terme ne soit mis en soen purchaz.

Brac. 253 *b*.

Brac. 254; Fle. 279 (§ 10); Reg. brev. orig. 224.

Brac. 261 *b*, 267; Fle. 286, 287.

[180 *b*.]

7. Sicum ceste assise est limité entre [6]certeynes persones, ausi est ele limité entre[6] certeins degrez. Car nous voloms, qe de la mort le piere et de la mort la mere et del uncle et del amyteyn[7] et del frere et de la soeur soit assise graunté,

1—1. soit primes en *N*. *sim*. *DA*. eit de ceo la primer *MCH*. 2—2. voille conustre a *L*. *sim*. *SF*. voille conustre le *ND*. luy voille conoistre pur *G*. voile reconustre le *M*. voille conustre al *CH*. 3—3. primes vaut la *D*. *sim*. *N*. a primes vaut la *A*. adeprimes tendra lu *M*. auera il *HC*. 4—4. sa pleuine *M*. la pleinte par sa mayn e *CH*. 5—5. les brefs qe a li *M*. 6—6. so *DM*. *sim*. *NG*. *om*. *LSC*. 7. *so LGS*. amite *N*. aunte *DMCAH*.

When the lord keeps out the heir, his remedy is by assise of Mortdancester.

6. If the lord obtains the first seisin, the heir being of full age, and the lord will not acknowledge him as heir, his first remedy is by assise of Mortdancester. And when any person wishes to proceed before our Justices for an inheritance thus detained from him, let him first find security by known pledges to prosecute his plaint, if he has such pledges ready; and if he has not, we will command the sheriff of the county to take security; and if the plaintiff be so poor that he cannot find security, the pledging of his own faith shall be sufficient; and such writs as his suit requires shall be forthwith granted to him. And if the plaintiff is under age, he need not find security to prosecute his plaint, nor need any term be mentioned in his writ[x].

Pledges to prosecute,

not insisted on, in case of poverty,

nor where plaintiff is a minor.

Degrees of kin, within which Mortdancester lies.

7. As this assise is limited between certain persons, so likewise it is confined within certain degrees; for assise is to be granted of the death of the father, mother, uncle, aunt, brother, and sister, and not ascending higher, as to the grand-

[x] That is, no term of limitation need be named, since, if his immediate ancestor died seised, the minority of the heir is itself a proof of the recent accruer of his title. See Bracton, f. 254.

et ne mie plus haut mountaunt, [1]sicum al[1] ael, ne plus bas descendaunt, sicum[2] al neveu; issi qe de la mort le ael, ne de la mort le neveu tauntsoulement, ne plus haut ne plus pas ne soit james graunté ceste[3] assise. Et pur plus clerement veer des queus auncestres tienent lu cestes assises, porra estre declaré par quatre degrez, dount piere et mere fount un degré, et uncle et amite[4] de part le piere fount un autre degré collateral, et uncle et anteyn[5] de part la mere fount le tierz degré collateral, et le fiz [6]del piere ou de la mere[6], le frere et la soeur de mesme le fiz fount le quart degré en la dreite line descendaunt del piere et de la mere. Et [7]cel quart degré neqedent est devisable[7] [8]en treis[8], sicum piert par ceste figure[9].

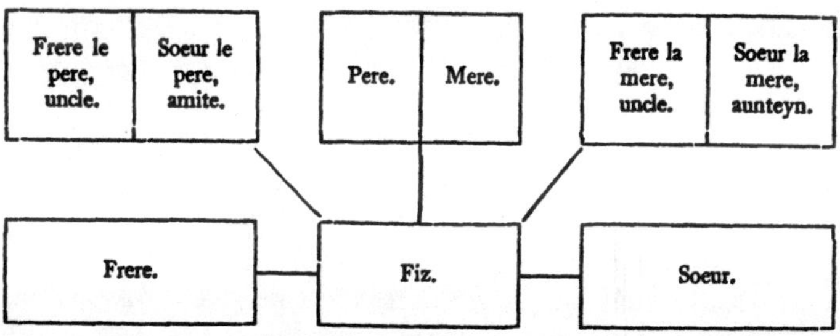

1—1. *so LN. sim. DGSAM.* qe *C.* ke *H.* 2. *conj.* qe *LNDGSMC.* ke *H.* si qe *A.* 3. ceste *om. ND.* 4. *so LS.* aunte *NMGCAH.* 5. *so LS.* aunte *NMGCAH.* 6—6. de pere ou de mere *HC.* del piere e de la miere e *ND.* 7—7. *so LM. sim. GS.* ces iiij. degreez neqedent sount diuisibles *ND. sim. A.* 8—8. en treis *om. M.* 9. figure purtrete *M.* *The figure is wanting in LM, and is variously given in other MSS.*

father, nor descending lower, as to the nephew; so that neither of the death of the grandfather nor of the death of the nephew alone[y], nor in any higher or lower degree is this assise ever allowed. And the more clearly to see of what ancestors this assise lies, let four degrees be set down, of which father and mother make one degree, uncle and aunt on the father's side the second degree collateral, uncle and aunt on the mother's side the third degree collateral, and the child of the father or of the mother, the son's own brother or sister, make the fourth degree in the right line descending from the father and the mother. And this fourth degree is divisible into three, as appears by the above figure.

[y] This word 'alone' appears to have reference to the exception afterwards stated concerning the case of a joint assise. See s. 10.

Brac 261 *b*; Fle. 286, 287.

8. [1]Et si le fiz deyve arramer ceste assise vers acun estraunge de saunc tenaunt, adounc tient bien lu ceste assise de la mort soen piere, et nient la reverse[2]. Car ceste assise suppose touz jours priorité del auncestre, ou a meyns parité[3];
[181.] et veut estre porté de plus bas vers plus haut, amountaunt et nient avalaunt, et ausi de pier en pier, sicum de la mort le frere par le frere ou par la soeur, et de la mort la soeur de
Brac. 254, 254 *b*; Fle. 279.
part le frere ou la soeur. Et si acun en plus loynteyn degré soit eydé par ceste assise, ceo serra plus pur autre persone qe
Post, s. 10.
fet la assise qe pur la sue, sicum apres serra dit. Et pur ceo voloms qe si autre assise [4]severale viegne[4] en jugement de autri mort qe entre [5]ceus deus[5] degrez, si chete l'assise, si autre persone ne soit ajoynte[6] qe face l'assise.

Glan. l. 13. s. 11; Brac. 278 *b*, 281 *b*,

9. Et voloms qe par ceste assise ne par nul bref de possessioun ne puse nule proscheineté de saunc estre trié, et

1. *A new chapter* (c. vij.) *commences here in NDGS, with the heading in N:* Del arramier assise. *So in AR, where the rubric is:* De mort de auncestre. 2. *so LGS.* ou de la mort sa miere e nient la reuerse *add. M. sim. NF.* 3. par alte *N.* 4—4. semblable soit leue *N. sim. DA.* auera qe veigne *C.* suera qe veigne *H.* 5—5. *so NDSM.* deus de ceo *L.* 6. aioynte assentue *ND.* assente *A.* enioynte *H.*

The ancestor must be in the ascending or equal line, not otherwise.

8. And if the son is to institute this assise against any stranger in blood, being tenant, then this assise may well be had of the death of his father, or of the death of his mother, and not in the reverse case[z]. For this assise always supposes priority in the ancestor, or at least equality; and requires to be brought by the lower of the higher, ascending and not descending, and also from equal to equal, as of the death of the brother by the brother or by the sister, and of the death of the sister on behalf the brother or sister. And if any one in a more remote degree is aided by this assise, it will be rather in consequence of some other person who makes the assise, than for himself, as shall be afterwards mentioned. Therefore we will that if any separate assise be brought to trial concerning the death of any person not within these two degrees, the assise shall fall, unless some person is joined who may make good the assise.

Question between persons claiming by

9. Neither by this assise nor by any other possessory writ shall any proximity of blood be tried; that is to say, between

z This appears to imply the possibility of a father claiming as heir to his son, though not by this assise. See post, l. vi. c. 4, s. 4, and note there.

nomément entre demaundaunt et tenaunt qi cleyment par une descente; einz voloms bien qe entre touz estraunges de saunc tiene lu ceste assise, taunt avaunt cum ele se porra [1]estendre. Et ceux procheyns, qi[1] par ceste assise ne porrunt estre succurruz, eynt remedie par nos brefs de cosinage de ael et de aele et de besael et de besaele; les queus brefs ne determinent rien del meer dreit, einz pernent nessaunce de ceste assise et determinent par jureez le dreit de la possessioun. Et ausi voloms qe ceste assise tiene lu entre privez del saunc, cleymauntz par diverses descentes, sicum entre deus freres de divers pieres ou[2] de diverses meres. Car le frere engendrez de autre piere est tut estraunge a demaunder rien de la mort le pere ou del auncestre le autre frere; et en mesme la manere de deus freres de diverses meres. Mes entre frere muylleré et frere bastard seisi del heritage le muylleré ne gist pas ceste assise. Car la proeve de la proscheineté de saunc ne put estre trié par nul plee de possessioun.

282, 283; Fle. 287 (§ 6, 7), 288, 307.

Brac. 267, 281; Fle. 306.

Brac. 267, 282 *b*, 283.

[181 *b*.]

Brac. 267, 280; Fle. 287 (§ 7).

10. Et acune foiz sount joyntz ensemble deus persones ou trois en divers degrez, as queus affiert remedie par assise de mort de auncestre, dount la nature est medlé de mort de

Brac. 254, 254 *b*; Fle. 279.

1—1. esteyndre entre proscheyns. E qi *ND*. 2. so *NDMCAH*. et *L*. e *SG*.

demandant and tenant claiming by the same descent; but between all strangers in blood the assise shall lie so far as it may extend. And such kindred as cannot be aided by this assise shall have their remedy by our writs of Cosinage, of Ael, Aele, Besael, and Besaele; which writs do not determine anything of the mere right, but spring out of this assise, and determine by means of juries the right of possession. The assise however takes place among privies of blood claiming by different descents, as between two brothers by different fathers or by different mothers. For the brother begotten by any other father is an entire stranger, so far as concerns the demanding of anything upon the death of the father or ancestor of the other brother, and so of two brothers born of different mothers. But this assise does not lie between a legitimate brother and a bastard seised of the other's inheritance, because the proof of the proximity of blood cannot be tried by any possessory plea.

the same descent, not tried by assise.

Writs of Cosinage for more remote degrees.

10. Sometimes two or three persons in different degrees are joined together, and obtain their remedy by assise of Mortdancester, where the plea partakes of the nature of an

Where of coparceners one only is in the first degree they may join in an assise;

auncestre et de cosinage; ausi cum un heritage descendeit de un cep a deus persones, qe fount[1] un heir par diverses lines, sicum a acune fille de une part, en qi persone tient lu assise de mort de auncestre, et a acun neveu de une autre fille en qi persone tient lu bref de ael, a quel degré assise de mort de auncestre ne se estent poynt. En queus cas nous voloms qe les reconisours del assise viegnent reconustre sur lur serment, si le piere ou la mere de[2] la fille, ou le ael [3]ou la aele[3] del neveu fust seisi en soen demeyne, etc.[4] Et ceo qe est dit de la [5]seisine le[5] ael ou [6]la aele[6] devers le neveu, purra estre dit et usé pur ley de lour freres et de lour soeurs, uncles et amites[7] la fille et cosins le neveu, desicum il sount en mesme le degré qe sount ael et aele; mes plus haut ne se estent point assise de mort de auncestre.

11. Et pur ceo qe il i ad plus hastif remedie en assise de
[182.] mort de auncestre qe en le plé de cosinage del [8]ael, voloms

1. *so GCH. sim. M.* sount *LNDSA.* 2. *so on eras. N.* ou *LDMGSCAHF.* 3—3. *so ND.* ou le ale *L.* ou le ael *M.* del aele G. ou le aele *SC. om. AH.* 4. cum de fee, etc. *N.* 5—5. assise de *ND.* 6—6. *so H.* le ael (*corrected* la aele) *L.* la ele *M.* aele *A.* de aele *ND.* de la aele *G.* del aele *S.* 7. *so LS.* auntes *NDMCH.* antes *A.* 8. ou de *NDAM.* ou del *GSCH.*

as daughter and grandson; assise of Mortdancester and of Cosinage; as in the case of an inheritance which descended from one stock to two persons, constituting a single heir, by different lines, as to a daughter on the one side, in whose person the assise of Mortdancester takes place, and to a grandson by another daughter on the other side, in whose person the writ of Ael lies, being in a degree to which assise of Mortdancester does not extend. In the which case we will that the recognitors of the assise come and make recognisance upon their oath, whether the father (or mother) of the daughter, and the grandfather (or grandmother) of the grandson was seised in his demesne, &c. And what is said of the seisin of the grandfather or grandmother as regards the grandson may also be said and reputed for law concerning their brothers and sisters, uncles and aunts of the daughter, and cousins[a] to the grandson, since they are in the same degree with the grandfather and grandmother; but higher the assise of Mortdancester does not ascend.

niece and great-nephew.

In such cases one party cannot proceed without the other

11. And because there is more speedy remedy in the assise of Mortdancester than in the plea of Cosinage de Ael, we will

[a] That is, as I understand, great-uncles and great-aunts.

nous qe tels pleintifs eynt remedie par assise de mort de auncestre, lequel qe il se voillent joyndre en une pleynte ou noun, issi qe la fille ne se puse purchacer par assise sauntz nomer le neveu el bref ou la issue del neveu, en quel degré qe il soit trové, ne qe le neveu ou sa issue se puse purchacer par bref de cosinage vivaunt la fille qe est sa parcenere[1] et plus proscheyne par un degré ou par plusours. Car la plus proscheyne persone fet l'assise et tret a sei la persone en plus loynteyn degré. Brac. 254 *b* (§ 4); Fle. 279.

12. Et sount autres brefs aukes semblables a ceste dreyne double accioun, ausi cum de la mort le uncle et la aunte[2] en heritage partable, ou en chescun cas deyvent estre joyntz en une accioun le neveu al uncle et al aunte[3] en assise de mort de auncestre, la quele accioun ne est mie medlé oveke cosinage; et ou les reconisours del assise deyvent venir reconustre sour lour sermentz, si le uncle ou la aunte de par le piere ou antein[4] de par la mere le neveu demaundaunt de Brac. 254 *b* (§ 5); Fle. 279 (§ 2).

1. parente parcenere *M.* aunte *H.* *om. NDA.* 2. amite *S G.* 3. amite *S.* 4. acon *M.*

that such plaintiffs have relief by assise of Mortdancester, whether the parties wish to join in one plaint or not, so that the daughter shall not be able to proceed by an assise without naming in the writ the grandson or his issue in whatsoever degree found; nor can the grandson or his issue proceed by writ of Cosinage in the lifetime of the daughter who is his co-parcener and nearer by one degree or more. For the nearest person makes the assise, and draws to itself the person in the more remote degree.

12. There are other writs somewhat resembling this last double action, as of the death of the uncle or aunt in a partible inheritance[b]; where in every case the nephew ought to be joined in the same action with the uncle and the aunt in an assise of Mortdancester, and this action is not mixed with Cosinage; and the recognitors of the assise ought to come and make recognisance upon their oath whether the uncle or the aunt on the father's or mother's side of the nephew demandant Similar joinder in assise for a partible inheritance.

b It will be remembered that in early times, by common custom, tenements in socage were partible or divisible among the sons. See Glan. l. 7, c. 3; l. 13, s. 11; Brac. 76; Fle. 309 (§ 2).

une part, et le frere ou la soeur le uncle ou la aunte [1]de par le autre[1] demaundaunt, qi heirs ceux deus demaundauntz sount, fust [2]seisi ou seisie[2] en soen demeyne.

Brac. 254 *b*; Fle. 279, 280.

13. Et si le heritage ne soit mie partable, et le uncle arrayme assise de mort d'auncestre de la mort soen piere ou sa meere ou soen uncle ou sa aunte [3]ou sa antein[3], et le [182 *b*.] neveu del frere porte bref de cosinage de mesmes les tenementz devers mesmes les estraunges persones, ou si ambideus eynt arramé assise de mort de auncestre vers une estraunge persone ceo est a saver, le neveu de la mort soen uncle, [4]et la antein ou[4] le uncle mesmes celi neveu[5] de la mort del frere ou de la soeur, en ambideus les cas est le neveu receivable al heritage plus tost qe le uncle. Et si acun des deus demaunde vers autre par assise ou par cosinage heritage descendaunt de un cep, en tel cas soit jugé pur le possessour, si le tenaunt cleyme par mesme la descente qe le demaundaunt fet, tut eit le demaundaunt majour[6] dreit; et puis se purchace par bref de dreit, le quel soul bref detrie la proscheineté del saunc et le dreit.

Brac. 254 *b*, 281 *b*, 282; Fle. 280.

1—1. del autre part *M*. 2—2. en seisine *ND*. 3—3. so *L*. *sim. SC*. *om. NDMAH*. 4—4. ou aunte e *ND*. e launte ou *A*. *sim. MH*. et la aunteine ou *C*. *sim. F*. 5. so *NDGAMCH*. uncle *LS*. 6. meur *NDA*. meillour *H*.

on the one part, and the brother or the sister of the uncle or the aunt on the side of the other demandant, whose heirs these two demandants are, was seised in his or her demesne.

Where an inheritance is not partible, the son of the elder son excludes his uncle.

13. Where the inheritance is not partible, and the uncle brings an assise of Mortdancester of the death of his father or mother, uncle or aunt, and the nephew by the brother brings a writ of Cosinage for the same tenement against the same strangers, or if both have instituted an assise of Mortdancester against the same stranger, that is to say, the nephew, upon the death of his uncle or aunt, and the uncle of the same nephew, upon the death of his brother or sister; in both these cases the nephew is to be received to the inheritance before the uncle. And if one of them either by assise or by Cosinage demands against the other an inheritance descending from the same stock; in such case it shall be adjudged in favour of whichever party is in possession, if the tenant claims by the same descent as the demandant does, although the demandant may have a better right; and let him afterwards proceed by writ of right, by which writ alone the proximity of blood and the right can be tried.

But if the uncle is in possession, the nephew must proceed by writ of right.

14. Et si acun estraunge deforce as parceners lour heritages, sicum chief seignur ou autre, et acuns soint diligentz de lour heritages[1] demaunder, et acuns negligentz, si covendra as diligentz, un ou plusours, fere sa pleynte [2]et soen[2] purchaz es nouns des trestouz les parceners, qi ne ount mie lour purparties, [3]pur la unité[3] del dreit qe remeynt en sa unité[4] avaunt la devisioun; adounc sue qi vodera; et ceux, qi sure voderount, averount remedie par ceste assise de la mort lour commun auncestre. Fle. 315 (§ 40).

15. Mes pur ceo qe ceste assise ne tient poynt lu par entre privez del saunc, et nomément par entre parceners, qi sount [183.] ausi cum un heir, voloms attamer en partie, par queles accioun et par queus brefs et coment un parcener deit chacer ses parceners a fere severalté de lour heritage qe il tienent en commun, issi qe chescun sache soen several, et qe chescun eit sa renable porcioun solom soen afferraunt; et si acun soit de tut deforcé par ses parceners, coment et par quel bref il deit aver soen recoverer, et par quel bref il deit recoverer

1. *so M.* homage *L.* heritage *NDSGACH.* 2—2. ou soen *LNS.* *sim. DG.* e son *M.* e si un *CH.* 3—3. *conj.* qi limite *LS.* qe limite *NDA.* *sim. F.* qe est limite *G.* qi la vnite *M.* limite *C.* limitez *HB.* 4. vertue *CHB.*

14. If any stranger, as, for example, the chief lord or other, deforce parceners of their inheritance, and some of them are diligent in demanding their inheritances and others negligent, it behoves the diligent, whether one or more, to make his plaint and purchase his writ in the names of all the parceners who have not their portions, by reason of the unity of the right, which remains united until division; after which any party who will may sue; and those who choose to sue shall have remedy by this assise of the death of their common ancestor.

Parcener must sue in the name of his co-parceners.

Secus, after partition.

15. Whereas this assise does not lie between privies of blood, and in particular between parceners who take as one heir, we propose, before more is said of the assise, in part to explain by what actions, and by what writs, and how one parcener may compel his other parceners to make severance of their inheritance which they hold in common, so that each may know his several, and that each may have his reasonable portion according to his due; and if any one be deforced of the whole by his parceners, how and by what writ he may

Proceedings between parceners, subject of following chapter.

partie, cum il soit de partie disseisi; einz ceo qe plus soit dit de ceste assise.

CHAPITRE VII. [LXXI.]

De Accioun mixte.

Brac. 102 *b*, 369 *b*, 443 *b*; Fle. 309.

1. Une manere de accioun i ad pledable en nostre court qe est appelé mixte, pur taunt qe ele touche la persone vers qi la demaunde est fete, et estre ceo touche la chose demaundé; et par taunt est ele pledable par personeles destresces et ausi par reales, sicum par le graunt *Cape* et par le petit; sicum est accioun a severer chose tenue en commun, et ou chescun est pleintif et chescun defendaunt, sicum en cas ou acuns estraunges persones sauntz affinité ou parenté ount [1]entre eus[1] acune chose a severer[2] qe il tienent en [183 *b*.] commun, sicum est des veisins qi voillent par plee[3] departer acun tenement entre eus, issint qe chescun i eyt severalté. Brac. 443 *b*; Fle. 309 (§ 2). Et si ad une autre manere de accioun mixte, qe est appelé

1—1. entree en *N*. 2. ceo *add. N*. 3. so *DMSGLAH*. *sim. N*. plee *om. L*.

have redress, and by what writ he may recover part if he be disseised of part.

CHAPTER VII.

Of a mixed Action.

Mixed action, partly real and partly personal.

1. There is a kind of action which may be tried in our court, called a mixed action, inasmuch it concerns the person against whom the demand is made as well as the thing demanded; and therefore is pleadable by personal distresses and by real also, as by the great and little *Cape*. Of such kind is an action to sever a thing held in common, wherein each party is plaintiff and defendant, as where strangers without affinity or kindred have something to be divided between them which they hold in common, as in the case of neighbours who proceed by action to divide some tenement between them, so that each may have severalty. Another kind of mixed action

Action for partition between strangers.

Partition between coheirs.

en la ley le Emperour, accioun [1]de la mesnee dame de Herciscunde[1], et tient lu entre ceux qi ount un commun heritage a departir.

2. Deus accciouns nequedent [2]ne nessent[2] mie tauntost cum le heritage ou autre chose est tenue entre ceux[3] parceners en commun, mes de tel tens qe acun de eus comence a chacer a[4] la divisioun. Et ceste accioun tient lu entre plusours parceners et un heir; sicum est en cas ou plusours freres ou soeurs ou lour issue tienent un heritage en commun sicum un heir, et voillent pleder a la divisioun, issi[5] qe chescun use[6] sa purpartie en severauté. Et ausi tient ele lu par entre parceners qi sount cum un heir de acun tenement commun qe il vodereint fere severer et qe est divisable par la resoun Brac. 443 *b*; Fle. 309.

1—1. *so S. sim. G.* de la mesme dame de hertisounde *L.* de la mesnee la dame de Herciscunde *M.* de meine la dame desheriteson *A.* la Meysnee la dame Hertisoun de mesme la descente del heritage *ND.* de la Monee dame de Hertescoumbe *CH. sim. B.* de la mesne dame deseritisoun de *F.* 2—2. sount qe ne ne suent *N. sim. D.* 3. tiels *N. sim. DH.* touz *M.* 4. a *om. ND.* 5. *so MF.* si *LNDSGA.* issint *CH.* 6. *so NDAMCH.* eust *L.* vst *SG.* eit *F.*

is that called in the Imperial law *actio familiæ herciscundæ*[c], which takes place between those who have a common inheritance to divide.

2. Nevertheless two actions[d] do not arise as soon as the inheritance or other thing is held between such parceners in common, but from the time that any of them begins to compel the others to a division. And this action obtains among several parceners and coheirs, as where several brothers[e] or sisters or their issue hold an inheritance in common as one heir, and wish to proceed for a division, so that every one may have his portion in severalty. It also lies between parceners who are as one heir in respect of a common tenement which they are desirous of having divided, and which is divisible by reason of Action, when it arises. Action between co-parceners.

c 'Nota hic de actione que dicitur Familia Herciscunde.' (Note in MS. *N.*) The word *herciscundæ*, (from *herciscere*, 'to divide,') which is scarcely found except in this connection, appears to have been taken for a proper name by our author or his transcribers.

d The word *cestes*, 'these,' appears to be wanting at the beginning of this sentence. In Bracton it is, 'Sed hæ duæ actiones;' but in Fleta we find, 'Sed duæ actiones.' Accepting the omission, we should perhaps translate the words, 'double or mixed action.' As to the relation of this work to Fleta, see the Introduction by the Editor.

e The words 'brothers or' seem to have crept into the text by mistake. The two cases intended in this and the following clause are, first, where a tenement is divisible by the common law among sisters; secondly, where a tenement is divisible by custom (par la resoun del tenement) among brothers. See the corresponding passage in Bracton and Fleta.

del tenement. Et cestes accioun sount appelez mixtes, pur ceo qe chescun est pleintif et chescun defendaunt. Car cist est pleintif qe primes se pleynt.

Brac. 443 *b*, 444; Fle. 309, 310.

3. Et en ces deus cas, si acun parcener demaunde devers autre sa renable partie, et le tenaunt, un ou plusours, face defaute, par taunt serra pris en nostre meyn [1]de tut le entier del[1] commun heritage solom la porcioun qe affiert al pleintif; [184.] et issi sera la destresce reale et ne mie personele. Et tiel deit estre le proces del plee de renable partie, et ceo plee tient lu en cas ou acun est dedit de estre parcener et deforcé de sa purpartie. Mes en cas ou touz sount conuz as heirs et as parceners, ne deit estre nul plee de renable partie, [2]coment qe plee neesse qe acun[2] eit meyns a sa purpartie qe aver ne deit.

Brac. 71 *b*; Fle. 310 (§ 4); Post, c. 9.

Brac. 71 *b*; Fle. 310 (§ 4).

4. Et pur ceo affiert[3] en tiel cas, qe tauntost cum tels parceners averount fet lour homages a lour chiefs seignurs, et voillent qe heritage[4] soit divisé par entre eus, issi qe chescun sache sa porcioun severale, soit la estente primes fete, et par

1—1. de tote leur terre del *C.* *sim. H.* 2—2. coment qe asqun se pleigne qil *A.* cum si aqun se pleygne *N.* *sim. D.* coment qe le plee cesse qasqun *C.* *sim. H.* 3. affiert a fere *N.* est a fere *A.* 4. so *LSM.* le heritage *NDGHC.* *sim. A.*

Mixed actions, second reason why so called.

the tenement. These actions are called mixed, because either party is plaintiff and either defendant, that party being plaintiff who first complains.

Process in action by parcener.

3. In these two cases, if any parcener demand against another his reasonable share, and the tenant or the tenants make default, there shall be taken into our hand, out of the entire common inheritance, the proportion which belongs to the plaintiff; and thus the distress will be real and not personal. And such shall be the proceeding in a plea *de rationabili parte*, which takes place where one is denied to be a parcener and is deforced of his share. But where all are acknowledged to be heirs and parceners, there should be no plea *de rationabili parte*, although an action may arise on account of one of them having less for his share than he ought to have.

Plea *de rationabili parte.*

Partition, how made.

4. It is proper therefore in such case, as soon as the parceners have performed their homage to their chief lords and are desirous to have their inheritance divided between them, so that each may know his several portion, that an extent

la resoun del estente soit fete entre eus la divisioun. Et si tels parceners voillent estre eydez par nous a cele divisioun fere, par quei gent jurgent de leaument fere, adounc maunderoms al viscounte, al purchaz de acun pleintif parcener, qe par chevalers et autres bones gentz del counté en presence des parceners, si il i voillent estre, face estendre totes les terres et touz les tenementz, qe furent a un tiel commun auncestre des parceners en tiel counté; et solom cele estente soit fete a chescun parcener la liveré de sa purpartie.

5. La estente soit fete en ceste manere. En primes soit enquis par serment des jurours, cum bien les edifices el chief maner et les fossez et les vivers et les hayes et les estaungs et les autres[1] pescheries vaillent par an de cleer, allouwé les reprises. Puis soit enquis de la verreye value des gardins curtilages columbers et des autres issues de eynz la court; et puis quantz des champs et des cutures sount en demeyne, et cum bien des acres chescune cuture tient, et cum bien chescune acre[2] vaut par an; et

Extenta Manerii (Stat. temp. incert.); Brac. 75; Fle. 157, 310.

[184 *b*.]

1. parties *add. D.* autres *om. G.* 2. cuture *H.*

should first be taken, and that according to the extent partition should be made between them. And if such parceners would have our aid in making the division, whereby an oath is taken to do it lawfully, then at the request of any plaintiff parcener we will command the sheriff that he do by knights and other good men of the county, in the presence of the parceners, if they will be there, cause an extent to be made of all the lands and tenements which were of such an one, (the common ancestor of the parceners,) in such a county; and according to this extent livery shall be made of his share to every parcener.

Writ of partition.

5. The extent shall be made in this manner[f]. First let an inquest be taken upon the oath of the jurors, how much the buildings in the capital manor, and the moats, vivaries, hays, pools, and other fisheries, are worth by the year, clear of outgoings. Then let the true value be inquired of the gardens, curtilages, dovecots, and the other issues within the court; then how many fields and closes of arable land there are in demesne, and how many acres each close contains, and how

Extent to be made of mansion and appurtenances;

Demesne lands.

[f] This section much resembles the ancient summary, called *Extenta manerii*, printed among the *Statuta temporis incerti*, in the Statutes at large.

quaunt des acres de pree i seynt [1]en demeyne et cum bien chescune acre vaut par an; et quaunt des acres i soint[1] de chescune manere de pasture et a quaunt des bestes suffisauntes, et a quele manere des bestes, et cum bien la pasture de une[2] beste vaut par an solom la manere de chescune beste. Et ceste article compreigne ausi bien commune de pasture as berbyz as porcs et as chevers cum pasture severale as boefs et as vaches et a genices et as harascz[3] des jumentz et des poleyns en boys ou en parcs ou en cloistures ou aylours en lour severals. Et puis soit enquis de mesmes les boys, cum bien chescune acre vaut par an, ou pur tener a boscage, ou pur assartir et cutefier[4]; et cum bien des acres les parcs et les autres demeynes boys contiegnent; et puis de la value de renables estovers en autri soil, cum bien vaillent par an, sicum de boys pur edifier, pur clore, pur arder, et de pescher en autri rivere[5], et de fouwer en autri soil ou en soil commun[6], et des autres choses necessaries. Et puis soit enquis

1—1. e quantz e cum bien *ND*. 2. chescune *NG*. 3. haras *N*. haraz *SGAMCH*. 4. cotiuer *SGMA*. coutiuer *C*. curtiner *H*. 5. viuer *N*. soil *G*. riuere combien vaile par an *M*. 6. E cum bien il vaillent par an sicum de pescherie en autri viuer e de syer en autri soyl ou en soyl commun *add*. *N*. *sim*. *D*.

much every acre is worth by the year; and how many acres of meadow there are in demesne, and how much every acre is worth by the year; and how many acres there are of every kind of pasture, and sufficient for how many beasts, and what kind of beasts, and how much the pasturage of one beast is worth by the year according to the kind of beast. Under this article is comprised as well common of pasture for sheep, hogs, and goats, as pasture several for oxen, cows, and heifers, and for studs of mares and colts in woods or parks, or in enclosures or elsewhere in their severals. Afterwards let inquiry be made concerning the said woods, how much each acre is worth by the year, to keep as wood, or to assart and improve; and how many acres the parks and the other demesne woods contain; then, of the value of the reasonable estovers from land belonging to others, how much they are worth by the year, as wood for building, fencing, and burning, and rights of fishing in another's river, and of digging turfs in another's soil or in some common soil, and other necessaries. Afterwards let inquiry be made of honey, and of pannage, and

Pastures. Woods. Estovers. Easements. Profits of forests and commons.

de mel et de pannage et de pesson [1]des glans[1] des noyz et de autre manere des fructz, et de tote manere de comodité issaunt de foreste, de boys, de mores[2], de brueres, de turberies, de gastines, et totes autres comoditez issauntes de commune, cum bien vaillent par an. Et puis de rentes issauntz des feez[3] apurtenauntz al maner, et des rentes dues al maner pur[4] commune [5]grauntee es[5] feez del maner, et de totes autres maneres de rentes. Et puis des molins, vivers foreyns, pescheries severales, cum bien vaillent par an. Et puis des plez et de purchaz des courtz, et de fraunchises, marchez, garrennes, conigers, travers[6], tolunes[7], custumes[8], vewes de fraunplege, et des issues annueles de chescune manere de fraunchises. Et puis des avowesouns des eglises, cum bien chescune eglise vaut par an; et des sutes des fraunes tenauntz, cum bien chescune sute vaut par[9] chescune defaute. Et ausi soit enquis des eydes, des presentz, [10]des herietz[10] et de chescun manere de annuel regard. Et puis des vileyns, et de villenages soint estenduz les mees several- [185.]

1—1. de glaan *ND.* de glaund *M.* 2. mareis *C.* Mareys *H.* 3. fiez e des tenemenz *M.* 4. *so SGMCH.* par *LNDA.* 5—5. *so LSG.* grauntee as *ND.* grauntee en *M.* graunt en *A.* 6. trauers *om. A.* 7. tolunes en feyres *ND.* tonuz *M.* tounues *HC.* 8. Weyfs *add. ND.* *sim. CH.* 9. pur *NMA.* 10—10. *om. LS.* des herietes *G.* de herreez *M.* des ayes *ND.* *sim. CH.* as heirs *A.*

of mast of acorns, nuts, and other kinds of fruit, and of all manner of profits arising from forests, woods, moors, heaths, turbaries, wastes, and every other kind of commodity issuing from commons, how much they are worth by the year. Then, of rents issuing out of the fees belonging to the manor, and of rents due to the manor for common granted in the fees of the manor, and of all other sorts of rents. Next, of mills, vivaries out of the manor, and several fisheries, how much they are worth by the year. Then, of pleas and perquisites of courts and of franchises, markets, warrens, rabbit-warrens, traverses, tolls, customs, and views of frank pledge, and of the yearly issues of every kind of franchise: and then, of the advowsons of churches, how much each church is worth by the year; and of the suits of freeholders, how much each suit is worth upon every default. It should also be inquired concerning aids, presents, heriots, and every kind of annual compliment. And afterwards, of villains, and of the villenages let every house be separately extended, and then their closes,

Rents.

Mills, foreign vivaries, several fisheries.

Profits of courts, and franchises.

Advowsons.

Suits of freeholders.

Aids, &c.

Villain tenements

ment, et puis lour cutures, lour pretz, lour pastures; et puis lour rentes, lour services, lour taillages, et lour custumes.

6. Et la greyndre estente soit enroullé ensemblement
[185 *b*.] oveke le verdit. Et pur le marc en la value del eglise, soit
Brac. 75 *b*; Fle. 158 (§ 10.) mis le soud en la estente, issi qe si la eglise vaille par an cent marcs, adounc soit la annuele value estendue a cent soudz. Et solom cele estente, soit fet a la vaillaunce de terre a ceux qi ne tendrount[1] mie le avowesoun del eglise. Car avowesoun ne est mie departable; mes si le avowesoun dust estre vendue, adounc serroit le[2] renable pris solom la value del eglise en un an. Et cele[3] estente, cum ele serra issi fete, soit enroullé et enselé desuth les seaus des estendours jurez.

Brac. 75 (§ 16); Fle. 312 (§ 11). 7. Et si les parceners soint en present, si lour soit demaundé si acun sache dire pur quei acun qi se dist estre parcener ne deit mie aver sa purpartie de cel heritage. Et cum declaré sera cum bien deverount departer le heritage, ou cum nul ne severa dire qe touz ne deyvent partir, ou si nul
Brac. 75 *b*; Fle. 312. des parceners ne viegne, si la somounse soit testmoigné, tauntost soit le heritage parti en taunt des parties cum il i

1. so *ND*. rendrount *L*. *sim*. *AMSCH*. 2. mis *ND*. 3. so *NGM*. tiele *L*. *sim*. *SCH*.

meadows, and pastures; also their rents, services, talliages, and customs.

Sum of extent. Mode of valuing advowsons. 6. The whole amount of the extent shall be entered on a roll, together with the verdict. And for every marc in the value of a church, one shilling shall be put in the extent; so that if the church be worth one hundred marcs a year, the yearly value shall be extended at a hundred shillings; and according to this valuation those who do not keep the advowson of the church shall be compensated in land. For an advowson is not divisible; but if it were to be sold, the reasonable price
Record of extent. would be according to the annual value of the church. This extent being so made, shall be enrolled and sealed under the seals of the sworn extendors.

Number of parceners ascertained. 7. If the parceners are present, they shall be asked whether any of them can show cause why any person who calls himself a parcener ought not to have his share of the inheritance. And when it is declared how many are to divide the inheritance, or where no cause can be shewn why all should not share, or if none of the parceners appear, and the summons is
Partition. proved, let the inheritance be forthwith divided into so many

ad parceners, solom la resoun del estente, issint qe chescune partie soit severé de autre par divises et par boundes.

8. Et puis soint les parceles [1]entrez et especefiez[1] en plusours escrowes, et celes escrouwes soint liverez a un lay homme qi rien de lettre ne seet ne del fet, et celi livere a chescun parcener un escrouwe. Et solom le sort de celes escrouwes se tiegne chescun parcener a sa purpartie. Et si acun i fet amendement ou enpirement, taunt cum la terre eit esté en sa meyn en partie ou en tut, cel damage soit allouwé en la estente a[2] celi qi le fist, et ausi soit sa porcioun encrue[3] solom le amendement qe il avera fet.

Brac. 75 *b*; Fle. 312 (§ 13).

[186.]

Brac. 75 (§ 16); Fle. 312 (§ 11).

9. Et si le viscounte sursete de ceo fere, si maunderoms dounc as Corouners [4]du pays[4], ou nous assigneroms acune Justice par nos lettres patentes de ceo fere. Car teles liverez si aerdent mout pres del dreit pur les boundes mettre; et pur ceo ad il mester qe sagement et bien et leaument soint teles devisiouns fetes.

Brac. 75 (§ 17); Fle. 312 (§ 12).

1—1. *so verb. ND.* entrez enteres especifiez *L.* enteres especefiez *G. sim. S.* entiers entreez e especefiez *M.* especefiez *C.* 2. *so DA.* et *L.* e *SGMC.* a *interl. N.* 3. *so verb. GMC.* entre *L. sim. S.* encrue e entree *ND.* 4—4. *om. M.*

parts as there are parceners, according to the extent, so that each portion may be severed from the other by divisions and bounds.

8. Afterwards let the parcels be entered and specified in several scrolls, and let those scrolls be delivered to some layman who knows nothing of letters or of the contents, and let him deliver one scroll to each parcener; and according to the lot of those scrolls let each parcener take to his share. And if any of the parceners has improved or damaged the land while it was in his hands, either in part or in the whole, let such damage be taken into account in the extent against the person who did it, and likewise let his portion be increased according to the improvement he may have made.

Allotment of parcels.

Allowance for improvement or damage.

9. If the sheriff be negligent in this matter, we will send our precept to the coroners of the district, or we will assign by our letters patent some Justice to execute it. For such delivery of shares touches very nearly upon the right of property by reason of the assignment of boundaries; and it is therefore necessary that such partitions be discreetly, properly, and lawfully made.

Precept for partition may be to coroner, or Justice.

Brac. 75 *b*; Fle. 312 (§13). 10. Et lequel qe teles liverez soint fetes par sort, ou par lour eleccioun, issi qe le eynznee parcener elise premerement, et issi chescun apres autre solom les degrez de lour ages, tauntost soint les parceles enbrevez [1]en roulle[1], quele[2] la parcele soit et cum bien, et par entre[3] queles boundes est [4]liveré la parcele et[4] a quel parcener par noun, issi qe totes les parceles de chescune purpartie soint enroullez ausi bien de demeynes cum de feez et de services et cum douwaries ou autres terres tenues en acune manere a terme de vie et qe deivent revertir apres le desces des tenauntz, et a qi celes terres deivent reverter, et a qi des parceners les services de tels tenauntz furent assignez. Et celi a qi acun service est assigné en purpartie tauntost prenge homage de celi tenaunt; et en le meen tens soit assigné a celi qi deit attendre la re-
[186 *b.*] versioun une porcioun de[5] tenement a tener, a la vaillaunce de[6] cele terre qe ly dust reverter, jekes au taunt qe cele terre ly eschete.

1—1. e enroulleez *N.* 2. quele qe *M.* 3. entre *om. M.* 4—4. liueree e *N. sim. A.* liuerez *M.* liuere *C. sim. H.* 5. *so NAMC.* de une *LH.* 6. del *AM.* dun *C.*

Parcels of each share to be enrolled. 10. And whether such deliveries are made by lot, or by election, the eldest parcener choosing first, and so one after the other according to their ages, let the parcels be presently imbreviated on a roll, that is to say, what each parcel is, and how much, and between what bounds the parcel is assigned, and to what parcener by name, so that all the parcels of each share be enrolled[g], as well demesnes as fees and services and dowers or other lands held in any manner for term of life, which are to revert after the death of the tenants, and to whom these lands are to revert, and to which of the parceners the services of such tenants are assigned. And he to whom any service is assigned towards his share shall forthwith take the homage of the tenant; and he who has to await the reversion shall have assigned to him in the meantime a portion of some other tenement according to the value of the land which is to revert to him, to be held until that land falls in.

Seigniories and reversions, how disposed.

[g] 'Upon a division being made, each parcener has a like title to his several. This title, when the division is made by the king's mandate, is a title of law, and requires to be vouched by record. But division made by assent of parties requires to be averred by specialty of writing, upon which issue shall be joined (le averrement se joyndra).' Note in MS. *N.*

11. Et cum acun des parceners moerge[1] apres la departie fete, et ne eit point des heirs de soen cors engendrez, adounc acrestra sa purpartie as autres parceners et a lour issue, a partir par[2] entre eus par ouweles porciouns, ne mie neqedent par successioun de heritage, car nul ne est autri heir, mes par dreit de accres. Brac. 77 b; Fle. 315 (§ 30) Ante, l. ii, c. 2. s. 11.

12. Et [3]si acun parcener soit[3], qe ne se tiegne mie apayé de tele partisoun, si froms nous venir le proces et le record devaunt nos Justices du baunc; et la die le pleintif en qi hom eit erré, et illucs soint les errours redrescez par novele estente si mestier soit; et[4] apres les assignementz fetz des purparties par sort ou par eleccioun, soit fete la seisine par jugement de nostre court. Brac. 75 b; Fle. 312 (§ 12). Brac. 77, 77 b; Fle. 314, 315.

1. murra *NH.* *sim. AMC.* 2. par *om. NMC.* 3—3. *so verb. NAMCH.* sicum parcener acun i soit *L.* 4. et *om. L.* e *NGC.*

11. If any one of the parceners die after the partition, not having any heir of his body begotten, then his share shall accrue to the other parceners or their issue, to be divided between them by equal portions, yet not by succession of inheritance, for none of them is heir to the other, but by right of accruer[h]. Accruer of shares.

12. And if any one of the parceners is not contented with the partition, we will cause the proceedings and the record to come before our Justices of the Bench; and the plaintiff shall there state what errors have been made, and the errors shall be there redressed by a new extent if need be. And after assignment of the shares, either by lot or election, let seisin be executed by judgment of our court. Unequal partition, how redressed.

h 'Whereas it is said that the parceners shall have the proportion of the one who dies by right of accruer, our companions say (si dient nos compaygnons) that this is not so. For after division, each parcener is inherited of his portion (est enhite de sa purpartie), as if he had purchased of a stranger; and if he had purchased of a stranger, and died without issue, his brothers or sisters would be his heirs.' (Note in MS. *N.*) The statement in the text, that the portion is taken *per jus accrescendi*, is derived from Bracton, who however does not say that the parceners are not heirs to each other.

CHAPITRE VIII. [LXXII.]

De Heritage devisable.

Brac. 75 b, 76; Fle. 312. 1. Touz heritages ne cheent mie uniement en divisioun ne en hochepot, a partir entre parceners; sicum sount chief maners ou chiefs chasteus de countez ou de baronies, et sicum parcs et vivers et avouwesouns de eglises. De heritage neqedent devisable avera le eynznee ou la eynzneesce pur la priorité de soen age le chief mees a sa purpartie, si cel mees
[187.] ne soit chief del counté ou de baronie, sicum desus est dit, pur le dreit del espeye, qe ne suffre divisioun, et[1] aventure qe la force del reaume ne defaille par taunt, la quele force fust primes establie [2]et devisé[2] [3]par countez et baronies[3].

Brac. 76 b; Fle. 313 (§ 16). 2. Mes si il eynt plusours chiefs mees, ou chasteus de countez ou de baronies, adounc porrount ceux chasteus ou ceux mees estre partiz, issi neqedent qe il remeignent en lour entierteez, sauve al eynznee ou a la eynznesce soen dreit de sa prerogative, issi qe la premere eleccioun soit sue. Car en teus cas sount les dreitz des espeyes gardez desblemies et

1. ou par *N.* e par *AM.* e en *H.* 2—2. en diuers leus *N.* *sim. A.* 3—3. par Countes e par Barouns *ACH.*

CHAPTER VIII.

Of the Division of Inheritances.

Some tenements not divisible. Heads of earldoms and baronies, parks, advowsons. Capital mansion assigned to eldest heir. Earldoms and baronies not to be dismembered.

1. All inheritances do not fall into partition or hotchpot, to be divided among parceners; as the capital manors or capital castles of counties or baronies, and as parks, vivaries, and advowsons of churches. But where the inheritance is divisible, the eldest brother or the eldest sister by right of seniority shall have the capital mansion for his share, unless this mansion be the head of an earldom or of a barony, as is said above, by reason of the right of the sword, which does not bear division, and of the risk that the strength of the realm may be diminished thereby, which strength was originally constituted and divided by counties and baronies.

Several castles of barony may be distributed.

2. But if there are several capital houses or castles of earldoms or baronies, then partition may be made of such castles or houses, yet so as to leave them in their entirety, saving to the eldest the prerogative of choosing first. For in such cases

desmembrez; mes issi ne [1]serroit il[1] mie, si un chief mees de counté ou de baronie fu parti entre plusours. Car s'il n'i eit qe un chastel ou un mees pur chief del counté ou de la baronie, celi remeigne enterement al eynznee ou a la eynznesce, issi qe as autres soit[2] fet proporcionelment a la vaillaunce del remenaunt del heritage.

3. Et si plusours chefs mees i[3] soint, adounc [4]eynt il la premere eleccioun[4], apres ceo qe le heritage sera severé en parties, et le autre eynznee ou eynzneesce apres ly la secunde eleccioun, et issi des autres degrez, [5]de degré en degré descendaunt[5]. Et si il i eynt plus des parceners qe des chefs mees, adounc soit liveré a celi a qi nul mees ne escheet en[6] purpartie a la vailaunce de un mees de tut le entier del heritage. Et si il eynt [7]plus des[7] chiefs mees qe des parceners, ceus mees soint departez entre eux par ouweles porciouns, si les parceners ne se assentent qe acun mees ou touz remeignent enterement a un ou a plusours issi qe as autres soit fet a la vailaunce proporcionelment. Et si n'i eit qe un [187 *b*.]

Brac. 76; Fle. 312, 313.

1—1. serroient i *M.* serrount *CH.* 2. so *NM.* soit *om.* *L C.* 3. i *om.* *M.* 4—4. soit la eleccioun premiere *M.* 5—5. et degrez en degrez descendauntz *L.* e de degre en degre descendaunt *N.* *sim.* *A.* de gre en gre descendaunt *M.* *sim.* *H.* e degree en degree descendaunt *C.* 6. del *M.* 7—7. *conj.* plusours *LNMGC.* *sim.* *S.*

the rights of the sword are preserved uninjured and undismembered, which would not be if one capital mansion of an earldom or barony was divided among several persons. For if there be but one castle or one house as head of the earldom or barony, that shall remain entire to the eldest, so that a proportionate allowance be made to the others according to its value, out of the remainder of the inheritance.

In partition of several mansions, eldest coheir has first choice.

3. If there are several capital mansions, then let the eldest have the first choice after the inheritance is divided into parcels, and the second next, and so of the other degrees, descending from degree to degree. And if there are more parceners than there are capital mansions, then let that parcener who has no house fallen into his share have the value of a house delivered to him out of the entire inheritance. And if there are more capital houses than parceners, let the houses in excess be divided among them in equal portions, unless the parceners agree that some or all of them shall remain entirely with one or more of the parceners, and that an allowance in proportion to the value be

chief mees, cel ne soit mie devisé, par quei qe il i eit plus del heritage dount satisfaccioun puse estre fete as parceners de la vaillaunce de lour porcioun, si le heritage soit departable de acun usage, et si noun, adounc remeygne[1] enterement al eynznee.

Brac. 76; Fle. 313 (§ 15). 4. Des terres de auncienes demeynes soit usé solom le auncien usage del lu; dount en acun lu tient hom pur usage, qe le heritage soit departable entre touz les enfauntz freres et soeurs, et en acun lu qe le eynznee fiz[2] avera trestut[3], et en acun lu [4]qe le pusnee de touz les freres eyt[4] tut.

Brac. 76; Fle. 313 (§ 18). Post, l. v. c. 3. s. 6. Brac. 76 b; Fle. 313 (§ 21). 5. Acune foiz avent, qe la sale de acun mees est [5]divisé en partie[5] en deus meytez ou en plusours parties, et acune foiz est la sale severé des chaumbres; et issi des autres mesouns, solom ceo qe dit serra es pletz de douwarrie. Mes avowesouns de eglises, ne servage de soils, [6]ne tele[6] manere des choses nient corporeles ne suffrent point de partisoun en lour singulerté. Plusours avowesouns[7] neqedent et plusours dreitz[8] suffrent divisioun entre parceners, issint qe chescun

1. remeygnent *L.* *sim. GSMC.* remeigne *N.* 2. fiz *om. N.* 3. tut *N.* tout *M.* tot *C.* 4—4. *so verb. M.* qe *om. L.* qe les puisnez aueroun*t N.* 5—5. deuisable en partie *N.* deuisez e departiz *M.* 6—6. *so M.* *sim. NA.* et en tele *LH.* nen tele *C.* 7. *so NGSMCAHF.* sount *add. L.* 8. *so NGSMCF.* qe *add. L.*

Mansion not to be divided, if there be sufficient other property. made to the others. And if there is but one capital mansion, let not that be subject to partition, provided that there is some other part of the inheritance out of which satisfaction can be made to the parceners of the value of their proportions, supposing that the inheritance is partible by custom. If otherwise, it will remain entirely to the eldest.

Customary rules of descent. 4. With regard to lands in ancient demesne, the ancient custom of the place shall be observed; for in some places it is held as a custom that the inheritance is divisible among all the children, both brothers and sisters; in some places, that the eldest son shall take all; and in others, that the whole shall go to the youngest brother.

Partition of a house. 5. Sometimes the hall of a house is divided into two halves, or into several parts; and sometimes it is separated from the chambers, and so of other buildings, as shall be mentioned in treating of pleas of dower. Advowsons not partible. But advowsons of churches, servitudes of soil, and such kinds of incorporeal things, are from their nature incapable of partition. Nevertheless several advowsons and several rights may admit of a partition among

dreit remeigne entier. Mes la avowesoun de une[1] eglise ne [188.] deit mie estre partie, tut soit acune foiz le cors del eglise Brac. 76 b; Fle. 314 (§ 21). divisible ou partable de antiquité par la resoun de diverses baronies. Car si eglise se[2] voide par la mort la persone, et plusours parceners soint patrouns cum un heir et un cors, pur l'unité del dreit qe il ount, nul ne ad resoun de presenter a tele eglise sauntz autre, einz[3] qe cele avowesoun soit assigné enterement a acun des parceners en sa purpartie, ou qe l'avowesoun soit limité par accord des parceners qe le un presente une foiz et le autre autre foiz et issi de [4]gré en gré[4]. Et si acun enceys[5] voille presenter par resoun de priorité de age, james neqedent ne ert le clerc receyvable al institucioun, taunt cum acun des parceners countrelute le presentement.

6. Et ausi des servages. Car si acun tenement, a qi Brac. 76 b; Fle. 314 (§ 23). est du acun servage, cheete en partie et en divisioun entre parceners, ja par taunt ne amenust le servage ne ne chaunge, eynz remeynt le servage en sa[6] unité quant a regard del soil chargé[7]. [8]Et tut soit un servage parti en plusours parties,

1. so *NSAMFH.* *sim. G.* une *om. L.* 2. seit *C.* 3. einz ceo *NMC.* 4—4. degre en degre *N.* gre en degre *M.* 5. en ceo cas *N.* einz ces *M.* ceo *C.* 6. so *NSMCAH.* la *LS.* 7. *conj.* chargé *om. LNGCH.* chaunge *MR.* changee *AW.* 8—8. so *verb. GAMCH.* *om. LNS.*

parceners, where each right remains entire. But the advowson of a single church ought not to be divided, although sometimes the body of the church may have become partible or divisible in ancient times by reason of different baronies. For if a church is void by the death of the parson, and several parceners are patrons as one heir and one body, by reason of the unity of their right, no one has a right to present to such church without the Parceners may agree to present alternately. others, until the advowson be wholly assigned to one of the parceners as part of his share, or so limited by agreement between them, that one shall present one turn, the second the next turn, and so on in succession. And if any one before such agreement offers to present by reason of seniority, the clerk shall not be admissible to institution, so long as any of the parceners oppose the presentation.

6. The like of servitudes; for if a tenement to which a ser- Effect of partition upon servitudes. vitude is due falls in partition and division among parceners, the servitude is neither diminished nor altered, but remains in its unity so far as regards the land charged. And although a servitude is divided into several parts, as regards the land to

quant a regard del soil[8] a qi il est du, pur la pluralité des parceners, et tut i ent plusours dreitz entiers, ja par taunt ne sera le soil chargé plus qe ne fust avaunt la partie, et issi remeint le servage en sa unité.

Brac. 76 *b*; Fle. 314 (§ 24). [188 *b*.]

7. Et sount acunes parceles de heritage qe ne soeffrent mie devisioun; par quei il les covendra enterement assigner a un des parceners, issint qe as autres soit fete satisfaccioun a la vaillaunce del remenaunt del heritage, sicum sount vivers pescheries hayes[1] et parcs, par quei qe[2] il i eit plus del heritage dount satisfaccioun puse estre fete as autres proporcionelement. Accorder se porrount il neqedent, et suffrable chose est, si les parceners se assentent, qe le un eit un tret et un pesson, ou une beste [3]el parc[3], et le autre un autre, et le tierz le tierz [4]et issi des autres.

Brac. 76 *b*, 77; Fle. 314 (§ 25).

8. De terre ou[4] de autre manere de heritage avaunt [5]doné ovek acun des parceners en fraunc mariage, voloms qe tiel soit le usage, qe si cele, a qi cel mariage avera esté doné, voille aver part del heritage dount lour commun auncestre

1. boys hayes *N.* *sim. CH.* so *M.* *sim. GAW.* lays *LS.* boyz *F.* 2. so *MG.* qe *om. LNSC.* 3—3. so *G.* el part *L.* ou vn peschun en parc [ou en viuer] *N.* en park *G.* en la [e] park M. en part *C.* 4—4. E si des autres terres e *N.* e issi des autres terres ou *M.* *sim. ACH.* 5. [la] diuision partie soit *add. N.*

which it is due by reason of the plurality of parceners, and although there may be several entire rights thereto, yet the land shall not be more burdened than it was before the partition, and thus the servitude shall remain in its unity.

Parks and fisheries not to be divided.

7. There are some parts of an inheritance which will not admit of a division, and therefore ought to be wholly assigned to one of the parceners, satisfaction being made to the others according to the value out of the remainder of the inheritance. Such are vivaries, fisheries, hays, and parks, provided there are other hereditaments whereout satisfaction may be made in proportion to the other parceners. Nevertheless the parties may come to terms, and it is allowable, if they so agree, that one of them shall have one draught or one fish, or one beast in the park, and the second another, and a third the third, and so on.

Land previously given in marriage to a parcener falls into hotchpot.

8. With respect to land or other hereditament before given with any of the parceners in frank marriage, the usage shall be this; that if she to whom the land was given in marriage chooses to share in the inheritance whereof their common

morust seisi en demeyne cum de fee, qe adounc rende sus et weyve ceo qe avaunt ly fust doné en mariage, et cel chete en hochepot ovek le remenaunt del heritage, et puis preigne sa purpartie solom la aventure de sort, sicum sa autre parcenere. Et si ele se tiegne a soen mariage pur sa purpartie, uncore fet a prendre garde si cele partie vaille plus qe ne[1] affiert a sa purpartie, ou noun. Et si plus, adounc soit fet amesurement, lequel qe ceo soit de heritage descendaunt de par piere ou de par mere, ou de purchaz, issint qe le[2] surplus soit parti [189.]
par ouweles porciouns par entre totes[3] les parceners. Et en mesme la manere soit usé [4]de doun[4] fet [5]par mere[5] a acune de ses filles en sa veduetė de tut soen mariage. Mes de pur Brac. 77; Fle. 314 (§ 26).
feffement ne tient james leu devisioun. Car ausi estables voloms qe tels douns de pur feffement sauntz[6] mencioun de mariage soint tenuz [7]en les[7] privez del saunc cum serreit en[8] estraunge persone. Et si piere ou mere ou ambideus doinent a une des parceners en mariage tut lour heritage, [9]en tel cas

1. so *NMH.* en *L.* *om. A.* 2. le exces e le *NCH.* *sim. A.* les encreez e le *M.*
3. touz *NAMCH.* 4—4. so *AM.* del doun *N.* doun *L.* dun *C.* de un *H.*
5—5. de Miere *N.* *sim. MCH.* par nefue *A.* 6. fere *add. NSAMCH.* *sim. G.*
7—7. entre les *MG.* 8. entre *M.* 9—9. e diuisioun *M.*

ancestor died seised in demesne as of fee, she shall yield up and relinquish that which was before given her in marriage, and it shall fall into hotchpot with the remainder of the inheritance, and then she shall take her share according to the chance of the allotment with her other parceners. And if she keeps to her estate in marriage for her share, still it must be seen whether this is worth more than belongs to her proportion or not. For if more, a measurement shall be made,—and this whether the land came by descent from the part of the father or of the mother or by purchase,—and the excess shall be divided by equal portions between all the parceners. The same usage shall hold where a mother in her widowhood gives to any of her daughters all her estate held in marriage. But where the feoffment is absolute, partition never takes place. For we will that such gifts by pure feoffment without mention of marriage shall be held as valid in the case of privies of blood as they would be in that of a stranger. And if either father or mother or both give to one of the parceners in marriage all their inheritance, in such case the inheritance shall

Parcener enfeoffed absolutely free from partition.

So where no inheritance is left to divide,

ne cherra mie cel heritage en divisioun[9], pur ceo qe rien remeynt a partir entre les autres parceners.

Brac. 77; Fle. 314 (§ 27).

9. Et si la eynznesce moerge, vivaunt soen piere ou sa mere, de qi le heritage deit descendre, la secunde avera sa prerogative, quant a la eleccioun, tut eit cele, qe morte est, lessé apres ly fiz ou fille de leale engendrure, pur ceo qe ele ne survesqi mie soen auncestre, qi heir ele dust aver esté. [1]Ore seut a detrier renable partie[1].

CHAPITRE IX. [LXXIII.]

De [2]Renable Partie[2].

Fle. 315 (§ 31, 32); Ante, c. 7. s. 3.

1. Cum acun parcener soit deforcé par ses parceners de tote sa renable partie del heritage lour commun auncestre, adounc tient lu bref de renable partie clos, et nient assise
[189 *b.*] de mort de auncestre. Car cest bref et nul autre detrie et determine le dreit de la possessioun entre parceners et[3] un heir, pur ceo qe chescun parcener el[4] point de la mort soen

1—1. *so verb. LSG. om. NAMCHF.* 2—2. remedie de parceners *ND.* 3. en *M.* 4. *so SGM.* en *LND.*

not fall into partition, because nothing remains to be divided between the other parceners.

If the eldest daughter be dead, the second has first choice.

9. If the eldest die in the lifetime of her father or mother from whom the inheritance is to descend, the second daughter shall have her prerogative of election, although the deceased have left behind her a son or a daughter lawfully begotten, because the eldest did not survive her ancestor, whose heir she would have been. We have next to deal with the action *de rationabili parte.*

CHAPTER IX.

Of the Plea de Rationabili Parte[1].

Parcener deforced by co-parceners; his remedy by writ *de rationabili parte.*

1. When any of the parceners is deforced by his coparceners of all his reasonable share of the inheritance of their common ancestor, the proper proceeding is by the writ close *de rationabili parte,* and not by assise of Mortdancester. For this writ, and no other, tries and determines the right of possession between parceners and coheirs, because at the instant of the

[1] The greater part of the materials of this chapter appears to be in Fleta, though not always in the same order, and not in Bracton.

auncestre [1]ad mesme le dreit uniement, et a chescun[1] descendi[2] le meer dreit ouwelement[3], autaunt al puisnee cum al eynznee; et ceo ne est mie en cas des freres ou de autres parentz nient[4] parceners, ou le meer dreit descent plus toust al un qe al autre.

2. Et autres maneres de brefs sount de renable partie; ceo est a saver, un de possessioun, et treis de dreit. Cel de possessioun ne tient james lu entre estraunges persones, eynz fet entre parceners et entre nuls autres, et est clos, autresi bien a fere plusours respoundre a un cum un a plusours, pur quei il lour deforce lour renable partie qe lour affiert del heritage qe fust a tel, lour piere, ou lour mere, ou lour frere, ou lour soeur, ou lour uncle, ou lour aunte, ou lour ael, [5]ou lour aele[5], ou lour cosin, ou lour cosine, qi[6] morust n'ad gers puis, sicum hom dist. Ou si acun parcener soit en plus loynteyn degré de autre, adounc issi: del heritage qe fust a tel, piere le avauntdite Heliz et ael la avauntdite Peronele, et issi outre[7] solom les degrez.

1—1. so *verb. ND.* om. *LMGSC.* 2. destent *M.* descent *C.* 3. uniement *M.* 4. so *NC.* sim. *GM.* om. *L.* 5—5. so *NA.* sim. *SG.* ou lour ael *L.* ou leur besael *C.* sim. *H.* om. *M.* 6. en qi *L.* e qe *NAG.* qe *M.* e qi *SCH.* 7. outre om. *M.*

ancestor's death every parcener has the same undivided right, and the mere right descended to each equally,—the youngest as well as the eldest,—which is not the case between brothers or other kindred, not being parceners, where the mere right descends sooner to one than to the other.

2. There are other kind of writs *de rationabili parte*, for there is one concerning the possession, and three concerning right. The possessory writ does not lie between strangers, but between parceners only, and it is a close writ. Its effect is to require an answer as well from several to one as from one to several, wherefore he deforces them of the reasonable share belonging to them of the inheritance which was of such an one their father, mother, brother, sister, uncle, aunt, grandfather, grandmother, or cousin, who lately died, as it is said. Or if any parcener be in a more remote degree than another, then thus: of the inheritance which belonged to such an one, father of the aforesaid Helice, and grandfather of the aforesaid Peronel, and so on according to the degrees.

Possessory writ *de rationabili parte.*

Fle. 315 (§ 37, 40). 3. Et ceo bref ne tient james lu for qe entre parcener pleyntif et parcener tenaunt; et se estent taunt cum le tens dure qe est limité en assise de novele disseisine, et ne mie outre, pur ceo mot, n'ad guers, qe ne suppose mie plus loung tens. Et ceo bref se estent a chescun auncestre, amountaunt
[190.] jekes a tresael, avalaunt jekes al dreyn neveu, taunt cum le tens avauntdit le soeffre. Et si ceo bref soit counté en le dreit, par taunt est le bref abatable, par la resoun qe serra dite el chapitre de cosinage.

4. De dreit i ount treis brefs, mes ceux deyvent estre overtz, et sount pledables en la court le chief seignur; dount les deus tienent lu quel houre qe hom veut, de eynz le tens avauntdit ausi bien cum apres; et dount le un sert a recoverer partie del heritage, en cas ou acun parcener est seisi de partie, et partie ly faut de sa renable porcioun, et le autre sert a recoverer les apurtenaunces en tut ou en partie, ou il est [1]deforcé des parceners[1]. Le tierz bref de dreit tient lu apres le tens avauntdit de tote la renable partie recoverer

1—1. aforcie des parceners *L.* deforcee des apurtenaunces *N.* *sim.* *GAMW.* afforcee dez apurtenances *S.* *sim.* *HF.*

Limitation in writ close de rationabili parte. 3. This writ lies only between parcener plaintiff and parcener tenant, and extends as far as the time limited in an assise of Novel Disseisin, and not further, by reason of the word 'lately[k],' which does not suppose a longer time. And this writ extends to every ancestor in the ascending line as far as the great-great-grandfather, and in the descending to the nephew in the lowest degree, so far as the time aforesaid will
Count must be of possession. permit. If the plaintiff in this writ count in the right, the writ is abatable for the reason which shall be given in the Chapter of Cosinage.

Three writs patent de rationabili parte, 4. There are three writs of right, and these ought to be open writs, and are pleadable in the court of the chief lord. Two of them lie at any time either within or after the term
one, for a partial deforcement; aforesaid; whereof one serves to recover a part of the inheritance, where a parcener is seised of part, and lacks the residue
another, for appurtenances; of his reasonable share; and the other serves to recover the appurtenances, in all or in part, where he is deprived of them
the third, for the whole share where plaintiff is barred by time in writ close. by his co-parceners. The third writ of right takes place after the time aforesaid, to recover the whole of the reasonable

[k] The Latin word in the writ is *nuper*. Fle. 315 (§ 40).

entierement, cum si acun parcener soit deforceour, et les parceners negligentz soeffrent a demaunder lour parties outre le tens limité en assise de novele disseisine, [1]des adounc[1] serrount [2]tels dormours[2] forclos de aver lour recoverir par le bref clos de renable partie, issint qe il ne averount james recoverer vers le parcener deforceour for qe par bref de dreit overt de renable partie; en quel bref tienent lu excepciouns sicum el graunt bref de dreit, bataille neqedent ne graunt assise ne tienent lu pur la proscheineté de saunc. Fle. 315 (§ 40).

5. Et cum le bref clos sera purchacé, et surté trové de sure, et la somounse fete et testmoigné, si le tenaunt parcener, un ou plusours, face defaute, tut soit qe ceste accioun semble personele, par la resoun qe nul certeyn[3] ne est demaundé, nul attachement neqedent soit fet for qe del entier del heritage a la vaillaunce de la porcioun le pleyntif par le graunt *Cape*. Fle. 315 (§ 34), 316 (§ 42). [190 *b*.]

6. Et cum plusours parceners soint tenauntz en commun ou en purparties, et le bref ne les compreigne mie touz, par taunt serra le bref vicious et abatable. Car lour dreit est issi Fle. 315 (§ 32).

1—1. adounc *L.* *sim.* *SG.* de soen afferaunt dounc *N.* des adonqes *M.* *sim.* *CF.* de cea *A.* 2—2. *so verb.* *AMCFW.* tels donours *LS.* touz les douns e tendroms *ND.* teus deforceours *GH.* 3. *so* *NMHW.* noun *add.* *GSF.* *sim.* *interl.* *LC.* certeine vewe *A.*

share; as, where one parcener is deforceor, and the co-parceners negligently omit to demand their portions beyond the time limited in an assise of Novel Disseisin; for thenceforth such sleepers shall be foreclosed of their recovery by the close writ *de rationabili parte*, so that they shall never recover against the parcener deforceor but by writ of right patent *de rationabili parte;* in which writ exceptions lie as in the great writ of right, but not battle, nor great assise, by reason of the nearness of blood.

5. When the close writ is obtained, and surety found to prosecute, and the summons made and proved, in case the tenant parcener or parceners make default, although the action seems to be personal, because no certain thing is demanded, yet no attachment shall be made except by the great *Cape*, of the bulk of the inheritance to the value of the share of the plaintiff. Process in the writ close, by great *Cape*.

6. If several parceners are tenants in common or in proportions, and the writ does not comprise them all, the writ is thereby defective and abatable. For their right is so far one, All the tenant parceners must be defendants.

un, qe nul ne deit respoundre sauntz autre pur la contribucioun. Et si acun le face, ceo ne chete mie en perjudice des
Fle. 315 (§ 33, 35). autres parceners tenauntz. Et si [1]plusours parceners[1] soint pleyntifs, si chescun ne[2] se pleyne severalment par sei, si serra le bref abatable, pur ceo qe tel bref purchacé sour commune pleinte ne chace james a ceo qe chescun eit sa renable
Fle. 315 (§ 35). partie. En cest plé ne gist point de vewe, ne voucher garraunt, ne abatement de bref par noun tenure.

Fle. 315 (§ 38, 39). 7. Et cum les parties vendrount en court, porra le deforceour dire, qe la terre ne est mie departable; ou qe le pleintif ne ad nul dreit en sa demaunde, pur ceo qe il ne est mie del saunc; ou, tut soit il del saunc, pur ceo qe il ne deit aver nule partie ne parcener estre al tenaunt par certeyne resoun; ou, tut dust il aver esté parcener, il fust neqedent forclos de la successioun par fourme de doun de soen auncestre.

[191.] 8. Et si acun soit feffé de commun auncestre de tut ou de
Fle. 315 (§ 41). partie del heritage, et soit de ceo enpledé, il ne vouchera mie tauntsoulement un des parceners a garraunt, einz fra trestouz

1—1. plusours *A.* parceners *H.* 2. ne *om. ND.*

that one ought not to answer without the rest on account of contribution. And if any one of them do so, it shall not pre-

Several parceners must make plaint separately. judice the other parceners tenants. And where several parceners are plaintiffs, unless each makes his plaint separately, the writ shall be abatable, because such a writ obtained on a joint plaint cannot lead to a judgment that every one shall

No view, nor voucher, nor abatement for non-tenure. have his reasonable share. In this plea there lies neither view, nor voucher to warranty, nor abatement of writ for non-tenure.

Various defences. 7. When the parties are come into court, the deforceor may plead that the land is not partible; or that the plaintiff hath no right in his demand because he is not of the blood; or, although he be of the blood, yet he ought not to have any share, or to be a parcener with the tenant for a certain reason; or although he should have been a parcener, yet he was excluded from the succession by the form of gift of his ancestor.

Where parceners are bound to warranty all must be vouched. 8. If any one who was enfeoffed of all or a part of the inheritance by the common ancestor of the parceners is impleaded thereof, he shall vouch to warranty, not one only, but

les parceners. Et si noun, et le voucher[1] soit chalengé, par taunt porra le tenaunt perdre pur soen fol voucher. Car puis qe il ne i ad for qe un dreit, tort serroit a fere un des parceners respoundre del entier del dreit, et a fere ly fere la garrantie ou les eschaunges, si trestouz les parceners ne[2] faisent contribucion solom chescuni[3] afferaunt; car autrement ne ly remeyndreit mie sa renable partie. Ne mie pur ceo qe si le un soit vouché soulement, et cil entre en la garrauntie sauntz demaunder eyde de ses parceners, en tel cas ne serrount mie les autres parceners tenuz a fere a ly nule contribucioun de sa partie s'il[4] meschiet.

9. Et tut soit la issue del une soeur engendré de vilein en matrimoigne, ja pur ceo ne soit ele barré a recoverer sa renable partie de sa amite[5]. Mes felonie et bastardie et autres teles generales excepciouns porrount tels pleintifs barrer de lour purparties recoverir. Cf. Fle. 315 (§ 36).

1. so *M.* vouchour *LSCH.* sim. *G.* 2. so *NG.* ne om. *LSAMCH.* 3. so *N.* sim. *DM.* chescun *L.* sim. *GSAHW.* 4. si a li *M.* 5. so *LS.* aunte *AGMCH.*

all the parceners; and if he do not, and the voucher be challenged, the tenant may lose by his foolish voucher. For since there is only one right, it would be unjust to make one of the parceners answerable for the entire right, and to oblige him to make warranty or exchange without the rest of the parceners making contribution according as belongs to each of them; for else he would not retain his reasonable share. Nevertheless where one alone is vouched, and he enters into warranty without demanding aid of his parceners, the other parceners, if he miscarry, shall not be bound to contribute to make up his share. But if one warrant and fail, he has no right to contribution.

9. Although the issue of one of the sisters be begotten in matrimony by a villain, yet such issue shall not thereby be barred from recovering his reasonable share from his aunt. But felony, bastardy, and the like general exceptions, may bar such plaintiffs from recovering their proportions. Exception of villenage not available; but exception of felony and bastardy, good.

CHAPITRE X. [LXXIV.]

[191 *b.*]

De Somounses.

Brac. 255; Fle. 280.

1. Purchacé le bref de mort de auncestre solom la nature de la querele, et moustré la patente a nos Justices, pur ceo qe assise de mort de auncestre et de novele disseisine ne sount mie pledables for qe en countez ou les tenementz sount, voloms qe nos Justices, vewes nos lettres patentes, assecent jour al pleyntif, et puis maundent al viscounte del lu par lour lettre, quel jour il vendrount[1] a ceo entendre[2], et en quel lu del counté. Et puis preigne le pleyntif cele lettre et noster bref clos, et les porte al viscounte, et retiegne la patente ove[3] ly jekes al jour del[4] play.

Glan. l. 13. c. 7; Brac. 255; Fle. 280.

2. Et le viscounte, resceuz noster bref[5], et pleges de sure, si noster bref le voille, tauntost face elire jurours del visné par assent des parties, si les parties voillent. Et cum il serrount esluz, soit enjoynt a deus frauncs hommes, terre te-

1. voilent *M.* vodront *GA.* *sim. SH.* ven [ol] drount *N.* 2. attendre *M.* 3. *so M.* vers *LNGSACH.* 4. de soen *N.* *sim. MACH.* 5. bref clos *MNA.*

CHAPTER X.

Of Summons, and other proceedings in the Assise of Mortdancester.

Proceedings in assise of Mortdancester.

1. The writ of Mortdancester being obtained according to the nature of the plaint, and the patent produced to our Justices, we will that, inasmuch as assises of Mortdancester and Novel Disseisin are pleadable only in the counties where the tenements lie, our Justices, upon sight of our letters patent, shall set a day to the plaintiff, and afterwards give notice by their letter to the sheriff of the county on what day and at what place in the county they will come to hear the plea. Then let the plaintiff take that letter and our writ close and carry them to the sheriff, and keep the patent by him until the day of plea.

Day of plea fixed by Justices.

Selection of jury.

2. The sheriff having received our writ, and taken pledges to prosecute, if required by our writ, shall forthwith cause jurors to be chosen of the neighbourhood by the assent of the parties, if they agree. And when they are chosen, let two

nauntz, qe ceux jurours somounent en lour propres persones, solom ceo qe dit serra en le chapitre des somounses el bref de dreit. Et le viscounte lour enjoyne qe il les somoignent, qe il seint a certeyns jour et lu devaunt nos Justices a reconustre si tiel homme soit mort, et si il morust puis le terme nomé en noster bref seisi del tenement en tele vile en soen demeyne cum de fee, et si tel pleintif soit soen proschein heir, et qe el meen tens veyent le tenement, issi cum dit est devaunt el proces de novele disseisine, issint qe chescun jurour [1]distingtement soit[1] garni en touz pointz, sur quel point il se deit aviser, avaunt soen vener en nostre court al meyns par xv. jours. Et les somenours soint chargez de estre illucs mesme le jour a testmoigner lour somouns. Et issi deit estre de touz somenours de totes somounses. [192.]

Post, l. 6. c. 5.

Glan. l. 13. c. 3; Brac. 253 b.

3. A quel jour les parties [2]porrount estre essoniez[2] de mal de venue. Et si le pleyntif se face essonier le premer jour, et le tenaunt se profre, adounc serra doné autre jour al tenaunt et al essoniour le pleyntif. A quel jour si le pleyntif ne viegne garraunter soen essoniour, chete le bref et soit

Glan. l. 13. c. 7; Brac. 255; Fle. 280.

1—1. soit distinctement *NAM.* seit destreitement *C.* *sim. H.* 2—2. se poent essoigner *M.*

freemen, terre-tenants, be enjoined to summon these jurors in their proper persons, as shall be mentioned in the chapter concerning summons in the writ of right. And the sheriff shall command them to summon the jurors to be at a certain day and place before our Justices, to make recognisance, whether such an one is dead, and whether he died since the time named in our writ seised of the tenement in such a vill in his demesne as of fee, and whether such plaintiff is his next heir; and that in the meantime they view the tenement, as before has been mentioned among the proceedings in novel disseisin, so that every juror in all particulars be distinctly warned, fifteen days at least before his coming into our court, upon what point he ought to inform himself. And let the summoners be charged to be there on the same day to prove their summons; as is the rule with all summoners upon every summons.

Summons of jurors; summoners.

Form of summons.

View.

Jurors to inform themselves of facts.

3. Upon the day named the parties may be essoined *de malo veniendi;* and if the plaintiff is essoined on the first day, and the tenant offers himself, then another day shall be given to the tenant and to the plaintiff's essoiner; at which day if the plaintiff does not appear to warrant his essoiner, the writ

One essoin *de malo veniendi* allowed.

agardé, qe le tenaunt [1]s'en voise quites[1] sauntz jour, et le pleintif et ses pleges de sure en la merci. Et si il viegne, et le tenaunt se face essonier de mal de venue, soit alouwable[2], si le tenaunt soit de plener age, et soit doné autre jour al pleyntif et al essoniour le tenaunt, issi qe en ceste assise eit lu un essoigne de mal de venue pur chescune partie, et nient plus de essoignes, tut soint plusours [3]demaundauntz ou plusours tenauntz[3], mes qe il demaundent ou tienent en commun.

Brac. 340 *b*; Fle. 384; cf. Glan. l. 13. c. 13.

Mes a nul de eynz age soit allouwé essoigne, par la resoun qe sera dite en le plé de dreit.

Glan. l. 13. c. 7, 12; Brac. 340 *b*; Fle. 384.

Ne ausi ne soit allouwé nul essoigne de[4] homme de plener age tenaunt encountre enfaunt de eynz age pleyntif; mes tauntost soit prise la assise par defaute le tenaunt, issi qe nule resomounse ne tiegne lu.

[192 *b*.]

Glan. l. 13. c. 13, 14; Brac. 340 *b*; Fle. 384.

4. Et si le tenaunt soit de eynz age, adounc fet [5]a prendre garde[5] coment et par quele title il est en seisine. Car si il en[6] est seisi[7] par title de purchaz en acune manere, tauntost courge l'assise, et en tel cas ly vaille essoigne, ausi cum a

1—1. voisse quites *N.* *sim. A.* voit *MC.* voet *H.* 2. alowe le essoigne *N.* *sim. A.* alowe *MH.* 3—3. *so verb. AS.* demaundez ou plusours tenaunt *L.* demaundauns e plusours tenauntz *N.* *sim. GMLH.* 4. a *NAMCH.* 5—5. *so NAMCH.* aprendre *L.* 6. en *om. NAMCH.* 7. en seisine *N.*

shall abate, and it shall be awarded that the tenant go quit without day, and that the plaintiff and his pledges to prosecute be in mercy. And if the plaintiff appears, and the tenant causes himself to be essoined *de malo veniendi,* it shall be allowed, if he is of full age, and another day shall be given to the plaintiff and to the tenant's essoiner; so that in this assise one essoin *de malo veniendi* lies for each party, and no more essoins are allowed, although there be several demandants or several tenants where they demand or hold in common. But let no essoin be allowed to any person under age for the reason which shall be given in the plea of right. Neither let any essoin be allowed to the tenant though of full age, as against an infant under age demandant, but let the assise be presently taken by default of the tenant, and no resummons take place.

No essoin where either party is an infant.

Infant tenant seised by purchase, may be essoined: assise not postponed to majority.

4. If the tenant is under age, regard must be had how and by what title he is in seisin; for if he is in any manner seised by title of purchase, the assise immediately lies; but in such case he may avail himself of an essoin as well as one of full

homme de plener age. Et si par title de successioun, uncore fet a prendre garde; car si soen auncestre en morust seisi en soen demeyne cum de fee, adounc ne respoundera point, eynz remeyndra l'assise jekes a soen age, coment qe il respoigne par cas al bref de entré de la disseisine soen auncestre; et si il ne morust mie seisi cum de fee, pur ceo qe il ne tint fors a terme de vie, ja par taunt ne remeygne l'assise a prendre. Mes s'il murt[1] seisi cum a certeyn terme par acune condicioun, ou par jugement de nostre court, en tels cas covendra saver si le aset de la condicioun soit fet ou noun, [2]ou si le jugement soit parfourni ou noun[2]; et solom ceo passera la assise ou remeyndra.

Stat. West. I. (3 Ed. I.) c. 47; Fle. 361 (§ 11).

5. Et si plusours soint pleintifs qe demaundent par ceste assise, ou si ceste assise seit arramé sur plusours tenauntz, si fet adounc[3] prendre garde lequel il soint parceners en[4] un heir, ou estraunges et divers, et lequel un ou plusours soint de eynz age ou qe touz soint de plener age, et lequel il tienent en severalté ou en commun. Et lequel qe acun pleintif soit de eynz age, ou touz ou plusours, ja pur lour noun age ne remeigne la assise a prendre des tenementz tenuz en severalté,

Stat. Glouc. (6 Ed. I.) c. 2.

[193.]

1. morust *NSGAMCH.* 2—2. *om. H.* 3. dunc a *A. sim. MCH.* 4. et *on eras. N.* ou com *A.* e *MG.* ou *CH.*

age. If by title of succession, another inquiry is necessary; for if his ancestor died seised in his demesne as of fee, he shall not answer, but the assise shall stand over till he is of age, however he may perchance answer to the writ of entry of the disseisin of his ancestor. But if he did not die seised in his demesne as of fee, inasmuch as he held only for term of life, the assise shall not stand over. And if he died seised for a certain term under a condition, or by judgment of our court, in such cases it will be necessary to know whether the condition is satisfied, or the judgment executed, or not; and the assise shall pass or stand over accordingly.

If his ancestor was seised in fee, assise is postponed.

Otherwise, if seised for life or term satisfied.

5. If there are several plaintiffs who demand by this assise, or if it is brought against several tenants, then it must be observed whether they are parceners entitled as one heir, or strangers to each other, and whether one or more are under age, or all of full age, and whether they hold in severalty or in common. And although one or all or some of the plaintiffs are under age, yet the assise shall not stand over respecting the tenements held in severalty, on account of their nonage,

Assise by or against several.

Minority of some of demandants.

fors qe soulement devers le chief seignur. Mes si un des tenauntz ou plusours soint de eynz age, ou touz, et lour tenementz ne soint mie deseverez, eynz soint tenuz en commun, en tel cas remeyndra la assise jekes autaunt qe le puisné eit atteint a soen age, et qe il soint tres touz deplener age. Et ceo est pur l'unité de lour dreit, qe unques uncore ne fust parti, et dount nul ne poit respoundre sauntz autre, taunt qe[1] le tenement est tenu en commun. Mes si chescun sceust soen several, adounc passereit l'assise en dreit de chescun qe serroit de age.

6. Mes si plusours filles et un heir eynt arramé ceste assise vers le chief seignur, si passera ceste assise pur celes qe serrount de plener age, par qei qe il i eit nule destaunce[2] de lour mariages. En dreit des autres de eynz age remeyndra l'assise jekes a lour age. Et cum eles atteyndrount a lour ages, si eynt lour renable partie ou par ceste assise vers le chief seignur, ou par bref clos de renable partie vers les autres soeurs, si eles en[3] soint deforceresces.

1. cum *N.* *sim.* *SGAMCH.* 2. defaute *SG.* 3. so *S.* ne *L.* *om.* *NGAMH.*

Minority of some of tenants. except only as against the chief lord. But if one or more or all of the tenants are under age, and their tenements are not severed, but are held in common, in such case the assise shall be stayed until the youngest has attained his age and they are all of full age; and this by reason of the unity of their right, which has not yet been divided, and concerning which one cannot answer without the other as long as the tenement is held in common. But if each knew his several, then the assise should pass so far as regards those that are of age.

Assise by several coheirs against their lord. 6. Where several daughters and coheirs have brought this assise against the chief lord, the assise shall pass for those that are of full age, provided there is no dispute respecting their marriages[1]; but with regard to the others who are under age, the assise shall stand over till they are of age; and when they have attained their age, they shall recover their reasonable shares either by this assise against the chief lord, or by writ close *de rationabili parte* against the other sisters, if they are deforceors.

[1] That is, provided the lord has no claim against the land for the value of the marriages of the several demandants. See before, l. iii. c. 3. s. 3, note.

7. Et si acun commun heritage soit parti entre parceners, si ne covendra ja purchacer for qe sour celi ou sour ceux qi tienent le tenement qe hom demaunde. Mes si acun par- [193 *b.*] cener soit somouns et viegne en court, et die qe il ne put respoundre sauntz ses parceners pur la unité del dreit qe est entre eus, ja par taunt ne chete le bref, mes les autres parceners serrount somouns qe il viegnent respoundre, issi qe si[1] celi de qi la pleinte est fet perde, il ne perdera mie qe touz les autres parceners ne soint tenuz a la contribucioun. Mes si touz tienent en commun, adounc cheet le bref si trestouz ne soint nomez.

8. Et si le tenaunt face defaute et le pleintif se profre, soit comaundé al viscounte qe le tenaunt soit resomouns, qe il soit devaunt eus a un autre jour, a oyer la reconisaunce del assise, et a respoundre pur quei il ne fu mie devaunt eus a tiel jour, sicum il fust somouns; apres la quele resomounse, ne soit james essoigné; mes qe le tenaunt se face essonier, ou tut autrement face defaute, soit prise la reconisaunce del assise par sa defaute. Ne apres essoigne ne gist james reso- Glan. l. 13. c. 7; Brac. 255; Fle. 280.

1. so *NM.* si *om. LSGCAH.*

7. Where a common inheritance is divided between parceners, the assise need only be brought against him or them who hold the tenement demanded. But if any parcener be summoned and appear in court, and say that he cannot answer without his parceners by reason of the unity of right which is between them, the writ shall not thereby abate, but the other parceners shall be summoned to come and answer, so that if he against whom the plaint is made shall lose, he shall not do so without all the other parceners being bound to contribute. But where they hold in common, the writ abates if all are not named. Assise against one of several parceners after partition. The other parceners may be summoned for contribution.

8. If the tenant makes default, and the plaintiff presents himself, command shall be given to the sheriff that the tenant be resummoned to be before the Justices another day to hear the recognisance of the assise, and to answer why he was not before them on such a day according as he was summoned; after which resummons he shall not be essoined. But whether the tenant cause himself to be essoined or otherwise make default, the recognisance of the assise shall be taken by Default of tenant. Resummons to hear recognisance.

mounse, car par le essoigne getté pur le tenaunt graunte le tenaunt la somounse[1].

Brac. 257 (c. 6. § 1); Fle. 281 (§ 6, 7). 9. Et cum le tenaunt vendra par resomounse en court, en primes respoigne de sa contumace. Et dounc il porra dire, qe il ne fu mie somouns, et sur ceo soint examinez les somenours; et si il soint trovez descordauntz par examinement
[194.] en les circumstaunces de la somounse, soit le tenaunt jugé quites quaunt a la defaute, et les somonours en la merci. Et si il soint trovez accordauntz, adounc[2] porra il defendre la somounse par sa ley; et pur plus haster[3] dreiture, face la ley meyntenaunt[4] a[5] sa soule meyn[6], qe il ne savoit de nule somounse avaunt le jour del autre sessioun, et soit quites de la defaute; et tauntost respoigne al assise. Mes si il eit esté essoynié, mes ne put dedire la somounse.

Brac. 257, 257 b; Fle. 281 (§ 7). 10. Et si le tenaunt viegne le premer jour, uncore porra il delayer la journee par excepcioun de noun renable somounse; cum si ele ly fust fete le jour avaunt la sessioun des Justices ou le secound jour, ou le tierz, ou meyns de xv. jours. Et cel

1. resomounse *MA.* 2. uncore *M.* 3. *om. NA.* 4. tantost *SM.* *sim. G.* 5. par *N.* od *G.* 6. tauntost *add. N.*

No resummons after essoin cast. default. Neither does a resummons ever lie after an essoin, for by the essoin cast for the tenant he admits the summons.

Tenant appearing on resummons must answer for his contempt. 9. When the tenant comes into court by resummons, first let him answer for his contumacy, as to which he may say that he was not summoned. And thereupon let the summoners be examined, and if upon examination they are found to disagree in the circumstances of the summoning, let the tenant be adjudged quit as to the default, and the summoners in mercy.
Summons may be denied by wager of law, without compurgators. And if they are found to agree, then he may defend the summons by his law; and for the more speedy dispatch of justice, let him forthwith make his law by himself alone, that he did not know of any summons before the day of the former session, and be quit of the default; and let him straightway answer to the assise. But if he has been essoined, he cannot afterwards deny the summons.

Exception of insufficient summons. 10. Where the tenant appears on the first day, he may still put off the day of assise by excepting that he had not a reasonable summons; as where it was made the day before the session of the Justices, or two or three days, or less than fifteen days before. This objection shall be tried by examination of

debat soit trié par examinement des soumenours, sicum desus est dit. Et si la somounse soit trovee nient renable, soint ajournez les parties et la assise jeques a un autre jour; a quel jour il porra estre essonié. Et si a tel jour face defaute, mes ne eit lu la resomounse; car le ajournement des Justices ne porra il mie dedire; eynz soit l'assise prise par sa defaute, si ele soit preste. Et si ele ne soit mie adounc preste, soit le pleintif ajornee jekes a un autre jour; et soit comaundé al viscounte, qe il [1]eit adounc[1] les cors [2]de eus a la assise[2]. A quel jour soint ceux del assise amerciez qi al autre jour ne furent mie, sicum il furent somouns, s'il ne [3]se pusent escoundire de[3] la somounse.

Brac. 256; Fle. 281 (§ 4).

Brac. 255 b; Fle. 280 (§ 3).

11. Et tut soit qe le tenaunt viegne a tel jour en court, et voille respoundre, ja pur ceo a respounse ne soit resceu pur le despit fet a nous et a nostre court de sa sursise, fors qe en cas especial, sicum de acune chartre moustrer, par quei les jurours pusent [4]estre meuz avisez, lemeyns[4] par quei qe[5] [194 *b.*]

Brac. 255, 255 b; Fle. 280 (§ 2).

1—1. adounc face venir *N.* *sim. A.* 2—2. *so L.* des Iurours de tiels prestez al assise *ND.* de ceus al assise prestes *AS.* *sim. GF.* de ceus del assise prestz *M.* de ceus al assise *C.* *sim. H.* 3—3. *so LM.* *sim. SG.* puissent esteyndre *ND.* *sim. A.* pussent mie countredire *C.* *sim. H.* 4—4. estre auisez lemeyns *L.* le meuz estre acertez auiseez *N.* *sim. D.* estre meuz auisez *A.* meuz estre auisez *G.* meuz auiser *M.* estre le meins auiseez *S.* estre meins auises *C.* *sim. F.* estre meuz auiseez *H.* vnqes estre auisez *W.* 5. qe *om. NMS.*

the summoners as above mentioned; and if it be found that he had not a reasonable summons, let the parties and the assise be adjourned to another day; at which day he may be essoined. And if at that day he make default, he shall not be resummoned; for he may not deny the adjournment of the Justices; but the assise, if ready, shall be taken by his default. And if it is not then ready, the plaintiff shall be adjourned to another day, and the sheriff shall be commanded that he then have the bodies of those of the assise. At which day let such of the assise as were not present on the former day pursuant to their summons be amerced, if they cannot excuse themselves respecting the summons.

Adjournment for insufficient summons.

Adjournment for absence of jurors.

Jurors amerced for default.

11. Although the tenant come into court on the adjourned day, and is ready to answer, yet he shall not be admitted thereto, for the contempt done to us and our court by his neglect, except in some special cases, as to produce some charter whereby the jurors may be better informed, or at the

Tenant in default; what defences are open to him.

il vouche acun a garraunt; ou nous voloms bien qe il soit a ceo resceu, mes a nule resoun dire pur ly, par quei la assise remeigne a prendre, [1]ne as excepciouns dilatories[1]; [2]ne as[2] excepciouns peremptories ne soit il point resceu, ou il pora dire par cas qe le auncestre, de qi mort l'assise est porté, ne tint[3] les terres for qe a terme de sa vie par fin fete en nostre court, ou excepcioun de felonie, ou autres peremptories; eynz[4] soit prise la reconisaunce del assise, et il soit agardé en nostre merci pur sa defaute.

Brac. 255 b; Fle. 280 (c. 3. § 3).

12. Et cum les parties serrount venuz en court sauntz defaute fere, tauntost le pleyntif rende sa patente as Justices; et si ele soit trové suffisaunte pur garraunt a eus, adounc facent lire en audience ceo bref, et le bref clos original, qe vint[5] al viscounte. Et puis die le pleintif sa entente solom les pointz del bref original, et die coment il est proschein heire tiel auncestre.

1—1. *om. A.* 2—2. ne en *L.* ne en autres *S.* ne as autres *GMCH.* mes as *A.* 3. *so MA.* tient *L.* auoit [mie] *N.* tent *CH.* 4. *om. M.* 5. *so SGAMCH.* vient *LN.*

least whereby he may vouch some person to warrant; in which case we allow him to be admitted thereto, but not to allege any reason to stay the assise, nor to plead any dilatory exceptions. Neither shall he be admitted to plead peremptory exceptions, wherein perhaps he might say that the ancestor of whose death the assise is brought held the lands only for term of his life by a fine levied in our court[m], or the exception of felony, or other peremptory exceptions; but the recognisance of the assise shall be taken, and it shall be awarded that he be in our mercy for his default.

Proceedings at the trial.

12. When the parties come in court without making default, let the plaintiff straightway deliver his patent to the Justices; and if it is found to be sufficient warrant for them, then

Reading of the patent and writ.

let them cause such writ, together with the original writ close which was sent to the sheriff, to be read in audience. And

Count of the plaintiff.

then let the plaintiff state his contention according to the articles of the original writ, and say how he is next heir to such ancestor.

m In this point our author differs from Bracton (f. 255), who states the exceptions here mentioned as those which might be pleaded by the tenant in default. Fleta appears to agree with Britton.

13. Et si le tenaunt rien desdie, ou denye la demaunde le pleintif, et desdie le gros de sa entente en tut ou en partie, soit enquise la verité par xii. jurours a ceo somouns et par nient meyns, et dount vii. al meyns eynt eu la vewe, et les queus ne sount mie remuables par verreis chalenges des parties. Et q'il facent le serment solom ceo qe dit est avaunt en assise de novele disseisine. Et solom lour[1] verdit soit rendu jugement pur le pleintif, ou pur le tenaunt.

Brac. 255 b; Fle. 280, 281.

[195.]

14. Et si l'assise eit esté prise sour le gros, et sour les articles del bref, et si la une partie se sente grevé par lour verdit, lequel qe l'assise eit esté prise par la defaute le tenaunt ou noun, et lequel qe le tenaunt se mist de cel article el verdit del assise ou noun, eit la partie grevé remedie par atteynte; et en mesme la manere sour lour faus serment fet sour[2] acun excepcioun, sicum sour excepcioun de villenage [3]et de[3] naifté, ou de fin fete en nostre court, ou de acun covenaunt, ou de jugement avaunt rendu en nostre court de mesme le tenement, ou sour autre aperte excepcioun sem-

Stat. West. I. (3 Ed. I.) c. 38; Brac. 256 (§ 3); Fle. 281 (§ 4).

1. so *NAM.* sim. *SGCH.* le *L.* 2. so *NAMCH.* sim. *SG.* par *L.* 3—3. ou *N.* ou de *GA.* de *M.* om. *CH.*

13. And if the tenant has nothing to object, or if he denies the demand of the plaintiff and contradicts the substance of his contention wholly or in part, let the truth be inquired by twelve jurors, and not less, summoned for that purpose, whereof seven at least shall have been present at the view, and none of whom are removable by just challenge of the parties. They shall take the oath, as hath been said before in the assise of novel disseisin; and judgment shall be given according to their verdict either for the plaintiff or for the tenant.

Plea of defendant. Trial by twelve jurors. Seven jurors must have had view. Oath of jury. Judgment.

14. If the assise has been taken upon the substance, and upon the points mentioned in the writ, and either party feels himself aggrieved by the verdict, whether the assise was taken by the tenant's default or not, and whether the tenant put himself as to the point in question upon the verdict of the assise or not, the party aggrieved shall have his remedy by attaint. The like upon a false oath by the assise touching any exception, as an exception of villenage and naifty, or of fine levied in our court, or of any covenant, or of a judgment before given in our court concerning the same tenement, or upon other like manifest

Verdict set aside by attaint.

blable. Mes en excepciouns sour les queles verditz sount pronounciéz en fourme des jurez et nient en fourme de assises, et en quels verditz les parties se sount mises par accord, et encountre [1]quels verditz[1] n'i ad nule evidente presumpcioun de faus serment, ne voloms mie qe atteintes soint grauntez, desicum les jurours sount fetz par assentement de

[195 *b*.] ambideus les parties ausi cum juges[2] arbitres.

Brac. 256 *b*, 257; Fle. 281 (§ 5).

15. Et si les parties soint accordez avaunt la reconisaunce del assise prise, soit le accord resceu et enroullé, et solom le enrouellement soit comaundé al viscounte de fere la seisine. Et voloms, qe parties pledauntz, priauntz coungé de accorder en nostre court, eynt a ceo cungé, for qe en felonies, en les queus gist peril de mort, sauve a nous les amerciementz, qe à nous appendent.

16. Et si acun recovere seisine de soen heritage par assise de mort de auncestre hors de la meyn le seignur del fee [3]clamaunt en[3] garde, cum le fee ne soit mie de chevalerie

Ante, c. 2. s 23. ne de graunt serjauntie, et ausi des parentz de acun enfaunt en garde, qi recoverent seisine del heritage le heir en garde

1—1. *so N.* *sim. AG.* qi verditz *LS.* queu verdit *M.* ky verdist *C.* *sim. H.* 2. *so NSGM.* *sim. CH.* Iugies *L.* iuges e *A.* 3—3. *so NAMCH.* en clamaunt *LSG.*

No attaint upon verdict taken by consent.

exception. But in exceptions upon which verdicts are pronounced by way of jury and not of assise, and upon which the parties have put themselves by consent, and against which verdicts there is no evident presumption of perjury, attaints shall not be allowed, inasmuch as the jurors are by the assent of both parties made as it were judicial arbitrators.

Judgment by accord.

15. If the parties agree before taking the recognisance of the assise, let the accord be received and enrolled, and according to the enrolment let the sheriff be commanded to deliver seisin. And we will that parties pleading, if they pray leave to accord in our court, shall have leave for that purpose, except in felonies in which a man's life is in peril, saving to us the amercements to us belonging.

Accord allowed in all pleas except appeals of felony.

Recovery of socage land of infant from lord.

16. If any one by assise of Mortdancester recovers seisin of his inheritance out of the hands of the lord of the fee claiming wardship, where the fee is neither held in chivalry nor in grand serjeanty, or if the kindred of any infant in ward recover seisin of the inheritance of the heir in ward on account of waste and destruction committed by the lord in the ward-

Forfeiture of wardship by waste.

par wast et destruccioun fet par le seignur en la garde, soit enroullé le proces del play, et solom le enroullement soit comaundé al viscounte, ausi cum de sus est dit.

CHAPITRE XI. [LXXV.]

[1]*Des Garraunties*[1].

1. Si les parties soint prestes[2] en jugement et les jurours, et le tenaunt eit acun garraunt qi ly est tenu a [3]garrauntir et a[3] defendre en sa seisine, meutz ly vaut del voucher, qe en soen peril [4]enprendre a[4] defendre le tenement encountre le pleyntif. Et s'il vouche, adounc fet a saver lequel le garaunt vouchee soit de eynz age ou[5] de plener age. Et si de eynz age, adounc covent al tenaunt, qe il moustre chartre al gardeyn, ou homage fet a soen auncestre qi heir il est, ou autre evidente resoun par quei il ly soit tenu a garrauntir; ou si noun, le garraunt vouché de eynz age ne ly respoundra nient.

Brac. 257 *b*; Fle. 281.

Heng. M. c. 13. p. 70, 71, 75.

[196.]

1—1. de garant vouchier *ND.* *sim.* *CH.* 2. *so* *NDGARC.* priez *L.* preez *S.* prest *MF.* prestz *H.* prestez *W.* 3—3. *so* *N.* *sim.* *AMCHF.* *om.* *LSG.* 4—4. prendre e *M.* 5. *so* *AGSCH.* ou noun ou *L.* ou noun *M.*

ship, the proceedings in the plea shall be enrolled, and according to the enrolment the sheriff shall be commanded to deliver seisin as aforesaid.

CHAPTER XI.

Of Warranties in Assise of Mortdancester.

1. When the parties are at trial and the jurors ready, if the tenant has any warrant who is bound to warrant and defend him in his seisin, it is more for his advantage to vouch him than at his own peril to take upon himself to defend the tenement against the plaintiff. And if he vouches, then it is material whether the warrant vouched be under age or of full age. If under age, the tenant must produce a charter to the guardian, or shew that homage was done to the infant's ancestor whose heir he is, or some other clear reason why he is bound to warranty; otherwise the vouchee under age shall not answer.

Voucher of warrant.

Infant vouchee need not answer unless upon presumption of liability.

Brac. 257 b, 258; Fle. 281; Heng. M. c. 13. p. 66.

2. Et si le garraunt vouché soit de plener age, adounc ne estora[1] mie moustrer chartre ne autre presumpcioun, eynz le porra voucher par eyde de la court, ou sauntz eyde, solom ceo qe sera dit en les garraunties en bref de dreit. Et si par eyde de la court, et le garraunt [2]soit manaunt[2] el counté, soit comaundé al viscounte, qe il le somoigne de estre devant mesmes les Justices a un autre jour a garrauntir solom ceo qe il serra vouché, ou a desdire. Et si le garraunt eit terre ayllurs et nient en cel counté, soit somouns par noster bref de jugement.

Heng. M. c. 13. p. 75.

3. Et si le tenaunt vouche a garaunt severalment [3]la ou il dust aver vouché plusours, ou plusours[3] la ou il ne dust voucher qe un, et les garauntz demaundent jugement del mauveis voucher, en tels cas cherrount les tenauntz en lour voucher, ausi cum il freynt en bref malement[4] purchacé.

1. estouera *SGMCH.* estut *N.* *sim. A.* 2—2. *om. M.* 3—3. *so verb. N. om. LGS.* la ou i dust voucher plusors ou plusurs *M.* *sim. A.* la ou il deust auer vouche plusours ou vouche a garaunt plusours *C.* 4. manueisement *M.*

Voucher by aid of court.

2. If the warrant be of full age, then there is no need to show a charter or other presumption; but he may be vouched by aid of the court, or without aid, as shall be said in treating of warranties in a writ of right[n]. If it be done by aid of the court, and the warrant resides in the county, let the sheriff be commanded to summon him to appear before the same Justices on another day, to warrant according as he shall be vouched, or to refuse. And if the warrant has land elsewhere, and none in that county, let him be summoned by our writ of judgment[o].

Summons to warrant.

Writ of judgment.

Objection for non-joinder or mis-joinder of warrants.

3. If the tenant vouches to warrant separately, where he ought to vouch more than one together, or many where he ought to vouch only one, and the warrants demand judgment of the bad voucher, in such case the tenant shall fail in his voucher, as he would have done in case of a writ ill purchased.

n The chapter here referred to is wanting in all the copies. See before, vol. i. p. 107, note; and see the last chapter of Britton, s. 5, where reference is made to the same chapter alluded to above. As to the incompleteness of the work, see the Introduction by the Editor.

o If the vouchee had land in the county, he was summoned without writ by precept of the Justices to the sheriff; if his land was in another county, it was necessary to obtain a writ out of the Chancery. See the parallel passages of Bracton and Fleta. The expression 'writ of judgment' is in Fleta, not in Bracton. The form of the judicial writ is in Reg. Brev. Judic. 46 *b*.

4. Et cum le tenaunt eit vouché acun a garraunt qi viegne en court et ly garrauntize, ou plusours tenauntz en commun cum un heir, qe ly garrauntisent, et ceux vouchent acun autre, et issi de garraunt en garraunt, si acun de touz face defaute, soit la assise prise par sa defaute, ausi cum trestouz fesoint defaute, lequel qe acuns soint de eynz age ou noun. Et ceo qe est dit[1] de un tenaunt, voloms qe soit tenu[2] de plusours. Brac. 257 b, 258; Fle. 282 (§ 2). [196 b.]

5. Et si le garaunt viegne al jour qe il serra somouns et le pleintif ausi, et le tenaunt nient[3], tauntost soit prise l'assise[4] par [5]la defaute le tenaunt[5], si les jurours soint presentz; et si noun, soit doné as parties autre jour. Et si le garaunt eit attendu [6]jekes al quart jour[6], soit agardé, qe il s'en voist quite de sa garauntie sauntz jour, et qe l'assise soit prise par la defaute le tenaunt, sicum de sus est dit. Et la resoun pur quei le pleintif ne recovere mie tauntost sa demaunde sauntz[7] reconisaunce del assise est pur ceo qe touz les articles de soen bref [8]ou en partie[8] porrount estre faus. Car tut cesse le tene- Brac. 258 (§ 5); Fle. 282 (§ 3). Brac 258 (§ 5); Fle. 282 (§ 4).

1. *so F.* *sim. CH.* dit *om. LSGAM.* fet *N.* 2. fet [tenu *interl.*] *N.*
3. *so NA.* *sim. M.* vient *LG.* vent *S.* veut *CH.* 4. *so NAC.* et *add. L.* *sim. MH.*
5—5. sa defaute *A.* 6—6. *so N.* *sim. SGAMCH.* autre iour *L.* 7. *so N.* *sim. AMCH.* par *LGSA.* 8—8. en *om. M.* ou *om. A.* en sa purpartie *CH.*

4. When the tenant has vouched to warrant any one who comes into court and warrants him, or several tenants in common as one heir, who warrant him, and these vouch some other, and so on from warrant to warrant, if any one of the whole number makes default, the assise shall be taken by his default, as if all had made default, whether they be any of them under age or not. And what is said concerning one tenant, shall be observed where there are several. Of several vouchees, upon default of any, assise is taken by default.

5. If the warrant appears at the day for which he is summoned, and the plaintiff also, but not the tenant, let the assise be forthwith taken by the default of the tenant, if the jurors are present; and if not, let another day be given to the parties. And if the warrant has waited until the fourth day, let it be awarded that he go quit of his warranty without day, and that the assise be taken by the default of the tenant, as above said. The reason why the plaintiff shall not straightway recover his demand without recognisance of the assise, is because all the points of his writ or some of them may be false; for although the tenement demanded ceases presumptively to If the vouchee appears and the tenant not, the assise is taken by default. And the vouchee is quit. Judgment not given for plaintiff without assise; reason of this.

ment demaundé estre par semblaunt al tenaunt par sa defaute, uncore covendra neqedent qe nostre court soit instructe del dreit al pleyntif. Car si l'assise die qe le pleintif ne ad nul dreit en sa demaunde, ne est mie resoun qe il la recovere, desicum il ne put prover les pointz de sa entente.

Brac. 258; Fle. 282 (§ 4). 6. Et si le tenaunt viegne, et les garrauntz ausi, et le pleintif face defaute, au quart jour soit agardé qe le tenaunt s'en voist quites de cel bref sauntz jour, et les garrauntz de lour garrauntie, et le pleyntif et ses pleges de sure [1]en la merci remeygnent en nostre court[1].

Brac. 258; Fle. 282 (§ 4). [197.] 7. Et si le tenaunt et le pleyntif viegnent en court, et le garraunt face defaute, soit prise l'assise par la defaute le garraunt, issi qe nule prise de terre ne soit agardé vers le garraunt jeqes autaunt qe hom sache par l'assise lequel le tenaunt deyve retener ou perdre. Car si il deive retener, adounc ne sera mie mester de passer outre al plee de la garrauntie.

Brac. 258, 258 *b*; Fle. 282 (§ 4). 8. Et si la prise de l'assise soit delayé jekes a un autre jour par cas, a quel jour, tut viegne le garraunt et voille garraun-

1—1. en la mercy *M*. remeygnent en nostre Merci *N*. *sim*. *SGAC*. seient en la mercy *H*.

be the tenant's by reason of his default, yet still it is necessary that our court be informed of the right of the plaintiff; for if the assise say that the plaintiff hath no right in his demand, there is no reason that he should recover, inasmuch as he cannot prove the points of his case.

Default of plaintiff. 6. If the tenant appears and the warrants also, and the plaintiff makes default on the fourth day, let it be awarded that the tenant go quit of that writ without day, and the warrants of their warranty, and that the plaintiff and his pledges of suit remain in mercy in our court.

Default of vouchee; no execution against him until after assise. 7. If the tenant and the plaintiff appear in court, and the warrant makes default, let the assise be taken by the default of the warrant, but let no caption of land be awarded against the warrant until it be known by the assise whether the tenant ought to retain the land or to lose it. For if he ought to retain it, then there will be no need of proceeding to the plea of warranty.

Vouchee in default not allowed to warrant until after assise. 8. And if the taking of the assise is delayed by any chance to another day, and the warrant comes on that day and is

ter, pur ceo ne soit il mie resceu a ceo, for qe as eschaunges fere, enceis[1] qe l'assise soit prise en forme de assise; et par tres resouns, dount une est, pur ceo qe il ne avoit nul jour a garraunter; le autre est, pur ceo qe il perdi ses excepciouns et totes ses defenses par la defaute qe il fist al autre jour; et la terce[2], pur ceo qe ne est mie mester qe il soit a ceo resceu eynz qe hom sache de la necessité, sicum de sus est dit. Et issi piert [3]qe ne ad[3] mie mester de sa presence eynz qe il viegne par distresce puis qe l'assise [4]encountre le tenaunt avera passé[4]. Car si il fust soeffert[5] qe il venist en court apres sa defaute et garrauntist et deist issi, jeo garrauntiz et reng[6] le tenement demaundé au pleintif, si freit le garraunt aperte disseisine al tenaunt[7], s'il le fist encountre le gré le tenaunt, et nomément [8]pur ceo[8] qe il ne avoit adounc nul [197 *b*.] jour en court. Car tut soit garraunt tenu a defendre soen tenaunt en sa possessioun, pur ceo [9]ne le[9] deit il mie disseiser

1. einz ceo *NSGAMCH*. 2. *so SG*. tierz *L*. 3—3. qe ne est *N*. *sim. H.* qil nest *SGAC*. *sim. M.* 4—4. auera passee encountre le tenaunt *N*. *sim. SGMACH.* 5. *so N*. *sim. AMCH*. surfet *L*. 6. *so LNF*. renk *M*. rend *GAC*. rende *H*. renc *S*. 7. *so NA*. et *add. L*. *sim. SGM*. 8—8. puis *CH*. 9—9. ne ly *N*. *sim. A*. ne *SGM*. nel *C*. ne lui *H*.

ready to warrant, yet he shall not be admitted thereto, except with a view to making the exchanges[p], before the assise is taken in form of assise; and this for three reasons; first, because he had no day given him to warrant; secondly, because he lost the benefit of his exceptions and all his defences by the default which he made on the former day; and thirdly, because there is no need of his being admitted thereto before the necessity of it is known, as hath been said above. Hence it is apparent that there is no need of his presence until he is caused to appear by distress, after the assise has passed against the tenant. For if he were allowed to come into court after his default, and to warrant and say, 'I warrant, and I restore the tenement demanded to the plaintiff,' the warrant would be guilty of a manifest disseisin against the tenant, if it were done against his consent, and particularly as the warrant had then no day in court. For although the warrant is obliged to defend his tenant in his possession, he ought not upon that pretence to disseise him by surrendering to the

Warrant need not appear till assise goes against tenant.

Warrant in default cannot admit plaintiff's right.

p See below, s. 16.

par[1] rendre la demaunde al pleintif, cum rendre et defendre sount contraries.

Brac. 258 *b* (§ 6); Fle. 282 (§ 5).

9. Et cum la prise del assise soit agardé par la defaute le garraunt, et l'assise soit passé encountre le tenaunt, dounc a primes soit [2]agardé la seisine[2] al pleintif, et qe le garraunt soit destreint a venir a un autre jour en ceste manere, qe le viscounte prenge en nostre meyn de la terre le garraunt a la vaillaunce de la terre demaundé, et qe le garraunt soit somouns, solom ceo qe dit serra el plee del dreit. Car garraunter, en un sen, signefie a defendre le tenaunt en sa seisine, et, en un autre sen, signefie, qe s'il ne le defende, [3]apres ceo qe en due fourme soit vouché[3], qe le garraunt ly soit tenu as eschaunges, et de fere soen gré a la vaillaunce. Et en ceste manere soit destreint, si il eit terre en mesme le counté.

Brac. 258 *b* (§ 7); Fle. 283 (§ 5).

10. Et si la terre perdue et la terre dount eschaunges deyvent fet soint en diverses countez, en primes soit fete la

1. pur *M*. 2—2. garde la seisine *L*. agardee seisine *D*. [a]gardee seisine *N*. agarde la seisine *GM*. *sim*. *SAF*. agarde lassise *H*. 3—3. so *N*. *sim*. *A*. *om*. *LGSCHF*. apres ceo qe en due manere soit vouche *M*.

plaintiff his demand, inasmuch as surrendering and defending are contraries.

Warrant summoned to fulfil the warranty.

9. When the taking of the assise is awarded by default of the warrant, and the assise passes against the tenant, then for the first time seisin shall be awarded to the plaintiff[q], and the warrant shall be distrained to appear on another day in the following manner.

Process by distress.

The sheriff shall take into our hand of the lands of the warrant as much as the value of the land demanded, and he shall be summoned, as will be mentioned in the plea of right[r].

Obligation of warranty.

For warranty in one sense signifies the defending of the tenant in his seisin, and in another sense it signifies that if he does not defend him after being properly summoned, the warrant is bound to exchange, and to make him satisfaction to the value. And in this manner let him be distrained, if he has land in the same county.

Process, when the warrant's land is in another county.

10. If the land lost and the land whereout exchange is to be made are in diverse counties, first let the tenant's land

[q] This statement about seisin being awarded at this stage of the proceedings is not found in the corresponding place of Bracton or Fleta, and appears inconsistent with s. 11 See also s. 23, 24. Perhaps we should read, gardé la seisine al tenaunt, the tenant's possession being undisturbed.

[r] See note above, s. 2

estente de la terre al tenaunt; et cum nos Justices serrount de la value certifiez, soit maundé par [1]bref de jugement[1] al viscounte, en qi baillie le garraunt ad terre, qe il prenge en nostre meyn a la vaillaunce solom l'estente, et le garraunt soit somouns de estre devaunt eux a un autre jour. Et si plusurs garrauntz deyvent issi estre destreyntz, et ceux eyent [198.] lour terres en diverses countez, adounc soit maundé as viscountes, qe chescun prenge en nostre meyn proporcionelment solom ceo qe[2] chescun afferra[3] de garrauntir solom l'estente de la terre au tenaunt.

11. La resoun pur quei [4]il ne recovere mie[4] sa demaunde tauntost apres la defaute del garraunt et[5] apres l'assise passé pur ly est pur ceo qe le garraunt porra par cas [6]sei escuser de la[6] defaute par acune desturbaunce, par la quele excusacioun deit le proces estre anienti jekes a la somounse, ausi cum en plee de dreit. Car defaute ne porra mie verrement estre jugé, taunt cum ele porra estre defendue par ley; et mal seroit si le garraunt perdiseit ses respounses vers le

Brac. 258 *b*, 259; Fle. 283 (§ 5).

1—1. nostre bref de Iugement *GAM*. nostre bref *CH*. 2. a *add. N*. 3. auera *A*. *sim. M*. 4—4. ne recouere mie *L*. ne recoure *S*. il ne recouera *NACH*. *sim. MA*. 5. et *om. N*. 6—6. *so M*. *sim. G*. sei *om. LSCH*. encuser la *N*. escuser la *A*.

be extended; and when our Justices shall be certified of the value, let the sheriff in whose bailiwick the warrant has land be commanded by writ of judgment to take into our hand to the value according to the extent, and let the warrant be summoned to be before them at another day. And if several warrants are to be thus distrained, having their lands in diverse counties, the sheriffs shall be commanded that each of them take into our hand proportionally as much as each ought to warrant according to the valuation of the land of the tenant.

Vouchee may excuse his default

11. The reason why the plaintiff shall not recover his demand immediately after the default of the warrant, and after the assise passed in his favour, is this, because the warrant may perhaps excuse himself for the default by alleging some hindrance; by which excuse the proceedings may be annulled as far back as the summons, as in a plea of right; for it cannot be properly adjudged a default so long as it may be defended by law; and it would be ill, if the warrant should lose his answer to the demandant, and give the tenant his exchange

demaundaunt et ly feist eschaunges, ou il avereit bones defenses. Et si le garraunt ne viegne en court, ou s'il viegne et ne se puse escuser de la defaute, adounc a primes soit prise l'assise par la defaute le garraunt. Et si trové soit qe le pleyntif ad dreit en sa demaunde, soit agardé qe le pleintif recovere sa demaunde vers le tenaunt, et le tenaunt [1]recovere a la vaillaunce de la terre le garraunt[1], et le garraunt remeigne en nostre merci. Et si le pleyntif ne eit nul dreit, soit jugé encountre ly, cum avaunt est dit.

Brac. 259 (§7); Fle. 283 (§7).

Brac. 259 (§7); Fle. 283 (§7). [198 b.]

12. Et pur ceo qe mal serreit qe le tenaunt recoverast vers le garraunt par la defaute le garaunt a la vaillaunce de la terre demaundé, et jalemeins tenist sa terre en pees, si[2] l'assise deist[3] encountre le pleintif, pur ceo voloms nous, qe l'assise soit[4] prise eynz qe nul play soit meu vers la garraunt. Et si le garraunt qi terre est prise en nostre meyn ne viegne al jour qe il autre foiz fu somouns, [5]et l'assise juree et leau-

1—1. *so verb. SG. sim. MCHF.* de *om. L.* a la vaillaunce vers le garraunt *N. sim. A.* 2. E si *N.* 3. *so HF.* deit *LGSAM.* die *N.* seit *C.* 4. *so N. sim. GAMCH.* soit *om. LS.* 5—5. *so L. sim. SG.* lassise soit passee pur *N.* e lassise eit passe pur *MH.* e lassise seit pur *AC.*

If he does not appear or does not save his default, judgment against him for exchange.

when he had a good defence. But if the warrant does not come into court, or if he comes and cannot excuse himself for the default, then and not before let the assise be taken[a] by the default of the warrant; and if it be found that the plaintiff has right in his demand, let it be awarded that the plaintiff recover his demand against the tenant, and that the tenant recover to the value of the land of the warrant, and that the warrant remain in our mercy. And if the plaintiff has no right, let it be adjudged against him, as before is said.

No judgment against warrant, unless the assise passes against the tenant.

12. And because it would be wrong for the tenant to recover against the warrant by his default to the value of the land demanded, and at the same time to hold his own land in peace, supposing the assise to declare against the plaintiff, therefore we will that the assise be taken before any plea is commenced against the warrant. And if the warrant, whose land is taken into our hand, does not appear on the day for which he is a second time summoned, and the assise, being

[a] This statement is difficult to reconcile with what is said before in s. 7, where the assise is directed to be taken immediately upon the first default of the vouchee. (See also s. 8, 12) The same apparent inconsistency is found in the parallel passages of Bracton and Fleta. Perhaps we should understand here, that the assise taken in the absence of the warrant should not be treated as taken by his default, so as to be binding upon him, until he had had an opportunity of clearing his default

mentes chargé eit passé pleynement pur[5] le pleintif, soit adounc[1] jugé encountre le garraunt, cum [2]plus plenerement est avaunt[2] dit.

13. Et cum le garraunt vendra en court, et die countrepledaunt la garrauntie, qe il [3]ne deit ne en nule manere porra[3] garrauntir par ceste[4] resoun, qe garrauntir est [5]defense de[5] tenaunt en sa seisine, pur ceo neqedent qe garrauntir, quant a un autre sen, signefie a fere [6]au tenaunt eschanges[6] a la vaillaunce si par defaute del garraunt eit sa terre perdue, voloms nous qe le pleintif recovere ses eschaunges. Et si il se puse neqedent defendre qe il ne ly face a la vaillaunce, soit agardé [7]par nos Justices[7], de aler ent[8] quites sauntz jour.

Brac. 259 (§ 8); Fle. 283 (§ 8).

Brac. 259, 259 *b*; Fle. 283 (§ 8).

14. Et si il entre en garrauntie, et vouche autre a garraunt, soit le autre garraunt somouns encountre un autre jour, a quel si il fet defaute, soit pris de sa terre a la vaillaunce de la demaunde[9] en nostre meyn, et soit somouns encountre un autre jour, a quel jour, si il [10]ne viegne, ou si il viegne et[10] ne

Brac. 259 *b*; Fle. 283 (§ 8).

1. adounc *om. NAMCH.* 2—2. auaunt est *NA.* deuaunt est *MCH.* 3—3. *so LGS.* ne puit *N. sim. AMCH.* 4. la *NAMCH.* 5—5. defendre le *M.* defense le *CH.* 6—6. taunt en eschaunges al tenaunt ceo est a sauer *N. sim. A.* 7—7. *so LSG. om. NAMCH.* 8. *so LS. om. NGAMCH.* 9. terre demaundee *N. sim. CH.* 10—10. *so M.* vient ou si il ne veint et *L.* ne veigne ne enueye par quei il *N. sim. A.* ne veigne ou sil vent e *C.* ne vint ou s'il vent e *G. sim. SH.*

sworn and lawfully charged, has passed for the plaintiff, let judgment then be given against the warrant, as is before more fully set forth.

No defence in a plea of warranty that vouchor is no longer seised.

13. If the warrant comes into court, and says by way of counter-plea to the warranty, that he ought not, neither is able to warrant, by reason that warranty is the defending of the tenant in his seisin, nevertheless, as warranty in another sense signifies the giving to the tenant an equivalent exchange, if he has lost his land by default of the warrant, we will that the plaintiff recover his exchanges. And yet if he can defend himself from the liability to make satisfaction to the value, it shall be awarded by our Justices that he go quit without day.

Second vouchee; process against him.

14. If he enter into warranty and vouch another to warrant, let the second warrant be summoned against another day; at which if he makes default, let there be taken into our hands of his land to the value of the land demanded, and let him be summoned against another day; at which day if he does not

Heng. M. c. 8. p. 35, c. 13. p. 70. puse saner[1] la defaute, soit jugé solom le proces del petit *Cape*, sicum plus plenerement et apertement serra dit [2]apres en le[2] plee de dreit.

[199.]

Brac. 259 *b*; Fle. 283 (§ 8). 15. Et si le autre garraunt viegne en court et countreplede la garrauntie, et die qe il ne deit garraunter, pur ceo qe il ne tient nient de ly, ne service ne ly fet, ne homage unqe ne ly fist; ou s'il die, qe il ne ly[3] est mie tenuz a garrauntir[4], pur ceo qe, tut fust il a ceo tenuz, si le[5] ad le vouchour defailli[6] et perdu eyde de ly par la defaute qe il fist, la quele [7]ly fust[7] prejudiciele, [8]qe la ou il dust[8] aver respoundu a la assise, si il fust venu al jour, la perdi il par sa defaute totes ses defenses et ses excepciouns, la quele perte[9] il porra retter[10] a sa negligence demeyne, et de ceo demaunde[11] jugement, voloms qe jugement se face encountre le voucheour. Et en mesme la manere si le tierz garraunt eit fet [12]mesme la respounse[12].

Brac. 259 *b*, 260; Fle. 283, 284 (§ 9); Ante, s. 8. 16. Et issi piert bien, qe cum le garraunt eit fet defaute le

1. *so LN.* sauuer *SMG.* 2—2. en *NACH.* el *M.* 3. ly *om. N.* 4. la garrauntie *N.* 5. *so L. sim. S.* le *om. NGAMCH.* 6. fet defaute *NAMC.* fet par defaute *H.* 7—7. fust si *N.* li fust si *M.* 8—8. *so MCH. om.* (*with an hiatus*) *LS.* qe il la ou il dust *N.* qil ne duit *A.* qe la ou il pout *G.* 9. *so NAMH.* partie *LC.* pert *G.* 10. arratter *A.* 11. *so N. sim. AMCH.* maunde *L.* 12—12. *so verb. NS. sim. MCH.* mes les respounses *L. sim. AG.*

appear, or if he appears and cannot clear his default, the judgment shall be by process of the lesser *Cape*, as shall be more fully and plainly said in treating of the plea of right[t].

Process by little *Cape*.

Defence of second vouchee, by denying the liability, or pleading first vouchee's default.

15. If the second vouchee comes into court and counterpleads the warranty, and says that he is not bound to warrant because the other holds nothing of him, nor does any service to him, nor ever did homage to him, or if he says that he is not now bound to warranty, because, although he were bound thereto, yet the vouchor has made default to him, and has lost his aid by such default, which was prejudicial to him, inasmuch as where he might have answered to the assise if he had appeared at the day, he by his default lost all his defences and exceptions, which loss he may impute to his own negligence, and if he thereof demands judgment, we will that judgment be given against the vouchor. So likewise, if a third vouchee gives the same answer.

Vouchee in default admitted to make exchange, but not to defend the title

16. Hence it plainly appears, that when the warrant makes

t See note ante, s. 2. The practice referred to is described in Bracton 384; Fleta 411. c. 25.

premer jour, par quei l'assise est jugé a prendre, et la reconisaunce del assise soit delayé [1]a prendre[1] jekes a un autre jour par acun cas, a quel jour le garraunt soit venu et voille garrauntir eynzces[2] qe l'assise soit prise, qe fere le porra, ne mie neqedent qe il die[3] acune resoun par quei l'assise remeigne, ou qe il defende le tenaunt en sa seisine, mes as eschaunges fere, si le tenaunt perde par l'assise, et mout plus fort apres la reconisaunce del assise, et qe rien ne vaudra a tiel garraunt de voucher autre garraunt. [199 *b.*]

17. Et si acun garraunt face defaute en court puis qe il avera vouché, et le pleintif et le tenaunt soint en court, tauntost soit prise la reconisaunce del assise, lequel qe le autre garraunt vouché viegne ou noun. Et en mesme la manere soit fet par la defaute le tenaunt, tut soit le garraunt present. Car tut poreit[4] le tenaunt [5]ou le[5] garraunt acune resoun dire a destourber l'assise, pur ceo ne serra mie le garraunt quite de la garrauntie. Car pur le dit le tenaunt ne Brac. 260; Fle. 284 (§ 9).

1—1. *om. AM.* 2. einz [ceo] *N.* einz ceo *MCH.* einz *A.* 3. ne die *M.* 4. prent *LGSMF.* puit *NDA.* poet *W.* preigne *CH.* 5—5. oue le *N.* ou lautre *M.*

default the first day, whereupon the assise is adjudged to be taken, but through some accident the recognisance of the assise is delayed until another day, and the warrant comes at that day, and, before the assise is taken, is ready to warrant, he may be admitted thereto, yet not so as to allege any reason for staying the assise, or to defend the tenant in his seisin, but in order to make the exchanges if the tenant should lose by the assise,—and much more after the recognisance of the assise,—and that a vouchee in that position will not be assisted by vouching another warrant.

17. If any warrant, after he has vouched another, makes default in court, and the plaintiff and tenant are in court, let the recognisance of the assise be immediately taken, whether the second warrant appears or not; and let the same course be taken, where the tenant makes default, although the warrant is present. For although the tenant or warrant might have some reason to allege for hindering the assise, yet the warrant shall not be therefore quit of the warranty [u]. For the assise If either vouchor or vouchee make default the assise is taken by default.

[u] I think there is some confusion here, arising from the compiler having followed Fleta's abridgment of Bracton, in which the sense of the latter is not truly represented. The reason given by Bracton for excluding the warrant from taking exceptions to the assise in the absence of his vouchor is that by the default of the latter he is quit of the warranty. Bracton afterwards supposes another case, in which the vouchee has appeared and

remeindra mie l'assise, cum il eit mis totes ses defenses en la bouche le garraunt, les queles il ne porra reprendre a sa volunté; ne al garraunt affiert rien for qe a defendre sei de la garrauntie.

Brac. 260 (§ 10); Fle. 284 (§ 9, 10).

18. Et si le garraunt ne face nule defaute, et entre en la garrauntie, adounc list a ly respoundre et dire encountre l'assise, par quei ele ne deit passer; cum totes les excepciouns et defenses sount alowables en sa persone, desicum il est fet ausi cum tenaunt par sa garrauntie, qe eussent esté alouwables al tenaunt. Ou celi garraunt porra voucher autre, et celi autre, et issi des plusours.

Brac. 260 b; Fle. 284 (§ 10).

19. Et cum plusours soint issi vouchez, et le drein ne puse defendre le tenaunt, ou si la assise soit prise par la defaute de acun garraunt, et le dreyn garraunt ne se puse defendre des eschaunges, soit agardé qe le vouchour eit de la terre de soen
[200.] garraunt a la vaillaunce, et issi de vouchour en vouchour, deques autaunt qe le pleintif recovere sa demaunde del tenaunt, et il a la vaillaunce de soen garraunt; et le dreyn garraunt remeigne en nostre merci.

Tenant having vouched cannot defend himself.

shall not be stayed for anything the tenant can say, forasmuch as he has put his whole defence in the mouth of the warrant, and cannot resume it at his pleasure; and the warrant has nothing to do but to defend himself as to the warranty.

Vouchee accepting warranty may defend the action;

18. If the warrant makes no default and enters into warranty, then he is allowed to answer and allege against the assise any reason why it ought not to pass, since all the exceptions and defences are allowed him which would have been allowable to the tenant, inasmuch as by his warranty he is put in the place of tenant. Or the first warrant may vouch a second, and he another, and so of several.

or vouch another.

Judgment against several vouchees in succession.

19. When several are thus vouched, and the last cannot defend the tenant, or if the assise is taken by default of any warrant, and the last warrant cannot defend himself from liability to exchange, let it be awarded that the vouchor have of the land of his warrant to the value, and so from vouchor to vouchor until the plaintiff recover his demand against the tenant, and he in value against his warrant, and the last warrant shall remain in our mercy.

denied his liability to warranty; then, he says, neither the tenant nor the vouchee are in a position to raise any objection to the taking of the assise, for the same reasons as are stated by Britton in the next sentence. Brac. 260; Fle. 284 (§ 9). As to the relation between Fleta and Britton, see the Editor's Introduction.

20. Et si acun garraunt ou plusours soint de eynz age, adounc remeigne la parole sauntz jour jekes a lour age. Et si un de plusours demaundauntz en commun moerge eynz qe l'assise soit prise[1], pur ceo ne chet mie le bref. Et en mesme la manere soit, si un moerge des plusours tenauntz en commun. Mes si le heritage soit departi entre parceners[2] qi avaunt[3] tyndrent en commun, et acun des parceners moerge, l' assise cherra pur le bref vicious. Et si le baroun et sa femme del dreit la femme soint enpledez, et le baroun moerge avaunt l'assise prise, pur ceo ne cherra mie l'assise, ne le bref; mes la reverse. Brac. 260 *b*; Fle. 284 (§ 11).

21. Mes si le pleintif ou tenaunt ou ambideus moergent avaunt l'assise, si cherra l'assise par defaute de foundement. Et si acun garraunt moerge puis ceo qe il serra vouché, eynz qe il eit garraunti, pur ceo ne chete mie l'assise, nel bref, mes recomence le tenaunt a voucher soen heir. Mes s'il moerge [4]apres ceo qe il eit[4] garraunti, si chete le bref par defaute de foundement, cum le garraunt par sa garrauntie se fist ausi cum Brac. 260 *b*; Fle. 284, 285.

1. passee ou prise *N.* *sim.* *CH.* 2. freres parceners *N CH.* 3. le *add.* *NSGAMCH.* 4. auaunt qe il eit *L.* apres ceo qe il auera *N.* *sim.* *SGAMCH.*

20. If one or more of the warrants are under age, the plea shall stand over without day until their age. Where of several demandants in common one dies before the assise is taken, the writ does not thereby abate. Neither shall it abate if one die out of several tenants in common. But if the inheritance has been divided between parceners who before held in common, and one of the parceners die, the assise shall abate on account of the writ being bad. And if husband and wife are impleaded of the right of the wife, and the husband dies before the assise is taken, neither the assise nor the writ shall abate; but otherwise in the reverse case.

Minority of warrant delays the plea. Death of one joint demandant, or joint tenant, does not abate the writ.

Death of tenant's husband, no abatement.

21. If the plaintiff or the tenant or both die before the assise, the assise shall fail for want of a foundation. And if any warrant dies after he is vouched, but before he has warranted, neither the assise nor the writ thereby abates, but the tenant must begin again to vouch his heir. But if he dies after he has warranted, the writ shall abate for want of a foundation, as the vouchee by his warranty has made himself, as it were, prin-

Abatement by death of plaintiff or tenant. Death of warrant

princepal tenaunt, et enprist sur ly les fetz[1] del principal plee.

Brac. 261; Fle. 285 (§ 12). [200 *b.*] 22. Et si acun tenaunt ou garraunt die pur respounse, qe il ne put respoundre sauntz nous, et sur ceo boute avaunt chartre de nous ou de nos predecessours, pur ceo ne remeigne mie l'assise a prendre. Mes si ele face pur le pleintif, soit jugement delayé jekes a la proscheyne sessioun, si par la chartre seoums obligez a la garrauntie par acuns motz[2] especials, tut ne soit mie la clause[3] de garrauntie leynz especefié, et en le meen tens soint nos Justices de nous counseillez sour le jugement. Mes si la chartre soit de confermement le roi Knout, ou de autre qe ne fu mie noster auncestre, ou si la chartre die, Nous avoms graunté[4] quaunt qe en nous est sauve chescuni dreit, en ceo cas et en cas semblables ne voloms mie qe jugementz soint delayez.

Brac. 261; Fle. 285 (§ 13). 23. Et si cas avient, qe acun fort plee et graunt debat chete en acun plee de garrauntie, par le quel debat l'assise deit estre delayé par un jour ou par plusours, en tiel cas[5] ne

1. fez *NM.* feez *CH.* fes *SA.* 2. so *NGM.* mez *LS.* moz *AC.* 3. so *NAMCHF.* cause *LSG.* 4. garanti *M.* 5 so *NSGAM.* cas *om. L.*

cipal tenant, and taken upon himself the conduct of the principal plea.

Plea that the king should be a party. 22. If any tenant or warrant shall say by way of answer, that he cannot answer without us, and thereupon puts forward a charter of us or some of our predecessors, the assise nevertheless shall not be stayed. But if it passes for the plaintiff, let judgment be deferred until the next session, in case by the charter we may be bound to warranty by virtue of some special words, although the clause of warranty may not be therein expressed, and in the meantime let our Justices be consulted by us upon the judgment. But if it be a charter of confirmation of king Canute, or of any other who was not our ancestor, or if the charter express that we have granted as much as was in us saving the rights of all other parties, in that and the like cases we will not have judgment delayed.

(Margin notes: King bound to warranty. — Charter of king Canute. — Charter with general saving.)

Assise not to be delayed for the decision of a question arising upon the warranty. 23. If it shall happen that some great[x] dispute or difficult question arises in a plea of warranty, by the discussion of which the assise is like to be delayed for a day or more, in such

[x] It would seem from this, that when the warrant appeared, the Justices were accustomed, in a simple case, to go into the question of warranty before deciding the original plea.

greve nient de prendre l'assise, par qi reconisaunce hom porra estre certefiez si mester soit a continuer le plé de la garrauntie ou noun. Car si [1]assise face[1] encountre le pleintif, adounc ne serra mie mestier a determiner[2] le play de la garrauntie.

24. Et si le frere puisnee soit entré en le heritage soen piere, et hors de sa seisine eit feffé acun estraunge, sur qi le frere eynznee eit arrami assise de mort de auncestre, et cel tenaunt vouche a garraunt le frere puisnee soen feffour, et celi viegne garrauntir, et die qe assise ne deit estre entre ly et soen frere eynznee, desicum il cleyme a tener le[3] tenement par mesme la descente, pur ceo ne remeigne mie l'assise. Car, tut soit le frere puisnee defendour del tenaunt par sa garrauntie, pur ceo ne est il mie verrey tenaunt; [4]car le tenaunt james ne partira[4] de sa seisine duraunt le play de la garrauntie, mes cum le garraunt [5]mes ne ly[5] porra defendre en sa seisine, et le jugement face encountre le garraunt, dounc a primes serra il engetté par jugement. Car si l'assise deyve

Fle. 285 (§ 14).

[201.]

Fle. 285 (§ 15).

1—1. *so LSG.* lassise face *NA.* lasise passe *M.* *sim. F.* assise se face *CH.* 2. terminer *M.* 3. meme le *M.* *sim. NA.* 4—4. car le tenant iames ne departise *M.* ne iammes le tenaunt departira *CH.* 5—5. *so G.* mes ne *LSACH.* ne le *N.* mes nel *M.*

case there will be no harm in taking the assise, by the recognisance whereof it may be ascertained, whether there be any need of continuing the plea of warranty or not; for if the assise passes against the plaintiff, there will be no need of determining the plea of warranty.

24. If the younger brother has entered into the inheritance of his father, and during the time of his seisin has enfeoffed a stranger, against whom the elder brother brings an assise of mortdancester, and the tenant vouches to warrant the younger brother his feoffor, and the latter appears to warrant, and says, that assise ought not to be between him and his elder brother, inasmuch as he claims to hold the tenement by the same descent, the assise shall not be thereby stayed; for, although the younger brother is bound to defend the tenant by his warranty, yet he is not very tenant, for the tenant shall never part with his seisin pending the plea of warranty; but when the warrant can no longer defend him in his seisin, and judgment is given against the warrant, then and not before he shall be ousted by judgment. For if the assise between

Assise by elder brother against feoffee of younger.

Younger brother being vouched pleads exception of same descent.

Exception disallowed; why.

cheier entre ceux deus freres par la excepcioun de mesme la descente, adounc covendreit accioun sourdre en la persone le[1] eynznee a demaunder mesmes les tenementz par bref de dreit, et ceo ne purroit[2] estre si le frere puisnee ne fust verrei tenaunt; et s'il deyve porter le bref de dreit sur le tenaunt, adounc list al tenaunt a defendre le dreit le frere eynzné par batayle ou par graunt assise. Et pur [3]ceste graunt inconvenience eschure[3] ne voloms mie, qe tele excepcioun soit alouwable, for qe entre le demaundaunt et le verrei tenaunt en nul bref de possessioun.

Brac. 261; Fle. 285 (§ 16). [201 *b*.] 25. Et si acun feffe autre de acun tenement, et celi feffé de cel tenement face acune intrusioun ou autre encoumbrement vers acune terce[4] persone, qe sour le feffé arraime assise de mort de auncestre; ausi cum si Johan feffe Piers, et Piers feffe Roberd de mesme le tenement, apres qi mort Piers entre en les tenementz cum chief seignur, et le heir Roberd portast assise sour Piers, si Piers [5]vousist de ceo[5] voucher Johan a garraunt, si Johan puse averrer qe Piers ne est mié entré en

1. so *NA*. le *om*. *L*. al *M*. del *CH*. 2. so *N*. *sim*. *AH*. porrount *LC*. porra *M*. 3—3. pur ceo qe graunt inconuenient ensiwereit *N*. pur cel grant inconuenient eschura *M*. *sim*. *M*. 4. certeyne *N*. *sim*. *M*. *om*. *A*. 5—5. vosist sor ceo *M*. sur ceo vousist *CH*.

these brothers were to fail by reason of the exception of the same descent, then a right of action ought to arise in favour of the elder to demand the same tenements by writ of right, which could not be unless the younger brother was actual tenant; and if he be required to bring the writ of right against the tenant, then it will be lawful for the tenant to defend the right of the elder brother either by battle or by great assise. Therefore to avoid this great inconvenience, we will not that this exception be allowed in any possessory writ, unless between the demandant and the actual tenant.

Trial by battle disfavored.

Warrant not liable where feoffee has parted with the tenement and re-entered by wrong.

25. If one enfeoff another of any tenement, and the feoffee makes an intrusion or other encroachment upon a third person, who brings an assise of mortdancester against the feoffee,—as suppose John enfeoffs Peter, and Peter enfeoffs Robert of the same tenement, after whose death Peter enters into the tenement as chief lord, and the heir of Robert brings an assise against Peter; if Peter thereupon wishes to vouch John to warrant, and John can aver that Peter did not enter into the tenement

les tenementz par le fet Johan, mes par sa intrusioun demeyne, en tel cas ne voloms nous mie qe Johan, ne nul es cas semblables, soit tenu a garrantir, [1]einz en tel cas voloms nous qe chescun respoigne[1] de soen personel fet.

26. Si acun deyve purchacer assise de mort de auncestre sour acun tenement qe est tenu a terme des aunz, et le fermer soulement soit nomé tenaunt el bref, [2]issi qe le terme soit a x. ou a xii. ou a plus ou a meyns[2], si porra le fermer dire en jugement qe il ne cleime rien el tenement for qe terme des aunz de le les un tiel; et si issi seit, si chete le bref. Et si [3]le lessour[3] soit soulement nomé pur tenaunt, si chete ausi le bref, issi qe assise ne passe en prejudice le fermer, qi ad ausi graunt dreit en soen terme cum le lessour[4] el fraunc tenement. Et si ambideus soint nomez el bref, estoise le bref; et le fermer soit a jour, et vouche soen lessour a garraunt de soen terme, si il quide bien fere. Brac. 261; Fle. 285, 286.

27. En cas nequedent covendra nomer le fermer[5] soulement el bref, cum si acun seignur eit vendu la garde de acune terre jekes a certeyn terme des aunz, avaunt quel terme le heir eit [202.] Brac. 261, 261 *b*; Fle. 286 (§ 17).

1—1. einz respoigne chescun *N.* *sim. AMCH.* 2—2. so *L.* *sim. GS.* *om. NDAMCHFW.* 3—3. so *A.* le fessour *LGS.* *sim. NMF.* il *H.* 4. so *H.* fessour *LNAGSMCF.* 5. so *NAGMCHF.* fessour *LS.*

by the act of John, but by his own intrusion, in such case John, or any one in like position, shall not be bound to warrant; but in such circumstances every one shall answer for his personal act.

26. If an assise of Mortdancester is to be brought for a tenement held for a term of years, and the farmer only is named tenant in the writ, the term being for ten or twelve years, or more or less, the farmer may say upon the trial, that he claims nothing in the tenement but a term of years under the lease of such an one; and if it be so, the writ shall fail. And if the lessor alone is named as tenant, the writ shall likewise fail, so that the assise may not pass to the prejudice of the farmer, who has as much right to his term as the lessor to the freehold. But if both are named in the writ, the writ shall stand; and the farmer shall be present at the day, and vouch his lessor to warrant his term, if he thinks fit to do so. For tenement in lease, assise must be against freeholder and termor.

27. Nevertheless, in some cases the farmer only needs to be named in the writ, as where a lord has sold the wardship of any lands for a certain term of years, before which term the heir Assise may be brought by heir of age against lessee of his wardship without the lord.

atteynt a soen age plener et eit arramé assise sur le fermer, si le tenaunt vouche le seignur a garraunt par acun escrit de covenaunt, qe testmoigne qe le seignur ly est tenu a la garrauntie jekes a certeyn terme outre le age le dreit heir, [1] en tiels cas voloms nous, qe soint[1] favorables as heirs pleintifs, issi qe de dreit de lour heritage ne soint mie delayez par tiels vouchers, et les fermers eyent lour recoverer vers lour garrauntz par bref de covenaunt.

Fle. 286 (§ 18, 19).

Stat. Marl. (52 Hen. III.) c. 13; Stat. West. 1. (3 Ed. I.) c. 42; Stat. West. 2. (13 Ed. I.) c. 27, 28.

28. Et si les parties se profrent en court et covendra delayer la journee par defaute des jurours, soint les parties ajourneez [2]a mesme lour jour[2] sauntz estre essoniez, sicum ordiné est en nos estatutz. A quel jour si l'assise passe, cum assise ou cum juree, pur le pleyntif en absence del tenaunt, soit le jugement delayé [3]taunt qe a[3] un autre jour, et le tenaunt soit somouns de venir a tiel jour a[4] oyer soen jugement. A quel jour, lequel qe il viegne ou noun, soit jugé pur le pleintif pur la defaute le tenaunt apres sa apparaunce. [202 *b.*] Mes s'il soit aconvenu[5] entre les parties, qe le premer jour

1—1. en tiel cas voloms nous qe il soint *N.* *sim.* *SGMCH.* teus cas voloms qe seient *A.* *sim.* *F.* 2—2. iekes un autre *N.* a vn autre Iour *AM.* a meisme le iour *G.* *sim.* *SCH.* 3—3. *so* *LGS.* iekes a *N.* *sim.* *DMAF.* 4. *so* *GAMCH.* de *LNDEF.* *om.* *S.* 5. *so* *NDA.* aconueu *L.* a conue *S.* aconuenuz *M.* conuenu *H.* *sim.* *C.*

attains his full age and brings an assise against the farmer, if the tenant vouches the lord to warrant by virtue of some deed of covenant, which witnesses that the lord is bound to warranty until a certain term extending beyond the majority of the right heir, we will that such cases be favorably viewed in relation to the heirs plaintiffs, so that they may not be delayed of their right of inheritance by such vouchers; and the farmers shall have their recovery against their warrants by writ of covenant.

Assise put off for default of jurors.

28. If the parties present themselves in court, but it is necessary to delay the day by the default of the jurors, let the parties be adjourned to their said day without further essoin, as is ordained in our statutes. At which day if the assise passes, whether as an assise or as a jury, for the plaintiff in the absence of the tenant, let the judgment be delayed until another day, and the tenant be summoned to come upon such day to hear his judgment; at which day, whether he come or not, judgment shall be given for the plaintiff, for the default of the tenant after appearance. But if it has been agreed

soit l'assise prise et jugement rendu, lequel qe le tenaunt viegne ou noun, soit fet solom ceo qe convent [1] entre les parties.

CHAPITRE XII. [LXXVI.]

Excepcioun de mesme la Descente.

1. As pointz del bref porra le tenaunt respoundre en plusours maneres. Car a ceo qe est contenu primes el bref, si tiel auncestre fust seisi, porra il dire, qe sicum mesme le auncestre fu pere ou autre auncestre al pleintif et de qi seisine il cleyme le heritage, en mesme la manere fust il autiel [2] auncestre al tenaunt, et par la mort cel auncestre se tient il en le heritage cum proschein heir; et s'il demaunde jugement, si assise deyve estre entre si privez de saunc clamauntz par une mesme [3] descente, en tiel cas voloms nous qe le tenaunt voise sauntz jour et le pleintif [4] prenge rien par soen bref, par les resouns dites desus, eynz remeigne en nostre

Brac. 266 *b*; Fle. 287 (§ 2); Heng. Parv. c. 8. p. 114.

Ante, c. 6. s. 9.

1. conuient *N.* conuint *S.* conuenist *A.* couynt *M.* 2. au tiel *L.* au tel *M.* a tel *M.* auxi *N.* *sim. A.* 3. mesme *om. N.* 4. ne *add. NM.*

between the parties that the assise be taken and judgment given the first day, then, whether the tenant come or not, the agreement between the parties shall take effect.

CHAPTER XII.

Exception of 'same Descent.'

1. To the points of the writ the tenant may answer several ways; for as to that which is first contained in the writ, namely, whether such ancestor was seised, he may plead, that as this ancestor was the plaintiff's father or other ancestor by whose seisin he claims the inheritance, so was he likewise ancestor to the tenant, and by reason of the death of such ancestor he holds himself in the inheritance as next heir; and if he demands judgment whether the assise ought to take place between such privies in blood claiming by the same descent, in such case we will that the tenant go without day, and the plaintiff take nothing by his writ for the reasons after men-

Exception that demandand and tenant claim by the same descent.

merci pur sa fause pleinte. Et il se purchace par bref de dreit a detrier la proscheinté du saunc, si il quide bien fere.

Brac. 266 *b*; Fle. 287 (§ 3).

2. En cas nequedent porra valer la replicacioun le[1] pleintif, cum si acun pleintif clamast le tenement par le feffement

[203.] lour commun auncestre, et de ceo moustrast chartres ou[2] tendist averrement, et deist qe il ne clamat rien par descente. Mes si le tenaunt respoigne a ceo en triplicant, qe cel feffement ne ly deit grever, pur ceo qe le donour unques ne chaungea soen estat, ne unques le pleintif de ceo ne fust en seisine, mes[3] qe le donour demorast[4] tous jours en seisine, et morust seisi,—et solom ceo qe il ceo[5] puse averrer, si[6] face le jugement.

3. Entre deus privez de saunc nequedent, freres ou cosins ou autres privez, tient bien lu ceste assise et bref de cosinage et de ael, si hom le eust en usage, ou le dreit heir est pleintif freschement apres la mort lour commun auncestre, eynz ceo qe les tenauntz pusent clamer title de fraunc tenement par

1. al *MF*. 2. *conj.* en *L*. e *NSGAM*. 3. *so LSG*. mis *NAMCHF*. seisine mis qe le donour ne demorra *N*. *sim*. *AM*. *sim*. *HF*. 4. *so G*. demorast mie *L*. ne demorra *N*. ne demorast *SMC*. *sim*. *HF*. 5. *so SGAM*. se *L*. *om*. *NCH*. 6. se *NACH*.

tioned, but remain in our mercy for his false plaint. And if he thinks proper, he may proceed by writ of right to try the proximity of blood.

Replication, that plaintiff claims by feoffment.

2. Nevertheless in some cases the plaintiff may have a valid replication, as where a plaintiff claims the tenement by the feoffment of a common ancestor of himself and the tenant, and thereof produces charters or tenders averment, and says that he

Rejoinder, that seisin was never given.

claims nothing by descent. But the tenant may answer by way of triplication, that the same feoffment ought not to prejudice him, because the donor never altered his estate, and the plaintiff was never in seisin, but the donor all along continued in seisin and died seised; and according as he can verify this, so let judgment be given.

Assise by custom between privies of blood.

3. Nevertheless between two privies in blood, brothers or cousins or other privies, this assise may lie, as also the writ of Cosinage and of Ael, if it has been customarily used[y], where the right heir is plaintiff immediately after the death of their common ancestor, before the tenants can claim title of free-

y The statement here made is not confirmed by anything in Bracton or Fleta

lounge et pesible seisine. Et cel tens fet alouwer solom ceo qe le dreit heir eit freschement demaundé soen heritage puis ceo qe il le savoit ou le poeit[1] saver, solom ceo qe il avera esté loynz ou pres, de cea la mer ou de la, ou en prisoun ou dehors, ou solom ceo qe il ad esté negligent en[2] suffraunt le tenaunt dormir[3] en sa seisine.

4. Et si parcener demaunde par ceste assise vers parcener, sicum soeur qe demaunde de sa soeur sa purpartie, si chiet le bref et l'assise, et tient lu entre eus bref de renable partie. Et [4]si le tenaunt[4] die, qe le pleintif aveit une soeur de qie sount issues enfauntz qi sount en pleyne vie, qi autaunt de dreit averoint[5] a demaunder cum ele, si ceo soit averree, si chete le bref et remeigne l'assise, lequel qe ceus enfauntz soint engendrez hors de matrimoignie [6]ou noun[6]. Et sicum ceste assise ne tient mie lu par entre parceners et un heir, ausi ne tient ele mie lu par entre parceners qi tienent en commun ou en severalté par la resoun de la terre qe est en sei partable; eynz tient lu soulement bref[7] de renable partie. Et

Ante, c. 6. s. 15.

[203 *b.*]

Ante, c. 7. s. 2.

1. *so MCH.* pust *L.* pout *NSGA.* 2. ou *NGCH.* e *SAM.* 3. *so LM.* demorer *NGSA. sim. CH.* 4—4. *so NAGMCH.* le tenaunt *om. L.* sil *S.* 5. *so N. sim. SAMCH.* auerount *L.* aueient *G.* 6—6. *so LSG.* ou de feloun *NMCH. sim. A.* 7. *so NDR.* bref *om. LGSMCFW.*

hold by long and peaceable seisin. The time allowed must be determined by considering whether the right heir demanded his inheritance immediately after he knew of it, or could know of it, according as he was far off or near, on this side or beyond the seas, in prison or out, or according as he shall have been negligent in suffering the tenant to sleep in his seisin.

Limitation of time.

4. If one parcener demand against another by this assise, as where a sister demands her share against her sister, the writ and assise shall fail; and the writ *de rationabili parte* lies. Where the tenant says that the plaintiff had a sister who had issue children, who are alive, and who would have as much right to demand the inheritance as she, if this be verified, the writ shall fail, and the assise be stayed, whether those children were begotten in matrimony or not. And as this assise does not lie between parceners and coheirs, so neither does it take place between parceners who hold in common or in severalty by reason of the land which is in itself partible; but only the writ *de rationabili parte*. And as it lies not between privies

Assise lie not between parceners.

Exception of non-joinder of co-parceners.

Assise lies not between co-parceners by custom,

sicum ele ne tient mie lu entre privez de saunc muyllerez, ausi ne tient ele mie lu par entre [1]frere bastard tenaunt[1] et frere mulieré pleintif, ne nul bref for qe bref de dreit qe detrie et determine la proscheinté [2]et le dreit del saunc[2].

CHAPITRE XIII. [LXXVII.]

De Excepcioun [3]de seysi[3].

Brac. 261 *b*, 262 *b*: Fle. 288 (§ 9, 10).

1. Et quaunt a cele parole [4]motié el bref[4], morust seisi, purrount sourdre plusours excepciouns. Car il porra morir seisi en diverses maneres, sicum par corporele presence, et ausi par volunté, tut ne soit il present en propre persone. Et en mesme la manere porra estre seisine purchacé[5]. Et hom porra retenir[6] seisine par presence de cors, tut ne eit il la
[204.] volunté de retenir seisine, sicum avent de ceux qi dounent et moergent seisiz eynzces qe les purchaceours eyent plenere seisine. Et par volunté put homme morir seisi, sicum est de

1—1. freres soeurs bastardz tenauntz *N.* 2—2 du sanc e le dreit *M.* 3—3. de seisine *ND.* de le Seysy *MA.* de sa seisine *CH.* 4—4. *so verb. S.* mortie el bref *L.* mettre en le bref *ND.* *sim. ARW.* notee el bref *M.* *sim. G.* notee *C.* notezie *H.* 5. *so verb. NGAMCH.* purchaz *LS.* 6. recouerir *N.* reservir *C.* resceiuere *H.*

nor between bastard tenant and mulier plaintiff.

of blood being legitimate, so does it not lie between a bastard brother, tenant, and a legitimate brother, plaintiff,—nor any writ except the writ of right, whereby the proximity and right of blood is tried and determined.

CHAPTER XIII.

Exception upon the word 'seised.'

Seisin by act and by intention.

1. With respect to the clause expressed in the writ, 'died seised,' many exceptions may arise. For one may die seised in several ways, as by bodily presence, and also by intention, although not present in person. And in like manner may seisin be acquired. A person may also retain seisin by bodily presence, although he has no intention to retain it, as happens with those who make a gift and then die seised, before the purchasers have had complete seisin. And a man may die seised by intention, as is the case with those who go on

ceux qi s'en vount en pelrinage, et ne lessent nul homme en lour tenementz, et moergent par chemin.

2. Ausi bien neqedent moergent seisiz par serjaunt ou attorné ou gardeyn, cum [1]tiel qi morust seisi[1] en sa propre persone; cum si acun gardeyn en noun de acun enfaunt de eynz age, ou autre procuratour ou attorné resceyve[2] seisine en acun tenement en autri noun, si cist en qi noun la seisine est prise moerge issi seisi, en tel cas voloms bien qe tels moergent seisiz, tut ne viegnent il a la seisine en [3]propres persones[3], et qe lour heirs tele seisine pusent demaunder par ceste assise [4]des mortz[4] lour pieres. Brac. 262; Fle. 288 (§ 11).

3. Plusours ausi porrount morir seisiz de un mesme tenement, qe il averount tenu cum de fee de divers feffementz. Et cum plusours assises de ceo soint [5]par eus arramez[5], si covendra primes terminer l'assise arramé de la mort del drein seisi, et issi de seisine en seisine arere meyn, jekes autaunt Brac. 262 b; Fle. 288 (§ 12).

1—1. cil qe moert seisi *N*. si i moert *M*. 2. reteigne *NCH*. *sim*. *AM*. 3—3. lur propres persones *G*. lur propre persone *M*. 4—4. *so S*. de mortz *L*. de la mort *NGMC*. 5—5. porteez *N*.

a pilgrimage leaving no one in their tenements, and die on their way.

2. A person may die seised by bailiff, attorney, or guardian, as well as if he died seised in his own person. Thus, where a guardian in the name of an infant under age, or any other procurator or attorney in the name of another receives seisin of any tenement, if he in whose name the seisin is taken die so seised, we are content that such persons be deemed to have died seised, although they do not come to be seised in their own persons, and that their heirs may demand such seisin by this assise on their fathers' deaths. Seisin by attorney and by guardian.

3. Again, several persons may die seised of the same tenement, which they have held as of fee by divers feoffments. And when several assises have been brought by them[1] for it, the assise brought for the death of the person last seised must be first determined, and so backwards from seisin to seisin, Several assises for successive abatements.

[1] That is, apparently by the heirs of the persons so dying seised (cf. Brac. 262 *b*). The case supposed is somewhat obscure, but appears to be that of several successive re-abatements. Upon the death of A seised in fee, B a stranger enters, and enfeoffs C in fee. C dies seised, and D a stranger enters and enfeoffs E, who dies seised. F a stranger enters. The respective heirs of E, C, and A bring several assises of the deaths of their respective ancestors. The assise of the death of E is taken first.

qe le dreit de la possessioun soit joynt par jugement al dreit de la propreté.

Brac. 262 *b*; Fle. 288 (§ 13).

4. Et si acun soit feffé a ly et a ses heirs par ly engendrez, ou a autres, si il ne eit point engendrure ou si sa engendrure moerge,—si tiel purchaceour moerge et eit engendrure, en [204 *b*.] cel enfaunt tient bien lu ceste assise. Mes si il n'eit point de enfaunt, ou s'il soint mortz, dounc descende le dreit as autres nomez en le feffement, en qi persones neqedent ne gist nul recoverir par ceste assise, mes par bref de fourme de doun.

Brac. [illegible]; Fle. 288, 289.

5. Et ausi porra acun si feffer, qe ses heirs ne porrount estre succurruz par ceste assise; ausi cum qi feffast autre a la vie le feffour; si le purchaceour survive le feffour et retiegne, as heirs le feffour ne vaille ceste assise [1], mes bref de entré a terme qe passé est. Et si acun face purchaz de tenement a sa vie soulement, le feffour eit soen recoverer apres le desces le purchaceour par mesme le bref de entré, si il en soit deforcé. Et si acun soit feffé a ly et a ses heirs taunt cum le feffour vivera, en tel cas tient bien lu ceste assise en les heirs le purchaceour, vivaunt le feffour, apres la mort lour piere;

1. riens *add.* *NDG.* *sim.* *SMRC.*

until the right of possession is united by judgment with the right of property.

Ass'se lies for heir in tail, but remainderman in tail must proceed by *formedon.*

4. Where any one is enfeoffed to him and his heirs by him begotten, and if he have no issue or if his issue die, then over to others, if the purchaser dies having issue, his child may proceed by this assise. But if he has no issue, or if the issue is dead, then the right descends to the others named in the feoffment; in whose persons however no recovery lies by this assise, but by writ of formedon.

Holding over after term of life; remedy by writ of entry.

5. A man also may make such a feoffment that his heirs cannot be aided by this assise. Thus, where one has enfeoffed another for the life of the feoffor, if the purchaser survive the feoffor and retain the seisin, the heirs of the feoffor shall not avail themselves of this assise, but of a writ of entry *ad terminum qui præteriit*. And if any one make purchase of a tenement for his life only, the feoffor shall have his recovery after the purchaser's decease, if he be deforced, by the same writ of entry.

Heir of tenant *pur autre vie* may have assise.

If any one be enfeoffed to him and his heirs so long as the feoffor shall live, in such case this assise will lie in favour of the heirs of the purchaser after their father's death during the

[1]et les heirs le feffour apres la mort lour piere[1] eynt lour recoverir par bref de entré, sicum devaunt est dit.

6. Ou le tenaunt porra traverser, et tendre[2] de averrer par l'assise[3] qe le auncestre ne morust unques seisi, ou s'il fust en acune manere seisi, ceo ne fust mie par sa persone, eynz fust en autri noun, ou a terme sauntz aver fee ou fraunc tenement. Et si le pleyntif die, qe il fust seisi par acun feffement, a ceo soit respoundu par triplicacioun, cum [4]desus est dit[4]. Fle. 289 (§ 16). Ante, c. 12. s. 2.

CHAPITRE XIV. [LXXVII.]

Excepcioun de dreyn seysi.

1. [5]Ou il porra dire, qe a tort demaunde il de la mort soen auncestre par ceste assise, car le pleintif mesmes ou autre fu de ceo en seisine pus la mort cel auncestre de qi seisine il demaunde. Car si le heir puis ceo qe il avera esté de plener [205.] Brac. 273; Fle. 297 (§ 25).

1—1. *so verb. MGS.* *om. LNDRCFW.* 2. *so NSGMC.* entendre *L.* 3. assise *NM.* 4—4. de ceo serra dit apres *N.* 5. *In L this chapter commences with the words preceding,* A ceo soit respoundu; *sim. S.* *In HF, as in the printed copies, there is no division of chapters.* *NGABW have a new chapter as above.*

life of the feoffor[a]; and the heirs of the feoffor after their father's death shall have their recovery by writ of entry, as aforesaid.

6. The tenant may traverse, and tender averment by the assise, that the ancestor did not ever die seised, or that if he died seised, he was seised not in his own right but in the name of another, or for a term without having fee or freehold. And if the plaintiff say that he was seised by virtue of some feoffment, to this it may be answered by triplication, as hath been said above. Seisin may be traversed.

CHAPTER XIV.

Exception upon the words 'last seised.'

1. The tenant may urge as another exception, that the plaintiff wrongfully demands by this assise as upon the death of his ancestor; inasmuch as the plaintiff himself, or another, was in seisin since the death of the same ancestor by whose Exception that the plaintiff has been in seisin.

[a] Compare below, c. 15. s. 2, and note there.

age, et avera ewe sa seisine apres la mort soen auncestre, alienast soen heritage et le vendist en fee, si il put [1]recoverer al purchaceour[1] par demaunder de la seisine soen auncestre, en tele manere serreit[2] le feffement aneanti et de nule force, et ceo serroit graunt incovenient.

Brac. 273 (§ 7); Fle. 297 (§ 6).

2. Et pur ceo fet a prendre garde, quele[3] seisine issint ewe apres [4]mort de[4] auncestre reboute l'assise et quele nient. Car la seisine del dreit heir en tens de vacacioun del heritage apres la mort soen auncestre, de quel age qe il soit, ly[5] serra touz jours barre[6] a recoverer par ceste assise, pur ceo qe assise de novele disseisine i tient lu. Mes si par cele assise ne puse averrer[7] sa seisine, adounc tient lu ceste assise de mort de auncestre. Mes si acun heir eit eu[8] torcenouse seisine et dount il ad esté freschement engetté, tele seisine [9]ne barre mie ceste assise[9], [10]si qe[10] ceste excepcioun ne est nient allouwable, si le tenaunt [11]ne die, qe il en morust un autre[11] plus tard seisi[12], sicum dreit heir le auncestre qi seisine est de-

1—1. recouerir e repurchacier *D.* recoueri[r] e repurchacee[r] *N.* recouerir a repurchaser *M.* *sim. W.* recouerer e repurchacer *C.* *sim. R.* recouerir del purchasour *G.* 2. *so S.* *sim. M G.* soreit *L.* serra *N.* 3. *so NSGM.* qe la *L.* 4—4. la mort le *NM.* 5. il *N.* 6. *so SGMC.* barree *LN.* 7. *so LSGC.* auer *NAMHF.* 8. *so SGMC.* eu *om. L.* 9—9. ne luy vaudra mye *G.* 10—10. qe si *SG.* 11—11. *so LSG.* die qe il morust un autre *ND.* *sim. A.* die qe vn autre i morust *M.* [ne] die qe il [i] morust *R.* ne die qil ne morust vnqes *C.* ne die *om. F.* en dye qe il en morust *W.* 12. seisi *om. C.*

seisin he demands. For where after the heir is of full age and has had his seisin upon the death of his ancestor, he aliens his inheritance and sells it in fee, if he could recover it from the purchaser by demanding it in respect of the seisin of his ancestor, the feoffment would be invalidated and ineffectual, and this would be greatly inconvenient.

What seisin, had by the heir, bars Mortdancester.

2. It is necessary therefore to observe what seisin thus had after the death of an ancestor excludes the assise, and what does not. For the seisin of the right heir at a time when the inheritance was vacant after his ancestor's death, of whatever age the heir may be, shall always bar him from recovering by this assise, because then the assise of Novel Disseisin lies. But if he is not in a position to aver seisin in that assise, then the assise of Mortdancester is in place. But if an heir has had a wrongful seisin from which he has been presently ejected, such seisin bars not this assise, so that this exception is not allowable, unless the tenant say that another died more lately seised

maundé, qi heir le pleintif est. Et si deus parceners et un heir, eint arramé ceste assise [1]en vers[1] acune estraunge persone de la mort lour auncestre, si le tenaunt[2] die qe un des parceners fu puis seisi, ja par taunt ne remeigne ceste assise, si cele seisine ne prist nul effect. [205 *b.*]

CHAPITRE XV. [LXXVIII.]

Excepcioun en[3] soen Demeyne.

1. A ceo qe dit est el bref, en soen demeyne, si[4] porra le tenaunt sei[5] eyder par excepciouns. Car en demeyne porrount estre tenuz terres et rentes, en fee et a terme de vie. Mes demeyne proprement est tenement qe chescun tient severalment en fee. Et ausi sount les tenementz tenuz en Brac. 263; Fle. 289.

1—1. et en vers *L.* *sim. SG.* vers. *NM.* enuers *C.* 2. so *NDAR.* ne *add. LSGMCHF.* 3. de en *M.* de *GF.* 4. si *om. M.* se *NG.* 5. so *M.* sei *om. LNSGC.*

as right heir of the ancestor whose seisin is demanded, and whose heir the plaintiff is [b]. And where two parceners, coheirs, bring this assise against a stranger upon the death of their ancestor, if the tenant say that one of the parceners was since seised, the assise shall not be stayed if this seisin took none effect.

CHAPTER XV.

Exception upon the words 'in his demesne.'

1. Whereas it is said in the writ, 'in his demesne,' the tenant may aid himself by exceptions. For in demesne may be held lands and rents, in fee and for term of life. But demesne is properly a tenement which is held severally in fee. Those tenements also which are held in villenage and farmed at will Demesne, what so called.

[b] The latter part of the above sentence is not easily intelligible; and the text appears doubtful. I do not find in Bracton or Fleta anything which throws light upon it. According to these authors, the objection, founded upon a former possession of the demandant, was held only where, being of age, he had been in lawful seisin for so long a time that he might have conveyed away the property. (Brac. 273, 273 *b*; Fle. 297.) Seisin by an infant was immaterial, since the objection was founded only upon the danger of one, who had aliened the land, recovering it by the assise against his own donee. (Brac. 273 *b.*) Where the demandant had had a tortious seisin from which he had been ejected, the seisin did not furnish in itself a valid exception to the assise; but another objection might be taken, namely, that the demandant had forfeited his right to the assise by usurping the possession without judgment. (Brac. 273.)

villenage, et a volunté [1]a ferme[1] de jour en jour, et a terme des aunz communement et en garde [2]les demeynes celi de qi eles[2] sount [3]issi tenuz. Et demeyne si[3] est dit a la difference de ceo qe est tenu en seignurie ou en service, ou en commun ovekes autres. Car nos demeynes sount [4]teles qe sount les

Brac. 262 *b*. vos[5] demeynes; issi[4] qe ceste assise chete si ele soit arramé sour la mort des plusours tenauntz en demeyne; desicum sa nature est tiele, qe ele veut touz jours estre porté de la mort le dreyn seisi, sicum apres serra dit.

Brac. 268, 268 *b*: Fle. 289 (§ 21).

2. Mes de nule manere de demeyne neqedent ne tient lu ceste assise for qe de cele dount le auncestre morust seisi

[206.] cum de fee, soit [6]de terre[6] ou de service; [7]car de la seisine[7] nul fermer[8] a terme des aunz, ne [9]de celi qi avera tenu[9] en villenage, ou en garde, ou en gage, ou a terme de vie, ou par

1—1. *so DGSMF*. afferme *L* a seruir [ferme *interl*] *N*. aferme *C*. 2—2. *so verb. SGAFW*. les demeynes *om*. *LND*. les demeynes celi qi des *M*. les demeines cely de qi eus *C*. 3—3. tenuz issi en demeyne. E si *ND*. *sim*. *A*. 4—4. a graunt difference de ceo qe nous tenoms en seignurie: e si vous dioms *R*. *sim*. (die *for* dioms) *A*. tenementz qe furent en aunciene temps annexes a nostre Corone et qe noz gentz tiegnent de nous en demeigne del doun de noz progenitours. Et voloms *Z*. 5. nos *ND*. noz *G*. 6—6. ceo de fee [terre] *N*. 7—7. *so LSGCF*. quar lassise ne tient liu vers. *N*. *sim*. *DW*. Car la seisine ne tient vers. *M*. 8. *so NGMC*. ferme *LS*. 9—9. de celi qi le auera tenu *L*. *sim*. *SG*. vers celi qe cleyme a tener *N*. deuers celi qe le aura tenuz *M*. de cely qe avera tenu *C*.

from day to day, and commonly for terms of years, and are in the care or custody of others, are the demesne of him of whom they are so holden. The word demesne is also used in distinction from that which is holden in seignory or service, or in common with others. For then my demesnes are the same as your

No assise of the death of several joint-tenants.

demesnes; so that this assise shall fail if it be brought upon the death of several persons tenants in demesne, inasmuch as its nature requires that it should be always brought in respect of the death of the person last seised, as hereafter shall be said.

The ancestor must have been seised in fee.

2. But this assise does not hold concerning any manner of demesne, save that whereof the ancestor died seised as of fee, whether it be land or service. For it lieth not concerning the seisin of any farmer for term of years, or of him who hath held in villenage, or in ward, or in gage, or for term of life[c], or

c 'A termor holding to him and his heirs and assigns for the life of the lessor shall recover by Disseisin, and his heir if ejected by the lessor or a stranger by Mortdancester. Which implies as it were the possession of a fee (qe sone tot en la p'on come de fee), which fee becomes extinct in the purchaser by virtue of the covenant, upon the death of the lessor, and not before. And it is to be understood, that he who hath only a term of years

condicioun en[1] fee ou les heirs sount forclos par la fourme del feffement jekes en tens ou a touz jours.

3. Mes si les heirs de acun creaunceour eint purchacé ceste assise, a qi le deforceaunt[2] die, qe lur auncestre ne tint[3] nient les tenementz demaundez for qe en gage, et les heirs[4] le creaunceour dient pur replicacioun, qe la terre fust engagé a lour auncestre qi heirs il sount jekes a un certeyn jour par tiele condicioun, qe si le dettour ne rendist a lour auncestre une summe de aver a certeyn jour passé, qe la terre remansist[5] al creaunceour et a ses heirs en fee; et si ceo pussent averrer par escrit ou en autre manere, adounc tiegne lu ceste assise de la seisine le creaunceour, si le deforceaunt ne puse averrer la soute, ou al meyns [6]qe lour fust offert al jour et moustré en lu certeyn de la soute fere en[6] presence de bones gentz tut a descovert tut pleynement sauntz nule defaute. Brac. 268 *b*; Fle. 289, 290.

1. so *NMC.* ou *L.* 2. so *NC.* sim. *SG.* deforceynt *L.* defendant *M.* 3. so *M.* tienent *L.* qi heirs il sount ne tient *N.* tent *SC.* tient *G.* 4. so *NMC.* heirs *om. L.* 5. remeyndreit *N.* sim. *MC.* 6—6. qe ele lour fust offerte al iour e moustre a acun qe fust a la soute en *N.* sim. (lour *om.*) *DR.* qe la seute lur fu offert al iour e mustre el lu de la sute en *M.* ke lour fust offert au iour e mustre el lu de la soute *F.* qe lur fuit offert au Iour e mustre e le lu de la soute *G.* sim. *S.*

by condition in fee, where the heirs are excluded by the form of the feoffment either for a time or for ever.

3. But if the heirs of a creditor proceed by this assise, and the deforciant pleads against them that their ancestor held the tenements demanded only in gage, and the heirs of the creditor reply that the land was engaged to their ancestor, whose heirs they are, until a certain day upon this condition, that, if the debtor did not pay to their ancestor a sum of money at a certain day since passed, the land should remain to the creditor and his heirs in fee, and if the demandants can aver this by writing or in any other manner, then this assise shall take place concerning the seisin of the creditor, unless the deforciant can aver payment, or at least that the making of such payment was offered at the day, and openly tendered at a certain place in the presence of lawful people, in full view and to the full amount without any default. For if a part is paid or tendered,

Assise by heirs of mortgagee. Plea of tenant. Replication of demandants.

Averment of payment.

hath barely (escharcement) a chattel; and shall therefore recover nothing but damages by the *Justicies* (le Iustice), or by the *Quare ejecit* But he who can in any way claim more than a term of years shall recover by assise of Novel Disseisin. For term of years and no more is chattel; and more than a chattel he cannot have without having a freehold.' (Note in MS *N.*)

Car si partie soit offerte a rendre ou rendue, si le tut ne soit rendu ne offert a rendre, ne vaille rien au dettour sa excepcioun. [1] Et mesme la resoun tiegne lu [1] si acun jour des plu-

[206 *b*.] sours soit enfreynt, si a plusours foiz [2] dust la soute aver esté [2] fete par parceles.

Brac. 268 *b*; Fle. 290 (§ 23).

4. Et si les heirs le dettour eint arramie l'assise ver le creaunceour ou ses heirs, et ceste condicioun chete en debat, et trové soit qe le aver ne fust point rendu ne offert solom la condicioun, si chete l'assise, et soit tenue la volunté le feffour. Et si l'assise soit arramé devant le jour de la condicioun, soit le [3] tenaunt agardé de aler [3] sauntz jour, et le pleintif en la merci pur sa fause pleinte, pur ceo qe houre ne vient mie uncore de [4] pleindre, en quel cas ne estovera mie al creanceour ou [5] soen heir receivere soen aver ne se demestre de soen gage devant le jour, si il ne voille.

Brac. 268 *b*; Fle. 290 (§ 23).

5. Et si la soute ne se estent mie as heirs le dettour, et le dettour moerge avaunt soen jour, si remeigne la terre al

1—1. *so verb. SF.* Et par mesme la resoun tiegne lu *L.* *sim. N.* E par mesme la reson tient lu ceste assise *M.* En mesme la reson teigne leu *C.* 2—2. soit due la soute qe dust estre *D.* *so* (qe *interl.*) *N.* seit due la soute dount soute deit estre *R.* 3—3. agardee al tenaunt qe il soit iugee quites *N.D.* *sim. R.* 4. prendre lenqueste ne de *add. NDRW.* 5. ne a *ND.* ou a *MW.*

but the whole is neither paid nor tendered, the debtor shall gain nothing by his exception. And the same reason shall hold, if a breach has been made of one day out of several, where the payment was to have been made by parcels at several times.

Assise by heir of debtor against mortgagee.

4. If the assise is brought by the heirs of the debtor against the creditor or his heirs, when this condition comes in question, and it is found that the money was not paid or tendered according to the condition, let the assise abate and let the intention of the feoffor be observed. And if the assise be brought before the day for fulfilment of the condition, let it be awarded that the tenant go without day and the plaintiff be in mercy for his false plaint, because the time for complaining is not yet come, and the creditor or his heir shall not be obliged to receive his money or part with his security before the day, unless he is willing so to do.

Creditor not obliged to receive his money before the day.

If the condition be on payment by the debtor himself, it cannot be fulfilled by his heir.

5. And if the condition of payment does not extend to the heirs of the debtor, and the debtor dies before the day, the

creaunceour solom lour covenaunt, tut soit le heir le dettour prest a rendre le aver enprompté, desicum il ne sount mie nomez el covenaunt. Et ausi de autre part voloms nous qe les covenauntz se teignent par la ou nule mencioun ne est fete des heirs le creaunceour; issint qe si les heirs le dettour arramient assise sur le creaunceour ou sour ses heirs, et les heirs al creaunceour respoignent al assise, et dient qe lour auncestre morust seisi en fee, et les heirs le dettour dient qe ne mie purement en fee mes en gage pur une summe de aver, la quele il sount prestz a rendre, et les deforceours dient, qe a ceo ne pount il avener pur le jour de la soute qe passé est, et [207.]
pur ceo qe la soute ne se estent mie a lour persones, et les pleintifs dient qe ausi ne se estent mie le gage as deforceours; si trové soit par les escritz de covenauntz, les quels ne porrount mie estre desditz, qe la terre fu engagé en ceste fourme, qe si le dettour ne rendist al jour passé qe la terre remeyndreit al creaunceour en fee, en tel cas ne pernent rien les pleintifs,

lands shall remain with the creditor according to the covenant, although the heir of the debtor be ready to pay the money borrowed, inasmuch as heirs are not named in the covenant [d]. And so on the other hand we will that the covenants shall be observed, where no mention is made of the heirs of the creditor; so that if the heirs of the debtor bring an assise against the creditor or his heirs [e], and the heirs of the creditor plead to the assise and say that their ancestor died seised in fee, and the heirs of the debtor reply that he was seised not purely in fee but in gage for a sum of money, which they are ready to pay, and the deforceors say, that they cannot be admitted thereto, because the day of payment is passed, and the payment does not extend to their persons, and the plaintiffs say, that neither does the gage extend to the deforceors—if it be found by the writings of covenant, which cannot be contradicted, that the land was engaged in the following form, that if the debtor did not pay the money at the day passed the land should remain to the creditor in fee, in such case the plaintiffs shall take nothing, although it is not specified in the writings

'Land to remain to one in fee' imports an inheritance.

[d] In the time of Littleton, a more liberal construction was put upon a conditional clause of this kind, the heirs, though not named, being allowed to perform the condition. Lit. Ten. s. 334; Co. Lit. 205 *b*.

[e] It should be, 'against the heirs of the creditor.'

tut ne soit il mie especefiez en les escritz, qe la terre remeigne as heirs le creaunceour, pur le fee qe[1] autaunt vaut.

6. Et si les pleintifs dient, qe equité les deit eyder pur la petitesce de la dette, ceo ne lour vaille rien, desicum chescun fraunc homme put ordiner de sa chose a sa volunté sauntz tort fere a ses heirs, hors pris en cas, [2]sicum en fourme[2] de doun, en mariages, et a gent de religioun ou a autre persone defendue.

Brac. 268 *b*; Fle. 290 (§ 124).

7. Et ausi voloms nous qe covenaunt soit tenu par entre dettour et creaunceour de terre lessé a ferme al creaunceour par ceste condicioun, qe s'il aviegne[3] le dettour morir[4] de eynz le terme, qe la terre engagé remeigne al creaunceour en fee, ou a tote sa vie; [5]et s'il[5] soit [6]aconvenu, qe si[6] le creaunceour moerge de eynz certeyn terme, adounc remeigne le [207 *b*.] tenement issi engagé a acune [7]autre terce[7] persone, si tiegne le covenaunt. Et tut eynt[8] les heirs le dettour acune colour de porter ceste assise de la mort lour auncestre, desicum il morust ausi cum seisi en fee, solom le covenant neqedent

1. *so NMGC.* qe *om. L.* 2—2. de fourme *M.* 3. *so M. sim. G.* auent *LS.* auient qe *ND.* auient *C. sim. W.* 4. moerge *ND.* 5—5. *so verb. SG.* et *om. LNC.* qe i *M.* ke i *F.* 6—6. *so LS. sim. F.* conuenu qe si *M.* aconuenu qe *G.* conu qe *N.* conue si *C.* 7—7. estraunge *MC.* 8. *so N. sim. MC.* ieynt *L.*

that the land shall remain to the heirs of the creditor, by reason of the word fee, which is equivalent thereto.

No equity to redeem a mortgage.

6. And if the plaintiffs say that equity ought to assist them, by reason of the smallness of the debt, that shall not avail them, since every freeman may dispose of his property at his will without doing any wrong to his heirs, except in particular cases, as in *formedon* or in marriage, or when the gift is to persons in religion or other prohibited persons.

General power of disposition as against heirs.

Condition to enlarge an estate.

7. We will also that the covenant be performed between the debtor and creditor concerning land let to farm to the creditor, where the condition is, that if the debtor happen to die within the term, the land shall remain to the creditor in fee, or for his whole life: or if it be covenanted, that if the creditor die within a certain term, then the tenement so engaged shall remain to some third person, such covenant shall stand good. And although the heirs of the debtor have some colour for bringing this assise of the death of their ancestor, inasmuch as he died in a manner seised in fee, yet their right must stand or fall by the covenant. And whereas a

preigne effect ou chete. Et puis qe simple covenaunt barre l'assise jekes en tens ou a touz jours, par plus forcible resoun deit ele remeyndre solom jugement de nostre court.

CHAPITRE XVI. [LXXIX.]

Excepcioun de fee.

Brac. 263 *b*, 261; Fle. 290 (§25-29).

1. A ceo qe est contenu [1]el bref,[1] sicum de fee,—porra un tener en fee solom le regard del service et nient en demeyne, sicum le seignur del fee, et un autre porra tener en fee et en demeyne et nient en service, sicum acun fraunc tenaunt. Et fee est ausi quant qe chescun homme tient a ly et a ses heirs, lequel qe ceo soit terre ou rente issaunt de terre. Et si est la tierce manere de fee, qe est un noun general a touz feez, sicum as feez de chivaler et de touz autres[2].

2. Le fee neqedent especefié[3] en ceste assise signifie touz jours terre ou rente qe le auncestre tint a ly et a ses heirs, el le quel il poeit aver vendu en sa vie en fee, sauntz fere a nulli prejudice ou tort. Et si assise soit porté de autre manere [208.]

1—1. *so MG.* en le bref *NC.* *om. LS.* 2. feez *add. N.* 3. *so MC.* *sim. N.* est petite fee *L.*

Creditor's estate under judgment.

simple covenant bars the assise for a time or for ever, there is much greater reason for its being stayed in pursuance of a judgment of our court.

CHAPTER XVI.

Exception founded on the words 'as of fee.'

Fee,—various senses of the word.

1. As to the words contained in the writ, 'as of fee,' one person may hold in fee in respect of the service and not in demesne, as the lord of the fee; and another may hold in fee and in demesne and not in service, as any free tenant. Fee is also whatsoever any person holds to himself and his heirs, whether it be land or rent issuing out of land. And there is a third kind of fee, which is a general name for all fees, as well for a knight's fee as all others.

Fee equivalent to seignory. Fee equivalent to inheritance. Fee descriptive of tenure.

What fee is subject to assise of Mortdancester.

2. But the fee specified in this assise always signifies land or rent which the ancestor held to himself and his heirs, and which he might in his lifetime have sold in fee without doing a prejudice or wrong to any one. And if the assise be brought

de seisine, sicum de terre tenue a terme de vie, ou a terme des aunz, si cheite l'assise. A ceo qe [1]dit est[1] el bref, ausi cum de fee, poet[2] estre entendu en deus maneres, issi qe cest mot, ausi, signefie colour de verité, cum est de disseisours et de intrusours et de autres, qe detienent autri dreit, et les quels moerent seisiz ausi cum de fee, ou qe il signefie pure verité, sicum est de tiels qe tienent par verrei title, dount nul ne ad meillour[3] dreit de eus, et moergent seisiz en fee. Et en ambideus ces cas voloms nous, qe ceste assise se[4] tiegne.

Brac. 264; Fle. 290, 291.

3. Ou il porra dire, qe [5]tut morust le auncestre[5] seisi ausi cum de fee, rien nequedent de ceo ne poeit descendre a ses heirs, pur ceo qe il fust bastard. Et, tut soit qe nul ne put estre atteynt pur bastard for qe en sa vie et en court Cristiene, si les parties neqedent se assentent qe hom enquerge[6] par l'assise en manere de juree, si le auncestre fust bastard ou noun, soit prise la reconisaunce, et solom le verdit [7]se face[7] le jugement. Et si acun ne se vodera mettre en le averrement, adounc se face le jugement encountre ly, lequel

Brac. 269; Fle. 294 (§ 50).

1—1. deit estre *LGS.* dist est *NM.* est dist *C.* 2. so *C.* poeit *L.* puit *NMG.* 3. so *ND.* *sim. C.* meur *LG.* mere *S.* 4. so *NSGM.* se *om. L.* 5—5. le auncestre tot morust il *M.* 6. le querge *M.* 7—7. so *NGC.* si face *LS.* si passe *M.*

of any other manner of seisin, as of land held for term of life or for term of years, the assise shall fall. The words in the writ, 'as of fee,' may be understood in two ways, according as the word 'as' imports an apparent truth, as in the case of disseisors intruders and others, who withhold another's right and die seised as of fee, or signifies the mere truth, when persons who hold by a good title, and than whom none has a better right, die seised in fee. In both these cases we will that this assise take place.

'As of fee.'

3. Again, the tenant may say, that although the ancestor died seised as of fee, yet no part thereof could descend to his heirs because he was a bastard. And, although no one can be attainted as a bastard except in his lifetime and in court Christian, yet if the parties consent that it shall be inquired by the assise, by way of jury, whether the ancestor was a bastard or not, let the recognisance be taken, and judgment be given according to the verdict. And if any one will not put himself on the averment, then let judgment be given against him, whether he be tenant or plaintiff. And let the

Exception that the ancestor was bastard.

Legitimacy tried by jury, by consent.

qe il soit tenaunt ou pleintif. Et en mesme la manere soit fet[1] en cas, ou mise[2] est avaunt[3] excepcioun, qe le auncestre morust bastard sauntz heir de tenement dount il fust feffé soulement a ly et a ses heirs. Ante, l. ii. c. 16. s. 3.

4. Ou il porra dire, qe il ne tient les tenementz demaundez for qe de bail, ou a la volunté, ou en garde de acune tierce persone, sauntz qi il ne poet[4] respoundre. Et si ceo soit averré, chete l'assise. Et ausi, s'il die qe le auncestre ne morust mie seisi de[5] demeyne, mes soulement del fee. Brac. 269; Fle. 294 § (51). [208 *b.*]

5. Ou le tenaunt porra bien graunter[6], qe le auncestre le pleintif en morust seisi cum de fee, mes[7] il nepurquant rien ne poet[8] prendre par ceste assise; car mesme cesti auncestre lessa a celi tenaunt le tenement a terme par condicioun, qe, si le lessour deviast avaunt le terme, le termer i averoit fraunc tenement a terme de vie, ou fee et fraunc tenement, Brac. 269; Fle. 295 (§ 57).

1. fet *om. M.* 2. mis *LSM.* mist *G.* 3. pur *add. NMC.* *sim. F.* 4. *so SMC.* poeit *L.* puit *NG.* 5. *so LSGC.* del *M.* en [sun] *N.* 6. *so NGM.* garrauntir *LS.* garaunter *C.* 7. *so NGMC.* mes si *LS.* 8. *so C.* *sim. NG.* poeit *LS.* *sim. M.*

like be done, in cases where it is put forward as an exception, that the ancestor died a bastard without any heir to the tenement, whereof he was enfeoffed only to himself and to his heirs[f].

4. Or the tenant may say that he holds the tenements demanded only as bailiff, or at will, or by wardship of some third person, without whom he cannot answer; and if this be proved, the assise shall fall. So, if he says that the ancestor did not die seised of the land in demesne, but only of the fee. Exception that tenant holds as bailiff of another. Exception that the ancestor was not seised in demesne.

5. Again, the tenant may grant that the ancestor of the plaintiff died seised as of fee, but say that nevertheless he cannot take anything by this assise, for that the same ancestor let the tenement to the tenant for a term on condition that, if the lessor died before the end of the term, the termor should have a freehold for term of life, or a fee and freehold, wherefore that which he held before as at farm, he holds now as his Exception of term with condition to enlarge it to a fee.

[f] It is not easy to see how the case added in this clause differs from the one first mentioned. The whole passage is paraphrased from Bracton or Fleta, where the expressions are somewhat different. The latter case may possibly be that, where a bastard enfeoffed to himself and his heirs (without 'assigns') gives to another in fee, and dies leaving no heir, upon which the lord enters. The question however in this case would not arise upon an assise of Mortdancester of the death of the bastard, as seems to be implied in the text. See vol. i. p. 312.

par quei qe ceo qe il out avaunt cum a ferme, [1]tient il ja[1] cum soen fraunc tenement, et le quel covenaunt averree si perist l'assise. Et en mesme la manere remeyndra de terre engagé, si le dettour point nel aquite al jour, ou al meyns tendu[2] de aquiter, solom ceo qe dit avoums avaunt; ou s'il tiegne la terre en gage par jugement en nostre court.

Brac. 269; Fle. 294 (§ 51). 6. Ou il pora dire, qe il n'i ad rien, ne rien ne cleyme a ceste foiz, for qe en seignurie, ou en noun de garde, ou a tener en autri noun del bail un tiel sicum fermer a la volunté soen lessour, qi point ne est nomé el bref; et si ceo soit averree ou nient dedit, et la jurree testmoigne qe il [3]ne ad rien clamé[3] en soen noun demeyne, par taunt est le bref
[209.] abatable. Et ausi, si le tenaunt se reconisse estre autri vileyn, et issi tener en autri noun.

Fle. 295 (§ 57). 7. Et si acun demaunde par ceste assise ceo qe femme tient outre sa dreite dowarie, pur ceo neqedent qe ele cleyme nient for qe dowarie, si cherra ceste assise, et tient lu [4]de remedie aver[4] par amesurement de dowarie.

1—1. tient il *L.* si tient il ialemeyns *N.* tint il *SG.* tient ia *M.* tent il ia *C.* 2. [ne] tendist *N.* tendi *SGMC.* 3—3. ne ad rien ne rien ne cleyme *N.* *sim. MG.* 4—4. remedie *NMC.* *sim. G.* de remedie *S.*

freehold; and if such a covenant be verified, the assise is at an end. In like manner it shall be stayed, where the land has been put in gage, if the debtor has not discharged it or at least offered to discharge it at the day, according as we have said before; or if he holds the land as a security by judgment of our court.

Exception of mortgage.

Exception that tenant holds in right of an absent party.

6. Again, the tenant may say that he has nothing and claims nothing at this time except in seigniory, or by title of wardship, or to hold in another's name by the lease of such an one, as a farmer, at the will of his lessor, who is not named in the writ, and if this be proved or not denied, and the jury testify that he has not claimed anything in his own name, the writ is thereby abatable. So, if the tenant acknowledges himself to be the villain of another, and thus to hold in another's name.

Excess of dower, not recoverable by assise.

7. If any one demands by this assise that which a widow holds in excess of her right dower, the assise shall fail, inasmuch as she claims nothing but her dower; and remedy shall be had by writ of admeasurement of dower.

CHAPITRE XVII. [LXXX.]

Excepcioun del jour qe il morust.

Brac. 264: Fle. 291 (§ 31), 294, 295.

1. A ceo qe est contenu el bref, le jour qe il morust, ou le jour qe il prist habit de religioun, ou le jour [1]qe il s'en partist[1] de mesoun en pelrinage [2]et enprist[2] le chemin el quel il morust, fet bien a prendre garde. Car il i ad jour soler et jour luner, solom ceo qe[3] Deu devisa clarté de tenebres; et ceux deus jours fount[4] un jour artificiel, qe est de jour fet et de la nuyt suaunte, et contient[5] xxiiii. houres; et si est devisable en quatre parties. Car une porra comencer en la nutié[6], et finer en la minuyt; la autre porra comencer a la minuyt, et finer en la journaunt; la tierce porra comencer a la journaunt et terminer a mydy; et la quarte a midy et [7]pur passer[7] a la nuté[8]. Et dounc si acun moerge ou de nuit ou de jour, si moert il en le jour artificiel; et pur ceo est dit en [209 *b*.]

1—1. de soen departir *N.* qe i departist *M.* 2—2. *so verb. NMC.* et ou prist *L.* *sim. S.* e ou il prist *G.* 3. *so NSGMC.* qe *om. L.* 4. *so NGMC.* sount *L.* *sim. S.* 5. *so NGM.* *sim. SC.* contiegnent *L.* 6. meridie *N.* nuytee *M.* nuyte *G.* 7—7. finir *ND.* passer *SG.* porpasser *M.* porra fyner *W.* [purra] finir *R.* 8. miere leuee *N.*

CHAPTER XVII.

Exception founded on the words 'the day whereon he died.'

Day, solar, lunar, and artificial.

1. With regard to the words in the writ, 'the day whereon he died,' or 'the day whereon he assumed the religious habit,' or 'the day whereon he departed from his house on pilgrimage and undertook the journey in which he died,'—it is necessary to attend to the following points. For there is a solar day and a lunar day, according as God divided the light from the darkness, and these two days make one artificial day, which is made up of the day and of the night following, and contains twenty-four hours, and is divisible into four parts. The first may begin at nightfall and end at midnight, the second may begin at midnight and end at daybreak, the third may begin at daybreak and end at noon, the fourth may begin at noon and continue till nightfall. Therefore whether any one dies in the night or in the day, he dies in the artificial day, and for this reason it is said in our writ,

Division of the day.

noster bref, le jour qe il morust, et ne mie, la nuyt qe il morust.

Brac. 264; Fle. 291.

2. Par quei qe ne mie soulement covent a cely, qi bye recoverer heritage par ceste assise, averrer qe soen auncestre, de qi mort il avera arramie ceste assise, fust seisi acune houre del jour qe il morust, einz covient qe il mette a veir qe il morust seisi. Car ceux deus resouns porrount estre ensemble, qe le auncestre fust seisi le jour qe il morust, et qe il ne morust mie seisi. Car acun porra estre seisi en [1]la journaunt[1] de acun tenement en soen demeyne cum de fee, et[2] avaunt midi[3] en mesme le quarter le pora il doner et mettre de ceo autre en seisine oveske bone volunté de sei demettre, et[4] le purchaceour de ceo porra prendre seisine oveke bone volunté de retener, par la unité de quel assent accrest al purchaceour fraunc tenement et fee et demeyne par la volunté le feffour, qi del tut se met hors de seisine, et rien ne ad en volunté de retener. Et si le feffour moerge tauntost en le secund quarter, et soen heir demaunde cele terre aliené par ceste assise, et le tenaunt die qe cel auncestre ne morust mie seisi,

1—1. le moriaunt *M.* le iournant *L.* *sim. S.* le eniournant *N.* son moriant *G.* 2. so *N.* et *om. LSGM.* 3. e *add. M.* 4. en *LN.* e *MC.*

'the day whereon he died,' and not 'the night whereon he died.'

Ancestor must die seised, not merely be seised the day of death.

2. It behoves him therefore who would recover his inheritance by this assise not only to aver that his ancestor, of whose death he has brought this assise, was seised some time of the day on which he died, but he must also shew that he died seised. For these two propositions may stand together, that the ancestor was seised on the day on which he died, and that he did not die seised; since one may be seised of a tenement in his demesne as of fee at daybreak, and yet before noon in the same quarter of a day he may give it away, and put another in seisin thereof with a full intention of divesting himself, and the purchaser may take seisin thereof with full intention to retain it, by the union of which assent there accrues to the purchaser a freehold and fee and demesne by the will of the feoffor, who put himself out of the seisin of the whole, and has no intention of retaining any part of it. And if the feoffor dies immediately in the second quarter, and his heir demands by this assise the land aliened, and the tenant says that the

If the ancestor conveyed away on the day of his death, the heir cannot recover.

sicom en le cas avauntdit, et de ceo moustre chartre de feoffament qe ceo testmoigne, tut die le pleintif qe le doun soen auncestre ne deit[1] rien valer al purchaceour, desicum il ne prist unques espletz en plenere seisine avaunt la mort le donour, pur ceo ne vaille mie al pleintif ceste assise, si la [210.] volunté le donour ne soit trové par l'assise contrarie a soen doun, ou si le pleintif puse averrer qe le auncestre ne fu mie [2] en bone memorie ne en dreit sen el tens del[2] feffement.

3. Car si le auncestre ne poeit aver[3] recoverer par assise de novele disseisine en le tens de ceste assise porté, si il [4] eust vesqui[4] et se fust[5] repentu de soen doun, a mal tort tendreit ceste assise lu en la persone soen heir. Mes par assise de novele disseisine ne le eust le auncestre james repurchacé, taunt cum par la reconisaunce del assise pout estre averré, qe de soen gré [6] le dona, et de soen gré s'en issi[6] et se demist, et de soen gré mist le tenaunt en seisine. Et solom ceste resoun piert, et verité est, qe si le donour fust demoré en vie et se fust repentu de soen doun, et lendemein ou le tierz

1. purra *M.* 2—2. *conj.* en bone momorie ne en dreite en le tens de *L.* en dreite memorie en tens del *N.* *sim.* *DGSMFW.* 3. [ew sun *interl.*] *N.* 4—4. eit vesqui *L.* vesqui[si]st *N.* vst vesqui *G.* *sim* *M.* eut vescu *S.* 5. *so* *NG.* fu *LS.* vst *M.* 6—6. sen eissist *N.*

ancestor did not die seised as in the case aforesaid, and thereof produces a charter of feoffment which witnesseth the same, although the plaintiff say that the grant of his ancestor ought not at all to avail the purchaser, inasmuch as he never took esplees in full seisin before the death of the grantor, yet the plaintiff shall not succeed by this assise, unless it be found by the assise that the intention of the donor was contrary to his gift, or the plaintiff can prove that the ancestor was not in good memory and right mind at the time of the feoffment.

3. For where the ancestor, if he had lived and had repented of his gift, could not have had his recovery by assise of Novel Disseisin at the time that this assise is brought, it would be unjust if this assise should lie in the person of his heir. But the ancestor could never have recovered by assise of Novel Disseisin, so long as it could have been proved by recognizance of the assise that of his own accord he made the gift, and of his own accord went out and dispossessed himself, and of his own accord put the tenant in seisin. And according to this reasoning it would appear, and it is true, that, if the donor had remained alive and repented of his gift, and the next day or

Where the ancestor, if living, could not recover seisin, the heir cannot.

jour ou tost apres le doun[1] eust engetté le purchaceour, qe le purchaceour eust recoveri par assise de novele disseisine pur la conjunctioun de lur deus voluntez qe fust en la transmutatioun de la seisine.

Brac. 264 *b*; Fle. 292 (§ 32).

4. Et issi piert, et verité est, qe deus hommes ou plusours porrount estre de un tenement severalment seisiz en un jour en lour demeyne cum de fee, [2]si chescun[2] puse prendre seisine des homages et de rentes et des terres mountauntz a demye marc ou plus, pur[3] les paroles del counte par cas en le dreit; et dounc si le donour moerge mesme le jour de soen doun, et ausi le purchaceour, un ou plusours, si plusours feffementz eynt esté fetz en un jour de meyn en meyn, si deverses assises soint portez de mesme cel tenement par les heirs le donour et par les heirs [4]les purchaceours[4], en chescune persone tendra lu ceste assise; [5]le heir[5] neqedent celi qi dreyn morust seisi mesme le jour [6]le retendra[6] par jugement.

[210 *b*.]

Brac. 265; Fle. 292 (§ 32.)

5. Et [7]ausi le piert il[7] par celi qi enprent chemin de pelrinage, qi se porra demettre de sa seisine et feffer acun

1. donur *M*. 2—2. so *NM*. sicum *L*. si qe homme *G*. sim. *S*. 3. so *NMG*. par *LS*. 4—4. le purchaceour *NG*. sim. *GM*. 5—5. qe le heir *N*. les heirs *M*. 6—6. recouera *N*. recouront *M*. 7—7. ausi piert *M*.

the third day or soon after the gift had ejected the purchaser, the purchaser might have recovered by assise of Novel Disseisin by reason of the conjunction of their two wills, which took place at the transferring of the seisin.

Several persons successively seised the same day. Query, whether esplees must be taken.

4. Hence it appears, and so it is, that two or more persons may on the same day be severally seised of the same tenement in their demesne as of fee, provided perhaps, by reason of the words of the count in the plea of right, that each can take seisin of the homages and rents and lands to the value of half a mark or more. Wherefore if the donor dies on the day of his gift, and the purchaser also,—or the purchasers, supposing several successive feoffments to have been made the same day from one to the other,—and diverse assises are brought of the same tenement by the heirs of the donor and by the heirs of the several purchasers, for every such plaintiff the assise will lie, but the heir of him who died last seised on the same day shall retain the tenement by judgment.

Feoffment by pilgrim on the day of beginning his journey.

5. The same rule appears from the case of him who undertakes a pilgrimage, for he may divest himself of his seisin and

estraunge, et[1] tauntost mesme le jour se porra mettre en chemin, et morir mesme le jour ou le autre; en quel cas, tut puse soen heir averrer par assise, qe soen auncestre fu seisi le jour qe il se mist en chemin vers soen pelrinage, pur ceo ne proeve il mie, qe soen auncestre ly lessa acune seisine ou acun dreit, puis qe il ne morust mie seisi corporelement ne par volunté. Et mesme ceste resoun porra estre assigné en celui qi doune et autre met en seisine, et mesme le jour prent habit de religioun. Et par cestes resouns piert qe ceste assise ne tient lu en nule persone for qe en tieles, qi auncestres [2]eynt moruz seisiz, ou ausi cum morutz[2] par les resouns avaundites.

6. Ou il porra dire qe le auncestre ne est mie uncore mort, Fle. 294 (§ 48). et si ceo soit averré, si chete l'assise.

CHAPITRE XVIII. [LXXXI.]

De taunt de terre ove les apurtenaunces. [211.]

1. Contenu est ausi en le bref, de taunt de terre ove les apurtenaunces en tiele vile; des qeles paroles porrount nestre

1. et *om. LSG.* e *NM.* 2—2. furent mortz *M.*

enfeoff some stranger, and straightway on the same day begin his journey, and die the same day or the next; in which case, although his heir can aver by the assise that his ancestor was seised on the day that he set out on his journey towards his pilgrimage, yet he doth not thereby prove that his ancestor left him any seisin or any right, since he neither died seised corporeally nor by intention. And the same reason may be assigned where a person makes a gift to another and puts him in seisin, and the same day assumes the religious habit. From all which considerations it appears that this assise lies only for those whose ancestors died or are treated as having died seised, for the reasons aforesaid. Feoffment by monk the day of profession.

6. Again, the tenant may say that the ancestor is not yet dead, and if this is verified, the assise shall fall. Plea that ancestor is not dead.

CHAPTER XVIII.

Exception founded on the words 'of so much land with the appurtenances.'

1. The writ also contains these words, 'of so much land with the appurtenances in such a vill;' from which words Exception for error in description of the thing demanded.

excepcions al tenaunt, cum de errour fet en le purchaz, ausi cum de tenement nomé pur rente, ou la reverse, ou rente pur services et custumes, ou deus carues de terre pur une, ou si acun demäunde service cum il deit demaunder annuele rente.

Brac. 272; Fle. 296 (§ 12–14). Et pur ceo si tenement soit demaundé de celi qi rien ne cleyme, ou riens for qe en autri noun, sicum gardeyn, ou fermer, ou vilein, ou baillif, ou el noun sa femme, et[1] tels nient nomez en le bref, ou riens for qe la seignurie et services, ou si[2] service soit demaundé ou tenement dust estre demaundé en demeyne en tut ou en partie, ou si le pleintif die qe il demaunde ceo qe le tenaunt tient en demeyne cum en demeyne, et ceo qe il tient en service cum en service, par taunt chiet le bref. Car il covendra a chescun demaunder par ceste assise solom [3]le tenor del[3] bref, et solom ceo qe le auncestre morust seisi.

Brac. 272, 272 *b*; Fle. 296 (§ 16). 2. Et si le pleyntif ne sache moustrer as jurours le tenement qe il demaunde, ne ou il le deit recoverir, par taunt

1. si *L.* e *NDSGM.* 2. so *NDM.* si *om. LSG.* 3—3. la nature de cest *N.* la tenure del *SGM.*

exceptions may arise in favour of the tenant; as, for an error in the demand, if 'tenement' is named instead of 'rent,' or the reverse, or 'rent' instead of 'customs and services,' or two carucates of land for one, or if any one demands service, when he ought to demand annual rent. Wherefore if a tenement be demanded of him, who claims nothing therein[g], or nothing but in the name of another, as guardian, farmer, villain, or bailiff, or in the name of his wife, where such others are not named in the writ, or nothing but the seigniory and services, or if service is demanded where tenement should be demanded in

The land must be distinctly specified. demesne in all or in part, or if the plaintiff says that he demands that as in demesne which the tenant holds in demesne, and that in service which the tenant holds in service, the writ thereby falls. For in this assise every one ought to make his demand agreeably to the tenour of the writ, and according as his ancestor died seised.

Plaintiff must point out the land to the jurors. 2. And if the plaintiff cannot shew the jurors the tenement which he demands, nor where he ought to recover, the assise

[g] 'Note, that when one demands by Mortdancester otherwise than as the defendant holds, the assise shall fall; thus, if the demandant supposes in the tenant other estate than he hath, as where he is not "tenant in his demesne as of fee." For one ought to demand of him that hath the thing demanded; for of him that hath nothing, nothing can be demanded.' (Note in MS. *N.*)

chete l'assise. Et en mesme la manere, si le tenaunt die, qe il ne tient mie tote la demaundé, si les jurours del assise dient, qe il ne sevent lequel il tient tut ou nient[1]. [211 *b.*]

CHAPITRE XIX. [LXXXII.]

De excepcioun puis le terme.

Et si est contenu el bref, si le auncestre morust puis un certeyn terme nomé en mesme le bref, dount excepcioun poet[2] nestre al tenaunt. Car si il puisse averrer, qe il ne morust mie seisi puis le terme en soen demeyne cum de fee, si chete la assise. Brac. 263 (§ 10).

CHAPITRE XX. [LXXXIII.]

De excepcioun de[3] proscheyn heyr.

1. Puis est contenu en le bref, si le pleintif est proscheyn heir; dount qi est plus proschein heir de autre est en partie dit de sus, et plus serra dit en le plé de dreit. Et quant a Brac. 265 270 (§ 5); Fle. 292 (§ 36–38). Post, l. vi. c. 2, 3.

1. noun *NDSGMBW.* 2. so *S.* poeit *L.* puit *NM.* pout *G.* 3. de plus *ND.* del M.

thereby falls. So, if the tenant says that he does not hold all that is demanded, and the jurors of the assise say that they do not know whether he holds the whole or not. Abatement when tenant does not hold all the land.

CHAPTER XIX.

Exception founded on the words 'after the term.'

It is also contained in the writ, 'whether the ancestor died after' a certain term named in the same writ, from which an exception may arise in favour of the tenant. For if he can prove that the ancestor did not die seised after such term in his demesne as of fee, the assise shall fall. If the ancestor died before the term named, the assise fails.

CHAPTER XX.

Exception founded on the words 'next heir.'

1. The next article in the writ is, 'whether the plaintiff is next heir.' Who is nearer heir than another has been in part mentioned above, and shall be more fully set forth in treating of the writ of right. And as to the proximity, the tenant Plaintiff's title as heir traversed.

la proscheyneté porra le tenaunt respoundre[1], qe un autre est plus proschein heir; ou[2] tut outrement traverser, qe il n'est mie plus proscheyn, et de [3]ceo descendre[3] en l'averrement del assise.

Brac. 270 (§ 5), 272 *b*; Fle. 292 (§ 38).

2. Ou il porra dire, qe il ne est mie plus proschein, car il i ad un autre ausi proschein, si la terre soit partable, nient nomee el bref; la quele excepcioun averré ou nient dedite, si chete l'assise. Et ausi en cas ou l'assise est arramie sour un parcener, ou plusours parceners tienent en commun, par taunt est le bref abatable. Et cum plusours parceners ou autres tienent en commun, et ceste assise soit arramé sour trestouz, si le un des tenauntz moerge, si chiet le bref.

Brac. 276; Fle. 299 (§ 36, 37). [212.]

Brac. 268, 271 *b*, 273 *b*; Fle. 292 (§ 39), 299 (§ 28).

3. Ou le tenaunt porra dire qe le pleintif ne porra[4] estre heir proschein, car le auncestre de qi mort il porte[5] l'assise ne tint mie les tenementz en soen noun[6] demeyne, eynz fist [7]en le noun[7] un tiel et fu soen vileyn; et le quel cas averree ou nient dedit, chete l'assise.

Brac. 271; Fle. 292 (§ 40), 303 (§ 57).

4. De assise arramie par une soeur vers une autre soeur de

1. e dire *add. M.* 2. *conj.* en *LS.* e *NMG.* 3—3. *so NSGM.* *sim. D.* sei defendre *L.* 4. puit *ND.* pout *R.* 5. *so NDMW.* porta *LSG.* 6. noun *om. M.* 7—7. *so NDRW.* en vn nuon *L.* el noun *SGM.*

may answer that another is nearer heir than the plaintiff, or he may absolutely traverse his being the next heir, and thereupon descend to averment by the assise.

Exception for non joinder of co-parceners

2. Or he may say, supposing the land to be partible, that the plaintiff is not the nearest heir, there being another as near not named in the writ; and if this exception is proved or not denied, the assise shall fall[h]. So if an assise is brought against one parcener, where several parceners hold in common, the writ is thereby abatable. And when this assise is brought against several parceners, or others holding in common, and one of the tenants dies, the writ falls.

Abatement by death of parcener.

Exception that ancestor was villain.

3. Again, the tenant may say that the plaintiff cannot be next heir, for that the ancestor of whose death he brings the assise did not hold the tenements in his own name, but in the name of such an one, and was his villain, which case being proved or not denied, the assise shall fall.

Assise does not lie between co-parceners.

4. As to an assise brought by one sister against another of

h See the entry of an assise 16 Edw. I, cited in Cowel's Interpreter, *s. v.* Partitione facienda.

tenement descendaunt de lour commun auncestre, voloums qe ne tiegne nul lu pur la perigalté del dreit possessorie entre eles, eynz tiegne lu bref de purpartie. Et cum deus soeurs eynt arramé ceste assise vers un tenaunt, et dount la une soit muleré et l'autre bastarde, tut die l'assise qe la une fu nee de eynz les esposailes et le autre devaunt, ja pur ceo ne remeigne, qe [1]la seisine ne[1] soit jugé al une et al autre, sauve a la muleré sa accioun a recoverer la partie de la bastarde par bref de dreit, puis qe ele avera age de ceo fere; et la soit dedute[2] la replicacioun de bastardie. Et mesme ceste resoun teigne lu entre parceners, dount acuns sount vileyns et acuns sount fraunes.

5. Ou il porra graunter[3], qe il est proschein heir, et nepurquant porra il dire, qe il n'en deit aver point uncore la seisine; car il la tient par feffement le auncestre a terme de vie, ou en gage, ou par condicioun, ou jekes a certeyn tens par jugement de nostre court, ou par la ley de Engleterre a — Brac. 271, 271 *b*; Fle. 294 (§ 56, 57). [212 *b*.]

1—1. lassise *L.* la seisine *SGM.* lassise ne *N.* *sim. D.* la seysine ny *W.* la seisine ne *corr. R.* 2. dedit *L.* deduct *N.* desdit *S.* desduit *G.* deduyt *M.* 3. *so NGM.* garraunter *L.* *sim. S.*

a tenement descending from their common ancestor, we will that such an assise shall not lie, by reason of the parity of the possessory right among them, but the remedy shall be by writ of partition. And where two sisters, one of whom is legitimate and the other is a bastard, have brought this assise against a tenant, although the assise say that one was born in matrimony and the other before, yet it does not therefore follow that the seisin shall not be adjudged to both, saving to the legitimate her action to recover the bastard's share by writ of right when she is of age to do so; and let the objection of bastardy be then determined upon replication. The same rule also holds among parceners, some of whom are villains and others free[1].

On assise by sisters, mulier and bastard, judgment for both.

So for sisters, free and villain.

5. Again, the tenant may admit that the plaintiff is next heir, but still may say that he ought not as yet to have the seisin, for that the tenant holds it by feoffment of the ancestor for term of life, or in gage, or upon condition, or for a certain time by judgment of our court, or by the law of England for

Exception of particular estate not determined.

Estate by the curtesy.

[1] The case in which this point would arise is explained by Bracton, by reference to a custom of Cornwall; according to which, if a freeman married a neif, half the children were free, and half were villains.

terme de vie. Mes a ceo covendra de averrer[1] engendrure, qe fust oy crier et qe avoit faceoun[2] de homme et ne mie de moustre, et la quele ne fust unques atteynte pur bastarde.

Brac. 271 b; Fle. 295 (§ 5). 6. Ou il porra dire, qe il i ad plus proschein heir; sicum en cas ou le puisnee frere de treys eit arramé ceste assise de la mort soen milueyn frere, si le tenaunt meyne en court acune issue del frere einznee, par taunt cherra l'assise.

Brac. 272; Fle. 296 (§ 10). 7. Ou il porra dire, qe, tut soit il proschein heir soen auncestre, neqedent ly [3]en ousta[3] par assignement en sa dreyne volunté par testament. Et si ceo soit averré, et le tenement soit devisable par usage et custume del lu, sicum est de burgages, si cherra l'assise.

Brac. 272; Fle. 296 (§ 11). 8. Ou, tut soit il dreit heir, cel bref neqedent ne suffit mie pur remedie pur la contrarieté[4] de usage, qe est, qe nul bref ne courge for qe le bref de dreit clos solom le usage del maner. Et si le tenement[5] soit [6]des auncienes[6] demeynes de nostre Coroune, et le pleintif et le tenaunt soint ambideus sokemans, ou si le pleintif sokeman eit arramé ceste assise

1. so *LS.* auer *NDGMWR.* 2. so *N.* face, ou *L.* fachun *M.* face *SG.* 3—3. ennoyta *M.* 4. so *SGMF.* contrarie ceo *L.* contrarie *N.* 5. Maner *NM.* 6—6. de acuns *L.* *sim. S.* des ascunes *G.* de auncien *N.* auncienes *M.* de auncienes *F.*

term of life. But for this he must prove that he had issue, which was heard to cry, and which had human form, and not that of a monster, and was never attainted as bastard.

Exception of nearer heir. 6. Again, he may say that there is a nearer heir, as where the youngest of three brothers brings this assise of the death of his second brother, if the tenant produces in court any issue of the eldest brother, the assise shall fall.

Exception of devise by will. 7. Or he may say, that although the plaintiff is the next heir to his ancestor, yet his ancestor excluded him by a disposition made in his last will by testament; and if this be verified, and the tenement be devisable by usage and custom of the place, as is the case with burgage tenements, the assise shall fall. (Tenements devisable by custom.)

Exception of ancient demesne. 8. Or the tenant may say, that although the plaintiff be right heir, yet he cannot have remedy by this writ by reason of an usage to the contrary, to wit, that no writ shall run, except the writ of right close according to the custom of the manor. And if the tenement is parcel of the ancient demesnes of our Crown, and both the plaintiff and tenant are sokemen, or if the plaintiff being a sokeman has brought this assise

vers le seignur del maner, par taunt cherra cest bref, si le pleintif ne puse moustrer coment le tenement soit chaungé par feffement hors de socage. [213.]

9. Ou il porra dire, qe, tut soit il proschein heir soen auncestre, neqedent ne en morut mie si seisi, qe le donour ne demora touz jours en seisine oveke ly, et uncore en est seisi. Et si ceo soit averré[1], si remeyndra l'assise[2].

CHAPITRE XXI. [LXXXIV.]

De excepcioun, qi la terre tient.

1. A ceo, qe [3]il dit[3] el bref, somonez tiel qi la avauntdite terre tient, ou rente [4]deforcé tient[4], fet a enquere si le tenaunt tiegne tut soul[5] ceo qe le auncestre tint[6], ou en partie. Car le entier porra estre en plusours maneres. Cum si le pleintif demaunde acun maner ove les apurtenaunces, ou une carue de terre ove les apurtenaunces, ou [7]x. liverez[7] de terre ove les

Brac. 266; Fle. 293 (§41).

1. ou nent dedit *add. M. sim. W.* 2. *so ND.* la seisine *LSGMWF.* 3—3. est dit *ND. sim. GW.* i dit *M.* dist *B.* 4—4. deforceour tient *N.* deforce *S.* deforce ou tient *M.* 5. solom *NMF.* soulement *SG.* 6. *so SGM.* tient *L.* tynt *ND.* 7—7. xl. li. *NM.*

against the lord of the manor, the writ shall thereby abate, unless the plaintiff can shew how by feoffment the tenement has been changed from socage.

9. Or he may say, that although the plaintiff is next heir, yet his ancestor did not so die seised, but that the donor always continued in seisin together with him, and still is seised; and if this be verified, the assise shall be stayed.

Exception that the ancestor's seisin was never perfect.

CHAPTER XXI.

Exception founded on the words 'who holds the land.'

1. As to the words in the writ, 'summon such an one who holds the aforesaid land,' or 'holds the rent deforced,'—inquiry should be made whether the tenant holds all according as the ancestor held it, or only part of it. For the whole may be of various kinds. Thus, where the plaintiff demands a manor with the appurtenances, or one carucate of land with the appurtenances, or twenty librates of land with the appur-

Statement of parcels in the writ.

apurtenaunces, dounc[1] solom la demaunde covent as jurours, qe il veient especialment quel tenement et cum bien le pleintif demaunde, lequel le entier solom ceo qe le auncestre [2]le tint[2], ou partie; et si le entier soit demaundé, et partie de cel entier soit aliené nient forprise el bref, chete l'assise.

Brac. 266; Fle. 293 (§ 42, 43). 2. Et si le pleintif face sa demaunde par parceles, issi sera chescune parcele un entier; et dounc si acun ne tiegne acune [213 *b.*] parcele entierement, si cherra le bref quant al entier de cele parcele, et se tendra quant as autres parceles entieres. Car, tut soit qe il n'i ad qe un pleintif devers plusours tenauntz, neqedent cherrount plusours accionns, tut soint eles semblables, pur la pluralité des parceles et des[3] tenauntz. Et si acun demaunde une parcele par plusours parceles vers un tenaunt, sicum une carue de terre[4] par plusours vergeez[5], ou une vergee par plusours acres, si le tenaunt ne tiegne mie le entier solom la demaunde, si chiete le bref, ou pur ceo qe le tenaunt ne tint[6] unques rien, ou pur ceo qe il aliena partie, dount nule mencioun ne est fete, avaunt le bref purchacé.

1. dounc *om. M.* dount *N.* 2—2. *so S* le tient *L.* le pleyntif tient *ND.* le tynt *M.* tient *G.* 3. *so NG.* des *om. L.* de *M.* 4. *so ND.* de plusours *add. LS.* vers plusours *add. G.* 5. *so NS.* verges *LG.* vergees *M.* 6. *so SG.* tient *L.* tynt *NDM.*

tenances, the jurors according to the demand must particularly view what tenement and how much the plaintiff demands, and whether the whole according as the ancestor held it or part only; and if the whole be demanded, and a part of that whole not excepted in the writ be alienated, the assise shall fall.

If tenant does not hold any parcel, the writ abates as to that parcel. 2. And if the plaintiff makes his demand by parcels, then every parcel is a separate whole, and therefore if the tenant does not hold the whole of any parcel the writ shall fall as to the whole of that parcel, and shall hold good as to the other entire parcels. For though there is but one plaintiff against several tenants, yet several (although similar) actions shall accrue, by reason of the plurality of parcels and of tenants. And where one parcel is demanded against one tenant by several particulars, as one caracute of land by several virgates, or one virgate by several acres, if the tenant does not hold the whole according to the demand, the writ shall fall, either because the tenant never held any part of it, or because he aliened part before the writ was obtained, of which alienation no notice is taken.

3. Et si acune alienacioun soit fete apres le bref purchacé, pur ceo ne remeigne mie l'assise pur presoumpcioun de la fraude le alienour; desicum graunt presumpcioun est en tels cas, qe tieles alienaciouns sount fetes a delayer les pleintifs de lour dreit, et pur escure[1] les jugementz de nostre court. Mes cum acune tele alienacioun soit fete, et le feffour moerge avaunt le jour de play, pur ceo ne chete mie le bref; mes viegne le tenaunt, et respoigne al assise, ou vouche a garaunt le heir le feffour. Et si le heir soit de eynz age, pur ceo ne remeigne mie la assise a prendre; car en tels cas voloms nous qe le heir respoigne, de quel age qe il soit, ausi cum [214.] ordiné est en nos estatuz qe il respoigne al bref de entré founde[2] sour disseisine. Et si le heir recovere, sauvé soit al tenaunt de sa garrauntie recoverer, quant le heir vendra a soen age, par resomounse hors des roules de nos Justices, ou nous voloms qe especiale mencioun soit de ceo fete.

Brac. 266; Fle. 293 (§ 43).

Stat. West. 1. (3 Ed. I.) c. 47.

4. Ou si le tenaunt die, qe il ne tient mie le entier, adounc covent qe il die, qi[3] tient le remenaunt. Car nous voloms, qe eynz ceo qe brefs se abatent par vice et par

Brac. 266 b, 270 b (§ 6); Fle. 293 (§ 44).

1. eschure *NDSG.* *sim. M.* 2. *so M.* *sim. SRW.* foundu de *L.* fundu *N.* foundu *G.* 3. *so MG.* qe il *LN.* qil *S.*

3. If any alienation be made after the obtaining of the writ, the assise shall not be thereby stayed, by reason of the presumption of fraud in the alienor, as in such cases there is a great presumption that such alienations are made to delay the plaintiffs of their right, and to evade the judgments of our court. But if any such alienation be made, and the feoffor die before the day of plea, the writ shall not abate; but the tenant must come and answer to the assise, or vouch to warrant the heir of the feoffor. And if the heir is under age, yet the assise shall not stand over to be taken; for in such cases we will that the heir shall answer of what age soever he be, as it is ordained in our statutes that he shall answer to the writ of entry founded on disseisin. And if the heir recover, let the tenant's right be saved to recover his warranty, when the heir shall be of age, by resummons out of the rolls of our Justices, wherein we will that special mention be made thereof.

Alienation, after writ purchased, does not stay assise.

Assise not stayed by non-age of heir of alienor.

4. If the tenant says that he does not hold the whole, then he ought to declare who holds the residue. For we will that before writs be abated for a fault or error, the tenants

Tenant pleading non-tenure of part, must state who holds.

errour, qe les tenauntz enforment les pleintifs coment il se purchaceront bons brefs. Et si le tenaunt die le noun de celi qi tient le remenaunt, a ceo par cas porra le pleintif respoundre qe par taunt ne se deit le bref abatre, car il mesmes tint[1] le entier le jour qe le bref fu purchacé.

Brac. 270 b (§ 6); Fle. 293 (§ 45).

5. Ou il porra dire, qe celi qe tiel remenaunt tient le tient a terme des aunz, ou a volunté, ou en villenage, ou[2] vileyn est celi qi est nomé tenaunt el bref; [3]et en tel cas estera le bref[3]. Et si le tenaunt die, qe le tenaunt del remenaunt est soen fraunc homme et cel remenaunt tient de ly fraunchement, si le pleintif ne eit presentement[4] sute del[5] saunc al vileyn a prover qe il soit vileyn, si chete le bref; et le pleintif se purchace bon[6] bref sour ambideus les tenauntz. Et si les teuauntz allegent noun tenure, et[7] ne sachent dire
[214 b.] qi[8] tient le remenaunt, si respoigne[9] de ceo qe il tient[10].

6. Ceste excepcioun de noun tenure tient lu proprement en ceste assise ensemblement oveske les autres excepciouns tochauntes les motz el bref. Car en autres brefs, si ele soit

1. so *M.* tient *LNG.* 2. e *SGMF.* 3—3. *om. M.* 4. prest *ND.* en present *G.* prestement *MF.* 5. so *NDM.* de *L.* 6. son *M.* 7. et *om. L.* e *MGF.* si il *NDW.* *sim. R.* 8. so *NM.* *sim. F.* qe il *L.* 9. respoignent *M.* 10. i tiegnent *M.*

Replication to such plea.

inform the plaintiffs how they shall purchase good writs. And if the tenant sets forth the name of him who holds the residue, the plaintiff may perhaps answer thereto, that the writ ought not thereby to abate, for the tenant himself held the whole the day that the writ was purchased.

Replication that the alleged tenant is the defendant's villain.

5. Or the plaintiff may say that the person who holds such residue holds it for a term of years, or at will, or in villenage, and is the villain of him who is named tenant in the writ; and in such case the writ shall stand.

Rejoinder.

And if the tenant says that the person who holds the residue is his freeman, and holds such residue of him freely, and the plaintiff is not prepared with suit of the blood of the villain to prove that he is a villain, the writ shall fall; and let the plaintiff obtain a good writ against both the tenants. If the tenants allege non-tenure, and cannot say who holds the residue, let them answer for what they hold.

Proof by suit of the villain's kin.

Exception of non-tenure may be pleaded with other exceptions.

6. This exception of non-tenure lies properly in this assise, together with the other exceptions concerning the words in the writ. For in other writs, if it be put forward with effect,

mise avaunt atteignaument, si ele est si chargeaunt, qe autres excepciouns ne i ount point de lu, eynz [1]se fra[1] jugement solom ceo qe averement se face de cele excepcioun. Et ceo diversement; car en bref de eschete et de entré et de fourme de doun et de cosinage et autres, en queus batayle ne gist ne graunt assise, si le verdit de ceste excepcioun se face pur le tenaunt, adounc chiet le bref, et issi est ele dilatorie,—et si encountre le tenaunt, le pleintif recovera sauve al tenaunt sa acciouen en le dreit; et si ele soit mise avaunt atteignaument en plee de dreit, si eirt ele peremptorie, encountre qi [2]qe unqe[2] passe.

7. Et si le pleintif se pleyne et demaunde tenement en demeyne, et le bref die, qe le tenaunt le deforce, par taunt est le bref abatable pur vice de cel bref; car il dust aver dit, qe le tenaunt tient. Et s'il ne demaunde mie terre ne tenement en demeyne, mes rente et service, et le bref die, qe le tenaunt tient, par taunt est le bref vicious et abatable, s'il en soit chalengé; car il dust estre, qi la avaundite rente [215.]
deforce. Et si il i eit errour el purchaz de noun de ville cum Fle. 293 (§ 46).

1—1. so *MF.* ceo serra *LS.* fra *N.* se fera *G.* 2—2. qe vnqes ele *NS.* qe ele *MG.*

it is of such force, that there is no room for other exceptions, but judgment must be given according as proof is made of this exception. And that in different ways; for in writs of escheat, entry, formedon, cosinage, and others, in which battle and the great assise do not lie, if the verdict upon this exception be given for the tenant, the writ abates, and so the exception is dilatory,—if against the tenant, the plaintiff shall recover, saving to the tenant his action in the right; but if it be put forward successfully in a plea of right, it will be peremptory against whomsoever it passes.

Otherwise, in other actions.

Exception of non-tenure, where dilatory, where peremptory

7. If the plaintiff makes his plaint and demands a tenement in demesne, and the writ says, 'whereof the tenant deforceth him,' the writ is thereby abatable for fault in such writ, for it ought to have said, 'which the tenant holds.' And if he does not demand land or tenement in demesne, but rent and service, and the writ says, 'which the tenant holds,' the writ, if it be challenged, is in that respect defective and abatable, for it ought to have been, 'who deforceth the aforesaid rent.' And if there is error in the writ as to the name of the vill, as where

Forms of writ for tenement in demesne,—and in service.

Misnomer.

si hamelet soit nomé pur vile, ou autre manere de errour, par taunt est le bref abatable.

CHAPITRE XXII. [LXXXV.]

Excepcioun de felonie [1]al accioun[1].

Brac. 276 b; Fle. 302 (§51). 1. Ou le tenaunt porra dire, qe assise ne deit estre, car celi auncestre qi seisine il demaunde fu feloun, si qe par mi ly ne poeit descendre seisine ne dreit a nuli autre, for qe a chief seignur cum eschete. Mes[2] ceo ne suffist mie, si dit ne soit coment feloun, sicum en excepcioun de bastardie covendra dire coment bastard. Et cum il avera dit coment feloun, adounc covendra ceo averrer par record, pur peril qe pora estre de la atteynte, si les jurours del assise feissent faus[3] serment. Car s'il die, qe il fust jugé cum feloun en tiel lu ou en tiel, uncore ne suffist mie, si pleine execucioun ne fust fete de jugement, et de ceo covendra voucher acun record

1—1. *om. NDBW.* 2. Sire Ieo vous die qe mes *N. sim. DR.* 3. so *NSGM.* sauntz *L.*

a hamlet is named, where it should have been a vill, or any other kind of error, the writ is thereby abatable.

CHAPTER XXII.

Exceptions of felony and bastardy, and other exceptions to the assise.

Exception of felony of ancestor. 1. Again, the tenant may say that assise ought not to be, for that the ancestor whose seisin he demands was a felon, so that no right or seisin could descend through him to any other, but to the chief lord[k] as an escheat. But this is not sufficient, unless it be said how he was a felon, as in an exception of bastardy, it must be set forth how a bastard. And when he has explained how he was a felon, then he must aver it by record, on account of the danger there might be of an attaint, if the jurors of the assise should make a false verdict. This exception must be vouched by record. For if he says that he was adjudged felon at such or such a place, yet this is not sufficient, unless the judgment was fully executed, and for this some record should be vouched as a

[k] The expression 'chief lord' denotes not the superior or sovereign, but the immediate lord; as the tenant in chief is the immediate tenant. See before, book ii. c. 8. ss. 5, 8.

a garraunt. Et par ceste resoun piert bien, qe nul jugement de felonie ne dust estre rendu sauntz presence de acun qe porte record. Et s'il die qe il fust utlagé, a ceo porra estre respoundu, qe cele utlagerie fust puis anienti par dreit, sicum de sus est dit.

Brac. 273; Fle. 302 (§ 52). Ante, l. 1, c. 14.

2. Et s'il die, qe il avoit un frere eynznee, qi fist felonie dount il porta jugement, par quei nul dreit porra descendre del auncestre si noun par mi ly, pur qi felonie il entra en les tenementz cum chief seignur en[1] sa eschete, pur ceo qe diverses oppiniouns sount en ceo cas, voloms nous qe hom sache la ley estre itele[2] en cest cas en touz brefs, qe si celi frere eynznee qi fu feloun survesqui le auncestre de qi seisine ceste assise est arramie, ou s'il morust devaunt le auncestre, et lessa acune engendrure qe uncore est en pleine vie, en tiel cas chete ceste assise, et autrement nient, eynz soit prise la assise par le dreit qe descendi del auncestre al fiz puisnee, puis qe le dreit ne trova nul eynzné frere ne issue de ly, ou il poeit descendre; et soit tenu en teu[3] cas ausi cum s'il ne eust unques esté engendré; ne james ne soit fete men-

Brac. 272 b; Fle. 302 (§ 51, 52). [215 b.]

1. so *GMWR.* et *L.* e *S.* cum en *ND.* 2. tiele *N.* tele *MGS.* 3. touz *LNG.* ceu *M.* toz *S.*

warrant. And for this reason it plainly appears that no judgment of felony ought to be given except in presence of some one to bear record thereof. If the tenant says that he was outlawed, to this it may be answered, that such outlawry was afterwards legally reversed, as is above mentioned.

Plea of outlawry.

2. If the tenant says that the plaintiff had an elder brother who committed felony for which he suffered judgment, so that no right could descend from the ancestor except through him, by reason of whose felony he, as chief lord, entered into the tenements as his escheat,—whereas there are diverse opinions upon this point, we will that it be understood that the law in such case as to all writs is this: that if the eldest brother survived the ancestor of whose seisin this assise is brought, or if he died before the ancestor and left any issue still living, this assise shall fall, and otherwise it shall not, but the assise shall be taken by virtue of the right which descended from the ancestor to the younger son, since the right never found any elder brother, or issue of him, to whom it might descend; and such case shall be treated as if he had never been born,

Felony of elder brother bars the assise, if he survived the ancestor or left issue; otherwise not

cioun de ly en counte countaunt en nule descente. Et si le counte soit chalengé pur le omissioun, a ceo soit respondu, qe il [1]ne attendi[1] unques qe acun dreit ly poeit descendre, et si acun ly descendi, celi neqedent resorti[2] al auncestre dount il vient, si qe del piere ou del autre auncestre descendi le dreit al puisnee frere sauntz nul meen, ausi cum nul eynzné[3] ne fust unques creé[4].

Brac. 278 (§ 2), 280; Fle. 305 (§ 62). 3. Excepcioun de bastardie mise[5] encountre acun pleintif ou acun tenaunt en ceste assise fet en touz cas remeyndre l'assise; et [6]la torne[6] acune foiz en juré; et acune foiz [7]en est enveié la conisaunce a dedure[7] en court Cristiene. De [216.] celi neqedent, qi est de eynz age et tenaunt, ne passera nul averrement sur excepcioun de bastardie eynzces qe il soit de plener age, pur ceo qe cele excepcioun detrie le dreit. Mes si la excepcioun soit mise encountre le pleintif, tut soit le pleintif de eynz age, ja par taunt ne remeyndra, qe juree n'en soit prise pur estre certefié del excepcioun. Et si le tenaunt

1—1. *so NDG. sim. MF.* nen tendi *LS.* 2. *so NMF.* resort *LS.* resorte *G.* 3. frere *add. NDMF.* 4. *so ND. sim. MF.* qe *LS.* oy crier *G.* 5. *so N.* mist *L.* mys *M.* mis *F.* 6—6. si tourne ele *M.* si ele tourne *F.* 7—7. en est enreie la conisaunce a dedire *L.* enueyee a dedure la conisaunce *N.* est enuoie la conoissaunce a dedure *G.* est enueyez la reconissance a dedure *F.* est la reconisaunce enueez a dedure *M.* en est enueye la conissance a dedire *S.*

Brother dead before the ancestor without issue, not named in counting of a descent. and no mention shall be ever made of him in counting of any descent. And if such a count be challenged for the omission, it shall be answered that he did not live until any right could descend to him; and that if any did descend to him, it nevertheless resulted to the ancestor from whom it came, so that the right descended from the father or other ancestor to the younger brother without any intermediate, as if no elder had ever existed.

Exception of bastardy. 3. Exception of bastardy being objected against any plaintiff or tenant in this assise stays the assise in all cases; and sometimes it turns it into a jury, and sometimes the cognizance Bastardy of infant tenant not tried during infancy. thereof is transferred to be decided in Court Christian. Nevertheless against one who is under age and tenant, no averment shall pass upon an exception of bastardy before he is of full Otherwise, as to infant plaintiff. age, because that exception determines the right. But if the exception be pleaded against the plaintiff, although he be under age, yet it does not follow that a jury shall not be had to ascertain the truth concerning such exception. And

die qe soen piere ne esposa unques sa mere, en tel cas covendra de ceo estre certifié par le Evask et[1] par les ordinaries. Et si ceste excepcioun soit mise avaunt encountre ambedeus, en teu cas covendra primes estre certifié de la legitimacioun le pleintif. Car si il ne puse prover legitimie, si remeyndra la possessioun ovek le tenaunt, lequel qe il soit bastard ou noun.

4. Ou le tenaunt porra dire qe, si le pleintif i eust unques acun dreit ou [2]auncestre qi ly[2] eust, cel dreit [3]ad il[3] relessé et quiteclamé. Mes a ceo ne suffist mie tauntsoulement[4] vive voiz, tut i eit il suffisaunte seute, eynz ceo covendra[5] moustrer par record de nostre court, ou par escrit ou chartre del pleintif; et uncore ne suffist mie cele quiteclamaunce, si le pleintif puse averrer qe nul[6] fee ne fraunc tenement ne dreit ne ly fut descendu quant il la fit, ou qe il fu de eynz age ou nient en soen dreit sen, ou qe celi, a qi la quiteclamaunce fust fete, ne fu mie adounc en seisine de ceo, eynz se bota puis en seisine par sa intrusioun ou par sa force.

Brac. 270 *b*; Fle. 294 (§51).

Ante, l. ii. c. 8. s. 9.

[216 *b*.]

1. ou *N*. 2—2. *conj.* auncestres qe il *L*. *sim*. *S*. auncestre iekes il *ND*. auncestre qe il *M*. *sim*. *G*. auncestre de ki il *F*. 3—3. so *M*. a il *L*. a li *S*. si le ount il *ND*. ad il luy *G*. ke il ad *F*. 4. tauntsoulement *om*. *S*. vne *add*. *N*. sa *add*. *GMF*. 5. so *NDM*. covendra *om*. *LGS*. 6. so *NDMG*. nulli *L*. *sim*. *S*.

if the tenant say that the plaintiff's father was never married to his mother, this fact must be certified by the bishop and ordinaries. And if the same exception is put forward against both, the legitimacy of the plaintiff must first be ascertained; for if he cannot prove his legitimacy, the possession will remain with the tenant, whether he is a bastard or not.

Fact of marriage certified by the ordinary.

4. Again, the tenant may say that if the plaintiff ever had any right, or if his ancestor had it, that right has he released and quitclaimed. In this case however it is not enough to plead this in words, although he may have sufficient suit, but he must make it appear by record of our court, or by writing, or charter of the plaintiff. And even this quitclaim will not avail if the plaintiff can prove that no fee or freehold or right had descended to him at the time of making it, or that he was under age, or not in his right mind, or that the person to whom the quitclaim was made was not at the time in seisin of the tenement, but afterwards thrust himself into seisin by intrusion or by force.

Plea of quitclaim.

Quitclaim, how pleaded. Release, when valid.

Fle. 294 (§ 52). 5. Ou il porra dire, qe a tort ly enplede il, car le auncestre le pleintif ly enfeffa, et obligea le pleintif a la garrauntie, et dounc, si il fust par autre enpledé, il le vouchereit a garraunt; et si ceo soit averree ou nient dedit, si chete la accioun;—par quei[1] le purchaceour i entra en voide seisine par le assent et la induccioun del feffour, ou par jugement de nostre court, et ne mie par sa intrusioun ne par sa force; ou tut eit esté le entré viciouse et defective, le pleintif neqedent, où autre qe autaunt de dreit i out, le ad puis ratifié par confirmacioun; et si ceo soit veirs[2], si chete la assise.

Brac. 272 (§ 3); Fle. 295 (§ 9).

Brac. 274; Fle. 294 (§ 53), 295 (§ 4). 6. Ou il porra clamer soen title par reversioun, ou [3]par mi fin[3] en nostre court, qe suppose reversioun pur defaute de engendrure, tut fut ele prejudiciele a ly; et si le pleintif ne deface la fin, si cherra la accioun, si le pleintif n'i eit acun

1. qi *SG.* ki *MF.* 2. auerre *G.* 3—3. par fin fete *NAM.* par my fin fete *G.* *sim.* *FH.*

Plea that plaintiff is bound to warrant. 5. Again, the tenant may say that the plaintiff wrongfully impleads him, for that the ancestor of the plaintiff enfeoffed him, and bound the plaintiff to warranty, and therefore if he were impleaded by another, he should vouch him to warranty;—and if this be proved or not denied the action shall fall[l];—wherefore the purchaser entered therein when the seisin was vacant by the assent and induction of the feoffor, or by judgment of our court, and not by his own intrusion or force; or, although the entry was wrongful and defective, yet the plaintiff, or another who had as great a right, afterwards ratified it by confirmation; and if this be true, the assise shall fall.

Plea of title by fine. 6. Again, the tenant may claim title by reversion, or through a fine in our court, which supposes a reversion in default of issue[m], although it be prejudicial to the plaintiff; and if the plaintiff does not avoid the fine, the action shall

l There appears to be an error or omission in the text at this point, which I have been unable to correct.

m There is a confusion here, which I am unable satisfactorily to clear up. The words *par reversioun ou* appear to have been slipped into the text by mistake. The words *fin qe suppose reversioun* are from Fleta, where the word *supponit* is perhaps used in the sense of 'suppresses' or 'destroys.' After the statute *De donis conditionalibus*, which is alluded to above, but is not noticed in Fleta, a reversion for default of issue could not be barred by fine, as had previously been the usage. But at the time when Britton and Fleta were written, such a plea might still be common with reference to a fine levied before the passing of the statute, it being expressly provided that this enactment should not be retrospective. The later operation of a fine to bar the

Stat. West. 2. (13 Ed. I.) c. 1. Stat. Modus levandi fines (18 Ed. I.)

fee taillé par acune fourme de doun. La fin porra hom defere en plusours maneres; car si cil, a qi ele est prejudiciele, eit esté detenu en prisoun, ou hors del[1] reaume de Engleterre, ou de eynz age, ou hors de soen dreit sen, ou sourd, ou muet, par quei il ne poeit cele fin reclamer de eynz le an et le jour.

Stat. de bigam. (4 Ed. I.) c. 1, 2; Brac. 270 b; Fle 294 (§ 54); cf. ante, c. 11. s. 22.

7. Ou si le tenaunt die, qe il ne porra point respoundre sauntz nous[2], et il de ceo moustre chartre par la quele nous [3]sumus obligez[3] a la garrauntie et as eschaunges, adounc remeigne l'assise et autrement nient. [217.]

Brac. 271 b; Fle. 295 (§ 7).

8. Ou il porra [4]clamer soen title[4] par jugement de nostre court, ou par rendre, ou par defaute fete par le pleintif ou par soen auncestre, ou en autre maniere. Ou il porra dire, qe, tut eust il dreit acune houre de aver porté[5] ceste assise, il neqedent ad cel dreit defet, pur ceo qe il ne ad gardé le dreit ordre de pleder; car il de mesmes ceus tenementz sei[6] est avaunt [7]ces houres pleint[7] de mesme le tenaunt[8] en la pro-

Brac. 271 b, 274; Fle. 295 (§ 8).

1. *so NMG.* de *LS.* 2. qe soumes obligeez *add. D.* 3—3. serroms tenuz *ND.* sumes tenuz *MG.* seyoms tenuz *F.* 4—4. *so NMF.* clamer soen *LS.* reclamer *G.* 5. *so MF.* *sim. N.* partie *L.* 6. ceo *L.* si *ND.* se *SM.* 7—7. *so N.* *sim. DSG.* ceux houres pleins *L.* ceste houre pleint *M.* 8. *so NDM.* *sim. F.* tenement *LSG.*

Fine how avoided.

fail, unless the plaintiff has a fee-tail by form of gift. The fine may be avoided several ways; for it is sufficient if he to whom it is prejudicial was detained in prison or out of the realm of England, or under age, or out of his right mind, or deaf or dumb, whereby he could not reclaim the fine within the year and day.

Plea of charter binding the king to warrant.

7. Where the tenant says that he cannot answer without us, if he produces a charter, whereby we are bound to warranty and exchange, the assise shall stand over, but not otherwise.

Exception of judgment; of writ of right formerly brought;

8. Again, he may claim title by judgment of our court, either by surrender or by default made by the plaintiff or his ancestor, or in some other manner. Or he may say, that although he had once a right to bring this assise, nevertheless he has defeated that right, inasmuch as he has not observed the proper order of pleading; for he formerly brought his plaint against the same tenant for the same tenements in the pro-

issue in tail was a consequence of the construction put upon the Stat. 4 Hen. VII. c. 24; see Coke, Inst. ii. 517, 518; Brooke, Abr. tit. Fine pl. 1; Blackstone, Comm. vol. ii. pp. 118, 354; Reeves, Hist. Eng. Law, vol. iv. pp. 135, 138; Hallam, Const. Hist. vol. i. p. 14.

preté par bref de dreit, par [1]quei mes[1] ne porra reverter a

Brac. 272; Fle. 296 (§ 17). pleder sour la possessioun. Ou issi: qe assise n'i deit estre, pur ceo qe assise passa avaunt entre mesmes les persones de mesme le tenement, et pur le tenaunt; et si ceo soit averré,

Fle. 296 (§ 18). si chete la secunde en totes maneres de assises. Et ausi si il i eit uncore autre assise pendaunte de mesme le tenement par entre mesmes les persones, sicum par la resoun de plee de bastardie pendaunt en Cristiene court, ou par autre resoun.

Fle. 296 (§ 19). Et ausi si le tenaunt puisse averrer, qe le pleintif tient [2]a la vaillaunce en eschaunges[2].

Fle. 297 (§ 23). 9. Ou il pora dire qe le tenement est autri dreit, qe il ne porra mie mener en jugement sauntz sa femme en qi le fraunc tenement repose, et il rien ne ad for joyntement oveke sa femme; et ceo[3] porra aver[4] treis veies[5] de verité; ou

[217 *b.*] pur ceo qe il furent feffez a tener en commun, et en teu cas covendra moustrer chartre ou voucher acun record; ou pur ceo qe il en trova sa femme seisie, enceys qe il la[6] esposa; ou pur ceo qe le tenement descendi a sa femme, puis qe la esposa, cum soen heritage.

1—1. *so NM. sim. DS.* qi mesmes *L.* quoi qe mes *G.* quey mesmes *F.* 2—2. *so NDF. sim. M.* a la volunte en eschaunges *L. sim. SG.* 3. *so NGMF.* ceo *om. LS.* 4. *so GM.* auerrer *LS.* 5. *so SGM.* voies *N. sim. F.* de veies *L.* 6. *so NMF.* la *om. L.*

perty by writ of right, wherefore he cannot come back after-

of former assise; wards to plead upon the possession. Or thus: that assise ought not to be, because an assise formerly passed between the same persons of the same tenements, and in favour of the tenant; and if this be verified, the second action in all kinds

of assise pending; of assises shall abate. So, if there is another assise concerning the same tenement between the same persons still pending, as by reason of a plea of bastardy pending in Court Christian, or

of exchange. for other reason. The like if the tenant can aver that the plaintiff holds to an equal value by exchange.

Exception that the tenement belongs to the tenant's wife. 9. Again, the tenant may say that the tenement is the right of another, which the plaintiff cannot bring in judgment without the tenant's wife, in whom the freehold rests, and that he holds nothing therein save jointly with his wife. And this he may verify three ways, either because they were enfeoffed to hold in common, in which case he must either shew a charter or vouch some record; or because he found his wife seised thereof before he married her; or because the tenement descended to his wife as her inheritance after his marriage with her.

10. Ou il pora dire qe il est soen vileyn et[1] soen astrer et demoraunt en soen villenage; et si ceo soit averré, si chete la accioun. Brac. 271, 273 b; Fle. 298 (§ 28).

11. Et si le tenaunt soit sourd et[2] muet naturelment, et nient de survenue par maladie, ou si il soit purement arragé, ou fol[3] nastre de nativité[4], issint qe il ne sache point de descrescioun, en tel cas remeyndra la assise jekes au meillour estat. Et en mesme la manere si le tenaunt soit de eynz age, si remeigne la assise jekes a soen age, si soen auncestre en morust seisi cum de fee, de quel fee qe le tenement soit, chivalerie ou fraunche ferme ou burgage ou autre. Et si le pleintif soit de eynz age, qi se pleigne de soen chief[5] seignur, en tiel cas remeigne la assise jekes a soen age, si le seignur ne cleyme rien for qe seignurie. Mes si ly ou autre i cleyme[6] fraunc tenement, si courge la assise. Brac. 274 b, 275; Fle. 298, 299.

1. ou *NDMW*. 2. ou *NDSGMRWF*. 3. *so NDW*. fust *L*. fut *S*. sot *G*. sol *M*. 4. nature *ND*. 5. *so NMG*. cheer *L*. chier *S*. 6. fee ou *add. N*. *sim. M*.

10. Or he may say that the plaintiff is his villain and his astrer, and abiding in his villenage[n]; and if this be verified, the action shall fall. Exception of villenage.

11. If the tenant is deaf and dumb naturally, and the same is not lately come upon him through sickness, or if he is a mere madman or an idiot from his birth, so as to be incapable of discretion, the assise shall stand over until he is in a better state[o]. In the same manner also where the tenant is under age, the assise shall stand over until his age, if his ancestor died seised of the tenement as of fee, of whatever kind of fee it be, whether knights' fee, free farm, burgage or other. And if the plaintiff who brings a plaint against his chief lord is under age, in such case the assise shall stand over until his age, if the lord claims nothing but the seigniory; but if he or another claims a freehold therein, the assise shall go. Incapacity of tenant. Infancy of tenant. Infancy of plaintiff.

[n] That is, as I understand it, in *the lord's* villenage, or upon his demesne. An astrer (Lat. *astrarius*) was a peasant householder, residing at the hearth or home (astre) where he was bred, 'villanus in veteri astro suo commorans.' (Fle. 217 (§ 8); Hengham Mag. c. viii. p. 103.) The word *astre*, in this sense, has been supposed to be connected with the English *hearth*, Anglo-Saxon *heorð*, but seems to be common to many of the medieval Roman dialects. See Spelman, Gloss. *s. v.* astre; Ducange, Gloss. *s. vv.* astre, stare.

[o] This appears to be one of those instances in which Bracton or Fleta has been carelessly paraphrased. The direction to put off the assise refers to the case where the incapacity arises from sickness. Compare Brac. 274; Fle. 298 (§ 29). In the other case, according to Bracton, *cadit assisa*.

CHAPITRE XXIII. [LXXXVI.]

De Assises tournez en Jurez.

[218.] Brac. 277 b, 278; Fle. 302 (§ 53). 1. Aucune foiz chiet[1] ceste assise hors de sa grosse nature, et tourne en une juree; et ceo par plusours enchesouns en mesme la manere cum assise de novele disseisine; et acune foiz par fourme de doun, ou heir femelle est resceyvable[2] al heritage plus toust qe le frere masle.

Brac. 278; Fle. 302 (§ 54). 2. Ou, si acun eit[3] arramé ceste assise vers soen seignur, et il respoigne qe il ne cleyme rien for qe garde, et a ceo soit respoundu qe garde [4]ne poet[4] il clamer, pur ceo qe le fee ne est ne chevalerie ne serjauntie, et le seignur die qe ly et ses auncestres ount eu[5] la garde del tens dount memorie ne court, si la partie[6] [7]le traverse et denye[7], en tiel cas serra la verité enquise par les jurours en fourme de juree.

1 *so NM.* chete *L.* chece *G.* 2. *so N. sim DGMW.* resounable *L.* 3. *so NGM. sim D.* soit *L. sim. S.* 4—4 poeit *L.* ne puit *NDM.* poet *S.* ne pout *G.* 5. *so NDGM.* euz *L.* 6. *so NDGM.* par tele *L.* parcele *S.* 7—7. *so G. sim. NDMF.* trauerse cleyme *L.* trauersee e le nie *S.*

CHAPTER XXIII.

Of Assises of Mortdancester turned into Juries.

Assise turned into jury; 1. Sometimes this assise descends from its comprehensive nature, and is turned into a jury; and this for many causes in the same way as the assise of Novel Disseisin[p]. Thus, it sometimes happens by reason of form of gift, where the heir female is to be admitted to the inheritance before the heir male. (by reason of form of gift.)

Jury to inquire concerning tenure. 2. So, where any one has brought this assise against his lord, and the lord answers that he claims nothing but wardship, and to this it is replied that he cannot claim wardship, because the fee is neither chivalry nor serjeanty, and the lord says that he and his ancestors have had the wardship thereof from the time whereof memory runneth not,—if the party traverses and denies this, in such case the truth shall be inquired by the jurors in form of jury.

p 'The first point in the writ is whether the ancestor died seised; the second, whether he died within the term; the third, whether the demandant is next heir. If the assise passes upon the substance (sus le gros) of these three points, it passes in its general nature (grosse nature). But if the tenant put forward an exception against the demandant, to which he answers, and says that it ought not to affect him, and for such a reason, and tenders averment by the assise, if then it passes, it is as a jury.' (Note in MS. *N*)

3. Et ausi par la excepcioun de vente[1], cum si acun pleintif Brac. 278; soit respondu, qe il out un frere [2]eynzné, qi[2] conu fust pur Fle. 302, 303. heir, et seisi del heritage, qi cele terre ly vendi, si le pleintif die qe celi frere n'en fu unques seisi, issi qe il poeit fere alienacioun, ou tut fust il en seisine, unques neqedent de ceo ne ly mist en seisine en sa vie, par juree serra enquise la verité. Et ausi en cas ou le tenaunt met avaunt la quiteclamaunce soen auncestre, et il dedit qe ceo ne fu unques le fet soen auncestre.

4. Et en mesme la manere soit, si le tenaunt die, qe il ne Brac. 278; cleyme rien si noun par la ley de Engleterre a terme de vie, Fle. 303 (§ 55). si le pleintif die qe il ne out unques engendrure de sa femme; [218 *b*.] en tels cas soit la assise tourné en juree, et en plusours autres cas, si les parties se assentent, et si noun, soit jugé countre[3] cely qe assenter ne se vodera.

5. Et ausi par enfaunt supposé, sicum en cas ou acun qi se Brac. 278 dist estre heir demaunde par ceste assise vers le verrey heir, (§ 4); Fle. 303 (§ 56). si le dreit heir die qe il ne fu mie engendré de celi qi seisine il demaunde, car en le tens de sa nacioun fu cely qi il dist

1. so *M.* verite *LGSF.* *sim. ND.* 2—2. eynz qe *L.* qe *S.* einzne qe *NM.* *sim. DGF.* 3. encountre *N.* *sim. M.*

3. So, upon the exception of sale, as where the plaintiff is Jury to inquire as to sale, answered, that he had an elder brother acknowledged as heir and seised of the inheritance, who sold the land to the tenant, if the plaintiff says that this brother was never seised, so as to be able to make alienation, or that although he was himself seised, yet he never put the tenant in seisin during his lifetime, the truth shall be inquired by jury. The same, where the or release. tenant puts forward a release from the plaintiff's ancestor, and he denies that it was ever the deed of his ancestor.

4. Likewise, if the tenant says that he claims nothing save by Title by curtesy. the law of England for term of life, and the plaintiff says that he never had issue by his wife; in such and in many other cases the assise shall be turned into a jury if the parties con- Consent of parties to jury, how enforced. sent, and if not, it shall be adjudged against him that will not consent.

5. So, on account of a supposititious child, as where any one, Jury, as to supposititious issue. pretending to be heir, demands by this assise against the true heir, if such right heir says that the plaintiff was not begotten by him whose seisin he demands, for that at the time of his

estre soen piere en parties de outre meer et avoit esté par deus aunz devaunt ou plus, ou escoillié, ou [1]de tele maladie grevé[1] qe nule presumpcioun ne poeit fere qe il [2]puse aver engendrure[2], einz ly remua cum autri engendrure hors de sa mesoun si tost cum il retourna, ou tut le avowast il, mes qe suwe chose fust et notorie qe il ne fu mie de tiel auncestre engendré; si les parties de ceo[3] countredient, si perist la assise, et serra enquise la verité par juree, et en plusours autres cas, qe sount sauntz noumbre.

CHAPITRE XXIV. [LXXXVII.]

De Jugement.

1. Et cum les parties averount pledez jekes al assise, adounc soint les jurours demaundez[4], et ceux qi ne i[5] sount
[219.] mie soint amerciez, et les autres voisent paumer le livre. Adounc soit demaundé des parties s'il sachent rien dire pur quei les jurours ne deyvent mie jurer [6]un et un[6], et alowez

1—1. tele maladie auoit si forte e si greuouse *N*. 2—2. poeit fere engendrure *ND*. le poeit auer engendre *GM*. *sim*. *S*. 3. se *add*. *SGMF*. 4. *so M*. *sim*. *N*. maundez *LGS*. 5. *so M*. *sim*. *S*. i *om*. *LNG*. 6—6. vij et vij *L*. vn e vn *MF*. vij *S*. *om*. *NG*.

birth the person whom he alleges to be his father was in parts beyond sea, and had been so for two years and upwards before, or impotent, or labouring under such an infirmity that he could not be presumed capable of begetting children, but that as soon as he returned he removed him from his house as the offspring of another, or that although he acknowledged him for his own, it was well known and notorious that he was not begotten by such ancestor; if this point be contested between the parties, the assise is at an end, and the truth shall be inquired by jury; and so in numberless other cases.

CHAPTER XXIV.

Of the Judgment in an assise of Mortdancester.

Jury called over. Absent jurors amerced. Challenge of jurors.

1. When the parties have pleaded to the assise, let the jurors be called, and let those who are absent be amerced, and the rest go and lay their hands on the book. Then let it be asked of the parties, whether they have anything to say wherefore the jurors should not be sworn one after another;

lur resouns solom ceo qe dit avoms avaunt en assise de novele Ante, l. ii. c 21. Cf. Brac. 184 b, 185.
disseisine, si il ne eynt mie deschalengez jekes a xii., soit cele journé respité, et soit comaundé al viscounte qe il face venir suffisaument a un autre jour.

2. Et cum il averount asetz des jurours, si voysent jurer Ante, l. ii. c. 21. s. 4.
solom la manere qe dite est en assise de novele disseisine. Et puis soint chargez, et sauvement gardez qe nul ne les prosche[1] jekes autaunt qe il eynt respoundu. Et solom lour verdit soit jugé pur le un ou pur le autre. Et puis soint taxez les da- Ante, l. ii. c. 22. s. 8.
mages par les jurours, ou solom ceo qe dit est avaunt.

3. Et si plusours portent ceste assise de la mort lour Brac. 272 b.
commun auncestre, et les jurours ne sevent dire[2] qi de touz est plus proschein heir, en tiel cas remeigne [3]la seisine[3] al tenaunt, si les pleintifs pur moustraunce de lour dreit [4]ne facent les jurours estre chargez de[4] acun point[5], ou qe[6] eus mesmes le dient, par quei les Justices soint ensensez[7] qi de touz ad greyndre[8] accioun de autre. Et si plusours assises soint arramez vers un tenaunt de un mesme tenement et de

1. approche *N.* *sim.* *GM.* 2. dire *om.* *MF.* 3—3. *so* *DMGSWF.* la assise *L.* lassise ne *N.* 4—4. ne *om.* *M.* ne sachent les Iorours esclarser en *G.* 5. point *om.* *M.* 6. qe *om.* *M.* 7. asensez *M.* escuseez *D.* 8. plus grant *MGS.* meyndre *W.*

and after their challenges are allowed, as we have said before in treating of the assise of Novel Disseisin, if there do not remain as many as twelve unchallenged, let that day be respited and let the sheriff be commanded to cause a sufficient number to come on another day.

2. When there are jurors enough, let them go and be sworn Jurors sworn.
in the manner described in assise of Novel Disseisin. Afterwards let them be charged, and safely kept so that no one come near them until they have given in their answer. And Verdict.
according to their verdict let judgment be given for the one Judgment.
party or the other. And afterwards let the damages be taxed Taxation of damages.
by the jurors, as before is said.

3. If several persons bring this assise of the death of their Several plaintiffs must shew how the title lies between themselves.
common ancestor, and the jurors cannot say which of them all is nearest heir, in such case the seisin shall remain with the tenant, unless the plaintiffs for the manifestation of their right cause the jurors to be charged upon some point, or they themselves declare it, whereby the Justices may be informed which of them has the best right of action. If several assises are brought against one tenant for one and the same tenement

diverses descentes, en tiel cas fet primes a prendre la reconi-
[219 b.] saunce de cele assise qe est aramé sour la dreyne seisine. Et s'il covendra fere puralé, soit fete cum de sus est dit. Et cil qi tort avera remeigne en nostre merci, simple ou greve, solom ceo qe il avera malice ou colour de dreit.

CHAPITRE XXV. [LXXXVIII.]

De Quod permittat.

Brac. 284; Fle. 316.

1. Aucune foiz avient, qe, tut deveynt[1] a acun dreit heir la seisine de soen heritage, il neqedent est destourbé de aver la seisine de acune commune ou de autre appurtenaunce qe a soen heritage est annex de autri soil, et dount soen auncestre morust seisi; et ou par ceste assise ne gist point de remedie al heir, einz[2] par simple juree issaunt par mi un bref purveu en

Brac. 284 b; Fle. 316; Reg. brev. orig. 155, 156.

tiel cas, qe hom appele *Quod permittat.* Et mesme le remedie est purveu pur successours sour defforceours de [3]teles apurtenaunces[3] dount les predecessours moerirent seisiz sicum del

1. deueigne *N.* auiegne *M.* *sim. F.* 2. fet *add. NM.* 3—3. so *M.* *sim. ND.* cels apurtenauntz *L.*

demanded by divers descents, in such case the recognisance must first be taken of that assise which is brought upon the

Perambulation. Amercement of losing party.

last seisin. If a perambulation is necessary, let it be made as hath been said above. The party which is in the wrong shall be moderately or heavily amerced, according as his claim was malicious or founded on a colour of right.

CHAPTER XXV.

Of the writ called Quod permittat.

Easement recovered by heir by *Quod permittat.*

1. Sometimes it happens that although the right heir has obtained the seisin of his inheritance, nevertheless he is hindered from having the seisin of some common or other appurtenance annexed to his inheritance, in another's soil, and whereof his ancestor died seised; in which case no remedy lies for the heir by this assise, but by a simple jury proceeding by virtue of a writ provided in this case, called *Quod permittat.* The same remedy is provided for successors against the deforceors of such appurtenances whereof their predecessors died seised as in right of their churches. And if

dreit de lour eglises. Et si il i eint plusours deforceours[1] qi tienent en commun, adounc covendra trestouz nomer [2]en le bref[2], ou le bref serra abatable, si il en soit chalengé.

2. Cest bref ne detrie for qe le dreit de la possessioun, et si est limité par mesme le terme, qe est assise de mort de auncestre, et entre mesmes les persones; outre quel terme ne tient [3]lu nul bref[3] en cest cas for qe bref de dreit overt pledable en la court le seignur del fee. Brac. 284 *b*. [220.]

3. Al premer jour gist essoigne en cest bref de possessioun, ausi bien pur le tenaunt cum pur le pleintif. Et si le tenaunt face defaute, si courge la distresce solom[4] le proces dit avaunt en le chapitre de *Quo Jure*. Et tienent lu en cest bref vewe demaunder, et garraunt voucher. Brac. 284 *b*; Fle. 316 (§ 2). Ante, l. ii. c. 28. s. 3. Fle. 317 (c. 10. § 4).

1. *so NDSGM.* deforceours *om. L.* 2—2. *so NDM. sim. SG. om. L.* 3—3. *so M.* nul lu nul bref *L. sim. S.* nul bref liu *NDG.* 4. *so NDGM. sim. S.* sour *L.*

there are several deforceors who hold in common, then all must be named in the writ, or the writ, if it be challenged, will be abatable.

2. This writ tries only the right of possession [q], and is therefore limited within the same term, and to the same persons, as the assise of Mortdancester; and beyond this term no writ lies in this case except a writ of right patent pleadable in the court of the lord of the fee. *Quod permittat*, a possessory action.

3. In this writ of possession an essoin lies the first day as well for the tenant as for the plaintiff. And if the tenant makes default, let the distress run according to the process before-mentioned in the chapter of *Quo jure*. Demand of view and voucher of warranty both lie in this writ. Essoins. Process. View, voucher.

q 'Sometimes the *Quod permittat* may be altogether in the Right, when it contains the words *habere debet;* sometimes altogether in the Possession, by reason of the word *solet*, and this when the demandant demands of his own seisin. But when one demands the seisin of his ancestor, this savours of the nature of Mortdancester, because the writ shall make mention that the ancestor was seised of the thing as of fee as appurtenant to his freehold in such a town the day whereon he died.' (Note in MS. *N.*) A writ of *Quod permittat* containing the words *habere debet* was treated as a writ of right, triable by battle or great assise; and accordingly it was decided in 32 Edw. I. that a parson could not prosecute such an action without aid of the patron and the bishop. Year Book, 32 Edw. I. pp. 117, 510. Compare Vetus Natura Brevium, 68 *b*. In the examples given by Bracton of this writ, which he, as well as our author, describes as affecting the possession and not the property, the action is founded upon the seisin of the ancestor of the plaintiff, or of the predecessor of a parson claiming in right of his church. For the forms of writ in which the demandant founded his claim upon his own seisin, and of those in which the words *debet* and *solet* were contained, see Regist. Brev. Orig. 155, 156; Fitzherbert, Nat. Brev. 123; and compare below, l. v. c. 14. s. 1.

CHAPITRE XXVI. [LXXXIX.]

De Cosinage.

Brac. 281; Fle. 306. 1. Sicum assise de mort de auncestre est limité de eynz[1] certeyns degrez, et de la mort de certeynes persones, et lu tient vers certeynes persones, et point ne [2]s'estent[2] outre, en eyde neqedent de ceste assise furent perveuz brefs en degrez Ante, c. 6. s. 10. joygnauntz, a quels ceste assise ne [3]s'estent[3] point si noun par resoun de autre persone joynte al pleintif; par ount hom ne estovera mie en touz cas de si tardive seisine coure al bref de dreit, ou[4] plusours delays sount et[5] perils; ceo est a saver de cosinage, et de ael, et de besael, si le tens le seoffre, par mi queus le dreit de la possessioun puse estre detrié.

Brac. 281; Fle. 306. 2. Et cum il soint purveuz en eyde de cele assise, bien est resoun qe il [6]en suent[6] la nature en graunt partie, sicum el terme; et pur ceo sount il touz de une limitacioun de terme; [220 *b*.] et sicum entre mesmes les persones hors de degrez, car ces

1. de deus *L.* de deinz *ND.* *sim. MG.* 2—2. *so G.* *sim. NDM.* cessent *LS.* 3—3. *so G.* *sim. NDM.* cessent *LS.* 4. e en *ND.* 5. en *L.* e *M.* *om. ND.* 6—6. *so NM.* *sim. DG.* entient *L.*

CHAPTER XXVI.

Of the writs of Cosinage, Ael, and Besael.

Writs of Cosinage, Ael, and Besael, supplemental to assise of Mortdancester. 1. As the assise of Mortdancester is limited within certain degrees, and holds only of the death of certain persons and against certain persons and extends no further, certain writs in degrees adjoining, to which that assise does not extend except by reason of another person joined with the plaintiff, have been provided in aid of that assise, whereby in all cases of so recent a seisin a plaintiff will not be compelled to have recourse to a writ of right, wherein there are many delays and risks. These writs are those of Cosinage, Ael, and Besael, by which, if the time allows, the right of possession may be tried.

Limitation of time and parties in these writs. 2. As these writs are provided in aid of that assise, it is reasonable that they should in a great measure follow the nature of it, as in respect of the term, and therefore the same limitation of term is fixed for one and the other; so likewise they hold between the same persons out of the degrees, for these

brefs tienent lu par entre les persones hors des termes del assise, entre queles la assise tient lu [1]de eynz[1], et ne mie entre autres [2]persones sicum entre[2] privez de saunc clamauntz par une descente, amountaunt jekes al tresael, si tens le soeffre, et descendaunt jekes a dreyn saunc.

3. Et fet a entendre qe trestouz ceux qi issent des uncles et des auntes, ausi bien de part de mere cum de part de piere, [3]et ceux ausi qi issent des freres et des soeurs,[3] et ceux ausi qi issent de lour issues [4]es degrez[4] a quels assise de mort de auncestre ne se estent mie, sount proprement cosins, chescun a autre. Et en la dreite line descendaunt sount cosins, ausi bien [5]cum sount es[5] traverseles. Car amountaunt sount il auncestres ou aels ou besaels, et en descendaunt sount cosins; pur ceo qe le besael ou le tresael poet[6] demaunder[7] la seisine [8]de plus basset[8] trové en la dreite lyne par bref de cosinage, et le ael et le piere ou la mere la seisine de soen fiz ou de sa file ausi par mesme le bref de cosinage, [9]et countremeyn[9]

1—1. de deus *L.* de deinz *ND.* denz *M.* deinz *G.* 2—2. *om. M.* 3—3. *om. M.* 4—4. et des grez *L.* en degrez *N.* es degrez *G.* es desgrez *M.* es des greez *S.* 5—5. cum sount *LNSG.* com es *M.* com est *A.* 6. so *SW.* poeit *L.* puit *M.* purra *ND.* pout *G.* pount *R.* 7. de *add. NDRW.* 8—8. *so MF.* de plus basset et *L.* *sim. S.* plus baas qe ne soit *ND.* de plus bas *G.* de plus bas qe seit *R.* *sim. AW.* 9—9. encountre meyn *N.* e countre mount *M.* *sim. F.*

writs take effect between the same persons beyond the limits of the assise, between whom the assise lies within the limits, (and not between other persons, as privies of blood claiming by the same descent), ascending to the grandfather's grandfather, if the time admits of it, and descending to the remotest blood.

Cousins, how understood.

3. It should be understood, that all those who issue from uncles and aunts, as well on the part of the father as on the part of the mother, and all those who issue from brothers and sisters, and those also who issue from their issue, in the degrees to which the assise of Mortdancester does not extend, are properly cousins to each other. And in the right line descending they are cousins, as well as in the collateral lines. For ascending they are ancestors, or grandfathers or great-grandfathers, and descending they are cousins, because the great-grandfather or the grandfather's grandfather may by writ of Cosinage demand the seisin of the lowest found in the right line, and the grandfather or father or mother by the same

tendreit lu assise de mort de auncestre ou bref de ael et[1] de besael et[2] de dreit.

4. Et pur ceo[3] apertement veer, en [4]quels degrez[4] sount cosins quant a regard del pierre ou des autres trovez en la dreite line, soit trete une line dreite countreval, et la eynz soint quatre degrez, chescun de sus autre, dount el premer soint mis besael et besaele, en le autre ael et aele, en le tierz
[221.] pere et mere, et en le quart fiz et file. De treis sovereins degrez soint treis lines traverseles, de une part et de autre, et pur chescun enfaunt masle soit fet un degré par sei de une part, et pur chescune enfaunt femelle[5] ausi de autre part, et pur chescun enfaunt [6]de ceux enfauntz[6] soit fet un degré plus lointz, et issi outre del issue de cel issue de degré en degré,

1. ou *NMF*. 2. ou *M*. 3. ceo *om*. *NMF*. 4—4. quels des grez *L*. *sim*. *N*. queu degre *M*. queus degres *F*. 5. *so* *NMG*. de la femelle *LS*. 6—6. *so* *N*. *om*. *L*. de ses enfaunz *M*. *sim*. *GS*. des enfanz *F*.

writ may demand the seisin of the son or daughter[r]; where in the other direction assise of Mortdancester, writs of Ael and Besael, and writ of right would lie.

Table of Consanguinity. 4. In order to see plainly in what degrees they are cousins in relation to the father or others found in the direct line, let a line be drawn straight down, and let there be placed therein four degrees, one above the other, in the first of which let great-grandfather and great-grandmother be placed, in the second grandfather and grandmother, in the third father and mother, and in the fourth son and daughter. From the three upper degrees let three cross lines be drawn on each side, and for every male child let a degree be made by itself on the one side, and likewise for every female child on the other side, and for every child of these children let a degree be made further down, and so on for the issue of that issue from degree to degree, the eldest always filling the degree adjoining the

r Our author appears to stand alone in asserting a right of inheritance in the ascending line. (See post, l. vi. c. 3. s. 4.) 'A has a son B, and no other of his blood; B purchases, and dies without issue. *Quæstio*. Whether his father can or ought to have the purchase. *Solutio*. The chief lord and not the father, because the son is of the blood of the father, but the father is not of the blood of the son. But the purchase shall ascend collaterally, as to uncle or aunt, and this is the first resort, for in every Cosinage the count must be by resort. The second resort is to the grandfather's or grandmother's brother or sister; the third to the brother or sister of the great-grandfather or great-grandmother. But the seisin of the grandfather's grandfather cannot be counted of, save in the writ of right; so that by the fourth resort demand can only be made in a writ of right.' (Note in MS. *N*.) For the purpose of limitation the degrees appear to have been counted back from the person whose seisin was demanded, not from the claimant. See Year Book, 32 Edw. I. p. 145.

sauve qe le eynzné face touz jours le degré joygnaunt al pierre ou a la mere, en la dreite line descendaunt. La manere de la purtreture est tele cum apert en ceste figure[1].

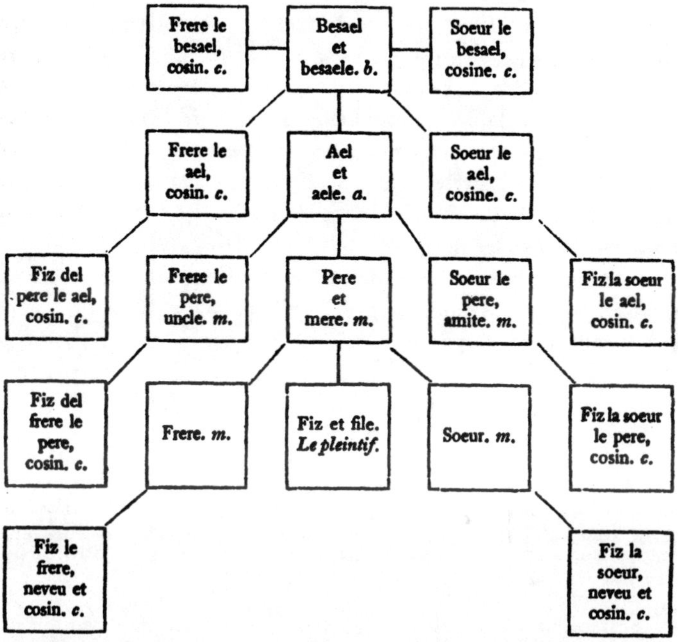

[2]Le degré trové [3]de suth[3] le besael signefie le fiz eynzné, et [4]es degrez[4] de costé le fiz, qi est appelé ael, sount les freres et les soeurs pusneez al ael, qi sount uncles et auntes al pierre

1. *This figure is wanting in LDSGMFC. It is variously given in NAR. The above is completed from that in N.* 2. *A new chapter commences here in NDGSW, with the title, in ND,* Des degrees del arbre. *sim. in W.* 3—3. de sus *L.* de suys *N.* suth *G.* de suz *S.* souz *M.* suz *F.* 4—4. *so M.* en degrez *L. sim. F.* en degre *N.* es grez *S.* ses degrez *G.*

father or mother in the right line descending. The manner of the drawing is such as appears by the above figure[*]. The degree found under the great-grandfather signifies his eldest son, and in the degrees at the side of the son, who is called grandfather, are the younger brothers and sisters of

[*] In the above figure the letters *m. a. b. c.* indicate the several writs of Mortdancester, Ael, Besael, and Cosinage, by which the son or daughter, the last persons in the direct line, might assert their right to an inheritance of which the several ancestors died seised. These letters have been added to carry out the apparent object of the introduction of the figure.

ou a la mere; et issi soit entendu de trestouz les autres degrez countreval par sotiveté de sen.

Brac. 283; Fle. 306. 5. Et trestouz ceux de qi mort ne tient mie lu assise de mort de auncestre ne bref de ael ne de besael sount cosins, et ou nul remedie ne gist par [1]tels brefs[1], si gist remedie par bref de cosinage, taunt cum le tens soeffre, outre quel tens ne gist nule manere de remedie for qe par bref de dreit, qe est [221 *b.*] dreyn remedie de touz remedies. La nature del[2] plee de co- Fle. 306 (§ 2). sinage sert[3] a fere conustre les descentes et les resortes[4], ausi bien de la dreite line cum des lines traverseles, et de la descente et [5]de la resorte[5] des parentz hors de la dreite line jekes en la traversele.

Brac. 283 *b*; Fle. 308 (§ 8). 6. En cest bref ne fet nient a fere mencioun de dreit en counte countaunt, ne en nul bref de possessioun, ou nule mencioun ne est fete el bref, car par variaunce del bref et de la demoustraunce seroit le bref abatable; eynz suffist a counter en ceo bref et en bref de ael [6]et de besael[6] de la seisine le cosin ou ael ou besael, qi en morust seisi en soen

1—1. cest bref *N.* touz brefs *M.* 2. *so NMG.* de *LS.* 3. *so Y.* soit *LS.* si est *NDA.* *sim. W.* fait *G.* est *MF.* 4. *so G.* resortz *N.* resources *MSF.* 5—5. *so G.* de la resource *LS.* del resort *N.* de la source *MF.* 6—6. *so verb. NDGWR.* *om. LS.* e de la besaele *M.*

the grandfather, who are uncles and aunts to the father or mother, and so by like reason it is to be understood of all the other degrees below.

Writ of Cosinage, in what cases it lies. 5. All those, of whose death neither assise of Mortdancester nor writ of Ael or Besael lies, are cousins, and where no remedy lies by these writs, it lies by writ of Cosinage, as long as the time allows, beyond which no kind of remedy lies but by Descents and resorts. writ of right, which is the last remedy of all. The nature of the plea of Cosinage serves to explain the descents and the resorts as well of the right line as of the collateral, and the descent and the resort of the kindred out of the right line to the collateral.

Count in writ of Cosinage; not of the right, but of the seisin. 6. In counting upon this writ no mention should be made of the right, nor in any writ of possession, where no mention is made thereof in the writ; for by variance between the writ and the declaration the writ would be abatable; but in this writ and in those of Ael and Besael it is sufficient to count of the seisin of the cousin or grandfather or great-grandfather, who died

demeyne cum de fee, sauntz rien parler del dreit. Car ceux deus motz, en soen demeyne cum de fee, meynent en jugement tut le dreit possessorie. Et cum cest mot, de dreit, est especifié en le counte, par taunt signefie qe le pleintif bie [1]a fere dedure[1] la proprеté, dount si le bref ne[2] fet mencioun, et le errour soit chalengé, par taunt cheet le bref.

7. Et estre ceo, ne est mie de la substaunce a counter en nul bref de possessioun de nule prise [3]des espletz[3], nient plus en pleez de cosinage ou de ael ou en autres brefs de possessioun qe en assises de novele disseisine ou de mort de auncestre ou autres. Car hom porra estre seisi tut ne prenge hom rien [4]des espletz[4], sicum le verrey heir apres la mort soen auncestre, vacaunt le heritage, par le mettre del pié, et sicum autre en qi persone repose la proprеté par simple conjunccioun del dreit a la possessioun, vacaunt le tenement; [5]et en quels[5] cas tel heir porreit morir eynz ceo qe il en prendreit point de espletz, et jalemeyns ne en morroit seisi en soen demeyne cum de fee; ne mie pur ceo qe si mencioun en soit fete et hom le puse averrer[6], plus aydent [7]les paroles[7] qe ne

Brac. 284; Fle. 308 (§ 9).

[222.]

1—1. a fere dedire *LM*. a fere desdire *NS*. dedire *F*. 2. *so NG*. ne en *L*. nent *M*. 3—3. *so verb. NG*. de ces pletz *L*. *sim. S*. de ses esplez *M*. 4—4. *so verb. NSGM*. des pletz *L*. 5—5. et quel *L*. en quel *N*. *sim. G*. e en quel *S*. *sim. M*. 6. enuerrer *M*. 7—7. *so G*. les parceles *L*. *sim. S*. celes paroles *NM*.

seised in his demesne as of fee, without speaking of the right. For these two words, 'in his demesne as of fee,' bring in judgment all the possessory right; and when the word 'right' is expressed in the count, it imports that the plaintiff intends to bring in question the property, whereof if the writ makes no mention, and the error is challenged, the writ thereby abates.

7. Moreover it is not essential to count in any possessory writ of any taking of profits, and this is no more necessary in pleas of Cosinage or Ael or other writs of possession, than in assise of Novel Disseisin or Mortdancester. For one may be seised without taking profits, as the right heir becomes seised after the death of his ancestor, the inheritance being vacant, by setting his foot thereon, and others in whose persons the property rests by a simple conjunction of the right with the possession, the tenement being first vacant; in which cases although such heir should die before taking any of the profits, yet he would nevertheless die seised in his demesne as of fee. If however the taking of esplees is mentioned and can be verified,

Not necessary to declare taking of esplees.

grevent, car par [1]ces motz[1] porra la seisine mout[2] estre declaree[3].

Brac. 283; Fle. 307 (c. 8. § 1, 4). 8. En cest bref tienent lu essoignes, les *Capes*[4] par defautes, vewe demaunder, garraunt voucher, et les excepciouns de mesme la descente, de seisine, de dreyn seisi, de soen demeyne [5]cum de fee[5], de taunt de terre, [6]de terme[6] de proscheineté, de noun tenure, de felonie, de errours, de bastardie, et les autres qe dites sount de sus en assise de mort de auncestre. Ante, cc. 12—22.

1—1. *so G. sim. MSW.* cas mentz *L.* ces motz moustrez *R.* ceo par cas mieuz *N. sim. D.* 2. *om. ND.* 3. esclarse *G.* 4. *so NS.* capies *L.* capez *M.* 5—5. *om. M.* 6—6. *so NSGRMW. om. L.*

these words are rather of service than otherwise, since they tend strongly to declare the seisin.

Essoins, process, and exceptions in writ of Cosinage.

8. In this writ lie essoins, process by *Cape* upon default, demand of view, voucher of warrant, exceptions of the same descent, of seisin, of last seised, of his demesne as of fee, of so much land, of term of proximity, of non-tenure, of felony, of errors, of bastardy, and the others mentioned above in assise of Mortdancester.

BRITTON.

LIVRE IV.[1]

CHAPITRE I. [xc.]

De assise de Dreyn Present.

1.

ASSISE de drein present est une reconisaunce de xii. jurours, la quele detrie le dreit de la possessioun del avowesoun de acune eglise, qi drein presenta en soen noun demeyne en tens de pes; et acune foiz est pledable[2] devaunt nous cum nous serroms[2] descenduz en le counté ou la eglise est, et acune foiz par devaunt nos Justices errauntz, acune foiz el baunc de Westmoustre par le establisement

Glan. l. 4. c. 1, l. 13. cc. 18–22; Brac. 237 b; Fle. 317.

[222 b.]

Mag. Chart. c. 63; Fle. 317 (§ 1), 318 (§ 7).

1. Incipit liber iiij. De Iure patronatus *N.* *sim. D.* *No division of books occurs at this point in LSGM.* 2—2. ou nous seoms *M.*

BOOK IV.

OF PLEAS RELATING TO ADVOWSONS AND THE PROPERTY OF CHURCHES; AND OF ATTAINTS.

CHAPTER I.

Of the Assise of Last Presentation.

1.

AN assise of last presentation is the recognisance of twelve jurors, which tries the right of possession to the advowson of any church, that is, who last presented in his own name in time of peace. This may sometimes be pleaded before us, when we are come down to the county where the church is situate, sometimes before our Justices Itinerant, sometimes in the Bench at Westminster by the ordinance of the Great

Assise of darreign presentment; before what judges taken.

de la Graunt Chartre, et acune foiz, pur dreit haster, par devaunt nos Justices a ceo especialment entitlez; et acune foiz comence en un lu et termine en un autre; et acune foiz comence hors del counté, et la reconisaunce ou la juré est prise el counté; et acune foiz sount les parties ajournez a oyer lour jugement, et acune foiz nient ajournez.

Brac. 237 b; Fle. 317.

2. Et pur ceo si acun eit presenté a acune eglise voide, a la quele ly ou ses auncestres eynt presenté en tens de pees, pur ceo qe chescun heir deit aver la seisine qe soen auncestre out, si le destourbour ou le deforceour ne sache dire par apertes resouns le contrarie, et le quel debat est terminable par ceste assise de dreyn present, fet primes a veer a qi affiert de arramer ceste assise. Car a nul ne affiert de arramer si noun a celi qi en soen noun demeyne i avera presenté sovent, ou une foiz ou plusours, ou soen heir par resoun de successioun en le heritage et el dreit de acun auncestre qi morust seisi del avowesoun.

Brac. 238; Fle. 317.

3. Et ceo qe dit est de un heir soit entendu de plusours qi sount parceners et cum un heir. Et si plusours parceners

Charter, and sometimes for the dispatch of justice before our Justices especially authorized for that purpose. Sometimes the assise is begun in one place and is ended in another; and sometimes it is begun out of the county, and the recognizance or jury is taken in the county; and sometimes the parties are adjourned to hear their judgment, and sometimes not adjourned.

Who shall have assise of dareign presentment.

2. Therefore where any person has presented to a vacant church to which he or his ancestors have presented in time of peace, inasmuch as every heir ought to enjoy the seisin which his ancestor had, unless the disturbor or deforceor can shew plain reasons to the contrary, which contest is determinable by this assise of last presentation, we must first see to whom it belongs to bring this assise. For it belongs only to him who has, once or oftener, presented in his own name, or to his heir by reason of his succeeding to the inheritance and the right of an ancestor who died seised of the advowson.

Coparceners may bring assise.

3. What is said of one heir may be understood of several who are parceners and as one heir. But if several parceners

recoverent l'avouwesoun de acune eglise par ceste assise, et [223.] la eglise soit voide, nul parcener neqedent ne porra presenter sauntz autre par nule [1]prerogaunce de einznescerie[1], ne par nule autre resoun. Mes [2]a ceux[2] qi tienent par feffement en commun et ne mie par descente james ne tendra lu ceste assise, eynz ceo qe il eynt esté seisiz del presentement; de sicum deus ne porrount james recoverer par ceste assise a demaunder de la seisine celi, ou de ceux, qi heirs il ne sount mie, nent plus qe en pletz de dreit; ne a ceux qi tienent a terme des aunz, ne a terme de vie par resoun de dowarie ou par la ley de Engleterre, ou en gage, ou par feffement, ou par eschete, ou par autre purchaz [3]qe par[3] successioun.

4. Et si le plé soit nient el baunc, adounc tient lu un essoigne saunt plus pur chescune partie, issi qe apres lour apparaunce [4]n'i eit[4] nul essoigne. Et si le deforceour face defaute, adounc teigne le proces qe dit est de sus el chapitre de somounse. Et si le plé soit en le counté, tut eit il esté commencé hors del counté, adounc ne tiegne mie lu reso-

Brac. 238 (§ 3); Fle. 317 (§ 4).

Ante, l. iii. c. 10. s. 8.

Brac. 238 *b* (§ 6); Fle. 318 (§ 7).

1—1. prerogaunce de einz necessarie *L.* prerogatif de age ne deyns necessarie *N.* *sim. D.* prerogance de einz nescerie *S.* prerogatiue de einz necerie *M.* prerogatiue de eignesserie *G.* 2—2. *so N.* *sim. M.* acuns *L.* *sim. GS.* 3—3. qe *om. M.* qe par autre *S.* ou par autre *G.* 4—4. ne i eit lu *M.*

recover the advowson of any church by this assise, and the church is void, no parcener can present without the other by any prerogative of seniority, or for any other reason. But this assise shall never lie for those who hold in common by feoffment and not by descent, before they have been seised of the presentation, since two persons can never recover by this assise who make their demand of the seisin of him or of them whose heirs they are not, any more than in pleas of right. Neither does it lie for those who hold for term of years, or for term of life by reason of dower, or by the law of England, or in gage, or by feoffment, or by escheat, or by any mode of acquisition other than succession.

Eldest parcener has no prerogative to present.

Assise does not lie for feoffee before presentation; nor for termor, nor for tenant by dower or curtesy.

4. If the plea is not in the Bench, then one essoin and no more lies for each party, so that after their appearance there is no essoin. And if the deforceor makes default, then the process above-mentioned in the chapter of summons takes place. And if the plea is in the county, although it commenced out of the county, no resummons after default shall lie, nor

Essoins. Process. Resummons. In what cases resummons is not allowed.

Brac. 239; Fle. 318 (§ 8). mounse apres defaute, ne nul essoigne, ne nul delay. Et si le pleintif soit de eynz age, james ne tiegne lieu essoigne ne resomounse, lequel qe le plee soit el counté ou dehors; car [223 *b*.] autaunt vaut la absence le tenaunt en cel cas cum sa presence. Brac. 239; Fle. 318 (§ 9). Et ausi ne tient resomounse point de lu en cas de contumace[1], cum si le tenaunt ou le destourbaunt perge en court, et despitousement s'en depart puis qe il avera esté [2]veu en court de[2] Justice; einz soit en tel cas la assise prise Brac. 239; Fle. 318 (§ 11, 12). tauntost sauntz nule resomounse fere; ne ausi ne tiegne james lu resomounse, si le defendaunt face defaute; ou s'il perge, et ne voille ou ne sache rien dire par quei la assise remeigne, tauntost soit la assise prise si les jurours soint presentz, et si noun, soit comaundé al viscounte qe il eit les cors a un autre jour.

1. *so M.* continuaunce *LNS.* 2—2. veu en Court deuaunt *ND.* veu de la *M.* *sim. GS.*

any essoin, nor any delay. And if the plaintiff is under age, neither essoin nor resummons ever takes place, whether the plea be within the county or without; for in such case the Contempt. absence of the tenant is as good as his presence. Neither does resummons lie in cases of contumacy; as, where the tenant or the disturbant appears in court, and contemptuously departs, after he has been seen by the Justice in court; but in such case the assise shall be forthwith taken without any resummons; also, if the defendant makes default[a], resummons shall not lie. So, when he appears, and will not or cannot allege any cause why the assise should be stayed, let the assise be presently taken, if the jurors are present, and if not, let the sheriff be commanded to have their bodies at another day.

a That is, default after resummons; see the parallel places in Bracton and Fleta. Perhaps we should read, 'defaute apres defaute.'

CHAPITRE II. [XCI.]

De Jour de Play.

Et cum les parties vendrount en court, adounc covendra al pleintif, apres le bref lu en audience, moustrer sa entente en tele manere qe il die coment il ad accioun et resoun de sei pleyndre, et de qi seisine il ad arramé ceste assise, lequel de sa seisine demeyne ou de autre. Et si de sa propre seisine, uncore ad mester qi il die outre, pur certifier la court de soen dreit, si il, quant il presenta, [1]tint rien[1] de glebee[2], sicum rente ou soil, a qi la avowesoun appendi, ou noun. Et si il [3]tient cele glebee[3], uncore ad mester qe il die coment il la tient[4], lequel en fee ou a terme de vie ou a autre terme. Et si il die qe il demaunde la seisine de acun auncestre, adounc covendra qe il enseigne coment il est heir cel auncestre, issint qe hom puse par ly estre instruct, lequel il ad severale

Brac. 240; Fle. 319.

[224.]

1—1. *so GS.* tient rien *L.* tynt rien *N.* *sim. F.* tient point *M.* 2. glebe *NMF.* 3—3. tient de glebe *N.* tynt cele glebe *M.* 4. tynt *M.*

CHAPTER II.

Of the day of Plea; and of the Count of the Plaintiff.

When the parties appear in court, it will then behove the plaintiff, after the writ has been read in audience, to declare his case in such a way as to shew how he hath right of action and reason to complain, and of whose seisin he has brought the assise,—whether of his own seisin or of that of another. If of his own seisin, it will be necessary for him, in order to certify the court of his right, to say further, whether, when he presented, he held any glebe, such as rent or soil, to which the advowson was appendant, or not, and if he holds such glebe, then he must set forth how he holds it, whether in fee or for term of life or for any other term[b]. If he says that he demands the seisin of some ancestor, then he must shew how he is the heir of such ancestor, so that it may appear by his statement whether he has a several action, or one in common

Count of plaintiff.

[b] The word 'glebe' is used for the land to which the advowson is appurtenant. 'Nota, quod verus advocatus dicitur ille, qui patronus est ut de feodo et recto ex descensu hæreditatis. Quasi advocatus est ille, qui possidet glebam, ad quam pertinet advocatio, non in feodo sed ad terminum.' (Note in MS. *N.*)

accioun ou[1] en commun ovekes acun parcener; et si il se pleigne en commune accioun, uncore fet a saver si soen tourn[2] soit a cele foiz de presenter ou noun.

CHAPITRE III. [XCII.]

De Excepciouns.

Brac. 239 *b* (§ 6); Fle. 318 (§ 12) 1. A quei covendra le deforceour respoundre. Car voucher garraunt ne tient mie lu, pur ceo qe le bref seert [3]a ceo, a[3] fere certifier par la assise, qi[4] ad plus de la possessioun el presentement. A ceste entencioun porra le deforceour respoundre par excepciouns, dount les dilatories sount primes a mettre avaunt.

Brac. 240; Fle. 320. 2. A ceo qe contenu est el bref, quel avowé, fet a entendre qe avowé est cist, a qi le dreit del avowesoun de acune eglise apent, issi qe a cele eglise puse presenter en soen noun demeyne; et pur ceo est dit avowé a la difference de ceux qi presentent acune foiz en autri noun, sicum des gardeins qi [224 *b*.] presentent en noun des enfauntz de eynz age qi terres sount

1. ou noun ou *M*. 2. so *NMF*. cours *LG*. 3—3. *conj*. a ces a *LS*. asetz a *ND*. *sim*. *RW*. asses pur *G*. asez de *M*. 4. qe il *L*. qe *M*.

with any parcener. And if his plaint is in an action upon a common right, it should be further known whether it be his turn to present this time or not.

CHAPTER III.

Of Exceptions in Assise of Last Presentation.

Voucher of warrant does not lie. 1. The deforceor must thereupon answer. For voucher of warrant does not lie, because the object of the writ is to ascertain by the assise, who has the best right to the presentation. Exceptions of deforciant. The deforceor may answer to the declaration by exceptions, of which the dilatory are first to be proposed.

Advocate or patron. 2. As to the words in the writ, 'who is the advocate,' it must be understood that the advocate is he to whom the right of the advowson of any church belongs, so that he may present to that church in his own name, and he is called advocate by way of distinction from those who have occasion to present in the name of another, as guardians do in the name of infants

en lour gardes, et ausi a la difference de ceux qi ne tienent le tenement à quel acune avowesoun est appendaunte for qe a terme de vie, ou a terme des aunz, ou par intrusioun, ou par disseisine, sauve qe ceux[1] unqes ne presenterent; car si tels i eynt presenté, et issi soint en seisine de la avowesoun, par taunt sount il ausi cum avowez, quant a la seisine del presentement, taunt cum il sount tenauntz del tenement a quel le avowesoun est annex. Car ences[2] qe le [3]disseisi ou[3] le verrei possessour eit recoveré le tenement qe est le cors principal, en[4] nule rien accessorie al cors ne poet il aver nule chalenge.

3. Ceo qe dit est ausi, en tens de pees, est dit a la difference de tens de guerre, desouth quels tens sount compris touz les tens des grevaunces, solom ceo qe veisin fet a autre[5] veisin par violence[6], et[7] par intrusions, disseisines, roberies, destourbaunces, grevaunces et par autres tortz fere, dount tens de pees porra issi estre noté et entendu, qe hom porra presenter devaunt le tens de guerre, el tens, et apres le tens, et Brac. 240 *b*; Fle. 320, 321.

1. *so NSGM.* qi *add L.* 2. einz ceo *NSGM.* 3—3. *so NDM.* disseisour *LS.* disseisi ouesques *G.* 4. e *M.* 5. autre *om. MF.* 6. *conj.* volunte *LGF.* *sim. NDSW.* volente *M.* 7. et *om. GSM.* ou *N.*

under age, whose lands are in their ward, and also from those who hold the tenement to which an advowson is appendant for a term of life or years only[c], or by intrusion or disseisin, provided these have never presented; for if they have presented, and so are in seisin of the advowson, they are thereby become in a manner advocates, so far as regards the seisin of the presentation, as long as they hold the tenements to which the advowson is annexed; for until the disseisee or the true possessor has recovered the tenement, which is the principal subject, he can have no claim to anything accessory thereto.

3. The words also 'in time of peace' are used in distinction from time of war, under which are comprehended all times of injuries done by one neighbour to another by violence, and by intrusions, disseisins, robberies, disturbances, oppressions, and other wrongs; whence time of peace may be thus distinguished and understood; for one may present before the time of war, or in the time, or after the time, and yet the pre- 'Time of peace,' how understood.

[c] See the note from MS. *N.* in p. 173.

issi serra le presentement neqedent suffisaunt et dreiturel; et ausi a la reverse porra hom presenter par extorsioun maugré le verrei possessour[1] par barat et par contek. Et ausi cum
[225.] l'autre est en touz pointz bon et leal[2], ausi est le torcenous presentement james de nul effect, pur ceo qe a tort et issi hors de tens de pees. Et de teles torcenouses [3]violences et[3] oppressiouns nescent touz jours al pleintif excepcious encountre le title le destourbour.

Brac. 241; Fle. 321 (§ 5).

4. A ceo qe est ausi contenu el bref, presenta, fet a prendre garde lequel la persone, qe adounc fust presenté, fu al[4] presentement tiel[5] resceu et institut par Evask, ou noun. Car

Brac. 241; Fle. 321 (§ 6).

autrement ne valut rien le presentement. Et si deus clercs soint presentez a une eglise par divers patrouns, ambideus neqedent ne sount mie a ceo receivables a une foiz, einz covendra al meyns refuser le un; et si porra il bien avenir qe le un ne le autre ne serra resceu, tut eit le un patroun dreit de presenter, par deus resouns; la une est, si la eglise demoerge[6] desconseilé outre vi. meys, adounc solom le Con-

1. tenaunt *MF*. 2. dreiturel *M*. 3—3. violentes *N*. e violentes *M*. 4. a cel *N*. a tel *G*. 5. tiel *om*. *NGM*. 6. *so G*. *sim*. *S*. de moere *L*. soit demoree *N*. moert *M*.

sentation will be sufficient and lawful; and so in the reverse case, a presentation may be made by extortion, in despite of the true possessor, by fraud and contention. And as the one is in all points good and lawful, so the wrongful presentation is never of any effect, because in wrong and so not in time of peace. And from such wrongful acts of violence and oppression there do always arise exceptions in favour of the plaintiff against the title of the disturbor.

Exception that presentation was not peaceable.

Presentation, not complete without institution.

4. With regard to the word also contained in the writ, 'presented,' care must be taken to see whether the parson who was then presented was upon the presentation of such an one admitted and instituted by the bishop or not; for otherwise the presentation was of no avail. And if two clerks are presented to the same church by different patrons, both of them cannot be admitted at the same time, but one at least must be refused; and it may also well happen that neither of them shall be admitted, although one of the patrons have the right

Collation by bishop on lapse.

to present, and this for two reasons. One is, that if the church remains unprovided beyond six months, then according to the

seil de Latran par la descord des parties, la fra le Evaske del lu conseiller et dorra la eglise a acun clerc[1], [2]de soen[2] office, sauve chescuni dreit. La autre resoun est pur le noun age de un des presentours, sicum en cas ou chartres des auncestres sount moustrez encountre acun presentour qi est de eynz age, a les queles chartres[3] il ne porra point respoundre avaunt soen age, en tel cas appent al ordinarie du lu la collacioun, si les parties ne se accordent el presentement de une persone, sauve chescuni dreit cum celi de eynz age vendra a soen age. Mes en tiel cas covendra ordiner par conseil des Justices, qe acune annuele pensioun soit liveré a tiel enfaunt, jekes a soen age, pur la sauvacioun de soen dreit de presenter quant il atteyndra a soen age.

Decretal. Alex. III. tit. Fil. c. 10; Brac. 241; Fle. 321 (§ 6).

[225 *b.*]

5. Et si porrount deus presenter[4] a une foiz, des queus le un avera dreit et le autre point, ou le un et le autre acun colour de dreit. S'il avent dounc, qe il se consentent en un clerc sauntz fere detrier le dreit, par tiel presentement [5]n'i eirt ja nuli[5] dreit menusee[6] ne chaungé, eynz fet a resorter a la seisine celi patroun, de[7] qi certeinté est qe dreyn presenta de

Brac. 241; Fle. 321 (§ 7); Post, c. 4. s. 12.

1. des clers *M.* 2—2. e de *N.* 3. *so NMG.* chapitres *LS.* 4. *so GSW. sim. R.* presentementz *L.* presentementz estre *ND.* 5—5. ne ert ia nully *N.* ne iert a nuli *M.* 6. amenusee *N.* men *M.* 7. *so NSGM.* et de *L.*

Council of Lateran, upon the disagreement of the parties, the bishop of the diocese shall provide for it, and shall *ex officio* give the church to some clerk saving every one's right. The other reason is the minority of one of the presentors, as where charters of his ancestors are produced against any presentor who is under age, to which charters he can give no answer before he is of age; in such case if the parties do not agree in the presentation of a parson, the collation belongs to the ordinary of the place, saving every one's right when the person under age comes of age; but in such case it should be so ordered by advice of the Justices, that some annual pension be reserved to the infant until he comes of age, for the saving of his right to present when he shall attain his age.

Pension reserved from a church to save right of infant.

5. Two persons may present at the same time, one having a right and the other none, or both of them some colour of right; and if it should happen that they both agree in one clerk, without trying the right, by that presentation the right of no one is diminished or altered, but resort must be had to the seisin of that patron, of whom it is certain that he last

Seisin of advowson how affected by presentation made by compromise.

dreit soul. Mes si acune foiz eit presenté sauntz countredit de nulli, et acun autre a une autre vacacioun eit [1]mise desturbacioun[1] et puis assentu al presentement le verrey patroun, pur cel assent neqedent ne est le estat del avowé nient blemie, quant a soen dreit de presentement a acune autre vacacioun. Car une chose est assenter, et autre consentir. Assenter est, cum acun qi ne ad nul dreit de[2] presenter dit, apres qe il avera mise[3] desturbaunce, jeo me assent a cest presentement sauve moen dreit apres; et cel assent ne est mie prejudiciel al verrei patroun; ne rien de dreit par taunt ne
[226.] accrest al destourbour. [4]Cum al consentir[4], est cum acun qi est en seisine del avowesoun consente al presentement celi qi plus ad de dreit; car le un porra estre en seisine del dreit possessorie et le autre de la propreté, [5]et qi[5] plus ad de la propreté plus ad del dreit. Et cel consentir porra estre fet simplement, [6]ou par[6] protestacioun; et si simplement, issi renuncie il tut soen dreit; et si par[7] protestacioun[8], par ceste parole, sauve a moi moen dreit[9] a autres vacaciouns, par

1—1. mis destourbaunce *N.* *sim. M.* 2. *so NSG.* del *L.* a *M.* 3. mis *NGSM.* 4—4. de benefice. Consentir *NG.* benefice. Consenter *M.* Com assentir *S.* 5—5. qe *L.* e qi *NG.* E qe *MS.* 6—6. *so M.* ou *LGF.* *om. S.* en *N.* 7. *so SGMF.* par *om. LN.* 8. soit fete *add. N.* 9. *so NMGF.* et *add. L.* *sim. S.*

presented of right alone. But if any one has once presented without opposition, and some person at the next avoidance makes a disturbance, and afterwards assents to the presentation of the true patron, by this assent the estate of the patron, as regards his right of presentation at another avoidance, is not prejudiced. For it is one thing to assent and another to consent. Assenting is where any person who has no right to present, after having made a disturbance, says, 'I assent to this presentation, saving my future right;' and such assent is not prejudicial to the true patron, nor does any right accrue thereby to the disturbor. Consenting is when any one who is in seisin of the advowson consents to the presentation of him who has a better right. For the one may be in seisin of the possessory right, and the other of the property, and he who has more of the property has the greater right. And such consent may be made simply, or with protestation. If made simply, he thereby renounces all his right; if with protestation in these words, 'saving to me my right at other avoidances,'

Assent and consent distinguished.

Consent with or without protestation.

taunt retient il soen dreit qe il ad, tel quel. Et mesme ceste resoun si[1] tient en avowesons des chapeles, provendes, vicaries, hospitals, abbeyes, priories et de autres lus a queus hom poet presenter en tens de vacacioun. Fle. 321, 322; cf. Brac. 241 *b*.

6. Et ceo qe est dit el bref, la persone qe morte est, est dit a la difference del vicarie a qi vicarie[2] nul ne poit presenter. Et[3] cest mot, morte, ad[4] double entendement, sicum de mort naturele, ou de mort quant al siecle, sicum est de cesti qi est profes en religioun et ad weyvé totes seculeres choses, ou de ceo qe vaut mort[5] en cest cas, sicum est de celi qi ad esposé femme, ou autre chose fete par quei il ne porra nule eglise retenir[6]. Brac. 241, 241 *b*; Fle. 322 (§ 8).

7. Contenu est el bref, a tiele eglise qe est vacaunte, et a ceo fet a prendre garde lequel ele est de tut voide, ou soulement le personage. [226 *b*.] Car si acune pensioun eit esté graunté par acchesoun de acun acord entre parties, ou en noun de simple benefice, et celi moerge qi cel benefice receut, ja pur ceo ne se voide la eglise ne le personage. Et mesme ceo fet a entendre de vicarie, [7]qi vicarie[7] ne est de nulli presente- Brac. 241 *b*; Fle. 322 (§ 9).

1. *so LS.* se *MG.* *om. N.* 2. *om. N.* 3. en *add. M.* 4. i ad *M.* 5. mout *M.* 6. *so SGM.* receiuere *L.* *sim. NDRW.* 7—7. *so M.* *sim. F.* qe *L.* qe vicarie *LS.* qe *ND.* qi vikerie *GM.* *sim. F.*

he thereby retains the right that he has, whatever it may be. The same rule holds in advowsons of chapels, prebends, vicarages, hospitals, abbeys, priories, and other places to which one may present on occasion of avoidance. Advowsons of abbeys, prebends, &c.

6. That which is said in the writ, 'the parson who is dead,' is said to distinguish him from a vicar, to whose vicarage none can present. 'The parson who is dead.' The word 'dead' has a double meaning, being used either of natural death, or death to the world, as in the case of him who becomes professed in religion, and has renounced all worldly things, or of that which in this matter is equivalent to death, as where a parson has married a wife, or done any other thing whereby he is unable to retain any church. Death, natural and civil.

7. It is contained in the writ, 'to such a church which is void;' and here it must be observed whether it is entirely void, or the parsonage only; for if any pension has been granted by virtue of some accord between parties or by way of a simple benefice, and he who received that benefice dies, the church and parsonage do not thereby become vacant. Avoidance, entire or partial. The same is to be understood of a vicar whose vicarage is not in Vacant vicarage merged in parsonage.

ment, [1]et qe, s'il[1] moerge, tut accrest a la persone, et ceo nomément de vicarie taxé par ordinaries a renable sustenaunce de acun vicarie. Eglise est ausi dite a la difference de chapele, et pur ceo si en le bref soit dit eglise, ou chapele dust estre dit, issi[2] est le bref[3] abatable. Mes lequel ele soit chapele ou noun, ne fet mie a trier en lays courtz, mes en Cristiene.

Brac. 241 *b*; Fle. 322 (§ 9). 8. Et si la assise soit arramie de tote la eglise, ou la meyté soulement est voide ou la tierce partie ou la quarte, et contek soit de la vacacioun, issi qe la une partie die qe ele est voide et la autre qe ele est pleyne, de ceo soit la verité enquise par la assise. Car si la conisaunce de ceo fust maundé al Evask, si porreit la eglise par ly estre encoumbré, ou par cas ne remaundereit nule verité, cum s'il eit resceu et institut acun clerc en tiele eglise al[4] presentement de acun qi nul dreit ne eust de presenter, issi purreit il remaunder, qe la eglise ser-

1—1 E sil *N.* E qe cil *G.* e qi si *M.* *sim. F.* 2. par tant *M.* 3. par taunt *add. N.* 4. so *NGM.* ad le *LS.*

any one's presentation, and which upon his death accrues entirely to the parson, and in particular of a vicarage endowed

'Church,' or 'chapel.' by the ordinary for the reasonable support of a vicar[d]. The word 'church' is also used by way of distinction from chapel, and therefore if in the writ it is said 'church' where it ought to have been 'chapel,' the writ is thereby abatable. But whether it is a chapel or not is not to be tried in lay courts, but in court Christian[e].

Fact of avoidance may be tried by the assise. 8. If the assise is brought of the entire church, where the moiety only or the third or fourth part is void, and there is a dispute about the avoidance, for that one side says it is void and the other that it is full, let the truth thereof be inquired

Danger of reference to bishop. by the assise. For if the cognizance thereof was referred to the bishop, the church might be encumbered by him, or the truth perhaps would not be returned; as suppose he had admitted and instituted any clerk in such church upon the presentation of one who had no right to present, in such case he

d There appears to be an error here. In the parallel passage of Bracton the case here mentioned is stated as an exception to the general rule, by which a vicarage became merged in the parsonage. 'Et hoc dico *nisi* taxata fuerit per ordinarios ad rationabilem sustentationem vicarii.' Brac. 241 *b*. The same error occurs in Fleta (as printed), where the words are, 'et hoc ubi taxata fuerit,' &c. Fle. 322 (§ 9).

e This question was treated in 32 Edw. I. as one determinable by the assise. Year Book, 32 Edw. I. pp. 107, 349. Compare Fle. 323 (§ 18).

reit[1] pleyne et conseillé, et ceo serroit prejudice al verrei patroun.

9. Et solom le verdit del assise soit maundé al Evaske, qe il resceyve le clerc presenté; et s'il ne voille, tauntost soit somouns a respoundre pur quei noun. Et issi porra l'encombrement le Evask estre atteynt, si point [2]en i ad[2], et ausi de autre ordinarie. Et si acun ordinarie soit atteynt de tiel encombrement, tauntost agardé soit, qe il delivre la eglise, ou autrement face le assetz al patroun, et le ordinarie remeigne en nostre merci. Et issi porra la eglise estre voide de dreit et nent de fet. Mes quant eglise est voide de dreit et de fet, tauntost courge l'assise; car adounc est ele voide verrement et dreitement[3]. [227.] Brac. 241 b, 242; Fle. 322 (§ 10, 11).

10. Et si acun clerc soit de sa propre folie plungé en la eglise en tens de vacacioun, ja par taunt ne remeyne l'assise, [4]ausi cum[4] ele fust tut voide et desconselé. Et si les jurours dient qe ele est pleine par la intrusioun de tiel clerc, tauntost soit la parole enveyé jekes en Crestiene court, qe le Evask del lu certifie nos Justices, lequel la intrusioun soit dreiturele Brac. 242; Fle. 322 (§ 11).

1. fust *M.* 2—2. ein iad *L.* iad *NS.* en i eyt *M.* en eit *G.* 3. so *LS.* dreitureument *M.* sim. *G.* 4—4. so *LGS.* Mes auxi soit prise cum *ND.* sim. *M.*

might return that the church was full and provided, which would be a prejudice to the true patron.

9. And upon the verdict of the assise let the bishop be commanded that he admit the clerk presented, and if he will not, let him be forthwith summoned to answer why he refuses; and thus the incumbrance of the bishop or other ordinary, if any there be, may be proved. And if any ordinary is found guilty of such incumbrance, let it be immediately adjudged that he set the church free, or otherwise make satisfaction to the patron, and let the ordinary remain in our mercy. Thus the church may be void in law but not in fact. But where it is void both in law and in fact, the assise shall run immediately, for then the church is truly and rightfully void. Remedy for incumbrance by bishop.

10. And if any clerk has of his own folly thrust himself into the church at the time of avoidance, yet the assise shall not be stayed, but shall be taken as if it was entirely void and unprovided. And if the jurors say that it is full by the intrusion of such a clerk, let the plea be immediately sent to the court Christian, that the bishop of the diocess may certify our Justices whether the intrusion be rightful or tortious, and upon Intrusion by clerk.

ou torcenouse; et sour ceo se face jugement. Car la conisaunce des espiritueles intrusiouns, lequel eles soint dreitureles ou noun, ne apent point a lay court, nient plus qe de autre manere de espirituauté. Tiels maundementz de Evask neqedent ne suffisent mie touz jours pleynement, sauntz autre
[227 *b.*] presumpcioun des monumentz ou de autres proves.

Brac. 242; Fle. 322 (§12). 11. Et pur ceo qe dit est el bref, qe [1]avowesoun tiel dist[1] a ly appendre, est dreit qe le pleintif enseigne par apertes resouns coment il ad dreit, et resoun de sei pleindre. Dit est ausi, et somonez tiel; et a ceo covent il al pleintif enseigner en la demoustraunce de sa entente, coment et par quele resoun il a tort le deforce. Brac. 242; Fle. 323 (§13).

Brac. 242; Fle. 323 (14, 15). 12. Et tut die le bref, qi la avauntdite avowesoun le[2] deforce, ne [3]entende ja nul[3] par ceo, qe le deforceour soit en seisine del avowesoun. Mes deforce i est dit, car asetz deforce qi destourbe en tut ou en partie, tut ne ly engette mie del tut, sicum [4]dit est de sus[4]. Et de[5] cestes resouns avantdites porrount estre tirez[6] excepcionns a fere perir l'assise ou delayer. Ante, l. ii. c. 23. s. 6.

1—1. *conj.* auowesoun tele deit *L.* *sim.* *NG.* tele auoueson deit *M.* 2. ly est *N.* li *S.* luy *M.* 3—3. *so MG.* tend[r]a ia nule *L.* tendra Ia liu [exception] *N.* 4—4. desouz est dit *M.* 5. *so M.* de *om.* *LSG.* 6. *conj.* tres [triez *corr.*] *L.* tiez *NGMR.* triez *D.* treyz *S.* treys *W.*

Spiritual intrusions cognizable in court Christian. this let judgment be given. For the cognizance of spiritual intrusions, whether they are rightful or not, does not belong to the temporal court any more than that of other spiritual matters. Yet such returns of bishops are not always fully sufficient, without further support from muniments or other evidence. Authority of bishops' certificates.

Plaintiff must state his title, and how disturbed. 11. Whereas it is said in the writ, 'which advowson such an one saith belongs to him,' it is right that the plaintiff should plainly show how he hath right, and reason for complaint. It is likewise said, 'summon such an one;' therefore the plaintiff must in the declaration of his case point out how and in what way the defendant wrongfully deforces him.

The word 'deforce' is used, although the deforciant is not seised. 12. Although the writ says, 'who deforceth him of the aforesaid advowson,' yet it is not to be understood thereby that the deforceor is in seisin of the advowson. But the word 'deforce' is used because he is sufficiently a deforceor who disturbs another in the whole or in part, although he does not actually eject him from the whole, as above is said. From the points aforesaid exceptions may be drawn either wholly to destroy the assise or to delay it.

CHAPITRE IV. [XCIII.]

De Excepciouns hors del bref.

1. Et tut graunte le destourbour touz les articles del bref, uncore porra il exceper encountre l'assise, et dire, a ceo qe le pleintif counte de la seisine et le presentement [1]de ses[1] auncestres, qe a tort se pleint, pur ceo qe apres soen presentement demeyne dona il a mesme celi destourbour un tenement a qi la avowesoun apendi, ou a[2] acun de ses auncestres, et par cele chartre; et dounc tut soit qe le pleintif ou acun de ses auncestres presenta, il neqedent mes ne deit presenter par le fet avauntdit. Brac. 242 *b*; Fle. 323 (§ 15); Ante, l. ii. c. 9. s. 14.

2. Et si le pleintif soit de plener age, si porra reconustre la chartre et graunter le doun, et dire encountre la excepcioun, qe puis cel doun fet presenta il un tiel par noun, qi a soen presentement fut resceu, par quei le doun est nul et la chartre voide. Et si ceo soit prové ou nient dedit, si perist la ex- [228.] Brac. 242 *b*; Fle. 323 (§ 15, 16).

1—1. so *MG.* et de ses *L.* *sim. S.* [de lui mesmes ou] des[es] *N.* 2. so *MGS.* a *om. L.* a *interl. N.*

CHAPTER IV.

Of Exceptions independent of the Writ.

1. Although the disturbor admits all the articles of the writ, yet he may except against the assise, and say, that, whereas the plaintiff counts of the seisin and presentation of his ancestors, he wrongfully complains, because after his own presentation, he granted to this same disturbor or to one of his ancestors a tenement to which the advowson was appendant, and that by such a charter; and therefore, although the plaintiff or any of his ancestors did present, yet he ought not to present on account of the aforesaid deed. Exception of a gift by charter since the last presentation.

2. If, then, the plaintiff is of full age, he may acknowledge the charter and admit the gift, and say in answer to the exception, that after the making of such gift he presented such an one by name, who was admitted on his presentation, whereby the gift is null and the charter void. And if this be Replication of presentation by plaintiff since the charter.

cepcioun, si le deforceour ne puse dire, qe, tut soit la chartre voide et le doun nul pur le drein presentement del donour, puis cel presentement neqedent ly fit mesme celi pleintif ou soen auncestre novel doun et novele chartre, [1]par ount[1] a ly apent le presentement. Ou il porra dire, qe il ly conferma la premere chartre, et ceo qe fust [2]primes endeblé[2] par defaute de seisine ly aforcea puis par confermement. Et si ceo soit averree ou nient dedit, si chete l'assise, si le pleintif ne puse enseigner de plus tardif presentement. Ou il porra graunter[3] le presentement estre issi fet par le pleintif ou par soen auncestre apres le doun et apres la confeccioun de la chartre, mes purchacea il sour ly un bref de garrauntie de chartre, a quei il fust somouns et en nostre court conust la chartre estre soen fet et graunta le doun, issi qe fin se leva et cirographe, et issi prendra le plee fin.

1—1. par quei *M.* 2—2. primer enfebli *M.* primes en doble *F.* 3. so *NMG.* garraunter *L* sim *S.*

proved or not denied, there is an end to the exception[e], unless

Rejoinder of new charter,

the deforceor can say that although that charter be void and the gift null for the last presentation of the donor, yet after such presentation this same plaintiff or his ancestor made a new gift and a new charter to him, whereby the presentation belongs to him.

or confirmation,

Or he may say that the plaintiff confirmed the first charter to him, and so that which was before weakened by want of seisin he did afterwards strengthen by confirmation; and if this be verified or not denied, the assise shall fall, unless the plaintiff can aver a later presentation.

or fine levied for warranty of charter.

Or he may grant that the presentation was so made by the plaintiff or his ancestor after the gift and after the making of the charter; but he may say that he purchased out against him a writ of warranty of charter, upon which the plaintiff was summoned, and in our court acknowledged the charter to be his deed, and allowed the gift, so that a fine was levied, and a chirograph made; and thus the plea shall be ended.

e 'A gives a manor with the advowson of a church to B; A dies. C, son and heir of A, is under age, and in ward of D. The church avoids. D presents in right of wardship, and his clerk is admitted and instituted. When C is of age, the parson dies. C presents, and B, the purchaser, presents also. C brings assise. B, the disturbor, alleges his purchase. C replies of the continuance of seisin by the last presentation. *Quæstio, quid fiet. Solutio.* C shall recover, and B take nothing; because purchase without fine levied is invalid (riens ne valt) without seisin. *Contra.* Induction of seisin of the principal substance (del gros e del principal), to which the appurtenances are appendant and accessory, suffices for seisin of both. But the glebe is a principal substance to which the advowson is appendant and accessory; therefore the induction of seisin of the glebe is sufficient for the principal and for the accessory.' (Note in MS. *N.*) See before, p. 173, note.

3. Et pur clerement veer en ceste [1]matere, posoms[1] qe acun eit doné a autre acun maner ovek la avowesoun de acune eglise, a ly et a ses heirs en fee; einz ces qe la eglise voide, doygne le purchaceour mesme cel maner oveke la avowesoun a un autre, et dounc apres[2] moerge la persone le premer donour, et presente le premer purchaceour, et[3] le drein[4] ausi. Le premer purchaceour ne ad nul dreit, pur ceo qe il ne fust unqes seisi, ne le dreyn ne ad nul dreit, car nul ne poeit doner chose qe il ne out nient; a force covendra dounc qe le dreit del presentement remeigne al premer donour, qi touz jours remist en possessioun del presentement, puis qe le purchaceour aliena soen dreit avaunt la seisine[5], ceo est a dire, avaunt qe il y presenta. Et issi tient lu ceste resoun de plusours alienours.

Brac. 242 *b*; Fle. 324.

[228 *b*.]

1—1. *so G.* nature pusoms *L.* *sim. SF.* le fet e la nature. Posoms *N.* matire le fet posoms *M.* 2. adeprimes *N.* 3. et presente et *L.* il presente e *N.* e presente *MS.* il presente *G.* 4. presente *add. N.* 5. *so NG.* *sim. M.* assise *L.*

3. In order to see this matter clearly, let us suppose that one has granted to another a manor, with the advowson of a church, to him and his heirs in fee, and before the church becomes void the purchaser gives the same manor with the advowson to another; then the parson of the first donor dies, and the former purchaser presents, and the latter also. The first purchaser has no right, inasmuch as he was never seised; neither has the latter any right, for no one could give a thing which he had not; so that the right of presentation must of necessity remain with the first donor, who always continued in possession of the right of presentation, inasmuch as the purchaser aliened his right before seisin, that is to say, before he presented[f]. And the same reason holds in case of several alienors.

Case supposed of successive alienations without seisin.

No seisin acquired without presentation.

Assise must be in favour of first donor.

f 'If one purchase a tenement to which an advowson is appendant, and alien the tenement before he has presented to the church, the second purchaser hath lost for ever his action to recover the advowson by reason of his purchase. *Probatio hujus.* Feoffor cannot make higher estate to his feoffee than he himself had; but the feoffor had no estate in the advowson. Therefore he could make none. *Contra.* Seisin of principal is seisin of accessory; but the purchaser, by means of the glebe, takes seisin of the principal; therefore of the accessory. *Responsio.* Seisin cannot be taken more largely than it is delivered, but seisin was never delivered of the advowson; therefore it could not be taken. *Solutio.* There are some appurtenances which may be severed by the owner; as a garden belongs to a house, but if the owner gives the house with its appurtenances, retaining the garden, there are two principal matters where before there was but one (sunt deuz gros qe avant ne furent fors qe un gros). So in the former case (Auxi par decha); the donor aliened the land with the advowson, but retained the advowson by the presentation after the gift; as,

Brac. 242 *b*; Fle. 324 (§ 2); Ante, l. ii. c. 9. s. 14.

4. Car si le drein purchaceour pout en acune manere voucher soen feffour a garraunt, si ne vaudreit, pur ceo qe le garraunt ne fust unques seisi. Car nul ne deit autre defendre en sa seisine for qe celi qi est trové en possessioun. Et si le garraunt garrauntist de fet, cum de dreit ne ly estovereit point fere, [1]et celi[1] vouchast le premer alienour, ja ne ly estovereit de garraunter, et ceo par deus resouns. Une est pur ceo qe le vouchour[2] ne est mie en seisine; et l'autre pur ceo qe le drein purchaceour ne porra mie reappeler ne reaver[3] ceo qe unques ne out ne qe aver pout. Et, tut soit qe le premer alienour confermast le doun al premer purchaceour,
[229.] ja pur ceo ne est le drein purchaz efforcié[4], cum le doun ne soit mie le fet le confermour ne de nul de ses auncestres, et pur ceo qe le doun ne fust unqes de nul effect. Et pur ceo si le premer donour i presente, et le drein purchaceour ausi, lequel qe il eit confermement de soen purchaz ou noun, la

1—1. *so verb. D.* et celi qi *L.* a cely qi *G.* *sim. MSF.* e [*on eras.*] cely [qe *oblit.*] *N.* a celi qi *R.* 2. *so M.* voucher *LS.* voucheur *N.* vouche *G.* 3. auoir *M.* 4. *so LMS.* enforcee *NDR.* aforce *GF.*

No bligation of warranty in the case supposed.

4. For if the last purchaser could in any way vouch his feoffor to warranty, it would not avail him, because the warrant was never seised. For no one is bound to defend any other in his seisin, except him who is found in possession[g]; and if the vouchee should warrant to him in fact,—since in law he would not be bound to do so,—and should himself vouch the first alienor, the latter would not be bound to warranty, and this for two reasons; first, because the vouchor is not in seisin; and, secondly, because the last purchaser cannot claim or have again what he never had or could have. And although the first alienor confirm the gift to the first purchaser[h], yet the last purchase is not thereby strengthened, since that gift is not the deed of the confirmor or any of his ancestors, and because the gift itself was never of any effect. And therefore if the first donor presents, and the last purchaser also presents, whether he has a confirmation of his

Effect of confirmation.

if I enfeoff you of two acres, and continue in seisin of one, the charter is void as to that acre. But if he who purchased the land with the advowson had not aliened the land, but had presented in time of avoidance, and had been disturbed by his feoffor or other, and had proceeded by law, he might have recovered the advowson. But since he did not do so, the right remains with the donor. Et sic nota, quod actio alienari non potest.' (Note in MS. *N.*)

g The text here is ambiguous, and the previous sentence might seem to show *celi* to be used in the nominative case. But the meaning is shown by the parallel places of Bracton and Fleta.

h The sense appears to require 'last purchaser;' compare Brac. 243, Fle. 324 (§ 2).

seisine serra agardé al confermour par l'assise pur la seisine dount unqes ne [1]s'en parti[1], puis qe la[2] seisine ne [3]sei comencea[3] unqes nule part aylours a esprendre[4].

5. Et si le drein purchaceour i presente de fet acun clerc qe soit receu a soen presentement, et puis en face alienacioun de meyn en meyn, et chescun eit esté en seisine del presentement; si eglise soit[5] voide, et le premer donour i presente, et le drein purchaceour ausi, si ambideus portent ceste assise, l'assise[6] de la dreyne seisine soit primes prise[7], et puis soit nule assise prise sour assise, eynz se purchace le premer donour par bref de dreit sour la proprété, si il quide bien fere; et a sa negligence demeyne purra il retter, qe il ad perdu soen recoverer en la possessioun. Brac. 243; Fle. 324 (§ 2).

6. Et si [8]chartre proferte[8] encountre ceste assise soit dedite, soit prové par les testmoignes leynz nomez, et par l'assise prise en manere de juree, si celi encountre qi ele est proferte ne soit de eynz age; car enfaunt de cel estat ne purra a nule chartre respoundre. Mes a fin et a[9] autre reconisaunce Brac. 243; Fle. 324 (§ 2).

1—1. fust departi *N.* se departi *M.* sen departist *G.* 2. sa *M.* 3—3. ceo comensa *L.* se comencea *N.* *sim. MS.* comensast *G.* 4. so *MGS.* respoundre [esprendre *corr.*] *L.* respoundre *N.* 5. se *M.* *om. N.* 6. so *MG.* *sim. S.* lassise *om. LN.* 7. lassise *interl. N.* 8—8. la chartre oferte *M.* 9. so *NSMGC.* a *om. L.*

purchase or not, the seisin shall be awarded by the assise to the confirmor on account of the seisin from which he never parted, since it never began to attach anywhere else.

5. But where the last purchaser in fact presents a clerk, who is admitted on his presentation, and then it is aliened from hand to hand, each purchaser being in seisin of the presentation, and upon the avoidance of the church, both the first donor and the last purchaser present, if both bring this assise, let the assise be first taken of the last seisin, and let no assise upon assise be afterwards taken, but let the first donor proceed by writ of right upon the property, if he thinks fit to do so; and he may impute it to his own negligence that he has lost his recovery in the possession. If the second purchaser once presents, the donor cannot recover by assise.

6. If a charter produced against this assise is denied, let it be proved by the witnesses therein named, and by the assise taken in the manner of a jury, unless he against whom it is proffered is under age; for an infant in that condition cannot answer to any charter; but to a fine or other recognisance Charter proved by witnesses named therein, and by jury.

[229 *b*] fete par auncestre respoundera chescun heir, de quel age qe il soit. Et en cas de noun age serra l'assise delayé jekes al age; Ante, c. 3. s. 4. mes par conseil de nostre court sera purveu a tet enfaunt une pensioun annuele a prendre jekes a soen age. Mes si nule chartre soit proferte, tauntost courge l'assise, tut soit une des parties de eynz age. Et si [1]fin ou[1] autre reconisaunce fete par le auncestre acun des parties i soit vouché, ja pur noun age del heir ne remeigne l'assise.

Brac. 243; Fle. 325 (§ 2). 7. Et si chartre de auncestre taunsoulement soit proferte, qe soit dedite, soit provee; et si ele soit graunté, et dit soit encountre, qe ele voide est et de nule force, pur le presentement suant, et del adverse partie soit denié le presentement fet puis la confeccioun de la chartre, tauntost courge l'assise en manere de juree par le assent des parties par celes paroles: lequel le donour qe porte la assise presenta a cele eglise puis qe il fist cel doun qe la chartre testmoigne a celi tiel, ou noun.

1—1. par fin ou par *M*. par fin ou autre *C*.

Infant not to answer to ancestor's charter; otherwise as to fine.

made by his ancestor every heir, of whatever age he may be, shall answer[h]. In case of nonage, the assise shall be put off until age; but by advice of our court an annual pension shall be provided for such infant, to be taken until he is of age. But if no charter is produced, the assise shall run forthwith, although one of the parties be under age. So where a fine or other recognisance made by the ancestor of any of the parties is vouched, the assise shall not be stayed by reason of the nonage of the heir.

Fact of presentation since the charter, tried by jury.

7. If a charter only of an ancestor is produced, and the same is denied, let it be proved; and if it is admitted, but it is objected against it that it is void and of no force by reason of the subsequent presentation, and the adverse party denies that there was any such presentation after the making of the charter, let the assise forthwith run in manner of a jury by the consent of the parties upon this question, whether the donor who brings the assise presented to the church, after he made the gift to such an one, which the charter witnesseth, or not.

Form of issue.

h 'Carta dedici poterit, finis vero dedici non poterit; unde minor ad finem respondere cogetur.' (Note in MS. *N*.)

8. Oú al assise porra hom respoundre, qe ele ne deit passer pur ceo qe celi qi porte l'assise, ou acun de ses auncestres, dona et aliena al autre partie, ou a acun de ses auncestres, tut le tenement oveske totes les apurtenaunces, sauntz rien retenir, par [1]resoun del quel[1] il ad [2]hore presenté[2], lequel qe il furent en possessioun [3]de presenter ou noun[3], sauntz nule forprise condicioun ou sauntz lees a terme de vie ou des aunz. Et ceste resoun porra acune foiz par chartre et par escritz estre declaré, les queus si il soint proferz en court, si courge la assise; et [4]s'il i eyt[4] acun contredit, si courge le averrement par la[5] assise prise en manere de juree, si les parties se assentent. Et touz jours sount chartres a mettre avaunt devaunt jugement rendu. Car apres ne tienent eles mie lu, for qe en certificaciouns et en atteyntes.

Brac. 243; Fle. 325 (§ 2).

[230.]

Brac. 243 *b*; Fle. 325 (§ 2).

9. Ou hom porra dire encountre la assise, qe celi qi porte la assise nul tenement ne ad en sa meyn a qi la avowesoun

Brac. 243 *b*; Fle. 325 (§ 3).

1—1. *so S. sim. G.* par resoun del quel [doun *interl.*] *L.* par resoun de quel doun *N.* la quele reson *M.* par resoun de quel *CF.* 2—2. heir [ore *interl.*] presentie *L.* ore presentee *N. sim. GMF.* presente *C.* 3—3. ou noun de presenter *M.* ou noun *C.* 4—4. sil ne eynt *L.* si ily eit *N.* sil ny eient *G. sim. SF.* si li eit *M.* 5. la *om. M.*

8. Again, it may be answered to the assise, that it ought not to pass, because he who brings the assise, or some of his ancestors, gave and aliened to the other party, or to some of his ancestors, the whole of the tenement in right whereof he has presented, with all its appurtenances[i], without retaining anything, whether they were in possession of the presentation or not, and without any exception or condition, or without any lease for term of life or years[k]. And this allegation may sometimes be manifested by charter and by writings, which being produced in court, the assise shall proceed, and if any of them be denied, averment shall lie by the assise taken in form of jury, if the parties consent thereto. Charters must always be produced before judgment given; for afterwards they are not admissible, except in certifications and attaints.

Exception of gift in special form without reservation; assise proceeds.

Charter to be produced before judgment.

9. Again, it may be excepted against the assise, that he who brings it hath not in hand any tenement to which the

Exception of non-seisin of tenement to which advowson belongs.

[i] 'Nota quod unum est dicere, Do tibi cum pertinentiis, et aliud, cum omnibus pertinentiis, vel, cum pertinentiis sine ullo retenemento; quia per hoc quod dico, cum pertinentiis, aliquæ possunt pertinentiæ transmutari, et aliquæ retineri.' (Note in MS. *N.*)

[k] The sense requires, 'or leased it for term of life or years;' compare Bract. 243, and Fle. 325 (§ 2).

fust unques apurtenaunt[1], pur ceo qe il le perdi par jugement, ou par disseisine, ou en acune autre manere, et dounc, tut eit il dreit en le tenement et en ses apurtenaunces, primes neqedent deit il recoverer le tenement [2]a qi avowesoun[2] apent, qe est[3] princepal, einz ces qe il eit resoun de presenter. Et de ceo est dit[4], qe si acun eit une foiz recoveri le presentement de acune eglise par ceste assise, et acun soit qe plus en ad dreit, qi demaunde par bref de dreit la avowesoun ou[5] le tenement a qi la avowesoun apent, et pendaunt le plee moerge la persone, le pleintif neqedent ne ad nul dreit de presenter einz ceo qe il eit desreiné la avowesoun, ou le tenement, en le plee de dreit.

Brac. 243 *b*; Fle. 325 (§ 4, 5). [230 *b*.] 10. Ou la partie porra dire encountre l'assise, qe celi qi la porte ne avoit unques en la avowesoun for qe terme de vie, ne nul de ses auncestres, ou autre terme, qe passé est. Et si acune femme, apres le desces de soen baroun, destourbe le

1. *so NSGM.* en purtenaunt *L.* 2—2. a qi lauowesoun *N.* *sim. SGC.* al quel lauoueson *M.* 3. le *add. MC.* 4. dit *om. M.* 5. *so CF.* e *on eras. L.* e *NSGM.*

advowson was ever appurtenant, inasmuch as he lost such tenement by judgment, or by disseisin[1], or in some other way, and therefore, even if he has a right in the tenement and in its appurtenances, yet he ought first to recover the tenement to which the advowson belongs, which is the principal subject, before he has any ground for presenting. And upon this point it is said that, if any one has once recovered the presentation of a church by this assise, and there is another having a greater right to it who demands the advowson, or the tenement to which the advowson belongs, by writ of right, and pending the plea the parson dies, still the plaintiff has no right to present before he has deraigned the advowson or the tenement in the plea of right.

Exception that plaintiff's ancestor had only a term. 10. The party may also except against the assise, that neither he who brings it nor any of his ancestors ever had any right in the advowson except for term of life or other term which is passed. And if any woman after the decease of her

1 'A man inherits a manor to which an advowson is appendant; and is disseised of the entire manor. The church avoids. The disseisee and disseisor both present. The disseisee brings assise, and the disseisor *Quare impedit*. The disseisor shall recover. *Contra*. The disseisor ought not to be in a better condition than a purchaser, but if a purchaser had purchased the manor with the appurtenances, without special mention of the advowson, the advowson had remained with the donor; with much stronger reason should it remain with the disseisee. *Responsio*. True it is, the disseisor is in a better condition *quoad hoc*.' (Note in MS. *N*.)

presentement le heir qe est garraunt de sa dowarie, et die qe le presentement apent a ly par la resoun de sa dowarie qe ele ad en mesme la ville ou la eglise soit eynz, et dount ele ad purchacé sour mesme cel garraunt le bref *Quare impedit*, dounc fet a prendre garde coment soen dowarie li fust assigné. Car si ele eit la terce partie de acune ville en dowarie ovek les apurtenaunces, et en noun de cele dowarie voille chalenger le tierz presentement, ja pur ceo ne [1]fet a soeffrer[1], si acune[2] especialté [3]n'eit qe[3] de ceo face mencioun, cum si la avowesoun ly eit esté assigné en cele tierce partie; ou autrement ne purra ele rien [4]clamer ne[4] chalenger, tut soit la eglise[5] en sa tierce partie. Et si ele soit dowé de tote la vile enterement ove totes les apurtenaunces sauntz nule forprise, issi ad ele dreit; et si la avowesoun soit forprise, si ad ele nul dreit.

11. Et si le Evaske deyve[6] acun clerc [7]receyvere al[7] presentement par parceles, cum si acun maner a qi apent la avowesoun de acune eglise soit aliené par parceles a divers

1—1. soit soeffert *N.* 2. de acune *LN.* *sim. SMC.* dautre *G.* 3—3. *so S.* *sim. NM.* ne qe *L.* nen eit qe *G.* eit qe *C.* 4—4. *om. NMC.* 5. eschete *add. M.* 6. deueie *M.* 7—7. *so N.* *sim. GCF.* receyuere [a *interl.*] le *L.* de receiure le *M.* receuir le *S.*

husband disturbs the presentation of the heir, who is warrant of her dower, and alleges that the presentation belongs to her by reason of her dower which she has in the same vill where the church is situate, and thereupon purchases a writ of *Quare impedit* against the same warrant, care must be taken to observe in what manner her dower was assigned to her. For if she has the third part of a vill with the appurtenances in dower, and in virtue of this dower claims the third presentation, the claim cannot be allowed, unless she has some specialty which makes mention thereof, as where the advowson has been assigned to her in her third part; for otherwise she cannot claim or challenge anything, although the church be situate in her third. And if she is endowed of the whole vill entirely, with all the appurtenances without any exception, then she has a right; but if the advowson be excepted, she has no right.

Claim of presentation in right of dower.

Quare impedit.

Dowager, when entitled to present.

11. If the bishop is asked to admit any clerk to a presentation by parcels, as where a manor, to which the advowson of some church is appendant, is aliened by parcels to divers

Claim of presentation by owners of parcels of manor.

tenauntz, dount chescun soit feffé de sa porcioun oveke les apurtenaunces, et trestouz les tenauntz eint severalment presenté al eglise cum ele soit voide, le presentement del te-
[231.] naunt del drein remenaunt est receivable, sicum devaunt est
Ante, l. ii. c. 9. s. 15. dit. Car touz jours demoert en tel cas la avowesoun oveke la porcioun retenue, puis qe especialment [1]ne est[1] point aliené.

Brac. 244; Fle. 326 (§ 6); Ante, c. 3. s. 5. 12. Et si acun presente a acune eglise, et celi presenté soit resceu, et acun de ceo moeve contek par acun autre clerc, et puis se accordent par entre les presentours qe cil qi moveit le contek autrefoiz de[2] fet presente[3] al Evask le clerc institut, et le Evask le receive en prejudice del dreit le premer presentour, et issi remeigne[4] cist clerc institut a tote sa vie, deus foiz presenté et deus foiz institut; si[5] cil qi drein presenta, vacaunte la eglise, se voille puis purchacer par ceste assise, il n'en deit point estre oy. Car presentement sur presentement de un mesme fet et de un mesme presentement n'est de nule vertue.

Brac. 244 b; Fle. 326 (§ 7). 13. Si acun presente a eglise, et ences qe ly presenté i soit

1—1. *so NS.* ni est *L.* nest *GM.* 2. *so NMG.* le *LS.* 3. presenter *SG.* 4. enremaigne *M.* *sim. S.* 5. *so NMS.* et *L.* e *G.*

tenants, each of whom is enfeoffed of his portion with the appurtenances, and all the tenants severally present to the church, when it becomes void, the presentation of the tenant of the last remaining parcel is to be taken, as before is mentioned. For in such case the advowson, not being expressly aliened, always remains with the portion retained.

Second institution of the same clerk, disregarded. 12. If one presents to a church, and such presentee is admitted, and another person raises a dispute by some other clerk, and it is afterwards agreed between the presentors that he who raised the dispute shall *de facto* a second time present to the bishop the clerk already instituted, and the bishop thereupon admits him in prejudice of the right of the first presentor, and so this clerk remains instituted all his lifetime, having been twice presented and twice instituted, and if upon a new avoidance the person who presented last desires to proceed by this assise, he ought not to be heard. For presentation upon presentation at one turn and one avoidance is of no force.

Presentation by ancestor, guardian, and heir, upon one avoidance. 13. If any one presents to a church, and before the pre-

resceu, pendaunt le presentement, moerge le presentour, et le gardeyn del heir par resoun del noun age del heir presente autre clerc par la resoun de la garde, et durraunt le contek par entre les clers presentez devient le heir de plener age, et presente le tierz clerc, en tel cas est le presenté le heir receivable al eglise.

14. Et si femme dowé de acune avowesoun presente soen clerc, et soit resceu, et le heir qi est garraunt de sa dowarie, doigne l'avowesoun vivaunt la femme, et, einces qe le purchaceour eit seisine del avowesoun par soen presentement, devie la femme, si qe la dowarie devent en la meyn le verrey heir, en tel cas est mester al purchaceour de fere renoveler ¹soen purchaz¹ ou confermer. Car einzces qe il puse parler de seisine, ne porra il james pleder en la propreté. Brac. 245; Fle. 326 (§ 8). [231 *b*.]

15. Et si plusours parceners et heirs soint, et acuns soint de eynz age et acuns de plener age, et en seisine de lour heritage acuns par gardeyns et acuns en lour noun demeyne, et il n'i eit qe une eglise vacaunte, trestouz joyntement i deivent presenter, et en un clerc consentir; et si il ne facent, Brac. 245; Fle. 326 (§ 9).

1—1. *om. M.*

sentee is admitted, the presentor pending the presentation dies, and the guardian of the heir by reason of the nonage of the heir and in right of the wardship presents another clerk, and during the litigation between the clerks thus presented the heir becomes of full age, and presents a third clerk; in such case the presentee of the heir is to be admitted to the church.

14. If a woman endowed of an advowson presents her clerk, who is admitted, and the heir who is the warrant of her dower makes a gift of the advowson in the lifetime of the widow; and before the purchaser has seisin of the advowson by presentation the widow dies, so that the dower falls into the hands of the right heir; in such case the purchaser must get his purchase renewed or confirmed; for until he can allege seisin, he can never plead in the property. Gift by heir during estate in dower.

15. If there are several parceners and heirs, some of whom are under age and others of full age, and some in seisin of their inheritance by their guardians and some in their own names, and there is only one church vacant, all ought to present thereto jointly, and to consent in one clerk; otherwise Presentation by coheirs, before partition;

le presentement ne tendra nul lu taunt cum il se desacorderount; et issi la dorra le Evesk, cum tens vendra. Mes, si trestouz soint de age et chescun sache sa purpartie[1] severale, adounc se tiegne solom ceo qe il se accorderount en la devisioun. Mes al Evesk ne apent point la collacioun, si chescun parcener severalment[2] presente soen clerc, cum trestouz soint de age et averount parti lour heritage, pur ceo qe le Evask [3]ne poeit[3] en tel cas nulli clerc receivere sauntz prejudice[4] des autres parceners. Autrement neqedent estre purroit, si un soul homme, qi [5]tut le[5] dreit avereit de presenter, presentast deus clers ou plusours, à une foiz ou par diverses.

Brac. 245; Fle. 326 (§10). [232.] 16. Pur ceo qe de une vacacioun et del presentement a une eglise se porrount plusours pleindre par[6] diverses resouns; —car deus ou plusours se porrount pleindre et porter ceste assise, et demaunder le presentement[7] par title de successioun de la seisine lour auncestres, ou de lour presentement de-

1. *so NMC. sim. F.* proprete [purpartie *interl.*] *L.* proprete *SG.* 2. ne *interl. N.* i *add. M.* 3—3. ne poet pas *M.* ne puit *N.* ne poet *S.* ne pout *G.* 4. assent *M.* 5—5. *om. N.* title de *M.* 6. e par *MC.* 7. de meisme la eglise *add. N.* de vne eglise *add. SGMC.*

the presentation shall not take place so long as they disagree, and the bishop when the time comes shall dispose of the church. But if all are of age, and every one knows his several share, then the presentation shall go according as they shall agree in the partition. Neither does the collation belong to the bishop if every such parcener severally presents his clerk, when they are all of age and have made partition of their inheritance[1], because in such case the bishop could not admit the clerk of one without prejudice to the other parceners. But it might be otherwise, if one single person who had the entire right of presentation presented two or more clerks at once, or one after the other.

after partition.

Various titles to one presentation.

16. Whereas in respect of one avoidance and of the presentation to one church several persons may be plaintiffs upon different grounds, for two or more may complain and bring this assise, and demand the presentation by title of succession as of the seisin of their ancestors, or of their own presentation,

[1] This clause, 'when they are all,' &c., appears to have slipped into the text by mistake. The sense intended appears to be, that where of several parceners each presents his own clerk, the bishop is not entitled to make his choice.

meyne, et ausi porra une femme douwé, ou plusours, par resoun de lour dowarie, ou [1]de autre manere de terme de vie ou des aunz, solom les diverses maneres de tenures, par le bref *Quare impedit* ou par *Quare non permittit*, ou pur ceo qe ele tient partie de la ville ou la eglise est eynz et[2] par diverses foiz puisse presenter, et par[1] plusours autres resouns; les queles covendra totes examiner ententivement par ordre, par quei hom puse estre certifiez a qi ou queus apent la accioun, et a qi nient. Et del proces en chescune persone covendra fere mencioun [3]en les lettres[3] maundables al Evask. Brac. 245, 245 *b*.

17. Et cum acune femme par resoun de sa dowarie eit presenté a acune eglise, et qi clerc soit receu del Evask, [4]et le[4] heir, qi garraunt est de sa dowarie, eit puis doné la avowesoun, et vacaunte autre foiz la eglise en la vie la femme, autre foiz [5]i eit[5] la femme presenté, si [6]soen clerc[6] soit resceu, par taunt est le presentement reservé al heir et a ses heirs; et issi ne vaudra le doun rien et remeyndra la chartre voide par defaute de seisine. Brac. 245 *b*; Fle. 327 (§11).

1—1. en autre manere solom diversete des tenures ou par *C.* 2. et *om. N.* 3—3. *so G.* en lettres *MW.* e lettres *NDCR.* et les autres [lettres *interlin.*] *L.* es lez autres *S.* 4—4. al *LGS.* e le *NMC.* 5—5. *so MGSC.* i est *L.* eit *N.* 6—6. *so N.* *sim. C.* un clerc *LSM.* soun presentement *G.*

and a widow endowed, or several widows, in right of their dower, or of any manner of term of life or years according to the different kinds of tenures, either by writ of *Quare Impedit* or *Quare non permittit*, or by reason that such a widow holds part of the vill where the church is situate, and therefore might present in turn, and upon several other grounds,—all these reasons should be carefully examined in proper order, so that it may be ascertained who has a right to the action and who not; and in the letters to be directed to the bishop mention should be made of the proceedings in the case of each person.

17. When a widow in right of her dower has presented to any church, and her clerk is admitted by the bishop, and the heir, who is the warrant of her dower, afterwards grants away the advowson, and the church being again void in the lifetime of the widow she presents again, if her clerk is admitted, the right of presentation is thereby reserved to the heir and to his heirs; and the grant will be ineffectual, and the charter void for want of seisin. Presentation by dowager after alienation by heir remits seisin to the heir.

Brac. 245 *b*; Fle. 327 (§11).

18. Et si acun die countre[1] ceste assise, qe cist qi la porte ne poeit presenter par resoun de doun et de feffement, et sur ceo moustre chartre, si la chartre ne puse estre dedite ne le feffement, si perist l'assise, et l'autre retendra la seisine, cum il soit issi cum en seisine apres le doun et apres la confec- [232 *b*.] cioun de la chartre. Et si le chartre et le doun soint deditz, [2]soint proveez; [3]et si il soint provez[3], mes ne porra soen presentement destourber. Et si le donour reconuse la chartre (Ante, s. 2.) et le doun, et il die qe il presenta puis, sicum avaunt est dit, ceo soit enquis par l'assise. Car sa soule voiz ne fet nient a crere, ne a[4] nule presumpcioun soulement, tut aporte il en testmoignage les lettres patentes le Evask [5]del lu[5] testmoignales[6], qe il resceut soen clerc a tiele eglise. Ne de la seisine le donour ne est mie mester en tiel cas de enquere par la assise. Car par [7]le graunt de la chartre[7] se forclost il de la seisine et de soen presentement, puis qe rien ne seet dire ne moustrer, qe il eit presenté puis soen doun ne puis la confeccioun de la chartre.

1. encountre *NMC*. 2. e eles *add. N.* si *add. GS.* 3—3. *om. LNGS.* e si i soient prouez *M.* e sil seient prouez *C.* 4. ad *MG.* 5—5. *om. M.* 6. testmoignables *NG.* temoignanz *M.* tesmoinaunces *C.* 7—7. *so M.* la graunt [garraunt de la *interlin.*] chartre *L.* la graunt chartre *G.* le garraunt de la *N.* le grant chartre *S.*

Gift by charter since last presentation bars assise.

18. When any one says, by way of defence to this assise, that he who brings it cannot present by reason of a gift and feoffment, and thereupon shows a charter, if the charter and feoffment cannot be denied, the assise is at an end, and the other shall retain his seisin, when he is thus as it were in seisin after the gift and the making of the charter. And if the charter and gift are denied, let them be proved; and if they are proved, the plaintiff cannot further hinder the presentation. And if the donor acknowledge the charter and the gift, and say that he afterwards presented, as aforesaid, let this be inquired by the assise, for his bare allegation is not to be believed, nor any presumption alone, although he should produce in evidence the letters patent of the bishop of the diocess testifying that he admitted his clerk to that church. Nor need the assise in this case inquire concerning the seisin of the donor; for by acknowledging the charter he has barred himself from the seisin and from his presentation, when he is unable to show that he has presented after his gift or after the making of the charter.

Presentation since the charter, how proved

19. Et cum le pleintif die [1]en counte[1] de sa seisine demeyne ou de la seisine de ses auncestres, et qe il presenta certeyne persone, qe fust resceu, et de ceo se met en les jurours del assise, si[2] les jurours dient qe n'en sevent nient qi presenta la dreine persone [3]ne l'autre[3], ou s'il dient qe eus outrement rien ne sevent, en tel cas ne prenge rien le pleintif, eynz remeigne en la merci. Et si en une vile soint deus seignurs et divers feez, et for qe une eglise, et les jurours ne sachent mie dire, qi dreyn presenta, ne en qi fee la eglise est, ou si le soil soit commun a ambideus les parties en quel soil la eglise est fete, en tel cas covendra dire as parties, qe il se accordent en une persone, ou nul ne emportera rien; einz remeyndra le pleintif en la merci, ne mie par defaute de dreit, mes pur la defaute de la prove de soen dreit.

Brac. 245 *b*, 246; Fle. 327 (§ 12).

Brac. 246; Fle. 327 (§ 13).

[233.]

1—1. e counte *NMG*. e conust *C*. 2. *so MGSC*. et si *L*. *sim*. *N*. 3—3. ne lautre ne lautre *M*.

19. When the plaintiff counts of his own seisin or of that of his ancestors, and says that he presented a certain parson, who was admitted, and thereof puts himself upon the jurors of the assise, if the jurors say that they do not know who presented the last parson, or the one before him, or if they say that they absolutely know nothing thereof, in such case let the plaintiff take nothing, but remain in mercy[m]. So, if in one vill there are two lords and diverse fees, and but one church, and the jurors cannot say who last presented, nor in whose fee the church is, or if the ground on which the church is built is common to both parties, in such case the parties must be told to agree upon a parson[n], or neither of them will take anything, but the plaintiff shall remain in mercy, not for want of right, but for want of proving his right.

If the jury profess ignorance, the plaintiff fails.

Where there are two manors in one parish, and the jury cannot decide, it is a proper case for accord.

m Bracton cites a case of the tenth year of Henry III. to show that in the above circumstances the parties without further writ might proceed upon the proprietary right, which would be tried by battle or the great assise.

n Bracton says they should agree to present alternately.

CHAPITRE V.[1]

De verditz et de jugementz.

Brac. 239 b; Fle. 318. 1. Cum les jurours serrount presentz en court, et les parties i eint pledez jekes al assise, si les jurours ne soint rebotez par chalenges des parties, si jurge le un apres le autre, issi: Ceo oyez, vous Justices, qe jeo verité dirray de ceste assise de[2] la eglise, ou de la chapele, dount jeo ay fet la vewe par le comaundement le Roi, et pur rien ne lerray qe verité ne dirray, si moi ayde Deus et les Sainctz. Et puis lour soit rehercé[3] le bref en[4] la manere coment les parties ount pledé, si mester soit.

Brac. 239 b; Fle. 318, 319. 2. Et cum eus averount entreparlé, et soint de un assent de lour verdit, si purrount dire qe le pleintif presenta la dreine persone, qe morte est, al avauntdite eglise en tens de pes, ceo est a saver, tel clerc par noun, qi drein morust per-

1. *This chapter is wanting in CHF, in the original print, and in Houard. It was printed by Wingate in his appendix of corrections.* 2. e de *NM.* 3. recite *M.* 4. e *ND.*

CHAPTER V.

Of the Verdict and Judgment in Assise of Last Presentation.

Oath of the Jurors. 1. When the jurors are present in court, and the parties have pleaded to the assise, if the jurors are not rejected by the challenges of the parties, they shall swear one after the other thus: 'Hear this, ye Justices, that I will speak the truth concerning this assise of the church (or of the chapel), whereof by the king's precept I have made the view, and that I will not fail for anything to speak the truth, so help me God and the Saints.' Then let the writ be rehearsed to them, and the manner in which the parties have pleaded, so far as necessary.

Verdict. 2. When the jurors have spoken together, and are agreed in their verdict, they may say that the plaintiff presented the last parson, who is dead, to the aforesaid church in time of peace, to wit, such a clerk by name, who last died parson in

sone en mesme la eglise; ou il porrount dire le contrarie, qe celi ne presenta mie le drein clerc, einz fit un autre, tel par noun; ou il porrount dire totes les resouns pur quei le presentement ne apartent point al pleintif qe le deforceour purroit dire, si il fust present, et porrount moustrer pur quei il ne deforce mie a tort, cum si le pleintif ou soen auncestre puis le drein presentement aliena la avowesoun en acune manere en fee ou a terme.

3. Et ne suffit mie as jurours dire tauntsoulement, qe le pleintif, ou soen auncestre, drein presenta, s'il ne enseignent coment le deforceour a tort ad destourbé cel presentement. Ne ausi ne suffit mie qe a tort, s'il ne dient qe a[1] celi soit fet le tort qi se pleint, eynz ceo qe le pleintif prenge[2] rien par l'assise, tut soit qe le verdit vaille pur acun autre qi dreit ad. Ou il porrount dire qe nule rien [3]il ne en[3] sevent; et adounc covendra enquere, qi presenta le autre persone devaunt, et issi de persone en persone taunt cum le tens limité le soeffre.

Brac. 239 *b*; Fle. 319 (§ 5, 6, 7).

1. *so NMS.* a *om. LS.* 2. enprengne *N.* en prenge *MS.* ne prenge *G.* 3—3. il ne *LN.* ne en *M.* ne *G.* en *S.*

the same church; or they may say, on the other hand, that he did not present the last clerk, but that another, such an one by name, did so; or they may give all the reasons which the deforceor himself might allege, if he were present, why the presentation does not belong to the plaintiff, and show that the other does not wrongfully deforce him, as where the plaintiff or his ancestor after the last presentation aliened the advowson in some manner in fee or for a term.

3. It is not sufficient for the jurors to say merely that the plaintiff or his ancestor presented last, but they must also declare how the deforceor has wrongfully disturbed the presentation. Likewise, it is not enough to say 'wrongfully,' without saying that the wrong was done to him who complains, since this must appear before the plaintiff can take anything by the assise, however useful the verdict might be to another person having the right. Or they may say that they know nothing of the fact; and then they must inquire who presented the next parson before, and so from parson to parson as long as the limited time permits.

Verdict must find fact of disturbance,

and in whose wrong.

If last presentor is unknown, former presentations to be found.

Brac. 239 b; Fle. 319 (§ 7, 8).

4. Et si les jurours dient qe le pleintif presenta, issi [1]se fra[1] jugement pur ly; et s'il dient qe ses auncestres drein i presenterent le autre persone, mes qi presenta la persone qi plus tard morust ne sevent, uncore se face jugement pur le pleintif, si nule resoun ne ouste les Justices de la presumpcioun, qe cesti pleintif, qi est dreit[2] heir celi qi drein presenta, ad meer[3] dreit par le title de successioun. Et si le presentement [4]neqedent fu fet avaunt[4] le terme limité en plee de mort de auncestre, si cheet l'assise, et le pleintif se purchace par bref de dreit, s'il quide qe bien soit. Et s'il soint en aweer et en doute, si remeigne la seisine en soen lu, et le pleintif en la merci. Et en mesme la manere soit en cas ou les jurours ne ount nule conisaunce de la persone le pleintif, ou, tut [5]eynt il la[5] conisaunce, il neqedent ne sevent mie certeynement s'il soit le proschein heir le auncestre qi dreyn presenta ou noun.

Brac. 251 (c. 8. § 2); Fle. 331 (c. 19. § 3).

5. Et si acun eit une foiz recoveri seisine de presenter par ceste assise, et cil, vers qi il ad recoveri, se purchace a demaunder la avouwesoun par bref de dreit, et pendaunt le plee

1—1. *so GS. sim. M.* se serra iugement *L.* serra iuge *N.* 2. *so NMG.* dit *LS.* 3. meur *ND.* maiour *MR.* meilliour *G. sim. SW.* 4—4. *so verb. MGS.* fu fet auaunt neqedent *L. sim. D.* fust fet [neqedent] auaunt *N.* 5—5. i eynt il la *N.* en eyent il *M.* en eient il la *GS.*

Judgment.

4. If the jurors say that the plaintiff presented, then judgment shall pass for him; and if they say that his ancestors presented the last parson but one, but they know not who presented the parson who died last, still let judgment be given for the plaintiff, unless there is any reason to exclude the Justices from the presumption that the plaintiff, who is right heir to him who last presented, has the mere right by title of succession. But if the presentation was made before the time limited in a plea of Mortdancester, the assise falls; and let the plaintiff proceed by writ of right, if he thinks fit to do it. And if the jurors are undecided and in doubt, then let the seisin remain where it is, and the plaintiff in mercy. The like where the jurors have no knowledge of the person of the plaintiff, or although they have some knowledge of him, yet they do not know for certain whether he is the next heir of the ancestor who last presented or not.

Assise falls where the jurors do not know the fact, or do not know the plaintiff, or whether he is heir.

Pending writ of right, the last presentor may present.

5. If any one has once recovered seisin of a presentation by this assise, and he against whom he has recovered proceeds to demand the advowson by writ of right, and pending the plea

se voide la eglise, et[1] le un et l'autre i presentent, le presenté celi qi la gayna par assise[2] deit estre resceu, sauve al pleintif soen dreit en la proprete.

CHAPITRE VI. [XCIV.]

De Quare impedit.

1. Touz iceux, a queus apent acune avowesoun, ne ount mie accioun a demaunder par assise de drein present de lour presentement demeyne, ou uncore de la seisine de lour auncestres, sicum dit est en assise de drein present. Car acuns sount qe purchacent avowesouns de eglises et dreit de presenter par verreis titles, sicum par title de doun en[3] fee ou a terme, ou par jugement en nostre court, et par disseisines et intrusiouns des tenementz as queus les avowesouns sount annexes, et plusours autres maneres, par ount, si[4] teles eglises se voident et teus purchaceours i presentent et il soint destourbez, en tel cas ne lour vaudra mie le remedie par la avauntdite assise. Car bref de dreyn present est un bref de Brac. 246 b; Fle. 328.

1. et *om. LMGS.* e *N.* ou *LMGS.* ou de *C.* 2. *so NGS.* et *add. L.* *sim M.* 3. *so on eras. N.* 4. [qe] si *N.* qe si *MC.*

the church becomes void, and both of them present, the presentee of the person who recovered by the assise ought to be admitted, saving to the plaintiff his right in the property.

CHAPTER VI.

Of the Action of Quare impedit.

1. Not all those to whom an advowson belongs have an action to demand it by the assise of last presentation, either in virtue of their own presentation or of the seisin of their ancestors, as hath been explained in treating of the assise of last presentation. For there are some who purchase advowsons of churches and a right to present by good titles, as by title of gift in fee or for a term, or by judgment in our court; also by disseisins and by intrusions in the tenements to which the advowsons are annexed, and in many other ways, whereby if such churches become void, and the purchasers present thereto and are disturbed, they can have no remedy by the aforesaid assise. For the writ of last presentation is a writ of pos- Remedy for recovery of advowson by person never seised, by *Quare impedit.*

possessioun; et tels purchaceours ne poent counter de lour possessioun. Et pur ceo fu purveu le bref de *Quare impedit*, pur remedie de tiels purchaceours, qe est pledable par so-
[233 *b*.] mounse et par attachementz et par destresces.

2. La force [1]de ceo[1] bref se tient tut el trespas de la torcenouse destourbaunce. Et pur ceo, si acun, qi ad dreit de presenter par acun verrei title, voille presenter, et autre i mette destourbaunce, qe meyns de dreit eit, par presentacioun de autre clerc, ou en autre manere, si celi qi est destourbé ne puse counter de sa propre seisine, ne de la seisine soen auncestre, adounc tient proprement lu cest bref, *Quare*
Brac. 247; Fle. 328. *impedit*; qe est autaunt a dire, [2]pur quei le destourbour[2] a tort met soen pié[3] el dreit le pleintif, qe il ad en la presentacioun; [4]et dount[4], tut ne fust il unques pleinement seisi del dreit possessorie, [5]de la proprete est[5] il seisi par le title de beau[6] purchaz. Et pur ceo vaut autaunt [7]le destourber qe del tut engetter[7], et autaunt greve; et issi tient lu remedie par cest bref.

1—1. en ceo *N.* en cest *M.* 2—2. *so verb. GC.* pur le destourber *L.* pur le destourbour *N.* por qei il le desturbeour *M.* 3. cleym *M.* 4—4. E dounk *N.* *sim. GS.* adonkes *M.* 5—5. *so MGS.* *ne* de la proprete [si *interlin.*] est *L.* de la propretee [neqedent] si est *N.* 6. bon *NDMGSC.* 7—7. *so verb. GSR.* le destourber [cum cely *interlin.*] qe del tut engetter *L.* le destourbour cum cely qi del tut engette *D.* *so* [qi *interl.*] *N.* le destourbour com del tut engettour *M.* *sim. W.* al destourbour del tot engettre *C.*

session, and such purchasers cannot count of their possession. And therefore the writ of *Quare impedit* was provided as a remedy for such purchasers; which writ is pleadable by summons, attachments and distress.

Nature of a *Quare impedit.* 2. The force of this writ lies wholly in the trespass of the tortious disturbance. Therefore where any one having a right to present by a good title desires to present, and another who has less right interposes a disturbance by presenting another clerk or in any other manner, if he who is thus disturbed cannot count of his own seisin or of the seisin of his ancestor, then this writ of *Quare impedit* properly lies, which is as much as to say, wherefore the disturbor wrongfully sets his foot in that right which the plaintiff has in the presentation, and whereof, although he was never fully seised of the possessory right, he is seised of the property by title of good purchase; and therefore the disturbing him is equivalent to ejecting him from the whole, and is equally injurious; and thus remedy lies by this writ.

3. Mes si le pleintif presentour ne eit nule manere de seisine ne del dreit possessorie, ne de la proprеté par nul colour de tenure de tenement, ne par autre title en soen dreit, ne purra nul mettre le pié a tort, pur ceo qe il n'i ad nul dreit ou hom puse le pié mettre a dreit ne a tort; et en tiel cas ne tient mie lu proprement le *Quare impedit*, eynz fet le *Quod permittat*. Et ceo bref de *Quod permittat* tient ausi lu en la persone le purchaceour encountre soen feffour, si il ly destourbe de user sa seisine del avowesoun qe il ly out doné.

Brac. 247 (§ 4); Fle. 328 (§ 3).

4. Et cum les parties serrount venuz en court, si porra le destourbour dire, qe il ad dreit del destourber par la resoun [234.] qe ly et ses auncestres touz jours i ount presenté, si qe il est seisi del un dreit et del autre. Ou[1] il porra dire qe il ne ad mie destourbé a tort, pur ceo qe il tient le tenement, a quel la avowesoun apent, ovek totes les apurtenaunces par vente

Brac. 247 b; Fle. 331 (c. 18. § 2).

1. so *NMGS.* cum *L.* e *C.*

3. But if the plaintiff presentor has no sort of seisin either of the possessory right or of the property by any colour of tenure of tenement, or other title in his right, there can be no setting foot wrongfully, because he has no right upon which a man can set his foot either rightfully or wrongfully; and in this case the writ of *Quare impedit* does not properly lie, but that of *Quod permittat*. This writ of *Quod permittat* also lies in the person of a purchaser against his feoffor, if he disturbs him in using his seisin of the advowson which he has given to him[o].

Remedy by *Quod permittat (Quare non permittit).*

4. When the parties have appeared in court, the disturbor may say that he has a right to disturb the plaintiff, by reason that he and his ancestors have always presented, so that he is seised both of the one right and the other. Or he may say that he has not wrongfully disturbed, because he holds the tenement, to which the advowson is appendant, with all its

Exception in *Quare impedit.*

o The above section is a perverted paraphrase of Bracton, whose text, as printed, is somewhat obscure, but appears to mean, that where the plaintiff had not had seisin and did not claim property, but only an usufructuary or possessory right, his remedy was by *Quare non permittit;* so that if the plaintiff or his ancestor had had actual seisin by a former presentation, his remedy was by assise of Darreign presentment; if he claimed the advowson, and had not had seisin by himself or his ancestor, his remedy was by *Quare impedit;* if he claimed only a possessory right as tenant in dower or by the curtesy, his remedy was by *Quare non permittit.* See before, c. 4. s. 16.

del pleintif, ou de soen auncestre, ou par acun autre title de reles ou de quiteclamaunce ou de autre.

Brac. 247 *b*; Fle. 331 (c. 18. § 1).

5. Et cum acun, qi le dreit del presentement eit perdu par jugement, ou autre[1] qi nule manere de dreit ne purra clamer, i eit[2] presenté, et eit fet somoundre le clerc institut a respoundre, pur quei il destourbe le pleintif de presenter, si porra respoundre, qe il ne deit point presenter si noun en tens de vacacioun, et la eglise est pleine et conseilé, par quei il ne deit [3]ore aparmesmes[3] presenter. Et si le pleintif die, qe ele est voide, de ceo soit la court certifié par le ordinarie del lu. Et solum le maundement del Evask serra la parole terminé.

Brac. 247 *b*; Fle. 331 (c. 19. § 1, 3).

6. Clerc porra travailler autre clerc a tort, puis qe il avera esté institut, et puis qe soen patroun avera conquis soen dreit del presentement par jugement de nostre court. Et pur ceo qe tele enquietacioun est prejudiciele a nostre digneté, a defere quant qe en ad esté dreiturelment fet en nostre court, voloms nous qe tels travaillez[4] soient eydez [5]par nous et nos[5]

1. autrement *M.* 2. *so G.* et eit *L.* e eit *NMS.* 3—3. ore par mesmes *LC.* a [*eras.*] ore apar meismes *N.* a ore a par meismes *D.* ore aparmeismes *G.* ore parmeimes *S.* point ore aparmeymes *M.* ore a par meimes *F.* ore *W.* aore *R.* 4. *so GCF. sim. MS.* trauals *LN.* 5—5. par nos *NMF. sim. GS.* par *C.*

appurtenances, by sale of the plaintiff or his ancestor, or by some other title, as by release, quitclaim, or otherwise.

Exception that the church is full.

5. And when any one, who has lost the right to the presentation by judgment, or any other person who has not any right presents, and causes the clerk who has already been instituted to be summoned to answer why he disturbs the plaintiff from presenting, the clerk may say that the plaintiff ought not to present save in time of vacation, and that the church is full and provided, wherefore he ought not now immediately to present. And if the plaintiff say, that the church is void, the court shall be certified thereof by the ordinary of the place; and according to the bishop's return the plea shall be determined.

Fact of plenarty to be certified by ordinary.

Proceeding in court Christian in opposition to judgment of civil court, prohibited.

6. One clerk may wrongfully molest another after he has been instituted, and after his patron has made good his right of presentation by judgment of our court. And because such molestation is prejudicial to our dignity, and tends to defeat that which has been legally done in our court, we will that such as are so troubled be aided by us and by our prohibitions,

prohibiciouns, et par attachementz qe en suent, ausi bien as juges, qe il ne tiegnent le plee, cum as parties, qe il ne suent. Brac. 250 b, 251.

7. Et ausi purroit le Evaske, pendaunt le plee en nostre court, a tort encombrer la eglise par acun de eynz les vi. mois. Et si acun doute ceo, si purchace noster bref de prohibicioun al[1] Evask, qe il point ne face, ou qe il ne receyve nul clerc [2]a nuli[2] presentement jekes a taunt qe le plee pendaunt en nostre court soit deduit[3], et noméement de eynz le tens de vi. moys. Et si le Evaske face encountre noster defens, tauntost seut[4] le attachement. Et si il ne receyve les clers presentez a noster maundement, tauntost soit somouns a respoundre pur quei il ne le ad fet. Brac. 247 b, 248; Fle. 331 (c. 19. § 2). [234 b.] Brac. 251 (c. 9); Fle. 331, 332.

1. so *NMGC.* et le *L.* 2—2. so *M.* sim. *N.* a nul *LGS.* al *C.* de dreit [dedut *interlin.*] *L.* deduct *N.* detrie de dreit *GS.* dedut *C.* 3. so *M.* 4. siwe *N.* sue *GS.* courge *M.*

and by attachments in pursuance thereof, as well to the judges, that they hold not such plea, as to the parties, that they do not prosecute the same.

7. The bishop also pending the plea in our court may wrongfully incumber the church by his clerk within the six months. Therefore if any one be apprehensive of this, let him purchase our writ of prohibition to the bishop that he do no such thing, or that he do not admit any clerk upon the presentation of any until the plea pending in our court be concluded, and in particular within the period of six months [p]. And if the bishop acts contrary to our prohibition, an attachment presently follows. And if he does not admit the clerks presented pursuant to our mandate, let him be immediately summoned to answer why he has not done so. Bishop prohibited from admitting clerk pending plea. *Ne admittas.* *Quare non admisit.*

[p] These words, which are derived from Bracton or Fleta, seem to imply some uncertainty as to the bishop's right to present by lapse where the suit is undetermined at the end of the six months. It has been held in later times, that if he is not a party to the action of *Quare impedit*, he may present by lapse. Consequently it is now the universal practice to make the bishop a party. See Lancaster *v.* Lowe, Croke's Reports, *t.* Jac. 93; Blackstone's Comm. vol. iii. p. 247. 'The bishop shall present in all cases, where there is disturbance and the king does not write to the bishop to certify him of the right patron within the term of six months. Which may be for diverse reasons; either because the court cannot take cognizance thereof so soon, or because the plea cannot be ended so soon, or cannot be ended at all for want of proof of right; and although the court may certify, yet the collation belongeth to the bishop where there are several parceners, and they cannot agree.' (Note in MS. *N.*)

CHAPITRE VII. [xcv.]

De Assise de Utrum.

Brac. 285 *b*; Fle. 332.

1. La quarte assise est de *Utrum*, qe mout ad de le un dreit et del autre, pur ceo qe ele termine le un et l'autre. Car apres le jugement de ceste assise ne ad nul recoverer for qe acune foiz par atteynte. Par ceste assise reconust hom, lequel le tenement dount le plé est meu soit lay fee le tenaunt, ou fraunche aumoyne appurtenaunte a la eglise le pleintif, lequel qe le pleintif soit clerc ou lay. Car en les[1] persones de ambideus tient bien lu, ne mie neqedent es[2] persones de touz clers, mes soulement de ceux qi sount persones et rectours[3] de eglises parochieles [4]qi i[4] sount institutz par Evask ou par autres ordinaries, et de ceux ausi qi
[235.] sount chanoynes en eglises cathedrales, et des Abbés et des Priours et des autres qi ount eglises en propres oes[5], qi sount

1. *so M.* les *om. LN.* 2. en *N.* 3. *so NM.* rentouses [rectours *interlin.*] *L.* rentiers *G.* renters *S.* 4—4. e qe *N.* qe *M.* qi *G.* 5. *so N.* eus *L.* oeps *G.* us *MS.* uses *C.*

CHAPTER VII.

Of the Assise of Utrum.

Assise to determine whether land is frankalmoigne, or lay fee.

1. The fourth assise is that of *Utrum*, which partakes very much of both rights, because both are determined by it. For after judgment in this assise there is no recovery except sometimes by attaint. By this assise recognisance is made whether the tenement, whereof the plea is brought, be the lay fee of the tenant or frankalmoigne belonging to the church of the plaintiff,—whether the clerk or the layman be plaintiff[q]. For the assise may well lie at the suit of either, yet not of all clerks, but for such only as are parsons and rectors of parochial churches instituted therein by bishops or other ordinaries, and also for canons in cathedral churches, and abbots and priors who have churches appropriated to their use, and are in the position of parsons; and this, although

Either party may be plaintiff.

Assise provided for parsons claiming in right of their churches.

q Bracton informs us, it had been at one time decided that this assise could only be had upon the plaint of the parson, but its extension was considered advisable, as it offered a means of avoiding the delays of a writ of right, and the decision by battle or great assise. Brac. 285 *b*.

autresi cum persones; tut [1]ne eynt il qe moités[1] par[2] resoun de divers feez et de divers avowez[3], et dount chescun avowé purra par sei estre[4] enpledé et pleder; et autre chose serroit de chose tenue entre eus en commun. Et si acune eglise soit doné a deus persones par un soul avowé, nul ne se purra pleindre par ceste assise, ne nul estre enpledé sauntz autre. Brac. 286; Fle. 332 (§ 4).

2. Le[5] bref de *Utrum* pur le clerc fu purveu pur soen bref de dreit, pur ceo qe il ne poeit[6] mie counter par descente el[7] dreit; et issi est il de la nature del plee de dreit, et pur ceo sount limitez par un terme. Le proces de cest bref est autretiel cum en le darein present. Le tenaunt neqedent purra voucher a garraunt. Fle. 323 (§ 2). Ante, c. 1, s. 4; Brac. 286; Fle. 332 (c. 20. § 7; c. 21. § 1).

1—1. *so LSGC.* [ne] eynt il la doneisoun [al' voweson] entiere tote Mes qe la moytee *N.* ne eient il qe la doneison *M.* 2. la *add. NM.* 3. *so C. sim. M.* diuerses auowesouns *L.* diuers avowesons *GS.* 4. en peril de pleder e estre *N.* 5. par le *M.* par *C.* 6. poet *M.* 7. en qi defaute *M.*

they have only moieties by reason of there being divers fees and divers patrons, for which moieties each patron may severally plead and be impleaded; though it would be otherwise of a thing held in common between them. And if any church is given to two parsons by one patron, neither of them can plead or be impleaded by this assise without the other[r]. Half-churches. Two parsons of one church.

2. The Writ of *Utrum* in favour of the clerk was provided as his writ of right, because he could not count by descent in the right. Thus, it is of the nature of a plea of right, and therefore they are limited by the same term[s]. The proceedings in this writ are similar to those in an assise of last presentation. Nevertheless the tenant may vouch to warranty. *Utrum*, the parson's writ of right. Same limitation as in writ of right. Process. Voucher of warrant.

[r] 'There are sometimes two parsons, or more; and this by reason that it was the original ordinance of the first patron, or because the church is founded upon divers fees, whereof each lord is patron and advocate of his own lordship.' (Note in MS. *N.*) Half-churches, and smaller fractions of churches, occur frequently in Domesday-book. Compare before, c. 3. s. 8.

[s] It was said by Brumpton, Justice, in the Cornish Iter, 30 Edw. I., that the right of action in this writ was not barred by prescription of time. Year Book, 30 Edw. I. p. 207.

CHAPITRE VIII. [XCVI.]

De Excepciouns.

Brac. 286, 286 *b*; Fle. 332, 333. 1. Le tenaunt se purra eyder par ses excepciouns generales et dilatories. Et si le tenaunt soit lay, si purra il dire qe la eglise ne fust unques en seisine del tenement demaundé; et, tut en fut ele en acun tens seisie, cist pleintif neqedent ne i purra rien conquestre[1]; car il ad resceu service et feuté de mesme le tenement. Et si ceo soit averré, ou nient dedit,
[235 *b*.] si chete l'assise, par taunt au meyns a tote sa vie. Car feuté prendre en cest cas barre[2] accioun, sicum homage prendre
Fle. 333 (§ 3). [3]en autres[3] cas; car homage forbarre demeyne. Et ausi perist l'assise, [4]si soen[4] predecessour eit aliené le tenement en fee au lay, qi en ad puis purchacé le confermement del feffement del Evask del lu, et del patroun.

Brac. 286 *b*; Fle. 333 (§ 4). 2. Et si perist [5]de tote manere de tenement doné[5] as eglises cathedrales et de religioun, si purchaz soit fet de tel

1. reconquere *N*. conquere *MC*. conquester *GSF*. 2. *so GF*. barra *LS*. barrira *N*. e le homage barre *M*. 3—3. entre autre *LSF*. entre autres *N*. *sim. M*. entres autres *G*. en autre *C*. 4—4. *so N*. *sim. MCF*. sicum *L*. 5—5. *so F*. *sim. NM*. de tote manere cest tenement *L*. de ceste manere le tenement *S*. tote manere dassise de tenement *C*.

CHAPTER VIII.

Of Exceptions in the Assise of Utrum.

Dilatory exceptions. Peremptory exceptions.

1. The tenant may aid himself by his general and dilatory exceptions. And if the layman is tenant, he may plead that the church was never seised of the tenement demanded; and that, although it were at any time seised, yet the plaintiff cannot recover anything therein, for he hath received fealty and service for the same tenement; and if this be verified or not denied, the assise shall fall at least for the parson's life. For in this case the taking of fealty bars the action, as in other cases the taking of homage, because homage excludes demesne. The assise is also at an end if his predecessor aliened the tenement in fee to a layman, who has since obtained a confirmation of the feoffment from the bishop of the diocess and the patron.

Taking of fealty by parson bars his action.

So, alienation with confirmation by bishop and patron.

No assise of *Utrum* for land belonging to cathedral or convent.

2. The assise also fails as to any kind of tenements given to cathedral or conventual churches, if the writ be purchased of

tenement, pur ceo qe tiele gent ount autel remedie [1]qe ount autre[1] gent. Mes es douns fetz as[2] eglises parochieles ne sount mie compris les persones, et pur ceo tient lu cest bref soulement en eus. De lour seisine demeyne neqedent, s'il soint engettez ou destourbez, averount il remedie par assise de novele disseisine, et par bref de entré de disseisine fete a soen predecessour, taunt cum le tens porra suffrer. Et si perist la assise, si tenement soit demaundé en demeyne ou la eglise ne fust unques seisie for qe de la seignurie. Et ausi [3]en cas[3] pur acune condicioun contenue et comprise el feffement dount la eglise estoit feffé.

Cf. ante, l. iii. c. 4. s. 9.

Brac. 286 b, 287; Fle. 333 (§ 4).

Brac. 286 b; Fle. 333 (§ 5, 6).

3. Et si lay homme se pleigne de clerc persone, ou il se pleint dounc par bref de possessioun par descente de acun auncestre, ou par bref de dreit; et si par bref de possessioun, adounc courge entre eus autel proces cum courrut[4] par entre autres gentz; et si par bref de dreit, ou le clerc dounc ad garraunt, ou noun; et s'il eit garraunt qe ly garrauntie, si [236.]

Brac. 287; Fle. 333 (§ 10).

1—1. qe ount laye *N.* *sim.* *GSF.* com laye *M.* com ount lay *C.* 2. so *MGSC.* es *LF.* des *N.* 3—3. so *NG.* en [cas *interlin.*] cum *L.* en cas ou *M.* *om.* *C.* [en cas *interl.*] ou *F.* 4. curreit *N.* court *SG.* correit *M.* serreit *C.*

such a tenement, because such persons have the same remedy as laymen; but in gifts made to parochial churches the parsons are not included, and therefore this writ lies only for them. In respect however of their own seisin, if they are ejected or disturbed, they shall have remedy by assise of Novel Disseisin; and by writ of Entry upon a disseisin done to their predecessor as long as the time will admit. The assise likewise fails, if the tenement be demanded in demesne where the church was never seised but of the seignory. So in some cases on account of a condition comprised and contained in the feoffment by which the church was enfeoffed[s].

Parsons may bring assise of Novel Disseisin or writ of Entry.

Exception that the Church was seised only of seignory.

Exception of condition.

3. When a layman complains against a clerk who is a parson, he does so either by a possessory writ by descent from some ancestor or by writ of right. If by a possessory writ, then the process between them shall be the same as it would be between other persons. If by writ of right, then the clerk has either a warrant or not. If he has a warrant who will

Proceeding by layman against parson, by possessory writ; by writ of right.

Warranty.

[s] The nature of the condition alluded to is more fully explained in Bracton. It was not uncommon for a layman to enfeoff a church on condition of being reenfeoffed to hold of the church; and thus to make the land feudally subject to the church in order to obtain its protection. (Brac. 286 b.)

courge le proces, ausi cum en bref de dreit, par bataile ou par graunt assise par entre le demaundaunt et le garraunt, ou autrement, sicum par entre autres[1] del people. Et s'il ne eit point de garraunt, [2]eynz soit defendant[2] et respoigne mesmes, en tiel cas ad il double remedie par le bref de dreit, et porra elire le quel qe il vodera; ou mettre sei en juree, lequel la terre demaundé soit fraunche aumoyne etc. ou lay fee, autresi cum lay homme [3]en eust[3] arramie l'assise; ne ja pur ceo ne se tourne[4] point la cause de la propreté jekes en la cause de possessioun, tut detrie la juree et termine la une cause et l'autre; ou il se porra defendre par bataille ou par graunt assise, si le poer le ordinarie et le consentement del patroun le soeffrent.

Fle. 334 (§ 11, 12). 4. Et si lay homme porte ceste assise, si purra le clerc respoundre et dire, qe le auncestre le pleintif n'en fust unques Ante, s. 2. seisi. Et s'il demaunde en demeyne ceo qe il deit demaunder en service, si chete l'assise, ausi cum avaunt est dit de la Brac. 287 b; Fle. 334 (§ 13). pleinte le clerc. Et si le tenement fu tenu avaunt de la eglise, et le pleintif ou soen auncestre le forfit par acun juge-

1. *so NMF.* eus *LS.* gentz *G.* 2—2. eynz defende *NF.* einz se defende *M.* adonq' defend *G.* en defendant e *S.* 3—3. *so N.* si en eust *L.* eust *M.* vst *G.* 4. *so N.* *sim. M.* attorne *L.* *sim. GS.*

warrant to him, let the proceedings be carried on between the demandant and warrant as in a writ of right by battle or Defence of parson. great assise or otherwise, as between any other persons. If he has no warrant, but defends the action, and answers for himself, in such case he has a double remedy by reason of the Trial either by assise, *Utrum, &c.* writ of right, and he may choose whichever he will; either he may put himself upon a jury, whether the land demanded be frank-almoigne, &c., or lay fee, just as if the layman had brought an assise;—not that the proprietary cause is thus turned to a possessory one, although the jury tries and deter- or by battle or great assise. mines both rights,—or he may defend himself by battle or the great assise, if permitted by the authority of the ordinary and the consent of the patron.

Exceptions of clerk to assise of layman. 4. Where a layman brings this assise, the clerk may answer and plead, that the ancestor of the plaintiff was never seised. And if he demands in demesne what he ought to demand in service, the assise falls, as before is mentioned in the case Exception of felony and forfeiture. of a plaint by a clerk. And if the tenement was aforetime held of the church, and the plaintiff or his ancestor forfeited

ment de felonie, en tel cas est le [1]tenement eschete[1] al eglise; et issi tient lu la excepcioun de felonie. Ou si le tenaunt moerge sauntz heir, ausi serra le tenement eschete a la eglise pur [2]le meer[2] dreit qe prent [3]refute et abri illoke[3] par defaute qe il ne trove ou il puse aylours descendre. Mes [236 *b.*] si la eglise, ou la persone en soen noun, rien ne eit resceu de cel tenement si noun en noun de aumoygne, rien ne porra par taunt escheer al eglise del tenement.

5. Et cum les parties averount pledé jekes al assise, [4]ou si l'assise[4] soit agardé par defaute le tenaunt, [5]et la resomounse[5] soit testmoigné, ou si ele soit demaundé pur contumace del tenaunt, qe fut veu en court par record [6]des Justices[6], et les jurours del assise [7]i soint[7] presentz et nul jurour soit chalengé, ou, s'il soint, apres les chalenges des parties triez, tauntost voisent jurer par cestes paroles. Ceo oyet vous [8]sires Justices[8], qe jeo verité dirray de ceste assise et de taunt de terre ove les apurtenaunces en N. dount jeo ai fet

Brac. 286 *b*, 287; Fle. 333 (§ 7).

Brac. 287; Fle. 333 (§ 8).

1—1. *so MGS. sim. N.* tenaunt le chete *L.* 2—2. *so LSG.* le meur *N.* meur *M.* 3—3. *so LS.* refute e abri qe le patroun resceust illucs *N.* refut ileques *M. sim. G.* refut al eglise ileok *F.* 4—4. *so NGCF.* ou lassise *M. om. L.* 5—5. al resomounse *L.* E si la resomounse *N.* e la somounse *M.* la resomons *G. sim. S.* e la resomouns *C.* a la resomounse e *F.* 6—6. de la Iustice *M.* 7—7. *so N. sim. GF.* et soint *L. sim. SC.* soint *M.* 8—8. *so GS.* sire Iustices *L.* Iustice *M.* Iustices *GF.*

it by some judgment of felony, in such case the tenement is escheated to the church, and the exception of felony holds. Again, if the tenant dies without heirs, the tenement will also escheat to the church by reason of the mere right, which takes refuge and shelter there for want of finding any other place where it may descend. But if the church, or the parson in its name, has received nothing from the tenement except a payment by way of alms, nothing can thereby escheat to the church.

Escheat.

5. When the parties have pleaded to the assise, or when the assise is awarded by default of the tenant, and the resummons is proved, or when the assise is demanded by reason of the contumacy of the tenant, having been seen in court by record of the Justices, if the jurors of the assise are present, and none of them is challenged, or, if they be, after the challenges of the parties have been tried, let them straightway be sworn in these words: 'Hear this, sirs Justices, that I will speak the truth of this assise, and of so much land with the

Oath of jurors.

la vewe par le comaundement le Roi, lequel la avauntdite terre ove les apurtenaunces soit fraunche aumoyne apurtenaunte a tele eglise dount le pleintif est persone, ou le lay fee le tenaunt (ou la reverse, si le lay soit le pleintif), et pur rien ne lerray, etc. Et puis soint instructz et enfourmez sur quel article il deivent certefier la court. Et solom le
Brac. 288; Fle. 334 (§ 15). verdit se face jugement. Et cum l'assise soit passé en manere de assise pur le lay, et le tenement soit jugé au lay pleintif, le clerc n'en avera james recoverer for qe par atteynte; [1]et la fourme coment[1] apparra en le chapitre suaunt.

CHAPITRE IX. [XCVII.]

[237.]

De Atteynte.

Fle. 334. 1. Serment est affermement [2]ou niement de[2] acune chose, dount homme est chargé en peril de sa alme de dire verité; et fu purveu pur mescreable gent qe [3]hom dust[3] jurer sour sainctz evangelies Deu pur [4]les maumeries[4] eschure. Et fut

1—1. *so LNSG.* en la forme qe *M.* en la fourme com *C.* 2—2. *so M. sim. G.* vniement de *LNS.* de Ioggement en *C.* ou jugement *F.* 3—3. dussent *C.* 4—4. mauuestee e maumeries *N.* les maus *C.*

appurtenances in N., whereof I have made the view by the king's precept, whether the aforesaid land with the appurtenances is frank-almoigne belonging to such a church, whereof the plaintiff is parson, or lay fee of the tenant' (or the reverse if the layman be plaintiff), 'and will not upon any account
Charge of jury. omit,' &c. Afterwards let them be instructed and informed
Verdict and judgment. upon what point they are to certify the court. And let judgment be given according to the verdict. And when the assise
Verdict final, unless falsified by attaint. has once passed in favour of the layman after the manner of an assise, and the tenement is adjudged to the lay plaintiff, the clerk shall never have any recovery but by attaint, the form of which will appear in the following chapter.

CHAPTER IX.

Of the nature of an Oath, and of the process of Attaint.

Oath, its nature. 1. An oath is an affirmation or denial of anything, whereby a person is charged upon peril of his soul to speak the truth; and it was provided on account of people difficult of belief that
Oath to be taken on the Gospels. oaths should be taken upon the Holy Gospels of God for

ausi ordeynez pur merite de bien aver; car par serment de gentz sount moutz des mauveistez[1] atteyntz et puniz, et meynt homme par serment fet graunt bien et graunt ayde a soen prosme. Et fu ausi purveu, qe hom dut jurer par Deu, et ne mie par ses creatures, ne par ses membres, pur eschure le pecché de blasfemie, et qe nul ne jurast [2]si noun for qe par entencioun de merite[2] aver par le serment, et en besoigne, et en cas honest. Et dounc est [3]il alouwable[3], quant la conscience deeynzime[4] se acord en chescun point a la bouche, et ne meyns ne plus; et s'il i eit descord, adounc [5]i ad il parjuri[5].

2. Et si acun soit fet parjurer a escient par acun sovereyn, ambideus sount a punir par une manere de peyne. Et cil qi fet ou procure [6]cely jurer[6] qe il seet bien qe jure faus, et cely ausi qi a escient resceit le faus serment, est quant devers Deu homicide, tut ne tue il mie le cors, einz est parcener de la felonie, quant il a escient perd la alme, qi a tel peril fet le serment; et tels par consequent perdent lour almes, qi sount consentauntz. Et en mesme la manere est de celi, qi est Fle. 335 (§ 5). [237 *b.*]

1. maufez *M.* maus *C.* 2—2. so *L.* *sim.* *NSG.* si noun for qe pur merite *M.* si noun par entencioun de Merit *C.* fors ke par ententioun de merite *F.* 3—3. so *L.* *sim.* *S.* le serment leal e alowable *N.* il loal *M.* il leal *GCF.* 4. dedeinzime *N.* denz *G.* *sim.* *S.* denzime *M.* demeine *C.* denz emue *F.* 5—5. est il pariurs *N.* *sim.* *G.* i est il pariors *M.* est pariours *C.* 6—6. cil pariurer *M.* e cely del Ioree e asquuns seient par asqun souerein *C.*

avoidance of idolatry. Oaths were instituted that men might thereby do good service; for by means of an oath many crimes are convicted and punished, and many a man doth by an oath great good and great service to his neighbour. It was likewise provided that one should swear by God and not by his creatures, or his members, to avoid the sin of blasphemy, and that none should swear but with an intention of doing service by the oath, upon necessary and just occasions. An oath therefore is allowable when the conscience within agrees in every point with the lips, without any addition or abatement; and if there be any disagreement, it is perjury. Expediency of oaths. Perjury.

2. If any one wilfully perjures himself in obedience to his superior, both of them are to be punished with the same penalty. And he who causes or procures another to take an oath well knowing that he swears falsely, as well as he who knowingly admits such a false oath, is in relation to God a homicide, although he do not kill the body, but is partner in the felony, forasmuch as he knowingly destroys the soul of him who at such peril takes the oath; and they consequently destroy Procuring of perjury, criminal.

present et escoute fere le[1] serment et s'en test sauntz ly reprendre. [2]Parjurie est mensonge afermé[2] par serment. Et si pecche hom en iii. maneres. Une est cum est de celi qi seet [3]ou quide[3] acun faus estre faus, et ceo dit estre verité par soen serment. L'autre est cum est de celi qi est descu et quide chose fause estre verité, [4]et issi le dit[4] estre sour soen serment. La tierce est cum de celi [5]qi dit[5] par soen serment [6]acune chose estre verité, et[6] purement est verité, en sa consience neqedent il la quide estre fause, cum del Jeu qi jura Saincte Marie estre la mere al fiz Deu. Mensonge est fause significacioun de voiz[7] oveke deceyvable entente; et ceo pecché est si venimous, qe nul ne deit voler menter pur autri vie rechater.

Brac. 288 *b*, 289; Fle. 334 (§ 3).

Fle. 335 (§ 6).

3. Des sermentz sount acuns promissories del tens avener, et de tels sermentz sount treis maneres. La une est, [8]qe promette[8] par serment, qe il ferra, [9]ou qe il eydera[9] acune chose [10]qe ne fet mie a fere, sicum de hom felonousement

Fle. 334 (§ 2, 4).

1. *so LS.* faus *add. NGMCF.* 2—2. *so MG.* pariuriz est mensonge ferme *L.* pariurs est. E mensonge est afferme *N.* pariury est meintenge ferme *S.* pariure est qe meyn ferme *C.* pariurc est mensoynge ferme *F.* 3—3. *so MGF.* qe de *L.* qi de *S.* *om. C.* e quide *on eras. N.* 4—4. *so NMF.* *sim. G.* issi le deit *LS.* 5—5. *so N.* qe deit *L.* qe dit *MGS.* *sim. F.* 6—6. cum chose est verite et *L.* acune chose estre veritee qe *N.* *sim. MGF.* 7. *so NSMC.* *sim. GF.* verite [voiz *interlin.*] *L.* 8—8. *so L.* qe qi promette *NS.* com qi promet *M.* *sim. GCF.* 9—9. *so LN.* *sim. DS.* ou eidera *G.* ou dirra *MF.* ou dorra *C.* 10—10. *om. M.*

their souls who are consenting. The like is true of him who is present and hears the oath without speaking and reprehending it. Perjury is a lie affirmed by oath. A person may be guilty of this sin in three ways; first, where he who knows or believes a thing to be false affirms it by his oath to be true; secondly, where one is deceived and thinks a thing to be true which is false, and declares it upon his oath; thirdly, where he who says upon his oath that something is true, which in fact is so, yet in his conscience believes it to be false, as when the Jew swore that Saint Mary was the mother of the Son of God. A lie is a false expression of the voice with an intent to deceive; and this sin is so poisonous that no one ought to be willing to lie, even to ransom another person's life.

Three cases of false swearing.

Lying, never permissible.

3. Of oaths some are promissory respecting the future, and of such oaths there are three kinds. The first is where any one promises by an oath that he will do or assist in something which ought not to be done, as feloniously to kill a man; and such an oath ought not to be kept. The second is where a per-

Promissory oaths.

tuer; et cel serment ne fet point a tener. L'autre est cum qui jure, qe il freit[1] acune chose[10] qe il porra bien fere, et ceo solempnement sauntz mester [2]et folement, et issi pecche le jurour. La tierce manere de jurer est qe vient[2] de legerté de jaungle et de [3]mauvesté de[3] usage; et issi pecche le jurour, mes meyns qe cil devaunt. Mes de ces treis maneres de serment ne [4]parle hom nient en[4] cest chapitre. Car nule [238.] terriene atteynte ne gist; ne en nul serment for qe [5]del assertorie, qe ne estent[5] fors qe al tens passé ou present.

4. Et pur ceo, si il avent qe les jurours de acune petite assise eynt fet faus serment, a la pleinte dounc celi qi[6] avera perdu par assise[7], purrount il estre atteintz en plusours maneres; [8]et acune foiz[8] par serment de xxiiii. jurours; acune foiz par lour propres conisaunces par examinement des Justices; et acune foiz par repentaunce et de lour gré; mes en tiel cas gist mitigacioun et merci. Et pur ceo, si acun bie a fere atteyndre acuns jurours, si fet a prendre garde quant des jurours et queus furent[9] en l'assise, issi qe chescun jurour

Stat. West. 1. (3 Ed. I.) c. 38; Brac. 288 *b*; Fle. 335 (§ 6, 7, 8).

1. *so LG. sim. S.* fra *CF. so on eras. N.* 2—2. *so verb. M. om. L.* et ceo ne fet nent *add.* (*after* folement) *S. sim. G.* 3—3. mauueis *NSGMC.* 4—4. parle nient *NC. sim. SG.* parout nient *M.* 5—5. *so M.* la qe ceo ne estent *L.* del autre qe ceo ne estent *N.* del feffour car ceo nestent *G. sim. S.* de la certeinete ne sestent *C.* 6. *so NMCF.* le *add. L. sim. G.* 7. *so NMGCF.* purement *add. L.* 8—8. si cum akune foiz *N.* alafiez *M. here and below.* 9. *so C.* sount *LNG.* sunt *MS. om. F.*

son swears that he will do something which he may lawfully do, and this solemnly, but without necessity or reason, and in so doing he is guilty of sin. The third kind of swearing is that which proceeds from a levity in talking and from a bad habit; this kind of swearing is sinful, but less so than the former. But of these three kinds of oaths we shall not speak in this chapter; for they are not subject to any earthly attaint, nor is any oath except that of assertion, which relates only to time past or present.

Unnecessary swearing, sinful.

Assertory oath.

4. Therefore if it happens that the jurors in any petty assise have taken a false oath, they may on the complaint of the losing party in the assise be attainted in several ways. Sometimes upon the oaths of twenty-four jurors, sometimes by their own acknowledgment upon examination by the Justices, and sometimes by their repentance and of their own free will; and in the last case there is room for mitigation and mercy. Therefore when any one desires to attaint any jurors, it must be seen how many and what jurors were upon the assise, so

Attaint of jurors in assise.

There must be two attainors to every juror.

eit deus atteignours al meyns; et [1]sil en eint plus, ceo ne nust point. Et affiert[1] qe il soint de ausi bone condicioun cum les jurours, ou de meillour.

Brac. 288 *b*; Fle. 335 (§ 8). 5. De ceo pecché est acune foiz [2]la Justice en la coupe[2], et acune foiz[3] les jurours. [4]Mes qi qe en soit en la coupe, touz jours[4] fet a crere[5] l'enroullement del record de la Justice, deques autaunt qe par jugement soit chaungee. Et pur ceo fet en [6]prime chief[6], eynz ceo qe les atteignours soint somouns, a examiner le proces et le record de la Justice. Car si il soulement soit trové en la coupe, ceo ne soit mie [238 *b*.] retté as jurours, ne la reverse. Apres dounc le record tauntost poet[7] hom aparceivere, et ne mie avaunt, lequel l'assise fust Cf. Brac. 288 *b*; Fle. 335 (§ 8); post c. 10. prise en manere de assise, ou en manere de juré. Et si en manere de juree, dounc tient lu a tote gent remedie par atteinte. Et si ele soit passé en manere de assise, dounc ne tient mie lu atteinte for qe a ceux soulement, et [8]a lour[8] heirs, qi furent en seisine en lour nouns demeyne, [9]tut i[9]

1—1. sil ne eint plus et ceo affiert *L.* *sim. S.* si il ni eynt plus a ceo affiert *N.* e si li eent plus ceo nen nuit point e il afiert *M.* e sil eient plus ceo nuyt point e ceo affiert *G.* e sil eient plus ceo ne nust point e affert *C.* *sim. F.* 2—2. *so NSCF.* *sim. G.* la Iustice en la Court [coupe *interlin.*] *L.* la coupe en la Iustice *M.* 3. en *add. M.* 4—4. *so verb. MGF. om.* [e pur ceo *interlin.*] *L.* E pur ceo *N.* *om. S.* 5. *so NGCF.* enquere *LN.* 6—6. *so NC.* premer bref [prime chief *interlin.*] *L.* primes chef *MF.* *sim. G.* primer chief *S.* 7. *so MC.* poeit *L.* puit *N.* 8—8. *so N.* de [a *interl.*] les *L.* de les *G.* *sim. S.* de lur *M.* a leur *C.* a lor *F.* 9—9. *so M.* *sim F.* dounc [tut *interl.*] *L.* tut *NGS.* *sim. C.*

that each juror may have two attainors at least; but if there Attainors to be of higher rank. be more, it is no harm. It is also proper that they be of equal or better condition than the jurors[t].

Examination of record. 5. Of this offence sometimes the Justice is guilty and sometimes the jurors. But whoever is in fault, credit must always be given to the enrolment of the record of the Justice until it be altered by judgment. Therefore in the first place, before the attainors are summoned, the proceedings and record of the Justice should be examined; for if he only is found to be in fault, it is not to be imputed to the jurors, nor the reverse. Therefore after examination of the record, and not before, it may be immediately seen whether the assise was taken as a jury, or as an assise. If it was taken by way of jury, then every one may have remedy by attaint; if by way of assise, then an attaint lies only for these persons and their

t 'The attainors ought to be persons of better condition than the jurors; and therefore the writ says: Summone xxiiii. milites; whereas it is said in the writ of assise: summone xii. legales homines.' (Note in MS. *N.*)

furent il en autri nouns, cum vileyns, ou termers, baillifs, ou gardeins.

6. Ne a touz[1] Justices ne appent mie de prendre atteyntes ou certificaciouns. Mes a ceus apent de prendre certificaciouns qi pristrent le verdit del assise, si[2], eynz ceo qe il soint remuez de lour office, le facent. Mes a ceux Justices qi pristrent la reconisaunce del assise ne apent james de prendre les atteyntes apres jugement rendu. Car les correccions de jugementz avoms reservé a nostre propre jurisdiccioun. Mes si les Justices [3]a acune assise prendre[3], avaunt jugement rendu [4]solom le verdit[4], soint requis de atteyndre les jurours del assise, tauntost par gage et plege de la partie porrount les Justices fere prendre la juree des xxiiii. atteignours, s'il soint presentz, ausi bien cum sour certificacioun. Car puis qe le plein poer lour est doné de oyer et de terminer totes les choses, par taunt sount grauntez qe mester lour est a saver pur clere veie fere al jugement. Et cum certificacioun

Brac. 291 *b*; Fle. 338 (§ 19).

Ante, l. i. c. i. s. 11.

[240.]

1. totes *SG*. 2. *so NMGCF*. si *om. L*. 3—3. *so C*. a acune acune assise prendrount *L*. as acunes assises prendre *N*. *sim. F*. ascune assise prendrount *G*. *sim. S*. acune assise prengnent *M*. 4—4. *om. C*.

heirs who were seised in their own names, and not for those who were seised in the name of others, as villains, termors, bailiffs, or guardians.

6. It is not the duty of all Justices to take attaints or certifications. For it belongs to those Justices who took the verdict of the assise, to take certifications, so as they do it before they are removed from their office. But it belongs not to those Justices who took the recognisance of the assise to take attaints after judgment given; because we have reserved the amendment of judgments for our own jurisdiction. But if the Justices at the taking of any assise are required before judgment given to attaint the jurors of the assise, they may immediately[u], upon security and pledge of the party, cause the jury of twenty-four attainors to be taken if they are present, as well as upon a certification. For since the full power is given them to hear and determine the whole matter, they are authorised to acquaint themselves with every thing necessary to clear the way to their judgment. And where certification or attaint is accessory to

What Justices shall take attaints and certifications.

Justice of assise may not take attaint after judgment,

but may take a certification or an attaint on the spot before judgment.

[u] See the note to chap. xi. s. 2, below.

[1]ou atteinte soit dependaunt[1] del assise, et les Justices veient qe sauntz certificacioun ou sauntz atteinte ne pusent mie aler al jugement pur terminer la assise, bien semble et veyrs est, qe a ceux apent de prendre atteynte et certificacioun, as queus apent pleine jurisdiccioun de terminer l'assise, si hastivement le facent, et si noun, mes ne apent cel office a eus, ne a ceux ne deit le poer estre graunté.

Mag. Chart. c. 12; Brac. 291; Fle. 338 (§ 19).

7. Et tut conteigne la Graunt Chartre des fraunchises, qe acunes assises soint prises en countez, pur ceo ne entende[2] nulli qe[3] certificaciouns ne atteyntes [4]i deyvent estre prises autresi[4]. Car ceo ne est mie mester, si noun en cas ou nuli poer est doné for qe sour l'assise. Mes, si acune Justice soit assigné par novel poer de acune atteynte prendre ou certificacioun, adounc ne covendra mie par force [5]de cel[5] estatut prendre la en mesme le counté. Car [6]assise, certificacioun, atteynte et juree[6] sount diverses en privilege et en nature.

1—1. ou atteinte *om. L.* e atteynte dount soint dependauntz *N.* *sim. G.* donc saient dependantz *S.* e ateinte soient dependaunz *M.* dunt atteintes seyent dependans *F.* 2. atende *M.* *sim. G.* 3. *so NMC.* *sim. F.* qe *om. L.* 4—4. *so LN.* *sim. GS.* i deiuent aillours estre prises *M.* deiuent autrefoiz estre pledez *C.* 5—5. *so M.* de *LNGS.* del *C.* de cest *F.* 6—6. *so verb. MGCF.* la assise certificacioun en Iuree *L.* assise certeficacioun e Iuree *N.*

the assise, and the Justices see that without certification, or without attaint, they cannot proceed to judgment to determine the assise, it appears, and true it is, that it belongs to those who have full jurisdiction to determine that assise, to take such attaints and certifications, provided it be presently done; for if not, this duty does not belong to them, neither ought this authority to be granted to them[x].

Attaints and certifications need not be taken in the county.

7. Although it is contained in the Great Charter of liberties that some assises shall be taken in counties, yet it shall not be understood that certifications and attaints must likewise be taken there. For that is not necessary except in cases where no authority is given but upon the assise. But if any Justice be assigned with fresh power to take an attaint or certification, then it will not be necessary by virtue of that statute to take it in the same county. For assise, certification, attaint, and jury differ in their privilege and nature.

x 'When the Justice, out of favour for one party, allows a false verdict to pass, how shall the falsehood be punished? *Responsio.* Either by the Judge himself, by resummoning the parties, or by another Justice; and this by attaint, or by bill to the king's council.' (Note in MS. *N.*)

8. Et cum la atteinte soit arramie, si fet bien examiner le verdit del assise, coment les xii. jurours pronuncierent lour verdit. Car acuns jurours jurent faus acune foiz dreit[1] a escient, et ceux sount parjurs plus apertement; et plus punisables sount qe ne sount tels qe[2] sount parjurs par acune folie. Car acuns mentent apertement, quant [3]conscience en la pensé ne repose[3]. Et acuns fount faus serment et mentent par fole hastivesce qe ne vient mie a dreit de la pensee, sicum est de ceux qi pronouncient le verdit eynz ceo qe il ount examiné lour pensee; et ceux sount meyns punisables, qe ne sount ceux qe de [4]mauveiseté purpensee[4] encountre lour conscience se parjurent. Et acuns sount parjurs par fole pronunciacioun, et si ne le quident mie pur[5] acune presumpcioun qe piert verité qe ne est mie; et si[6] ceo porrount moustrer apertement, coment il furent desceuz, en tiel cas covendra estre merciable quant a lour penaunce, mes ne mie quant a lour jugement redrescer.

Brac. 288 *b*; Fle. 336 (§ 9).

[240 *b*.]

1. *so NG.* [e *interl.*] dreit *L.* de dreit *M.* saunz dreit *C.* 2. *so MGCF.* ne *add. LN.* 3—3. *so LNSG.* il responignent el qe nest en lur conscience e en lur pensee *M.* il Ioergent gen la concience e en la pense nen est repose *C.* il dyent autrement ken la conscience ou en la pensee repose *F.* 4—4. *so M.* mauueise purpense *LG. sim. S.* mauueyses purpenseez *N.* mauueis pense *C.* mauues se porpensee *F.* 5. par *M.* 6. *so NSMCF.* sil *G.* si *om. L.*

8. When the attaint is brought, the verdict of the assise ought to be thoroughly examined, in what manner the twelve jurors pronounced their verdict. For jurors sometimes swear falsely with full knowledge of what they do; and then are more openly perjured and are more severely to be punished than those who are forsworn through some indiscretion. For some persons lie openly, when conscience does not rest in their thoughts. Others swear falsely, and lie through a foolish hastiness, which does not come directly from their thoughts, as in the case of those who pronounce their verdict before they have thoroughly examined their thoughts, and these are less punishable than such as perjure themselves with malice aforethought against their conscience. And some are forsworn by a foolish verdict, not being aware of it on account of a presumption that appears true, but is not so; and if they can make it plainly appear how they were deceived, some extenuation should be had as to their punishment, but not as to the redressing of their judgment.

Various degrees of perjury.

Brac. 289; Fle. 336 (§ 10). 9. Et si les jurours eint trop poi dit par defaute de examinement des Justices, ou trop obscurement[1] eynt pronouncié lour verdit, ou nient pleynement respoundu, ou s'il eynt concelé acune verité[2] pur ceo qe il furent menez par acun errour, en tiel cas[3]est meutz[3] remedie par certificacioun qe par atteynte, par quei les jurours facent certeyn de noun certeyn et verité de chescune doute et de chescun errour. Mes si le record ne soit mie trové defective ne meyns suffisaunt, mes plener et suffisaunt, adounc ne vaut rien la certificacioun; car les jurours ne porrount mie countredire ne chalenger le record.

CHAPITRE X. [XCVIII.]

[241.]

Ou gist Atteynte.

Brac. 289 b; Fle. 336 (§ 11). 1. En la examinacioun de chescun record, einz ceo qe atteinte soit graunté ou tiegne lu, fet a prendre bone garde, lequel l'assise passa en fourme de assise sour acun gros point del bref, ou en manere de juree, et lequel ele fust prise en la presence le tenaunt ou noun. Et si ele passa sour acune ex-

1. *so MW.* outrement *LNDCR.* *sim. GS.* 2. *so MCW.* verdit *LNDGS.* 3—3. est meyns [-eutz *interlin.*] *L.* git meins *M.* gist meins *C.* est mieuz *N.* *sim. D.* gist meuz *G.* est meins *S.* *sim. W.*

Incomplete verdict rectified by certification. 9. Where the jurors have said too little for want of examination by the Justices, or have given their verdict too obscurely, or have not answered fully, as, if they have concealed any part of the truth, being induced thereto by some mistake, in such case the better remedy is by certification than by attaint, that by such certification the jurors may render certain what is uncertain, and reduce to truth what was doubtful and erroneous. Otherwise, if it appears complete on the record. But if the record is not found defective or insufficient, but full and sufficient, then there is no room for certification; for the jurors cannot gainsay or challenge the record.

CHAPTER X.

In what cases an attaint lies.

Matters to be regarded upon the question whether an attaint lies. 1. In the examination of every record, before the attaint is granted or takes place, it must be carefully observed whether the assise passed in form of assise upon some material point in the writ, or by way of jury, and whether it was taken in the presence of the tenant or not. And if it passed upon any

cepcioun, adounc fet a prendre garde, lequel la excepcioun fust dilatorie ou peremptorie; [1]et si peremptorie[1], lequel peremptorie del bref soulement et ne mie del accioun par acun errour de noun de vile ou de homme, qe ne touche mie l'assise, ou peremptorie del assise et del bref[2] ensement. De la premere manere ne tient mie lu atteynte, tut eynt les jurours erré en lour verdit, ou mentu, pur l'assise et pur la accioun qe remeynt entiere. En la secunde manere, cum en cas si acun demaundast par assise[3] tenement, ou il dut demaunder rente, si les jurours dient pur le pleintif, en tiel cas tient lu atteinte pur le mensonge.

2. Et si le bref soit covenable et bon, si covendra al pleintif tendre de averrer tote sa entente par ceux del assise. Et si le tenaunt se assente et se mette tauntost en l'assise, et les jurours facent faus serment, en tiel cas [4]tient lu la[4] atteinte, [5]cum si il eint dit qe il ly[5] disseisi, ou[6] il ne ly disseisi point. Et ausi bien gist la atteinte acune foiz en lour verdit des choses qe touchent[7] l'assise, cum en le gros, cum s'il eynt dit

Brac. 289 *b*; Fle. 336 (§ 11, 12).

[241 *b*.]

1—1. *so G. sim. MC. om. LNSF.* 2 e de Ioggement e del assise *add. C.* 3. *so SGMCF.* le *add. LN.* 4—4. *so L.* la *om. NSG.* gist *MCF.* 5—5. sicum il eint [dit *interlin.*] il est *L.* sicum si il eynt dit il est *N.* si com il eyent dit il est *S.* sicom il eient dit qil le *G.* si com est devaunt dit qe il le *M.* 6. *conj.* qe *add. LNSGMC.* 7. *so GS.* touchent [nient] *L.* [ne] touche nient *N.*

exception, then it must be seen whether the exception was dilatory or peremptory; and if peremptory, whether peremptory of the writ only, and not of the action, by reason of some mistake in the name of a vill or of a person, which does not affect the assise, or peremptory of the assise as well as of the writ. In the former case attaint does not lie, although the verdict of the jurors may have been mistaken or false, on account of the assise and the action remaining entire. In the latter case, as, where any person demands by the assise a tenement where he ought to have demanded a rent, if the jurors find for the plaintiff, an attaint lies by reason of the falsity.

No attaint lies if verdict passed upon a dilatory exception.

2. If the writ is suitable and good, the plaintiff must offer to prove the whole of his case by the jurors of the assise; and where the tenant consents, and straightway puts himself on the assise, if the jurors make a false verdict, it is a proper case for attaint; as if they find that the tenant disseised the plaintiff, where he did not disseise him at all. Sometimes also an attaint may be brought upon their verdict as to matters which touch the substance of the assise, as where they find that the tenant

Attaint lies of a false verdict by assise upon the whole case,

or upon a matter essential to the assise,

qe le tenaunt ad disseisi le pleintif de soen fraunc tenement, ou il [1]ne tint[1] unques for qe en villenage, et en cas semblables. Et ausi gist en le point de lour verdit qe touche acune excepcioun, tut ne touche il la accioun ne l'assise, ne [2] mie simplement neqedent [3]pronunciaunt, mes[3] oveke acune enchesoun, issi qe le pleintif fraunc tenement aver ne put, pur ceo qe il est vilein et en villenage le tient, et eynt mentuz pur ceo qe il est fraunc et fraunchement le tient, et ausi de le la reverse, si celi pleintif puis par xxiiii. se put prover fraunc, et qe les premers jurours eynt mentuz, issi gist la atteinte, pur ceo qe l'assise fust chargé del gros de la pleinte, et ne mie sur nule juree incidente.

Brac. 193, 290; Fle. 336, 337 (§ 12, 13).

3. Et si le pleintif par cas deniast simplement la excepcioun le tenaunt, et dit qe il fust fraunc et ceo fust prest de averrer par les jurours del assise, lequel qe la prove se feit[4] encountre le pleintif par les jurours ou par[5] sute de prove des parentz ou noun, en tiel cas ne gist point de atteynte, tut i eynt il fet faus verdit, pur ceo qe les parties de lour assent se mistrent [242.] en lour verdit, ausi cum en une juré a prover la excepcioun;

Brac. 192 b, 193, 198, 290; Fle. 238, 336, 337.

1—1. ne la tient *N.* ne le tint *S.* *sim. GM.* 2. ne est *N.* 3—3. *so verb. MCF.* pronunciaunt *L.* *sim GS.* Mes si il la pronuncient *N.* 4. *so GSF.* soit *L.* fet *N.* face *M.* feist *C.* 5. defaute de *add. M.*

hath disseised the plaintiff of his freehold, whereas he never held except in villenage, and in like cases. It lies also upon a point of their verdict concerning some exception, although not concerning the action or the assise, where the verdict does not pronounce simply, but adds a reason, as that the plaintiff could not have a freehold, because he is a villain, and holds the tenement in villenage, whereas this is false, because the man is free and holds freely,—and in the reverse case;—if this plaintiff can afterwards by four-and-twenty jurors prove himself to be free, and that the first jurors gave a false verdict, attaint lies, because the assise was charged with the substance of the plaint, and not with an incidental matter for a jury.

or upon a matter introduced as a reason for the verdict.

3. If the plaintiff had simply denied the exception of the tenant, and said that he was free, and was ready to verify the same by the jurors of the assise, in such case, whether the proof were made against the plaintiff by the jurors or by evidence of suit of kindred or not, although the jurors gave a false verdict, yet no attaint would lie, because the parties of their own consent put themselves upon their verdict, as upon a jury,

Attaint does not lie upon matter referred to the jury by consent.

et coment qe il eynt[1] dit pur le pleintif ou encountre ly, ja pur lour dit ne est soen estat amendé ne empiré ne chaungé en nul point. Et en tel cas touz jours apent al tenaunt la prove. Et si le pleintif respoigne al excepcioun de villenage et die qe il est fraunc, uncore apent al tenaunt de prover sa excepcioun, si le pleintif ne voille prover la negative; et si nule sute de ses parentz ne soit amené al excepcioun prover, a force ly covendra dounc prover par les jurours.

Ante, l. ii. c. 18. s. 8.
Brac. 193.
Post, s. 5.

4. Et tut[2] graunte le tenaunt tote la resoun le pleintif en tesaunt, uncore porra l'assise remeindre par acune excepcioun; sicum par mettre avaunt acun fet encountre le pleintif, sicum soen escrit de covenaunt, ou par acune condicioun ou par acun autre title. Et s'il tende cest escrit averrer pur le fet le pleintif, ou de soen auncestre qi heir il est, et ceo soit averré ou nient dedit, issi cheet l'assise [3]et la[3] accioun. [4]Et si le fet soit dedit, issi cheet l'assise et la accioun[4], et [5]comence un[5] novel play sour la prove del covenaunt; qe purra estre prové en plusours maneres; acune foiz par fet et par[6] testmoignes

Brac. 289 *b*; Fle. 337 (§ 12).
Ante, c. 4. s. 6.

1 *om. LND.* eit *SGMCW.* eyent *F.* 2. dounc *L.* *sim. GS.* si a dounc *ND.* tout *MW.* tot *CF.* 3—3. al *M.* e nient *C.* 4—4. *so verb. NMCF.* *om. LGS.* 5—5. *so MGC.* couent un *LS.* coment de *N.* 6. *so MC.* par *om. LNS.*

to prove the exception; and whether they find for or against the plaintiff, yet his condition is not rendered better or worse or in anywise altered by their verdict. In such cases the proof always lies upon the tenant; and if the plaintiff in answer to the exception of villenage says that he is free, still it lies on the tenant to prove his exception, unless the plaintiff chooses to prove the negative; and if no suit be brought of the kindred of the plaintiff to make good his exception, then of necessity it must be proved by the jurors.

If villenage is excepted, the burden of proof is upon the tenant.

4. Although the tenant should tacitly admit the declaration of the plaintiff, yet the assise may be stayed by some exception, as by setting up some deed against the plaintiff, such as his writing of covenant or some condition or other title. And if the tenant offers to aver this writing to be the deed of the plaintiff or of his ancestor whose heir he is, and this is either verified or not denied, the assise and the action fall. And if the deed is denied, in that way the assise and the action are brought at an end, and a new plea begins upon the proof of the covenant. This may be proved in several ways; sometimes by

Exception of deed of covenant.
Proof of covenant,

leinz nomez, et acune foiz par jurours del assise par defaute de chartre, et ceo serra en manere de juree, si les parties se
[242 *b*.] assentent, ou nule atteynte ne gist. Et si le pleintif ne se voille assenter, rien ne prenge par sa pleinte; et si le tenaunt ne le voille, si remeigne noun defendu.

Brac. 192, 192 *b*, 290; Fle. 236 (§ 4), 337 (§ 13).

5. Et mesme ceste resoun se tient en la excepcioun de villenage. Car en tiel cas covendra al tenaunt prover le villenage; et solom ceo qe la prove se fra pur le pleintif ou encountre, serra la accioun terminé. Par les parentz le pleintif ne[1] bosoigne neqedent mie de fere la prove del excepcioun, si [2]le tenaunt le die[2] estre soen vilein. Car cele prove poroit estre prejudiciele al seignur, si la prove [3]se feit[3] encountre ly, et issi nestrereit[4] forte excepcioun al pleintif en [5]play de[5] naifté, si james le[6] vousist le seignur chalenger pur soen vileyn. Mes si le seignur soit seur, qe la prove [7]se fra[7] encountre le vileyn, qe il fust soen astrer reseaunt en soen villenage, et il en seisine de ly et des ses chateus et de sa sute ausi cum de

1. E ne *ND*. 2—2. *so verb. SGM*. le [tenaunt de- *interlin.*] die *L*. le tenaunt dedie *N*. 3—3. *so ND*. se fait *LS*. seit *MCF*. se freit *G*. 4. *so M*. mettrast *L*. mettreit *NC*. *sim. S*. nestreit *G*. ne sereit *F*. 5—5. pleinte de *SG*. proue de la *M*. 6. *so SMCF*. le *om. LG*. 7—7. *so C*. ne fra mie *LS*. ne se fra mie *N*. ne se freit mye *G*. ne fra *M*. ne sera *F*.

by witnesses, by jury.

the deed and the witnesses therein named, and sometimes where there is no charter, by the jurors of assise, and this will be done in the form of a jury, if the parties consent, and then no attaint will lie; and if the plaintiff will not consent, let him take nothing by his plaint, and if the tenant refuses, let him be treated as without defence.

Exception of villenage need not be proved by suit of kin.

5. The same reason holds in the exception of villenage; for in such case the tenant must prove the villenage, and according as the proof turns out for or against the plaintiff the action will be determined. Yet when the tenant alleges that the plaintiff is his villain, it is not necessary to prove the exception by the kindred of the plaintiff; for such proof, if made against the lord, might be prejudicial to him and would afford the plaintiff a strong exception in a plea of Naifty, if ever the lord chose to claim him as his villain [y]. But if the lord is sure that the proof will be made against the villain, that he was his astrer [z], reseant in his villenage, and he in seisin of him, with his chattels and

But if the plaintiff is in the tenant's seisin, such a proof is proper,

y This agrees with Fleta, p. 337. It would appear from Bracton, that the objection to the proof by suit of kindred, where the alleged villain was not actually in his lord's seisin, was rather founded upon consideration for the villain than for the lord. (Brac. 290.)

z See before, p. 155, note.

soen villein de eynz le an[1], en tiel cas purra bien la prove passer par les parentz et par les jurours del assise, et issi serra terminé et le estat et la assise, si le pleintif se assente.

6. Mes s'il die qe il est fraunc et de fraunc estat, et demaunde agard [2]et jugement[2], s'il deive mettre soen estat en la assise avaunt plenere restitucioun de touz ses biens moebles et nient moebles, en tiel cas cesse la assise; et covendra al tenaunt overer par bref de Naifté, si le vileyn ly defuie et ne puse mes estre trové en le fee le seignur. Et si la excepcioun de villenage soit trié et prové par la assise par commun assent des parties, ja pur ceo ne soit tele proeve prejudiciele al estat le pleintif, ne nul atteinte ne gist. Car la excepcioun [3]ne sert[3] mie a proever le pleintif vileyn, eynz[4] a barrer ly qe il ne prenge rien par sa pleinte. Et issi piert qe en ces deus excepciouns de covenaunt et de villenage remeint la assise entiere, tut se chaunge ele par acune juree [5]en costé[5].

Brac. 191, 290; Fle. 337 (§ 13).

Hengham Parva, c. 8. p. 103.

[243.]

7. Et si l'assise soit prise en absence le tenaunt, ou tut

Brac. 290; Fle. 337.

1. e le Iour *add. C.* 2—2. *om. SGMCF.* 3—3. ne fet *LNSG.* na siert *M.* ne fiert *C.* ne affert *F.* 4. fet *add. MCF.* fait *add. G.* 5—5. en cost *L.* encoste *M.* de couste *ND.* par ceste assise e de couste *G.* *sim. S.* e coste *C.* de coste *IF.*

his suit, as of his villain within the year, in such case the proof may well pass by the kindred and by the jurors of the assise, and thus, if the plaintiff consents, both the status and the assise will be determined.

and determines the question of status.

6. But if the plaintiff says that he is free and of free condition, and demands award and judgment, whether he ought to put himself concerning his condition upon the assise, before full restitution of all his goods moveable and immoveable, in such case the assise shall cease, and the tenant will be forced to proceed by writ of Naifty, supposing that the villain is a run-away, and not to be found within the lord's fee. And if the exception of villenage be tried and proved by the assise by common consent of the parties, yet such proof shall not be prejudicial to the condition of the plaintiff, neither does any attaint lie. For the effect of the exception is not to prove the plaintiff a villain, but to bar him from taking anything by his plaint. And thus it appears that in these two exceptions of covenant and of villenage the assise remains entire, although it be altered by some collateral matter determined by jury.

Plaintiff, being fugitive, may refuse to try his status by assise before restitution of goods;

and if the exception be tried by jury, the question of status is not prejudiced.

7. Where the assise is taken in the absence of the tenant,

Where assise is taken upon the general issue, attaint lies.

soit il present et rien ne die neqedent par quei l'assise deive remeyndre a prendre, mes tauntost se mette, coment qe les jurours dient pur la une partie ou pur l'autre es [1] articles [2]del bref[2], mes qe il eint[3] dit faus, ou s'il eint dit qe il [4]i out[4] covenaunt, sicum avaunt est dit, ou point ne out, ou qe le pleintif soit le villein le tenaunt, cum il soit fraunc, ou qe il soit bastard, cum il soit muelleré, ou autre chose semblable,
Brac. 291 b; Fle. 338 (§ 20). en touz tels cas tient lu atteinte. Et pur ceo qe la vertue del bref[5] original deit estre contenue el bref de atteinte, piert et veirs est, qe atteynte ne tient mie lu proprement si noun sour les articles del bref original.

CHAPITRE XI. [XCIX.]

[243 b.]

De Excusaciouns.

Brac. 290; Fle. 337.

1. Si le tenaunt soit absent a la prise del assise, adounc purrount les jurours[6] plus largement errer[7], pur ceo qe il ne sount par nuly enfourmez[8] a dire pur le tenaunt; et s'il soint

1. so *SGF.* en *L.* as *N.* en les *MC.* 2—2. so *NG.* *sim. M.* des brefs *LCF.* *sim. S.* 3. ount *LN.* eient *GC.* *sim. MS.* 4—4. so *NMS.* out eu *L.* out *GC.* 5. so *NMGC.* *sim. S.* bref *om. L.* 6. so *NMGC.* le *add. LSF.* 7. so *GICF.* ouerer *LNMS.* 8. attournez *C.*

or if he is present and alleges no cause why the assise ought to be stayed, but forthwith puts himself thereupon, in such case, whether the jurors find for the one party or the other upon the points of the writ, supposing they find what is false, or if they say that there was a covenant, as aforesaid, where there was none, or that the plaintiff is the villain of the tenant, when he is free, or that he is a bastard, when he is legitimate, or other like thing,—in all these cases an attaint will lie. And whereas the substance of the original writ ought to be contained in the writ of attaint, it follows, and it is true, that an attaint does not properly lie except upon the points of the original writ.

CHAPTER XI.

Of the Excuses of Jurors in mitigation of Attaint.

Absence of party may excuse a mistake of the jurors.

1. Where the tenant is absent at the taking of the assise, the jurors are then more liable to err, inasmuch as they are not instructed by any one how to find for the tenant; and if

parjurs, provable errour les deit escuser en la atteinte, issint qe mitigacioun lour soit fete de la peyne en partie ou en tut, solom ceo qe le errour [1]avera esté gras ou megre[1], ou dreiturel ou coluré.

2. En la graunt assise ne tient james atteinte lu, pur ceo qe le tenaunt se met par sa eleccioun. Mes en petite assise ad sovent besoigne. Et sount plusours sermentz fetz, ou nule atteinte ne gist, sicum serment fet de un soul homme a autre; car illucs ne gist nule vengeaunce[2] for qe de Deu. Estre ceo ne gist nule atteinte sour le verdit des damages, [3]ne es[3] certificaciouns, ne en purgaciouns, ne en defences encountre sutes par ley, [4]ne en enquestes[4] generalment ne en jurez ne gist james atteinte, si noun par noster especial comaundement. Brac. 290 *b*; Fle. 337, 338; ante, l. ii. c. 11. s. 1.

3. En cas de jurours fet a prendre garde, a ceo qe la mitigacioun de la peyne de la atteinte [5]deive estre graunté[5] as jurours, si le errour soit apert ou privé. Car, si il soit privé[6], Brac. 290 *b*; Fle. 338 (§ 17, 18).

1—1. seit graunt ou petite *C.* 2. so *verb. SGMCF.* atteinte *L.* vengeaunce ne atteynte *N.* 3—3. mes *LNGS.* *om. M.* nen *C.* 4—4. so *NG.* ne en questes *LS.* ne enquestes *M.* *sim. C.* 5—5. so *MG.* de mettre garrauntie *LNDS.* 6. *conj.* apert *LNMICF.* *sim. SG.*

they should forswear themselves, a probable error ought to excuse them in the attaint, so that they may be spared the penalty either in part or entirely, according as the error has been gross or slight, rightful or colourable.

2. Attaint never lies in the great assise, because the tenant puts himself thereon by his own election. But in petty assises there is frequent occasion for it. Many oaths are taken upon which no attaint lies, as an oath taken by one man alone to another, for in that case vengeance belongeth only to God. Moreover no attaint lies upon the verdict concerning damages[z], nor in certifications, nor in purgations, nor in defences by wager of law against the suit produced by the plaintiff, nor generally in inquests or juries, except by our special command. No attaint lies of great assise, nor concerning damages, nor of certification, wager of law, or jury.

3. With respect to jurors, in order that the punishment upon attaint may be mitigated, it must be observed whether the error be patent or secret; for if it be secret, as it fre- Error by jury as to a secret contract, excusable.

z So Bracton and Fleta say that an error in damages is not a case for attaint, but for certification by the jurors. But in the Cornish Iter, 30 Edw. I., Berewick, Justice, being dissatisfied with the verdict of an assise upon the point of damages, warned the jury, that there might be an attaint as well for the damages as for the principal matter, and that immediately, without issuing a writ out of the Chancery. (Year Book, 30, 31 Edw. I. p. 124.) As to the immediate attaint, see before, c. 9. s. 6.

cum est de plusours contractz fetz privément[1] par entre parties, si qe nul ne seet[2] for qe deus ou treis, en tiel cas pur-
[244.] rount les jurours legerement estre desceuz pur lour ignoraunce del contract; et tel errour est escusable. Mes de chose fete apertement, ou tut le plus del pays le sevent[3], ne deit nul errour estre escusable.

Brac. 290 *b*; Fle. 338 (§18).

4. Et si les jurours countent tote la verité del fet sicum il avint, et solom le verdit soit rendu jugement, et si en le jugement soit trové errour, en tiel cas sount les Justices plus en la coupe pur lour fol jugement qe les jurours [4]pur nul[4] faus serment. Et pur ceo [5]fet bosoigne a la[5] Justice de fere bone[6] examinacioun en chescun verdit, par ount qe les doutes et les errours soint amenez[7] en clere verité. Et si difficulté chete en le jugement, [8]a plus sage[8] bosoigne de conseiller; car estre en acunes doutes de totes choses est plus [9]sure chose[9] a la Justice qe [10]estre trop sur a soen propre sen[10]; et conseut[11] sovent repentaunce hastif counseil, et plus sovent hastif jugement.

1. *so MI. sim. C.* priuez *L.* ou priuez *G. sim. S. om. N.* 2. soit *LN.* siet *M.* seit *GC.* set *S.* 3. siet *M.* 4—4. *so G.* pur lour *LN. sim. S.* par nul *MC.* 5—5. *so LS.* bosoygne la *N.* bosoingne ben a la *M. sim. C.* est busoigne a les *G.* 6. diligent *M.* diligence *C.* 7. meuz *MC.* 8—8. *so LN. sim. SG.* ad le plus sage *M.* ou plus sage *IC.* ad plus sages *F.* 9—9. seur *M.* sein *IC.* 10—10. sei trop affier en son propre sen *M. sim. I.* il ne pout estre plus seure en sen *G. sim. S.* 11. *so M.* conte *with eras. L.* contient *NA.* conceut *C.* content *GSI.*

quently happens in contracts made secretly between the parties where two or three only are privy to it, in such case the jurors, from their ignorance of the contract, may be easily mistaken, and such error is excusable. But of a thing done openly, so that the greatest part of the country knows it, an error is not excusable.

Where a wrong judgment is given upon a verdict at large, the Judge is to blame.

4. Where the jurors relate the whole truth of the fact just as it happened, and judgment is given according to the verdict, if error be found in the judgment, the Justices are in fault for the folly of their judgment rather than the jurors for any false oath. Therefore the Justice must needs make diligent examina-

Duty of the Judge.

tion into every verdict, whereby matters which are doubtful or erroneous may be reduced to certainty and truth. And if any difficulty arises in giving judgment, it is needful to advise with one more learned. For it is safer for a Justice to be in some doubt as to all matters than to be too confident in his own opinion; and repentance often follows upon rash counsel, and still oftener upon rash judgment.

CHAPITRE XII. [c.]

De Proces de Jugement.

1. Purchacé dounc le bref de atteinte, et la partie somounse, bien porra il estre essoignié al jour. Et cum les parties al autre jour soint presentz en court, et les atteignours nient, soit doné autre jour as parties, et les atteignours soint mis par gage et plege, qe il soint a mesme le jour. Et si la partie somounse face defaute, soit attaché de estre a un autre jour. Et si le pleintif face defaute, et la partie attachee ou somounse se profre, si chiet le bref, et les jurours s'en voisent sauntz jour, et le pleintif et les pleges de sure en la merci remeignent. Brac. 291 *b*; Fle. 338 (§ 21). [244 *b*.]

2. Et cum les parties et les jurours et les atteignours soint presentz en court, et la partie somounse ou attaché ne die nule excepcioun pur quei la atteinte ne deive passer, adounc a primes soit oy le record del assise, saver moun coment ele passa. Et puis soit enquis del pleintif en queus pointz les jurours del assise sount parjurs, ou en les articles del bref, ou Brac. 291 *b* (§ 7); Fle. 339 (§ 22).

CHAPTER XII.

Of the Trial and Judgment in Attaint.

1. The writ of attaint being obtained, and the party summoned, he has a right to be essoined at the day. And when the parties on the second day are present in court, but the attainors are not, let another day be given to the parties, and the attainors be required to find security and pledges to appear at the same day. And if the party summoned makes default, let him be attached to be there some other day. And if the plaintiff makes default, and the party attached or summoned offers himself, the writ falls, and the jurors shall go without day, and the plaintiff and his pledges to prosecute remain in mercy. Process in attaint. Essoin. Process in Default, of attainors, of defendant, of plaintiff.

2. When the parties, the jurors, and the attainors are present in court, and the party summoned or attached alleges no exception why the attaint ought not to pass, then in the first place let the record of the assise be heard, to wit, how it passed. Next, let the plaintiff be asked in what points the jurors of the assise are perjured, whether in the articles of the Proceedings on trial of attaint.

en acune excepcioun, ou nule excepcioun fust mise avaunt par le tenaunt, mes soulement par les jurours del assise en
Ante, c. 10. s. 1, 2. lour verdit, la ou il ne furent chargez for qe [1]a dire[1] le gros del assise. Et sur ceo soint les atteignours chargez par lour serment a dire verité; et ne soint mie chargez par serment de assise, mes par serment de juree. Et apres lour serment tauntost lour soit moustré la fourme de la querele, sur[2] quels pointz il deivent dire verité, [3]et ceo est a saver, si[3] celi, qi se pleint, a tort eit esté disseisi ou noun. Et ausi lour soit dit la resoun le pleintif.

Brac. 292; Fle. 339 (§ 23, 24). [245.] 3. Et cum il soint retournez et deivent lour verdit pronuncier, si sount lour resouns a examiner estreitement, si qe[4] aperte verité ou au meyns presumpcioun overe pur eus, et qe par provables resouns proevent lour verdit; et solom ceo se face jugement. Car il purrount acune foiz legerement estre desceuz par acun provable errour, ausi bien cum les premers jurours, et issi porroit[5] par defaute de bon examinement des Justices [6]estre doné un faus[6] jugement.

1—1. sur *MCF*. 2. [en] cel cas sour *N*. e sur *SGMF*. 3—3. le quel ceo est a sauer *M*. le quel cest a sauer *CF*. 4. *so MC*. par *add. LNS*. par *interl. G*. 5. *so MG*. *sim. S*. purrount *LNC*. 6—6. sure fol *M*. sur fol *C*.

writ, or upon some exception, such exception not having been put forward by the tenant, but only by the jurors of the assise in their verdict, when they were charged to find upon the whole

Oath of attainors. matter of the assise. Thereupon let the attainors be charged by their oath to speak the truth; and the oath whereby they shall be charged shall not be the oath of assise, but the oath of jury. And after they are sworn, let the form of the plaint be forthwith shown to them, and upon what points they are to speak the truth; as for instance, whether he who complains has been wrongfully disseised or not. And let them be informed of the plaintiff's case.

Reasons of verdict to be examined. 3. When the jurors are returned, and are ready to give in their verdict, their reasons ought to be strictly examined, so that manifest truth or presumption at least may be on their side, and their verdict grounded on probable reasons; and according thereto let judgment be given. For sometimes they may be as easily deceived by some probable error as the first jurors, and thus for want of good examination by the Justices a false judgment may be given.

4. Et si les atteignours ne se purrount acorder de un assent, soint afforceez par autres. Et si il dient, qe il ne sevent riens, ou qe[1] il soint en doute, issi qe il ne sevent dire nule plenere verité, si remeigne [2]la seisine[2] en soen lu. Et s'il soint de un acord et dient encountre le pleintif, en mesme la manere cum les jurours del assise, si remaigne [3]la seisine[3] en soen lu, et serra agardé qe les xii. firent leal serment, et qe le pleintif soit mis en la gaole, et illucs puni par prisoun et par fin. Brac. 292; Fle. 339 (§ 24).

5. Et si le derreyn verdit soit contrarie al premer, issint remeindrent les premers jurours atteintz de faus serment; et serra agardé qe le pleintif recovere sa seisine, et le tenaunt soit en la merci, et les primers jurours s'il soint presentz perdent fraunche ley [4]a remenaunt[4], issint qe mes ne soint cruz par nul serment, et qe lour terres et lour chateus soint pris en nostre meyn, et qe il soint enveez a la gaole et de[5] illucs reyntz. Et s'il soint absentz, adounc soint comaundez [245 *b*.] a prendre. Acune foiz sount neqedent acuns jurours escusables, quant a la perte de fraunche ley, tut ne seint il quant Brac. 292 *b*; Fle. 339, 340.

1. si *MC*. 2—2. *so LSAIC*. lassise *G*. *sim. M*. 3—3. *so LSGMA*. lassise *NIC*. 4—4. *so MC*. et remeignent *LN*. *sim. SG*. 5. de *om. M*.

4. If the attainors cannot agree in one opinion, let them be afforced by others. And if they say that they know nothing of the fact, or that they are in doubt, so that they cannot fully declare the truth, let the possession remain undisturbed. So, if they are agreed, and find against the plaintiff in the same way as the jurors of the assise, the possession shall remain as before, and it shall be adjudged that the twelve made a lawful verdict, and that the plaintiff be committed to gaol, and there punished by imprisonment and fine. Afforcement of jury. If no verdict be given, the assise stands; if against the plaintiff, the assise stands, and the plaintiff is committed.

5. If the last verdict is contrary to the first, it follows that the first jurors will be attainted of a false oath; and it shall be awarded that the plaintiff recover his seisin, and the tenant be in mercy, and that the first jurors, if they are present, do for ever after lose their free law, so that thenceforth they shall not be credited upon any oath, and that their lands and chattels be taken into our hand, and they be sent to gaol, and there put to ransom. And if they are absent, it shall be commanded that they be taken. Some jurors however may be sometimes excused with regard to the loss of their free law, Judgment on attaint. Plaintiff recovers seisin. Jurors lose their law, and are put to ransom. Loss of law excused, if jurors have confessed before plaint.

a la raunceoun, nomément, ceux qe par tendresce de lour conscience de lour gré avaunt la moustraunce de acune pleinte reconisent qe il ount fet faus serment par enchesoun de acun provable errour, et prient qe il se pusent amender; et en tiel cas ne covendra mie passer la atteinte par bref, si trestouz les jurours prient de lour verdit amender, einz fet apeler les parties al[1] jugement reverser. Les jurours neqedent sount punisables soulement par simples fins. Et si trestouz ne se repentent, au meyns vaille as repentauntz lour bounté.

Brac. 293; Fle. 340 (§27). 6. Et acune foiz est atteinte barré qe ele ne put passer; et ceo est en plusours maneres; sicum en cas ou jugement ne fut unques rendu en le proces del assise, si les Justices soint divers; ou[2] tut fut il rendu unqe neqedent ne fut fete execucioun; ou tut en fut fete execucioun en partie, partie[3] Fle. 340 (§25). neqedent remeint uncore a fere. Et ausi remeynt ele sovent par acord des parties; et en tiel cas soit fete la seisine par jugement solom le record des Justices. Et ausi deit ele re-

1. e le *MGC.* 2. so *M.* et *L.* sim. *NCS.* 3. so *MC.* partie *om. LNSGC.*

although they be not as to the ransom, namely, those who through tenderness of conscience before the exhibition of any plaint confess they took a false oath by reason of some probable error, and pray that they may amend; and in such case, if all the jurors pray to amend their verdict, the attaint need not pass by writ, but the parties should be called to reverse the judgment[a]. The jurors however are punishable by simple fines only; and if all the jurors do not repent, yet those who do so shall have the benefit of their goodness.

Exceptions to attaint; 6. An attaint may be barred from passing in several ways, as where judgment was never given upon the proceedings in Judgment of assise not executed; the assise, the Justices being divided; or although it was given, yet it was never put in execution; or although it was partly put in execution, part of it still remains to be performed. Accord; It is likewise often stayed by agreement of the parties, and in that case let seisin be executed by judgment Error in procedure. according to the record of the Justices. It ought also to be

a '*Casus.* A parson brings assise of *Utrum* against a lay tenant. The twelve jurors, against their conscience or by a misguided conscience, (ou de conscience blesmie,) say that the land is frank-almoigne belonging to the church. The parson takes possession. Then the jurors, except two who are dead, come before Justices, and acknowledge of their own accord that they made false oath. *Quid juris?*' (Note in MS. *N.*)

meindre en cas ou la coupe est en la Justice; et ceo porra estre ou pur fol jugement ou pur errour del enroullement, ou pur ceo qe la Justice ne voleit allower a la partie ses resounables excepciouns ou ses resounables chalenges des jurours; et en tiel cas fet le proces a repeler deqe en cel estat mesmes cum il fut [1]en tens[1] qe il mist[2] avaunt cele excepcioun. Et ausi deit atteinte remeindre en cas ou le pleintif est tenaunt del tenement q'il perdi, ou de partie del tenement, par sa intrusioun ou par redisseisine, pur ceo qe il deservi[3] de recoverer par jugement chose qe il ad conquis par sa propre force en despescaunt[4] la ley.

Fle. 340 (§ 26). [246.] Brac. 293; Fle. 340 (§ 27, 28).

7. Et sicum assise ne fet mie a prendre sour assise, ausi ne fet atteinte prendre sur atteinte, nomément par entre unes[5] mesmes persones et de un fet et de une chose. Deus atteintes neqedent[6] purrount sure une assise, sicum en cas ou les jurours del assise duissent tut aver doné ou tut tolet, ou il ne donerent ou[7] ne tolirent for qe partie; et en teus cas pur-

Brac. 295 *b*; Fle. 340 (§ 29).

1—1. einz ceo *MF*. 2. *so NGMCF*. vient [mist *interlin.*] *L*. 3. *so LS*. [ne] deserui [mie] *N*. ne deserui mie *D*. defuist *G*. ne deit *M*. defui *IC*. desmeri *F*. 4. despisant *MG*. *sim. ICF*. *sim. on eras. N*. 5. *so NDF*. vne *LMCW*. 6. *so MF*. ne *add. L*. si *on eras. add. N*. 7. ou *om. L*. ne [ne] *N*. ou il *MCF*.

stayed where the fault is in the Justice, which may be owing either to a foolish judgment or to error in the enrolment, or because the Justice would not allow the party his reasonable exceptions or his reasonable challenges of the jurors; and in such cases the proceedings are to be restored to the state they were in at the time of the exception being put forward. An attaint ought likewise to be stayed where the plaintiff is tenant of the tenement which he lost, or of part of it, by his own intrusion, or by redisseisin, because he has lost his right to recover by judgment a thing which has obtained by his own force in despite of the law.

Forcible entry by plaintiff.

7. As an assise is not to be taken upon an assise, so neither is an attaint to be taken upon an attaint, that is, between the same persons, of the same fact, and of the same thing. Yet two attaints may follow one assise, as where the jurors ought to have given or taken away the whole, when they gave or took away part only[b]; not however by different attainors, but

Attaint upon attaint not allowed. But there may be two attaints upon one assise.

[b] In this case each party might complain of the verdict, and therefore there might be two attaints. See Bracton, f. 295 *b*.

rount passer deus atteintes, [1]ne mie neqedent par divers atteignours[1] [2]mes par [3]uns mesmes[3] jurours pur eschure le peril qe en porreit avenir si contrarieté avenist par cas entre divers atteignours. Et[2] tut soit atteinte acune foiz passé, uncore purrount les atteignours[4] estre eydez par certificaciouns, en mesme la manere et pur autel cas cum en verdit de assise.

1—1. *so N. sim. SGMCF. om. L.* 2—2. *so verb. F. sim. SGMC. sim. in marg. N. om. L.* 3—3. mesmes les *in marg. N.* une mesme *MGC. sim. S.* vns meymes *F.* 4. atteins *F.* Iurors *G.*

by the same jurors, to avoid the peril which might ensue if there should happen to be a contrariety between the different attainors. And although an attaint should have once passed, yet the attainors may be aided by certifications in the same manner and in the like cases as in verdicts of assises.

BRITTON.

LIVRE V.

[1]CHAPITRE I.[1] [CI.]

De Dowaries. [246 *b.*]

I.

MATRIMOIGNE ne est autre chose qe assemblé de femme a homme a lour deus assentz par joyngture de saincte eglise, pur demorer ensemble, ausi cum une char, a totes lour vies sauntz espeir de departir. Pur ceo dounc il bosoygne as femmes esposez de estre dowez pur doner meillour talent a femmes de amer matrimoigne, tut soit dowarie prejudiciele as seignurs des feez, ceo est a Brac. 92; Fle. 340.

1—1. Incipit liber v. de Iure dotium. Cap. I. *N.* *sim.* *D.* *No division of books occurs at this point in LSGM.*

BOOK V.

OF PLEAS OF DOWER, AND ENTRY.

CHAPTER I.

Of the Nature of Dower.

I.

MATRIMONY is no other thing than the union of a woman with a man with the consent of both by junction of Holy Church, to live together as one flesh all their lives without expectation of separation. Therefore it is expedient that married women should be endowed, in order to give women the better disposition to love matrimony, although dower is prejudicial to the lords of fees, that is to say, such dowers as are incident to

Matrimony.

Dower, prejudicial to lord.

dire de dowaries qe sount accessories a matrimoigne. Dowarie est ceo qe fraunc homme doune a sa espouse al us del mouster pur la charge de matrimoigne et pur le mariage aver, a la susteinaunce de la femme et la nurture des enfauntz a[1] engendrer, si la femme sourvive le baroun.

Brac. 92 (§ 4); Fle. 340 (§ 4). 2. Dowarie ne est mie assigné en touz lus, ne en totes houres, mes as certeins, sicum en[2] le comencement [3]del contract, et soulement[3] al us del mouster en solempneté des testmoignes, et ne mie en muscettes. Car sicum[4] privéz[5] esposailes fetes en muscettes sount prejudicieles [6]en successioun quant as heirs, ausi sount eles prejudicieles[6] as femmes quant a lour dowarie recoverer. Nature dounc de dowarie est, qe par la ou esposaile est solempnement fete al mouster en presence del poeple, en tiel cas tient lu dowarie demaunder, et [247.] ne mie autrement. Et si le matrimoigne se deface en acune

1. *so SGM.* et a *L.* [engendrez] e a *N.* 2. entour *G. sim. S.* 3—3. *so verb. SGHF. interl. N. sim. C. om. L.* 4. especials fetz e priuez feffementz fet en muscettes sunt preiudicieles quant a la succession as heirs auxi *add. in marg. N.* 5. *so MGCF.* primes *LNS.* 6—6. *so M. sim. SGC. om. LN. ins. in marg. F.*

Dower, what. matrimony. Dower is that which a freeman gives to his wife at the church door in regard of the charge of matrimony, and by way of consideration for the marriage, for support of the wife and nurture of the children to be begotten, if the wife shall survive the husband.

Dower to be appointed at marriage and at the church door. 2. Dower is not assigned in all places nor at all times, but at certain, to wit, at the commencement of the contract and at the door of the church only, with the solemnity of witnesses, and not in private. For as secret marriages, performed in private, are prejudicial to heirs with reference to the succession, so are they prejudicial to wives with respect to the recovery of their dowers. The nature of dower then is such, that where espousals are solemnized at the church in the presence of the people, in such case and not otherwise dower may be demanded[a]. And if the marriage be in any way dissolved

a 'Every contract of marriage, at which there is present a parish priest (prestre parochiel) and his clerk, is at the church door, and sufficiently solemn; for it is *in facie ecclesiæ*. And because usage of dower is become law, a wife is sufficiently endowed though her husband say nothing. But suppose that the husband protests distinctly and solemnly at the time of the marriage, that he does not intend that his wife shall be in any way endowed after his decease, and this is a known and notorious fact; *quæstio*, whether she ought to recover dower or not. *Responsio.* It seems not, for if the husband had established her dower in certain, however much less than might have been proper (qe ne affierreit), and she had agreed thereto, she would be barred; so in the other case, when she agreed to the marriage without having dower, she cannot have her action for dower.

manere par jugement en lour vies, mes ne porra la femme aver accioun a recoverer dowarie, si noun par especiale clause graunté par le baroun en premer contract, qe si devorce avigne, qe ele avera acun certein a terme de sa vie ou autrement; et[1] cele especialté fete pur dowarie hors de general assignment de dowarie, la[2] dorra accioun.

Glan. li. 6. c. 17; Brac. 92 (§ 4); Fle. 340 (§ 4).

3. [3]Dowaries se fount[3] acune foiz[4] par le piere ou le ael ou autre parent ou amy la femme, de certeine terre [5]ou tenement ou de partie de lour chateus. Et acune foiz est terre[5] ou tenement ou chatel doné par la feme ou par acun [6]de ses[6] parentz ou de ses amis pur le mariage. Et acune foiz est[7] la resounable dowarie encru par acun encrees de acun parent[8]; et ceo purra avener ausi bien apres les esposailes duraunt le

Brac. 92, 92b; Fle. 341 (§ 4, 5, 6).

1. a *LMGSCF.* e *on eras. N.* 2. qe *GS.* 3—3. des dowaries se sount *L. sim. S.* des dowar'. Si sount *N.* de soun dowar'. Si sount *D.* doweire qe funt *M.* des doweires qe fount *G.* Dowaires se sount *I.* Doweirs se fount *C.* Dowaries ke sunt *F.* 4. donez *add. I.* femmes dowees *interl. N.* 5—5. *so verb. DGS. sim. MCF. sim. in marg. N. om. L.* 6—6. *so MCF.* des *LNGS.* 7. *so NMG. sim. F.* est *om. LS.* 8. part *MF.* partie *C.*

by judgment in their lifetime, the wife has no right of action for recovery of dower, unless there was a special clause granted by the husband in the first contract, that if a divorce should happen, she should have a certain provision for the term of her life or otherwise; and such specialty made for dower beyond the general assignment of dower, shall entitle her to an action.

Dower defeated by divorce, unless there be a special contract.

3. Dowers are sometimes given by the father, grandfather, or other kinsman or friend of the wife, of certain land or tenement, or of part of their chattels. And sometimes land, tenement, or chattel is given by the wife or some of her kindred or friends for the marriage. Reasonable dower is sometimes increased by an addition from some kinsman, which may happen as well after the espousals during the marriage, as

Dowry of wife.

Frank-marriage.

Absolute gift to wife.

Contra. Dower is accessory to marriage, and, the principal established, the accessories are also established. (*Verum est*, if it had not been contradicted by the husband.) Further, dower was ordained by common constitution of people; and cannot be undone by any single person. For if by one, then by another, and so the constitution would be destroyed; *quod non est permissum, ne pereat lex approbata.*' (Note in MS. *N.*) The reasons here stated against permitting the common rights of the wife to be taken away by private agreement so far prevailed, that before the time of Littleton it became an established rule, that the wife might, if she pleased, after the death of her husband refuse the dower established *ad ostium ecclesiæ*, and fall back upon her common law right. (Vet. Nat. Brev. 6. *b.*; Litt. Ten. s. 41.) The restriction of dower *ad ostium ecclesiæ* to a third, had also at that time been abolished. (Litt. Ten. s. 39; Co. Litt. 34*b.*; Fitzherbert, Nat. Brev. 150 P.) The Statute 27 Hen. VIII. c. 10, by which a jointure might be made in bar of dower, was a restoration of the old law in another form.

matrimoigne cum en les esposailes mesmes. Et cel encrees ne cheet point en divisioun ne en partie, lequel qe le doun soit fet a la femme soulement ou al baroun et a sa femme joynctement, par quei le doun soit[1] simple et peur et nient par enchesoun del mariage.

Mag. Chart. c. 7; Glan. li. 6. cc. 1, 2; Brac. 92 *b*, 93; [247 *b*.] Fle. 341 (§ 11); Hengh. Parv. c. 3. pp. 85, 87.

4. Renable dowarie del fee de chevaler et de graunt serjauntie est la terce partie de totes les terres, ensement feez et services, qe le baroun tint en soen demeyne cum de fee le jour qe il la esposa et [2]dount puis[2] il la pout dower. De[3] socages, [4]fraunches fermes[4], petites serjaunties et de autres feez soint les dowaries fetes solom le usage. Et a plus haut ne se estent mie renable dowarie; mes de meyns porra la femme estre dowé si de taunt se tiegne apayé. Et si exces i soit, sicum avient acune foiz par trop large liveré des gardeyns, taunt cum les heirs soint de eynz age, tel exces porra estre repelé par bref de amesurement de dowarie.

1. est *M.* 2—2. so *LSA.* puis dont *M.* *sim.* *GFK.* dount *IC.* donk' *Y.* 3. e des franchises *G.* 4—4. fraunchises seruices *LNMSA.* e seruices *G.* fraunchises demeines *C.* franche demeynes *K.* franches demeynes *F.* *sim.* *I.* franche seruices *Y.* fraunche fermes *print.*

at the time of the espousals; and this increase, whether the gift be made solely to the wife or to the husband and wife jointly, does not fall into division or partition, provided the gift be simple and absolute, and not in consideration of the marriage[b].

Reasonable dower, third of husband's land at time of marriage.

4. Reasonable dower in knights' fees and grand serjeanties is the third part of all the lands, together with the fees and services, which the husband held in his demesne as of fee on the day of his marriage, and whereof he could afterwards endow his wife[c]. In socages, free farms, petty serjeanties, and other fees, let dowers be granted according to custom. Reasonable dower does not extend beyond this, but the wife may be endowed of less, if she is contented to be so. And if there should be any excess, as sometimes happens from too large an assignment by guardians, while the heirs are under age, such excess may be revoked by writ of admeasurement of dower.

Socage regulated by custom.

Dower may be of less than third.

Excess recovered by admeasurement.

[b] This must be understood by reference to book iii. chap. 8. sect. 8, where it is said that a coheiress claiming her part of the inheritance is bound to bring her estate in marriage into hotchpot. Compare Bracton f. 92, 92 *b*.

[c] The right of the wife to be endowed of land acquired after the marriage is somewhat ambiguously stated. Compare below, chap. 2. s. 4; Hengham Parva, cap. 3. p. 87. This right, which did not exist in the time of Glanvill, and is not admitted by Bracton or Fleta, was held to have been given by Magna Charta, cap. 7. See the Year Book, Mich., 5 Edw. II. p. 133.

5. Et ne mie soulement sount femmes dowables des terres et des tenementz dount lour barouns eint esté seisiz en lour demeyne cum de fee, eynz purrount estre dowez des acunes terres qe deivent reverter al heir le baroun par la mort de acun tenaunt qi ne tient for qe a terme de vie. En tiel cas la femme attendera la mort de teus tenauntz, si en le premer contract ne soit autrement aconvenu, qe acun tenement luy soit assigné especiaument a tener en tenaunce deqe autaunt qe cele terre, issi apres autri mort assigné, chiete[1]. Brac. 93; Fle. 342 (§13); Hengh. Parv. c. 3. p. 87.

6. Et tut soit qe dowarrie puisse al comencement estre assigné ausi bien de maners entiers cum de la tierce partie de touz les maners, le maner neqedent qe est chief de la baronie, ou del counté, remeyndra entierment al heir, si ele puisse aylours aver sa dowarie. Si plusours neqedent soint [248.] chiefs maners de plusours baronies ou countéz, et la femme ne puisse par ailours pleynement estre dowé, en tiel cas covendra qe ele en soit dowé par la necessité, qe veynt ley et usage. Mag. Chart. c. 7; Brac. 93; Fle. 342, s. 14.

1. eschete *MGCF.* *sim. S.*

5. Wives are not only dowable of the lands and tenements whereof their husbands were seised in their demesne as of fee, but they may be endowed also of any lands which are to revert to the heir of the husband upon the death of a tenant holding only for term of life[d]. And in that case the widow shall wait until the death of such tenants, unless it was otherwise agreed in the first contract, that some tenement should be specially assigned to her to hold in tenancy until the land so assigned to her after the other's death should fall in. Dower may be assigned of reversions.

6. Although dower may in the first instance be assigned as well of entire manors as of the third part of all the manors, yet that manor which is the head of the barony or county shall remain entire to the heir, if the widow can elsewhere have her dower. But if there are several capital manors of several baronies or counties, and the widow cannot elsewhere be fully endowed, in such case she must be endowed thereof by necessity, which overcomes law and usage. Heads of baronies and counties not generally assigned in dower. *Necessitas vincit legem.*

d This should be understood of an express establishment of dower, not of dower by common right. Compare the parallel passage in Bracton f. 93. '*Case.* A. has four carucates of land, and aliens one carucate to D. for his life. A. afterwards takes wife, and dies. His heir B. enters, and assigns one carucate to the wife in dower. D. the termor dies. *Quæstio.* Shall the wife have the third of this land? She shall not, for the husband had nothing of the demesne the day he married or ever after.' (Note in MS. *N.*)

CHAPITRE II. [CII.]

[1]*De Establisement de Dowarie*[1].

Brac. 92 (§ 11).

1. Dowarie proprement par les barouns as femmes est establi, et par les heirs est assigné solom le establisement le auncestre. Et purra issi estre establi del comencement, qe le baroun purra assigner a sa femme acun certein pur sa dowarie, si ele se paye, issint neqedent si cel certein suffise pur renable dowarie, [2]entierment dounc remaigne[2], et si rien le [3]defaille, si le[4] soit parfet, et si il eit surplusage[5], si soit rendu al heir. Et sicum les femmes purrount estre dowez de certeyns tenementz, ausi purrount eles estre dowez en certeine soumme de deners, ou de darrez, mes qe[6] eles se tienent apaez; et[7] si les femmes neqedent sourvivent lour barouns, si ne purrount eles mie plus demaunder pur lour dowaries[8] for qe solom la premere constitucioun; et si[9] les

(Margin: Brac. 93 *b*; Fle. 342 (§ 7). — Brac. 94; Fle. 342 (§ 16).)

1—1. *so verb. NMGSCF. om. L.* 2—2. a ly ensement dunc qe le remaine *M. om. C.* ensemement dounc le remeyne *F.* 3. la *N.* ly en *M. sim. GS.* la *C.* 4. ly *NM.* 5. *so M. so on eras. N. so corr. G.* simple vsage *LSCF.* 6. *so MC. sim. on eras. N.* si *LF.* si qe *GS.* 7. et *om. LNSG.* e *M.* 8. doweires de teles doweires *M. sim. F.* 9. *so NMSGCF.* si *om. L.*

CHAPTER II.

Of the Establishment of Dower.

Establishment and assignment of dower distinguished.

1. Dower, properly speaking, is established by husbands on their wives, and is assigned by the heirs in pursuance of the establishment of the ancestor. And it may be so established from the beginning, that the husband may assign to his wife some certain thing for her dower, if she is satisfied therewith, yet so that if such certain thing be sufficient for her reasonable dower, it shall remain entire; if there be any deficiency, it shall be made up to her; and if there be any excess, it shall be restored to the heir. And as wives may be endowed of certain tenements, so they may also be endowed in a certain sum of money or goods, so as they be contented therewith; and if such wives survive their husbands, they cannot demand for their dower more than according to the first appointment.

(Margin: Conditional establishment. — Dower of money or chattels.)

chateus as mortz ne suffisent, adounc soit lour recoverer del sourplus.

Brac. 94; Fle. 342 (§17). [248 *b*.]

2. Et ne mie soulement purra dowarie estre establie de un baroun a une soule femme, mes a plusours femmes, ausi bien cum a une, lequel qe totes soint en pleine vie, ou a chescune apres autri mort, ou apres le divorce entre eus celebré. Car acune foiz ad esté qe un homme par sa mauvesté ad esposé plusours femmes, qe totes furent a une foiz en pleine vie. Saincte eglise neqedent dit qe de teles femmes qe nule ne est sa femme a dreit for qe la premere, par quei [1]ley ne tient[1] les autres femmes for qe essomauntes[2] et concubines; et pur ceo sount eles forcloses de accioun de lour dowarie. [3]Acune foiz neqedent enporte cele dowarie qe drein est trové seisie del baroun[3]. Acune foiz [4]nule ne avera[4] dowarie, sicum apres

Brac. 94; Fle. 342 (§17).

1—1. *so M.* il ne tienent nient *L. sim. N.* ele ne teint *C.* il ne tient *GF.* il ne tenent *S.* 2. *so LGM.* essoinauntes *ND.* essoynantes *S.* assoignauntes *I.* assoinances *A.* 3—3. *so verb. M. om. LNSGA.* E pur ceo qe cel auera doweir qe drein est trove seisi de baroun *C.* E por ceo ke tele dowarie ke drein est troue seysi del baroun *F.* Ascune fetz nequedent teles femmes recouerent doware qe dereyn est seisi del Baroun *T.* 4—4. *so verb. GS.* nule manere de *L.* de nule manere de [nauera *corr.*] *N.* nule ne ad *M.* nen ad *C.*

And if the chattels of the deceased are not sufficient, their recovery shall be for the difference[d].

Of several wives, one only can claim dower.

2. It may happen that dower is established by a husband not on one wife only, but on several, whether they be all living, or on one after the death of another, or after a divorce pronounced between husband and wife. For it has sometimes been, that a man from wickedness has married several women, all living at the same time; but Holy Church says that of such women none but the first is his lawful wife; wherefore the law regards the others only as false wives or concubines; and therefore they are excluded from any action of dower. Sometimes however she takes the dower who was found last seised of the husband; and sometimes none of them have dower, as will be mentioned afterwards[e]. So, on the other hand, one

Validity of marriage determined by Holy Church.

[d] The expression here is obscure. Bracton says in effect, that when a burgess, or other, endows his wife with a sum of money, whether he has lands or not, she can ask no more out of his tenements or chattels, but may insist on having the full amount named, quamdiu ibi fuerit unicus obolus, so far as the chattels of the husband will extend. And Fleta says, more distinctly, that such dowers cannot be demanded except so far as the chattels of the deceased suffice to pay them. See the passages cited in the margin above.

[e] It appears from Bracton that the last possession prevailed where there was no proof of the legality of another marriage. But where no wife was in possession, and no sufficient evidence which claimant was the lawful wife, no dower was assigned. Bracton, f. 94.

serra dit. Et ausi de autre part purra une femme estre esposé a plusours hommes[1] vivauntz eus touz. Pur ceo neqedent ne avera mie dowarie de trestouz, tut ly soit [2]establie par chescun baroun. Car a un soul est ele femme, et as autres essomaunte[3] et concubine.

Brac. 94, 94*b*; Fle. 342 (§18). 3. Et si [4]dowarie desceivablement[4] soit establie de trestouz les tenementz qe le baroun purchacera, [5]pur ceo qe bien porra estre qe le baroun james terre ne purchacera[5], et la femme ne deit mie estre sauntz dowarie, si[6] le baroun out terre en demeyne et en fee, en tiel cas est tele[7] constitucioun [8]renable de[8] dowarie solom la nature des feez et le usage del lu. [9]Car as desceuz eyde dreiture et ne mie as desceivauntz[9].

4. [10]Ne de nul tenement[10] ne purra dowarie estre establie
[249.] si noun del tenement qe le baroun tint le jour qe il esposa sa femme ou avera tenu puis en fee a ly et a ses heirs, lequel[11] les heirs soint compris al[12] purchaz en generalté ou en espe-

1. barons *M.* *sim.* *CF.* 2. doweire *add.* *GM.* *sim.* *SF.* *sim. interl.* *N.* doweyr a cel *add.* *O.* 3. *so* *SGM.* essoniaunte *LD.* 4—4. de dowarie de tenement *L.* doware de tenement *ND.* *sim.* *GS.* doweire deceiuablement *M.* le doweyr le *C.* dowarie desceiuaument *F.* 5—5. *so* *D.* *sim.* *MSGHCWF.* *sim. in marg.* *N.* *om.* *LNR.* 6. *so* *MCF.* et si *L.* *sim.* *NDSG.* 7. *so* *MSGF.* cele *LMD.* cel *C.* 8—8. de *om.* *MSG.* renable et renable *IC.* renable a renable *F.* receyuable *W.* 9—9. *so verb.* *G.* *om.* *LNDSRW.* Car a de teus e de dreiz e ne mie as desceiuance *M.* Car a ceus *C.* Car ad desceus eyde dreit e ne mye as desceyuans *F.* 10—10. *om.* *C.* 11. qe *add.* *NGMC.* 12. en le *GM.* el *I.* au *C.*

Woman married to several men can have dower only of one. woman may be married to several husbands all living at the same time; yet although dower may have been established on her by each husband, she shall not have dower of them all. For she is the wife of one only, and concubine to the others.

Dower of tenements 'to be purchased,' more largely assigned. 3. If dower be deceivably established of all the tenements which the husband shall purchase, yet whereas it may happen that he may never purchase any land, and the widow ought not to be without dower, if the husband had lands in demesne and in fee, such an appointment is treated as an appointment of reasonable dower according to the nature of the fees and the custom of the place. For the law assists the deceived rather than the deceivers.

Dower of tenements held by husband in fee; 4. Dower can be established only of such tenements as the husband held on the day of his marriage, or shall afterwards have held in fee to him and his heirs, whether the heirs be comprehended in the purchase generally or specially, and

cialté, et lequel qe[1] par privé condicioun en fee ou par especiale mencioun, issi, a tel baroun et a ses heirs qe il engendra, et si nul[2] ne engendre ou si la engendrure moerge et defaille, qe la terre issi doné apres le desces le purchaceour retourne al donour et a ses heirs. Et[3] s'il eit engendrure, tut[4] moerge et defaille, ja pur ceo ne soit la femme barré qe ele ne eit dowarie. Car tut [5]fust le doun[5] al comencement condicionel et le fee en balaunce, par la engendrure neqedent devient le feffement[6] simple et peur; et issi acrest accioun de dowarie a la femme. Et en mesme la manere est de tenementz purchacez en touz autres cas[7] ou le fee est en balaunce et depent solom aventure; qe si le aventure nomé el feffement chiete, ja par taunt accrest fee al purchaceour, par ount le doun est devenu simple et peur qe primes fut aventurous et condicionel, solom ceo accrest accioun a la femme de dowarie demaunder, ou [8]de lesser a[8] demaunder.

1. qe *om. N.* 2. heir *add. GMF.* 3. Et *om. LNSGM.* E *C.* 4. ele *add. M. interl. N.* 5—5. *so NM.* soit la dowarie *L.* fut le doweir *S. sim. G.* ne feust le doun *C.* 6. *so SGMCF. so on eras. N.* tenement *L.* 7. *so SGMCF.* maneres et en cas *L. sim. N.* 8—8. *so LSG.* nient *C.* nent *I.* del lessur a *F.*

whether by a tacit condition in fee[f] or by being specially named, as thus: to such a husband and to his heirs which he shall beget, and if he shall have no issue, or if such issue shall die or fail, that the land thus given shall, after the decease of the purchaser, return to the donor and his heirs. In such a case, if the husband has issue, although such issue die and fail, the wife shall not be thereby barred from having her dower; for, although the gift was in the beginning conditional and the fee in suspense, yet by the birth of issue the feoffment becomes simple and absolute[g], and thus an action of dower accrues to the wife. So is it as to tenements purchased in all other cases where the fee is in suspense, and depends upon an event; for if the event named in the feoffment happens, then a fee thereby accrues to the purchaser, so that the gift which was at first contingent and conditional, becomes simple and absolute; and according to the event an action accrues to the wife to demand her dower or not.

of tenements descendible to heirs special;

of conditional fees, if the condition happens.

[f] These words possibly refer to an estate given in frank-marriage, which was subject to a tacit condition in favour of the donor and his heirs. See Stat. West. 2. (13 Edw. I.) c. 1.

[g] The Statute *de donis conditionalibus* (Stat. West. 2. (13 Edw. I.) c. 1.) had recently been made when this was written, and the doctrine here stated appears to be that which prevailed before the judicial exposition of that statute. See Coke, Inst. pt. ii. p. 335.

Brac. 94 *b*; Fle. 343 (§ 19, 20).

[249 *b*.]

Brac. 95; Fle. 343 (§ 21).

5. Estre ceo ne vaut nient le dowement qe establi est des terres et des tenementz qe le baroun a tort tient, sicum autri dreit, si en sa vie sauntz fraude les perd par acun jugement, ou soen heir apres ly. Et sicum homme put dower sa femme de[1] certeyn ou de[2] noun certeyn de soen propre, ausi le purra il fere de autri terre, sicum est de ceux qi dowent lour femmes de renable dowarie del heritage qe le piere ou la mere al[3] baroun tient[4], par lour assent; mes autrement ne vaudra rien cel dowement, si celi a qi la terre est ne soit en present et se assente solempnement al us del mouster. Et tut i soit escrit fet qe ceo testmoigne, uncore ne vaut rien si al us del mouster ne fust fet ou graunté al meyns par le tenaunt de la terre, et pur la parole del counte, qe covendra dire, dount il la dowa par le assent de soen auncestre al us del mouster; car s'il counte qe il assenti[5] aillours, le counte est vicious, et pur la variaunce par entre le bref et le counte serra le bref abatable. Mes acune foiz est renable dowarie establie de homme a[6] femme; et si le heir, vivaunt le auncestre et sa

1. en *MCF*. 2. en *MCF*. 3. *so M*. *so on eras. N*. ou *LSF*. ou le *GC*. 4. *so NGF*. tint *LS*. tynt *M*. 5. *so GMC*. ne sente *L*. se assenti *N*. nen sente *F*. 6. *so SGMF*. et de *LN*. e de *C*.

Establishment of dower out of land held in wrong is void.

Dower may be established out of ancestor's land, by his assent at the church door.

5. Moreover, dower which is established out of lands and tenements which the husband wrongfully holds, as being the right of another, is invalid, if without fraud he loses them by judgment in his lifetime, or his heir after his death. But as a man may endow his wife out of his own property whether definitely or indefinitely, so he may do it out of lands belonging to others, as where a husband endows his wife with a reasonable dower of the inheritance held by his father or mother, with their consent; for such endowment is ineffectual unless the owner of the land is present, and solemnly assents thereto at the church door. And although there be a deed witnessing the act, yet it is invalid unless it be made or at least allowed by the tenant of the land at the church door, and this by reason of the words in the count, which ought to say, 'whereof he endowed her by assent of his ancestor at the church door;' for if she counts that he assented elsewhere, the count is defective, and the writ will be abatable for the variance between it and the count. But reasonable dower may sometimes have been established by a man on his wife; and if the heir in the

Endowment by heir is subject to dower of ancestor's wife.

femme, dowast [1]sa femme[1] de tote la tierce partie des terres [2]soen auncestre par le assent[2] le auncestre, tel douwement serreit[3] prejudiciel [4]a la premere[4]; a force la covendra dounc dower [5]de la tierce partie des deus parties, et del tierz[5] de la tierce partie cum ele escherra. Et ausi de la reverse, si le auncestre prenge femme, qe il deit dower, apres qe le heir avera dowé sa femme de la tierce partie del entier par le assent le auncestre. Brac. 98; Fle. 345 (§ 14); Hengh. Parv. c. 3. p. 89. [245.]

6. Et puis qe dowarie avera esté [6]a dreit establie[6], mes ne porra tele dowarie estre encru en prejudice del heir pur nul contract qe purra estre fet par entre le auncestre et sa femme, [7]puis ceo[7] qe il la avera esposé. Et sicum ele ne purra mie estre encru en prejudice del heir, ausi ne purra mie estre amenusé en prejudice de la femme. Brac. 95 b; Fle. 343 (§ 22).

1—1. *so GCF. interl. N. om. LSM.* 2—2. *so verb. M.* le auncestre par le assent *S. sim. GC. om. LNF.* 3. *so GC. sim. SM.* serra *LN.* seit *F.* 4—4. al premer *LG.* al primer *SMF.* al [a femme] primer [e] *N.* 5—5. *so verb. MF. sim. SG. sim. in marg. M. om. L.* 6—6. establi auant *C.* 7—7. *so NGM.* pur ceo *LSF.* puis *C.*

lifetime of the ancestor and his wife, with the assent of the ancestor, endows his wife of the third part of all the lands of the ancestor, such endowment will be prejudicial to the first wife. He must of necessity therefore endow her only of the third part of two parts, and of the third of the third part when it shall fall in. So in the reverse case,—if the ancestor take a wife whom he has to endow after the heir has endowed his wife of the third part of the whole by the assent of the ancestor[h].

6. When dower has been once legally established, it cannot be increased to the prejudice of the heir by any agreement between the ancestor and his wife after the marriage. And as it cannot be increased to the prejudice of the heir, so neither can it be diminished to the prejudice of the wife. Dower cannot be increased to the preju-dice of heir.

[h] 'If the father be sole and without a wife at the time when his son endows his wife by the father's assent, and the father take a wife afterwards, he cannot endow her except of the third of two thirds; and on the death of the father and son, the son's wife shall have her action to have dower out of the whole. And where the father and mother are joint purchasers, and the son endows his wife by their assent, *constat*, that this is of a third of the whole, and if the mother dies, and the father takes another wife, the endowment of this wife takes nothing from the son's wife's dower first established. But suppose the father dies, and the mother takes another husband, who has issue by her, and the mother and son die in one day; *qu.* whether the second husband shall hold the whole by the curtesy, or the son's wife have her dower.' (Note in MS. *N.*)

CHAPITRE III. [CIII.]

De Assignement de Dowarie.

Mag. Chart. c. 7; Brac. 96; Fle. 344.

1. Apres le disces des barouns[1], dounc a primes sount establisementz de dowarie confermez. Et pur ceo soint les dowaries tauntost assignez et deliverez as femmes, solom ceo qe il furent establiz, sauntz nul fin demaunder, et sauntz duresce fere, et ne mie soulement de lour dowaries mes des tenementz ausi qe lour furent donez en mariage. Et pur ceo qe il ne affiert mie qe tieles femmes soint[2] botez hors ovek les cors de lour barouns, ne qe eles ne eynt ou herberger, est graunté pur ley et pur usage, qe eles[3] en les chiefs mees qe furent a lour barouns par xl. jours apres la mort lour maris [4]puissent demorer[4], et qe en le meen tens lour soint lour dowaries assignez, si[5] le chief mees ne[6] soit
[245 *b.*] chief del counté ou de baronie ou chastel; et[7] en tel cas soint purveus acunes [8]honestes mesouns as mansiouns[8] par ayllours,

1. ou riens ne vaudra le dowement si le ami le voile contrepleder par ceste parole el bref al huis du Mouster *add. M.* 2. *so verb. GMF.* ne soint mie *L. sim. NS.* 3. demoergent *add. G. sim. MCF.* 4—4. *om. GMCF.* 5. et si *L.* E si *N.* e liuerez. E si *S.* e lyuerez si *G.* e deliuerez Si *M. sim. CF.* 6. ne *om. SM. eras. N.* 7. et *om. NM.* 8—8. honestes mansions *SG.* honestez manauntises *M. sim. F.* manaunces *C.*

CHAPTER III.

Of the Assignment of Dower.

Dower to be assigned without fine or duress.

1. After the husband's death, the establishment of dower is first confirmed. Wherefore let the dowers of widows be forthwith assigned and delivered to them according as they were established, without asking any fine or using any oppression, and not only their dowers, but also the tenements which were given to them in marriage.

Quarantine.

And because it is improper that such wives should be thrust out of doors with their husbands' bodies, without having a place to lodge in, it is allowed by law and custom that they may abide in the capital messuages which belonged to their husbands forty days after their husbands' deaths, and that in the meantime their dowers be assigned to them, unless the capital messuage be the head of the county or of a barony, or a castle; in which case some other decent house shall be provided for their dwelling, where they

ou eles purrount demorer lour quarenteines. Et ou qe eles demoergent, qe eles eint del issue del entier des terres lour covenable[1] susteinaunce [2]ci la[2] qe lour dowaries lour soint deliverez et assignez solom ceo qe al us de mouster lour fust establi le jour qe eles furent esposez, en mesme le estat en touz pointz, oveke les fruiz[3] et les rentes et[4] ovek totes les apurtenaunces cum eles furent le jour de la mort lour barouns; et ceo qe serra pris et coilli en le meen tens, ceo lour soit rendu.

2. Mes en cas ou acun mari avoit aliené soen heritage en sa vie par feffement et par fermes en partie ou en tut, en tel cas ne estut mie qe les tenauntz tauntost rendent dowarie a la femme, si il ne voillent, pur ceo qe il ount graunt resoun pur eus [5]de la retener[5] jekes autaunt qe il eint a la vaillaunce, taunt cum ley lour porra suffrer. Mes si acun delaye a tort de dowarie rendre, il est tenuz a fere aseez a la femme de ses damages; mes ne mie en touz cas. Car si la femme[6] se pleigne par bref de dowarie overt, nomément des tenementz

Brac. 96, 96*b*; Fle. 344 (§ 4).

Stat. Mert. (20 Hen. III) c. 1; Brac. 96*b*; Fle. 344 (§ 4, 5); Hengh. Parv. c. 2. pp 85, 86.

1. renable *M.* 2—2. ci e la *LS.* si la *NGCF.* ci la *M.* 3. *conj.* fins *LMGI.* feez *on eras. N.* finz *S.* 4. et *om. LN.* e *SGMCF.* 5—5. del tener *L.* *sim. N.* del retenir *SMF.* de la retenir *GC.* 6. *so F.* ne *add. LSGMC.* *eras. N.*

may keep their quarantine; and that wheresoever they abide they shall have suitable maintenance out of the profits of the whole of the lands until their dowers be assigned and delivered to them, according to the appointment made at the church door on the day of marriage, in the same state in all points, with the fruits, rents, and all the appurtenances, as they were on the day of the death of their husbands; and that which has been taken or gathered in the meantime shall be restored to them.

Maintenance during quarantine.

Mean profits.

2. But where any husband has aliened his inheritance in his lifetime by feoffment or farms either in part or in the whole, in such case the tenants are not obliged, whether they will or no, immediately to render to the wife her dower, because they have great reason for retaining it, until they are compensated to its value, so far as the law will permit. But if anyone wrongfully delays the rendering of dower, he is obliged to make satisfaction to the wife for her damages, though not in all cases. For if the wife brings her plaint by writ of dower patent demanding the tenements aliened in the lifetime of her

Where husband has aliened, donee not bound to surrender without plea.

Damages recovered from detainor,

not by writ of dower patent against alienee of husband.

alienez en la vie soen baroun, par mi ceo bref ne deit ele
Fle. 344 (§ 7). mie recoverer damages, sicum parra[1] en soen lu. Mes si ele[2]
[246.] se pleigne par le commun bref de dowarie clos, et demaunde sa renable dowarie, par mi ceo bref recovera ele la tierce partie de touz les tenementz qe furent a soen baroun en demeyne et en fee cum soen propre dreit le jour qe il la esposa, et ausi de touz ceux tenementz qe soens furent puis[3] qe il la esposa; et si ele puisse averrer qe hom ly ad delayé a tort de sa dowarie rendre, en tiel cas ele recovera damages, et ne mie en cas ou le deforceour ad bone resoun[4] del dowarie retener, sicum avaunt est dit. Et cil rende les damages, [5]qi de la injurie serra[5] atteint.

Fle. 344 (§ 7); Hengh. Parv. c. 2. p. 85. 3. Et acune foiz recovera ele plus qe le tierz, solom la nature del fee, et solom le usage del soil. Car plusours tenementz sount, dount resounable dowarie se estent a la meité des tenementz, sicum de acuns sokages; et en tiel cas soit le usage del pays et del lu tenu pur ley.

Brac. 299 *b*; Fle. 344 (§ 8). 4. Et acune foiz deit ele recoverer une certeine quantité

1. *so* *MG*. purra *LS*. aparra *N*. apparera *C*. porra *F*. 2. *so* *MGF*. ne *add*. *LSC*. *eras*. *N*. 3. le iour *G*. 4. encheson *M*. 5—5. *so* *G*. qe de la Iuree serra *L*. *sim*. *NS*. qe del iniurie serrunt *M*. qe del tort serra *C*. ke del iniurie serra *F*.

husband, by this writ she ought not to recover damages, as
but generally by writ of dower close. will appear in its proper place. But if she complains by the common writ of dower close, and demands her reasonable dower, she shall by this writ recover the third part of all the tenements which her husband held in demesne and in fee as his own right on the day of his marriage with her, and also of all such tenements as were his after he married her; and if she can prove that she has been wrongfully delayed in obtaining her dower, in such case she shall recover damages, but not where the deforceor has a good reason for keeping back the dower, as before is mentioned. And let him restore the damages who shall be found guilty of the wrong.

Dower by custom may extend to half. 3. In some instances the widow shall recover more than the third part, according to the nature of the fee and the custom of the land. For there are many tenements in which reasonable dower extends to a moiety of the land, as is the case in some socage tenements; and in such cases the custom of the country and of the place is to be observed as law.

4. Sometimes also she has a right to recover a certain

pur sa dowarie solom ceo qe sa dowarie fust establie. Et en tiel cas recovere ele par bref de dowarie nomé[1]. Et si cele dowarie issi nomé en certein passe la value [2]de renable dowarie[2], le[3] sourplus porra le heir purchacer[4] par bref de amesurement de dowarie. Et si tiel certein ne s'estent mie a la value de la tierce partie, ou[5] a la value de renable dowarie, de taunt se covendra apayer[6]. Car plus qe dowarie nomé ne [246 *b.*] purra ele mie chalenger, puis qe ele se paya al establisement. Mes si ele ne se paya mie al establisement et ceo puisse averrer, adounc recovera ele le sourplus deqes a la value de renable dower; et ausi si ele puse averrer, qe en le establisement fut fete tele condicioun, qe si tiele dowarie nomee ne mountast a la value de renable dowarie, qe le sourplus ly soit assigné deques a la value de renable dowarie. Et par mi ceo bref recovera ele ausi damages de celi qi tort[7] le avera fet, quant ele recovera dowarie. Et en mesme la manere de dowarie delayé a tort qe fut establi [8]de autri[8] tenementz recoverount femmes damages.

1. *om. LNSG.* nomez *M.* nome *CF.* 2—2. *om. SG.* 3. *so MCF.* et *L.* [l]e *N.* E *S.* e le *G.* 4. *so LNSG.* *sim. F.* repurchacer *C.* recoverir *M.* 5. *so MF.* cum *LN.* com *SG.* 6. tener apaye *M.* *sim. SGF.* 7. *so GMF.* A tort *LNS.* 8—8. *so M.* *sim. C.* des autres *LNG.* de autres *SF.*

quantity for her dower pursuant to the establishment of her dower; and in that case let her recover by writ of dower named. And if the dower so specifically named exceed the value of reasonable dower, the heir may recover the excess by writ of admeasurement of dower. But if that specific dower does not amount to the value of the third part, or to the value of reasonable dower, she must be contented with what there is. For more than the dower named she cannot claim, since at the establishment of it she was contented to take it. But if she was not so contented at the establishment, and can verify her dissent, then she shall recover the difference to the extent of the value of reasonable dower. So likewise if she can aver that in the establishment a condition was made, that if the dower named did not amount to the value of reasonable dower, the difference should be assigned to her to the extent of the value of reasonable dower. And by means of this writ she shall also recover damages against the wrong doer when she shall have recovered her dower. And in like manner shall widows recover damages for the wrongful detainer of dower established out of the tenements belonging to another.

Recovery of established dower by writ of dower named.

If it exceed a third, the heir may recover excess;

if it fall short, the widow has no remedy,

unless she dissented at the establishment,

or the dower was subject to conditional enlargement.

Damages for delay of dower.

Brac. 96 b; Fle. 345 (§ 11). 5. Dowarie deit estre assigné entierement et ne mie par parcelerie[1], ceo est a saver [2]la tierce[2] de [3]touz les[3] tenementz qe lour maritz tindrent en demeyne et en fee, ausi bien des villenages, feez de chivalers, services de fraunces hommes, Brac. 96 b, 97; Fle. 345 (§ 11, 12). [4]et de[4] avowesouns de eglises, cum de [5]demeynes terres. Si especial mencioun neqedent ne fut fete [6]en le[6] premer establisement de dowarie [7]des avowesouns ou tierz presentementz[7], autrement[8] ne purra la femme rien demaunder pur dowarie en la avowesoun ne en le presentement, pur ceo qe avowesoun de eglise ne est mie partable, ne receivereit point [247.] de divisioun. Mes en[9] cas ou la dowarie fust establi de acun maner entier ovek totes les apurtenaunces, sauntz rien retener, si[10] avowesoun de eglise apend, en tiel cas apent[11] la avowesoun a [12]la dowarie, [13]et a[13] la femme apendra[14] de presenter, cum la [15]eglise se voidera. Car ceo mot, sauntz rien retener, suffist a la femme pur especial establisement [16]del avowesoun[16].

1. parceles *GMF.* parcele *C.* 2—2. *so LN.* le tierce *M.* *om. SG.* 3—3. totes les terres e les *SGC.* *sim. MF.* 4—4. *so verb. MCF.* et *om. LNS.* et de *om. G.* 5. *so NGM.* de *om. LS.* des *CF.* 6—6. *so NMS.* en *L.* el *GF.* 7—7. *om. LNS.* des auouesouns ou tierce presentement *M.* *sim. GF.* dauoesones ou tierce presentment *C.* 8. outreement *S.* 9. *so MGCF.* tiel *add. LN.* 10. *so MGF.* qe *LS.* a qi la *on eras. N.* 11. *so MF.* apent *om. LNSGC.* 12. e *SG.* 13—13. et a *om. LSG.* appendra e a *N.* e a *MCF.* 14. *om. N.* 15. *so SGMF.* la *om. L.* *interl. N.* 16—16. de presenter la voeson *M.*

Dower, how to be assigned. 5. Dower ought to be assigned as a whole, and not by parcels; that is to say, the third of all the lands and tenements which the husbands held in demesne and in fee, as well of villenages, knights' fees, services of freemen, and Advowsons, when assigned. advowsons of churches, as of demesne land. Unless however in the original establishment of the dower special mention was made of advowsons or third presentations, the widow cannot demand anything for dower in an advowson or presentation, because the advowson of a church is not partible, neither would it admit of division[1]. But where the dower was established of an entire manor with all the appurtenances, without any reservation, if the advowson of a church be appendant to the manor, the advowson belongs to the dower, and the widow will have a right to present when the church becomes vacant. For these words 'without any reservation' are equivalent to a special establishment of the advowson on the wife.

[1] Bracton states, that, where there were several advowsons, the widow should have her share of them as entireties; but where there was only one, it should not be divided, but she should have satisfaction for its value. If not so satisfied, he suggests that she ought to have the third presentation. Compare Butler's Coke Litt. 32 a, 32 b, note 197

6. Et[1] en le assignement de dowarie ne poent les femmes rien chalenger en mees ne en chasteus[2] qe sount chiefs de baronies ou de countez, ne ausi en autres feez ou nul chief meez en est for qe un soul, ne ausi [3]en cervoires ne[3] en vivers ne en haies[4] ne en estangs ne en parcs ne en gardins ne en fossez del mees, ne en riens qe est de eynz le [5]clos del[5] chiefe mees, fors qe sa quarenteine[6], taunt cum hom ly puse assigner par aylours a la vaillaunce en terre ou en rente ou en autre chose, si le heir ne le voille; eynz luy soit assigné pur mees acun mees des villenages, et de ceo se[7] tiegne apayé. Et si nul tiel i eit, adounc luy soit purveu une place en lu covenable, et soit assigné en loungure et [8]en leure[8] a la quantité del tierz del mees, ou ele porra fere edefier[9] et demorer, mes ne mie a la vaillaunce de la tierce partie del mees, et des issues del entier del heritage luy soit fet un mees suffisaunt. Mes si le heir ne luy puisse assigner aillours a la vaillaunce, adounc ly estovera par force dower de la [247 *b*.] tierce partie de quant qe il ad, sauve de avowesoun de eglise,

Brac. 97 *b*; Fle. 345 (§ 13, 14).

1. Ou *L*. e *SG*. E *MF*. Ne *on eras*. *N*. 2. chateus *LS*. chatels *N*. cha[s]teus *M*. cha[s]teaus *F*. chasteaus *G*. 3—3. *so M*. *om*. *LNGS*. en seruurs ne *F*. 4. *so GF*. lais *L*. lays *NSM*. 5—5. *so MGF*. *om*. *LNS*. 6. *so verb*. *GMF*. rente *LNS*. 7. *so NSGMCF*. se *om*. *L*. 8—8. la leure *LN*. en leour *SF*. en laeur *G*. en laour *M*. en laure *C*. 9. *so SGMF*. edifice *LN*. [e de] fere *C*.

6. In the assignment of dower widows cannot claim anything in mansions or castles which are heads of baronies or counties, nor in mansions in other fees where there is but one capital messuage, nor in preserves of deer, vivaries, hays, stanks, parks, or gardens, nor in the fosses of the messuage, nor anything within the close of the capital messuage beyond her quarantine, unless the heir chooses, so long as the value of her dower can be assigned to her in land, rent, or other thing elsewhere. But let one of the houses of the villain tenements be assigned to her to dwell in, and let her be content therewith. And if there be no such, let her be provided with a plot of ground in some convenient place to build and dwell in, and let that be assigned to her in length and breadth in proportion to the third part of the messuage, but not to the value of the third part of the building; and let a sufficient messuage be erected for her out of the issues of the entire inheritance. But if the heir cannot assign her the value elsewhere, then of necessity he must endow her of the third part of whatever he

Things excluded from dower. Capital mansions. Parks. House to be provided, or built.

si especiale mencioun ne soit fete en le establisement. Mes de deyms ne de autre veneisoun, ne de autres bestes en parcs ne en chaces, ne de pessoun en ewes, ne de homages[1] ne deit james dowarie estre assigné. En pescheries neqedent, ou les comoditez dependent en cas de aventure, tient bien lu assignement acune foiz del tierz treit, issi qe [2]le heir[2] i pesche deus foiz, et la femme la tierce foiz.

Brac. 98 (§ 4); Fle. 346 (§ 16).

7. Mes si bref de dreit deive estre dedut et pledé, ceo ne apent nient al dowarie, ne en nuli court[3] qe ne tient for qe a terme de vie, eynz covendra estre dedut en la [4]court a[4] celi de qi le pleintif deit tener le tenement demaundé par le homage, coment [5]il ne deive[5] tener de autre par feauté. Ne ausi ne apent point a dowarie de aver poer de tener vewe de fraunc plege, ne pleder pleez de vee[6], ne de aver[7] estray ne weif, ne de aver les amendes de assises enfreintes[8], ne la fraunchise de infangenthef ne wrek, ne nule fraunchise reale issaunte de la dignité de nostre Coroune. Car ceux pleez sount pledables par le heir et ses bailifs, tut[9] soint les

1. *so MCF.* homage *LNSG.* 2—2. *so MC. sim. F.* hom *LN.* lem *SG.* 3. *so GMCF. so corr. N.* tort *L.* cort *S.* 4—4. tort a *LN.* court *SGMCF.* 5—5. *so LS. sim. M.* qe il deyue *on eras. N.* qil deiue *G. sim. F.* qil ne deit *C.* 6. de nam *add. G. sim. C.* 7. *so GMC. sim. F.* autre *LNS.* 8. de payn e de cerueyse *add. C.* 9. *so verb. MCF.* Si *LSG.*

has, saving the advowson of a church, unless special mention was made thereof in the establishment. But dower shall never be assigned of deer or other game, nor of other beasts in parks or chases, nor of fish in waters, nor of homages. Yet in fisheries where the profits are casual, sometimes the third draught may be assigned, so that the heir may fish twice and the widow the third time.

Deer in parks. Homages. Fisheries.

Jurisdiction of dowager's court.

7. If a writ of right is to be brought and pleaded, this jurisdiction does not belong to the dower, nor indeed to the court of any one who holds only for term of life; but it must be determined in his court of whom the plaintiff claims to hold the tenements demanded by homage, although he may hold of some other person by fealty. Neither does it belong to dower to have authority to hold view of frank-pledge, or to take cognizance of pleas *de vetito namio,* or to have estray or waif, or the correction of assises broken, or the franchise of infangthef, or wreck, or any regal franchise derived from the prerogative of our Crown. For such pleas are pleadable by

femmes dowez de entiers maners as queus celes fraunchises apendent.

8. Assigné issi dowarie as femmes par certeines merches et par certeins boundes, lour[1] serrount gardes[2], mariages, releefs, eschetes, et les purchaz de courtz et de pletz de lour tenauntz, et totes maneres de commoditéz issauntes del dowarie, si especiale forsprise ne les forbarre. Les eschetes neqedent ne serrount lour for qe al terme del dowarie. Et pur ceo qe dowarie deit estre purement fraunche, si n'ert la femme rien tenu des dettes le baroun aquiter, eynz ert le heir. Et si il ne suffit a nostre dette ou a [3]noster service[3] rendre, ou [4]a autri service ou[4] dette qe par le auncestre avera esté [5]conue en nostre court[5], adounc covendra estendre [6]les bras[6] al dowarie. Et si nul ne voille rendre dowarie a la femme de soen gré, adounc covendra qe ele soit eidé par plee.

[248.] Brac. 98 (§ 3); Fle. 345 (§ 15).

Brac. 98 (§ 4); Fle. 345 (§ 15).

1. *so MC. sim. SGF.* Et lour *L. sim. N.* 2. *so F.* agardez *LM. sim. SG.* gardez *C.* agardez [de auer les seruices e gardes] *N.* 3—3. nostre ferme *N.* 4—4. *om. LNGS.* autri seruice ou *M.* al autre seruice ou *C.* autre seruice ou *F.* 5—5. *so verb. G.* conue *LNS.* reconue en nostre Court *M. sim. F.* 6—6. les bleez *L.* les bleez [al. braz *int.*] *N.* le bras *SF.* les Bras *G.* lez braz *M.* le braz *C.*

the heir and his bailiffs, although the widows be endowed of the entire manors to which the franchises belong.

8. Dower being thus assigned to widows by certain limits and bounds, the wardships, marriages, reliefs, escheats, perquisites of courts, and pleas of their tenants, and all manner of profits issuing out of the dower, shall belong to them, unless they are barred by some special exception. The escheats however shall be theirs only for the term of the dower. And whereas dower ought to be absolutely free, the widow is not bound to discharge the debts of her husband, but that lies upon the heir. And if he is not able to satisfy our debt, or to perform our service, or the service or debt owing to another which the ancestor shall have acknowledged in our court, then the hand must be extended to reach the dower[j]. If any one refuses to allow dower to the widow of his own accord, she must be aided by plea.

Profits of dower.

Heir bound to acquit dower from ancestor's debts.

[j] This provision, making the dower to some extent liable for the husband's debts in case of the deficiency of his remaining property, is not derived from Bracton or Fleta. It finds however some support, so far as regards debts due to the Crown, in one of the forms of writs, *quod mulieres non distringantur*, given in the Register. See Regist. Brev. Orig. f. 142 b, 143; Fitzherbert, Nat. Brev. 150 Q; Coke, Litt. 31 a.

CHAPITRE IV. [CIV.]

De Remedie de Dowarie.

Glan. li. 6. c. 14; Brac. 296, 296 *b*; Fle. 346.

1. Play de dowarie est terminable en nostre court; et par [1]graunt resoun[1]. Car si deus femmes ou plusours estrivasent ensemble entour dowarie, et chescune se dit aver esté la femme espousé al baroun mort, et nous ou autres vousisoms estre certifiéz, la quele de totes fut la dreite femme, cum
[248 *b*.] nule ne put estre for qe une a une foiz, sicum avaunt est dit, [2]de ceo ne put homme[2] estre certefié [3]for qe par la court Cristiene[3]; et dounc, si autre de nous maundoit al Evask de estre[4] sour tel debat certifié, et le Evaske ne vousist, si ne averoit[5] nul poer de amener le Evask [6]a ceo[6] fere, s'il ne vousist fere, for qe nous; et par[7] plusours autres resouns[8].

Brac. 296 *b*; Fle. 346.

2. Et si acune femme dounc se voille pleindre de torcenouse detenue de sa dowarie, si fet a prendre garde et de

1—1. mouz des resons *M.* 2—2. e si ne porreit nul *M.* si purra nule *C.* 3—3. si noun par maundement de crestiene Court *M.* *sim. CF.* 4. *so MCF.* seur et *add. L.* enseur e *add. N.* 5. il *add. GM.* *so interl. N.* 6—6. *so M.* de *LNCF.* de le *S.* del *G.* 7. *so SGMCF.* par *om. LN.* 8. sount *add. N.*

CHAPTER IV.

Of the Remedies for recovery of Dower.

Plea of dower *unde nihil habet*, held in the king's court only; reason for this.

1. Plea of dower is determinable in our court, and that for good reason. For if two or more women should contend together about dower, each alleging herself to have been the espoused wife of the deceased husband, and we or any other person desired to be certified which of them all was his lawful wife, since one only can be so at one time, as before has been said, this point can be certified only by the court Christian; and therefore if any other than ourselves should direct a mandate to the bishop to be certified upon such a question, and the bishop should refuse, no one except ourselves would have any jurisdiction to compel the bishop to certify against his will. And there are several other reasons.

Various remedies for detainer of dower, in what cases proper.

2. If any widow then would complain of a wrongful detaining of her dower, care must be taken to examine narrowly

examiner estreitement, lequel tort est fet a la femme par le heir ou par autre, et lequel de tote la renable dowarie nomee especialment en le premer establisement, et lequel de tenementz dount soen mari fust seisi ou de tenementz le auncestre soen mari par soen assent, et lequel ele tient [1]partie ou nient; et si ele en tiegne[1] partie, [2]lequel partie le en faut[2] del princepal ou des apurtenaunces. Et en chescun point gist divers remedie. Car si ele ne fust unqe de rien seisie, et le establisement lui fut fet de renable dowarie, illuc tient lu le commun bref de dowarie clos de renable dowarie dount ele rien ne ad. Et si le establisement ly fut fet en certein, adounc i ad remedie par autre[3] bref. Et si[4] par assent [5]le auncestre[5] des terres le auncestre, adounc ele avera autre remedie. Et si ele eit partie del tenement et demaunde le
remenaunt, adounc tient lu le bref de dreit de dowarie overt [249.]
pledable en la court le heir[6]. Et [7]si ele eit[7] sa renable dowarie del princepal et de acune des apurtenaunces soit deforcé,

1—1. *so verb. SGMF. sim. C. sim. in marg. N. om. L.* 2—2. *conj.* la qele partie le enfaunt *L. sim. GS.* le quel la partie soit *on eras. N.* le quel partie del enfaunt *M.* le quel luy defaute *C.* len fant *F.* 3. manere de *add. GMC. sim. SF.* 4. *so SGMCF.* si *om. LN.* 5—5. *so MG.* lautre *L. sim. S.* del au[ces]tre *N.* de lautre *C.* del autri *F.* 6. *so SMCF. so on eras. N.* Roi *LG.* 7—7. *so GMCF. so on eras. N.* sil soit *L. sim. S.*

whether the wrong is done to her by the heir or by any other person, and whether by detainer of all the reasonable dower specially named in the original establishment, and whether of tenements whereof her husband was seised, or of tenements of the ancestor of her husband whereof she was endowed by his assent, and whether she has part or not; and if she has part, whether the deficiency be in the principal subject, or in the appurtenances. On each of these points there lies a different remedy; for if she has never been seised of any part, and the establishment made upon her was of reasonable dower, then the common writ of dower close, 'of reasonable dower whereof she hath nothing,' lies. And if the establishment made was in certain, then there is remedy by another writ. And if of lands of the ancestor by his assent, then she shall have a different remedy. And if she has part of the tenement and demands the residue, then the writ of right of dower patent pleadable in the court of the heir is in place. And if she has her reasonable dower of the principal, but is deforced

adounc tient lu le bref de [1]dowarie overt, qe est apelé bref de dowarie de[1] renable partie [2]la femme[2].

Brac. 296 *b*; Fle. 346 (§ 2, 7). 3. Et si plusours deforceours soint en un counté, trestouz purrount estre compris en un bref. Ceo play est real, et pledable[3] apres defautes[4] par destresces reales, [5]sicum par *Capes*[5], et [6]si est ausi[6] pledable par essoignes al premer jour et ausi apres chescune apparaunce. Et ausi si le deforceour face defaute apres essoigne, et[7] en cas ou le deforceour ad vouché a garraunt, et ne eit mie sui de fere somoundre soen garraunt countre l'autre jour, tient lu le petit *Cape*. Ceste accioun [8]ad comaunde a[8] estre la plus favorable qe soit de touz brefs de possessioun nient pledables par assise, et[9] pur ceo fet [10]il le[10] plus a haster.

Stat. Marl. (52 Hen. III.) c. 12; Fle. 347 (§ 8).

Brac. 296 *b*, 297; Fle. 347 (c. 25). 4. Le plus commun bref de dowarie est[11] le bref clos dount femme rien ad; et pur ceo fet a comencer de ceo bref, dount

1—1. *om. C.* dowarie de *NF.* 2—2. *om. C.* 3. par defalte *interl. N.* 4. *so MCF.* et *add. L.* *sim. NSG.* 5—5. *conj.* sicum [les *interlin.*] parties *L.* sicum les parties *N.* *sim. SGMF.* *om. C.* 6—6. *so SGMF.* si ausi *L.* si est *C.* 7. si *LS.* si [come] *N.* sicom *G.* e *MCF.* 8—8. [est *on eras.*] comaundee a *N.* est comaunde de *M.* *sim. G.* est demaunde a *IC.* est comandee a *S.* *sim. F.* 9. *om. LNSG.* e *M.* E *C.* 10—10. *so M.* ele *LNSF.* ele le *C.* *om. G.* 11. *so MGF.* qe est *LNS.* qest *C.*

of some of the appurtenances, then the writ of dower patent, called writ of dower *de rationabili parte mulieris*, lies[k].

Process in writ of dower. 3. If several deforceors are in the same county, they may be all comprised in one writ. This plea is real, and pleadable after default by distresses real, as by *Cape's;* and essoins are allowed on the first day, and also after each appearance. And if the deforceor makes default after essoin, and also where the deforceor has vouched to warrant, and not caused his vouchee to be summoned against another day, the petty *Cape* lies. It is intended that this action shall be the most favoured of any of the writs of possession not pleadable by assise, and therefore there ought to be greater dispatch therein.

Action of dower favoured.

Count in writ of dower *unde nihil habet.* 4. The most common writ of dower is the writ close whereof the widow hath nothing, and therefore we ought to begin with

k 'The writ of dower, *unde nihil habet*, and the two possessory writs, *de dote certa* and *de dote de assensu patris*, are pleaded only in the Bench on account of the precept to the bishop. But the writs of right are pleadable in the lord's court, because the cause of dower, that is, the marriage, cannot be denied after the plaintiff has been recognized as lawful wife by the delivery of all or part of her dower, whether this was done by plea or without plea.' (Note in MS. *N.*) For the form of these several writs, see Regist. Brev. Orig. f. 3, 170; Fitzherbert. Nat. Brev 8 G, 148 A.

[1]counte est[1]: Ceo vous moustre Peronele, qe fust la femme Johan, qe Piers a tort la deforce de la tierce partie de taunt de terre ove les apurtenaunces en tele vile, [2]a ses[2] damages de x. li., et pur ceo a tort qe le avauntdit Johan, jadis soen baroun, de ceo la dowa al us del mouster le jour qe il la esposa, [3]cum celi qi dower la pout[3], et si ceo reconisse, beal luy est, et si il le dedie, a tort le dedit, car ele en ad sute [249 *b.*] bone et suffisaunte.

5. Et cum ele avera issi moustré sa entente, et le deforceour ne voille rien dire ne sei defendre, si remeyndra en la merci cum noun defendu, et la femme recovera sa demaunde en[4] autel estat cum les tenementz furent le jour qe soen mari morust, et ses damages. Et s'il[5] defende tort et force, et les damages la pleintife, et les autres motz defensables, puis[6] se purra eyder en mout des maneres par excepciouns [7]generales et dilatories[7], et [8]par especiales[8] peremptories, sicum apparra Post, c. 6–10. apres.

1—1. *so LG.* est countee *N.* contee est *S.* le counte est tel *MCF.* 2—2. *so GCF.* et a ces *L.* *sim. NS.* e sez *M.* 3—3. e qe ben la poeit dower *M.* *sim. ICF.* 4. *so SGMF.* et *L.* e[n] *N.* 5. *so MG.* *sim. SF.* il *LN.* 6. et puis *L.* *sim. NSG.* *om. MCF.* 7—7. generaus dilatoires *M.* *sim. F.* 8—8. *om. C.*

that writ; in which the count is thus: 'This sheweth to you, Peronel, who was the wife of John, that Peter wrongfully deforces her of the third part of so much land with the appurtenances in such a vill to her damage of ten pounds, and herein wrongfully, in that the aforesaid John, formerly her lord, endowed her thereof at the church door on the day when he married her, as he that lawfully so might do, and if he admit this, he does well, and if he deny it, he denies it wrongfully, for she hath thereof suit good and sufficient.'

5. When the widow has thus declared her case, if the deforceor will not say anything or defend himself, he shall remain in mercy as undefended, and she shall recover her demand in the same state as the tenements were on the day that her husband died, and also her damages. And if the deforceor defends the wrong and force and the damages of the plaintiff, and so on, according to the proper words of defence, he may then aid himself several ways, either by general dilatory exceptions, or by special peremptory exceptions, as will afterwards appear.

Judgment, where no defence is made.

General words of defence.

Exceptions.

CHAPITRE V. [cv.]

Des Garaunties.

Brac. 297; Fle. 350.

1. Si le deforceour vouche a garraunt, adounc se tiegne le proces qe serra dit des garraunties en le play de dreit, quaunt as [1]jugementz de[1] defautes. Et si le garraunt viegne al jour qe il avera esté somouns [2]et garrauntise[2], adounc soit le toyl par entre la pleintive et le garraunt; et en le meen tens remeigne le tenaunt a mesoun en sa seisine deques autaunt qe le play de la garrauntie soit dedut. Car solom la fin de cel play retendra[3] le tenaunt ou perdera. Et si ceo soit de dowarie qe fu nomé a la femme en certein en le premer establisement, et le tenaunt ceo deive perdre[4], la femme
[250.] recovera sa demaunde tut outre, et le tenaunt a la vaillaunce del garraunt. Mes[5] de renable dowarie demaundé [6]ne est mie[6] issi. Car de cele dowarie recovera la femme a la vaillaunce del garraunt, et le [7]tenaunt remeyndra[7] en tenaunce de la demaunde.

1—1. *om. C.* 2—2. *so verb. SGMF. so corr. N.* a garrauntie *L.* e garaunt *C.* 3. *so MCF.* recouera *LNSG.* 4. *so GMCF.* et *add. L. sim. S. eras. N.* 5. en cas *add. C.* 6—6. nen est iammes en nul leu *IC.* 7—7. verrey tenaunt remeindra peisiblement *IC.*

CHAPTER V.

Of vouching to Warranty in Pleas of Dower.

Voucher of warrant.

1. If the deforciant vouches to warranty, then the like process shall hold as shall be mentioned of warranties in a plea of right, so far as regards judgments upon defaults[k].

Process on appearance of warrant.

And if the vouchee appears on the day of the summons and enters into warranty, then let the contest be between the plaintiff and the warrant; and in the meantime the tenant may remain at home in his possession until the plea of warranty is determined, for according to the event of that plea the tenant shall hold the land or lose it.

Judgment, where dower in certain is demanded;

And if the demand be of dower which was named in certain to the wife upon the first establishment, and the action goes against the tenant, the widow shall recover her demand in full, and the tenant to the value from the warrant.

where reasonable dower is demanded.

But where reasonable dower is demanded it is not so; for of that dower the widow shall recover to the value of the warrant, and the tenant shall remain in tenancy of the land demanded.

k The passage referred to is not found in Britton, but the process is stated in Bracton, f. 384, Fleta, p. 411. See Introduction, p. xlii.

2. Tut soit le garraunt[1] de eynz age, pur le favour neqedent de vedues ne est mie[2] usage ne dreit, qe les femmes[3] attendent jekes [4]as ages[4] des garrauntz, pur ceo[5] qe dowarie garrauntir ne est mie[6] prejudiciel as heirs par quei il deivent encoure desheritesouns[7], ne mie pur ceo qe il[8] covendra a teus[9] tenauntz de moustrer acune chartre ou acun[10] fet par ount la court soit certefiez, qe l'enfaunt soit lié a la garrauntie par[11] soen auncestre; et lequel ceo soit de renable dowarie ou de certein, le heir respoundra, de quel age qe il soit. Et si la femme recovere sa demaunde, et le heir [12]vodera mettre chalenge, si se purchace[12] le heir, [13]cum il vendra a soen age. Et si purra il regayner[13] la terre [14]qe il mesmes[14] perdi. Et s'il ne puse, adounc estoise le premer jugement. Brac. 299 b, 300; Fle. 350 (§ 4).

3. Et fet a entendre[15] qe en chescun jugement de seisine fere a femme pleintive de renable dowarie nient nomez, sount touz jours a forprendre les bleez cressauntz et les feins faucheez. [250 b.] Fle. 350 (§ 4).

1. qe deit garraunter *add. IC.* 2. a la Court le Rey *add. IC.* 3. doweir demaundaunz *add. C. sim. I.* 4—4. al plener age *IC.* 5. qe la Court le Rey ad bien perceu *add. IC.* 6. si *add. MCF.* 7. par la tenaunce des femmes qe tenent en doweyr *add. IC.* 8. *so LNSGC.* ne *add. MF.* 9. *so GCF.* touz *LN.* teuz *M.* 10. autre especial title ou *add. IC.* 11. le fet *add. C. sim. I.* 12—12. face le eschaunge si repurchace *M. sim. C.* face leschaunge e si le porchace *F.* 13—13. quant il serra de age si i puise. E si il dounc le puisse purchacer si regaingnera *M. sim. F.* quant il serra de plener age sil pusse repurchacer si le remeigne e regainera *C.* 14—14. mesme qe il *M. sim. F.* 15. tenir *GMF.* sauer *C. sim. I.*

2. Although the warrant be under age, yet, out of favour to widows, it is not the custom or law that the women shall wait until the full age of the warrants, because warranty of dower is not so prejudicial to heirs as to involve disherison. Nevertheless such tenants must show a charter or deed, whereby the court may be certified that the infant is bound to warranty by his ancestor; and whether the demand be of reasonable dower or of dower in certain, the heir shall answer of whatever age he be. And if the widow recovers her demand, and the heir is disposed to dispute it, he may take proceedings when he comes of age. And so he may possibly regain the land which he himself lost; but if he cannot do so, then the first judgment shall stand. Infancy of warrant does not delay the action. If a charter be produced. But when of age, he may recover.

3. It should be understood that in every judgment awarding seisin to a widow plaintiff of reasonable dower not named, the corn growing and the grass mowed are always to be excepted. Growing corn and hay excepted in the judgment.

Brac. 300 *b*; Fle. 351 (§ 5). 4. Et tut soit l'enfaunt en garde, et la garde aliené de meyn en meyn, ceo ne greve nient al voucheour, pour ceo qe il vouchera touz jours le heir a garraunt, et nient soen gardeyn, tut soit qe soen gardein est tenu de presenter l'enfaunt en court, qi qe unques en soit gardeyn. Et ceo qe est dit de un heir de eynz age, est ausi a entendre de plusours heirs de eynz age qe sount parceners et ausi cum un heir.

CHAPITRE VI. [CVI.]

De Excepciouns de Mort.

Brac. 301 *b*; Fle. 351. 1. Des articles en le bref purrount nestre[1] excepciouns al tenaunt. Car de ceo qe dit est en le bref, qe fu femme jadis un tel soen baroun, porra il dire qe il fust jadis soen baroun[2] et uncore est, et pur ceo qe soen baroun est uncore en pleine vie, ne ly est mie tenu a respoundre sauntz soen baroun. Et si ceo soit averree ou nient dedit, si perist la accioun, pur ceo qe [3]douns pur noeces[3] sicum des douns donez en mariage,

1. *so GMCF.* estre *LNS.* 2. mariz *M. sim. G.* 3—3. douns *om. LNGS.* douns pur neces *M.* deus purrount deus Mees doner *C.* deus por neces *F.*

Wardship of infant transferred. 4. Although the infant is in ward, and the wardship aliened from one to another, this does not prejudice the vouchor, because he shall always vouch to warranty the heir, and not his guardian; but the guardian, whoever he be, is bound to produce the infant in court. Coheirs. And what has been said with regard to a sole heir under age, is also to be understood of several heirs under age who are parceners and considered as one heir.

CHAPTER VI.

Of Exceptions respecting the husband's death.

Exception that the husband is not dead. 1. Exceptions may arise to the tenant from the articles in the writ. For whereas it is said in the writ, 'who was the wife of such an one, formerly her husband,' the tenant may answer, that he was formerly her husband and is so still, and inasmuch as her husband is still alive, he is not bound to answer her in the absence of her husband. And if this be proved, or not denied, the action is at an end; because gifts for marriage, as in the case of lands given in marriage

et[1] establisementz de dowarie ne se conferment james fors qe par la mort de maritz.

2. Et si la femme die, qe il ad resceu le habite de professioun, et le tenaunt die qe noun, [2]par le ordinarie del lu covendra[2] estre certefié; et taundis[3] remeigne le play original[4] en respit. Et[5] solom la certificacioun de le ordinarie soit fourni le jugement. Brac. 301 *b*; Fle. 351 (§ 1). [251.]

3. Et si ele die qe soen mari est mort de sa mort naturele, en tiel cas apent acune foiz la prove a la femme, si le tenaunt la charge de la prove, ou il dirra simplement qe il n'est nient mort. Car al pleintif generalment si apent [6]la prove de[6] sa entente, si le defendaunt ne se peyne de prover la reverse. Et si le deforceour die, qe il est en pleyne vie, et ceo est prest de prover, et la femme ne die for qe simplement qe il est mort sauntz ceo tendre de averrer, si apent la prove al tenaunt, pur ceo qe il apent al excipiaunt de prover sa ex- Brac. 301 *b*; Fle. 351 (§ 2).

1. et *om. LNGS.* en *M.* e *CF.* 2—2. *so verb. M.* ceo couendra *LNGS.* donk couiendra as ordinaries as queus Iurediccion est done de cele chose examiner e trier e *C.* 3. tut dis *L.* *sim. N.* taundys *M.* tandiz *S.* endementers *I.* *sim. C.* *om. G.* 4. *om. C.* 5. Et *om. L.* e *NMGC.* 6—6. de prouer *MCF.*

and establishments of dower, are not confirmed until the death of the husband.

2. If the wife says that her husband has taken the habit of profession, and the tenant says that he has not, this must be certified by the ordinary, and the original plea shall be in the meantime respited. And according to the certificate of the ordinary let judgment be given[1]. Replication of civil death by profession. Fact certified by ordinary.

3. If she says that her husband is dead by natural death, the proof sometimes lies upon the plaintiff, if the tenant puts her upon proving the same; in which case he shall only say that the husband is not dead. For in general it belongs to the plaintiff to prove his case, unless the defendant undertakes to prove the contrary. And if the deforceor says that the husband is alive, and that he is ready to prove the same, and the wife only says that he is dead, without tendering averment, then the proof lies on the tenant, inasmuch as it belongs to the Replication of natural death. Onus of proof on plaintiff, unless the deforciant* undertakes it.

[1] '*Casus.* A man takes a wife, and afterwards goes to a foreign country, and there enters into religion and is professed. The wife brings her writ of dower. The tenant answers, that the husband is alive; and she, that he is dead in law (solum ley de terre), and sets forth how and in what place. *Quaestio, quid juris?*' (Note in MS. *N.*) It was subsequently held that if a husband entered into religion, although the heir succeeded to the inheritance, the wife should not be endowed until the husband was naturally dead. See Coke, Littleton, f. 33 *b.*; Perkins, Profitable Book, p. 61.

cepcioun. Et si ambideus neqedent se profrent a la prove, en tiel cas apent al un de prover qe il soit en vie, et al autre qe il soit mort; et purra avener par cas qe ambideus provent lour entente. Mes en tiel cas fet[1] a crere a la plus renable [2]partie de[2] prove. Et tut eit la femme prové la mort, pur ceo ne [3]li deit mie uncore seisine de dowarie estre jugé[3] sauntz autre respouns del tenaunt eynz ceo qe [4]ele eit assigné[4] coment ele ad dreit et accioun en sa demaunde; car bien porra estre, qe ele ne ad nul dreit a demaunder dowarie.

Brac. 302 (c. 7); Fle. 352 (§ 3). [251 b.] 4. Et si la prove soit trové[5] meyns suffisaunte de une part et[6] de autre, en tiel cas deit le jugement fere pur la pleintive, en favour des femmes vedues, mes par condicioun neqedent, qe si soen baroun vive [7]et soit mené et moustré en court[7], qe la femme [8]rendra la[8] dowarie ovek totes les issues del meen tens, si a ceo fere puise trover surté tiele cum la court agardera; et si noun, si remeyndera la seisine en soen lu, [9]jekes

1. *so M.* soit *LN.* fait *G.* sait *S.* seit *CF.* 2—2. *so L. om. NSGMCF.* 3—3. *so verb. MF.* deit il mie vncore estre seisi de dowarie *L. sim. NS.* ly deit mye vncore seisine de doweire estre estably *G.* 4—4. *so I.* il eit assigne *L. sim. N.* ele assigne *SG.* ele ad enseigne *M.* il eit ensigne *C.* 5. *so MF.* proue *L. sim. NSG.* 6. qe *LSG.* e *MF.* e *on eras. N.* 7—7. *so verb. F.* et ne soit mie moustre et en tort *L.* e ne seit menez e mustrez en Court *M.* e seit mene a moustrer en Court *C.* e ne seit mye mustre en Court *G. sim. S.* 8—8. *conj.* recouera *LNGS. sim. MIF.* 9—9. *so verb. SGM. sim. CF. sim. in marg. N. om. L.*

person excepting to prove his exception. And if both undertake the proof, it is for the one to prove the man to be alive and for the other to prove that he is dead, and it may happen that both parties furnish proof of their case; but then credit should be given to the most reasonable proof. And although the widow proves her husband to be dead, yet seisin of dower ought not to be adjudged to her without further answer of the tenant, before she has shown how she is entitled and has right of action in her demand; for it may well be that she has no right to demand dower.

Upon disproof of this exception judgment does not immediately follow.

Conditional judgment for widow.

4. If the proof be found insufficient on both sides, in such case, on account of the favour granted to widows, judgment ought to be given for the plaintiff; but on this condition nevertheless, that if her husband be alive and be produced in court, the wife shall restore the dower with all the profits in the meantime, provided she can find such security to perform this as the court shall award; and if not, the tenant will continue

autaunt qe la court soit meuz certefié de la mort le mari. Et en le meen tens soit suspendu le plé[9] [1]jekes autaunt qe mester soit de[1] resomouns.

CHAPITRE VII. [CVII.]

De Excepcioun de Concubinage.

1. Dit est ausi en le bref, tele qe fust femme tiel. A ceo purra le tenaunt dire, qe ele ne fust unques sa femme, pur ceo qe ele ne ly fust unques esposé, einz la tint en concubinage; et tut fut ele esposé[2], unqe neqedent par leal matrimoigne, pur ceo qe il avoit avaunt esposé une autre, la quele fust en pleine vie el[3] tens qe il la[4] esposa, issi qe si ceste pleintive fut sa femme, ceo fut de fet et ne mie de dreite fourme[5] pur l'autre qe fut sa femme de dreit. Deus femmes ne pout il mie aver a une foiz, sicum piert par la difinicioun de matrimoigne, ou est dit, qe matrimoigne est assemblé de femme a homme, et ne dit mie, de femmes as hommes, mes [252.]

Brac. 302; Fle. 352 (§ 4).

1—1. e enroule quaunt mester sera par *M*. e renouele quant mester sera par *C*. *sim*. *F*. 2. sa espouse *GMF*. sa espose *S*. sa femme espose *C*. 3. *so MG*. en *LNF*. en le *SC*. 4. *so NMGSC*. *sim*. *F*. la *om*. *L*. 5. *so LNSGM*. de femme *F*.

in seisin until the court is better certified of the husband's death. The plea in the meantime shall be suspended, and renewed by resummons when there shall be occasion.

CHAPTER VII.

Of Exceptions founded on the invalidity of the marriage, and on the dower established being different from that claimed.

1. It is also said in the writ, 'such an one who was the wife of such an one.' To this the tenant may answer, that she never was his wife, inasmuch as she was never married to him, but he had her as his concubine; or if she was married to him, yet she never was so by lawful matrimony, because he had before married another who was living at the time he married the plaintiff, so that if she was his wife, she was so in fact only and not in lawful form by reason of the other, who was his wife in law. That he could not have two wives at one time appears by the definition of matrimony, where it is said, that matrimony is the union of a woman to a man, and not of

Exception that plaintiff was not lawful wife.*

singulerement, de femme a homme. Et si plusours femmes soint assemblez a un homme, vivauntes totes, nule neqedent ne est sa femme de dreit for qe la premere, et les autres de fet a tort.

Brac. 302; Fle. 352 (§ 4).

2. Ou tut fut ele sa femme de dreit, uncore porra il dire, qe ele ne deit dowarie aver par la reule de ley, qe est: duraunt matrimoigne remaint la accioun de dowarie, et [1]definaunt le[1] matrimoigne s'estent; et divorce fut celebré par entre ly et soen mari, par ount le matrimoigne cessa, et par consequent s'estent ja accioun de dowarie demaunder. Car divorce ne est autre chose for qe severalté[2] de lit par entre espous et espouse. Et si ceo soit averré ou nient dedit, la femme recovera nule dowarie. A ceo purra la femme respoundre par cas, qe tut [3]eust il toil de court de la partie[3] fere en acun tens par entre soen mari et luy, unques neqedent ne vint tel toil al jugement, vivaunt le mari; ou tut fut le divorce agardé, ele[4] neqedent encountre cel agarde apela, et par le apel fut cel agard anienti et repelé, et passa jugement

Brac. 298 *b*; Fle. 349 (§ 23).

1—1. *so LS.* diffinaunt le *ND.* deseaunt *M.* desuant le *G.* 2. seuerale *L.* *so S. sim. GMF.* seueral[te]e *N.* seueraunce *C.* 3—3. ne eint il toil de tort de la partie *L. sim. S.* eust il toyl de Court de la departie *D. sim. corr. N.* i out il toil e plee en de departir *M.* i vst il toil en Court de la departie *G.* y out il tel plee de Court a la partie *C.* i vst il toil e plee de court de la partie *F.* 4. *so SGMF.* cele *L.* cele [femme] *N.*

women to men, but in the singular. And if several women, all living at the same time, are united to one man, yet none of them but the first is in law his wife; the others being so in fact and wrongfully.

Exception of divorce.

2. Again, although she was his lawful wife, yet the tenant may say that she ought not to have dower by that rule of law which says that the marriage subsisting action of dower remains, but the marriage failing the action is extinct, and a divorce was pronounced between her and her husband, whereby the marriage ceased, and consequently her action to demand dower is extinguished. For a divorce is no other thing but a separation of bed between man and wife. And if this be verified, or not denied, the wife shall not recover any dower. To this the widow may perhaps answer, that although there was once a question in court concerning a separation between her husband and her, yet it never came to judgment in the lifetime of the husband; or, that although the divorce was awarded, yet she appealed against the award; and by that

Replication of judgment not given in life of husband; of appeal.

pur la femme, issi qe [1]soen baroun fu seisi de luy le jour qe il morust cum de sa femme, et ele de ly cum de soen baroun[1]. Et a ceo porra le tenaunt dire qe tut apelast[2] ele de cel agard, uncore ne deit ele mie dowarie aver, pur ceo qe le mari morust einz ceo qe le jugement passa en le play del apel. [252 *b.*]

3. Ou il porra dire, qe tut fust ele sa femme de dreit, uncore ne deit ele dowarie aver, pur ceo qe ele ne fut unques solempnement esposé al us del mouster, et par consequent ne luy fut unqes dowarie establi illuc. Et si ceo soit averré, ele ne recovera nule dowarie pur la parole [3]del bref[3], al us del mouster. Brac. 302; Fle. 352 (§ 4).

4. Et si les Justices voillent estre certifiez sour acun divorce, par maundement del ordinarie covendra estre certefié. Car[4] tiele conisaunce ne apent point a lay court, nient plus qe de matrimonie, cum le un depent del autre. Et pur ceo en tiel cas fet maunder par noster bref al ordinarie del lu, qe, apelez les parties et autres qe covendra apeler[5], enquerge la Brac. 302, 302 *b*; Fle. 352 (§ 5, 6).

1—1. *so* *LN*. *sim*. *SG*. ele fu seisie de son baroun si com sa femme de dreit el tens de la mort le mari *M*. *sim*. *CF*. 2. *so* *S*. *sim*. *GF*. apele *L*. apel[ast] *N*. aselast *M*. 3—3. *so* *M*. *om*. *LNSG*. en le bref *C*. el bref *F*. 4. *so* *SGMCF*. par *L*. 5. *so* *SGMF*. et *add*. *L*. *sim*. *N*.

appeal the award was annulled and repealed, and judgment given for the wife; so that the husband was seised of her as his wife the day he died, and she of him as her husband. To which the tenant may say, that although she appealed from such award, yet still she ought not to have dower, because the husband died before any judgment was given in the plea of appeal.

3. Again, the tenant may say, that although she was his lawful wife, yet she ought not to have dower, because she was never solemnly married at the church door, and consequently dower was never established upon her there. And if this be verified, she shall not recover any dower on account of the words of the writ, 'at the church door.' Exception that marriage was not at church door.

4. If the Justices would be certified concerning any divorce, they must be certified by letters of the ordinary; for the cognizance thereof belongeth not to the lay court,—no more than of matrimony, since the one depends upon the other. Therefore in such case our writ must be directed to the ordinary of the place, that after calling the parties and other Fact of divorce to be certified by ordinary. Writ to bishop.

verité de la chose, et solom ceo qe il trovera, si certefie as[1] Justices. En ceo cas deit le ordinarie fere somoundre le tenaunt qi mist avaunt la excepcioun, en quel lu[2] qe il soit demoraunt, qe il soit a certein jour et lu devaunt ly a moustrer[3], si il voille ou sache dire encountre le matrimoigne. Et puis qe il avera esté solempnement somouns, lequel qe il
[253.] vienge al jour ou noun, soit resceue la proeve la femme par les testmoignes qe ele avera amené, [4]issi qe eus[4] ne soint mie chalengeables; et tele prove solempnement par serment des testmoignes resceu, tauntost solom [5]la enqueste[5] remaunde le ordinarie as Justices ceo qe il avera trové, et en tel cas ne git nul apel de nul des parties, par quei [6]le plee[6] en nostre court ne prenge [7] nule manere plus[8] delay.

Brac. 302 *b*, 303; Fle. 353 (§ 7).

5. Mes ore purroit [9]asqun aver demaundé[9], qe si un[10] tenist une amie en concubinage et engendrast de ly un enfaunt, [11]et puis la esposast privément aylours qe al us del mouster, et puis teles esposailles[12] engendrast de ly un enfaunt[11], et puis la

1. noz *GM.* les *CF.* 2. *so LNSG.* euesche *MCF.* 3. *so verb. SGMCF.* Westmouster *L.* 4—4. qe eus *L.* qe els *N.* qe *SG.* issi qe i *M.* 5—5. *so M. sim. CF.* ceo *LNSG.* 6—6. *so verb. MF. sim. corr. N.* la pel *L.* le apel *S. sim. GC.* 7. en *add. M.* 8. de *G.* 9—9. *so L. sim. I.* aucun autre demander *S. sim. MGF.* 10. homme *add. MC. sim. F.* 11—11. *so verb. GMF. sim. C. om. LNS.* 12. priuement *add. C.*

necessary persons, he do inquire the truth of the matter, and according as he shall find certify the same to the Justices.

Proceedings before ordinary.

In such case the ordinary ought to cause the tenant who propounded the exception, in whatever diocese he resides, to be summoned to be at a certain day and place before him to show whether he can or will say anything against the marriage. And after he has been solemnly summoned, whether he come at the day or not, let the widow's proof by the witnesses she shall produce be admitted, so as such witnesses be not liable to challenge; and such proof being solemnly admitted upon the oath of the witnesses, let the ordinary forthwith according to the inquest make a return to the Justices of the fact as found; and in such case no appeal lies by any of the parties, that the plea in our court may not in any way be longer delayed.

Proof by witnesses in court Christian.

A secret marriage may legitimate the issue, but not give right to dower.

5. But now it may be asked, whether if a man kept a mistress in concubinage, and begot a child by her, and afterwards secretly married her elsewhere than at the church door, and after such marriage had another child by her, and then

esposast solempnement al us del mouster et illuc la dowast, et puis engendrast de luy un autre enfaunt, le quel enfaunt serroit receivable a la successioun del heritage le piere, et par resoun de quel enfaunt deit la mere estre dowé apres le desces le piere. Et en tiel cas fet[1] a respoundre, qe [2]le milueyn[2] deit estre resceu a la successioun del heritage le piere, et sera counté pur mulieré, tut fuessent les esposailes privez, quant en dreit de la nacioun, mes qe il puisse averrer qe il fust né de eynz esposailles, lequel qe les esposailes furent [3]fetes solempnement ou privément[3]. Et si ne avera mie la mere dowarie par la resoun [4]de cel enfaunt, eynz la [253 *b.*]
avera, par la resoun del tierz fiz, et par les[4] solempnes esposailes, ou ele fut dowé al us del mouster. Et issi piert et veirs est, qe la mere ne avera [5]acune foiz[5] point de dowarie, tut soit soen fiz receivable a la successioun del heritage soen piere; ne qe james ne accrest accioun a nule femme de dowarie demaunder, si establisement ne luy eit esté fet al

Brac. 304; Fle. 353 (§ 12).

1. *so SMCF.* soit *L.* fait *G.* 2—2. *so LS.* si le muluen fiz *G.* le Milu ein fiz *M.* muluein fiz *CF.* 3—3. solempnes ou priuees *M.* 4—4. *so verb. M.* *sim. CF.* del enfaunt eynzne mes par la resoun del mulueyn et par *L.* *sim. NS.* de tiel fiz mes par la reson del tierz fiz e par les *G.* 5—5. *om. LN.* acune feiz *M.* *sim. CF.*

publicly married her at the church door, and there endowed her, and after that had a third child by her, which of these children would be admissible to the succession of the inheritance of the father, and by reason of which of them the mother shall be entitled to dower after the decease of the father. The answer in such case is, that the middle son ought to be admitted to the succession of the inheritance of the father, and shall be accounted legitimate in respect of his birth, although the marriage was secret, provided he can aver that he was born within wedlock, whether the espousals were publicly or privately performed. And yet the mother shall not have dower by reason of that child, but she shall have it by reason of the third son, and of the solemn espousals wherein she was endowed at the church door. Hence it appears, and true it is, that sometimes the mother shall not have dower, although the son may be admissible to the succession of the inheritance of his father, and that no right ever accrues to any woman to demand dower,

Dower not allowed unless established at the church door.

us del mouster, lequel qe ceo soit en tens de[1] entredit ou en autre.

Brac. 303; Fle. 353 (§ 8, 9). 6. Et cum le ordinarie ad fet solempnement ceo qe a soen office apent [2]entour la enqueste fere[2] de sour les pointz de noster maundement[3], et sour ceo eit remaundé et certifié nous ou nos Justices, a la seute dounc la pleintive soit le tenaunt resomouns[4], qe il soit devaunt nos Justices a certein jour et lu. A quel jour les parties purrount estre essoniez. Et si le tenaunt face defaute, et la resomounse soit testmoignié, tauntost soit la demaunde[5] prise en nostre meyn par le petit *Cape*, et soit autre foiz somouns a estre a un autre jour a oier soen jugement.

Fle. 353 (§10). 7. Et si le tenaunt soit trespassé einz ceo qe il soit resomouns, en tiel cas covendra a la femme resusciter novel bref sur[6] novel tenaunt. Et si autre foiz soit mise encountre la excepcioun avauntdite, autre foiz ne ly covendra point

[254.] estre veiez[7] a la court Cristiene, puis qe une foiz eit juge-

1. *so MCF. sim. G.* de *om. LNS.* 2—2. *so M. sim. CF.* en co[u]rt et enqueste fete *L.* en Cort e enqueste fete *S. sim. NG.* 3. *so MCF.* comaundement *LNSG.* 4. *so MC.* somouns *L. sim. SG.* [re]somouns *N.* 5. terre *add. M.* [la terre] *interl. N.* 6. le *add. SGMCF.* 7. enuoyee *N. sim. GC.* veie *S.* enueez *M.*

unless it was established to her at the church door, and this,

Interdict. whether in a time of interdict or not[m].

Proceedings in action after certificate. 6. When the ordinary has solemnly performed the duty of his office with regard to the making of the inquest upon the points comprised in our mandate, and has thereupon made his return and certified us or our Justices, the tenant at the in-

Resummons. stance of the plaintiff shall then be resummoned, that he be

Essoin. before our Justices at a certain day and place. At which day

Process on default. the parties may be essoined. And if the tenant make default, and the resummons be proved, let the land demanded be forthwith taken into our hand by the petty *Cape*, and let him be again summoned to appear at another day to hear his judgment.

If tenant dies, a fresh writ is required; 7. If the tenant dies before he is resummoned, the widow must revive her action by a fresh writ against the new tenant; and if the aforesaid exception be again alleged, it will not be necessary to send it again before the court Christian, after judgment has once passed in her favour, but

m The meaning seems to be, that though there was an interdict upon the ceremonies of the church, dower could still be 'established' at the church door. Compare Bracton, f. 304

ment overé pur luy; eynz suffit une foiz prover le matrimoigne en court Cristiene pur touz jours mes. Et issi ne vaudra cele excepcioun en nuli bouche; eynz le covendra autre chose dire, ou la femme recovera sa demaunde. Et en mesme la manere si acune femme demaunde acun homme en baroun et jugement soit fet en Cristiene court pur la femme, lequel qe le homme eit apelé del[1] jugement ou noun, [2]si il[2] moerge neqedent eynz ceo qe le jugement soit reversee, la femme recovera dowarie; et suffisera[3] cel jugement [4]pur prover leal[4] matrimoignie a touz jours mes. Brac. 303 *b*; Fle. 353 (§ 10).

8. Et si le tenaunt die pur excepcioun, qe ele ne fut unqes dowé al us del mouster, solom ceo qe ele dit en counte countaunt, et la femme die la reverse, par pays purra la verité estre enquise. Et si ele ne die les motz, al us del mouster, le bref est abatable pur le vicious counte. Et si la femme demaunde plus qe ne ly fust establi al us del mouster au comencement, tut [5]la creut[5] soen baroun apres le premer establisement par acune fole gelousie, de ceo sourplus ne deit Brac. 303 *b*, 304; Fle. 353 (§ 11, 12). Brac. 304; Fle. 354 (§ 13).

1. de *N.* a defere le *MF.* a defere *C.* 2—2. et si ele *L.* *sim. NSG.* si i *M.* si ele *C.* sil *F.* 3. suffit *SG.* suffira *M.* 4—4. assez pur la femme pur proue de *M.* assez proue del *C.* 5—5. la crust *N.* la encrust *G.* la encresce *M.* le creit *C.* laccrest *F.*

but the marriage need not be proved again.

it is sufficient to prove the marriage in court Christian once for all. Therefore that exception will thenceforth be of no avail in the mouth of any one; but some other defence must be made, or the widow shall recover her demand. In like manner if a woman demands a man as her husband, and judgment is pronounced for the woman in court Christian, whether the man has appealed from the judgment or not, yet if he dies before the judgment is reversed, the woman shall recover dower, and that judgment shall for all future time be a sufficient proof of the marriage.

Endowment at church door denied. **Fact proved by the country.** **Words 'at the church door' must be in the count.** **Dower fixed at church cannot be increased.**

8. If the tenant by way of exception says that she was never endowed at the church door in the manner she has declared in her count, and the widow says the contrary, the truth may be inquired by the country. And if she omits the words 'at the church door,' the writ is abatable for the defect in the count. And if the widow demands more than was at first established upon her at the church door, although her husband from some foolish fondness afterwards increased it, she shall not be en-

[254 b.] ele estre respoundue. Car ausi cum dowarie ly fust establi al us del mouster nomé[1] en certein, ou de la tierce partie et issi en noun certein, en mesme la manere deit soen dowarie estre assigné, et de taunt demaunder ad ele accioun, si ele en soit deforcié, et nient plus.

Brac. 304 b; Fle. 354 (§ 14).

9. Et si la femme demaunde dowarie nomé[2] ausi cum ceo qe luy fust establi al us del mouster en certein, et le tenaunt respoigne et die qe a tort demaunde ele dowarie nomé[3], de sicum ele ne fust point dowé en le establisement for qe de renable dowarie, et si de noun certein ou de la tierce partie de acun certein[4], en tel cas apent a la femme la prove. Et si[5] le tenaunt tende atteignaument de averrer la negative, adounc apendra a ly de prover sa excepcioun, ausi cum a la femme appendera de prover sa entente. Et si la femme amene testmoignes qi fuerent al establisement, ou tende escrit qe de ceo luy fut fet le jour del establisement, et le tenaunt nient for qe le[6] pays, en tiel cas, et[7] ausi en le cas de la prove de la mort, serra plus receivable et de greinure

1. *so corr. N.* ne mie *LSGM.* 2. *so verb. GMCF. om. LNS.* 3. *so verb. MCF. om. LNGS.* 4. *so GMCF.* et *add. L. sim. NS.* 5. *so MCF.* issi *LS.* issi si *N.* iussint *G.* 6. *so SGCF.* del *LN. om. M.* 7. et *om. L.* e *NSGMCF.*

titled to be answered in respect of that increase. For as dower was appointed her at the church door, whether in specie, or of the third part, and so not in specie, in that form dower shall be assigned to her, and she has an action to demand so much, and no more, if she be deforced thereof.

Exception to claim of dower named, that the establishment was of reasonable dower.

9. If the widow demands dower named, as being that which was established upon her at the church door in certain, and the tenant says in answer, that she wrongfully demands dower named, inasmuch as at the establishment she was endowed only of reasonable dower, and therefore uncertain, or of the third part of something certain; in such case the proof lies on the widow; and if the tenant expressly tenders averment of the negative, then it shall belong to him to prove his exception, as well as to the widow to prove her case. And if the widow produces witnesses who were present at the establishment, or tenders a writing which was made to her thereof on the day of the establishment, and the tenant offers nothing but averment by the country, in such case, as well as in cases where the death of the husband is to be proved, the widow's proof shall

Proof lies on widow.

Proof by suit of witnesses, or by deed, preferred to proof by the country.

substaunce la prove de la femme qe del tenaunt. [1]Et si la femme amene la prove, et nul de la prove ne fut al establisement, ne en l'autre cas al enterrement del baroun, [2]en nul cas est[2] sa prove resceivable[3] encountre la seute le tenaunt[1]. Et si nul ne tendra seute, mes simple averrement par pays, en tiel cas soit la verité enquise par pays.

CHAPITRE VIII. [CVIII.]

De [4]Excepcioun de[4] pluralité des femmes. [255.]

1. Si plusours femmes demaundent dowarie a une foiz del dowement un soul mary, par taunt [5]nest la excepcioun al deforceour[5], qe il ne deit point a une foiz as plusours femmes demaundauntes dowarie de [6]la mort[6] un soul homme respoundre. Brac. 306; Fle. 355.

1—1. *om. M.* 2—2. *so verb. ICF.* et nul ne eit *L.* *sim. N.* ne nul ne est *S.* en nul nest *GS.* 3. *so verb. GICF.* resounable *L.* resnable *S.* 4—4. *so M.* *sim. CF.* *om. LNSG.* 5—5. est la excepcioun al deforceour *L.* *sim. NS.* nest excepcion al deforceur *G.* *sim. F.* neit le deforceour excepcion *M.* 6—6. *om. C.*

be more admissible and of greater weight than that of the tenant. But if the widow brings her witnesses, and none of them were present at the establishment of the dower, or, in the other case, at the burial of the husband, her proof is in neither case to be admitted against the suit of the tenant. And if neither of them tenders suit, but simply averment by the country, in such case let the truth be inquired by the country.

CHAPTER VIII.

Of the pleadings where several women claim dower of one husband.

1. If several women at one time demand dower by the establishment of a single husband, an exception thereby arises to the deforciant, that he ought not at the same time to answer several women demanding dower by reason of the death of one man. Exception, where several claim dower of one husband.

Brac. 306; Fle. 355.

2. Et si une femme eit recoverie dowarie, et un autre la demaunde, [1]fet adounc[1] a destincter, lequel ele se pleint del tenaunt soulement, ou de ly et de sa femme dowé, et [2]la quele[2] ad vouché le tenaunt a garraunt. Car si le tenaunt soit entré en garrauntie, adounc apent al garraunt a defendre la voucheresce vers la pleintive. Et si il ne eit mie uncore garraunti, adounc purra la dowé respoundre[3] par ly mesmes, qe ele ne deit mie dowarie aver [4]ne nule for qe cele qe dowé est, quant ele[4] fut la femme espousé a cely de qi mort ele est dowé, et de ly fust seisie[5] en le tens qe il morust ausi cum de soen mari, et pur ceo fust ele dowé, et par graunt dreit. Et a ceo purra la pleintive respoundre et dire, qe [6]la tenaunte[6] a tort ceo [7]dit, car[7] ele ne fu mie sa femme, et [8] parut bien par ceo qe ceste pleintive en acun tens enpleda mesme cely mari en Cristiene court, et ly demaunda a [255 *b.*] baroun en tiel lu par devaunt tiels juges, et en la presence de

1—1. soit adounc *LN.* *sim. SG.* adonc fet *M.* *sim. CF.* 2—2. le quel *SG.* ausi la ou ele *C.* 3. issi *add. MCF.* 4—4. so *M.* *sim. F.* for que tiele qe ad esproue qe ele *L.* *sim. NS.* fors qe cele qe ad proue qe *G.* ne nule chose fors qe cele qe dowe est Car *C.* *sim. I.* 5. feffe *LS.* seysie *corr. N.* seisi *MGC.* *sim. F.* 6—6. le tenaunt *LMC.* *sim. SG.* la tenaunte *corr. N.* 7—7. desdit qe *L.* *sim. NG.* se dit Car *F.* dit qe *M.* dedit Car *C.* 8. ceo *add. MGCF.* *sim. interl. N.*

Action by wife claiming dower against wife endowed.

2. If one woman has recovered dower, and another demands it, a distinction must then be made, whether the plaint is against the tenant alone or against him and the wife endowed, she having vouched the tenant to warrant. For if the tenant has entered into warranty, then the warrant is bound to defend the voucheress against the plaintiff. And if he has not yet entered into warranty, then the dowee may answer by herself to the following effect: that the plaintiff ought not to have dower, nor any one except herself, forasmuch as she was the espoused wife of him of whose death she is endowed, and was seised of him as of her husband at the time when he died, and she was therefore endowed, and that rightfully[n]. To which the plaintiff may in answer say, that the tenant saith wrongfully, for she was not his wife, as plainly appears, inasmuch as this same plaintiff heretofore impleaded the same husband in court Christian and demanded him as her husband

Answer of tenant in dower.

Replication of judgment in court Christian.

n In Bracton this pleading is given as that of the warrant, who is there called tenant. In Fleta, as here, it is the pleading of the woman endowed, and she is called tenant, *mulier tenens.*

mesme [1]cele tenaunte[1] ly dreyna[2] a baroun, ou ceste unqes en nul point ne le reclama ne le countredit. Et si [3]la tenaunte[3] ne le dedie, la pleintive recovera dowarie de ceo qe ele tient. Et si ele dedie par la affirmative ou[4] la negative, sourd une doute dount la certeinté fet a enquere del ordinarie, et solom soen maundement soit la parole resomounse et le jugement fourniz; [5]et plee pendaunt[5] en la court Cristiene soit le plee original endormi. Si replicacioun soit fete de apel et de jugement reversé, soit ausi cum dit est desus de cele replicacioun. Ante, c. 7. s. 2.

3. Ou tut ne die ele pur excepcioun for qe issi, qe ele ne pout estre sa femme, pur ceo qe ele [6]se tust[6] ou ele dust aver reclamé, sicum as baans de secundes esposailes qe solempnement [7]furent demaundez[7] par trois foiz en la eglise [8]mesmes ou la tenaunte fut presente[8], par la negative de la tenaunte serrount ambideus enveez a court Cristiene [9]pur fere les Brac. 307 (s. 2); Fle. 356 (§ 3).

1—1. *so S.* celi tenaunt *LM.* *sim. NG.* cel tenaunt *C.* *sim. F.* 2. desrena *SM.* deserua *CF.* 3—3. *so MG.* le tenaunt *LC.* *sim. F.* la tenaunt *corr. N.* 4. e *M.* en *SGC.* e *F.* 5—5. plee pendaunt *L.* [e le] plee pendaunt *N.* E pendant le ple *MF.* *sim. SGC.* 6—6. *so M.* *sim. G.* fut *LS.* fust *N.* ne sout *C.* ne out *F.* 7—7. *om. LNSGCF.* sunt demaundez *M.* 8—8. *so verb. GM.* *sim. C.* ou commun fut present *L.* ou [la tenaunte] commun fust present *N.* memes ou le tenant fut present *S.* *sim. F.* 9—9. pur certefier les Iustices *M.* pur fere certifier les Justices *G.*

in such a place and before such judges, and in the presence of the same tenant deraigned him as her husband, on which occasion she did not make any counterclaim or opposition. And if the tenant does not deny this, the plaintiff shall recover dower of that which she holds. But if she denies it by affirmation or negation, a doubt arises, which must be ascertained by inquiry of the ordinary, and according to his return the parole shall be continued by resummons, and judgment given; and pending the plea in court Christian, the original plea shall be at rest. And if replication be made of an appeal and judgment reversed, the effect shall be as is above mentioned concerning such a replication. Proof by certification.

3. Again, if the tenant in dower says only, by way of exception, that the plaintiff cannot be his wife because she held her tongue when she ought to have claimed her husband, as, when the banns of the second marriage were three times solemnly asked in the church where she was present, upon the negation of the tenant both of them shall be sent to court Exception that plaintiff heard the banns without claim. Fact referred to court Christian.

Justices certifier[9] sur tiel debat, la quele fut femme al mari de dreit, et la quele de fet. Et solom la certificacioun le ordinarie soit fourni le jugement.

Brac. 307 (s. 3); Fle. 356 (§ 4, 5). 4. Et tut fut la une sa femme a dreit, uncore purra cel dreit perir par defaute de prove, cum si ele fust esposé hors de noster poer. Et ausi par sa negligence [1] en sa entente [1],
[256.] sicum en cas ou la dreite espouse ne encusa unques le secunde contract vivaunt soen baroun qi la weyva [2], en ceo cas perit [3] la accioun de la dreite espouse, qe ele ne deit dowarie aver, nomément si la secounde femme se tint [4] ovek soen baroun jekes a sa mort. Et en mesme la manere perit sa accioun, tut encusast ele le secound matrimoigne, si le baroun morust entre les bras de la secunde femme avaunt le jugement de divorce. En touz ces cas neqedent averount les primeres femmes dowarie, si lour enfaunt puisse recoverer successioun del heritage lour piere.

1—1. e par sa nicete *M.* *om. F.* 2. dowa *F.* veyua *S.* 3. *so SM.* *sim. GCF.* *sim. corr. N.* piert *L.* 4. *so MG.* tient *L.* tynt *N.* tent *C.* tyent *F.*

Christian in order that the Justices may be certified upon this question, which of them was the wife of the husband in law, and which only in fact; and according to the certification of the ordinary judgment shall be given.

Lawful wife may fail, for want of evidence; or by laches. 4. Although one of the women was lawfully his wife, yet her right may be lost by default of evidence, as where she was married out of our jurisdiction. Also by negligence in her claim, as where the rightful wife never disputed the second contract in the lifetime of her husband who abandoned her; in which case her right of action is lost, and she ought not to have dower, especially if the second wife remained with the husband until his death. And in like manner her action is lost, even though she disputed the second marriage, if the husband died in the arms of the second wife before judgment of divorce. But in all these cases the first wives shall have dower, if their children are able to recover the succession of their father's inheritance.

CHAPITRE IX. [CIX.]

[1]*De Excepciouns par le assent le piere*[1].

1. Acune foiz sount escritz fetz, et sagement, del establisement de dowarie, et les queus s'il soint profertz en jugementz, par taunt purra la demaunde de la femme estre [2]meuz clarifié[2]. Et s'il serreint[3] deditz, par collacioun[4] de seals, ou par les testmoignes leynz nomez, ou[5] par pays, et en plusours autres maneres purra la doute estre trié, et lour leauté estre prové. Mes de touz establisementz de dowarie si ad plus de mester [6]de escrit qe de nules autres terres, ou aucun[6] assent i est corru. En tele manere neqedent purra le escrit estre fet, qe rien ne vaudra quant a la prove de la entente la femme; car [7]s'il soit[7] contenu qe soen baroun la dowa, [8]et l'assent[8] le possessour de la terre ne soit trové[9], rien ne ly

Brac. 305; Fle. 355.

[256 *b.*]

1—1. *so verb. CF. sim. MG. In LNDS there is no division or heading of this chapter, but the words* par assent lour piere *are by error introduced into the text before* acune foiz. 2—2. enclarifi *M.* enclarfi *C.* mut estable *F.* mieuz enclarifie *S.* le meuz esclarfie *G.* 3. serrount *N.* seent *M.* seient *GC. sim. F.* 4. *so verb. GMF. sim corr. N.* collusioun *L. sim. SC.* 5. *so M.* et *L.* e *NGSF.* 6—6. *so LNDSG.* de escriz de establicemenz de doweire dacune terres ou autri *M.* descrit destablissement de doweir e dautre terre ou autri *C.* de escrit destablisement des dowaries ke des autres terres, ou autre *F.* de escritz qe de nules aultres maneres establicementz de dowaries des acunes terres ou autri *W.* 7—7. *so verb SG.* sil eit *L.* si il est *MF.* il eit *C.* 8—8. *so verb. N. sim. F.* al assent *LGS.* oue lassent *M. sim. C.* 9. proue *F.*

CHAPTER IX.

Of Exceptions relating to the Assent of the Father.

1. Sometimes writings are made of the establishment of dower, and that wisely; for if such writings are produced at the trial, the wife's demand can be more clearly made out. And if they should be denied, this doubt may be tried and their legality proved by comparison of seals, by the witnesses named in the writings, by the country, or in several other ways. But of all establishments of dower, there is most need of writing where the assent of a third party has concurred. The writing may however be so made as to be useless in proving the wife's case; for if it is said, that her husband endowed her, and the assent of the possessor of the land is not mentioned, the writing

Deed of establishment of dower;

especially necessary, where the assent of a third party is to be shown.

vaudra en cel cas le escrit de la prove de sa demaunde. Et[1] ausi, si contenu i soit, qe autre del baroun la dowa.

Brac. 305; Fle. 355. 2. Bien bosoigne dounke qe en chescun tiel escrit soint cestes resouns especefiez, qe baroun la dowa al us del mouster de la tierce partie de la terre soen piere ou de autre parent ou [2]de autre[2] ami, et qe mesme celi ami ou parent se assenti en mesme le lu et en mesme le houre. Et a ceo qe le escrit soit [3]de atteignaunte[3] value, et[4] tut soit le escrit aillours fet, uncore le covendra graunter et confermer par assent al us del mouster; ou rien ne vaudra le dowement, si le ami le voille countrepleder, par ceste parole en le bref, al us del mouster. Par ceste resoun apiert et veirs est, qe femme ne recovera mie dowarie maugré le tenaunt, si ele ne mette a veir par escrit, ou par testmoignes qi furent al establisement et as esposailles, ou par pays, qe ces deus choses convinrent[5] a les esposailes, establisement [6]de par[6] baroun, et assent de cel ami, ou de soen auncestre, de qi terre ele demaunde dowarie,

1. ne *MCF*. 2—2. *om. MF*. 3—3. *so M. sim. GSF.* de atterminaunte *LN*. 4. et *om. M.* ou *G*. 5. conuendrount *L.* conuiendrent *N.* tenerent *C.* corurent *GF*. 6—6. de son *M.* par le *SG*.

will not avail in evidence of her demand. So likewise, if it is stated in the writing, that some other person than the husband endowed her.

Requisite contents of such a deed. 2. It is necessary therefore, that in every such writing these points should be specially mentioned, that the husband endowed the wife at the church door of the third part of his father's land, or of that of some other kinsman or friend, and that the same friend or kinsman assented in the same place and at the same time. And although the writing be made elsewhere, yet in order that it may be of effectual value, it should be granted and confirmed by assent at the church door, or the endowment will be worth nothing, if the friend choose to dispute it, on account of the expression in the writ, 'at the church door.' By this reasoning it appears, and it is true, that a woman shall not recover dower against the will of the tenant, unless she make it appear by writing, or by witnesses present at the establishment and at the marriage, or by the country, that these two things concurred at the marriage, namely, an establishment of dower by the husband and an assent of that friend, or his ancestor, of whose land she demands dower, and

et illuc se assenti al dowement, lequel [1]qe eit escrit[1] ou noun. [257.]
Car aylours assenter ne vaut rien.

CHAPITRE X. [cx.]

De Excepciouns communes.

1. A cel qe est contenu en le bref, dount ele rien ad, purra le tenaunt dire, qe ele ad partie. Mes a ceo covendra destincter, lequel la pleintive eit resceu partie de sa dowarie avaunt le purchaz del bref, ou puis. Car si puis, et de mesme le deforceour de qi ele se pleint, en mesme la vile qe est nomé en le bref, ja par taunt ne est le bref abatable; car ele purra dire, qe del sourplus fut fet soen assetz. Et si ele eit resceu partie avaunt le bref purchacé, si est le bref abatable, ne mes ne tendra lu nul bref for qe bref overt sour le dreit. Brac. 311 *b*; Fle. 347 (§ 1); Stat. West. 1 (3 Ed. I.) c. 49.

2. Ou le deforceour purra dire qe la femme pleintive ne deit dowarie aver, car soen baroun ne tint point le tenement Brac. 309 *b*; Fle. 347 (§ 5); Hengh. Parv. c. 3. p. 87.

1—1. qili eit escrit *S.* qil eit contenu *M.*

that he assented to the endowment, whether there be writing or not, at the church door; for an assent at any other place is useless.

CHAPTER X.

Of common Exceptions in Actions of Dower.

1. To those words in the writ 'whereof she hath nought,' the tenant may answer that she hath part. But then it will be necessary to distinguish, whether the plaintiff has received part of her dower before the purchasing her writ or after. For if after, although from the same deforceor of whom she complains, and in the same vill named in the writ, yet the writ is not thereby abatable; for she may say that satisfaction was made to her for the difference[o]; but if she received part before the writ was purchased[p], then the writ is abatable; and no writ shall lie but the writ patent upon the right. Exception, that the widow has part of her dower.

2. Again, the deforceor may say that the plaintiff ought not Exception, that husband did not hold in demesne;

[o] That is, she may say by way of replication, that at the time of purchasing the writ she had nothing of her dower, but that an assignment has since been made to her in satisfaction of part of her demand. Compare Bracton, f. 311 *b*.

[p] This must be understood, if the part was received from the same deforciant and in the same vill. See Statute of Westminster 1. c. 49; Fleta, p. 347 (§ 4).

dount ele chalenge dowarie [1]en demeyne[1] le jour qe il la esposa ne puis, ou, s'il [2]le tint[2] en demeyne, il neqedent ne
Brac. 310 (§ 8); Ante, c. 1. s. 5. la pout dower mie, pur ceo qe il ne out rien del fee. Mes si le mari la femme eut le fee de acun tenement qe deust retourner[3] a ly ou a ses heirs apres le desces de acun qe le
[257 *b*.] avera tenu a terme de vie, en tote manere de tel tenement purra la femme bien demaunder dowarie, tut [4]en fut le fraunc tenement[4] aliené avaunt qe le mari la esposa, si al us del mouster en fut dowé.

Brac. 311 *b*; Fle. 347 (§ 6); Hengh. Parv. c. 3. p. 87. Ante, l. i. c. 6. s. 5. 3. Ou il porra dire, qe ele ne deit point dowarie aver, par la resoun qe soen baroun fut feloun et porta jugement de la felonie, de quei il fust pendu, ou decolé, [5]ou faleisé[5], ou demembré, [6]ou neyé[6], ou [7]a acune autre[7] mort condempné, ou forjura la terre, ou fut utlagé; et dounc covendra le record voucher a garraunt. Et quant le record serra venuz, uncore purra la femme dedire le record, si ne soit testmoigné par

1—1. *so M. sim. C.* mesme *L. sim. NGS.* auer en demeyne *F.* 2—2. ne tient *L.* le tynt *corr. N.* la tint *M.* ne tent *GSC.* nel tint *F.* 3. *so GF. sim. MSC.* recouerer *L.* reuertir *N.* 4—4. *so verb. M.* fut le tenement *LGS. sim. N.* feust le fraunk tenement *C.* en fust le tenement *F.* 5—5. *so M.* faleste *C. om. LNGSF.* 6—6. *so F. om. LNGS.* ou nee *MC.* 7—7. ou en autre manere a la *M.* ou en asqune manere a *C. sim. F.*

to have dower, for that her husband did not hold the tenement, whereof she claims dower, in demesne either on the day on which he married her or afterwards, or that if he did hold
or not in fee. it in demesne, yet he could not endow her, as he had no fee
Wife may be expressly endowed of a reversion. therein. But if her husband had the fee of any tenement which was to return to him or his heirs on the death of some person who held it for term of life, in all such kinds of tenements although the freehold was aliened before the husband married her, a wife may demand dower if she was endowed thereof at the church door.

Exception of felony of husband. 3. Again, he may say that she ought not to have dower by reason that her husband was a felon and suffered judgment of
Various forms of execution. felony, for which he was hanged, or beheaded, or buried in the sands, or dismembered, or drowned, or condemned to some other death[q], or abjured the realm, or was outlawed; in which case
Proof by record. the record must be vouched to warrant. And when the record is produced, the widow may dispute the record unless it is

q As to the various modes of execution mentioned above, and the places where they were customary, see Hengham Parva, p. 87, and Selden's notes thereupon.

acun qe porte record[1] par auctorité de nous. Car ele purra dire qe acun li pendi par haunge, et ou il ne fust unques acoupé de nule felonie, et par tel et [2]tiels autres qi[2] encolourerent sa mort par une manere de jugement. Et si ceo soit averré par pays, ja pur cel jugement torcenous ne deit la femme estre barré de sa dowarie, ne le heir de la successioun del heritage. Ne ausi ou la felonie ne amounta mie a xii. deners, ne ausi ou la utlagerie fut pronouncié [3]avaunt le quart Counté, ou pronuncié[3] en autres countez qe par la ou [4]il ne dust aver pecché[4]. Ne[5] en nul cas ou la utlagarie est defensable par dreit. Ne ausi en nul cas de[6] jugement de mort, ou la felonie par examinacioun est trespas et nule felonie, ne [258.] ausi en abjuracions pur trespas, sicum pur parcs ou pur vivers ou par autre trespas semblable.

4. Et tut eit le baroun suffert jugement de felonie et par sa decerte, uncore purra ele dire, qe pur ceo ne deit ele mie estre barré de sa demaunde; car en le tens qe il fit sa[7]

1. *so verb. MGSF.* *sim. in marg. N.* *om. L.* kar ceo couiendra estre tesmoine par asqun qe port record *C.* 2—2. *so N.* *sim. G.* tieles autres qe *L.* *sim. S.* teuz autres e *M.* teus autrs *C.* deus autres *F.* 3—3. *om. GMCF.* 4—4. ne *om. NG.* ou le peche fu fet *M.* ou il nauoit peche *C.* ou il auoit pecche *F.* 5. ausi ou la utlagerie fu pronuncie deuaunt le tierz counte ne *add. M.* *sim. CF.* 6. *so SGMCF.* en *L.* ou *N.* 7. la *SGM.* *so corr. N.* cele *CF.*

proved by some one authorised by us to bear record. For she may say that some one out of hatred caused her husband to be hanged, when in fact he was never found guilty of any felony, and that this act was done by such an one, and by certain others who coloured his death with a sort of judgment. And if this be verified by the country, the widow ought not by such a wrongful judgment to be barred of her dower, nor the heir of the succession to the inheritance. So neither where the felony did not amount to 12*d*, nor where the outlawry was pronounced before the fourth county court or pronounced in any other county than in that where the offence was supposed to have been committed. Nor in any case where a lawful defence may be made to the outlawry. Nor in any case of judgment of death, where the supposed felony is found on examination to be a trespass and not felony, nor in the case of abjurations for trespass, as in parks or fishponds, or other like trespasses.

Replication of colourable judgment; larceny under 12*d*.; informal outlawry.

4. Although the husband suffered judgment of felony and that deservedly, yet she may say that, notwithstanding this, she ought not to be barred of her demand, for at the time he

Replication that the felony was not done during the marriage.

felonie, ne ly out ele mie entre ses bras, ne point ly fut esposé, ne en fut assentaunt, ne rien [1]ne sout. Et de sicum[1] femme a feloun ne deit mie perdre sa dowarie for pur ceo qe hom deit[2] supposer qe ele savoit de la felonie soen mari, et [3]dunc ele ne le dust point encuser[3], ou[4] la felonie ne fut unques fete en le tens qe ele fut sa femme, en tiel cas[5] deit ele aver dowarie des terres le heir qe furent[6] en la garde soen seignur.

Ante, l. i. c. 25. s. 9.

Brac. 92, 302; Fle. 348 (§9); Hengh. Parv. c. 3. p. 88.

5. Et ausi ne avera femme renable dowarie, si ele ne puisse averrer par pays ou en autre manere, qe ele pout dowarie aver deservi, vivaunt soen baroun, tut soit ele pucele, ou tut soit ele de xx. aunz ou de c.[7]; ne ausi ou les maritz morirent si joevenes, ou de autre estat, qe il ne poeint consenter. Mes ja pur ceo ne soint eles barrez a recoverer autre manere de dowarie. Ne ausi ne deit point femme recoverer dowarie

1—1. *so verb. M.* ne sout de ly par quei *LN. sim. GS.* nen eust ne seust E de si qe *C.* nen sout e de ci ke *F.* 2. dust *N.* deit bien *MC. sim. F.* 3—3. *conj.* dunc ele ne dust point excuser *L. sim. SG.* dunt ele ne dust point escuser *M. sim. NEFC.* 4. e *M.* 5. *so NSGMCF.* cas *om. L.* 6. sunt *MF.* sount *C.* 7. anz *add. GS.*

committed his felony she was not united with him nor married to him, neither was assenting or privy thereto. And inasmuch as the wife of a felon ought not to lose her dower, except by reason that she may be fairly supposed to know of the felony of her husband, and even then she is not bound to accuse him, therefore, where the felony was not committed during the time that she was his wife, she ought to have dower of the lands of the heir which are in the custody of his lord[q].

Widow not entitled to reasonable dower unless she was *capax viri* during marriage, nor if husband was incapable of consent.

5. The widow shall not have her reasonable dower unless she can aver by the country or in some other manner, that she was capable of deserving dower in the lifetime of her husband, whether she be a maid or not, and though she be twenty or a hundred years old; nor where the husbands died so young, or in any other such condition as to be incapable of consenting to matrimony[r]. They are not however barred from recovering

[q] These last words should apparently be understood of the felon's lands escheated to the lord. 'A man commits a felony which is not discovered; afterwards he purchaseth land, and afterwards taketh a wife. Although he be sentenced for the felony, the wife shall recover dower. Dubium tamen est, quia quicquid acquiritur inter feloniam commissam et ipsius feloniæ convictionem, fit ac si ante feloniam perpetratam propter convictionem ob quam nomen felonis subibit.' (Note in MS. *N.*) I do not find, that in later times an exception was made in favour of the wife of a felon, when the crime was committed before the marriage. See Perkins, Profitable Book, s. 387; and compare Coke Litt. 31 *a.*

[r] It would appear from the above, that reasonable dower could not be claimed unless the husband was of an age before his death to consent to the marriage. This was not the

en nule avowesoun de eglise en tut ou en partie, si ele ne[1] puisse averrer, qe ele en fut douwé. Uncore luy[2] purra barrer sa negligence, qe ele suffri puis, sauntz debat et sauntz cleym mettre, qe le heir soen mari, ou autre en soen noun, presenta puis la mort soen mari. Et si le bref soit purchacé sour le heir et sour le gardein joyntement, si cheit le bref, si il soit chalengé; pur ceo qe le gardein fet touz jours a somoundre qe il eit avaunt l'enfaunt qe la pleintive [3]dist estre[3] en sa garde.

Fle. 348 (§ 12). [258 *b.*] Fle. 348 (§ 10).

6. Ou purra dire qe ele ad dowarie deservi[4] et forfet par soen avouterie, car ele s'en ala [5]de soen mari[5] a autri lit puis

Stat. Westm. 2. c. 34; Fle. 348 (§ 13).

1. so *NGMC.* ni *S.* ne *om. LF.* 2. so *LNC.* li *S.* la *M.* le *G.* 3—3. so *print.* dust entrer *LNDMCF.* *sim. GSBW.* 4. so *LNGS.* desmeri *MF.* 5—5. par son auouterie *M.*

other kinds of dower. Neither ought a widow to recover dower in the advowson of any church in whole or in part, unless she can aver that she was endowed thereof; and still she may be barred by negligence, if she afterwards without question or claim permitted the heir of her husband or some other in his name to present after the death of her husband. And if the writ be obtained against the heir and the guardian jointly, the writ falls if it be challenged, because the guardian must always be summoned to produce the infant whom the plaintiff alleges to be in his ward.

No dower of advowson, unless named.

Joint writ against heir and guardian, bad.

6. Again, the tenant may say that the plaintiff has forfeited

Forfeiture of dower by adultery.

rule of later times. 'If the wife be past the age of nine yeares at the time of the death of her husband, she shall be endowed, of what age soever her husband be, albeit he were but four yeares old.' (Coke Litt. 33 *a.*) And I do not find any authority for the doctrine of the text in Bracton or Fleta. The former says that the minority of the husband or the wife did not impede dower, provided the wife was of ability 'dotem promereri et virum sustinere.' (Bracton, f. 92.) And Fleta fixes the required age of the wife at nine years and a half. (Fleta, p. 340, c. 23. § 3, 348, § 9; compare Littleton, Ten. s. 36; Coke Litt. 33 *a.*) But the doctrine of Britton is supported by Hengham (Hengham Parva, p. 88); and by the Register, where it is said, that a woman will lose her dower if her husband die under age. (Regist. Brev. Orig. 170.) And the annotator in MS. *N.* says that in all cases where the husband was incapable of consenting to the marriage, either because he was 'infra annos nubiles, i. e. ad xiiii. annos,' or from any other cause, although there was no default in the wife, she should not have dower. So, it is said to have been held in the 13th Edw. I., that a wife would lose her dower if her husband died under nine years. (Fitzh. Abr. *Dower.* 172. citing 13 Ed. I. Iter North.; but *qu.* whether it should not be read *ele* for *il;* that is, if *the wife* died under nine years.) In 12 Ric. II. dower was allowed where the husband was ten years of age, and the wife eleven at his death. Fitzh. Abr. *Dower.* 54. The clause which follows in the text refers apparently both to the wives of infants, and to widows of tender age, who, as it seems, might claim dower certain, but not 'reasonable dower.' 'Although the wife be not of ability to deserve dower, yet she shall have it, provided that the assent of the husband was given at their espousals; because establishment of dower is a kind of purchase which is not forbidden by the nonage; and is therefore permissible.' (Note in MS. *N.*) This distinction is also found in Hengham, but does not appear to have been recognised in later times. Compare Coke Litt. 33 *a.*

ceo qe il la esposa, et issi forfit ele dowarie. Et si la femme a ceo respoigne, et die, qe ceo ne luy deit barrer ne grever, car ele fust puis a ly recouncilé, si qe il la resceut[1], et en sa seisine morust, a ceo purra le tenaunt respoundre, qe ja pur ceo ne deit ele uncore aver dowarie, car il ne la resceut[2] unques de soen gré; einz fit maugré soen par cohercioun[3] de Saincte Eglise, et par jugement de Cristiene court. Et si ceo soit averré la pleintive ne enportera[4] nient.

Fle. 348 (§14). 7. Et si la femme se pleingne del heir, issi purra il respoundre, qe il la deit garraunter de soen dowarie, si ele fut dowé et de sa dowarie enpledé, mes [5]s'il ne eit les[5] chartres, qe furent a soen auncestre, qe[6] ele ly detient, [7]car autrement par cas purra il[7] estre desherité, issi qe il ne fut unques encountre de fere luy sa dowarie [8]par si qe ele[8] deliverast les
[259.] chartres qe a ly apendent de soen heritage. Et si ceo puse averrer, soit agardé qe la femme rende les chartres, et qe il

1. recoillist *C.* 2. recoillist *C.* 3. coaccion *MC.* *sim. F.* 4. prendra *MCF.* 5—5. sil ne eint les *L.* si il ne eit *N.* *sim. D.* sil ne eust les *G.* *sim. SMW.* sil moustre *C.* si ele nust les *F.* 6. les queus *MCF.* 7—7. purra il par cas *M.* purra par cas *C.* si porra il par cas *F.* 8—8. issint qe ele ly *G.*

and lost dower by adultery, inasmuch as she left her husband after he married her for the bed of another, by which act she forfeited her dower. If to this the wife replies that it ought not to bar or affect her because she was afterwards reconciled to him, so that he received her again, and in her seisin died, the tenant may say in answer that notwithstanding this she still ought not to have dower, for that he did not receive her of his own accord, but against his will by coercion of Holy Church and by sentence of court Christian. And if this be proved, the plaintiff shall take nothing.

Replication of condonance.

Rejoinder, of ecclesiastical coercion.

7. If the widow brings her plaint against the heir, he may answer thus, that he is bound to warrant her dower to her in case she was endowed and was impleaded of her dower, provided he has the charters delivered to him, which were his ancestor's, and which she detains from him; for otherwise he may perhaps lose his inheritance; so that he was never against assigning her dower, provided she would have delivered up to him the charters which belong to him, relating to his inheritance. And if he can verify this, let it be awarded that the widow restore the charters, and that he assign and deliver to

Exception that widow detains the title deeds.

assingne et delivere sa dowarie; et la femme remeindra en la mercie pur sa fause pleinte.

8. Ou il purra dire qe ele ne deit estre dowé, car de acune dowarie qe ele tient fut ele en acun tens [1]enpledé, et ou[1] ele ly[2] dut aver vouché a garraunt, sicum le garraunt de sa dowarie, la voucha ele un autre, tel[3] par noun, en disheritesoun del dreit heir. Et si ceo puisse le dreit heir averrer, si ad ele [4]perdu recoverer de tut le remenaunt de[4] dowarie pur sa malice. Fle. 348 (§ 15).

9. Ou il purra dire, qe a tort se pleint ele, car satisfaccioun luy fut fete, dount ele se paya, par la vaillaunce de terre ou de deners[5]. Et si la femme le graunte, ou ne le dedie mie, mes die qe unques [6]del plein ne[6] luy fut fete satisfaccioun, adounc cesse la demaunde de dowarie, et se pleigne par bref de covenaunt, si ele quide bien fere. Ou il purra dire qe autre foiz recovera ele dowarie de mesme les tenementz et devers ly mesmes par semblable bref, et si ceo soit averré ou nient desdit, si cheete le dreyn bref, et la femme sue le jugement del premer bref, si ele voille. Fle. 348 (§ 16). Fle. 348 (§ 17).

1—1. *so verb. MF.* plede ou *L.* enpledee ou *N.* *sim. GS.* 2. *so G.* *sim. C.* *sim. interl. N.* ly *om. LMSF.* 3. *so SMCF.* *sim. G.* *sim. in marg. N.* tel *om. L.* 4—4. forfet de recouerir de tut le remenant de *G.* forfet tut le recouerir a demaunder *M.* 5. *so MF.* *sim. C.* tenement *LGS.* tenement [ou de deners] *N.* 6—6. *so MF.* del plein *LS.* de pleyn ne *N.* del pleine *G.* de la pleinte *C.*

her her dower; and the widow shall remain in mercy for her false plaint.

8. Again, the tenant may say that she ought not to be endowed, for that she was once impleaded of part of the dower which she holds, and whereas she ought to have vouched him as the warrant of her dower, she vouched another, such an one by name, in disherison of the right heir. And if the right heir can verify this, she has forfeited all recovery of the residue of her dower for her malice. Exception that widow has vouched another to warrant.

9. Or he may say that she wrongfully complains, forasmuch as satisfaction was made to her for her dower by the value in land or money, wherewith she was contented. And if the wife admits the agreement, or does not deny it, but replies that satisfaction was never fully made to her, the demand of dower shall thereby cease, and she may proceed by writ of covenant if she thinks proper. Or he may say that heretofore she recovered dower against him of the same tenements by a like writ, and if this be verified or not denied, the last writ shall fall, and the wife, if she pleases, may sue judgment on the former writ. Accord and satisfaction. Former judgment.

Brac. 298 *b* (§ 5); Fle. 349 (§ 23, 24). [259 *b*.]

10. Et purra avener, qe plusours femmes demaundereint dowarie a une foiz del dowement de un soul mari[1]; totes neqedent ne deivent mie estre dowez; car une fut sa dreite femme, et cele deit dowarie enporter. [2]Mes, qe[2] fut sa dreite espouse et qe[3] concubine, ne [4]poet nul seculer[4] juge enquere; car la conisaunce de matrimoigne et de testament apent a Cristiene court. Ne james ne fet dowarie a graunter[5], taunt cum debat est entre deus femmes ou plusours, jekes autaunt qe [6]prové soit[6] en Court cristiene quele de totes fut la dreite femme al mari.

Brac. 298 *b*, 299; Fle. 349 (§ 26, 27).

11. Ne james ne fet a graunter[7], en cas ou le dreit heir plede pur soen heritage, et la femme pur sa dowarie a une foiz, deques autaunt qe le plé de la successioun soit terminé, pur le inconvenient qe purra sure[8]. Car si deus femmes toillauntes[9] entour dowarie fuessent enveez en Cristiene court, [10]pur veer[10] illuc, la quele [11]des deus femme soit[11] al mari et

1. baroun *MC*. *sim*. *F*. 2—2. *so LGS*. Mes qe[le] *N*. mes quele *M*. pur ceo qele *C*. mes ky *F*. 3. *so GC*. qi *LS*. [la] qe[le] *N*. quele *M*. 4—4. *so MC*. *sim*. *GF*. puisse nul voler *L*. purra nul seculer *corr*. *N*. 5. *so M*. *sim*. *GF*. garraunter *LC*. *sim*. *S*. garraunter [al' graunter *in marg*.] *N*. 6—6. *so M*. *sim*. *CF*. la proue *L*. la proeue [soit finie *in marg*.] *N*. la proeue seit *G*. *sim*. *S*. 7. *so MGF*. *sim*. *corr*. *N*. garraunter *L*. 8. sourdre *F*. 9. qe toilent *M*. toillent *C*. toillaunt *F*. 10—10. a prouer *MCF*. 11—11. de deus femmes soit *L*. *sim*. *S*. des deus femmes soit [droite espouse] *N*. des deus femme seit *G*. de deus femmes fuisse dreite femme *M*. de eus feust la dreyte femme *C*. des deus fust dreite femme *F*.

Where several claim dower, the question of marriage is first determined in court Christian.

10. It may also happen that several wives at one time demand dower of the endowment of one husband, whereas they ought not all to be endowed, for one only was his lawful wife, and she ought to obtain the dower. But which was his lawful wife and which his concubine, no secular judge can inquire, for the cognizance of marriage and of testaments belongs to the court Christian; and so long as there is a dispute between two or more wives, dower is not to be allowed, until it be proved in court Christian which of them was the lawful wife of the husband.

Of two pleas, for dower and for the inheritance, the latter must be determined first.

11. So where the lawful heir brings an action for his inheritance and the wife for her dower at the same time, dower is not to be granted until the plea relating to the succession is determined, on account of the inconvenience which might ensue. For if two wives who are contending about their dower were to be sent into court Christian, there to determine which of them was the lawful wife of the husband, and which

la quele concubine,[1] purroit par cas avener, qe [2]cele se proveroit[2] pur dreite espouse, qe[3] ne serroit mie mere a celi qi se averoit[4] provė pur dreit heir en nostre court, et qe le fiz cele qe serroit provė concubine en Cristiene court, se averoit provė pur dreit heir en nostre court. Et pur ceo covent il en ceo cas quant plusours heirs toillent entour heritage, et plusours femmes entour la dowarie, qe les plez de dowarie soint suspenduz deques autaunt qe discus soit en nostre court, a quel heir serra ajugé la successioun. Et solom le semblable cas [5]de tiel toil eu[5] par entre clers en Cristiene court fut [260.]
primes purveu la prohibicioun del *Indicavit*, a fere suspendre le play en Cristiene court jekes autaunt qe discus soit en nostre court par entre les avowez, pur le peril qe purra [6]nestre al un des avowez[6] sour la avowesoun, si le play prist primes fin en Cristiene court par entre les clers qe par entre les lays del avowesoun. Et tauntost cum il avera soen heritage recoveri, soit la dowarie assigné a sa mere, sauntz

1. *so MCF.* et *add. L.* *sim. GS.* ceo *add. on eras. N.* 2—2. *so verb. F.* ele qe se profert *L.* ele qe se [ad] profert *N.* cele se profreit *M.* cele qe se proeue *G.* cele qe se profreit *S.* *sim. C.* 3. qe *om. G.* 4. ad *LN.* auereit *MCF.* 5—5. de tiel toil et *L.* *sim. NS.* de toil *M.* detoille eu *F.* en tiel toil e *G.* 6—6. a vn des auowes sourdre *C.*

his concubine, it might perhaps fall out that she should prove herself to be the lawful wife, who was not the mother of him who might prove himself in our court to be the lawful heir, and that the son of her who in the court Christian was found a concubine, might prove himself in our court the lawful heir. Therefore in the above case where several heirs are disputing about their inheritance and several wives about their dower, it is proper that the pleas of dower should be suspended until it be decided in our court to whom the succession is to be adjudged. And accordingly, in the like case of a dispute between two clerks in court Christian, the prohibition by *Indicavit* was first provided, to cause the plea in court Christian to be suspended, until the question between the patrons be decided in our court, by reason of the risk which might arise to one of the alleged patrons in respect of the advowson, if the plea in court Christian between the clerks was determined before that between the laymen concerning the advowson. And as soon as the heir has recovered his inheritance let dower be assigned to his mother, but without

Analogous case of two pleas by clerk and patron of advowson.

agard neqedent de damages pur le delay, car le delay vient del garraunt de la court et nient del tort le heir. Et cum le heir serra issi en seisine del heritage a dreit ou a tort, et la femme issi dowé, et autre femme viegne demaunder dowarie, [1]et soen fiz[1] le heritage, en tiel cas soit dit a la femme, qe ele face soen fiz primes prover a dreit heir, et puis serra ele respoundue de sa dowarie et ne mie avaunt.

Brac. 299; Fle. 349 (§ 29). 12. Et lequel qe femme qe demaunde dowarie eit enfaunt ou noun, touz jours est[2] cil garraunt de sa dowarie a qi la dowarie deit reverter apres le desces de la femme, lequel qe il soit heir ou chief seignur a qi les deus parties sount eschetes en acune manere par defaute de saunc, ou par felonie en cas, ou par revercioun. Un cas neqedent est forpris, sicum en cas de la femme qe ad recoverie dowarie de acun qi [3]feffé en fust[3] par le mari, ou par soen heir, et rien [260 *b.*] ne soit demoré al heir dount il puse garraunter la dowarie, ne fere a la vaillaunce, en tiel cas deit la dowarie reverter la dount il vient; et si li ne serra mie neqedent garraunt de cele dowarie.

1—1. *so verb. MCF.* de soen fiz qi ad *LN. sim. GS.* 2. *so MGCF.* eit *L.* soit *N.* 3—3. feffe enfaunt *L. sim. N.* en fu feffe *M. sim. GSCF.*

awarding any damages for the delay, inasmuch as the delay was warranted by the court, and did not proceed from the wrongful act of the heir. And when the heir is thus in seisin of the inheritance, whether rightfully or wrongfully, and the wife endowed, and another wife comes and demands dower, and her son demands the inheritance, in such case let the wife be told that she should first cause her son to be proved lawful heir, and that then, and not before, she shall be answered as to her dower.

The reversioner is the warrant of dower, 12. Whether the wife who demands dower has a child or not, that person is always the warrant of her dower to whom the dower ought to revert after the death of the wife, whether it be the heir or the chief lord, to whom the two other parts are escheated in any way either by failure of blood, or perhaps for felony, or by reversion. There is a case however excepted, unless the land has been aliened. where a wife recovers dower of one who was enfeoffed by the husband or his heir, the heir having nothing left whereout he could warrant the dower or make satisfaction in value; in this case such dower shall revert to him from whom it came, and yet he shall not be warrant of the dower.

13. Ou il purra dire qe ele ne deit dowarie aver, pur ceo qe soen mari n'out nent de dreit en cele terre, de sicum ele fut le heritage ou le mariage de sa premere femme. Ou issi, [1]pur ceo qe[1] [2]par soen eyndegré a sa fraunche[2] volunté en sa [3]lige veftee[3] relessa et quiteclama tut le dreit qe ele out[4] ou aver pout [5]en dowarie[5]. Ou issi, pur ceo qe ele est sa neyve, et tenaunt de ly villenage sicum astrer[6], et ly seisi de luy et de ses chateus et de sa sute. Ou pur ceo qe le mari perdi le tenement[7] par jugement, sicum autri dreit. Ou pur ceo qe nule femme ne soleit unqe estre douwé pur le usage del pays, qe [8]s'il ne eussent escritz[8]. Ou pur ceo qe le mari ne out unqes en sa vie fee ne demeyne[9] en cel tenement dount ele demaunde dowarie. Ou[10] pur ceo qe autrefoiz s'en parti quites par jugement de mesme la demaunde vers mesme la pleintive. Ou[11] pur ceo, qe il ne tient rien del tenement, dount ele demaunde dowarie, le jour del bref purchacé ne puis. Ou pur

Brac. 308, 308 *b*; Fle. 357 (§ 1).

1—1. *so M. sim. F.* purra ceo qe *L.* purra estre qe *G.* purra ceo estre qe *S.* purra [il] dire qe pur ceo qe *N.* purra cesti *C.* 2—2. a son eide gre oue sa bone *M.* par son einz degre e sa propre *G.* 3—3. pure e lige veduete *M.* lige veduetee *N. sim. GSCF.* 4. a doweir demaunder *add. M.* a doweyr auer *C. sim F.* 5—5. *om. MCF.* 6. astre *M.* 7. dount ele demaunde dowerie *add. M. sim. CF.* 8—8. ne le soeffre *M. sim. F.* luy nestut estre *C.* 9. *so M.* nient *LNCF. sim. GS.* 10. *so SGM. so corr. N.* Et *LECF.* 11. *so SGMF. so corr. N.* et *L.* e *C.*

13. Or he may say that she ought not to have dower, because her husband had not any right in the land, inasmuch as it was the inheritance or the estate in marriage of his first wife. Or thus: because she of her own accord and by her free will in her absolute widowhood released and quitclaimed all the right which she had or might have in her dower. Or thus: for that she is his nief holding of him in villenage as an astrer[s], and he seised of her and of her chattels and her suit. Or thus: for that the husband lost the tenement by judgment as the right of another. Or, for that by the custom of the country no widow was ever wont to be endowed unless there were writings. Or, for that the husband never in his lifetime had fee or demesne in the tenement whereof she demands dower. Or, for that the tenant was heretofore acquitted by judgment of the same demand at the suit of the same plaintiff. Or, for that he held nothing in the tenement whereof she demands dower on the day of the writ purchased, or since. Or, for that he does not claim any freehold therein, but holds

Exceptions. Land belonged to first wife; Release; Villenage; Judgment against husband; No dower by custom; Husband had no fee; Previous acquittal; Non-tenure; Tenure in another's right;

[s] See p. 155, note.

ceo, qe il ne cleyme nul fraunc tenement, eynz le tient en autri noun, sicum gardeyn ou baillif ou termer ou vileyn.

[261.] Ou pur ceo qe il tient le tenement joyntement[1] en commun oveke autres sauntz queus il ne purra respoundre.

Fle. 357 (§ 1). 14. Et si acun die qe il ne ad nul fraunc tenement si noun[2] par condicioun jekes autaunt qe il eit taunt levé des issues, ou jekes autaunt qe [3]tele chose chete[3] ou aveigne ou tele, ja par taunt ne cherra le bref, einz estoise, [4]et il en[4] vouche a garraunt, si il quide bien fere. (Stat. West. 2. (13 Ed. I.) c. 4; Brac. 310 (§ 10); Fle. 357 (§ 3).) Et a ceo qe le tenaunt dit, qe ele ne deit dowarie aver pur ceo qe soen baroun perdi par jugement le tenement, a[5] ceo purra il estre respoundu par replicacioun, qe ceo fut par fraude et collusioun, et par gré le baroun; et si ceo soit averré, si ne vaudra rien la excepcioun.

Brac. 310 (§ 8); Fle. 357 (§ 3). 15. Ou il purra dire qe soen[6] baroun aliena la terre qe ele demaunde en dowarie einz ceo qe il la espousa. Et si ele die[7], qe cele alienacioun fut a terme de vie ou autrement retournable al feffour, si qe cele terre ly fust assigné en sa dowarie en le premer establisement, quel houre qe ele[8]

1. *om. M.* 2. par an ou *add. M.* 3—3. cele chete *L.* tele [chose] cheite *N.* tele chose achiete *M.* cele chose chece *G.* tele chose chiete *S.* cele chose eschete *F.* 4—4. et sil *L.* *sim. N.* e si *S.* e il le *G.* e il en *MF.* 5. *so M.* et *add. L.* *sim. NGSC.* 6. soen *om. L.* son *MS.* *sim. G.* le *N.* 7. *so M.* dedie *L.* le dedie e *GS.* 8. *so MGC.* *sim. S.* le *L.*

it in another's right as guardian or bailiff or termor or villain.

Joint-tenure. Or, for that he holds the tenement jointly, in common with others, without whom he cannot answer.

Conditional fee, no bar. 14. If any one say that he has only a freehold upon condition until he has levied so much out of the profits, or until such or such an event happens, yet the writ shall not thereby abate but stand, and he may vouch to warranty if he thinks proper. (Replication as to judgment against husband;) And as to the tenant's exception, that she ought not to have dower because her husband lost the said tenement by judgment, she may answer by way of replication, that it was (Judgment by collusion.) by fraud and collusion, and by consent of the husband; and if this be proved, the exception will not avail.

Plea of alienation by husband. 15. Again, the tenant may say that her husband aliened the land which she demands in dower before he married her; and (Replication.) if she reply, that such alienation was for term of life or otherwise revertible to the feoffor, and that this land was appointed to her for dower in the original establishment thereof, as soon

voidast; et si le tenaunt ceo desdie, par pays soit la verité enquise.

16. Ou il purra dire, qe ele ne deit point dowarie aver, car le baroun de qi mort ele demaunde dowarie avoit une autre femme qe il avoit esposé avaunt qe il esposa ceste qe ore se pleint, la quele il dowa de mesmes ces tenementz, et la quele est uncore en pleine vie. En tiel cas seura le tenaunt bref de fere venir en court si nule tiele i soit, a reconustre si ele cleyme riens. Mes si la femme pleintive voille averrer la negative, q'il ne out[1] autre femme, ou s'il out autre femme nule neqedent ne est en vie, en ambideus les cas serra la parole remuable[2] en Cristiene court; et solum le maundement le ordinarie se fourmera[3] le jugement. Fle. 357 (§ 4). [261 *b.*]

17. Et de dowarie qe femme recovereit de fermer a terme des aunz, de office de Justice [4]soit agardé[4], qe [5]al termer[5] remaignent les deus parties qe demorent [6]de la terre[6] jekes autaunt [7]qe en soit[7] resceu a la vaillaunce de la tierce partie qe il en avera perdu. Et issi avera une manere de fraunc Brac. 312; Fle. 357 (§ 5, 6).

1. vnqes *add. M.* 2. enueiable *M. sim. C.* 3. fournera *N.* fournira *G.* fornerait *S.* 4—4. *so M. sim. GSC. om. L.* serra iuge *interl. N.* 5—5. al terme *M.* a terme *C.* 6—6. *so GS. so corr. N.* en la terre *L.* de terre *M.* des terres *C.* 7—7. *so LS.* qil eit *G.* qe il eyt *on eras. N.* qil en eit *M.*

as it became vacant; and if the tenant denies this, let the truth be inquired by the country.

16. Or he may say that she ought not to have dower, for that the husband of whose death she demands dower had another wife, whom he had married before he married her who now complains, and that he endowed that wife of these same tenements, and that she is yet alive. In such case the tenant shall sue out a writ to cause the woman, if any such there be, to come into court to acknowledge whether she makes any claim. But if the plaintiff will aver the negative, to wit, that her husband had not another wife, or that if he had another wife, there is none now living; in both cases the plea shall be removable into court Christian; and according to the return of the ordinary judgment shall be given. Plea of former wife living. Alleged wife to be produced. If the plaintiff avers the negative, plea removed to court Christian.

17. With respect to dower which a wife recovers from a farmer holding for a term of years, let it be awarded by the Justice *ex officio* that the termor shall retain the other two parts of the land until he has received the value of the third part which he has lost. And thus he will have a kind of free- When dower is recovered from termor, he shall retain the residue until satisfied for his loss.

tenement, ou avaunt point ne out. Mes si la femme recovere tote la terre qe le fermer tient, ausi cum cele dount ele fut dowé en certein, en tiel cas deit le fermer recoverer par jugement [1]par mi le[1] play de la garrauntie a la vaillaunce de la terre soen lessour. Et si soen lessour ne eit point de terre dount il puse garraunter soen terme, par office des Justices serra agardé, qe il [2]recovere a[2] la vaillaunce de ceo de soen lessour, quant terre escherra de tele dowarie, ou de autre dount il puise[3] fere satisfaccioun; et tiel agard soit enrouellé, si qe il puisse aver remedie par bref de jugement par mi cel enrouellement, quant houre serra.

CHAPITRE XI. [CXI.]

[262.]

De Jugement[4].

Brac. 312 b; Fle. 358 (c. 31, § 8).

1. [5]Cum il ne purra estre dedit[5], qe femme ne deit dowarie aver, tauntost soit agardé, qe ele recovere seisine de sa dowarie, et ses damages par taxacioun de jurours en la manere qe dit est avaunt.

Ante, c. 3. ss. 2, 4.

1—1. *so M. sim. G.* par nul *LS.* e par mi *corr. N.* 2—2. *so MGSCF.* recouera *LN.* 3. *so M. sim. SG.* poit *L.* 4. de doweyre *add. M.* 5—5. *so verb. M. sim. W. so corr. R.* Ou purra dire *L.* La ou lem ne purra dire *D. sim. corr. N.* Acun poera dire *S.* E com il ne purra dedire *G.* Asqunefoiz purra estre dedit *C.*

If termor loses all, he has judgment against his lessor.

hold where before he had not. But if the wife recovers all the land which the farmer holds, as land whereof she was endowed in certain, in such case the termor ought to recover from his lessor by judgment in the plea of warranty to the value of the land. And if the lessor has no land wherewith he can warrant his term, it shall be awarded *ex officio* by the Justices that he shall recover of his lessor to the value when the land included in the dower shall fall in, or any other out of which he can make satisfaction; and let this award be enrolled, so that when the time comes he may have remedy by writ of judgment upon such enrolment.

CHAPTER XI.

Of the Judgment in an Action of Dower.

Judgment for dower and damages.

1. When it cannot be denied that the widow ought to have dower, let it forthwith be awarded that she recover seisin of her dower, and her damages to be assessed by the jury, as before mentioned.

2. Et tut recovere femme dowarie, en plusours maneres [1]la purra ele[1] perdre, cum si soen garraunt perd par jugement les deus parties sauntz collusioun, adounc perdera ele sa dowarie. Et ausi par usage del pays, et nomément en Kent,—et acune foiz le soleit hom[2] en Loundres et en plusours autres lues,—[3]si toust cum [4]la femme[4] se lessa esposer a autre baroun, ou qe ele devenisist enceinte de autre qe de soen premer baroun, tauntost purra ele estre engetté de sa dowarie.

Brac. 313; Fle. 358 (§ 9, 10).

Prerog. Reg. (Stat. temp. incert. temp.) c. 18.

3. Et ausi si acune femme soit disseisie de sa dowarie, et ele apres loung entreval et apres pesible seisine del disseisour prenge la seisine par sa propre force, refusaunt jugement, si le disseisour puisse seisine recoverer par assise de novele disseisine, la femme ne recovera mes dowarie, si noun par mi le eyde le heir, ou par bref de dreit de dowarie countaunt de sa seisine demeygne.

Brac. 313; Fle. 358 (§ 11).

1—1. ele purra *LN*. le porra ele *M*. *sim. SGF*. 2. fere *add. N*. vser *add. F*. 3. qe *add. MC*. *sim. F*. 4—4. femme [vedue] *N*. la vedue *GS*. tele uefue *M*. tele vedue *C*.

2. But although the widow recover dower, she may lose it in several ways, as where her warrant loses the two other parts by judgment without any collusion, then she will lose her dower. So she may be deprived of it by the custom of the country, as particularly in Kent, and sometime there was such an usage in London and in many other places[a], that as soon as the widow is married to another husband, or becomes with child by any other than her first husband, she may be immediately ejected from her dower.

Dower may be lost by judgment against the warrant; by second marriage, in customary tenements.

3. So if a widow is disseised of her dower, and after a long interval and peaceable seisin of the disseisor she takes the seisin by her own force, refusing to proceed by judgment,—if the disseisor can recover seisin by assise of novel disseisin, the widow shall never recover her dower except by the aid of the heir, or by writ of right of dower wherein she shall count of her own seisin.

Seisin lost by assise after forcible entry, recovered only by writ of right.

[a] The form of expression, which seems to imply that the custom was no longer enforced in London, is not found in the parallel places of Bracton and Fleta.

CHAPITRE XII. [CXII.]

[1]*De plee de Dreit de Dowarie*[1].

Brac. 313, 313 *b*; Fle. 358.

1. Treis cas sount ou femme ne ad nul recoverer a sa dowarie for qe par mi le bref de dreit de dowarie overt pledable en la court le garraunt. Le un cas est ou la femme [262 *b*.] ad perdu sa seisine par assise de novele disseisine, cum avaunt est dit. L'autre est ou la femme demaunde partie de terre ou de tenement en dowarie, sicum de sa[2] renable partie, et ou ele est del[3] sourplus en seisine. Le tierz cas[4] est ou ele est deforcé de acune chose qe est apurtenaunte a sa dowarie.

Brac. 313 *b*; Fle. 359 (§ 1, 2).

2. Ces plays soint [5]comensables et pledables[5] sicum en le graunt bref de dreit overt, mes nient [6]par disreyne, ne[6] par essoigne de mal de lit, et[7] remuables jekes en counté, et de[8] illuc par devaunt nos Justices en totes maneres cum dit serra

1—1. *so verb. GS. om. L.* Des caas de dreit *N. sim. D.* De dreit de plee de doweyr *C. sim. MF.* 2. *so MGF. so corr. N.* la *L. om. C.* 3. *so MGCF. so corr. N.* de *L.* 4. cas *om. GMCF.* 5—5. comensables [et punisables *interlin.*] *L.* comenceables e punisables *ND. sim. S.* pleidables e comensables *G.* comensables e prouables *MW. sim. CF.* 6—6. par deresne ne *M.* par disreyne [al' destresce] ne *N.* de perdre son iour *C.* 7. est *LGS.* e *M.* 8. *so M.* de *om. LNGSCF.*

CHAPTER XII.

Of the Plea of Right of Dower.

Writ of right of dower patent, when it lies.

1. There are three cases in which a widow has no recovery for her dower, save by writ of right of dower patent pleadable in the court of the warrant. The first is where the widow has lost her seisin by assise of novel disseisin, as before is mentioned. The second, where the widow demands part of the land or tenement in dower, as of her reasonable share, and is already seised of the rest. The third case is where she is deforced of anything which is appurtenant to her dower.

Process in this writ.

Deraignment not admitted.

2. These pleas shall be commenced and tried in the same manner as the great writ of right patent, but not so as to admit of deraignment[1] or of essoin *de malo lecti*, and are removable into the County, and from thence before our Justices, in all

[1] This word 'deraign' appears to be used here of the mode of trial used in the ordinary or 'great' writ of right, namely, battle or great assise. The proof in writ of right of dower was by 'the country.' See Bracton, f. 313 *b*; Fleta, p. 359 (§ 1, 2).

apres en le play de dreit par le graunt bref; et ausi par vewes demaunder et par garraunt voucher.

3. Et si le tenaunt se voille defendre, ou soit garraunti par autre qe ly voille defendre, issi purra respoundre et dire, qe a tort demaunde ele dowarie, pur ceo qe ele li delivera ou rendi le tenement de soen eindegré, et soen dreit relessa et quiteclama; ou autrefoiz se retret devaunt tele Justice de autel bref; ou qe le tenement demaundé ne apent mie a sa dowarie; ou tut fut ele en acun tens seisie, si[1] ne fut mie sicum de dowarie; ou qe ele ne fut unques dowé, einz fut de autre terre en certeyn; ou qe ele fut dowé de meyns qe de la tierce partie, et dount ele se paya; ou qe ele ad plus [2]qe a sa dowarie[2] ne apent [3]a ly de aver[3]. Et si la femme ne voille le amesurement, et le tenaunt [4]voille averrer ceo, cum[4] sa excepcioun, en tiel cas ne prenge la femme rien par soen bref, einz remeigne en la merci; et le tenaunt se purchace de amesurer la dowarie de la quele ele fut dowé, sicum en certein, ou sicum del tierz.

Brac. 313 *b*, 314; Fle. 358, 359.

Fle. 359 (§ 4).

[263.]

1. ceo *M C.* 2—2. de son dowere qe *M.* en doweir qe *C.* a son dowere ke *F.* 3—3. *om. G.* 4—4. le voille auer sicom *G.*

the ways that shall be hereafter mentioned in the plea of right by the great writ. Demand of view and voucher of warrant also lie.

Defences of tenant or vouchee.

3. If the tenant desires to defend himself, or is warranted by another who defends him, the answer may be, that the plaintiff wrongfully demands dower, for as much as she of her own free will delivered up or surrendered the tenement to him, and released and quitclaimed her right; or that she heretofore withdrew herself from a like writ before such a Justice; or that the tenement demanded does not belong to her dower; or that although she was sometime seised thereof, she was not so seised as of her dower; or that she was never endowed thereof, but of other land specially named; or that she was endowed of less than the third part, and was contented therewith; or that she has more than belongs to her to have for her dower; and in the last case if she will not consent to admeasurement, and the tenant is ready to verify this as his exception, the widow shall take nothing by her writ, but remain in mercy; and let the tenant proceed for admeasurement of the dower whereof she was endowed, whether in certain or of the third part.

Plaintiff put to admeasurement.

CHAPITRE XIII. [CXIII.]

[1]*De Amesurement de Dowarie*[1].

Brac. 314, 314 *b*; Fle. 359 (§ 4).

1. Amesurer ne est autre chose qe remener en mesure ceo qe avaunt fust hors de mesure, et ausi bien chose qe ne apent mie a dowarie cum le exces ou la superfluité. Mes lequel qe la femme tient en dowarie trop, [2]ou chose[2] qe a ly ne apent point de tener, saunt jugement neqedent ne la fet point de oster ne de engetter. Et pur ceo affiert de purchacer remedie par bref de amesurement de dowarie.

Glan. li. 6. cc. 17, 18; Brac. 314 *b*; Fle. 359 (§ 5).

2. Et cum le viscounte avera resceu[3] pleges de sure la pleinte, si apent a ly de[4] somoundre la femme qe ele soit a certein jour; et il deit ausi fere somoundre le Corouner et les chivalers et autres fraunes hommes del visné. Al quel jour si la parole n'en soit remué par *Pone*, apent al pleintif moustrer sa pleinte solom le tenour del bref, si la femme i soit. Et si noun, ou tut soit ele, et ne sache rien dire par quei le amesurement ne deit estre, tauntost soit le amesure-

1—1. *so verb. SGMC. sim. F. om. L.* De amesur' *N.* 2—2. *so MCF.* en clos *LS.* en cloes [ou chose] *N.* en chose *G.* 3. le bref et *add. C.* le pleintif e *F.* 4. fere *add. SMCF. sim. G.*

CHAPTER XIII.

Of Admeasurement of Dower.

Remedy for excess or usurpation of dower by admeasurement.

1. Admeasurement is nothing else but the reducing to measure what before was out of measure, and extends as well to a thing which does not belong to dower as to the excess and superfluity of it. But whether the widow holds in dower too much, or a thing which she ought not to hold, yet she is not to be ousted or ejected without judgment. Therefore it is proper to proceed for remedy by writ of admeasurement of dower.

Proceedings by the sheriff.

2. When the sheriff has taken pledges for the prosecution of the plaint, it is his duty to summon the widow to appear on a certain day. He ought likewise to summon the coroner and the knights and other freemen of the neighbourhood. At which day, if the plea is not removed by *Pone*, it is the duty of the plaintiff to set forth his plaint according to the tenor of the writ, if the widow is present. And if she is not there, or if she is there and cannot say anything wherefore the ad-

Admeasurement, how made.

measurement ought not to be had, let the admeasurement be

ment [1]fet par serment de[1] prodes hommes presentz par bone et leale estente. Puis soit enquis coment sa dowarie luy fust [263 *b.*] establi, ou en certein ou del tierz, et solom ceo prenge le amesurement fin, issi neqedent qe le amendement[2] qe la femme avera fet ne chiete point en le estente, einz[3] chiete cel amendement enterement a la femme.

Brac. 315; Fle. 360 (c. 34. § 3).

3. Et si la femme voille[4], plusours respouns purra ele dire pur quei le amesurement ne se deit fere; sicum pur ceo qe le heir fut de plein age quant il la dowa; ou pur ceo qe ele ad tenu[5] dowarie avaunt le terme nomé en assise de novele disseisine; ou, tut la douast le heir par soen gardein, ou[6] tut la douast noster eschetour [7]ou autre taunt[7] cum le heir fut de eynz age, il neqedent, apres qe il [8]esteit atteint a soen[8] age, cel assignement out [9]a gré[9] et estable. Et pur plusours autres resouns purra ele destourber le amesurement.

Brac. 314 *b*, 315; Fle. 360 (c. 34. § 2).

4. Et si la parole soit en nostre court et le defendaunt face defaute, si courgent les destresces et les attachementz sicum

Stat. West. 2. (13 Edw. I.) c. 7.

1—1. *so M.* *sim. C.* pris par *G.* fet *om. LS.* fet *interl. N.* 2. *so NM.* *sim. F.* comaundement *L.* maundement *C.* demande *GS.* 3. *so MGSCF.* en *L.* [einz] en *N.* 4. aueigne a *M.* y veigne *C.* *sim. F.* 5. en *add. MCF.* le *add. G.* 6. *so NMGWF.* et *L.* 7—7. *so verb. GMF.* et autre au taunt *L.* *sim. S.* e autre taunt *ND.* 8—8. auint de plener *M.* 9—9. *so S.* agre *LMF.* agree *NC.* ferme *G.*

straightway made upon the oaths of freeholders then present by good and lawful extent. Then let it be inquired, in what manner her dower was established on her, whether in certain, or of the third part, and according thereto let the admeasurement be finished, yet so that any improvement which has been made by the widow be not included in the extent but fall entirely to her.

Widow to have the benefit of improvements made by her.

3. If the widow chooses, she may say in answer many reasons why the admeasurement ought not to be taken; as, that the heir was of full age when he endowed her; or, that she has held dower before the time named in the assise of novel disseisin; or, although the heir endowed her by his guardian, or, although she was endowed by our escheator or other when the heir was under age, yet that since he has attained his age he has agreed to and confirmed the said assignment; and by several other exceptions she may hinder the admeasurement.

Defences of widow.

Time of limitation.

4. If the plea is in our court, and the defendant makes default, distresses and attachments shall run as in personal

Process in king's court.

en personele accioun, et puis outre sicum dit est en [1]noster estatut[1].

Brac. 315; Fle. 360 (c. 34. § 4). 5. Et cum la femme avera par dreite mesure ceo qe a ly apent de aver pur dowarie, [2]ele ne[2] purra fere de cele dowarie ne de rien qe a luy[3] apent nule vente outre sa vie, ne nul exil as vileins, [4]ne eus enfrauncher, ne[4] nul wast. Et si ele face, si courge le remedie ordinee par nos estatutz. Stat. Glouc. (6 Edw. I.) cc. 5, 7.

CHAPITRE XIV. [CXIV.]

De Entreez.

Fle. 360. 1. [5]Acunes causes[5] sount[6] [7]de possessioun[7] qe mult saveu-

[264.] rent del dreit de la proprieté, sicum accioun[8] de entrez, et de custumes [9]et de services[9], ou[10] sount contenuz [11]touz ces[11] deus motz, *solet* et *debet*; et de *Quo jure*, et de renables de-

1—1. noz estatuz *M.* *sim. CF.* 2—2. *so MGCF.* *so corr. N.* ne la *L.* 3. ceo *M.* cel *G.* 4—4. *so M.* fraunca ne *L.* [ne des] fraunca ne *N.* enfranchir en *F.* ne *GS.* 5—5. *so M.* *sim. F.* Acuns cas *L.* *sim. NG.* Aucunes cases *S.* 6. *so MGS.* diuers *add. LN.* 7—7. *om. G.* 8. *om. M.* 9—9. *om. MC.* 10. e *N.* 11—11. touz [en *interlin.*] ces *L.* touz en ceux *N.* ces *GMF.* sez *S.*

actions, and such further process as is mentioned in our statute.

Widow not to make sale or waste. 5. When the widow has by just measurement that which belongs to her for her dower, she has no power to make any sale of the dower or anything that belongs to it beyond her life, or to make exile of villains, or enfranchise them, or commit any waste; and if she does so, the remedy provided by our statutes shall be pursued[u].

CHAPTER XIV.

Of the Actions founded on Writs of Entry.

Some possessory causes allied to property. 1. There are some possessory causes which savour much of the right of property, as the action of entry, the writ of customs and services, where both the words *solet* and *debet*

u 'Note, that waste, sale, and exile, are three things that touch disherison; wherefore termor doing them justly loses his tenancy as one who disinherits another: for by his act he proves himself to claim an estate which he ought not to have, and by consequence shall lose all, as it is said in reprobation (en reprover): Often michel yerne bringeȝ littel hom.' (Note in MS. *N.*)

vises, et de renables estovers de chescun aver, [1]et autres semblables[1].

2. Et en ceo play de entré sount treis degrez. Le un est, ou hom demaund [2]terre ou[2] tenement de sa seisine demeyne, apres le terme du les passé. L'autre est, ou hom demaund terre ou tenement apres le terme passé [3]de autri les[3]. Le tierz est, cum tenement est demaundé de acun tenaunt, qe out entré par cely, a qi acun auncestre le pleintif le lessa a terme qe passé est. Et solom ces degrez se varient les brefs de remedies. Et si ad uncore la quarte fourme, qe est hors de degrez, et [4]issaunt hors[4] de plus loingteine seisine, ou les autres treis degrez ne se estendent point; issi qe en le second degree si est [5]*per*; el tierz *per* et *cui*; et[5] en la fourme de hors, si est contenu *post*[6], ceo est a dire, puis le lees, ou puis la disseisine, qe tel fit a un tel. Et si acun bref de entré soit conceu[7] hors de soen cas, si ke une fourme soit purchacé pur[8] une autre, si est le bref vicious, et par taunt abatable.

Brac. 317 *b*, 318; Fle. 360 (c. 35. § 2).

1—1. *so verb. SF. sim. GMC. sim. corr. N.* a autre semblable *L.* 2—2. *so SGMCF. so corr. N.* de terre ou de *L.* 3—3. *so verb. GMFC.* [del] autre les *L.* del autr[y *on eras.*] lees *N.* 4—4. en cas *MGCF.* issantz *S.* 5—5. *so verb. M.* le terce pere *L. sim. N.* per tenters per e *S.* parel al tierz par encui *F.* per le tierce e per ou *C.* 6. *so SGMF. so on eras. N.* puis *L.* per *C.* 7. *so print.* contenu *LNGSMCF.* 8. *so MGS. sim. F. so on eras. N.* puis *L.*

are contained, of *Quo jure*, of reasonable bounds, of reasonable estovers of each kind, and others like.

2. In the plea of entry there are three degrees. The first is, where one demands land or tenement of his own seisin after a term of lease expired. The second is, where one demands land or tenement after the expiration of a term of lease created by another. The third is, when a tenement is demanded of any tenant who had entry by one to whom some ancestor of the plaintiff leased it for a term which is expired; and according to these degrees the writs of remedy are varied. There is still a fourth form, which is out of the degrees, and is derived from a more remote seisin to which the other three degrees do not extend. The second degree contains the word *per*; the third the words *per* and *cui*; and the form beyond the degrees the word *post*, that is to say, after the lease, or after the disseisin which such an one made to such an one. And if any writ of entry is not framed agreeably to the case, so that one form is obtained instead of another, the writ is defective, and therefore abatable.

Writ of entry *ad terminum qui præteriit.* Several cases where it lies.

Entry in the *per*; in the *per* and *cui*; in the *post*.

Brac. 318; Fle. 361 (§ 7–10); Reg. brev. orig. 227 *b*, 228.

3. La fourme del premer degré est tele. Comaundez a W. qe il rende a P. le maner de C.[1] ove les apurtenaunces, le quel il ly lessa a terme qe passé est. L'autre [2]fourme est tele[2]. Comaundez a J. qe il rende a P. le maner de C. en le quel il ne ad entré for qe par [3]E. mere[3] ou cosin ael ou
[264 *b*.] besael mesme celi P. qi le avauntdit maner ly lessa a terme qe passé est. La tierce forme est tele. Comaundez a J. qe il rende a P. le maner de O. en le quel il ne ad entré for qe par T. a qi un tiel, pere ou mere[4] cosin ou ael ou besael, qi heir mesmes celi P. est, [5]cel maner[5] lessa a terme qe passé est. Et la forme hors de degrez est tele: en le quel il ne ad entré si noun puis le les qe un tel, pere ou mere, [6]fit, etc. qi heir il est[6]. Et de ces [7]quatre sount tretes totes[7] les fourmes de totes maneres de entrez, qe sount hors de certein sauntz noumbre.

Fle. 363 (§ 25).

4. Cest bref tient lu ausi bien vers estraunges persones qe ount entré par disseisours, un ou plusours[8], taunt cum les

1. Eltham *M.* Bondon *C.* soun doun *F.* 2—2. est *MGCF.* 3—3. T. [pere ou] miere [ou autre auncestre] *N.* B. mere ou auncestre *S.* *sim.* *G.* un tel pere ou mere ou autre auncestre *M.* *sim.* *F.* pere ou mere aunte *C.* 4. ou autre auncestre ou *add.* *M.* *sim.* *CF.* 5—5. li *M.* le maner ly *F.* 6—6. *so* *LN.* si com deuant qi heir il est de ceo fist a tele a terme qe passe est *M.* *sim.* *SGCF.* 7—7. *conj.* treis sount tres tous *L.* *sim.* *ND.* quatre sount totes *GS.* *sim.* *MW.* iiij. degrees sount passes *C.* iiij. degre sunt totes *F.* 8. *so* *MCF.* et cum vers ceux qi entrent *add.* *L.* *sim.* *SG.* *sim.* (et *om.*) *N.*

Several forms of writs of entry.

3. The form in the first degree is as follows. 'Command W. that he render to P. the manor of C. with the appurtenances, which he demised to him for a term which is past.' The second form is thus. 'Command J. that he render to P. the manor of C. in which he hath not entry save by E. mother (or uncle, cousin, grandfather, or great-grandfather) of the same P. who leased the aforesaid manor to him for a term which is past.' The third form is as follows. 'Command J. that he render to P. the manor of O. in which he hath not entry save by T. to whom such an one, father, (or mother, cousin, grandfather, or great-grandfather, &c.), whose heir the same P. is, leased the said manor for a term which is past.' And the form beyond the degrees is thus:—'in which he hath not entry save after the lease which such an one, father (or mother, &c.) whose heir he is, made, &c.' And from these four are drawn the forms of all kinds of writs of entry, which are of infinite number.

Writ upon entry by means of heir of disseisor.

4. This writ, so long as the degrees and term will permit, lies as well against strangers who have entered by disseisors,

grez et le terme le[1] soeffrent, cum vers les heirs [2]de disseisours et cum vers ceux qi entrent par[2] tels heirs, deques a la tierce persone, sicum par ceste fourme. Comaundez a P. qe il rende a J. le maner de E. en le quel il ne ad entré si noun par T. fiz et heir S. qi mesme cel maner ly lessa puis qe mesme celi [3]S. de ceo[3] a tort avoit [4]disseisi ja[4] le avauntdit J. Ou si le disseisi soit mort, et [5]soen heir[5] demaunde vers le heir le disseisour, adounc issi: en le quel il ne ad entré si noun par T. fiz et heir S. qi mesme cel maner ly lessa puis qe mesme celui S. a tort avoit disseisi E. pere ou mere ou autre auncestre le avaundit J. qi heir il est. [265.]

5. Mes si acun [6]fist disseisine[6] de acun tenement qe fu le dreit sa femme demeyne, et le disseisour deviast et la femme[7] demorast[8] et continuast sa seisine tele cum soen baroun out en sa vie, et issi deviast seisie, et soen heir entrast apres ly et[9] continuast[10] mesme la seisine, et le disseisi portast sour mesmes le heir bref de entré, tut fut qe le heir respoundi qe Fle. 363 (§ 25).

1. *so MC.* ne *L.* les *F.* 2—2. *so verb. M.* *sim. CF.* par le disseisour *L.* *sim. N.* le disseisour par *G.* *sim. S.* 3—3. *so MC.* *sim. F.* *om. LN.* 4—4. *so S.* seisi ia *L.* [dis]seisi Ia *N.* ja *om. CHF.* 5—5. *so verb. SGF.* heir *om. L.* sen [heir *interl.*] *N.* I. heir *M.* 6—6. *so verb. MCF.* soit disseisi *LN.* fet disseisine *SG.* 7. *so NSGMCF.* et *add. L.* 8. vesquist *F.* 9. et *om. LSG.* e *NM.* 10. continuant *SG.*

whether one or more, as against the heirs of the disseisors and against those who enter by such heirs as far as the person in the third degree, as for example in this form. 'Command P. that he render to J. the manor, &c., in which he hath not entry save by T. son and heir of S. who leased the same manor to him after the same S. had wrongfully disseised the aforesaid J. thereof;' or, if the disseisee is dead, and his heir brings the action against the heir of the disseisor, then thus:—'in which he hath not entry save by T. son and heir of S. who leased the same manor to him after the same S. had wrongfully disseised E. father (or mother or other ancestor) of the aforesaid J. and whose heir he is.'

Writ of heir of disseisee.

5. But if one commits disseisin of a tenement which was the right of his own wife, and the disseisor dies, and the wife abides therein, and continues the like seisin as her husband had in his lifetime, and dies so seised, and her heir after her death enters and continues the same seisin, and the disseisee brings a writ of entry against the same heir, although the heir

Defective entry transmitted by disseisor to true owner.

il ne eust point de entré par nule disseisine qe soen piere ou soen auncestre fit, einz out par descente de sa mere, qe de ceo morust seisie en soen demeyne cum de fee et de dreit, [1]il deit[1] respoundre[2] al vicious entré le auncestre de qi la mere ne fut for qe entrebat[3]. Car tut moerge la mere en soen demeyne cum de fee, ele neqedent avoit torcenous entré par la disseisine de soen baroun, et pur ceo [4]qe par mi tiel[4] vicious entré [5]est cele terre devenue[5] al heir, tut soit par entrebat, est le heir tenu en ceo cas a respoundre al[6] entré.

Brac. 318; Fle. 363, 364 (§ 25, 26). 6. Et si le [7]tenement passe[7] le tierz degré del[8] saunc par successioun, mes ne vaudra remedie par bref de entré. Tel bref neqedent soleit estre fet en tel cas. Comaundez a P. qe il rende a J. le maner, dount T. disseisi mesme celi J. ou autres de ses auncestres, qi heir il est, saunt fere mencioun

1—1. et *L.* e *SG.* adounk purra hom *N.* [il *interlin.*] deit *M.* *om. CF.* 2. respoigne *G.* 3. entreabat *M. here and below.* 4—4. qe nul tiel *LN.* *sim. SG.* qe parmi cele *M.* *sim. F.* *om. C.* 5—5. so *M.* *sim. CF.* qe cele terre deuiegne *L.* *sim. NSG.* 6. a la vicious *G.* 7—7. passe *om. L.* teñ passe *SG.* tenaunt passe *M.* *sim. F.* tenaunt soit en *N.* 8. el *MF.*

should make answer that he had not entry by any disseisin which his father or ancestor made thereof, but by descent from his mother, who died seised thereof in her demesne as of fee and of right, yet he is bound to answer to the entry of the ancestor from whom his mother's seisin was merely derivative. For although the mother die in her demesne as of fee, yet she had a tortious entry by the disseisin of her husband; and because by means of such defective entry, although derivative, the land is come to the heir, the heir is bound in such case to answer to the entry.

Form of writ where the tenement has passed by inheritance for three degrees. 6. If the tenement pass the third degree of blood by succession, the remedy by writ of entry will not avail[x]. But in such cases a writ is used to be framed as follows. 'Command P. that he render to J. the manor, whereof T. disseised the same J. or others of his ancestors, whose heir he is,'—without

x '*Nota*, that if the tenements be come to several hands, as to five, or ten, or twelve, the writ of entry still lies, because nothing has accrued to the last purchaser more than to the first. But if they be come to four heirs in lineal succession, or to three, *secundum quosdam*, so that each has been seised, and the last is in possession, he is as it were inherited (come enherité) in the right, although the mere right be in another. And also if a grandfather has leased a tenement for a term, and the grandfather, his son, his son's son, and his son's son's son, die before the term be passed, so that the demandant is in the fourth degree, he cannot recover by writ of entry; because it is a writ of possession mixed with the right, and he ought not to be in better condition in this case than if his ancestor, i. e. the great-grandfather, had died seised.' (Note in MS. *N.*)

del entré. Ou si acun disseisist le disseisour, et cel tenement puis alienast, dounc il ne puit mie dire en ceo cas, qe le [265 *b.*] premer disseisour ly lessa, et pur ceo soit dit issi: en le quel il ne ad entré si noun par celi qi disseisi tiel puis qe mesme celi tiel avoit disseisi le pleintif, ou soen heir proschein ou remué, ou sauntz mencioun de entré.

7. Ceste accioun tient lu soulement vers tenauntz tenementz outre le terme qe il serrount lessez, et vers lour heirs et lour assignez, et vers ceux qi averount entré en acun tenement par intrusioun ou par disseisine, et ausi vers les[1] heirs et les[2] assignez les disseisours et les intrusours, qi par eus [3]i avoint entré par successioun ou par les ou par feffement; et vers eus qe avoint entré[3] par les ou feffement[4] des baillifs et des gardeins [5]et des vileins[5] et des autres qi nient ne avoint for qe terme des aunz ou terme de vie ou simple tenaunce, [6]ou par enfauntz de eynz age, ou par feffementz fetz a force en prisoun, ou par gentz aragez, ou par persone de eglise ou

Brac. 318; Fle. 361 (§ 5, 6).

Brac. 318, 323 *b*.

Brac. 318, 323.

1. *so MCF.* lour *LN.* *sim. GS.* 2. *so MCF.* lour *LN.* *sim. GS.* 3—3. *so verb. M.* *sim. S.* *sim. in marg. N.* *sim.* [*om.* ou par les] *F.* a escient entre *L.* a escient entrent *N.* i avoient entre *G.* 4. par succession *M.* 5—5. *om. M.* 6—6. *so verb. M.* *sim. GSCF.* *sim. in marg. N.* *om. L.*

making mention of the entry. Again, if any one disseised the disseisor, and afterwards aliened that tenement, he cannot in such case say, 'which the first disseisor leased to him;' and therefore let it be said thus: 'in which he hath not entry save by such an one, who disseised such an one, after the last-named had disseised the plaintiff,' or his heir[y], near or remote; or the entry need not be mentioned.

Form where there have been successive disseisins and then a conveyance.

7. This action lies only against those who hold tenements beyond the term for which they are leased, and against their heirs and assigns, and against those who had entry into any tenement by intrusion or by disseisin, and also against the heirs and assigns of the disseisors and intruders, who had entry therein by them by succession, lease, or feoffment; and against those who had entry by feoffment of bailiffs, guardians, villains, or others who had nothing save for term for life or years, or a simple tenancy, or of infants under age, or by feoffments made by compulsion in prison, or by mad persons,

Against whom action of entry lies.

[y] This word should apparently be 'ancestor.' The error, if it be so, is probably derived from Fleta, where the word is *hæredem*.

moigne[6] ou chanoigne remuable sauntz assent del Evask et de avowé, et par felouns et bastardz et par autres qi ne poeint mie aliener del dreit; et ausi vers ceux qi desceivauntment ount purchacé tenement sour purparlaunce de fere tele chose ou tele, et point ne le voillent fere quant il [1]en serrount[1] feffez.

Brac. 318; Fle. 363 (§ 24). [266.] 8. Ceo mot, terme, se estent ausi bien a terme de vie cum a terme des aunz. [2]Mes cil qi ne lest for qe a terme des aunz[2], tut feist il le les a terme de C. aunz, si il ne[3] lest for qe les esplez, et retient vers ly le [4]fee et le dreit et le[4] fraunc tenement, [5]si avaunt le les le out; et[5] ceo qe il retient lerra a soen heir cum il morra; ou sauntz tort fere al fermer porra il doner et aliener [6]a estraunge[6] persone; ou al fermer mesmes purra il relesser chescune manere de dreit et quiteclamer, et feffer, sauntz oster primes le fermer de sa seisine tele quele; et ausi ne purra il mie fere a autre estraunge per-

1—1. *so verb. SG.* eurent *L.* en furent *MC.* 2—2. *so verb. M.* *sim. F.* *om. LN.* mes cil qe ne eyt for ke a terme des ans *S.* *sim. G.* 3. *so GMCF.* ne *om. LS.* *interl. N.* 4—4. dreit del fee e del *M.* dreit le fee e le *F.* 5—5. *so verb. F.* si auaunt le les tut *LN.* *sim. SG.* si auaunt le lessent e *M.* si asqun le lesse *C.* 6—6. *so GM.* *sim. F.* et estre lige *LNC.* *sim. S.*

or by the parson of a church, or a monk or canon removable[z], without the assent of the bishop and the patron; or by felons or bastards, or by others who cannot alien anything of the right. So likewise against those who have deceivably purchased tenements upon a promise to do such or such a thing, and when they are enfeoffed thereof, refuse to perform it.

'Term,' for life or years. Nature of estate of lessee for years, and of lessor. 8. The word 'term' extends as well to a term of life as to a term of years. But he who leases only for a term of years, although he make the lease for a term of a hundred years, leases the profits only, and retains to himself the fee and the right and the freehold, if he had them before the lease; and all that he retains he will leave at his death to his heir; or he may, without doing any wrong to the farmer, give and alien it to a stranger; or he may release and quitclaim every sort of right to the farmer himself, and enfeoff him, without first ousting the farmer of his seisin, such as it is. This he cannot do

Lessor may enfeoff lessee without resuming possession.

[z] See vol. i. p. 159, and the note there; and compare Year Book, 31 Edw. I. p. 454. The words in Bracton are, 'a canon without the assent of the bishop and chapter, an abbot without the consent of his chapter, or a cellarer clerk or other *procurator* without the consent of his abbot or prior.' (Bracton, f. 318.)

sone, si le fermer de soen gré ne se cheve[1] al purchaceour; car [2]la seisine del[2] alienour [3]sei continue[3] touz jours par[4] le fermer, qi use sa seisine en le noun soen lessour.

CHAPITRE XV. [cxv.]

De Proces.

1. Le tenaunt, cum il serra somouns, se purra fere essoignier de mal de venue, et le pleintif ensement. Et le tenaunt purra demaunder la vewe de la demaunde; et[5] voucher a garraunt, lequel qe mencioun soit fete en le bref de entré ou noun, issi neqedent qe si mencioun soit fete, [6]adounc soit fet[6] le voucher de persone en persone, et de garraunt en garraunt, des persones nomez en le bref par ordre jekes al premer disseisour, ou [7]al autre entrour[7], ou a soen heir. Car autres garrauntz ne deivent point estre vouchez qe en le bref sount nomez. Et si nule mencioun Brac. 318, 318 b, 321; Fle. 364 (§ 27), 365.

1. *so LSC.* acheuast *M.* acheue *F.* 2—2. *so GMCF. sim. S.* sa seisine de *L.* la seisine de *N.* 3—3. *so on eras. N. sim. M.* si counte mie *L.* se contenue *S.* conteigne *G.* si est continue *C.* 4. *so MCF. so corr. N.* par *om. LSG.* 5. ou *SGMCF.* 6—6. *so verb. MF. om. LSG.* 7—7. *conj.* le autre entrer *L. sim. N.* le autre entre *S. sim. G.* lautre intrusour *M.* a lautre entier *C.*

to a stranger, unless the farmer of his own consent will attorn to the purchaser; for the seisin of the alienor is all along continued by the farmer who enjoys his seisin in the name of his lessor. Otherwise, as to stranger, unless lessee attorns.

CHAPTER XV.

Of the Proceedings in an Action of Entry.

1. The tenant being summoned may cause himself to be essoined *de malo veniendi*, and the plaintiff the like. The tenant may also demand view of the thing in demand; and may vouch to warrant, whether mention be made of entry in the writ or not; so nevertheless that if such mention be made, the voucher shall be from person to person, and from warrant to warrant, of the persons named in the writ in order up to the first disseisor, or other entror, or his heir. For other warrants than those named in the writ ought not to be vouched[a]. And Essoins. View. Voucher.

[a] That is, if the tenant does not deny the entry to have been as stated by the plaintiff. Compare below, c. 16. s. 2; Bracton, f. 321; Year Book, 31 Edw. I. p. 336.

[266 *b.*] ne soit fete del entré en le bref de degrez, adounc purrount plusours estre vouchez autres qe ne sount nomez en le bref, si les vouchours eint par quei.

Brac. 327; Fle. 365 (c. 36. § 1).

2. Et si le pleintif founde sa resoun [1]en le dreit, countaunt en le dreit[1] par descente ou par resortz, ausi cum en le play de dreit, descendaunt en la fin de soen counte al entré, en tiel cas purra le [2]defendaunt ou le[2] tenaunt aver deus maneres de defense. Car [3]s'il s'aforce a defendre la entré sour la[3] possessioun, dounc gist le averrement par juree [4]ou autre excepcioun[4]. Et s'il voille defendre la descente del dreit, adounc se purra defendre en treis maneres, ou par le cors du un soen fraunc homme, ou mettre sei en la graunt assise, ou fere terminer le play par juree. Et si[5] soit defendu par bataille ou par graunt assise, et le pleintif eit tendu disreyne, ou s'il soit assentu[6] a la graunt assise, adounc se purra le tenaunt al autre jour sei fere essoignier de mal de venue sicum apres apparaunce, et le autre jour de mal de lit, et issi purra il giser en langour par un an, et en tel cas fet a fere en touz

1—1. *so verb. M.* en le bref countaunt en le dreit *LN.* countant el bref *F.* 2—2. *om. MF.* 3—3. *so M.* *sim. F.* *sim. corr. N.* si sa force defende le autre sour la *L.* si sa force defendre le autre sur lautre *S.* *sim. G.* 4—4. *so verb. MF.* en autre excepcion *G.* autre excepcioun *LS.* *om. N.* ou par autre excepcion *C.* 5. *so S.* si *om. LN.* si ceo *M.* si il *CF.* 6. *so SGM.* sentu *L.*

if no mention is made of the entry in the writ of degrees, then others who are not named in the writ may be vouched, if the vouchors have sufficient ground for doing so.

Where plaintiff counts upon both right and entry, tenant may defend either property or possession.

2. If the plaintiff founds his case upon the right, counting in the right by descent or by resort, as in the plea of right, and coming down at the end of his count to the entry, in such case the defendant or tenant has two modes of defence. For he may undertake to defend the entry upon the possession, in which case he tenders averment by a jury, or pleads an exception.

If he defends the property, the process is as in writ of right.

If, on the other hand, he chooses to defend the descent of the right, he has three ways of defending himself, either by the body of one his freeman, or by putting himself upon the great assise, or by having the plea determined by a jury. If he be defended by battle, or the great assise, where the plaintiff has tendered deraignment, or agreed to the great assise, then the tenant may on the second day of plea have himself essoined *de malo veniendi* as after appearance, and at the next day be essoined *de malo lecti*, and so he may lie for a year *in lanquore*. And in this case the proceedings shall

pointz sicum dit serra en le play de dreit, pur ceo qe al eleccioun et par defense le tenaunt est vein en tut le dreit de la possessioun; si qe le entré[1] est tut outrement chaungé deques en la nature de play de dreit. Mes ceo [2]n'ust james avenu[2] par eleccioun le pleintif; et pur ceo remeynt [3]tote la force en le[3] defendaunt a[4] defendre sei en le dreit de la pro- [267.] preté en chescun plee qe savoure de ambideus les dreitz par bataille ou par graunt assise, ou a defendre sei en le dreit de la possessioun; et [5]ausi de[5] fere le plee de dreit chaunger jekes en[6] possessioun par cas, [7]sicum apres serra dit[7]; mes si mencioun el[8] plee de dreit soit fete del[9] entré en counte countaunt, et le defendaunt voille weyver les defenses el[10] dreit et defendre le entré, et issi la possessioun, adounc est la nature del bref de dreit si chaungé, qe mes ne tendra lu bataille ne graunt assise ne essoigne de mal de lit, einz serra le plee terminé par juré.

3. Acuns brefs de entré sount neqedent, et[11] de customes Brac. 326; Fle. 365 (§ 2).

1. *so GMCF.* autre *LS.* *sim. N.* 2—2. *so verb. GMF.* *sim. C.* moustra *LN.* 3—3. tote la force ou *L.* tote la force ou [e *eras.*] le *N.* tote la force en *SG.* tut al *M.* tot en le *C.* tot el *F.* 4. *so SGMF.* ad *LN.* 5—5. par cas sicum apres serra dit poet il *M.* 6. dreit de la *add. SMC.* *sim. F.* le plee de la *G.* 7—7. *om. M.* 8. *so MCF.* en le *G.* de *LNS.* 9. el *MF.* *sim. C.* al *LNG.* 10. *so MF.* ou *LNS.* en *G.* e le *C.* 11. et *om. LS.* et *om.* [come *interl.*] *N.* e *GM.* e ausi *CF.*

be in all points as will be stated concerning the plea of right; because at the tenant's election and by his defence the right of possession is disregarded, so that the action of entry is entirely changed to the nature of a plea of right. But this never happens upon the election of the plaintiff; therefore in every plea which savours of both rights it is entirely in the defendant's choice either to defend himself in the right of property by battle or by great assise, or to defend himself in the right of possession. And in some cases also it is in his power to cause the plea of right to be changed into one of possession, as shall afterwards be noticed; for if mention be made of the entry in counting in the plea of right, and the defendant chooses to waive the defence in the right and to defend the entry, and so the possession, the nature of the writ of right is so changed, that neither battle, nor great assise, nor essoin *de malo lecti* will lie, but the plea shall be determined by jury.

Election by tenant, not by plaintiff.

Similarly a writ of right is sometimes defended as a possessory action.

3. Nevertheless there are some writs of entry, and of cus-

Some writs of entry concern the possession only.

et de services, qe en nule manere ne se purrount chaunger hors de la possessioun jekes en la nature de plee de dreit; cum si acun eit lessé a terme des[1] aunz soen tenement qe il avera tenu a terme de sa vie ou a greynur terme des aunz, et demaunde arere[2] sa seisine demeyne apres le les[3], ou qe il demaunde[4] par bref [5]de entré[5] tenement qe il lessa a terme, ou il out fee sauntz prendre unques espleez; et ausi le bref de customes et de services, ou le *debet* est forpris.

Brac. 326 *b*; Fle. 365 (§ 3).

4. Et fet bien noter[6], [7]qe en trestouz[7] pleez del mound, ou le bref fet[8] mencioun de ambideus les dreitz, et en la [267 *b*.] demoustraunce est counté par mi le dreit ausi [9]bien cum[9] tochaunt la possessioun, coment qe le plee prenge fin par juré ou en autre manere, mes qe la defense courge par mi le dreit, [10]en tel[10] cas ne ad james resort a bref de dreit, pur ceo qe tut le dreit est terminé. Mes si la defense del[11] dreit soit lessé, et[12] la possessioun soulement soit defendu, en tiel

1. *so SGMCF.* de dus *L.* de xij. *N.* 2. *so SGCF. sim. M.* aver *L.* auer [ariere] *N.* 3. terme del lees *GMC. sim. S.* terme de les auns *F.* 4. *so MCF.* demaunda *LS.* demaundast *N.* 5—5. *so MCF. om. LNSG.* 6. a nostre *S.* a conoistre *G.* 7—7. *so G. sim. MF.* entre touz *L.* encountre touz *N.* qe tretouz *C.* 8. *so SGMCF.* fit *L.* fist *N.* 9—9. *so verb. MCF. om. LNS.* bien *G.* 10—10. *so S. sim. GMCF.* et cel *L. sim. N.* 11. *so GMCF.* de *LN.* de‿le *S.* 12. a *LSMC.* e *NGF.*

toms and services, which will nowise admit of being changed from a possessory nature to that of a plea of right; as, where a person has leased for a term of years his tenement which he held for term of his life or for a greater term of years, and at the end of the lease demands back again his own seisin; or if he demands by writ of entry a tenement which he demised for a term, and in which he had a fee without ever having taken esplees; so, the writ of customs and services where the *debet* is omitted.

Where the property is defended, no writ of right can be afterwards brought.

4. It is to be well observed, that in all pleas whatsoever, where the writ makes mention of both rights, and the plaintiff in his declaration counts by means of the right as well as concerning the possession, if the defence proceeds upon the right, however the plea is ended, whether by a jury or in any other manner, there is no resort to the writ of right, because all the right is determined. But if the defence of the right is waived and the possession only is defended, there will be a further

cas i avera uncore refute et remedie par bref [1]de dreit[1], tut ne[2] face la juré pur le pleintif ou pur le defendaunt[3].

CHAPITRE XVI. [CXVI.]

De Excepciouns.

1. En ceo play purra le tenaunt sei eyder par excepciouns generales dilatories et peremptories. Et issi purra graunter le entré par terme, mes de eynz le terme [4]li fut la terre[4] relessé et quiteclamé ou doné en fee. Mes dounc fet a destincter, si la excepcioun puisse estre prové par chartre ou par escrit, ou noun. Car si par escrit qe[5] soit prové ou[6] nient dedit, le jugement est cler. Et si [7]noun, et[7] ambideus se soint descenduz en juré[8] sour le entré par counte countaunt, et[9] par defense ausi par mi le dreit, adounc soit la reconisaunce de la juree prise en lu de graunt assise, par ces motz, a reconustre sour lour sermentz, si le avauntdit P. autre dreit ou autre entré[10] avoit en la avauntdite terre qe Brac. 320; Fle. 365.

1—1. so *SGMCF.* *interl. N.* *om. L.* 2. se *SMF.* *om. GC.* 3. tenaunt *MCF.* *sim. SG.* 4—4. neqedent li fu le tenement *M.* *sim. CF.* 5. so *MC.* *sim. F.* qe se *L.* *sim. S.* qe ceo *NG.* 6. so *NSGMCF.* et *L.* 7—7. *om. C.* et *om. SG.* 8. ou *add. M.* 9. ou *M.* 10. so *SGMCF.* *sim. interl. N.* entre *om. L.*

expedient, and a remedy by writ of right, whether the jury find for the plaintiff or for the defendant.

CHAPTER XVI.

Of Exceptions in the Action of Entry.

1. In this plea the tenant may aid himself by general dilatory and peremptory exceptions. General Exceptions. Thus he may admit the entry by the term, but say that within the said term the land was released and quitclaimed, or given to him in fee. Exception of release within the term, proved by charter, But in this case, it must be distinguished whether the exception can be proved by charter or writing, or not. For if by writing, which is proved or not denied, the judgment is clear. And if not, and both parties have gone to a jury upon the entry by the count and by defence also through the right, or by jury. then instead of the great assise let the recognisance of the jury be taken in these words:—to recognise upon their oaths whether the aforesaid P. had other right or other entry in the aforesaid Form of issue.

[268.] par J. qi cele terre luy lessa a terme qe passé est, ou si le avauntdit P. out entré en cele terre par mesme celi J. qi cele terre ly vendi ou dona ou quiteclama en fee, sicum mesme celi P. dit, et dount il conust[1] qe le avauntdit dit J. cele terre primes ly lessa [2]a terme, mes il en dist outre qe duraunt soen terme cele terre ly lessa[2] en acune manere en fee.

Brac. 320 *b*; Fle. 366 (§ 4).

2. Ou il purra dire qe il ne out mie le entré par tiel, einz out par autre tiel; et[3] en tiel cas ne covendra mie le tenaunt voucher celi a garraunt, einz suffit [4]a ly de abatre[4] le bref. [5]Et si il weyve[5] la excepcioun, [6]ceo ly purra par cas[6] grever.

[7]Ici finist le dreit de la Possessioun, et comence le dreit de la Propreté[7].

1. so *SGMCF.* couent *L.* couient [al' conust] *N.* 2—2. so *verb. SG.* *sim. MCF.* *om. LN.* 3. et *om. L.* e *SGMCF.* 4—4. so *verb. MCF.* de abatre *G.* *om. LNS.* 5—5. so *verb. GMCF.* sil veigne *L.* *sim. NS.* 6—6. so *verb. MCF.* *sim. G.* ne ly purra point *L.* ne ly purra [point] *N.* ne ly pora *S.* 7—7. so *verb. SGCF.* Ici comence le dreit de la proprete *L.* *sim. N.* Ci finist le drayt de la possessioun *M.*

land save by J., who demised the land to him for a term which is passed, or whether the said P. had entry in that land by the same J. who sold or gave or quitclaimed the same to him in fee, as the said P. says, and whereof he acknowledges that the abovesaid J. the same land first demised to him for a term, but further says that during his term he released the same to him in fee.

Exception denying the entry as alleged.

2. Again, the tenant may say that he had not entry by such an one, but by another person named; and in such case the tenant is not obliged to vouch the latter to warranty, but it will be sufficient for him to abate the writ. And if he waive the exception, it may perhaps prejudice him.

Here ends the Law of Possession, and begins the Law of Property.

BRITTON.

[1]LIVRE VI.

[CHAPITRE CXVII.][1]

TERMINÉ la fourme et la manere de pleder le dreit possessorie, ore fet a treter de la manere de pleder el dreit de la proprieté, qe est le drein remedie de touz recoverers [2]entre touz[2] ordres de pleez, issi qe de bref de dreit ne purra nul descendre al bref de plus basse nature, tut puisse hom fere la reverse. Brac. 327 *b*, 328; Fle. 370.

1—1. Lib. vi. De mero Iure c. i. *N. This paragraph is not numbered as a chapter in LSGM.*
2—2. *so LNC.* en trestuz *M. sim. GF.*

BOOK VI.

OF PROPRIETARY ACTIONS.

INTRODUCTION.

Of the Plea of Right.

HAVING finished the form and manner of pleading the possessory right, we must now treat of the manner of pleading upon the right of property, which in the order of pleas is the last of all remedies; so that none can descend from a writ of right to a writ of a lower nature, although the reverse may be done. Proprietary action, the last of all remedies.

CHAPITRE I. [CXVIII.]

[268 *b.*]

[1]*De plus Proscheynté.*[1]

Brac. 62 b; Fle. 370 (§ 3, 4). 1. Ceste accioun soulement detrie en counte countaunt la plus proscheineté des heirs quant a la successioun [2]de lour[2] heritage. Car heritage est successioun de heir en chescun dreit dount le auncestre morust seisi. Et de heritage est dit heir, qi est successour en chescun dreit qe le auncestre out en tens de sa mort. Et cel dreit acune foiz descent, ausi Glan. li. 7. c. 1, cum chose pesaunte, et acune foiz remounte[3]. Et, tut soit qe la possessioun ne sue mie acune foiz le meer dreit, a la fin neqedent i[4] recovera, si le dreit heir face dreite seute. Car a chescun verrei heir descent le meer dreit qe soen auncestre out quant il morust, ou qe le heir soit en le tens de la mort soen auncestre de cea la meer ou de la, en le ventre sa mere Brac. 63, 64; Fle. 370 (§ 5, 6, 7). ou de hors.

2. Touz enfauntz ne sount mie receivables al heritage.

1—1. Ci comence le drayt de la propretee *M.* 2—2. so *N.* de soen *L.* sim. *SGMC.* del *F.* 3. amounte *M.* 4. il *NSGCF.*

CHAPTER I.

Of Proximity of Heirs.

Proximity of heirs tried by writ of right. Inheritance, what. 1. This action alone by the manner of counting tries the proximity of heirs with respect to the succession to the inheritance. For inheritance is the succession of the heir to every right of which the ancestor died seised. And from inheritance is derived heir, who is the successor to every right which the ancestor had at the time of his death. And this right sometimes descends like a weighty body, and sometimes ascends. And although the possession does not always follow the mere right, yet in the end it will return to it, if the right heir proceeds in a proper manner. For to the right heir descends the mere right which his ancestor had when he died, whether the heir at the time of his ancestor's death be in the country or beyond sea, and whether he is in his mother's womb or already born.

Children, legitimate and bastard. 2. All children however are not admissible to the inherit-

Car acuns sount naturels et mulerez. [1]Des mulerez et naturels[1] sount acuns fiz et heirs, et acuns fiz et ne mie heirs; et acuns heirs lour pieres, et acuns heirs lour meres, et acuns de une part et de autre; et acuns ne sount nuli heirs, tut soint mulirez et naturels; et acuns comencent[2] de estre heirs et cessent par cas del estre, et acuns ne cessent nient. Et des naturels heirs et mulerez sount acuns proscheins heirs, et acuns plus proscheins, et acuns remuez; [3]et auns plus remuez[3]. Car touz freres de part lour pere sount proscheins heirs lour pere pur la partie[4] qe il ount en la possessioun; et ceo ne put estre dedit; pur ceo [5]qe si[5] le puisnee frere teigne soen frere einznee hors de soen heritage et de ceo eit resceu les espleez et pesible seisine, l'einzné ne avera nul recoverer en dreit de la possessioun, sicum avaunt est dit, eynz [6]le estoit[6] a demaunder soen heritage par mi le bref de dreit, quel bref soulement detrie le saunc, qi est plus proschein heir. Et

Glan. li. 7. c. 3; Brac. 64; Fle. 370 (§ 8, 9, 10, 11).

[269.]

1—1. e des natureus *M.* 2. *so GM.* [ount *interlin.*] le comencement *L.* ount le comencement *N.* le comencent *SF.* 3—3. *so verb. SGMCF.* *om. LN.* 4. *so LNSGMF. qu. read* parité. 5—5. *so G.* si *L.* qe *S.* *om. MCF.* 6—6. *so L.* *sim. SG.* le estut *N.* *sim. M.*

ance, for some are natural and legitimate[a]; and of those who are both legitimate and natural, some are sons and heirs, others sons and not heirs; and some are heirs of their fathers, some of their mothers, and some on both sides, and others are not heirs to either, although they are both legitimate and natural; and some begin by being heirs and afterwards perhaps cease to be so, and others not. And of natural and legitimate heirs, some are near and some again nearer, and some remote and others more remote. For all brothers on the father's side are near heirs of their father by reason of the share they have in the possession. This is undeniable, because if the younger brother keeps his elder brother out of his inheritance, and has taken the profits and peaceable seisin thereof, the eldest shall have no recovery in the right of possession, as before is mentioned, but he is driven to demand his inheritance by means of the writ of right, which writ alone tries who is nearest heir in

Heirs, near and remote.

All the sons are near heirs, but the eldest the nearest.

All the sons are equal as to possession, but not as to right.

[a] A clause appears to have been left out by the copyist here, owing to the repetition of the same word. The text should probably stand thus: Car acuns sount naturels et mulerez, et acuns sount naturels et nient mulerez, et acuns ne sount ne naturels ne mulerez. See the parallel places in Bracton and Fleta, referred to above. According to Bracton, a natural child is one born of parents between whom at the time of intercourse a legal marriage is possible, as between a bachelor and a maid not of kin to each other. And children born *ex prohibito coitu* are neither legitimate nor natural. (Bracton, f. 64.)

solom ceo qe serra trové par counte countaunt de la plus procheinté des freres, si serra le jugement. Mes en touz cas[1] est cist plus proschein heir de dreit, a qi le meer dreit plus toust descent.

CHAPITRE II. [CXIX.]

De Successioun.

Glan. li. 7. c. 3; Brac. 64; Fle. 370 (§ 11). 1. Trestouz ceux, qi descendent premers[2] del commun cep de degré en degré par dreite line jekes sauntz fin, sount dreitz heirs et verreis. Et cum defaute iert trové en la dreite line, dounc sount dreitz heirs ceux qi serrount trovez plus procheins en degrez collateraus jekes sauntz fin. Et al drein, cum defaute serra trové en la line transversele descendaunt, si serrount ceux resceivables qi serrount trovez plus proscheins [269 *b.*] amountaunt en acune line transversele. Et tut soint touz heirs issi amountaunt jekes sauntz fin dreitz heirs et verreis, trestouz neqedent ne sount mie pur ceo resceivables a la successioun a une foiz, pur ceo qe le einznee qi est plus proschein forclost le puisnee qe est le proschein, et le pros-

1. *so G. so interl. N.* cas *om. LSMCF.* 2. primer *M.* primes *SGC.*

blood. And according as it shall be found by counting of the proximity among brothers judgment shall be given. But in all cases that person is next heir at law to whom the mere right soonest descends.

CHAPTER II.

Of Succession, and the Law of Inheritance.

Order of descent. 1. Right line descending. 1. All those who first descend from the common stock from degree to degree in the direct line for ever are lawful and true heirs; and when default is found in the direct line, then those 2. Collateral line descending. who are found to be the nearest in the collateral degrees for ever are the right heirs; and lastly, when default is found in 3. Collateral line ascending. the transverse line descending, those who appear to be nearest in any transverse line ascending shall be admissible. But although the heirs so ascending for ever are lawful and right heirs, yet they are not all admissible at the same time to the succession, because the eldest, being nearest, excludes the youngest who is near, and he who is near excludes the remote,

chein forclost le remué, et le remué le plus remué. Et cum trestouz ceux defaillent, sicum par lour saunc[1] esteint, ou sicum par lour dreit esteint par jugement de felonie, a force resortist le tenement al seignur del fee, sicum a luy dount il primes sailli[2], pur ceo qe il ne troeve nule part ou ayllours coure. Et en tiel cas [3]cessent les homages resceuz[3] del tenement. Brac. 64, 66 *b*.

2. Plusours choses fount procheinté, et rendent heritage et dreit de successioun; ceo est a saver, lingné, age, line, heritage partable, pluralité des femmes, fourme de doun, et saunc. Lingné, pur ceo qe le masle est receyvable et la femme rebotable, taunt cum il ad masle apparaunt de[4] piere et de une mere; mes si[5] la file engendré de la premere femme est plus toust receivable a la successioun en[6] mariage graunté oveke sa mere, qe ne est le masle engendré de mesme le piere et de la secounde femme[7]. Brac. 65; Fle. 371 (§ 12).

3. Age, pur ceo qe[8] est plus toust receyvable cist qe primes est nee qe le puisnee de un pere et de une mere, et puisnee Brac. 64 *b*; Fle. 372 (§ 21).

1. *so SGMCF.* fraunc saunc *L.* *sim. N.* 2. *so MF.* *so corr. N.* failli *L.* *sim. SC.* issist *G.* 3—3. cessent [al' se esteinent *in marg.*] les homages resceuz *N.* se esteint le homage resceu *S.* *sim. MF.* *sim.* (se *om.*) *G.* 4. *so LMC.* vn *add. SGF.* *so interl. N.* 5. si *om. SGM.* 6. al *M.* 7. mere *M.* 8. *so NMF.* qe *om. LSG.*

and the remote one more remote. And when all these fail, either by their blood becoming extinct, or by their right being forfeited by judgment of felony, the tenement must of necessity return to the lord of the fee, as to the source from which it first issued, for want of any other direction in which it can go; and in such case the homage received for the tenement is extinguished[b]. The lord's right by escheat.

2. There are many things which constitute proximity, and confer an inheritance and right of succession, to wit, sex, age, line, a partible inheritance, plurality of female heirs, form of gift, and blood. Sex, because the male is to be received and the female rejected, so long as there is a male heir apparent of the father by the same mother; but the daughter begotten on the first wife is to be preferred in the succession to the marriage granted with her mother to the male begotten by the same father on the second wife. Sex, how it affects the descent. Estate in marriage.

3. Age is material; because he who is the first born is admissible before the younger son of the same father and Primogeniture.

[b] See above, pp. 33 and 34, and the note there.

frere remeindra le plus proschein heir al frere einzné, ou al
[270.] meyns proschein, solom ceo qe le einznee eit engendrure ou noun. Et si le einzné frere moerge sauntz heir de sei vivaunt soen pere, le frere puisnee tendra soen lu, et comencera de estre plus proschein heir al commun pere, et les autres puisneez proscheins; et issi de plus[1] remuez[2] jekes a sauntz fin.

Glan. li. 7. c. 3; Brac. 64 *b*, 65; Fle. 372 (§ 22).

4. Et si le frere einznee moerge vivaunt soen piere, et eit [3]engendré heirs[3], cele engendrure remeint en le poer le-ael, et serra le plus proschein heir al ael, pur le meer dreit qe a ly descendi par la mort soen pere fiz le ael, tut ne attendi[4] soen fiz nul estat; et le uncle, ou la aunte, sera proschein,[5] tut soit il un degré plus pres qe le neveu, qi est plus proschein. Et dounc si le uncle, ou la aunte, hors de seisine demaunde la seisine soen piere par assise de mort de auncestre, ou par bref de dreit, vers le neveu, la excepcioun de plus procheinté li forbarra; et en mesme la manere, si il demaunde vers estraunge persone. Et si le uncle ou la aunte soit en seisine

1. plus *om. M.* 2. iueuenes *F.* 3—3. engendrure *MF.* engendrure heirs *C.* 4. so *MF.* *sim. C.* attende *LN.* entendy *G.* *sim. S.* 5. *so print.* car *add. LMGCF.* *sim. NS.*

mother, and the younger brother will remain nearest heir to the elder, or at least a near heir, according as the elder shall have issue or not. And if the elder brother dies without heir of his own in the lifetime of his father, the younger brother will take his place, and begin to be next heir to their common father, and the other younger ones will be near; and so of those more remote, without end.

Representation of deceased eldest son by his issue.

4. If the elder brother dies in his father's lifetime, having begotten an heir, this issue remains under the authority of the grandfather, and shall be next heir to the grandfather by reason of the mere right which descended to him by the death of his father, the grandfather's son, although the son did not live to attain any estate; and the uncle or aunt shall be only near heir, although he is one degree nearer than the grandson, who is next heir. Therefore if the uncle, or aunt, being out of seisin, demand the seisin of his father by assise of Mortdancester, or by writ of right against the grandson, the exception of proximity shall bar him; and in like manner if he demand against a stranger. And if the uncle or aunt is in seisin,

et tiegne hors le neveu, [1]le neveu[1], qi est plus proschein heir, [2]recovera par mi le bref de dreit par counte countaunt. Et ceo qe est dit de frere puisnee, uncle proschein heir, soit entendu estre ensaumple de touz heirs proscheins en semblables cas.

5. Line, pur ceo qe la file trové en la dreite line descendaunt plus toust est receivable qe ne est le masle trové en la line transversele. Brac. 65; Fle. 371 (§ 12).

6. Heritage partable, sicum est avaunt dit, autaunt avera le puisnee fiz qe le einznee; et en tel cas soit le usage del lu tenuz. Brac. 66 b.

7. Pluralité des femmes, sicum est de soeurs parceners[3], lequel qe eles soint engendrez de une mere ou de plusours, qe se presentent totes en lu de une heir, et ou[4] nule ne est plus receivable qe autre, ne nule ne purra estre autri heir; car issi serroit supposé plus de procheinté en une qe en autre, qe point ne est; car totes sount ouelement plus proscheines. Et si la une moerge, les porciouns des autres serrount par taunt encruz, mes ne mie par dreit de suc- [270 *b.*] Brac. 66 b; Fle. 372 (§ 17); Ante, l. iii. c. 7. s. 11.

1—1. *so C. om. LNMGS.* 2. i *add. M.* il *F.* il *interl. N.* 3. *so MCF.* et *add. L. sim. NSG.* 4. ou *om. C.*

and keeps out the grandson, the grandson, being next heir, shall recover by means of the writ of right by pleading his descent. And what is here said of the younger brother, uncle to the near heir, may be taken as an example of the position of near heirs in all like cases.

5. Line is material; because the daughter found in the direct line descending is to be preferred before the male found in the transverse line. Direct line preferred to collateral.

6. Of a partible inheritance, the younger son, as before has been mentioned, shall have as great a share as the elder; and in this case the custom of the place shall be observed. Inheritance by custom partible.

7. Plurality of female heirs affects the succession, as in case of sisters parceners, who, whether they are begotten of one or of several mothers, all present themselves in the place of one heir, and no one of them is to be preferred before another, neither can one be heir to the others; for that would imply a nearer proximity in one than in another, which there is not, since they are all equally nearest. And if one of them dies, Sisters are coheirs. Co-parceners are not heirs to each other. Right of accruer.

cessioun, mes par une manere de dreit qe est apelé dreit de accres.

Brac. 68 *b*, 69; Fle. 372 (§ 19). 8. Fourme de doun, sicum piert en feffementz ou estraunges persones sount plus toust[1] receivables a la successioun qe ne sount les plus proscheins heirs, qi par les feffours en sount forclos. Stat. Westm. 2. (13 Ed. I.) c. 1. Car les volunteez des donours sount a garder en quant qe ley le purra suffrir. Et tut ne soint mie celes estraunges persones dreitz heirs, il serount neqedent en lu des heirs. Et ausi serrount en lu des heirs touz ceux a queus terre ou tenement escheit par acune manere de reversioun ou par eschete, lequel qe ele cheite[2] par defaute de saunc ou par forfeture.

Brac. 65; Fle. 371 (§ 13). 9. Dreit de saunc fet acune foiz la femele forclore le masle. Car si A. engendre de une femme fiz et file, et de une autre femme fiz, le fiz einznee iert plus proschein heir le piere et [271.] la mere; et si il devie sauntz heir de sei, plus proschein iert al frere mort la soeur, qe le puisné frere de l'autre femme ou

1. toust *om. LNSCF.* tost *GM.* 2. eschiete *M. sim. SF.* escheist *C.*

the shares of the rest shall be thereby increased, but not by succession, but by a kind of right called that of accruer[b].

Form of gift, excluding ordinary descent. 8. The form of gift is also material, as appears in the case of feoffments, whereby strangers are admissible to the succession in preference to the next heirs, who are excluded by the feoffors. For the wills of donors are to be observed as far as the law can permit; and although such strangers are not right heirs, yet they shall be in the place of heirs. And so shall all those stand in the place of heirs to whom lands or tenements fall by any manner of reversion or of escheat, whether it be by default of blood or by forfeiture.

Whole blood preferred to half blood. 9. Right of blood sometimes causes the female to exclude the male. For if A. begets by one wife a son and a daughter, and by another wife a son, the eldest son is next heir to the father and the mother, and if he dies without issue of his own, the sister is nearer heir to the deceased brother than the younger brother by the second or third wife. And so likewise

[b] It appears to follow from the doctrine of the text, that if an inheritance descended to several daughters by two wives, the share of one coparcener dying without issue would go by survivorship or accruer to all the others, and not by descent to her sisters of the whole blood. A similar doctrine is to be found obscurely expressed in Bracton, f. 66 *b*. (Compare Bracton, f. 77 *b*; and see above, p. 73, and note there; Blackstone, Commentaries, vol. ii. p. 231, note.) In modern times no *jus accrescendi* has been admitted between parceners. (Blackstone, Commentaries, vol. ii. p. 188.)

de la tierce. Et ausi la issue de la soeur. Mes les premers[1] ne purrount rien demaunder del heritage lour marastre jekes apres le disces de sa engendrure, et si ele ne eit nule engendrure de lour piere, james ne purrount rien demaunder del heritage lour marastre; ne ausi, tut eit ele engendrure de lour piere, si le heritage la marastre ne eit descendu a lour freres ou a lour soeurs engendrez de [2]un piere de[2] lour marastre. Mes si le heritage cheite a lour freres ou a lour soeurs de mesme le piere et de diverses meres, et la issue defaille de lour marastre, tauntost crest accioun a la premere engendrure ou a lour issue a demaunder la seisine de la dreine engendrure [3]ou de lour issue.

10. Et de engendrure[3] fete de une mere et de divers pieres, plus proscheins sount et plus toust resceivables al heritage les fiz et lour issue del premer piere a chescun heritage de par lour mere ausi bien qe de part lour piere, qe les fiz puisneez; et cum ceux moergent[4] seisiz et ne eient point de engendrure,

1. heirs primers *GM.* *sim. SCF.* premers heirs le piere *on eras. N.* 2—2. lur pere e de *G.* 3—3. so *SG.* *sim. MCF.* *sim. interlin. N.* *om. L.* 4. so *G.* *sim. MF.* morirent *LNC.* *sim. S.*

the issue of the sister. But the first issue shall never demand any part of the inheritance of their step-mother until after the decease of her issue, and if she has no issue by their father, they can never demand any part of the inheritance of their step-mother; nor, although she has issue by their father, if her inheritance did not descend to their brothers or sisters, the children of their common father by their step-mother. But if the inheritance falls to their brothers or sisters, the children of the same father by a different mother, and the issue of their step-mother fails, an action immediately accrues to the first children, or to their issue, to demand the seisin of the last children or of their issue[c].

A child may succeed to the inheritance of his step-mother through his half-brother.

10. Of issue begotten upon the same mother by different fathers, the son by the first father and his issue are nearer, and are sooner to be admitted to every inheritance on the part of their mother, as well as on the part of their father, than the younger sons; and if they die seised and without issue,

Possessio fratris in maternal inheritance.

c I do not find any authority in Bracton for the succession of the half-brother to an inheritance descended from his step-mother, a stranger in blood. But see the Year Book, 33 Edw. I. p. 444. Bracton allows a man to be heir to his half-brother in respect of land purchased by him, in default of brothers or sisters of the whole blood. And in respect of land descended from their common father, he appears to doubt whether the half-brother would not be preferred to the sister of the whole blood. (Bracton, f. 65, 65 *b*, 66 *b*.)

plus toust sount receyvables les soeurs de un pere et de une mere, qe les freres de une mere et de divers pieres.
[271 b.] Mes si nul masle del premer baroun ne lour issue ne attende le heritage lour mere, adounc sount plus toust les masles del autre baroun receivables al heritage la mere, qe les femeles del premer baroun; et si acun masle de premer baroun eit engendrure masle ou femele, cele engendrure est plus toust resceivable al heritage la mere qe les masles del autre baroun.

Brac. 65; Fle. 371 (§14).

11. Et acune foiz forclost la soeur puisnee le frere einzné; cum si Johan engendrast de sa premere femme un fiz et de sa secunde femme fiz et file, et le fiz puisné se purchaceast terre ou tenement et se lessast morir sauntz heir de sei, la soeur le purchaceour enportera le heritage, et forsclora le frere einznee. Al heritage neqedent descendaunt de la persone Johan, le commun piere, seroit plus tost receivable le frere. Et si Johan eit engendrure deus fiz et deus files de diverses meres, le einzné frere est plus proschein heir Johan, et[1] apres ly le puisné, si le piere sourvive le fiz einznee. Mes si un de ces freres face purchaz et moerge sauntz heir de sei, la soeur de

1. et *om.* *LM.* e *SGCFN.*

the sisters by the same father and mother are to be preferred to the brothers by the same mother and by different fathers. But if no male child of the first husband, or his issue, survive to attain the inheritance of his mother, then the males by the second husband are admissible to the inheritance of the mother before the females by the first husband; but if any male of the first husband has issue, male or female, this issue is to be admitted to the inheritance of the mother before the males by the second husband.

Right of representation.

Sister of the whole blood succeeds to brother's purchase before an elder half-brother.

11. Sometimes also the younger sister excludes the elder brother, as where John begets by his first wife a son, and by his second wife a son and a daughter, and the younger son purchases lands or tenements, and dies without heir of his own body, the sister of the purchaser shall carry off the inheritance and exclude the elder brother, although the brother would be sooner admitted to the inheritance descending from the person of John the common father. And if John has issue two sons and two daughters by diverse mothers, the elder brother is nearest heir to John, and after him the younger, if the father survive the eldest son; but if one of

mesme le ventre del purchaceour serra soen plus proschein heir et forsclora le frere et la soeur del autre ventre, si homage [1]ne le[1] forbarre.

12. Et si treis freres ou plus soint de un pere et de une mere, et le puisnee de touz face purchaz et se[2] moerge sauntz heir de sei, le eynzné frere serra soen plus proschein heir et forsclora le piere et la mere tut soint il plus proscheins de saunc, pur ceo qe le frere est trové le plus proschein en mesme le degré, et issi ne sount mie le pere ne la mere, et ausi forsclora il les autres freres et soeurs, tut soint il trovez en mesme le degré. Et tut en soit le milueyn ou autre en seisine, le einznee neqedent le conquera par bref de dreit. Et si le frere eynznee moerge sauntz heir de sei, adounc [3]serra le[3] einznee[4] frere apres[5], et issi de frere en frere jekes as soeurs. Et si frere ne soeur ne nule issue de eus ne perge, adounc serra[6] le commun piere, ou la commune mere, si le piere

Fle. 371 (§16).

[272.]

1—1. *so SG.* ne lour *L.* nel *MC.* 2. *so LSCF.* se *om. NGM.* 3—3. ⌜serra heir soen *N.* *sim. SG.* le serra le *MCF.* 4. einznee *om. SG.* 5. apres ly *N.* 6. ly serra heir *N.* ly serra *S.* *sim. G.* le serra me *F.*

these brothers makes a purchase, and dies without heirs of his own body, the sister of the same venter as the purchasor shall be the nearest heir, and shall exclude the brother and sister of the other venter, if not barred by homage[c].

Inheritance may be barred by homage.

12. If there are three or more brothers by the same father and mother, and the youngest of them all makes a purchase and dies without heir of his own body, the eldest brother shall be his next heir, and shall exclude the father and mother, although they are nearer in blood, because the brother is found to be the nearest in the same degree, which the father and the mother are not; and he shall also exclude the other brothers and sisters, although they are found in the same degree. And even if the intermediate or other brother be in seisin, yet the eldest shall obtain it by a writ of right. And if the eldest brother dies without heir of his own body, then it shall go to the next eldest brother, and so from brother to brother, until it comes to the sisters. And if neither brother nor sister nor any issue of them appear, then it shall go to

Eldest brother succeeds to purchase of youngest before father.

Succession in the ascending line.

[c] It is probably meant that an elder brother of the half blood will be excluded in favour of a sister of the whole blood, even where the relation of homage between the two half-brothers does not present an obstacle to the descent to the brother, as would be the case where the tenement of the deceased was derived by gift from the common father. Compare Glanvill, li. vii. c. 1; Bracton, f. 65 *b*; Fleta, p. 371 (§ 15, 16); and see above, p. 34, note.

soit mort, et nul autre soit trové en nul degré plus pres devers le piere, et issi de touz les autres degrez countremount. Et coment les degrez se esparpillent, piert par l'arbre de parentee suaunt [1].

CHAPITRE III.

[2]De Degreez[2].

Brac. 67; Fle. 372. 1. Des parentz sount diverses degrez, sicum parra en la figure suante[3]; dount fet a entendre qe nul ne est receivable a successioun qe ert trové en nul degree en line belive, mountaunt ou descendaunt, masle ou femelle, taunt cum acun est trové en vie en la dreite line descendaunt. Mes cum nuli n'i ert trové, adounc a force estovera quere les degrez en lines belives.

Brac. 67 b, 68; Fle. 372, 373. 2. Et touz jours fet a comencer a counter del commun cep drein seisi de ambideus les dreitz; et issint descendaunt en [272 b.] la dreite line de degré en degré sauntz nuli transsailler jekes

1. Hic deficit arbor *in marg. LC.* Hic fiet figura S. *The tree is taken with slight alteration from N, and is wanting in LSMCF.* 2—2. Des degrez de parente N. De successiouns M. *om. SGFC. In C, and the printed edition, this is not divided as a separate chapter.* 3. *om. NMF.*

the common father[d]; or if the father be dead, and no other be found in any degree nearer on his side, to the common mother; and so of all the other degrees ascending. In what manner the degrees branch out will appear by the following tree of kindred.

CHAPTER III.

Of Degrees of Kindred.

Table of kindred. Direct line taken first, then collateral. 1. There are various degrees of kindred, as will appear in the following figure. It must be observed, no one, whether male or female, found in any degree in the collateral line, either ascending or descending, is admissible to succeed, so long as any person is found alive in the direct line descending; but when no one is found there, then we are driven of necessity to seek the degrees in the collateral lines.

Descent, how to be traced, in the direct line. 2. It is always proper to begin to count from the common stock last seised of both rights, and so descending in the direct line from degree to degree, without stepping over any, to the

d See note, p. 325.

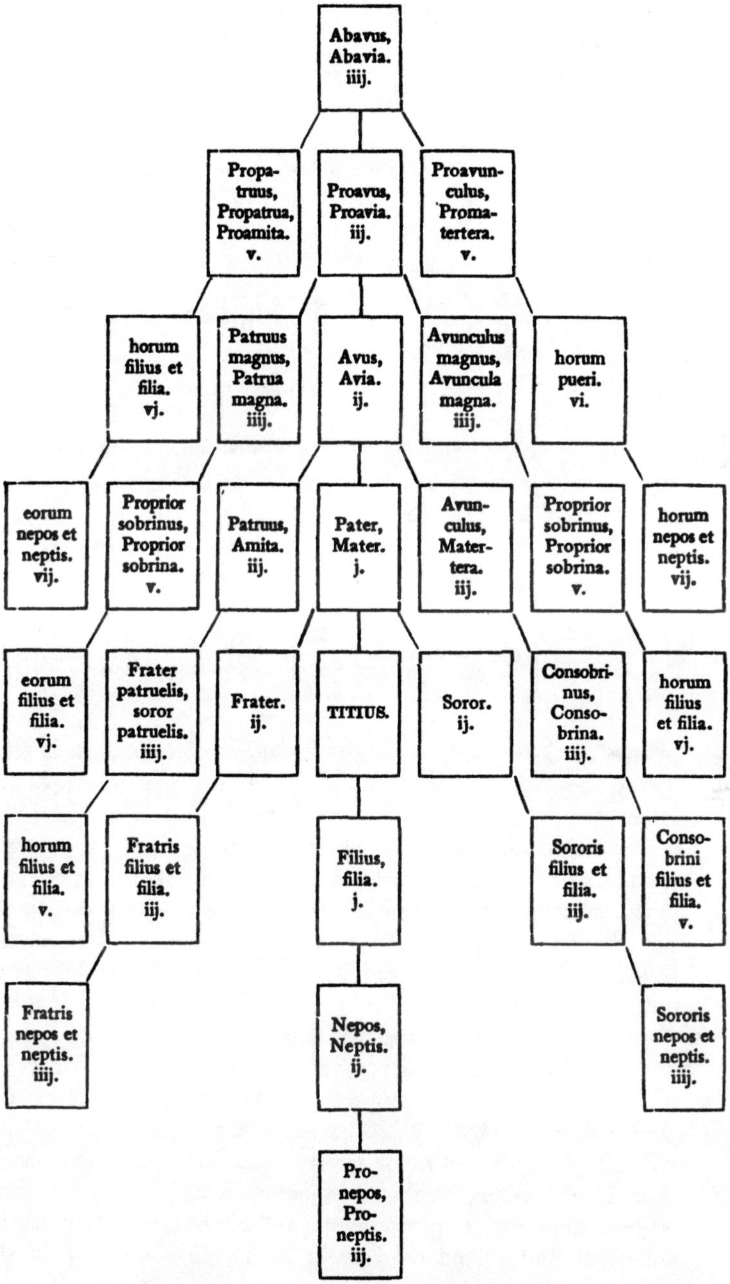

ARBOR CONSANGUINITATIS.

al pleintif; et ne mie soulement par mi touz les degreez pleyns trovez en la dreite line, einz[1] covendra acune foiz counter par mi les degrez voides; sicum en cas ou le fiz einzné, qi ad engendrure, se lest morir avaunt soen auncestre. Brac. 68; Fle. 373 (§ 4); Ante, p. 150. Et acune foiz sount les voides degreez transsaillez[2] en countaunt par descente, sicum en cas ou les fiz einzneez moergent sauntz heirs de lour cors, vivauntz lour auncestres. Car si acun fiz einzné moerge sauntz heir de sei, vivaunt soen auncestre, par mi celi ne[3] covendra james a counter, pur ceo qe il ne attendi unques qe acun estat ly descendist, eynz est[4] tel degree tut voide; et ausi, tut[5] eit il heir qi moerge sauntz heir de sei; et le plus proschein frere occupe soen lu pur le meer dreit qe [6]se esprent[6] en ly, sicum en le plus proschein del saunc; et si[7] nul frere n'i soit, adounc [8]se esprendra[8] le dreit de la successioun en la soeur, une ou plusours; et si nule soeur i soit, adounc resortera al proschein degré trové plein devers le auncestre de qi le heritage moet en acune line belive. Brac. 67 *b*; Fle. 373 (§ 2). Et si toust cum celi serra seisi del un dreit et del autre, si comence a fere dreite line quaunt as heirs de ly

1. *so NSGMCF.* et *L.* 2. a tressailler *GC.* *sim. MSF.* 3. *so NGMCF.* ne *om. L.* ny *S.* 4. *so SGMCF.* est *interl. N.* *om. L.* 5. *so NS.* *sim. GCF.* toust *L.* tost *M.* 6—6. *so SM.* *sim. NF.* ceo esprent *L.* se prent *C.* 7. *so NSGMCF.* issi *L.* 8—8. *so MF.* ceo esprendra *L.* se prendra *NSGC.*

Vacant degrees, when to be named. plaintiff, and not only through all the occupied degrees in the direct line, but sometimes through the vacant degrees; as in case where the eldest son, having issue, dies before his ancestor. Sometimes in counting by descent the vacant degrees are passed over, as, where the eldest sons die without heirs of their bodies in the lifetime of their ancestors; for if an eldest son dies without issue in the lifetime of his ancestor, it is never necessary to count through him, because he did not survive until any estate descended to him, but such degree is quite vacant; so also if he had an heir who died without issue; and in such case the next brother occupies his place by reason of the mere right, which attaches to him as the next of blood. **Collateral descent.** And if there is not any brother, then the right of succession will attach to the sister or sisters; and if there is no sister, then it will resort to the next occupied degree on the side of that ancestor from whom the inheritance moves in some collateral line. And as soon as he becomes seised of both rights, he begins to make a direct line as to issue begotten

engendrez, et comencera de estre commun cep [1]a regard[1] de ses heirs. Et [2]qi vodera[2] neqedent counter par mi celi, ou ses enfauntz, qi unqes ne attendirent qe acun estat lour descendist par la mort le commun auncestre, ne greve nient. Mes adounc ne deit il mie dire, qe le dreit de la successioun descendi, einz deit dire qe de Johan dust le dreit aver descendu a Piers, et de Piers a Thomas, cum a neveu et heir, mes pur ceo qe cel fiz ou neveu ne attendi mie qe dreit ly descendist, pur ceo qe il morust vivaunt le commun auncestre, descendi le dreit al secound frere ou al autre plus proschein heir. Et acune foiz cheit counte en branches pur pluralité, sicum est de soeurs parceners, et ou covendra primes counter par mi touz les degrez del issue del une et puis del autre, et issi des autres. [273.] Brac. 68; Fle. 374 (§ 7). Brac. 67 b, 68; Fle. 373 (§ 6).

3. Et en eyde des prentiz[3] soit fete une figure pur plus apertement demoustrer les degrez et les lines directes et belives par ount homme se puisse meuz conustre[4] en le dreit de successiouns; et seit tendu une line[5] countreval, et en mi lu Brac. 68, 68 b; Fle. 374, 375.

1—1. *so MCF.* a regarder *L.* quaunt a regard *N.* *sim. SG.* 2—2. *so NF. sim. SGC.* qi vendra *L.* si vodra *M.* 3. autres aprentis *N.* aprentiz *M.* *sim. S.* parentez *CF.* 4. *so NSMCF.* *sim. G.* counter *L.* 5. dreite *add. N.* *sim. SG.*

by him, and to be a common stock with regard to the heirs derived from him. Yet if any one chooses to count through a person, or his children, who did not live until any estate descended to them by the death of the common ancestor, it does no harm; but in such case he ought not to say that the right of succession descended, but that from John ought the right to have descended to Peter, and from Peter to Thomas as his grandson and heir; but inasmuch as such son or grandson did not live until such right descended to him, because he died in the lifetime of the common ancestor, the right descended to the second brother or to the other next heir. And sometimes the count is divided into branches by reason of plurality of heirs, as in case of sisters parceners, where it is proper first to count through all the degrees of the issue of the first, and then of the second, and so of the rest. Mode of pleading descent through vacant degrees. Descent traced through several lines.

3. For the assistance of learners, a figure may be made to show more plainly the degrees and the lines direct and collateral, whereby a person may be better acquainted with the law of successions. Let therefore a perpendicular line Table of descents.

soit fet un degré void, qe suppose le pleintif, qi pere ou mere soit mis en sus de ly sicum premer auncestre, et celi le premer degré; et en sus del pere ou de la mere soit mis le ael ou la aele le pleintif, sicum en le secound degré; et[1] en suis
[273 *b.*] del ael soit mis le besael ou la besaele, sicum en le tierz[2] degré; et en suis del besael le tresael, et issi [3]plus haut et[3] plus haut par divers degrez taunt cum tens limité el bref de dreit le vodera suffrer. Et countreval de suth le pleintif soit mis ou[4] fiz ou file, et[5] celi face le premer degré avalaunt; et de suth soit mis neveu ou nece, et celi i face le secund degré; et de suth uncore le fiz ou la file le neveu ou la nece, et celi face le tierz degré; et issi descendaunt de [6]gré en gré[6] jekes a sauntz fin.

Brac. 68 *b*; Fle. 375 (§ 12–19). 4. Et si nul pleintif ne soit trové en la dreite line a qi le dreit de la successioun puisse descendre, a force covendra dounc descendre a degrez de costé, sicum as plus proscheins del piere ou de la mere sicum al uncle le pleintif ou al aunte, et puis descendaunt en cele line de degré en degré taunt cum

1. et *om. LC.* e *SGMF.* 2. so *GMF.* quart *LC.* *sim. S.* quart [iij. *interl.*] *N.* 3—3. de plus haut en *GM.* 4. vn *GM.* 5. ou *L.* e *MCF.* 6—6. de degre en degre *GM.* degre en degre *NS.* *sim. C.*

be drawn, and in the middle of it let a void space be left for the supposed plaintiff, and let his father or mother be placed above him as the first ancestor, and that will make the first degree. Above the father or mother let the grandfather or grandmother of the plaintiff be put as in the second degree, and above the grandfather the great-grandfather, or the great-grandmother, as in the third degree; and above the great-grandfather the great-great-grandfather, and so higher and higher by different degrees as far as the time limited in a writ of right will allow. And directly under the plaintiff let son or daughter be placed, which will make the first degree descending; and under him grandson or granddaughter, to make the second degree; and lower again the son or daughter of the grandson or granddaughter to make the third degree, and so descending from degree to degree *ad infinitum*.

Collateral descent. 4. If there be found no plaintiff in the direct line to whom the right of succession can descend, then of necessity it must descend to the collateral degrees, that is, to the nearest to the father or the mother, as, to the uncle or aunt, and so on, descending in that line from degree to

il durent; et puis, par defaute de degrez trovez en la premere line bilive, covendra resorter al ael qe est en la dreite line, et puis resortaunt par defaute al frere ou a la soeur le ael en la line bilive, et issi de degré en degré taunt cum il serrount trovez pleins; et issi de trestouz les autres degrez plus hautz, issint qe a ceux qe serrount trovez en la dreite line escheite le dreit de la successioun, si nul ne soit [1]de suth[1] ly nule part ou le dreit purra descendre. Et par defaute de celi qi fit [274.] un degré en la dreite line descende le dreit a acun qi serra trové en la line bilive. Et, par defaute [2]de degré[2] [3]en la bilive[3], resorte autre foiz le dreit a la dreite line a un degré plus haut. Et s'il troeve degré plein, se tiegne; et si noun, courge dounc descendaunt en la bilive; et issi de touz autres degrez.

1—1. desus *L.* trouee souz *N.* troue desuz *SCF.* *sim. GM.* 2—2. *om. SF.* de gree *interl. N.* 3—3. trouee en la lyne belyue *N.* *sim. MF.* troue en la beliue *S.* *sim. G.*

degree so far as they continue, and then for default of degrees found in the first collateral line, it must resort to the grandfather in the direct line, and afterwards for default there, resort to the brother or sister of the grandfather in the collateral line, and so from degree to degree so far as they shall be found full; and so of all the other higher degrees, so that the right of succession shall fall to those who shall be found in the direct line, if none can be found anywhere below him to whom the right may descend[e]. And for default of him who would have made a degree in the direct line the right shall descend to one who shall be found in the collateral line, and for default of a degree in the collateral line the right shall resort again to the direct line at a higher degree, and if it find that degree full, it shall attach there; if not, it shall go on descending in the collateral line, and so of all the other degrees.

Lineal ascendant admissible to inheritance.

[e] It will be observed, that the writer admits succession by lineal ascendants, contrary to the generally received opinion, and without authority from the writers whom he generally follows. See before, p. 164, note, pp. 319, 320; and compare p. 312; Glanvill, l. vii. c. 1; Bracton, f. 62*b*. Coke, who frequently in his margin cites Britton upon this very subject, does not appear to have understood him as contradicting the received doctrine; 'I never read,' he says, 'any opinion in any booke, old or new, against this maxime,' (that an inheritance lineally descends, but does not ascend,) 'but only in *Lib. Rub.*, where it is said, Si quis sine liberis decesseret, pater aut mater ejus in hæreditatem succedat, vel pater et soror, si pater et mater desint.' (Coke Litt. 11 a.) The authority cited by Coke as *Liber Ruber* is the Collection of Anglo-Saxon Laws known as *Leges Henrici I.* c. lxx. § 20.

Glan. li. 7. c. 17; Fle. 375 (§ 18); Ante, p. 52.

5. Et si nul degré ne soit trové ou le dreit purra resposer, ou tut trove il degré, al seignur del fee apent de seisir soen fee jeques autaunt qe cil veigne demaunder, en qi persone respose le meer dreit de la successioun; et en le meen tens serra il en lu del heir.

6. Coment les degrez se tiegnent en parentage piert[1] par ceste figure dount la moité suffireit, et adunc resemblereit une banere, mes ele est desplié de une part [2]pur signefier de une part[2] la issue [3]des auncestres masles[3], et de autre part en signefiaunce del issue des auncestres femeles.

CHAPITRE IV. [CXX.]

De Court de Baroun.

Glan. li. 12. cc. 2, 7; Brac. 329, 329 b; Fle. 375, 376; Hengh. Mag. c. 3. pp. 9, 10.

1. Les brefs de dreit overtz deivent estre portez en courtz des seignurs des queus les pleintifs cleyment a tener. Et issi[4] en autres courtz si[5] soint portez ou purchacez qe en courtz des chiefs seignurs des feez, les chiefs seignurs des feez averount lour courtz hors de nostre court, quel houre qe eus le

1. so *GMC.* piert *om. LNS.* 2—2. *om. M.* 3—3. del saung masle *N.* 4. si *NSGMCF.* 5. si *om. NSGMCF.*

The lord may seise and hold his fee until the heir is found.

5. And if no degree be found where the right may rest,—or even if any be found,—the lord of the fee may seize his fee until he in whose person the mere right of succession rests shall come and demand it, and in the meantime the lord shall stand in the place of the heir.

Figure of consanguinity.

6. How the degrees are placed in consanguinity, appears by the above figure, whereof the half might suffice, and then it would resemble a banner; but it is displayed on the one side to show the issue of male ancestors, and on the other to show the issue of female ancestors.

CHAPTER IV.

Of the proceedings in a Plea of Right before the Court Baron and County Court, and of its removal into the Royal Court.

Writ of right patent to be brought in the lord's court.

1. Writs of right patent ought to be brought in the courts of the lords of whom the plaintiffs claim to hold; and therefore if they are brought or purchased in any other courts than those of the chief lords of the fees, such chief lords shall have their courts out of our court, as soon as they make demand

demaundent et puissent averrer les feez lour; et periroune les brefs et les proces, et remeindrount les pleintifs en nostre merci. [274 *b*.]

2. Et cum le pleintif avera soen bref purchacé, il le deit porter et moustrer a cely a qi le maundement est fet; et cil tauntost, sauntz seurté demaunder de sure, ly deit asseer jour a sa premere court, qe deit estre de eynz les treis symeyns sour mesme le fee. Et qe tiel bref soit moustré [1]et lu[1] en plein court et enroulé, et qe le tenaunt soit somouns par agard de la court.

3. Et si le pleintif eit plus delay, et le puisse prover, sicum apres serra dit, par pleinte et par proeve, pur[2] tel tort purra il weyver la court soen seignur pur ceo qe soen seignur ly ad defailli de dreit, et pleder en Counté, lequel qe le seignur eit la fraunchise de retourn de bref ou noun. Et issi par cas purra la parole estre remué [3]et remené[3] hors de une court jekes en mesme la court. Et avaunt la prove fete ne serra mie la parole ausi cum el Counté, et puis tendra lu le *Pone* a remuer la parole jekes par devaunt nos Justices, et ne mie avaunt.

Brac. 329 *b*; Fle. 376.

Brac. 329 *b* (c. 4); Fle. 375 (§ 6).

1—1. bien *LN.* e lu *GMF.* *sim. C.* *om. S.* 2. *so M.* par *LGF.* par tiel iour e par *N.* 3—3. *so verb. SGM.* *om. L.* e estre remuee *N.* e remuee *F.*

thereof, and can prove the fees to be theirs; and the writs and proceedings shall fall to the ground, and the plaintiffs shall remain in our mercy.

2. The plaintiff, having purchased his writ, ought to carry and show it to him to whom the mandate is directed; and he forthwith, without demanding pledges to prosecute, is bound to appoint him a day at his first court, which ought to be within three weeks, upon the same fee; and the writ should be produced and read in full court, and entered on the roll, and the tenant summoned by award of the court.

Proceeding in the lord's court.

3. If the plaintiff be longer delayed, and can prove the same, as hereafter mentioned, by plaint and proof, he may by reason of such wrong, and because his lord has failed to do him right, waive the court of his lord, and plead in the county court, whether the lord has the franchise of return of writs or not. And thus in some cases the plaint may be removed out of a court, and afterwards brought back into it again. And before proof made of default the plaint shall not be considered as in the county, but after that, and not before, a *Pone* will lie to remove it before our Justices.

Removal of plea into county, for defect of right.

Reclaimer of court.

Removal into king's court by *Pone*.

Brac. 329 *b*; Fle. 375 (c. 3. § 1).

4. En moutz de maneres est neqedent la parole remuable jekes en Counté, cum si le seignur ne se voille entremettre, ou pur ceo qe il ne ad nule court, ou pur ceo qe il ad relessé sa court par ses lettres patentes, et ausi pur la [1]noun pusaunce[1] del seignur et de sa court, sicum par garraunt vouché[2] hors
[275.] de soen poer, qe il ne porra point fere venir, ou si le tenaunt se face aillours essoignier de mal de lit qe[3] en le poer de soen seignur, ou pur ceo qe il ne ad poer de enveer les quatre chivalers de juger de mal de lit, ou si le tenaunt se met en la graunt assise, et en plusours autres maneres. Et acune foiz par le tenaunt, cum s'il ne tiegne rien de ly a qi le[4] maundement del bref est fet.

Glan. li. 12. c. 8.

Glan. li. 12. c. 6; Brac. 329 *b*; Fle. 376 (§ 1).

5. De sommouns, et de soursises, et de essoignes en courtz des fraunes hommes deit[5] estre solom la manere de chescun pays. Mes de vewes demaunder, et de garraunt voucher, de counter par descentes et par resortz, et de defendre, et de excepcioner, et de batailes joyndre soit mesme le ordre tenu de pleder[6] en court de fraunc homme cum[7] est agardé[8].

1—1. noun suffissaunce *GM*. *sim*. *F*. 2. voucher *NMC*. *sim*. *F*. 3. *so MF*. qe est *LSC*. *sim*. *G*. que *on eras*. *N*. 4. *so NSGMCF*. le *om*. *L*. 5. *so GMF*. de *LC*. deyt *on eras*. *N*. 6. *so MC*. cum *add*. *LN*. cume *F*. 7. *so MC*. *sim*. *SGF*. ou *L*. *om*. *N*. 8. *so LNSGM*. en la court le seignur *add*. *print*.

Causes for removal from the lord's court.

4. There are many ways besides in which a cause is removable into the county court, as, where the lord refuses to intermeddle therein, or because he has no court, or because he has released his court by his letters patent; also for want of authority in the lord and his court, as where the tenant vouches a warrant out of his jurisdiction, and whom he cannot compel to appear, or if the tenant cause himself to be essoined *de malo lecti* elsewhere than in the jurisdiction of his lord, or because he has not authority to send the four knights to judge of the sickness for which he is essoined, or if the tenant put himself upon the great assise, and for many other reasons. Sometimes also the plea is removable by the tenant, as where he does not hold anything of him to whom the writ is directed.

Practice in courts baron fixed by custom, or follows king's court.

5. As to summonses and defaults and essoins in the courts of freemen, the practice ought to be according to the custom of the country; but in the demanding of view, vouching to warranty, counting by descents and resorts, defending, excepting, and joining in battle, let the same order of pleading be observed in the court of a freeman as is awarded in our court.

Glan. li. 12. s. 7; Brac. 329 *b*, 330; Fle. 376 (§ 2); Hengh. Mag. c. 3. p. 10.

6. La court de seignur deit hom prover fause, ou le seignur mesmes, ou le baillif a qi le maundement [1]fust enveé, avera[1] defailli de dreit fere, en ceste manere. En primes se deit le pleintif pleindre al viscounte et moustrer le bref en plein Counté, et par agard de sutours, sauntz surté trover de sure, deit estre comaundé al baillif del houndred ou a autre, qe en presence des veisins voist prendre le serment del pleintif a sa tierce meyn en la court le seignur, si il eit court, ou en sa manauntise, ou sour[2] la terre mesmes, si le seignur ne eit nule court ne manauntise, qe le seignur ly ad defailli de dreit. [275 *b.*] Car a prover qe la court ad defailli de dreit fere, ne suffist point, einz estoit[3] prover qe cist a qi le comaundement est fet ad defailli de fere dreit, pur[4] la parole en le bref qe dit, et si tu ne feas[5], le viscounte le fra.

7. Et pur ceo se deit chescun pleintif pleindre a celi, a qi le bref va, de la court, eynz ceo qe la parole soit remuable jekes en Counté. Et le seignur dounc tauntost, oyé la pleinte, deit veer et examiner le proces et oyer le pleintif en presence

1—1. *so verb. G.* enuee auer *L.* *sim. SC.* est fet auera *NM.* fust enueye auer *F.* 2. *so N.* sus *LS.* sur *GMC.* 3. *so LF.* *so on eras. N.* *sim. S.* estuit a *G.* estut *M.* 4. *so NSGMC.* par *L.* 5. faiz *N.* fes *S.* faces *GMC.*

Proceeding to remove the plea into the county.

6. The manner of proving the lord's court false, where the lord himself or the bailiff to whom the mandate was directed, has failed to do justice, is as follows. In the first place, the plaintiff should complain to the sheriff, and produce the writ in full county court, and then, by award of the suitors, and without any security to prosecute being found, the bailiff of the hundred or some other shall be commanded that in the presence of the neighbours he go and take the oath of the plaintiff and two others, in the court of the lord, if he has a court, or at his mansion, or if he has neither court nor mansion, then upon the land itself, that the lord has failed to do him right; for it is not sufficient to prove that the court has failed to do right, but it must be proved that he to whom the mandate is directed failed to do right, the words in the writ being, 'And if thou do it not, the sheriff shall do it.'

Oath of defect of right to be taken in the court or on the manor.

Default to be shewn in the lord himself.

Appeal from the court to the lord.

7. Therefore every plaintiff, before the plaint is removable into the county, ought to complain of the court to him to whom the writ is directed. And then the lord, having heard the plaint, ought straightway to see and examine the proceed-

de suiters, en quel point les suiters ly ount fet tort. Et si il troeve errour, il ad poer del amender et de amercier les suiters. Et si il ne le face, adounc tendra lu la pleinte al viscounte.

Brac. 330, 330 b; Fle. 376 (§ 3). 8. Et cum le serjaunt avera pris le serment del pleintif et des conjurours, tauntost deit il fere somoundre le tenaunt par deus fraunes hommes terre tenauntz, qe il soit al proschein Counté a respoundre a tiel pleintif sur une demaunde qe il ly feist de taunt de terre ove les apurtenaunces en tele ville, solom le purport del bref; et deit enjoyndre as somenours, qe il soint a tiel Counté a testmoigner la somounse, et mesme le jour deit il asser al pleintif de suire la pleinte. Et si acun viscounte, ou [1]tenaunt lu le viscounte[1] en Counté ou en fraunchise, soursece[2] de fere dreit al pleintif, si il soit viscounte fermer, par taunt est punisable [276.] par prisoun et par fin, sicum despisour de noster maundement, et s'il soit viscounte de fee, par taunt ad deservi de perdre la fraunchise, s'il soit atteint, et de fere le gré al pleintif de ses damages.

1—1. le liu tenaunt le viscounte *N.* *sim.* *G.* sun lieu tenaunt *S.* 2. sil ne face *LN.* sursesse *S.* surcese *G.* sorsiete *M.* sursise *F.*

ings, and to hear the plaintiff in the presence of the suitors, in what point the suitors have done him wrong; and if he finds an error, he has authority to amend it, and to amerce the suitors. And if he neglects to do so, then the complaint shall be made to the sheriff.

Summons in the county court. 8. When the bailiff has taken the oath of the plaintiff and his cojurors, he is straightway to cause the tenant to be summoned by two freemen terre-tenants to appear at the next county court to answer to such a plaintiff upon a demand made against him of so much land with the appurtenances in such a vill, according to the purport of the writ; and he ought to enjoin the summoners to be at such county court to prove the summons, and also to appoint the plaintiff the same day to prosecute his plaint. When the sheriff, or any deputy of the sheriff in a county or franchise, fails to do right to the plaintiff, if he farms his office, he is punishable by imprisonment and fine as a despiser of our mandate; and if he be sheriff in fee, he hath deserved, if convicted, to lose the franchise, and to make satisfaction to the plaintiff for his damages.

Neglect of sheriff, how punished.

9. Et cum la parole soit issi ajourné al Counté, si le seignur del fee veigne al Counté et se pleigne del pleintif et tende de moustrer[1] [2]et de enseigner[2], qe le pleintif ad fet mal a entendre al viscounte et al Counté, et qe il ne defailli unques de dreit, coment qe sa court feist, seit oy, si il veigne einz ceo qe nul essoigne soit ajourné en Counté pur le pleintif ou[3] pur le tenaunt. Mes s'il attende taunt qe essoignie soit entré et alowé et ajourné, si qe la parole soit en le Counté par taunt de tens qe le *Pone* puisse trover aucune estencele de parole en Counté, mes ne purra le seignur del fee reaver sa court. Et si le viscounte remaunde maliciousement, qe il ne ad nule parole en le Counté solom la tenure del *Pone*, ja par taunt ne perisse le *Pone*, si presumpcioun overe pur le pleintif par les dates en le bref overt et en le *Pone*, qe la parole poeit aver esté en le Counté; et puis voise[4] avaunt le plee solum sa[5] nature.

Glan. li. 12. c. 7; Brac. 330 *b*; Fle. 376 (§ 5, 6); Hengh. Mag. c. 3. p. 10.

1. auerrer *SM.* 2—2. *om. S.* 3. *so NSGMCF.* et *L.* 4. *so NM.* *sim. S.* voeit *L.* voit *GC.* voyst *F.* 5. *so GMCF.* la *LNS.*

9. When the plaint is thus adjourned into the county, if the lord of the fee comes into court and complains of the plaintiff, and offers to show and instruct the court that the plaintiff has misinformed the sheriff and the county, and that he himself never failed in doing right, whatever his court may have done, he shall be heard, provided he comes before any essoin is adjourned in the county either for the plaintiff or for the tenant. But if he waits till an essoin is entered, allowed, and adjourned, and the plea has been so long in the county, that upon the arrival of the *Pone* the least spark of a proceeding in the county court can be discerned, the lord of the fee cannot afterwards insist upon his jurisdiction[f]. If the sheriff maliciously return that there is no plaint in the county court according to the tenor of the *Pone*, yet the *Pone* shall not be lost, if by the dates of the writ patent and of the *Pone* it may be presumed in favour of the plaintiff that the plaint may have been in the county; and afterwards the plea shall take its course according to its nature.

Proceeding of lord to reclaim his jurisdiction.

Court cannot be reclaimed after any proceedings in the county.

[f] It may be seen from the above, that although the jurisdiction of the lord was in theory maintained, the utmost facility was afforded for evading it. And it was found that in practice most lords were contented to waive their jurisdiction respecting the title to land, for an important reason, which we learn from Hengham, namely, that little or no profit accrued to the lord from holding such pleas in his court. Hengham Magna, c. 3. p. 11.

Brac. 330, 330 *b*; Fle. 376 (§ 3). 10. Al jour de la somounse al Counté purrount les parties estre essoigniez, et a celi qi serra essoignié serra doné un autre jour jekes al autre Counté par soen essoigneour. A quel jour cil qi avaunt apparust se purra fere essoignier, et issi apres chescune apparaunce, si il eint [1]mile apparaunces[1],
[276 *b*.] forspris especial cas, sicum appara apres en le chapitre de
Post, c. 9. essoignies de mal de venue. Et si le pleintif face defaute
Glan. II. 1. cc. 32, 33. et le tenaunt pierge, [2]si ert[2] agardé, qe le tenaunt s'en voise sauntz jour, et le pleintif ne prenge rien par soen bref, einz remeigne en nostre merci[3], si la defaute soit fete devaunt la vewe fete; et si ele soit fete apres vewe, si ert agardé qe le tenaunt remeigne en sa seisine quite del pleintif et de ses heirs a touz jours mes, et[4] le pleintif en la merci. Et si ambideus facent defaute, adounc purra la une defaute estre alowé encountre l'autre, puis qe le tenaunt ne [5]s'en passa[5] mie sauntz jour par jugement.

Brac. 330; Hengh. Mag. c. 8. pp. 34, 35; Fle. 376 (§ 4). 11. Et si le tenaunt face defaute et la sumounse soit testmoigné par les somenours, si ert agardé, qe la terre demaundé

1—1. nule apparaunce *L.* *sim. GC.* nules apparaunces *NF.* *sim. S.* miles apparaunces *M.* 2—2. *so SGCF.* *sim. M.* et si eit *L.* si soit *N.* 3. *so GMCF.* Et *add. L.* *sim. NS.* 4. et *om. L.* e *NSGMC.* 5—5. *so F.* sen passe *L.* passe *NC.* se passe *S.* se passa *GM.*

Process in county. Essoins. 10. At the day of the summons at the county court the parties may be essoined, and to him who shall be essoined another day shall be given by his essoiner at the next county court. At which day the person who before appeared may cause himself to be essoined, and so after each appearance, though it happen a thousand times, except in special cases, as
Judgment on default of plaintiff,— before view, will appear in the chapter of essoins *de malo veniendi*. If the plaintiff makes default, and the tenant appears, let it be awarded that the tenant go without day, and that the plaintiff take nothing by his writ, but remain in our mercy, that is, if
after view. the default be before view; but if default be made after view, let it be awarded that the tenant remain in his seisin quit of the plaintiff and his heirs for ever after, and the plaintiff be in
Default by both parties. mercy. And if both make default, then one default may be set against the other, the tenant not having had judgment to depart without day.

Default of tenant before appearance. 11. If the tenant makes default, and the summons is witnessed by the summoners, it shall be awarded, when the de-

soit prise en nostre meyn solom fourme del graunt *Cape*, si la defaute soit fete devaunt apparaunce, ou autrement solum le usage del lu. Et en mesme la manere iert, si le tenaunt face defaute al premer Counté, si le baillif testmoigne la somounse [1]oveke les somenours; la quele somounse[1] le tenaunt ne[2] purra mie defendre par sa ley; et issi porte le baillif record en les somouns oveke le testmoignage des somenours. Et si le tenaunt face defaute apres defaute, freschement adounc iert jugé pur le pleintif, sauve al tenaunt soen dreit de recoverer quant il quidera qe bon soit. Et en mesme la manere ert, si le tenaunt ne[3] replevisse sa terre prise en nostre meyn de eynz les xv.[4] jours, si deceyte ne courge[5]. Et ceo qe [6]defaut issi des defautes[6] en general, serra accompli plus especialment apres.

Hengh. Mag. c. 4. p. 14.

Cf. Glan. li. 1. c. 9; Hengh. Mag. c. 5. p. 26, c. 8. p. 37.

[277.]

12. Et si les parties apergent en court, et le pleintif eit counté soen counte vers le tenaunt, et le tenaunt eit defendu le tort par motz defensables, adounc purra il voucher a gar- Brac. 331; Fle. 377.

1—1. *om. M.* 2. nel *M.* 3. *so print.* *om. LNSGMCF.* 4. *so NM.* premers [xv. *interlin.*] *L.* primers *CF.* primers xv. *G.* xx. *S.* 5. en la Court *add. N.* *sim. S.* 6—6. *so G.* *sim. M.* defaut issi qe defautes *L.* *sim. SCF.* estoit de defaute apres defaute *N.*

fault is before appearance, that the land demanded be taken into our hand according to the terms of the great *Cape*, or otherwise according to the usage of the place. So likewise, where the tenant makes default at the first county court, if the bailiff with the summoners attest the summons; and this summons the tenant cannot defend by his law; and thus the bailiff, with the testimony of summoners, bears record of summonses. And if the tenant makes default after default, judgment shall be immediately given for the plaintiff, saving to the tenant his right to recover when he thinks good. In like manner it shall be, if the tenant does not within fifteen days replevy the land taken into our hands, unless the case is affected by deceit. What is here wanting upon the subject of defaults in general shall be more particularly supplied hereafter [g].

Process by *Cape.*

Default after default; judgment for plaintiff.

Non-plevin after *Cape*; judgment.

12. When the parties have appeared in court, and the plaintiff has counted his count against the tenant, and the tenant has defended the wrong by proper words of defence, Voucher of warrant.

[g] The further explanation of the law of defaults here promised is not found in the treatise as it now exists. The same observation applies to the description of trial by battle referred to in s. 14. See the Editor's Introduction, p. xlv. The subject of defaults is more fully treated in Bracton, f. 364 *b*–380; Fleta, p. 395–400.

raunt, si il ad qi; et si celi garraunt ne soit mie en la destresce le viscounte de cel pays, adounc covent al vouchour estre eydé par tiel bref al viscounte del lu ou le vouchee[1] avera sa terre. Comaundez a tiel qe il garrauntise a tiel taunt de terre ove les apurtenaunces en tiele ville, et s'il ne face, qe il soit as premeres assises, quant Justices eyrent[2] en celes parties, a moustrer pur quei il ne ad garraunti.

Brac. 331; Fle. 377.

13. Et dounc s'il ly voille garraunter en Counté, bien est; et si noun, si remeigne[3] la parole jekes en heyre, si avaunt ne soit remué jekes par devaunt nos Justices. Car en tel cas ne avera le Counté nul poer de aler avaunt en la parole. Et cum le plee de la garrauntie serra dedut[4] devaunt Justices en heyre, adounc list a eus de terminer la parole, ou de remuer [277 *b.*] la parole a terminer el Counté. Et si la parole soit remué en le meen tens jekes par devaunt nos Justices, adounc [5]s'esteint[5] le ajornement en heyre, et issi vouchera le tenaunt autre foiz a garraunt en plee del *Pone*. Et si le garraunt soit de eynz

1. *so N.* *sim. G.* viscounte [vouchee *interlin.*] *L.* vouchee *N.* garaunt *M.* viscunte *S.* *sim. CF.* 2. erraunz vendrunt *M.* erront *SG.* *sim. CF.* 3. donques *add. M.* *sim. SGCF.* 4. dedit *LSGF.* desdut *N.* descendu *M.* dit *C.* 5—5. cessent *L.* cesse e seste[y]nt *N.* se estent *M.* sestent *SC.* sestend *G.* sesteint *F.*

then he may vouch to warranty, if he has any one to vouch, and if the warrant does not live within the distress of the sheriff of that county, then the voucher must be aided by the following writ directed to the sheriff of that county where the warrant has his land. 'Command such an one that he warrant to such an one so much land with the appurtenances in such a vill; and that, if he does not do it, he be at the first assises when the Justices make their eyre in those parts to show why he has not warranted.'

Writ to compel warranty.

Question of warranty tried by Justices of Eyre, unless the plea be first removed by *Pone.*

13. If the vouchee will thereupon enter into warranty in the county, it is well; if not, let the plaint stand over to the eyre, if it be not first removed before our Justices. For in such case the county court will have no authority to proceed further in the action. And when the plea of warranty is tried before our Justices in eyre, then they may either determine the principal plea themselves, or send it to be determined in the county. But if the plea be in the meantime removed before our Justices, then the adjournment in eyre is annulled, and the tenant shall vouch to warranty again in the plea of

le age de xxi. aunz, et veigne en court pur prover soen age, adounc est le princepal plee suspendu en le Counté, et le plee de garrauntie ausi par devaunt les Justices en heyre, jekes al age le garraunt.

Hengh. Mag. c.13.pp.71,75.

14. Et si le tenaunt se defende par bataille, adounc soit fet solom ceo qe apres serra dit. Et si par la graunt assise, adounc soit doné jur al autre Counté, et en le meen tens se purchace lettre de la Chauncelerie, qe il est tenaunt, et par mi sa bouche covendra dire par queles paroles il soit mis en la graunt assise; et adounc avera bref al viscounte a fere la parole cesser jekes en heyre; et cel bref serra enroullé, en aventure pur le attachement qe enseut si le viscounte ne voille par taunt cesser. Et cum il avera purchacé cel bref, adounc se purchace un autre bref al viscounte de fere somoundre la graunt assise encountre la avenue[1] de Justices a touz pleez. Et si le tenaunt ne eit purchacé la prohibicioun avauntdite, al proschein Counté ou al jour doné al essoignour[2]

Glan. li. 2. cc. 7. 8; Brac. 331, 331 *b*; Fle. 377.

Reg. brev. orig. 7 *b*, 8.

Reg. brev. orig. 8.

Glan. li. 2. c. 10; Brac. 331 *b*; Fle. 377; Reg. brev. orig. 8.

Hengh. Mag. c.4.pp.12,13.

1. venue *SGMCF*. 2. *so verb. S.* seignur *L.* *sim. GMF.*

Pone. Where the warrant is under the age of twenty-one years, and comes into court to prove his age, the principal plea and the plea of warranty also before the Justices in eyre, are suspended until the warrant is of age.

Minority of vouchee suspends the plea.

14. If the tenant defends himself by battle, the proceedings shall be as hereafter mentioned. If by the great assise, then let a day be given at the next county court, and let the tenant in the meantime obtain a letter from the Chancery; and by his own mouth he is required to say that he is tenant, and by what words he has put himself on the great assise[h]; he shall then have a writ to the sheriff to cause the plea to cease until the eyre, which writ shall be enrolled by way of precaution, on account of the attachment which follows, if the sheriff refuses to cease thereupon. And when the tenant has purchased this writ, then let the plaintiff sue out another writ to the sheriff to cause the great assise to be summoned against the coming of the Justices for the hearing of all pleas. If the tenant has omitted to obtain the prohibition aforesaid, then at the next county court, or at the day given to the essoiner of the tenant,

Defence by battle; by great assise.

Writ *de pace habenda.*

Writ *de magna assisa eligenda.*

h The text of this sentence, either from corruption or otherwise, is somewhat dislocated. I have restored it in the translation to what appears to have been the proper order. See Bracton, f. 331; Fleta, p. 377.

le tenaunt, le pleintif recovera seisine de sa demaunde par la defaute le tenaunt.

Brac. 332; Fle. 377. 15. En plusours maneres sount les paroles remuez hors del Counté. Acune foiz a la requeste le pleintif, et ceo se purra fere sauntz signefier nule enchesoun. Et acune foiz a

[278.] la requeste le tenaunt. Mes ceo ne se deit mie fere sauntz affermer[1] la enchesoun [2]en mesme le bref del *Pone*, la quele enchesoun[2] ne deit[3] point estre allowable einz ceo qe ele eit esté detrié en plein Counté par le serment le tenaunt a sa tierce meyn.

Brac. 332 *b*; Fle. 377. 16. Et si le tenaunt a sa requeste eit fet remuer la parole jekes par devaunt nos Justices, et il face defaute le premer jour, et le pleintif se profre et demaunde jugement de la defaute, le pleintif recovera seisine de sa demaunde, et le tenaunt remeindra en la merci. Et si la parole soit remué hors del Counté a la requeste le pleintif, et le pleintif face defaute le premer jour, et le tenaunt se face essoignier, et

1. assigner *S.* 2—2. *so verb. NSG. so interl. L. om. MC.* 3. *so NSGMCF.* deuient *L.*

the plaintiff shall recover seisin of his demand by the default of the tenant.

Plea removed into the king's court by *Pone*. 15. Actions are removed out of the county court in several ways; sometimes at the instance of the plaintiff, and this may be without assigning any cause; and sometimes at the request of the tenant; but this ought not to be done without affirmation of the cause in the body of the writ of *Pone*, which cause ought not to be allowed before it has been tried in full county by the oath of the tenant with two cojurors[i].

If by tenant, he must assign cause by oath *tertiâ manu*.

Default before Justices. 16. If the cause be removed before our Justices at the request of the tenant, and he makes default upon the first day, and the plaintiff proffers himself and demands judgment of the default, the plaintiff shall recover seisin of his demand, and the tenant remain in mercy. And if the cause is removed out of the county at the instance of the plaintiff, and he makes default on the first day, and the tenant is essoined, and his

[i] The reason for making this difference between the plaintiff and the tenant seems to have been, that while the latter might desire to remove the cause for the purpose of delay, the former could have no interest in so doing. (Hengham Magna, c. iv. p. 14.) The cause assigned by the tenant might be a connexion between the sheriff and the plaintiff, or the predominating influence of the latter in the county, or that the tenant was abroad, or too infirm to attend the county court. (Bracton, f. 332 *b*; Hengham Magna, c. iv. p. 14.)

soen essoniour s'en soit parti de la court sauntz jour par jugement, tut eit le pleintif retenu le bref overt vers sei, si autrefoiz se purchace le *Pone* a fere remuer la parole hors del Counté, cel *Pone* vaudra nient, einz est retournable en ceste manere, qe nule parole n'en est pendaunte en Counté solom [1]le tenour[1] del bref, pur ceo qe par autre tiel bref fust ele avaunt remué hors del Counté jekes par devaunt les Justices. Et issi serra tut le plee a recomencer de novel, mes ne mie par mesme le bref.

17. Et acune foiz est la parole remué hors del Counté par necessité a la requeste le pleintif, sicum pur privilege le tenaunt, sicum sount Templers et Hospitelers et autres, qi sount enfraunchiz[2] par chartres des Rois, qe il ne respoignent nule part de nul plee for qe par devaunt nos Justices. [3]S'il soint[3] neqedent acune part entré[4] en respounse, mes ne se purrount repenter ne retrere. Et ausi acune foiz par necessité, quaunt le Counté ne ad nul poer de aler plus avaunt en la parole, sicum en cas ou bastardie est mise avaunt, ou matrimoignie soit dedit, ou en autre cas ou le

Brac. 332 *b*; Fle. 377, 378.

[278 *b*.]

1—1. la nature *S*. la tenure *GM*. 2. so *NMCF*. *sim*. *G*. fraunes *L*. 3—3. sil ne soint *L*. *sim*. *S*. si bral ne [lur] soit *N*. E sil ne seient *G*. si ne seent *M*. *sim*. *CF*. 4. Si il entrent *N*.

essoiner leaves the court, having judgment to go without day, although the plaintiff keeps by him the writ patent, if he brings a fresh *Pone* to remove the plaint out of the county, this new writ will be of no avail, but must be returned in this manner, that no plaint is depending in the county court according to the tenor of the writ, inasmuch as by another like writ it was removed out of the county before the Justices. And thus all the plea will have to be begun afresh, but not by the same writ.

17. Sometimes the action is by necessity removed out of the county court at the instance of the plaintiff, as, where the tenant is privileged, as the Templars, Hospitallers, and others are, who have this franchise by royal charters, that they need not to answer any plea elsewhere than before our Justices. If nevertheless they have anywhere entered upon their answer, they cannot afterwards change their minds or withdraw. Sometimes also of necessity, when the county court has no authority to proceed further in the plea, as where bastardy is alleged, or marriage is denied, or in other cases to the cogni-

Where the action must necessarily be removed. Privilege of Templars, &c.

Want of jurisdiction.

poer del Counté ne [1]s'estent[1] point a la conisaunce. Et acune foiz par la folie des suitiers del Counté, sicum el cas ou bataille soit agardé et ajoynte encountre commune ley et les communs usages de cest reaume. Et acune foiz ausi pur
Ante, vol. i. p. 313. la difficulté de jugement; et en plusours autres maneres. Mes le petit bref de dreit, ou est contenu, solom les usages del maner, et qe fust purveu pur sokemans, james ne est remuable par devaunt Justices.

CHAPITRE V. [CXXI.]

De Somounse.

Brac. 333; Fle. 378; Hengh. Mag. c. 5. p. 24. 1. Remenee[2] issi la parole jekes a la graunt court a la requeste le pleintif, si covendra[3] somoundre le tenaunt qe il soit a certeyn jour a respoundre al pleintif solom la fourme de la pleinte. Et si ad somounse, apres-somounse, et re-somounse. Et si ad maundement, qe ne est mie proprement
[279.] somounse, cum si nous maundisoms a acun qe il venist, ou

1—1. cesseint *L.* se estent *NSM.* *sim. CF.* sestend *G.* 2. so *NM.* *sim. S.* Remeigne *LC.* Somone *G.* Remeyne *F.* 3. fere *add. SMCF.*

zance of which the jurisdiction of the county does not extend.
Removal for error of the suitors in the county court, **Sometimes also the plea is removed on account of the folly of the suitors of the county, as where battle is awarded and joined contrary to the common law and the common usages of this realm.**
for difficulty of judgment. **Sometimes also by reason of the difficulty of judgment, and for many other causes.**
Writ of right close not removable. **The petty writ of right, which contains the clause, 'according to the custom of the manor,' and which was provided in favour of sokemen, is never removable before the Justices.**

CHAPTER V.

Of Summons in a Plea of Right.

Summons. **1. The plaint being thus removed into the great court at the instance of the plaintiff, the tenant must be summoned to be there at a certain day to answer the plaintiff according to the form of the plaint.**
Various kinds of summons. **There is summons, after-summons, and resummons. And there is also a precept which is not properly a summons, as where we should command any one**

si nous maundisoms al viscounte qe il feist vener, ou qe il eust tiel ou attachast, ou feit a saver qe il fust a tiel jour en tiel lu. Mes de dreite somounse est acune generale et acune especiale. Generale est qe touche acune université, sicum est de commune somounse de heyre, dount solempne crie est fete par citez bourgs et marcheez, et en autres cas semblables; et tieles somounses ne purra nule singulere persone desdire ne defendre par sa ley. Especiale est sicum somounse fete sour certein plee as certeines persones. Et si purreit un essoigne par cas tener lu en ambideus les somouns; cum si acun enpledé eit soen jour de plee le premer jour del heyre, et il se face essoignier, cel essoigne excusera sa absence ausi bien de la generale somounse cum de la especiale.

2. Somoundre neqedent ne purra hom mie totes gentz. Car enfaunt de einz age [1]ne seet a[1] receivere nule somounse, for qe par mi soen gardein, ne homme ausi qi est detenu en prisoun, tut le puisse il fere somoundre sauntz gardein; ne ausi homme arragé ne autrement sauntz sen, sicum sount fols nastres; ne ausi sourdz ne mutz; ne femmes esposez Brac. 336, 336 *b*; Fle. 381 (§ 21, 22).

1—1. ne soit a *LN*. ny fet *S*. ne siet *GM*. ne set *C*. ne seit *F*.

to come, or command the sheriff to cause him to come, or that he have or attach such an one, or cause him to know that he be on such a day in such a place. But of proper summonses, some are general and some special. A general summons is one which concerns an entire community, as the common summons in eyre, which is solemnly proclaimed throughout cities, boroughs, and markets, and in other like cases. Such summonses no single person can deny or defend by his law. Special summons is, for example, where summons is made upon a certain plea to certain persons. And so possibly one essoin might lie for both summonses; as if any one who is impleaded has his day of plea on the first day of the eyre, and he causes himself to be essoined, the essoin will excuse his absence as well for the general as the special summons. Summons general and special. One essoin may excuse a general and special summons.

2. All persons ought not to be summoned. For an infant under age is not capable of receiving any summons except through his guardian; nor a person detained in prison, although he may cause a summons to be made without guardian; nor a madman, nor one otherwise deprived of sense, as an idiot; nor deaf and dumb persons; nor married women with- Who may be summoned.

sauntz lour barouns; ne chanoyne[1] remuable sauntz le deen [279 *b.*] [2]et le[2] chapitre; ne autres religious remuables sauntz le Abbé ou lour[3] Priour.

Brac. 333 *b*; Fle. 378 (§ 4).

3. Cum acun dounc a dreit deive estre somouns, ou qe il soit trové en le Counté ou la demaunde est fete, purra il renablement estre somouns par deus fraunes hommes terre tenauntz en le Counté a sa propre persone. Car hors de la purceynte del Counté ne est nul tenu a receyvere somounse, si de bouche de Justice noun. Et si il ne soit mie trové, adounc suffit de la fere a sa mesoun[4], [5]pur ly fere[5] a saver cum il serra retournez. Et si il eit plusours mesouns, adounc soit ele fete a cele qe soit sour la[6] terre demaundé, si il [7]i soit[7] demurraunt, ou meisnee eit qe de la somounse ly purra fere a saver. Et si nule terre ne soit demaundé, adounc soit ele fete a cele mesoun ou il plus est conversaunt. Et si il ne eit nule mesoun en le Counté, adounc suffist de la

1. seculere *add. G.* 2—2. del *NS.* 3. le *NSGMCF.* 4. mesoun e a sa meisnee *N.* *sim. S.* meisnee *GF.* *sim. MC.* 5—5. qe il ly facent *N.* *sim. S.* 6. *so NSGMF.* cele *L.* 7—7. esteit *L.* soit *N.* seit *SG.* i seit *MF.*

out their husbands; nor a canon removable without the dean and chapter, nor other persons in religion removable without the abbot or their prior[k].

Summons, how made.

3. When any one then is to be lawfully summoned, wherever he be found in the county where the demand is made, he may be reasonably summoned in his proper person by two freemen terre-tenants of the county. For no one is obliged to receive a summons out of the precinct of the county, unless from the mouth of a Justice himself. And if he is not found, then it is sufficient to make the summons at his house, so that he may be informed thereof when he returns. And if the tenant has several houses, let it be made at that which is upon the land demanded, if he be resident there, or has any family there who can inform him of the summons. And if no land is demanded, let it be made at that house where he chiefly resides; and if he has no house in the county, then it is sufficient to

Summons made at the house of tenant,

or in his fee.

k The word 'removable' appears to be applied to the officers of a religious house holding office during the pleasure of their superior. See l. i. c. 29. s. 6, and note there, vol. i. p. 159. The parallel passage in Bracton points to the existence in some cases of an irremovable officer charged with the duty of representing the religious foundation in court. 'Item viri religiosi' [summoneri debent] 'per procuratores sindicos et actores perpetuos et non amotibiles, et qui tales sint, quod possint lucrari et perdere et rem in judicium deducere.' Bracton, f. 336 *b*.

fere en le fee ou il purra estre destreint oveke graunt testmoignage des veisins.

4. Et si acun deit estre renablement somouns, il deit aver espace de xv. jours al meyns de sei garnir de ses respounses. Et si meins de tens eit, et ly somouns le voille chalenger, la somounse ne ert de nule force, einz i deivent les somenours remeindre en la merci, si il soint atteintz de lour disresounable somounse. Acunes causes neqedent sount si favourables, qe renable somounse ne deit tener lu, sicum en causes tochauntes nos mesmes ou nos parentz ou nostre cumpayne, ou ses parentz, ou messagers des estraunges terres, ou marchauntz[1], ou croicez; et sicum en nos heyres [2]ou en heire[2] des Justices, et sicum en disseisines et en intrusiouns et en abatementz, et en fresches forces. Mes neqedent si acun se face essoignier apres tele disresounable somounse, ou pierge et ne chalenge mie, ou s'il[3] prenge jour de amour, mes ne purra chalenger la somounse estre disresounable. Et cum acun avera esté issi renablement somouns, mes ne se purra absenter hors del reaume ne aylours, tut procure[4] il puis nos

Brac. 334; Fle. 378 (§ 11).

[280.]

Stat. de Protectionibus. (temp. incert.); Fle. 378 (§ 5), 381 (§ 5).

1. amis *M.* 2—2. *om. C.* 3. *so NSGMCF.* ne *add. L.* 4. *so GSMCF.* portast *L.* porte *N.*

make the summons in the fee where he is distrainable, with a great number of neighbours for witnesses.

4. When any person is to be reasonably summoned, he ought to have fifteen days at least to prepare his defence. If less time is given, and the person summoned chooses to challenge the summons, it is of no force; but the summoners ought to be in mercy, if they are convicted of their unreasonable summons. Yet there are some causes which are so favoured, that reasonable summons is not required in them, as in causes touching ourselves or our kindred, ambassadors from foreign countries, merchants, and crusaders. So likewise in our eyres, or in the eyre of our Justices, and in disseisins, intrusions, abatements, and fresh force. Nevertheless if any one after such unreasonable summons causes himself to be essoined, or appears without challenging the summons, or if he accepts a day of grace, he cannot afterwards challenge the summons as unreasonable. When the tenant has thus been reasonably summoned, he may not from that time absent himself out of the realm or elsewhere, though he afterwards

Reasonable summons must allow fifteen days.

Cases where reasonable summons is not required.

Objection, how waived.

After reasonable summons tenant cannot justify absence by letters of protection.

lettres de proteccioun, qe le pleintif ne recovere sa demaunde, si la parole ne[1] soit defendue par le tenaunt ou par soen attourné.

Fle. 378 (§ 8). 5. En chescune somounse fet a aver le garraunt ou le transescrit enselé de soen[2] seal conu, si qe hom puisse saver devaunt quel juge, et qe hom se puisse armer des excepciouns encountre les acciouns le pleintif; ou autrement serra cele somounse disresounable et de nul effect; et covendra par la chalenge le tenaunt estre autrefoiz somouns par les Justices mesmes en court ou autrement par somenours[3]. Devaunt quel juge, est dit pur ceo qe par devaunt chescun qi se fet juge ne fet mie apparer. Car nul ne put aver la auctorité de fere somoundre for qe de nous; et tut le eit il de acun Justice, ceo ne vaille nient, pur ceo qe nul Justice ne put fere Justice, ne nul homme assigner de porter record ne de nul jugement fere sauntz garraunt de nos mesmes. Et generale rule est de ley, qe jugement pronuncié par cely qi ne est mie

Brac. 333 b (§ 4); Fle. 378 (§ 6, 7, 8).

Ante, vol. i. p. 7.

[280 b.]

1. so F. ne om. LMGSC. interl. N. 2. alcun N. om. M. 3. so N. sim. GSMF. somouns LC.

procure our letters of protection; but the plaintiff shall recover his demand, unless the plea be defended by the tenant or his attorney.

Transcript of summons to be produced.

5. In every summons it is proper to have the warrant or transcript sealed with his known seal[1], so that the tenant may know before what judge he is summoned, and may be able to arm himself with exceptions against the action of the plaintiff; otherwise such summons shall be unreasonable and of no effect, and the tenant, upon challenging the summons, must be summoned again either by the Justice in court or else by summoners. It is said, before what judge, because one is not obliged to appear before every one who pretends to be a judge; for no one can have authority to cause any to be summoned except from us; and though he should have authority from some Justice, that is of no value, because a Justice cannot make another Justice, nor authorize any person to bear record or pass judgment without warrant from us. And it is a general

Judge to be specified.

Judicial authority must be derived immediately from the Crown.

1 The written warrant for summons is not mentioned in Bracton; and in Fleta, although the warrant is mentioned, there is no notice of its bearing any seal. The seal required would appear to be the seal of the sheriff of the county where the appearance was to be, whether in the county court or before the Justices Itinerant.

soen verrey juge, ne deit a nuli[1] grever. Cum acun dounc soit renablement somouns par devaunt tiel qe eit poer et auctorité de nous de juger, si deit apparer.

6. Et pur ceo qe le viscounte purra par cas estre coupable de blame, fet bien a saver, qi est en la coupe, ou le viscounte ou les somenours. Et si hom puisse trover qe le viscounte ne amonesta[2] la somounse a nulli fere, soit puni pur la negligence, si il ne puisse renablement sei excuser, sicum pur ceo qe le pleintif ne trova nule seurté de seure sa pleinte, ou pur ceo qe le bref vint si tard qe il ne poeit fere nule execucioun, ou pur ceo qe il resceut soen bref hors de soen Counté, et ences[3] qe il vint [4]a ly covenist il[4] ayllors aler en loynteynes parties par tel maundement; et par plusours autres resouns si[5] purra le viscounte sei[6] excuser renablement. Et si le jour contenu en le bref soit passé, adounc coveint al pleintif purchacer novel bref; et ausi ou[7] les somenours ne firent mie la somounse, tut lour fust ele enjoynt as somenours a fere. La

Glan. ii 1. c. 30; Brac. 336; Fle. 380 (§ 21).

1. nul home *N.* ly *M.* 2. *so C.* amoneste *LSM.* 3. einz ceo *NGMC.* *sim. S.* einzceis *F.* 4—4. ly couient primes *N.* ly couendrait *G.* ly couenist il primes *S.* ly couenist *M.* *sim. F.* 5. se *LMGS.* si se *N.* 6. sei *om. NMGS.* 7. com *GM.* *sim. F.*

rule of law that no one shall be affected by a judgment pronounced by one who is not truly his judge. When any one therefore has had a reasonable summons to appear before a person who has power and authority of judging from us, it is his duty to appear accordingly.

Judicium non sui judicis non obligat.

6. And because it may happen that the blame ought to fall upon the sheriff, it is proper to know who is in fault, whether the sheriff or the summoners; and if it be found that the sheriff did not direct any one to make the summons, let him be punished for his neglect, unless he has a reasonable excuse, as that the plaintiff did not find any security to prosecute his plaint, or that the writ came so late that he could not execute it, or that he received the writ out of his county, and before it came to him he was obliged by such a precept to go elsewhere into some distant place; and by many other reasons the sheriff may reasonably excuse himself. And if the day contained in the writ is passed, then the plaintiff must purchase a new writ. So likewise where the summoners did not execute the summons, although they were enjoined to do so. This fact the

Neglect of sheriff to summon, punishable.

Sheriff may excuse his neglect.

Where summons is omitted, new writ required. Summoners may deny the order to summon by their law.

somounse les somenours[1] purrount defendre par lour ley, tut eit le viscounte seute.

CHAPITRE VI. [CXXII.]

[281.] *De Essoignies.*

Glan. li. 1, c.10,11,26,29; Brac. 336 b, 337; Fle. 381.

1. [2]Nul ne[2] deit departer [3]despuniz qi[3] renablement avera esté somouns et ne deigne apparer en court, si noun par renables excusaciouns, dount essoignies nescent, sicum de services Deu, et de nous, encusement de crime, maladie, force. Service Deu, sicum pelrinage, qe deit estre graunt enchesoun et favourable solom sa nature, sauve qe nule somounse [4]ne vient avaunt l'enchiminer[4]. Noster service, sicum estre [5]en nostre force a[5] la defense de nous et de noster poeple ou de noster reaume. Encusement de crime,

1. lour *add. N.* *sim. S.* se *add. G.* 2—2. so *MGCF.* Nuli *L.* Nul ny *S.* 3—3. [despriz *interl.*] de puis qe *L.* despuni qi *N.* despunisk *S.* despuni de puis qil *M.* de puis qe *GC.* de la curt puis ke *F.* 4—4. ne vient [auaunt] len chimener *L.* ne veigne auaunt le chemyner *N.* ne vint auant le cheminer *M.* *sim. GSF.* out auant le chemin *C.* 5—5. en noster efforz [estours] a *L.* en nos estours a *N.* en nostre efforz a *S.* nostre effortz a *G.* *sim. F.* nostre essorz *M.* en nostre force e de *C.*

summoners may defend by their law, although the sheriff brings suit to prove it[m].

CHAPTER VI.

Of Essoins.

Various excuses for not obeying summons.

1. No person ought to depart unpunished after he has been reasonably summoned, and does not think fit to appear in court, unless upon some reasonable excuse, whence essoins arise, as the service of God, or of ourselves, accusation of crime, sickness, force.

Service of God.

Service of God, such as pilgrimage, which ought to be an important excuse, and favoured according to the nature of it, provided that no summons arrived before the journey.

Service of king.

Our service, as where a man is in our forces for the defence of us, our people, or our realm. Accusation of crime,

[m] This is probably not to be understood of the case where the summons was publicly ordered in the county court; in which case, according to Glanvill, Bracton, and Fleta, the suitors bore record, which could not be contradicted by the summoners. Possibly the practice of ordering summons in the county court, which in the time of Glanvill was the regular course, had now become unusual. See Glanvill, li. 1. c. 30; Bracton, f. 336; Fleta, p. 380.

cum, si acun soit endité ou appelé de vie et de membre, james en perte de terre ne de chatel ne est tenu a respoundre si la qe de la greynure cause se soit defendu. Maladie, sicum est de ceux qi se moevent vers la court, et sount en chiminaunt suppris de maladie. Force, sicum est de ceux qi sount destourbez par enprisounement, ou de larouns ou des autres enemis par chemyn, ou [1] brusure des pountz ou des autres passages, ou [2] trop de tempest, ou [3] defaute de batels ou de neefs.

2. Si acun dounc voille[4] excuser sa absence, hastivement enveye acun excusour, qi nuncie en court la destourbaunce soloum ceo qe ele est avenue. Et si celi ne face entrer [5]le excusement[5] mesme le jour qe especefié est el bref ou qe doné ly fust autrefoiz en court, mes ne tendra lu nule excusacioun. [281 *b.*] Et tieles excusaciouns sount appellez essoignies et les excusours essoigniours.

3. Et coment qe essoignie soit enroulé[6], tiel[7] deit estre le entendement. Johan le essoignour Piers vint[8] le premer Brac. 339; Fle. 382 (§ 12).

1. par *add. NSGMF.* 2. par *add. MF.* de *add. G.* 3. par *add. GM.* 4. adounk fere *add. N.* fere *add. SMCF.* *sim. G.* 5—5. la excusacioun *N.* *sim. SGMCF.* 6. entre en roule *M.* 7. *so N.* *sim. GSMF.* et cel *L.* e tel *C.* 8. *so GM.* vient *LNS.*

for if any person be indicted or appealed of life and limb, he is never obliged to answer in a matter involving loss of land or of chattels, until he has defended himself in the more weighty matter. Sickness, as in the case of those who put themselves in motion towards the court, and are seized with sickness by the way. Force, as in the case of those who are hindered by imprisonment, or by robbers or other enemies on the road, or the breaking of bridges or other passages, storms, or want of boats or ships. Accusation of felony. Sickness. Force.

2. If any one therefore desires to excuse his absence, let him presently send some excuser, who may relate in court the impediment as it has occurred. And if the latter does not cause the excuse to be entered on the same day as is specified in the writ, or as was before given to the party in court, the excuse will not afterwards be allowed. Such excuses are called essoins, and the excusers essoiners. Excuses must be made in court on the day of return of summons. Essoin, and essoiner.

3. However the essoin is enrolled, the purport ought to be as follows: 'John, the essoiner of Peter, came the first day, Enrolment of essoin.

jour et moustra, qe cum Piers soen seignur fust somouns qe il fust en ceste court a cest jour a respoundre a Robert de plee de terre, mesme celi Piers, avaunt qe nule somounse ly fust fete [1]si estoit[1] departi de sa mesoun en pelrenage en le service le Roi Celestre vers les parties de outre meer a Sainct Sepulcre de Jerusalem en general passage ovekes autres croicez, si general passage soit[2] en cel tens, ou simple passage; ou, ences qe nule somounse ly estoit fete, ala il en real service par maundement, sicum par service qe il deit pur sa terre: et issi se fet il essoignier del service le Roi Celestre ou Terestre; ou tiele maladie ly prist en chiminaunt vers ceste court, qe il ne poeit avaunt pur gayner ou[3] pur perdre, einz se fist carier arere a sa mesoun ou ayllours; ou tele autre destourbaunce ly sourvint par chemin, qe il ne poeit avaunt pur gayner ne pur perdre; et issi se excuse il [4]par voie del[4] essoigne de mal de venue; et ceo deit le essoigniour tendre de averrer.

1—1. *so N. sim. S.* se soit *L.* se estoit *M. sim. F.* estoit *G. sim. C.* 2. eit este *M.* 3. ny *S.* ne *GMCF.* 4—4. *so G.* par motz [qu. mi *interl.*] del *L.* parmi del *N.* par moy del *S.* par my del *M. sim. F.* parmie *C.*

and showed, that whereas Peter his master was summoned to be in this court on this day to answer to Robert of a plea of land, the same Peter, before any summons was made to him, had set out from his house on a pilgrimage in the service of the Heavenly King towards parts beyond sea to the holy sepulchre at Jerusalem, in a general passage with other crusaders,' if there was a general passage at the time, or else, 'on an ordinary passage;' or, 'before any summons was made upon him, he went upon the king's service, in pursuance of a precept in that behalf, as upon a service due for his land.' In the above form he may cause himself to be essoined of the service of the Heavenly or Earthly King. Or thus: 'such a sickness overtook him in journeying towards this court, that he could not come forward to gain or lose, but had himself carried back to his own home or elsewhere.' Or, 'such other hindrance came upon him by the way, that he could not proceed to gain or lose;' and thus he excuses himself by way of essoin *de malo veniendi;* and thereof the essoiner ought to tender averment.

Essoin, *de servitio Regis æterni,*

de servitio Regis,

de malo veniendi.

Averment.

4. Mes pur ceo qe la prove apent a soen seignur a fere, et ne mie al essoigniour, et pur ceo qe hom ne est mie uncore certifié, lequel il soit verrey messager ou faus, ou qe soen seignur ly voille avower ou noun, est usee qe les essoigniours[1] des riches gentz pusauntz, sicum des countes et des barouns et de touz autres qi tienent en baronie, truissent pleges de aver avaunt lour seignurs al autre jour, issi qe tels essoigniours ne soint mie despuniz si il ne soint garrauntiz de lour message. Mes pur ceo qe ceo serroit grevouse chose a fere as essoigniours de poveres gentz, est suffert en favour des poveres, qe les essoigniours de tote manere de autre gent plevisent, sauntz plus fere[2], de aver avaunt lour garraunt al autre jour. [282.] Glan. li. 1, c. 12; Brac. 337 b; Fle. 382 (§ 12), 388 (§ 15).

CHAPITRE VII. [CXXIII.]

De Essoignies de Outre meer.

1. Breve[3] divisioun est des essoignies, la une de mal de venue, et l'autre de mal de lit. Mes [4]la premere est la une[4] Brac. 339; Fle. 382.

1. so *N.* essoignies *L.* essoignes *MGCF.* *sim. S.* 2. so *MF.* *sim. G.* de foiz *L.* *om. NSC.* 3. Breue e courte *N.* Bref de *MGSCF.* 4—4. le premer e le vn est *N.*

4. But because the proof of the essoin is the business of his master and not of the essoiner, and because it is not yet ascertained whether he is a true or a false messenger, or whether his master will acknowledge him or not, it is customary for the essoiners of rich and powerful persons, as earls, barons, and all others holding by barony, to find pledges to produce their lords at the day appointed, so that such essoiners may not escape unpunished, if they are not warranted in their message. But inasmuch as this would be oppressive if it were done with the essoiners of poor people, it is permitted, out of favour to such persons, that the essoiners of all other sorts of people do promise only, without more, to produce their warrants at the day appointed.

Pledges for production of principal.

Pledges not required, except from magnates.

CHAPTER VII.

Of the Essoin de ultra mare.

1. Essoins are briefly divided into essoins *de malo veniendi* and essoins *de malo lecti*. But the first division is again divided

Division of essoins.

de outre meer, et l'autre de cea la meer. Et de ceux de outre meer est acun de outre la meer de Grece, et acun simplement de outre meer, sicum a Rome ou a Sainct Jake. Et de ceux[1]
[282 *b*.] de outre[2] meer de Grece est acun en simple pelrinage al sepulcre de Jerusalem, [3]et acun en mesme le lu en general pellerinage[3].

Brac. 363; Fle. 394.

2. Et de ceux[4] de cea la meer nest acune destourbaunce [5]de maladie, et acune de autre destourbaunce[5]. Et de ceux[6] de maladie nest acun de maladie sourvenaunt par chemin, et [7]acun de[7] langour qe est appelé le mal de lit, et [8]acun de mal[8] sourvenaunt en la ville ou la court est tenue. Et de autre destourbaunce nest acune destourbaunce de sen, sicum est de fols nastres et de sourdz et de mutz et des autres [9]qi ount male[9] discrecioun de somounse receivere; et acune de destourbaunce de prisoun ou de passage; et acune del service le Roi terestre; et acune de encusement de felonie.

Brac. 338 *b*; Fle. 382, 383.

3. En le essoigne de outre la meer de Grece en general

1. *so N.* tels *L.* teles *G.* celes *SMF.* ceus *C.* 2. la *add. NMGS.* 3—3. *om. MF.* 4. *so N.* cels *L.* teles *MG.* ceus *C.* celes *SF.* 5—5. *so verb. MGS. sim. N. om. L.* 6. tiels *L.* celes *NGS.* tele *M.* ceus *C.* teles *F.* 7—7. *so M. sim. NGSCF.* acune foiz de *L.* 8—8. akune maladie *N.* 9—9. qe ne ount nule manere de *N.* qe ne vnt nule *G. sim. SMC.*

Essoin de ultra mare.

into those *de ultra mare* and those *de citra mare.* And of those *de ultra mare*, some are beyond the Grecian sea, and some simply beyond sea, as at Rome or at Saint James. And of those beyond the Grecian sea, some are in a simple pilgrimage to the sepulchre of Jerusalem, others to the same place in a general pilgrimage.

Pilgrimage.

Essoins de citra mare.

2. In essoins *de citra mare* the impediment sometimes arises from sickness, and sometimes from other hindrances. And of those from sickness, some arise from sickness overtaking the party on the road, and some from disease, which is called *malum lecti,* and some from an illness coming on in the town where the court is held. Of other impediments, some arise from the senses, as in cases of idiots, persons deaf and dumb, and others who are not of sufficient capacity to receive a summons; some arise from hindrances of imprisonment, or of roads; some from the service of the earthly king; and from accusation of felony.

Essoin of general pilgrimage.

3. In the essoin beyond the Grecian sea in a general pil-

pelrinage, fet a prendre garde si nul general passage de acun Roi Cristien fut de einz le an, ou de autre homme enveyé par le Apostoile ovek graunt host des Cristiens; adounc est cel essoignie alowable; et issi remeindra la parole sauntz jour en favour des [1]pellereins Deu[1], pur le privilege[2] des croicez jekes al retourn le[3] pelerin ou jekes a sa mort. Acune gent neqedent se purchacent nos lettres de proteccioun patentes durables a un an ou a deus ou a treis aunz; et jalemeins fount attournez generals ausi par nos lettres patentes. Et ceux [4]qi ensi fount si fount[4] bien et sagement. Car [283.] nul graunt seignur ne chivaler de noster reaume ne deit enprendre chemin sauntz noster coungé. Car issi purroit le reaume remeindre desgarni de forte gent. Mes celes lettres deussent estre hastivement moustrez en plein Counté ou en Hundred ou[5] en solempnes leus. Et si nul tiel general passage[6] eit esté jekes en la terre saincte de einz le an, adounc soit cel essoigne tourné jekes en le essoigne de outre meer de Grece jekes en la terre saincte en simple pelerinage. Et cest essoignie est le premer de touz les autres. Car si il

Brac. 338, 339 *b*; Fle. 383 (§ 6).

1—1. Crestiens *G.* 2. *conj.* pelereinage *L.* *sim. GMF.* perilinage *S.* 3. *so M.* de *LC.* del *GF.* 4—4. *so N.* qi en fount *L.* en fount *MGCF.* *sim. S.* 5. *so NSF.* et *L.* *om. MGC.* 6. ne *add. NS.* *sim. GMF.*

grimage, it must be observed whether there has been within the year a general passage of any Christian king, or other person sent by the Pope with a great host of Christians; for then this essoin is allowable, and the plea will stand over without day, out of favour for the pilgrims of God, on account of the privilege of those who have taken the cross, until the return or death of the pilgrim. There are some however who obtain our letters patent of protection to be in force for one, two, or three years, and who nevertheless by virtue of our letters patent do also make general attorneys; and such persons do well and wisely. For no great lord or knight of our realm ought to travel forth of it without our licence, since by that means the kingdom might be left destitute of able persons; and such letters ought to be presently shown in full county or hundred court, or at public places. And if there has not been any general passage to the Holy Land within the year, then let this essoin be turned into the essoin beyond the Grecian sea to the Holy Land in simple pilgrimage. This essoin is the

Plea stayed *sine die.*

Letters patent of protection.

General attorney.

Essoin of simple pilgrimage beyond the Grecian Sea.

soit getté apres nul autre, james n'iert dounc alowable solom sa nature.

Brac. 339; Fle. 383 (§ 2). 4. En le essoignie de outre meer de Grece en simple pelrinage soit graunté terme de un an et un jour. Et si le essoigniour veye qe il ne put a chief del an estre garraunté, Brac. 339; Fle. 383 (§ 7). uncore tendra lu[1] essoigne de outre meer simplement, qe singnefie pelrinage simple, sicum a Rome ou a Sainct Jake, et cel essoinge fet alouwer, et deit [2]le enjournement[2] aver le tens de xl. jours et de un flod et de un retret de la meer. Et si le essoigniour se aparceyve, qe soen seignur ne ly veigne uncore garraunter, uncore tendra lu le essoigne de mal de venue [3]en le quel[3] deit estre doné xv. jours de[4] terme au meins. Et si uncore ne puisse vener pur destourbaunce [283 *b*.] de maladie, adounc fet[5] a distincter si il est gisaunt en la maladie par chemin, ou en la ville ou la court est. Car si par chemin, de ceo nest essoignie de mal de lit, et cel essoigne Brac. 345; Fle. 387 (§ 4). covendra estre fet par deus messagers ou deus amys, et ne mie par essoigniours, solom ceo qe dit serra apres. Et si il

1. la *L.* liu *N.* lu le *MF.* *sim. GS.* leu *C.* 2—2. lour iournement *L.* leniournement *NCF.* *sim. GS.* le en iournement *M.* 3—3. *so GS.* et la quele *L.* a quel *NC.* en la quele *MF.* a la quele *S.* 4. *so NMGS.* a *L.* 5. *so NMSC.* soit *L.*

Essoin *de ultra mare* lies before other essoins. first of all the essoins; for if it be cast after any of the others, it will, from its nature, never be allowed.

On essoin *de ultra mare Græciæ*, a year and day allowed. 4. In the essoin beyond the Grecian sea in simple pilgrimage the term of a year and a day is to be granted. And if the essoiner sees that he cannot be warranted at the end of the Then on essoin *de ultra mare*, forty days. year, then again the essoin *de ultra mare* simply shall take place, which signifies a common pilgrimage to Rome or Saint James; and such essoin shall be allowed, and the adjournment shall be for the period of forty days, and one flood, and one Then on essoin *de malo veniendi*, fifteen days. ebb of the sea. And if the essoiner perceives that his master does not come to warrant him, then again the essoin *de malo veniendi* shall lie, in which a term of fifteen days at least Then essoin *de malo lecti*, ought to be given. And if he is still prevented from appearing by sickness, then a distinction must be made, whether he lies sick on his road, or in the town where the court is held, for if on the road[n], this gives rise to an essoin *de malo lecti;* and this essoin must be made by two messengers or friends, and

[n] I should prefer to read *a sa mesoun*, 'at home,' here and in the line above; but I find no authority for it.

gise en la ville ou la court est, adounc tient lu cest essoignie de mal de la ville, solom ceo qe dit serra en soen lu. Et si adounc ne viegne [1]ly essoniez[1] garrauntir [2]soen essoingniour[2], adounc primes est la terre pernable en nostre meyn en noun de destresce, si nous ne eioums rescu ses possessiouns en nostre protecccioun[3] par nos lettres patentes, [4]les queles suspendent[4] touz pleez for quatre. Fle. 383 (§ 2), 384 (§ 8).

5. La manere [5]del entré de tiels essoignes[5] est ceste: Johan, qi est passé en passage general de pelrins jekes a la terre saincte, vers Pieres, de plee de terre, par tiel. Et si en simple pelrinage, dounc issi: Johan qi est passé en pelrinage jekes a la terre saincte vers Pieres, de play de terre, par tiel. Et si en plus simple, adounc issi: Johan, qi est passé la meer en pelerinage, vers Piers, de play de terre, par tiel, la quele [6]meer qe il soit passé[6], de Fraunce, de Hirlaund, ou de Escoce. Brac. 339; Fle. 383 (§ 5, 6, 7); Hengh. Mag. c. 6. p. 27.

1—1. le seignur *N.* son essoneur *C.* 2—2. les essoignes *C.* 3. *so SGMCF.* ou *add. L.* 4—4. les supposent [la quele suspent *interlin.*] *L.* la quele suspend *N.* *sim. SA.* les queus supposent *GCF.* qe supposent lui estre quites de *Z.* 5—5. *so verb. S.* de celes essoignes *del* entre[r] *L.* de entrer tiels esson si *N.* de entrer celes essoignes *GM.* del Entree des essoines *C.* dextree de celes essoignes *F.* 6—6. *om. M.*

not by essoiners, as shall be hereafter mentioned. If he lies in the town where the Court is, then the essoin *de malo villæ* takes place, as shall be noticed in its turn. And if the essoinee does not then appear to warrant the essoiner, then and not before the land is to be taken into our hand by way of distress, unless we have received his possessions under our protection by our letters patent, which suspend all pleas but four[o].

Or *de malo villæ*.

Then, on default, process of *Cape*.

5. The manner of entering essoins is as follows: 'John, who is gone over in a general passage of pilgrims to the Holy Land, against Peter, of a plea of land, by such an one.' And if in a simple pilgrimage, then thus: 'John, who is gone in a pilgrimage to the Holy Land, against Peter, of a plea of land, by such an one.' And if in a more ordinary pilgrimage, then thus: 'John, who is gone across the sea in a pilgrimage, against Peter, of a plea of land, by such an one,' whether it be the sea of France, Ireland, or Scotland, which he has crossed.

Forms of entering essoins.

[o] Five kinds of actions are mentioned in Fleta as not being stayed by letters of protection, namely, the assises of novel disseisin, mortdancester, and last presentation, and the actions of *quare impedit* and dower *unde nihil habet*. (Fleta, p. 383. § 2.) A note in MS. *Z* mentions the same actions, omitting the assise of mortdancester, and adding plaints commenced before Justices in eyre.

Et si de mal de venue, quele qe la destourbaunce soit, ou
[284.] de maladie, ou de enprisounement, ou de passage, ou autre, adounc issi: Johan vers Pieres, de play de terre, par tiel.

Brac. 341 *b*, 343 *b*; 385 (§ 8), 386 (§ 13). 6. Et si plusours tenauntz en commun ausi cum un dreit soint essoigniez, adounc soit le essoigne entré, le quel qe hom voille, issi: Johan vers Pieres et les autres nomez en le bref, ou vers chescune persone severalment. Par un essoigniour neqedent purrount trestouz estre essoigniez. Et si partie se fount essoignier et partie nient, adounc covendra nomer les nouns de les essoigniez, et lesser a fere mencioun des autres nient essoigniez; ou issi: Johan et les autres nomez en le bref vers Pieres, ou vers P. M. et R. Mes issi ne ert mie des essoignes de plusours tenauntz par divers dreitz, tut tiegnent il ou demaundent en commun. Car en tiel cas covendra issi dire: Johan vers Piers, Thomas, et Symon de tiel play par tiel; ou issi: Piers vers Johan, Thomas vers Johan, et issi severalment de touz les autres, et en tiel cas covent, qe chescun qi se fet essoignier eit several essoigniour.

If it be an essoin *de malo veniendi*, whatever the hindrance be, whether sickness, imprisonment, hindrance of passage, or other, then thus: 'John against Peter, of a plea of land, by such an one.'

Entry of essoin of jointenants. 6. If several holding in common by one title are essoined, then let the essoin be entered according as they please, either thus, 'John against Peter and' the others named in the writ, or against each person severally. Nevertheless they may be all essoined by one essoiner. And if part cause themselves to be essoined and part not, then it will be necessary to mention the names of those who are essoined, and take no notice of the others who are not essoined, as thus: 'John and the others named in the writ against Peter, or against P. M. and R.' But it is otherwise with the essoins of several persons holding by different rights, although they hold or demand in common. For in such cases the entry must be thus: 'John against Peter, Thomas, and Simon, of such a plea, by such an one;' or thus: 'Peter against John, Thomas against John,' and so severally of all the rest; and in that case every tenant who causes himself to be essoined must have a separate essoiner.

CHAPITRE VIII. [CXXIV.]

De Essoigne de Service le Roi Terestre [1].

Le essoigne de service le Roi est en touz tens resceivable [2]par la ou il est alouwable[2]; [3]car il est acune foiz alouwable, et acune foiz nient[3]. Car il ne est james alouwable en nule des quatre petites assises; ne en nul plee de dowarie, ou la femme se pleint qe ele rien ad del dowarie; ne en atteintes, ne en certificaciouns; ne en nul plee ou le pleintif est de einz age; ne en nule persone ne tient lu qe nous ne seert mie en chief, tut face il soen service a acun [4]des nos[4]; ne es persones de ceux qi nous servent ne est il alouwable for qe en teles qe sount par noster maundement[5] oveke nous pur nous fere lour service a qi il sount tenuz par resoun de acun tenement; et as tieles gentz deit noster Chaunceler graunter bref de lour essoigniours garraunter et lour absence excuser, taunt cum ceux demorrount ovekes nous en tiels services. Et si acun bref soit autrement graunté, si voloms qe ceux brefs soint chalengez et tenuz a faus.

Stat. de Protectionibus (temp. incert.); Glan. li. I. c. 27; Brac. 338 b, 339 b, 340; Fle. 383, 384; Ante, p. 351.

[284 b.]

Glan. li. I. c. 27; Brac. 338 b.

1. Terestre *om. NS.* 2—2. *om. C.* 3—3. *om. MF.* Car ele est asqune foiz nient resceivable *C.* 4—4. de nous *LGMF.* des noos *S.* den oz *corr. N.* 5. comaundement *NMGC.*

CHAPTER VIII.

Of the Essoin founded on the King's Service.

The essoin *de servitio regis* may be received at any period in those cases where it is allowable; for it is in some cases allowable, and in some not. It is never to be allowed in any of the four petty assises, nor in a plea of dower where a widow complains that she has nothing of her dower, nor in attaints, nor in certifications, nor in any plea where the plaintiff is under age. Neither does it lie for any person who does not serve us in chief, although he performs his service to some one belonging to us; nor is it to be allowed to those who do service to us, unless they are with us by our command in order to perform the service to which they are bound by reason of some tenement. To such persons our Chancellor ought to grant a writ to warrant their essoiners, and excuse their absence, so long as they continue with us in such services; and if any writ be otherwise granted, we will that such writs be impeached and held bad.

Essoin *de servitio regis*, where not allowed;

to whom allowed.

Warrant of king's service.

CHAPITRE IX. [CXXV.]

De Essoigne de Mal de venue.

Brac. 340 *b*, 341; Fle. 384, 385.

Le essoignie de mal de venue, ne nul autre essoigne, ne tient lu en nule persone qe est de eynz age, pur ceo qe enfaunt de eynz age ne put nul essoigniour garraunter. Car garraunter essoigne ne est autre chose qe jurer sur saintz, qe la cause de sa absence fust verreye, solom ceo qe il en estoit essoignié al autre jour. Ne ausi en encusement de felonie; ne ausi en persones de disseisours ne de redisseisours; ne as enpledez de hamsokne, ou de fresche force, ou de enbatement; ne en pleez de vee de name es persones defendauntz; ne ausi
[285.] en persones de tels qi sount lessez par bail a acuns a respoundre pur eus, cors pur cors; ne en persones de ceux des queus le viscounte ad comaundement de les fere vener, ou de
Post, p. 358. fere les a saver [1]qe il i soint[1] si il voillent; ne en persones de ceux, qi ount fet attournez en court, si les attournez ne soint ausi essoigniez; ne en la persone de un attourné, ou [2]deus attournez sount[2] fetz par disjointe[3] en une parole, si

1—1. qe il soint *L.* *sim. GSF.* quels il sount *N.* qe eus i seent *M.* qil yseient *C.* 2—2. *so verb. MGF.* de deus attournez [qe *interl.*] sount *L.* de deus attournez forfetz par desceyte qi sount *N.* 3. difficulte *C.*

CHAPTER IX.

Of the Essoin de Malo veniendi.

Essoin de malo veniendi.

Neither the essoin *de malo veniendi* nor any other essoin lies for any person under age, because an infant cannot warrant any essoiner.

Warranty of essoin.

For warranty of essoin is nothing else but swearing upon the evangelists that the cause of his absence was true, according as he was essoined at the former day.

Where essoin does not lie.

Neither does it lie in an accusation of felony; nor in the person of disseisors or redisseisors; nor for those impleaded of hamsoken, or of fresh force, or of abatement; nor in pleas *de vetito namio* in the person of the defendants; nor for such as are let by bail to be answered for by others, body for body; nor in the persons of those whom the sheriff is commanded to cause to come, or to cause to know that they be there if they will; nor of those who have made attorneys in court, unless the attorneys be also essoined; nor for one

ambideus ne soint essoigniez; ne en persones de ceux, qi adversaries sount mortz, ou ne sount[1] mie pursuiz lour brefs ou lour pleintes; ne en cas ou [2]le bref[2] ne se acorde mie al essoigne; ne en cas ou comaundé est al viscounte qe il destreigne par [3]terre et par[3] chateus; ne[4] en cas ou les parties sount[5] ajournez de jour en jour; ne en cas ou les parties [6]grauntent de[6] venir sauntz essoigne; ne apres jour de amour doné par assent des parties; ne en cas ou la parole est suspendue par defaute des jurours, for qe al defendaunt, et ceo uncore for qe une foiz; ne en cas ou la partie essoignié, ou soen attourné, furent veews en court par [7]record des[7] Justices en le meen tens avaunt l'enjournement del essoigne; ne ausi ne tient james essoigne lu freschement apres defaute, si la partie ne se assente.

Stat. West. 2. (13 Edw. I.) c. 27.

Stat. West. 1. (3 Edw. I.) c. 42; Stat. West. 2. c. 28; Ante, p. 172.

1. *so verb. LNMGSC.* vnt *F.* 2—2. la pleinte *G* 3—3. *so M. om. LNGSCF.* 4. *so NMGSCF.* Mes *L.* 5. *so NGC. sim. SMF. om. L.* 6—6. grauntient *L.* ount grauntee de *N. sim. M.* eient grante de *G. sim. SF.* se acordent *C.* 7—7. *so MG.* cors des *LNSCF.*

attorney, where two have been made in one plea with several powers, unless both be essoined; neither does the essoin lie where the adverse parties are dead, or have not pursued their writs or plaints, or where the writ does not agree with the essoin[p]; nor in those cases where the sheriff is commanded to distrain by land and chattels; nor where the parties are adjourned from one day to the next; nor where they have agreed to come without essoin; nor after day of grace given by consent; nor where the plea is suspended for default of jurors, except for the defendant, and that only once; nor where the party essoined, or his attorney, hath been seen in court in the meantime before the adjournment of the essoin, and the Justices have taken notice thereof; neither does an essoïn ever lie immediately after default, unless by consent.

[p] This appears to be mistaken rendering of the words of Bracton, ubi breve non convenit petitioni. The meaning in Bracton seems to be, that when the whole proceeding is void, as where the plaintiff has not obtained a writ suitable to his plaint, the essoin is null. See Bracton, f. 341; Fleta, p. 384 (§ 4), 385 (§ 6).

CHAPITRE X. [CXXVI.]

[285 b.]

De Attournez.

1. Chescun ne put mie fere attourné. Car enfaunt de eynz age, ne sourd, ne muet, ne fol nastre, ne homme purement aragé, ne autrement sauntz descrescioun, ne homme acusé de felonie, ne nul de qi nous le defendoms, ne mesel ousté de commune de gent, ne put mie fere attourné.

Ante, vol. i. p 306.

2. Des attournez sount acuns generals, acuns especials. Les generals sount fetz en deus maneres, ceo est a saver, par nos lettres patentes, et par constitucions des gentz devaunt Justices en heires. Ceux attournez qi sount fetz par nos lettres patentes ount acune foiz poer plus des autres generals; pur ceo qe acune foiz lour est graunté le poer de attourner autres en lour leus. Et touz attournez generals purrount lever fins et cirographer, et accorder finalement[1] en touz pleez taunt avaunt cum çeux mesmes qi attournez il sount; et issi ne poent mie especials attournez. Car si toust cum

Stat. West. 2. (13 Edw. I.) c. 10.

Glan. li. 11. c. 1.

1. *so M.* *sim. NGSCF.* fin seurement *L.*

CHAPTER X.

Of Attorneys.

Who may make attorney.

1. Attorneys cannot be made by every one; for an infant under age, a deaf and dumb person, an idiot, a man simply mad or otherwise without discretion, a person accused of felony, or any one who is forbidden by us to do so, or a leper expelled from society, cannot make an attorney.

Attorneys, general and special.

2. Of attorneys, some are general and some special. General attorneys are made in two ways, that is to say, either by our letters patent, or by appointment of parties before Justices in eyre. Those attorneys who are made by our letters patent have sometimes more authority than other general attorneys, because they have sometimes the power granted them to attorn others in their place. All general attorneys may levy fines and make chirographs, and final accords in all pleas as fully as those whose attorneys they are. This cannot be done by special attorneys; for as soon as parties are at accord in

Powers of an attorney made by letters patent.

Powers of a general attorney.

Special attorney cannot make accord or fine.

parties sount acordez en nule manere de plee, si cesse la parole; et si nul contract[1] se deive fere sour le acord, par la comence une autre manere de plee et de une autre nature. Et tut soit fet acun attourné en la parole qe est, pur ceo ne est mie fet attourné en la parole qe serra, si le attourné ne soit fet general en touz plees moeuz et a mover.

3. Les attournez par nos lettres patentes ne [2]poet nul[2] receyvere for qe nous et noster Chaunceler. Ne autres attournez generals ne deyvent estre resceus for qe par devaunt nos Justices en [3]heires et en[3] pleine court. Les especials attournez ne poet[4] nul receyvere for qe nous, ou noster Chaunceler, ou autre qe nous avom assigné especialment a ceo fere par noster bref, ou les juges[5] en pleine court, quels il soint, viscountes ou autres hommes fraunces, par devaunt quels il deit pleder par noster bref. Et ou la parole est mue sauntz bref, ne purra nule tele court de seutours porter record de attourné, et pur ceo ne deit nul attourné estre resceu en tele court sauntz noster bref, for qe par la ou le plee est meu par bref. Les quatre chivalers, qi sount [286.] Glan. li. 11. c. 1. Glan. li. 11. cc. 1, 2.

1. so *LNGSF.* *sim. M.* *qu.* contek. 2—2. so *MG.* *sim. NF.* pount nuli *L.* *sim. S.* poet nul homme *C.* 3—3. Eyres en *NS.* eyre en *MGCF.* 4. so *M.* *sim. NGF.* pount *LSC.* 5. Iugementz *L.* Iuge *M.* Iugemenz *SGM.* *sim. F.* queus *C.*

any sort of plea, that proceeding is at an end; and if any question is to be made upon the accord, thereupon begins another sort of plea, and of another nature. And though one be made attorney in the existing proceeding, he is not thereby made attorney in the future proceeding, unless he be made general attorney in all pleas commenced and to be commenced.

3. No one can admit persons as attorneys by our letters patent, except us and our Chancellor. Neither ought other general attorneys to be admitted save before our Justices in eyres and in full court. Special attorneys cannot be admitted except by us or our Chancellor, or other person whom we may especially assign by our writ in that behalf, or the Judges in full court, whoever they be, sheriffs, or freemen, before whom the party is bound to plead by our writ. Where the proceeding is commenced without our writ, a court of suitors cannot bear record of attorney; and therefore no attorney can be admitted in such a court without our writ, except where the proceeding is commenced by writ. The four knights, who are

General attorneys, how constituted.

Special attorneys.

Glan. li. 1. c. 19; Brac. 353. enveez as malades en essoignies de mal de lit et de mal de ville, purrount[1] ausi receyvere attournez. Et si acun se profre pur attourné pur nous ou pur autre, et ne soit mie resceu attourné en nul des cas avauntditz, et il soit chalengé de la partie adverse, en tiel cas est le attourné comaundable a la prisoun. Et cum acun soit issi fet attourné, mes ne se purra remuer pendaunte[2] la parole sauntz la volunté de soen client. Glan. li. 11. c. 3.

Glan. li. 11. c. 3; Fle. 385 (§ 9, 10). 4. Et coment qe attournez soint fetz generals ou especials, et deus ou plusours soint fetz attournez [3]en disjoynte[3], tut eit chescun le poer soen seignur, ja par taunt ne vaudra le essoigne [4]del un[4] attourné si trestouz les attournez ne soint essoigniez, pur la fraude qe le attourné qi point ne se fist essoignier purreit fere, apres qe la partie adverse avereit resceu jour et parti de court encountre le essoiniour le autre attourné. Et cum acun eit fet dounc attourné et puis soit apparu en court et pledé, et eit resceu autre jour en sa propre persone, en tel cas ne suffit mie si il soul soit essoignié al autre jour, pur ceo qe il i ad attourné, ne qe le attourné soul [286 b.] Brac. 342, 342 b; Fle. 345 (§ 9).

1. so N. il add. LMGSCF. 2. pendant GSF. om. M. 3—3. om. C. 4—4. so NMG. de lour [un] L. de lour S.

The four knights in essoin *de malo lecti* can admit attorney. sent to the sick persons in essoins *de malo lecti* and *de malo villæ*, can also admit attorneys. If any person offers himself as attorney for us, or for any other, in any of the aforesaid cases, and being challenged by the adverse party, is not admitted as attorney, such person may be committed to prison. And when any one has been thus made attorney, he cannot retire pending the proceeding without the consent of his client. Attorney rejected by the court may be punished. Attorney cannot retire, plea pending.

Joint and several attorneys must be essoined together. 4. When two or more are made attorneys disjunctively, whether they be made general or special attorneys, although each has the power of his master, yet the essoin of one attorney will be invalid, unless all the attorneys be essoined, on account of the fraud which might be practised by the attorney who is not essoined, after the adverse party has had a day given him as against the essoiner of the other attorney, and has thereupon left the court. So, when any one has made an attorney, and has then appeared in court and pleaded, and had another day given him in his own person, it is not sufficient at the next day that he alone should be essoined, because there is If one make attorney and receive day in person, both must be essoined.

soit essoignié, pur ceo qe le attourné ne resceut[1] avaunt nul jour; [2]et pur ceo[2] plus seure chose est, qe ambideus soint essoigniez.

5. Et cum acun[3] eit fet attourné especial vers certeine persone tenaunt, et cel tenaunt vouche a garraunt, cest attourné ne tient mie lu vers le garraunt; einz covendra al pleintif fere novel attourné el plé de la garrauntie, ou il perdra soen bref, si le garraunt le chalenge, sicum[4] serra dit del baroun et sa femme pleintifs en le chapitre de garraunties; et[5] en tiel cas serroit le attourné comaundable a la prisoun. Et ausi en touz[6] cas ou nul se profre pur attourné [7]qi fust fet attourné[7] einz ceo qe nule parole fust [8]de quei il fust[8] fet[9] attourné, sicum en cas ou acun fust fet attourné einz ceo qe le bref fust liveré al viscounte, ou eynz ceo qe nule somounse soit fete; car avaunt somounse, ou qe autaunt vaille, ne est [287.] Brac. 334; Fle. 379 (§ 14).

1. *The last folio of MS. L, which has been heretofore followed, is wanting; and from this point the text is taken verbally from M, except where otherwise mentioned, the orthography of L being retained.* 2—2. *so N. om. MGS.* 3. il *N. om. S.* 4. *so N.* E com *M. sim. CF.* 5. et *om. SGC.* 6. tiel *NW. sim. S.* 7—7. *so verb. NGC. sim. S. om. MF.* 8—8. *so NS. sim. GCF. om. M.* 9. fet *om. N.*

an attorney; nor that the attorney alone should be essoined, because it was not the attorney that had day given him. It is therefore safer for both to be essoined.

5. When any has made a special attorney against a certain person tenant, and the tenant vouches to warranty, the attorney does not keep his place as against the warrant, but the plaintiff should make a new attorney in the plea of warranty, or else he will lose his writ, if the warrant take the objection, as will be said of husband and wife plaintiffs, in the chapter upon warranties[q]; and the attorney would in such a case be liable to be committed to prison. So likewise in all cases where any one offers himself for attorney, who was so made before any proceeding existed for which he was made attorney, as where the attorney was appointed before the writ was delivered to the sheriff, or before any summons was made. For before summons, or something equivalent to it, the pro-

Special attorney in original plea must be reappointed for the plea of warranty.

Special attorney cannot be made before the plea is commenced.

[q] This is another reference to a future chapter either never supplied or lost. The same chapter is referred to before, li. iii. c. 11. s. 2. The point intended to be mentioned may be found in Bracton, f. 381; Fleta, p. 408 (§ 9).

Fle. 385 (§ 7). nule parole. Et ausi, en cas ou le viscounte ad fet simplement a saver qe il soit en court a certein jour, si il quide bien fere, si[1] nul se profre pur attourné tel, eynz ceo qe il soit apparu en court, le attourné est chalengable; et ausi celi qi se profre pur[2] attourné de acun qi ne est mie nomé el bref ou en la principale pleinte, eynz ceo qe cist soit apparu en court qi attourné il se fet, sicum sount acunes gentz qi ount purchacé acuns tenementz puis les brefs purchacez sour les feffours, et qi ount amis en court, et se profrent pur attournez des tenauntz pur defendre le dreit des pleintifs, [3]en tiel cas sount ausi les attournez chalengables, lequel qe il eint garraunt ou noun; car einz ceo qe tiels tenauntz apiergent en court en lour propres persones, lour tendra lu nul attourné. Et ausi sount ceux attournez chalengeables en nostre court, [4]coment qe il[4] ne sount mie en la Cristiene ley, qi se profrent a fere la ley pur lour seignur, ou a jurer en lour almes[5]; et ausi en touz[6] cas ou acun se profre pur attourné el plee de *Pone*, [7]ou il fust fet attourné avaunt le *Pone*[7] purchacé.

1. E si *NS*. 2. *so NGS.* le *add. M.* 3. e *add. SGC.* 4—4. *so N. sim. GSCF.* com ceus *M.* 5. absence *C.* 6. cel *D.* teu *S.* 7—7. *so verb. NGC. sim. SF. om. M.*

Party, not directly made defendant, cannot make attorney until after appearance.

ceeding is not begun. So, where the sheriff merely informs a person that he is to appear in court on such a day, if he think proper to do so, if any one offers himself as the attorney of such person before he has appeared in court, the attorney is liable to challenge. So also is he who offers himself as attorney of one not named in the writ or the principal plaint, before the party whose attorney he represents himself to be has appeared in court; as where people have purchased tenements after the writs have been sued out against their feoffors, and have friends in court, who put themselves forward as attorneys of the tenants, to make a defence against the right of plaintiffs,—in such case the attorneys are liable to challenge, whether they have warrant or no; for before such tenants have appeared in court in their own persons, they will not be allowed an attorney. And in our court, however the practice may be in the law Christian, such attorneys are challengeable as offer themselves to make their law for their masters, or to swear upon their souls. So also in all cases where any one offers himself as attorney in the plea of *Pone*, having been appointed before the *Pone* was sued out.

Attorney cannot wage law or take oath for principal.

Practice in courts Christian.

6. Et si acun attourné moerge pendaunt le play, adounc fet a destincter, si cist, a qi le attourné fust, soit passé la meer ou noun. Car si il ne soit point en Engleterre ou en Hirlaund, si le plee i soit, adounc est la parole suspendable sauntz jour jekes al retourn celi[1]. Brac. 343 (§ 10); Fle. 385 (§ 11).

1. qi attorne il est *add. P.* etc. *add. F.* qi attorne il est. E comenceant le plee en bref de dreit chescun se puruei des excepcions qe li purront valer entre les excepcions auant dites en les plez de possession qar ausi bien sount il barree de accion en ceo plai com illoqes si com est excepcion de felonie bastardie quite clamance e autres chescun qi est encontree de partie. Dit auoms la fourme e la nature des plez pur ioeuenes genz en senser e les autres mentiuer *add. A.* *sim. B.*

6. If an attorney dies pending the plea, a distinction is to be made, whether he whose attorney he was is gone across the sea or not. For if he be not in England,—or not in Ireland, supposing the plea to be there,—the action may be suspended without day until his return[r]. Effect of death of attorney.

[r] It is plain from the above abrupt conclusion, as well as from the references, occurring in several parts of the work, to future passages and chapters which are not found in the existing treatise, that Britton in its present form is incomplete. See before, vol. i. p. 107; vol. ii. pp. 98, 102, 359. The few additional lines, which are found in two manuscripts of no great authority, do not appear to me to be a part of the original work, which, if continued, would probably have consisted of several more chapters following the arrangement of the latter part of Bracton and Fleta. See the Editor's Introduction, p. xlv.

GLOSSARY

OF

OBSOLETE FRENCH WORDS.

THE following GLOSSARY is intended to comprise the words found in Britton which are out of use in modern French, or of which either the form or the sense has materially changed. Mere peculiarities of spelling and slight alterations of form are not noticed. The following abbreviations and signs are employed in the Glossary.

A. S. = *Anglo-Saxon.*
adj. = *adjective.*
adv. = *adverb.*
art. = *article.*
Duc. Gloss. = *Ducange, Glossarium mediæ et infimæ latinitatis.*
cond. = *conditional tense.*
conj. = *conjunction.*
fem. = *feminine.*
Fr. Gloss. in Duc. = *the French Glossary printed at the end of the Glossary of Ducange.*
fut. = *future tense.*
lat. = *Latin.*
masc. = *masculine.*
med. lat. = *medieval Latin.*
m. fr. = *modern French.*
Ménage = *Ménage, Dictionnaire Etymologique de la Langue Françoise.*
part. = *participle.*
prep. = *preposition.*
pret. = *preterit tense.*
Roq. Gloss. = *Roquefort, Glossaire de la langue Romaine.*
s. v. adeser = *under the word* adeser.
subst. = *substantive.*
v. va. vn. = *verb, verb active, verb neuter.*
var. read. = *various reading.*

The sign = is placed between two forms of the same word, or two words used with the same sense.

The sign * is placed before some of the rarer words which are not found in the general Glossaries.

GLOSSARY

OF

OBSOLETE FRENCH WORDS.

***A saver moun,** ii. 43; **saver moun,** ii. 229, to wit. *This expression occurs in the contemporary histories of St. Louis, Recueil des Historiens des Gaules, vol. xx. pp.* 117 *e,* 159*b.*

Abandoner, abaundoner, to give freely, i. 208; to leave, i. 164. *See Roq. Gloss. s. vv.* abandon *and* abandonné, *which Roquefort derives from lat.* abundanter.

Abatable, abatable (of a writ), i. 328.

Abatement, abatement, usurpation (of a tenement), i. 336, ii. 3; abatement (of a writ), i. 334.

Abatre, *elsewhere* **enbatre; se abatre en un tenement,** to usurp possession of a vacant tenement, i. 336, ii. 2; to abate (a writ), i. 314.

Abbeter, to abet, set on, i. 16.

Abevrour = beverour (*m. fr.* abreuvoir), a watering place for cattle, i. 176, 400.

Able (*m. fr.* habile), fit, able, ii. 5.

Accres, accretion. accruer, i. 219.

Achater, to become feudally subject, i. 269. *See Duc. Gloss. s. v.* **accaptare**; *Ménage, s. v.* achepter.

Acherir (*m. fr.* enchérir), to make dear, raise the price of a thing, i. 193.

Achesun, *more commonly* **enchesun** (*lat.* occasio), occasion, cause, i. 32.

***Achever,** *also* **chever,** to transfer one's homage, or that of his tenant, ii. 23, 32, 47, 303. *See* **achater;** *and see Duc. Gloss. s. v.* **accaptare.**

Aconvenir, acovenir = convenir, to agree, i. 302, ii. 114, 128.

Acouper = encouper, to accuse, indict, bring to trial, i. 31, 63, 110.

Acuni, ascuni, aucuni, of any one, i. 312.

Adeprimes = enprimes, first, at first, i. 45.

Adessier, to touch, approach, ii. 15. *See Roq. Gloss. s. v.* adeser; *Duc. Gloss. s. v.* adatictus.

Adirree, *part.* lost, i. 57, 68. *See Bracton, f.* 150 *b; Fleta, p.* 55 (§ 1), 63 (§ 5); *Duc. Gloss. s. v.* adirare.

Adounc, adunc, then, in that case, i. 14; at that time, i. 53.

Adresces, a dresces, *adv.* straight, i. 364, 400. *See Roq. Gloss. s. vv.* dré, dreche, dres, drez.

Aferaunt, afferraunt, belonging; **soen afferraunt,** his due, ii. 63, 85.

Affiaunce, affiance, confidence, i. 166, ii. 37.

Affier, to trust, assure; **se affier de luy,** to trust him, i. 40; **ne affie mie,** it does not prove, i. 367. *See Duc. Gloss. s. v.* affidare (2).

Affiert, afeert, it belongs, i. 3, ii. 52; *fut.* **affera,** i. 109.

Aforcer, afforcer, (1) to force, compel, i. 159, 251, ii. 24; **s'aforcer** (*m. fr.* s'efforcer), to exert oneself, ii. 304; (2) to strengthen, reinforce, ii. 184; **afforcer les jurours,** to afforce the jury, *that is,* to increase its number, ii. 231.

Agard, judgment, award, i. 283.

Agarder, to adjudge, award, i. 123, 127.

Aherdre, aerdre (*qu. lat.* adhærere), to grow, attach, i. 264, ii. 71.

Al = a le, to the, i. 8, 10.

Aleggeaunce, allegiance, ii. 29.

Alienaunce = alienacioun, alienation, the process of aliening or conveying away property, i. 54.

Alloigner, Aloygner = esloigner (*m. fr.* éloigner), to remove, eloin, i. 44, 67. *also* to alien, i. 69, *where perhaps we should read more correctly* **alienes.**

Aloygneour, alienour = **esloigneour,** eloiner, one who removes, i. 67.

Ambedeus, ambideus (*lat.* ambo, duo), both, i. 38, 284.

Amenuser = **menuser** (*lat.* minuere), to lessen, diminish, restrict, i. 2, 374; to become less, ii. 77.

Amerciement, amercement, i. 154.

Amercier, to amerce, fine, i. 38.

Amite, aunte (*lat.* amita), aunt, ii. 57, 60, 61.

Amonester, to admonish, command, i. 152, ii. 343.

Amounter, to rise, to amount, ii. 51; **amountaunt et nient avalaunt,** ascending and not descending, ii. 58, 82.

***Amyteyn, anteyn, antein** (*lat.* amitina), aunt (*qu.* on the mother's side), ii. 56, 57, 61, 62.

Anel, ring; **anel del uihs,** door-handle, i. 261.

Anientir, anentir (*m. fr.* anéantir), to annihilate, i. 373.

Annex, annexed, i. 262, ii. 175.

Apaé, apayé (*lat.* pacatus), appeased; **s'apayer, se tenir apayé,** to be satisfied, ii. 73, 240, 249. *See* **payer.**

Aparmesmes (*qu. lat.* ad partem ipsam, on the spot), immediately, without delay, ii. 204. *See Roq. Gloss. and Fr. Gloss. in Duc. s. v.* aparmain.

Apel, *pl.* **apeaus,** i. 3, an appeal, an ancient form of criminal trial. *See* i. 97.

Aperge, *subj. from* apparer, to appear, i. 118, ii. 32.

Apert, apiert, appears, ii. 276.

Apparer (*m. fr.* apparaitre), to appear, ii. 343.

Apposer, to question, i. 300. *Certain exercises at St. Paul's school are. or were until lately, called* Apposition; *see Pepys's Diary, vol. i. p.* 7.

Aprompter, apromter = **enpromter** (*m. fr.* emprunter), to borrow, i. 156, 173.

Aramer, arramer, arramir (**une assise**), to institute or commence, i. 286, 356; ii. 111; *subj.* **arrayme,** ii. 62, 112. *See Duc. Gloss. s. v.* adramire.

Arere meyn, backwards, ii. 119.

Arerier (*m. fr.* arriérer), to hinder, i. 89.

Arerisement, hindrance, i. 95.

Aresouner, to arraign, i. 26.

Armure, arms, armour, i. 37, 105, 107.

Arrer (*lat.* arare), to plough, i. 368.

Arrure, arure, ploughing, i. 369.

As = **a les,** to the, i. 10, 65.

Asetz, aset, asset, *adv.* (*m. fr.* assez), enough, i. 245; **fere le asetz a ascun,** make satisfaction, i. 60; **fere le asset de la condicioun,** satisfy the condition, i. 240, ii. 89.

Assaer, assayer (*m. fr.* essayer), to try, essay, i. 329; to assay, try (of weights and measures), i. 4.

Assartir, assartier, to clear or enclose (waste land), i. 382, ii. 68.

Asseer, asser, *subj.* **assece** (*m. fr.* asseoir), to set, fix, assess, i. 101, ii. 86.

Assiduelment, continually, i. 26.

Assigner, to designate, declare, show, ii. 262.

Assise, 1. law, assessment, **assise de pain,** the law fixing the price of bread, i. 186; 2. a mode of trial by jurors, **graunt assise,** ii. 305, **petite assise,** i. 271; 3. an action determined by a petty assise, i. 19, 274.

Assoudre, *part. pass.* **asoutz, assouz** (*lat.* absolvere, absolutus), to acquit, discharge, resolve, i. 167, ii. 27.

***Astre,** hearth, home, i. 392; *see also* ii. 155 *note; Duc. Gloss. s. vv.* astre, stare; *Consuetudines Cantie, Statutes of the Realm, vol. i. p.* 224.

***Astrer, astrier, homme astrier,** a peasant having his hearth and home (astre) upon the manor, i. 392, ii. 155 *note,* 224, 287.

Attamer = **entamer** (*m. fr.* entamer), to touch upon, begin, i. 203, 204, 307, ii. 63.

Atteignaument (*adv. from* atteignaunt), effectually, i. 221, 223, ii. 146.

Atteignaunt, effectual, ii. 276.

Atteignours, attainors, jurors upon an attaint, ii. 216, 234.

Atteinte, conviction, attaint, ii. 216.

Atteyndre, to attaint, convict, i. 125; prove, i. 271.

Attirer, to prepare, i. 78, 105.

Attornement, attornment, transference of service, i. 269.

Attourné, attournez (*lat.* attornatus), attorney, ii. 356.

Attourner, attorner, to transfer or turn over to another the homage and service of a tenant, i. 269.

Auge, *subj. from* **aler,** let him go, i. 9.

Aukes, *adv.* (*lat.* aliquid), somewhat, to some extent, i. 219, ii. 61.

Aumoyne, aumoygne, alms, a species of tenure, i. 4, ii. 12; **fraunche aumoyne,** frank almoign, ii. 12, 51.

Aunir, to unite, i. 31.

Ausmee (*lat.* æstimatio), valuation, i. 332.

Ausmer (*lat.* æstimare), to value, i. 332.

Aust, August, harvest, i. 91, 201, 392.

Autiel, autel, such, i. 286, ii. 115.

Autresi = ausi (*m. fr.* aussi), so, as, ii. 207.

Autretaunt, *adv.* as much, i. 288.

Autretiel = autiel, such, i. 343, ii. 207.

Avenue, arrival, ii. 335; **avenues,** means, ways, i. 354.

Aver, property, money, i. 79, ii. 125, 126; cattle, i. 137, 364; **aver de pois,** goods sold by weight, dry goods, i. 96, 189.

Avouterie, adultery, i. 280, 284.

Avouwesoun, avoweysoun (*lat.* advocatio), advowson, i. 69.

Avowé (*lat.* advocatus), the patron of a church, ii. 174.

***Awer,** i. 32; **aweer,** ii. 200; **eoyr,** i. 336; **ewer,** *var. lect. ib.*, doubt: *perhaps from the lat.* æquare: *see Roq. Gloss., and Gloss. Fr. in Duc. s. v.* ewer. *The word* awere *was used in English with the same meaning; see* Promptorium Parvulorum, *and Mr. Riley's Glossary to* Liber Albus.

Bacberinde (*an English word*), backbearing, carrying on his back, i. 182.

Bail, baill, delivery, i. 259.

Bailie, baillie (*lat.* balliva), bailiwick, the limit of the authority of a sheriff, bailiff, or other officer, i. 12, 18, 22.

Banir, bannir, to ban, to outlaw, i. 53.

Barat, barretry, fraud, chicane, ii. 176; *see Duc. Gloss. s. v.* baratum, barata.

Baroun, 1. Baron, i. 2; 2. husband, i. 223.

Basset, *qu.* low, ii. 163.

Bat, boat, i. 39.

Baud, 3 *pers. sing. pres. indic.* from **bailler,** to deliver, i. 243, 260.

Baudement, boldly, i. 362; *see Duc. Gloss. s. v.* baldantia.

Baunc, baunk, bench; **Justices du baunk,** Justices of the Bench, *i. e. generally* of the Common Pleas, i. 19, 133, ii. 73; **el baunc,** in the Court of Common Pleas, ii. 169, 171; *cf. Bracton, f.* 108; *Foss. Judges of England, vol. ii. p.* 161; **clercs del un baunc et del autre,** clerks of the Common Bench or King's Bench, i. 94.

Beal, beul (*m. fr.* beau), handsome, ii. 37.

Beal pleder, correct pleading, i. 80.

Begger, to beg, exact, i. 91, 93.

Belif, belive, collateral, transverse, ii. 320. *See Gloss. Fr. in Duc. s. v.* belline, et bellivant.

Berbyz (*lat.* vervex, *m. fr.* brebis), a sheep, ii. 68.

Bercherie (*m. fr.* bergerie), sheepcote, i. 279.

Besael (*m. fr.* bisaïeul), great-grandfather, i. 206.

Besoigne; *see* **bosoigne.**

Beverour = abevrour (*m. fr.* abreuvoir), a watering-place, i. 400.

Bier, byer, to gape, *hence* to wish, intend, i. 350, ii. 134, 167. *See Duc. Gloss. s. v.* beare *and Gloss. Fr. in Duc. s. v.* beer, baer, beier.

Bille, a bill, a legal instrument by which an action is commenced, i. 83; *see Year Book,* 30 *Edw. I.*, p. 157.

Blemir, to injure, i. 327.

Blemure, a blemish, disfigurement, i. 123.

Bon estre; plus del bon estre qe de la substaunce, more of the form than of the substance, i. 254.

Bosoigne, bosoygne (*m. fr.* besoin), need, i. 61; business, i. 254; **ad besoigne, fet bosoigne,** it is necessary, ii. 227, 228.

Bosoigne, *v.* it needs, ii. 224, 228.

Bounde (*m. fr.* borne), a boundary, i. 81, ii. 71.

Bouter, boter, to push, thrust, compel, i. 45, 58; **se boter eynz, se boter,** to take possession, i. 266, 311, ii. 54; **bouter avaunt,** to put forward, ii. 110.

Bozoun, a kind of arrow, ii. 11; *see Duc. Gloss. s. v.* Bolzonus.

Bref, 1. a writ; 2. an action commenced by writ, ii. 161.

Broche, a brooch, pin, ii. 11; *see Duc. Gloss. s. v.* Broca; *Spelman, Gloss. s. v.* brochia. *Spelman interprets* brochia *in Bracton f.* 35 *b*, a can or jug, *but this is probably an error; see* ii. 11, *note.*

Bruser (*m. fr.* briser), to break, break into (enter with force), i. 42, 78.

Brusure, a breaking, a bruise, i. 122.

Bultel (*m. fr.* bluteau), a bolter or sieve for flour, i. 186, 188.

Burgesour, burgeysour, burglar, i. 42.

Bussel (*m. fr.* boisseau), a bushel, i. 186.

Carier (*m. fr.* charrier), to cart, to carry, i. 360, 365.

Carue de terre (*med. lat.* carucata terræ), a carucate or ploughland, ii. 143, 144.

Cendal, silk, i. 96.

Cep, stock of descent, ii. 320, 323.

***Cervoire**, a preserve of deer, ii. 251.

Cessioun, session, sitting, i. 298.

Chace, 1. a chace, a district devoted to hunting, i. 358; 2. a drift or drove-way, right of driving cattle through another's land, i. 301, 302, 363, 398; *see Termes de la Ley, s. v.* chase; *Co. Lit.* 56 *a*; **chemin de chace**, a drift way, i. 407.

Chaleng, chalenge, a challenge, objection, claim, i. 14, 30, ii. 95, 342.

Chalenger, 1. to challenge or object (to a juror), i. 30, ii. 85; 2. to challenge or claim, i. 69, ii. 25.

Chalis (*m. fr.* calice), chalice, i. 214.

Champart, chaumpart, champerty, division of profits, i. 94, 215.

Chanele, chanel (*m. fr.* canal, chenal), channel of a river, i. 218.

Charette (*m. fr.* chariot), cart, i. 15.

Chargeaunt, weighty, forcible, ii. 147.

Charnelé (*med. lat.* crenellatus), furnished with battlements, fortified, i. 78.

Charneus amis, kindred, i. 347. *See Duc. Gloss. s. v.* carnalis.

Chatel, *pl.* **chateus**, chattel, i. 27.

Chauciage, a toll or tax for maintaining a causeway or high road, i. 92.

Chaunceler, to cancel, i. 314.

Chayt, chayst, chei (*pret. from* cheyer), fell, i. 15.

Chef; *see* **chief**.

Chefage, chevage, head-money, money paid by a villain in recognition of the lord's right to his service, i. 201.

Chef plege, headborough or tithingman, i. 181.

Cheminage, a kind of toll; *see* i. 75.

Chescuni, every man's, i. 85, ii. 53.

Chever; *see* **achever**.

Cheus (*past part. from* **cheyer**), fallen, i. 16.

Cheyer, cheer (*lat.* cadere, *m. fr.* choir), to fall, i. 16, 39.

Chief, chef, head; **en prime chief**, in the first place, ii. 216; **tener en chief de ascun**, to hold of him immediately, i. 254, 256; *so* **chief seignur**, the immediate lord, i. 252, ii. 148, 155. *But in Glanvill, lib.* 9. *c.* 1, capitalis dominus *is the liege lord; compare Britton, vol. ii. p.* 41; *Fleta*, p. 10 (§ 7), 344 (§ 1).

Ci la qe, si la qe, until, i. 124, 128, ii. 247, 345. *See Roq. Gloss. s. vv.* si la que, ferlin.

Cirographe, chirograph, the record of a fine, i. 95, 310.

Cirographer, to make a chirograph, ii. 356.

Cirographer, a writer of chirographs, i. 94.

Cist, he, this, i. 268.

Cloaunt (*part. from* **clore**, to close), closing, concluding, i. 103.

Coket, cokette; payn de coket, a kind of bread of middle quality, inferior to wastel, i. 186.

Colueré (*m. fr.* coloré), coloured, ii. 277.

Comaunde; ad comaunde a estre, is commanded to be, ii. 256.

Comensable, that may be begun, ii. 292.

Coment il ne deive, although he ought, ii. 252.

Commune, community, common right, i. 369, 373; **commune de gent**, human society, ii. 356.

Communer, a commoner, or person enjoying a right of common, i. 343, 371.

Communer, 1. to communicate, i. 65, 322; 2. to common, enjoy a common right, i. 371.

Compasser, to compass, contrive, i. 40.

***Condouner**, to attribute, adjudge, ii. 4.

Coniger, rabbit warren, i. 357, ii. 69.

Coniys, conys (*lat.* cuniculi), conies, rabbits, i. 85.

Conquestre, *var. read.* **conquere** (*m. fr.* conquérir), to acquire, recover by action, ii. 208, 319.

Conrey, correy, *pl.* **conreiz** (*lat.* conredium), a corrody, or allowance for board in a monastery, i. 280.

Conseiler, conseiller, to provide with counsel, *used of a church to which a parson is instituted*, ii. 177, 204; *see* **desconseilé**.

Consense, *subst. fem.* consent, i. 99, 108.

Conseut, *from* **consure** (*lat.* consequi), it follows, ii. 228.

Contecker, to contest, i. 283.

Contek, contest, i. 283, ii. 176.

Conversaunt, conversant, living, i. 184.

Corner, corner, i. 107.

Corsue, large, coarse, i. 367. *See Fr. Gloss. in Duc. s. v.* corsus.

Cortiner, i. 372. *Carpentier, in Duc. Gloss. s. v.* incortinare, *citing this place of Britton, interprets* **curtiner** *as meaning* to enclose, *connecting it with* incortinare, to curtain in; *but perhaps the better reading is* **cotiver** *or* **coutiver**, to cultivate. *See* **cutefier**.

Costié, costé (*m. fr.* côte, côté), side, coast, i. 219, ii. 165.

Cotel (*m. fr.* couteau), knife, i. 37, 354.

Counter, to count, *used of the plaintiff's pleading*, i. 101, 204. **en counte countaunt**, 1. in pleading, i. 72, ii. 150; 2. to account; 3. to deem, i. 123, ii. 267.

Countour, accountant, i. 347.

Countre ester, to resist. *See* **encountre ester**.

Countrefere, to destroy, i. 401.

Countreluter (*lat.* contra luctari), to struggle against, ii. 77.

Countremeyn, on the other hand, ii. 163.

Countremount, ascending, ii. 320.

Countrepan, counterpart, corresponding obligation, i. 237.

Countreroullour (*med. lat.* contrarotulator), controller, keeper of a counter-roll, i. 17.

Countreval, below, downwards, ii. 164, 166.

Countrevaler, to countervail, to be equivalent to, i. 260.

Coupe (*lat.* culpa), fault, i. 157, ii. 216.

Couperie des bourses, cutting of purses, i. 60.

Coute (*lat.* cubitus, *m. fr.* coudée), a cubit, i. 189.

Covenable, suitable, ii. 247.

Covenir = **convenir**, to agree, to be agreed, ii. 115.

Covert; **chevaus covertz**, war-horses, horses armed for battle, i. 354, ii. 10.

Coveytise (*m. fr.* convoitise), covetousness, i. 32.

Cowe (*m. fr.* queue), tail, i. 68.

Coyne; *see* **cyre de coyne**.

Crampu de goute, cramped or disabled by gout, i. 90.

***Creysurz** (*var. read.* **cressours, croysurs**), i. 220. *The phrase*, **engendrure de creysurz**, *is used with reference to acquiring a title by the curtesy of England. Possibly it may mean* crying children (auditos infra quatuor parietes, *Glanvill, li.* 7. c. 18, *Bracton, f.* 438), *from the old French verb* croissir, *or* croistre (*lat.* crepere, crepitare), to squeak or creak; *see* i. 341, ii. 142.

Crie, crye, proclamation, i. 107.

Curtilage, the court-yard or curtilage of a house, i. 279.

Custage, costs, expenses, i. 68, ii. 15.

Cutefier, to cultivate, ii. 68; *but* quære, *whether we should not read* **coutiver**, *or* **cotiver**. *See* **cortiner**.

Cuture (*lat.* cultura), a plot of cultivated land, ii. 67, 70.

Cyllour des bourses, cutpurse, i. 62, 179.

Cyre de coyne, *qu.* sealing-wax, i. 96, *var. read. See Duc. Gloss. s. v.* cognus.

Damasche, damesche, tame, domesticated, i. 122, 216.

Dareyn, derreyn, dreyn (*m. fr.* dernier), last, i. 24, ii. 231; **dreyn present**, last presentation, ii. 169.

Darré (*med. lat.* denariata, *ital.* derrata, *m. fr.* denrée), money's worth, goods, merchandise, ii. 240.

Debarrer, to exclude, i. 305.

Deboter, debouter, to thrust out, i. 249, 292. *See* **bouter**.

Debruser, to break, break out of (prison), i. 43.

Decert, merit, desert, i. 52. *See* **deservir**.

Deceyte, *subst. fem.* (*lat.* deceptio), deceit, ii. 333.

Deceyvable, deceptive, ii. 214, 242.

Decyrer (*m. fr.* déchirer), to tear.

De eynz, deynz, within, i. 10, 12.

Deeynzime, internal, ii. 213.

Defamé (*lat.* defamatus), degraded, infamous, i. 61.

Defens, *subst. masc.*, prohibition, i. 152, 205.

Defere, to undo, defeat, i. 302, ii. 153; *qu.* to deny, i. 141.

Defforcer, deforcer, to deforce, eject by force, i. 73, ii. 143.

Definer, to cease, ii. 264.

Defuyr (3 *pers. sing.* **defut**, *pret.* **defuy**), to fly, desert, i. 204.

***Degez**, *part. pl.* (*qu. lat.* dejecti), *used only of lepers*; **mesels degez**, lepers put out of society, i. 227, 347. *See also* i. 224, *var. read.*

Deguerpir, to abandon, i. 200, 214. *See* **guerpir**.

Del, *for* **de le**, of the, i. 2.

Delayer, to delay, i. 95, 243.

Delit de peché, sinful excess, i. 227.

Deloyaunce, illegality, i. 252.

Demaunt, 3 *pers. sing. subj. from* **de-**

maunder, to ask, demand. *Compare* **graunt** *for* **graunde.**

Demesne, demeyne, *subst.* (*lat.* dominium, terra dominica), demesne, domain, ii. 123; **auncienes demeynes,** ancient demesne, i. 69.

Demeyne, demeene, *adj.* (*qu. lat.* dominicus), own; **nos ministres demeynes,** our own officers, i. 80, 314, ii. 140.

Demoustraunce, declaration or count, the plaintiff's statement of his case, ii. 166; **demoustrance de sa entente,** ii. 182.

Dené (*lat.* decanatus, *m. fr.* doyenné), deanery, i. 317.

Deodande (*lat.* deodandum), a deodand, i. 16, 39.

Departable, divisible, subject to partition, ii. 76.

Departer, departir, to withdraw, ii. 41; to divide, ii. 65, 75.

Deprecatif, precarious, i. 362.

Deques, deqe, *more commonly* **jekes,** until, i. 290, 342.

Des *is used as a negative prefix, as* **despuniz,** unpunished, i. 29; **despris,** untaken, i. 86; **desgarni,** unprovided, i. 26.

Desafoeblir, to disconnect, i. 76. *See Duc. Gloss. s. v.* affibulare, diffibulare; *Bescherelle Dict. Fr. s. v.* désaffubler.

Desassenter, to disagree, i. 334.

Desatamé, not begun, i. 133.

Desavisé, unadvised, inconsiderate, i. 282.

Desblemi, uninjured, ii. 26, 75.

Deschalenges, unchallenged, i. 30.

Desconseilé, desconselé, deprived of counsel, disconsolate (*used of a vacant fief or benefice*), ii. 49, 176, 181.

Desconuz, unknown, i. 139.

Descovenable, inconvenient, i. 158.

Descovert, uncovered, i. 64, ii. 125.

Desdire, dedire, to refuse, i. 34, ii. 98; to deny, i. 135, ii. 95, 127.

Desenfower, to dig out, disinter, i. 9.

Deservir (*med. lat.* deservire), to deserve, merit, ii. 280; to forfeit a right, ii. 233, 281.

Deseverer, to dissever, ii. 90.

***Desgager** (*med. lat.* disvadiare), to release upon security (for damage done by trespassing), i. 381. *See Duc. Gloss. s. v.* vadium, desgagium; *compare Leg. Hen. I. c.* 57.

Desheritisoun, disheritesoun, disherison, i. 41, 280.

De si qe = de sicum, inasmuch as, i. 222.

De sicum, desicum, inasmuch as, i. 207, &c.

Desleal, illegal, ii. 17.

Desmembrer, to dismember (*used of the division of a barony or lordship held* in capite), i. 71, 73, ii. 76.

Desnaturel, unnatural, i. 208.

De sour, upon, ii. 268.

Desouth, desuth, de suth (*lat.* sub, subtus), under, i. 23.

Desparager, to match unequally, disparage, ii. 24.

Despeiré, unexpected, i. 358.

Despescaunt, despising, ii. 232.

Despiser, to despise, i. 414.

Despit; en despit de lour defaute, by way of punishment for their default (in odium defaltæ, *Fleta, p.* 226), i. 305; *so* **en despit de sa force,** by way of punishment for his violence, i. 414.

Despitousement, contemptuously, ii. 172.

Desplaer (*m. fr.* déployer), to unfurl, display, i. 354.

Despris, unapprehended (*of a prisoner*), i. 86.

Desreyner, disreyner, dreyner (*med. lat.* disrationare), to prove, deraign, to recover by deraignment, i. 105, 249, 324, ii. 190, 273. *The word* deredner *occurs in this sense in the French laws of William the Conqueror, c. ii.*

Destaunce, difference, dispute, i. 320, ii. 41.

Desterminé, undetermined, i. 133, 318.

Destincter (*m. fr.* distinguer), to distinguish, i. 410, ii. 277.

Destourbaunce, hindrance, disturbance, i. 275, 361.

Destourber, desturber, to hinder, i. 116; to disturb (*in legal sense*), i. 375.

Destreindre, destreyndre, to distrain, i. 126, 146, 160.

Destresce, distress, seizure of goods, i. 136.

Destrescer = estrescer, to straighten, narrow, i. 81, 279.

Destreynable, distrainable, subject to distress, i. 12, 142,

Desusez, disused, i. 79.

Detrier, to try, determine by judgment, i. 326, ii. 80.

Devaunt meyn, beforehand, in advance, i. 270.

Deveier, to deny, refuse, i. 400. *See* **vier.**

Devier, to die, i. 242, ii. 193.

Devisable, 1. divisible, ii. 57; 2. devisable, that may be given by will, i. 142, 198.

Devises, divises, *pl.* divisions, boundaries, i. 81, ii. 71.

Dimissioun, a demise or lease, i. 225.

Discus, *part. pass. from* **discuter,** to discuss, ii. 44.

Disjointe; par disjointe, en disjointe, disjunctively, severally, ii. 354, 358.

Disparagacioun, disparagement, ii. 23.

Disreyne, dreyne, deraignment, proof, i. 391. ii. 292, *note.*

Disseisine, disseisin, dispossession, i. 212.

Disseisir, to disseise, dispossess, i. 272.

Dizeiner, dizeyner (*med. lat.* decennarius), a tithingman, headborough, i. 48, 49.

Dizeyne, dixeyne (*med. lat.* decenna), a tithing, or ten-mens-tale, i. 13, 48, 181.

Dorra, dourrount, *fut. from* **douner** (*m. fr.* donner), to give, i. 215.

Dotaunce, doubt, i. 252, ii. 53.

Dounc, dunc, then (of time), i. 408; in that case, i. 12; therefore, ii. 33.

Dowarie, dowarrie, *subst. fem.* dower, i. 331, 332. *So in MS.* L; *in other MSS.* doweir *or* doweyre *subst. masc. is more common; see* i. 37.

Dras *pl.* (*m. fr.* draps), cloth, clothes, i. 83, 93.

Dreit (*m. fr.* droit), 1. right, law, i. 45, 360, 362; 2. subject, matter, **en plus haut dreit,** in higher matter, i. 30; **en dreit des Justices,** in reference to the Justices, i. 3; **ou en dreit** (*m. fr.* dans quel endroit), in what place or direction, i. 332.

Dreyn = dareyn (*m. fr.* dernier), last, i. 79, ii. 61.

Dreyne; *see* **disreyne.**

Dreyner; *see* **desreyner.**

Duresce, hardship, oppression, ii. 246.

Ees (*lat.* apes), bees, i. 215.

Efforcier, to strengthen, ii. 186.

***Eindegré; par soen eyndegré, de soen eindegré,** voluntarily, ii. 287, 293. *Compare Roq. Gloss. s. v.* aingréer.

Einz; *see* **eynz.**

Eirt; *see* **ert.**

El = en le, in the, ii. 115, 133.

Embatement, enbatement = abatement, abatement, usurpation of a tenement, ii. 4. *See* **enbatre.**

Emprover, enprouwer, to cultivate, employ for profit, ii. 14, 24. *See Duc. Gloss. s. v.* appruare; *Fleta, p.* 164, 170; *Stat. Westm.* 2, *c.* 46.

***Enaumoyner,** to give land to religious uses, ii. 13, *var. read. So in the Coutumier de Normandie en vers, chap. xlii,*

> L'en dit ceux tenir teneure
> Par omosne, qui terre pure
> Tiennent, qui furent ausmonées
> A Dieu et a ses Sains donnés.
>
> *Houard, Dictionaire de droit Normand, tome iv, supplément, p.* 81.

Enbatement, abatement, ii. 354.

Enbatre (*elsewhere* **abatre**), to abate, usurp possession; **sei enbatre en le heritage,** ii. 2.

Enbeverer, (*m. fr.* abreuver), to water cattle, i. 395, 400.

Enbeverer = abevrour (*m. fr.* abreuvoir), a watering-place, i. 279.

Enbrever (*med. lat.* imbreviare), to imbreviate, enroll, i. 14, 17, 18, 303, ii. 72.

Encepper (*med. lat.* incippare; *see Duc. Gloss. s. v.* cippus), to put in the stocks, i. 323.

Ences, enceys; *see* **eynz.**

Enchacer, to drive away, i. 139, 275, 381.

***Encheminer,** to travel, i. 65, ii. 344.

Enchesoun = achesun (*lat.* occasio), cause, occasion, i. 15, 16.

Enchesouner (*med. lat.* occasionare, *Bracton, f.* 75 *b*, *Fleta, p.* 35, § 7), to call in question, i. 182.

Enclousture, inclosure, shutting in, i. 215.

Encountre ester, to resist, i. 418, ii. 282.

Encountrer, to meet, i. 308.

Encouper = acouper (*m. fr.* inculper), to indict, i. 26, 59.

Encoure (*m. fr.* encourir), to incur, to run against, i. 246.

Encousture, the act of closing (of a door), i. 261.

Encres, encrez, increase, i. 218.

Encuser = acuser, to accuse, i. 33, 98; to dispute, ii. 274.

Endeblé (*lat.* debilitatus), enfeebled, ii. 184.

Endementers (*ital.* mentre), meanwhile, i. 19, 26.

Endenté, *part.* indented, written in the form of an indenture, in two or more parts, i. 24, 251.

Enditer, to indict, i. 30.

Engetter, engeter, engitter, engiter (*lat.* ejicere), to eject, i. 226, 228.

Englescherie, Englishery, the fact of a murdered man being an Englishman, i. 17, 38.

Engyn, contrivance, i. 25, 165, 314.

Enhauncer, enhaucer, to exalt, raise, enhance, i. 106, 302.

Enke (*med. lat.* incaustrum), ink, i. 314.

Enmaladir, to fall sick, i. 112.

Ennuyer, to injure, i. 398.

Enoyter, to increase, extend, i. 2.

Enparkement, impounding, ii. 384.

Enparker, to impound, i. 90, 381.

Enparler, entreparler, to emparl (*a term used of the consultation of a jury*), i. 350, ii. 198.

Enpleder, empleder (*med. lat.* implacitare), to implead, sue at law, i. 169, 267.

Enprendre, to undertake, ii. 97, 110, 136.

En present, present, i. 182, ii. 244.

Enprimes, **en primes**, **a primes** (*lat.* imprimis), first, ii. 20, 56.

Enprouwer; *see* **emprover.**

Enpurtenant = apurtenant, appertaining, ii. 190, *var. read.* 1.

Ens, es = en les, in the, i. 225, ii. 163, 165.

Ensample, example, i. 154.

Enseler (*m. fr.* sceller), to seal, i. 23.

Ensemblement, together, i. 230, ii. 146.

Ensement, likewise, ii. 221, 303.

***Ensenses** (*m. fr.* enseigné), informed, i. 32, 300, ii. 159.

Ensint, ensi = issint, issi (*m. fr.* ainsi), so, i. 36, 80.

Ensure (*m. fr.* ensuivre), to follow; *subj.* **ensue**, ii. 162.

***Ent = en** (*lat.* inde, *m. fr.* en), therefrom, thereof, thence, ii. 105. *With the form* **ent** *compare* **dount, par ount.**

Entencioun = entente (*lat.* intentio), the contention or demand of the plaintiff in an action, i. 126, ii. 174.

Entendant, attendant, subordinate, i. 4, 5.

Entendre (*lat.* intendere), to contend, ii. 34; **si le tenaunt le voille entendre**, if the tenant chooses to accept the challenge, *qu.*, ii. 34.

Entente = entencioun (*lat.* intentio), the contention or demand of the plaintiff in an action, ii. 94, 95, 173, 274.

Ententivement, attentively, i. 32.

Entitler (*med. lat.* intitulare), to authorize, i. 5, 7, 315, ii. 170.

***Entrebat**, *a term used of a seisin derived from the tortious entry of another*, ii. 300.

Entrepreter, to interpret, i. 414.

Enveer, enveier, enveyer (*m. fr.* envoyer), to send, i. 133, 152, ii. 250.

Ercevask, ercevesk, archevak, arcevasqe, archbishop, i. 21, 131.

Erent (*lat.* erant), were, i. 207.

Errauntz = heyrauntz, itinerant, i. 3, 20.

Ert, eirt, iert, *pl.* **erunt** (*lat.* erit, erunt), will be, i. 53, 209, 267.

Eschaete, eschete, escheat, i. 32, 36.

Eschalere (*m. fr.* échalier, *or qu.* escalier), fence (*or qu.* steps); *see* i. 63, *note.*

Eschap (*m. fr.* échappée), an escape, i. 44, 87.

Escharcement, barely, scarcely, ii. 125, *note.*

Eschauder (*m. fr.* échauder), to scald, *qu.* to suffocate; *see p.* 9, *note.*

Eschere, escheer (*m. fr.* échoir), to fall in, to escheat, i. 37, 70, ii. 75.

Eschetour, escheator, i. 85.

Eschure, escure, to eschew, avoid, i. 15, ii. 145.

Escient (*lat.* sciens, scienter), conscious; **a escient**, knowingly, i. 48; **a lour escient**, i. 30; **a sa escient**, i. 294; **as escienz les disseisiz**, i. 296; **al escient des seignurs**, i. 374.

Esclaundre (*med. lat.* scandalum), slander, i. 32, 121.

Escoillé, escoillié, disabled from procreation, impotent, ii. 16. *See Duc. Gloss. s. v.* excoliatus.

Escorger (*lat.* excoriare, *m. fr.* écorcher), to skin, flay, i. 84.

Escoundire, to excuse, ii. 93. *See Duc. Gloss. s. v.* excondicere.

Escrouwe, escrowe, scroll, ii. 71.

Escumengé, excommunicated, i. 322.

Esmer (*lat.* æstimare), to value, i. 45.

Especialment, especiaument, expressly, by special mention, i. 253.

Especialté, especiauté, specialty, peculiarity, express mention, i. 220; **especiaulté de fet, especiauté de escrit**, express mention in deed, or writing, i. 224, 279.

Espeye, espee, sword, i. 354, ii. 74.

Espleis, espletz (*med. lat.* expletia), esplees, profits of land, i. 260, ii. 49, 135.

Esporoun (*m. fr.* éperon), **uns esporouns**, *qu.* a pair of spurs, ii. 11.

Esprendre (*m. fr.* éprendre, *or qu.* épreindre); **sei esprendre**, to take effect, vest, ii. 187, 322.

Esprist (se), took effect, vested, i. 268.

Espurger (*lat.* expurgare), to clean out, i. 364.

Esquacher (*lat.* quassare), to break, disfigure, i. 314, *var. read.*

Essoigne, essoyne, essoignie (*med. lat.* essonium), essoin, excuse for non-appearance in court, i. 20, ii. 88.

***Essomaunte**, a pretended wife, a concubine, ii. 241, 242.

Essonier, essoiner, to essoin, i. 139, ii. 88.

Essoniour, an essoiner, ii. 88.

Estaunc, estaunck, estaung (*lat.* stagnum, *m. fr.* étang), pond, pool, stank, i. 398, 399, ii. 67.

Estable, stable, firm, ii. 295.

Estaundard, a standard of weight or measure, i. 186, 189.

Esteins=**esteynt**, extinct, i. 39, 262.

Estendre (*law lat.* extendere), to value, i. 86, ii. 67, 70.

Estente (*law lat.* extenta), an extent or valuation of land, ii. 67.

Ester (*lat.* stare), to stand; *subj.* **estoyse**, i. 101; **ester a dreit** (*med. lat.* stare ad rectum), to submit to justice, i. 140, 150.

Esterling, an English penny, a penny sterling, i. 188, *note.*

Estil (*m. fr.* style), style, manner of drawing writs, i. 314.

Estoper, estouper, to stop (a road or river), i. 81, 183.

Estor, farming stock, ii. 21; military stores, ii. 10, *var. read.*

Estora=**estovera**, it will need, ii. 98, 251.

Estorer, to stock, store, ii. 21.

Estovera, estovereit, it will, would, be necessary, i. 35, ii. 112, 186. *See* **estut.**

Estovers, materials, provisions, estovers, i. 395, 396.

Estray, an estray or animal strayed, i. 67, 216; the right to appropriate such animals, ii. 252.

Estrayer, to stray, i. 216.

Estre (*lat.* extra), beyond, beside; **estre ceo**, moreover, i. 5.

Estreper (*lat.* exstirpare), to root out, destroy, i. 36.

Estrescer, estrescier (*m. fr.* étrécir), to limit, narrow, restrict, i. 254, 399.

Estretes (*med. lat.* extracta), estreats, extracts from the exchequer rolls, i. 89, 193.

Estrif, strife, i. 335.

Estriver, to strive, ii. 254.

Estut, estoit, it needs, ii. 247; *fut.* **estovera, estora**, it will be necessary, ii. 98, 251.

Evask, evak, bishop, i. 21, 131.

***Eve; de eve et de treve** (*lat.* ab avo et tritavo), from generation to generation, i. 196, *note.*

***Eweresce**, of water; **molin ewerescе**, water-mill, i. 360. *Compare* ventresce.

Exceper, exciper, to except, exclude, i. 311, ii. 183.

Exigende, exigend or exigent (*a part of the process in outlawry*). *See* i. 13, *note.*

Exil (*lat.* exilium), exile; the driving away of villains from an estate, ii. 6, 22.

Eyndegré; see **eindegré.**

Eynz, einz, *conj.* but, ii. 81, 84, 225.

Eynz, de eynz, deynz (*lat.* intra), within, ii. 225.

Eynz, *prep.* (*lat.* ante), before; **eynz ceo, eynz ces**, ii. 190, **eynzces**, ii. 107, 118, **enceys, enceis**, ii. 77, 101, **ences**, ii. 175, *adv.* (*lat.* antea), before.

Eynznee, eynzné, eyné, *fem.* **eynzneesce** (*med. lat.* antenatus, *m. fr.* aîné), elder, eldest, i. 49; earlier (*of a writ*), i. 290.

Eynznescerie (*m. fr.* aînesse), seniority, birthright, i. 171.

Eyrer, heyrer (*lat.* itinerare), to hold the eyre, ii. 334.

***Faleisé** (*med. lat.* infalistatus, *from fr.* falaise), put to death by burial in the seashore (*a form of execution used at Dover, Hengham Parva, p.* 87).

Faude (*lat.* falda), a fold, i. 279. *The nusance of 'fold,' spoken of in this passage, is the damage done to a lord by erecting a fold for sheep in derogation of his right of faldage, i. e. to have the tenant's sheep to manure his land. See Spelman, Gloss. s. v.* falda; *Domesday of St. Paul's, pp. lxxxix,* 105.

Fausener, a falsifier, forger, i. 25.

Fausenerie, fausine, the crime of falsification, forgery, i. 25, 33.

Fee, fé, fié, *pl.* **feez, fiez** (*lat.* feodum), fee, feud, fief; *used in various senses:* 1. seigniory, lordship, i. 229, 381; **de qi fee qe les terres soint**, in whose lordship soever the lands be, ii. 7; 2. tenure, ii. 5, 11; **tener par fee de chivaler**, to hold in chivalry; 3. land held by feudal tenure, heritable land, ii. 6, 129; 4. an annual payment granted for service, i. 270; 5. a fee or sum of money taken by a public officer, i. 47.

Fee ferme, *pl.* **fee fermes** *and* **feez fermes** (*lat.* feodi firma), fee farm, a free tenure the services of which were rendered in money, i. 4, ii. 8, 11. *In later times, when socage was free, fee farm was undistinguishable from socage: see Coke, Inst. part ii. p.* 44; *Co. Lit.* 143 *b.*

Feffement, feoffament, feoffment, ii. 135.

Feffer, to enfeoff, ii. 136.

Felounesse, *adj.* felonious, i. 43.

Felounousement, feloniously, i. 42.

Fere qe sages, to act wisely. *So in Les Tournois de Chauvenci, line* 1234.

Ferling, the quarter of a denarius, a farthing, i. 186.

Fet (*m. fr.* faut), it is necessary, i. 370.

Feuté, fealty, i. 185.

Feyre, feire (*m. fr.* foire), a fair, i. 75.

Filaz (*med. lat.* filacium), a file or tape upon which writs or other documents were strung together, i. 321.

Finiement, end, i. 306.

Firges, fyrges, fers, fetters, irons, i. 27, 35.

Foer (*lat.* forum), market, price, i. 193; **a foer de franc homme**, on the level of a free man, i. 200, *note.*

Fol nastre, an idiot or natural fool, i. 42, 52, 98, 223; **fol nastre de nativité**, ii. 155. *The word* **folnastre** *appears to be wrongly interpreted in Roq. Gloss.*, archifou. *See* **sot nastre.**

Forbarrer, to shut out, ii. 319.

Forcelette, a fortress, fortlet. *See Duc. Gloss. s. v.* forcellettum.

Forclore, forsclore, to exclude, ii. 316, 319.

Foreyn (*lat.* forinsecus), foreign, out of the manor, ii. 69; **el foreyn**, out of the lord's jurisdiction, i. 57.

Forjuger, to forjudge, deprive by judgment, i. 51, 65.

Forjurer, to abjure, i. 65.

Fornage (*from lat.* furnus), payment for an oven, i. 188.

Forner, fornir, fournir, to perform, furnish, i. 21, 353, ii. 273.

Fornier (*med. lat.* furnire, *from* furnus), to bake, i. 191.

Forprendre, to except, exclude, i. 311.

Forprise, exception, i. 308.

Forstallour, forstaller, one who buys goods for the purpose of raising the price, i. 84.

Founs (*m. fr.* fonts), font, i. 111.

Founs (*m. fr.* fond), bottom, i. 16.

Fourme de doun (*lat.* forma doni), formedon, gift in tail, writ of formedon, ii. 120, 128.

Foyer, fouwer (*m. fr.* fouir), to dig, to take turf, i. 395, ii. 68.

Fra, frount, *fut. from* **fere**, to do, i. 63.

***Frape des gentz**, multitude of people, i. 93. *Compare Duc. Gloss. s. v.* frappa; *Roq. Gloss. s. v.* frapail.

Fraunc plege, fraung plege (*lat.* francus plegius), frankpledge, i. 7, 9, 181. *The French and Latin terms appear to have arisen from a misunderstanding of the Anglo-Saxon* Friðborh *or* Friborh, pledge of peace. *See* i. 181, *note.*

Freit, freynt, *cond. from* **fere**, to do, ii. 98, 101.

Fresche, fresh, recent, i. 36.

Furment, forment (*m. fr.* froment), wheat, i. 186, 188.

Fust, *pl.* **fustz** (*lat.* fustis), wood, i. 64, 93.

Futif (*lat.* fugitivus), fugitive, serf residing out of his lord's jurisdiction without leave, i. 200.

Gager sa ley, to wage his law, *that is*, to pledge his faith supported by cojurors, i. 151.

Garbe (*m. fr.* gerbe), sheaf, i. 91.

Garnir, to warn, i. 126, 350.

Gast, guast (*med. lat.* vastum), waste, i. 290, 344.

Gastel (*m. fr.* gâteau), wastel, the finest kind of wheaten bread, i. 186.

Gayner, to till, i. 368, ii. 9.

Gaynerie, tillage, i. 344, 357.

Gaynour, tiller, ii. 13.

Gelousie, excessive fondness, ii. 269.

Gers; *see* **n'ad gers puis.**

Gilour, deceiver, cheat, i. 60.

Glebee, glebe, land to which an advowson is appurtenant, ii. 173. *Compare Year Book,* 30 *Edw. I. p.* 207.

Graunt, *masc. and fem.*, great, i. 271, ii. 112.

Gravele (*m. fr.* gravier), sand, shingle, i. 216.

Greable, voluntary, i. 259.

Gree, gré, agreement, intention, i. 71, ii. 135; **fere soen gre**, to make him satisfaction, ii. 102; **fere gree de soen mariage**, to compound for his marriage, ii. 25; **aver a gré et estable**, to consent to, confirm, i. 263, ii. 295.

Greef, gref, greve, heavy, i. 14.

Greynure, i. 31; **greinure**, ii. 270; **greynur**, ii. 306; **greyndre**, ii. 159; (*lat.* grandior), greater.

Guerpir (*A. S.* weorpan, *Germ.* werfen), to throw away, to abandon, i. 214.

Hamsokne (*an English word*), hamsoken (homeseeking), attack on a man's house, i. 84, 180.

Handhabbynde (*an English word*), handhaving, having in hand, i. 182.

Harascz, *pl.* (*m. fr.* haras), studs or breeds of horses, ii. 68.

Haspe (*A. S.* hæps, *m. fr.* happe), hasp, i. 261.

Hastivesce (*m. fr.* hâtiveté), haste, ii. 219.

Haunge, hayne (*m. fr.* haine), hatred, i. 22, 122.

Haye, haie (*A. S.* haga, *m. fr.* haie), a hay, or inclosure for deer in a park, ii. 67, 78.

Heiret, *pl.* **heireez**, heriot, i. 71.

Herberger (*m. fr.* héberger), *va.* to harbour, entertain, i. 49; *vn.* to lodge, i. 93, ii. 246.

Heu et cri, hue and cry, an alarm raised for the pursuit of felons, i. 37.

Heyr (*lat.* hæres), heir, i. 35.

Heyr (*lat.* aer), air, i. 213.

Heyre (*lat.* iter), the eyre or circuit of the Justices Itinerant, i. 18.

Heyrer, to make the eyre, i. 20; **Justices heyrauntz**, Itinerant Justices, i. 75.

Hochepot, hotchpot, common property, i. 305, ii. 74, 79.

Hom, *short form of* **homme**, man, *is found where in modern French* on *or* l'on *is used*, i. 1.

Hors (*m. fr.* lors); **hors de sa seisine**, at the time of his seisin, ii. 109.

Host, ost, host, warlike expedition, i. 99, ii. 10.

Houre, hore (*lat.* hora), hour, time, i. 1, ii. 153; **quel houre**, as soon as, i. 275, 277.

Huteys (*med. lat.* hutesium), hue and cry, i. 179.

Idle (*lat.* insula), island, i. 219.

Iert=**ert** (*lat.* erit), will be, i. 267.

Illoekes, illucs (*lat.* illic, illuc), there, i. 19.

Impetracioun, claim, demand, i. 209.

Infangenthef (*an English word*), Infangthef (a franchise so called), i. 56, 222, 228.

Inlagerie, inlawry, restitution to law, i. 51.

Institut, *part.* instituted to a benefice by the bishop, i. 267, ii. 176.

Interpretisoun (*lat.* interpretatio), interpretation, i. 252.

Issi, issint, so, thus, i. 96, 252, ii. 103.

Issir, to issue; **s'en issi**, went out, ii. 135.

Istrai, *qu. fut. from* **issir**, I will depart, i. 64.

Itel, such, ii. 149.

Ja (*qu. lat.* jam), now, henceforth, i. 30, 47, ii. 132, 264; **ja ne**, never, i. 330; still, yet, ii. 182, 186; **ja pur ceo ne remeyndra**, yet it does not follow, i. 380, ii. 141.

***Jalemeyns, jalemeyns ne**, nevertheless, i. 9, 141, 264, 318.

Jaungle, careless talk, ii. 215.

Jekes, jeqes, *also* **deqes, deques** (*lat.* usque, *m. fr.* jusques), until; *followed by the prep.* **a** *and* **en**, i. 333, 334, ii. 86; **jekes autaunt**, until, ii. 100.

Jeuparti, gambling, *hence* risk, jeopardy, i. 318. *See Duc. Gloss. s. v.* jocus partitus; *Bracton, f.* 212 *b*; *Hengham Magna, c. iv. p.* 13.

***Journaunt**, dawn, ii. 133, 134.

Joyr, joyer (*m. fr.* jouir), to enjoy, i. 28, 294.

Jue (*m. fr.* Juif), Jew, i. 311.

Juise, juyse (*lat.* judicium), 1. punishment, i. 61, 182; 2. instrument of punishment, such as gallows, pillory, or tumbrell, i. 79, 180, *note*, 191; 3. jurisdiction implied by the possession of such instruments, i. 75, 181. *In the French laws of William I.* § 14, *the ordeal* (judicium aquæ vel ignis) *is called* juise.

Jurz, *pl.* of **jur**, a day, i. 63.

Justice, *subst. fem.* (*med. lat.* justicia, *used for* Justiciarius), Justice, Justiciary, i. 19, 20.

Justicer (se), to submit to justice, i. 161.

Justizable, amenable to justice, subject to the jurisdiction of a court, i. 222.

Juvene (*m. fr.* jeune), young, ii. 37.

Keus (*lat.* coqui), cooks, i. 83.

La eynz=**leynz**, therein, i. 264, ii. 164.

Latoun, latten, a mixed metal, i. 60.

Lays (*qu. lat.* laquei), nets, snares, i. 78, *var. read.* 1.

Le *is frequently used for* **la** (*fem. art. and*

pron.) *before a vowel*, i. 8, 219, 259, ii. 152.

Le, to him, to her, ii. 106, 182, 240, 273.

Lees, les, lease, i. 225, 276, ii. 113.

Legitimie, legitimacy, ii. 151.

Lequel, *conj.* whether, i. 15.

Lerray, lerra, lerrount, *fut. from* **lesser** (*m. fr.* laisser), to let, permit, omit, ii. 48.

Lers, liers, thief, i. 57.

Lesser (*m. fr.* laisser), to let, to release; **lesser par plege, lesser par meynprise**, to bail, i. 14, 87.

Lestage, a kind of toll. *See p.* 75, *note.*

Leure, breadth, width, i. 410, ii. 251.

Ley (*m. fr.* loi), law, i. 1.

Leynz, therein, i. 15, ii. 110.

Li, ly=**le**, *pron.*, he, it, ii. 152.

Li, ly=**le**, *art.* the, i. 57, 264, ii. 42, 193.

Lige (*med. lat.* ligeus, ligius), absolute, entire, liege; **seignur lige**, liege lord, ii. 37, 41; **lige veffee**, absolute, or free, widowhood, ii. 287.

Ligeaunce, leggeaunce = **aleggeaunce**, allegiance, ii. 6, 28, 29, 41.

Linge, made of linen, light, slight, i. 107. *See Duc. Gloss. s. v.* lingius; *Roq. Gloss. s. v.* linge.

***Ligné**, *qu.* sex, ii. 313.

List, lit (*lat.* licet), it is allowed, i. 293, 401, ii. 4.

Liveré, delivery, i. 396.

Liveré de terre (*lat.* librata terræ), land worth one pound a year, ii. 143.

Loints, loinz (*m. fr.* loin), far, i. 364, ii. 164.

Lower, louwer (*m. fr.* loyer), hire, payment, i. 8, 86.

Lue, liuwe (*m. fr.* lieue), league, mile, i. 23, 413. *See Spelman Gloss. s. v.* leuga.

Madle, masle, male, i. 71, ii. 22.

Mahaigné, maheyné, maheygné, maimed, i. 90, 100, 105, 122,

Maheyn, maheygn, mayhem, maiming, i. 98, 122.

Mal de venue (*law lat.* malum veniendi), illness by the way, a cause of essoin or excuse for non-appearance in court, ii. 88.

Manace (*lat.* minæ, minatio), threatening; **bref de manace** (*lat.* breve de minis), i. 11; *Regist. brev. orig.* 88 *b.*

Manaunt (*lat.* manens), residing, ii. 98.

Manauntise, habitation, mansion, i. 184, ii. 329.

Mangeusent (*lat.* manducent), *subj. from* **manger**, to eat, i. 27.

Marchauscie (*m. fr.* maréchaussée), marshalship, office of Marshal, ii. 10.

Marché (*med. lat.* mercheta), merchet, i. 247. *See* i. 196, *note.*

Marlere, marler (*med. lat.* marlaria, *m. fr.* marnière), marl-pit, i. 81, 179.

***Mascecref** (*lat.* macellarius, *med lat.* macecrarius, macegrarius, *Leg. Edw. Conf.* c. 39, *Stat. Walliæ,* 12 *Edw. I.*, c. 4.), a dealer in meat. *Spelman interprets* **macegref** *to mean* **a stealer of meat**, *referring the last syllable to the French* griffer, *A. S.* ræfan, to seize; *Coke has a similar explanation, Inst. part. iii. p.* 110.

Maumerie, idolatry, ii. 212.

Mauvesté, wickedness, crime, i. 22, ii. 213.

Mayle, a halfpenny, a weight equal to half a denarius, i. 29, 186.

Maynpast; *see* **meynpast.**

Medler (*m. fr.* mêler), to mix, ii. 59.

Meen (*m. fr.* moyen), mesne, middle, intermediate or mesne tenant, i. 71, 146, 344; one that is intermediate in a transaction, i. 230.

Meer (*lat.* merus), mere, absolute; **le meer dreit**, the mere right, *that is*, the property as distinguished from the possession, ii. 59, 200, 211.

Mees, mies, house, ii. 248, 251.

Meité, meyté (*m. fr.* moitié), half, ii. 248.

Mellif, *var. read.* **medlif**, affray, i. 180.

Menee; menee de corns et de bouches, the hue and cry, i. 49.

Menour (*lat.* minor), less, inferior, i. 21.

Menuser = **amenuser**, to diminish, ii. 177.

Merche, boundary, landmark, ii. 253.

Merci (*lat.* misericordia, miseratio), mercy, pity, ii. 215; **estre en la merci, remeyndre en nostre merci**, to be in mercy, to be subject to amercement, i. 31, 304, 306.

Merciable, merciful, ii. 219.

Merim, merime, merrym (*med. lat.* materiamen, meremium), timber, i. 93, 217.

Mes (*qu. lat.* magis), 1. but; **mes qe**, provided that, ii. 4, 226, 306; provided that not, *qu.* i. 224; **mes si il ne eit**, provided he has, ii. 281; 2. for the future; **pur tous jours mes**, for ever after, ii. 269; **mes ne porra**, cannot in future, ii. 111, 154, 196.

Mescheaunce, accident, mischance, i. 113.

Meschiet, fails, *from* **mescheer**, ii. 85.

Mescreaunt, misbeliever, heretic, i. 42.

Mescreable, incredulous (*qu.* incredible), ii. 212.

Mescreu, mescru (*med. lat.* malecreditus), suspected of crime, i. 13, 35.

Mesel, meseyl, *pl.* **meseeus**, leper, i. 98, 223, 322, 347.

Mesfet, misdeed, i. 178.

Mesnage, household, i. 109.

Mesnee, meyné, family, i. 93, 263, ii. 65.

Mester, mestier, 1. office, duty, i. 4; 2. necessity, i. 101; **il ad mester**, it is necessary, i. 39, ii. 101; **pur mestier**, upon occasion, ii. 43.

Mettre a veir, mettre a voir, to prove, i. 117, 121, ii. 134.

Mettre (se), to put himself (upon a jury, &c.), *that is*, to accept that mode of trial, ii. 227.

Mettre sur, to accuse, i. 104.

Meuthz, meutz, meuz (*m. fr.* mieux), better, i. 22, 351, ii. 97.

Meyn, hand; **ove sa duzime meyn**, i. 150; **a lour xii. meyn**, i. 339 (*med. lat.* duodecima manu, *Glanvill, l. i. c.* 9.), at twelfth hand, *that is*, with eleven sworn compurgators; **a sa soule meyn**, alone, ii. 92; **arere meyn**, backwards, i. 356; **devaunt meyn**, beforehand, in advance, i. 270; **countre meyn**, on the other hand, ii. 163.

Meynovere (*m. fr.* manœuvre), act, handywork, i. 405.

Meynoverer, to work, do, i. 265, 405.

Meynpast, household, i. 13, 181; member of a household, i. 41, 181. *See Bracton, f.* 124 *b.*

Meynpernour (*med. lat.* manucaptor), mainpernor, one who makes himself responsible for the appearance of another, i. 11.

Meynprise, mainprise, the responsibility of a mainpernor, i. 87; **lesser par meynprise, mettre par meynprise**, i. 18, to bail.

***Meyntefoiz**, however, ii. 7.

Meys (*m. fr.* mois), month.

Mi (*lat.* medius), middle; **le mi leu**, the mid place, middle, i. 279; **par mi**, by means of, i. 269; **par mi et par tut**, in the whole and in every part, i. 386.

Mie, *in the phrase* **ne mie**, not, i. 1.

Mies=**mees**, house, i. 261.

Milueyn (*from* **mi lu**), middle, ii. 142, 267.

Mireus, *qu.* intermediary, i. 230, *var. read.*

Misprisioun (*m. fr.* méprise), mistake, i. 317.

Moeller (*m. fr.* molaire), molar (tooth), i. 123.

Moist, i. 400, *should probably be read* **moust** (*from* **moudre**), grinds.

More (*A. S.* mor, *fr.* marais), moor, ii. 69.

Morer, morir (*m. fr.* mourir), to die, i. 232; *subj.* **moerge, murge**, ii. 233; *pret.* **morust**, ii. 1.

Moster, mouster, mousteer (*lat.* monasterium), minster, church, i. 17, 62.

Mot=**mout**, much, i. 277.

Motié, moté (*qu. from* mot, a word), expressed, mentioned. *See Duc. Gloss. s. v.* motire, ii. 118.

Motz de la court, the formula of pleading adopted by the court, i. 111; **motz defensables**, the formula of defence, i. 116, 119.

Moun; *see* **a saver moun.**

Mounture, *qu.* a riding-horse, i. 89, 344.

Mouster; *see* **moster.**

Moustraunce, mustraunce = **demoustraunce**, declaration or statement of plaintiff, i. 101, 348.

Moustre (*lat.* monstrum), monster, ii. 142.

Moustrer, to shew, ii. 143.

Mout, moutz, much, many, i. 40, 139, ii. 168.

Munter, mounter (*m. fr.* monter), to amount, i. 56.

Murage, a tax for repairing town walls, i. 75.

Muscer, muscier, to conceal, i. 8, 107.

***Muscesces, mussesses**, secrecy, i. 362.

Muylliré, muylleré, mulieré (*law lat.* mulieratus), legitimate (child), i. 234, ii. 59, 118.

Naam (*A. S.* name), a distress, i. 137.

Nacioun, birth, ii. 157, 267.

N'ad gers puis, n'ad guers (*m. fr.* naguère), lately, ii. 81, 82.

Naufrer (*m. fr.* navrer), to wound, i. 8.

Nayf, neyf, *fem.* **nayve** (*med. lat.* nativus, nativa), a naif and a nief, a male and female villain, i. 195, 198.

Nayfté (*med. lat.* nativitas), naifty, the condition of a naif or villain, i. 194.

Nece (*lat.* neptis), granddaughter, ii. 324.

Nel=**ne le**, i. 80, ii. 55, 109, 132.

Nepurquant, nevertheless, ii. 141.

Neqedent, nequedent, nevertheless, ii. 65, 153.

Nestre (*m. fr.* naître), to be born; **neest**, is born, arises, i. 205.

Neveu (*lat.* nepos), grandson, nephew, ii. 314, 324.

Neyer (*m. fr.* noyer), to drown, i. 15.

Niement, denial, ii. 212.

Nient, nent, nothing, ii. 98, 132; not, ii. 97, 129.

Noun (*m. fr.* nom), name; **nouns nomables**, *qu.* Christian names, i. 317.

Nounsachaunce, ignorance, i. 217.

Noveleries, news, rumours, i. 84.

Nul, none, *also* any; **si ren nous soit arere de nul service**, if anything be in arrear of any service, i. 71.

Nuli, none, ii. 320; of no one, of any one, ii. 2, 252.

Nuncier (*lat.* nuntiare), to tell, relate, ii. 345.

Nurri, one bred in a house, fosterchild, i. 111. *See Duc. Gloss. s. v.* Nutritus.

Nurture (*m. fr.* nourriture), nurture, ii. 236.

Nust (*lat.* nocet), hurts, ii. 216.

***Nutauntre, de nutauntre**, by night, i. 180, 313.

Nuté, nutié, the commencement of night, ii. 133.

Ny (*m. fr.* nid), nest, i. 215.

Oceye, *subj. from* **ocir**, to kill, i. 64.

Oes=us (*lat.* usus), use, i. 85, 285.

Oesé (*m. fr.* aisé), easy, i. 364.

Office; de soen office, ex officio; **par office des Justices**, i. 105; **de office de Justice**, ii. 289; **par office de juge**, i. 326, as of course, by the discretion of the court without reference to the demand or consent of the parties. *See the Index to Coke's Reports, s. v.* Office of Court.

Onkes; *see* **unkes**.

Ordinarie (*med. lat.* ordinarius, judex ordinarius). 1. ordinary, immediate ecclesiastical superior or judge, ii. 151; *also* 2. one who ordains or admits to holy orders, *unless we should read* **ordinour**, i. 208.

Ore, now, i. 97, 368.

Orrount, *fut. from* **oyer**, to hear, i. 270.

Otreyer, ottreyer (*m. fr.* octroyer), to grant, authorise, i. 258, 299.

Ounehyne (*an English term*), hoghenhine, a man's own hind or domestic, i. 49.

Ouster, oster (*m. fr.* ôter), to oust, remove, i. 44, 264, 284, 332.

Outfangenthef (*an English word*), outfangthef. *See i.* 229, *note.*

Outrement; tut outrement, utterly, entirely, i. 141.

Ove, ovek, ovekes, oveske (*m. fr.* avec), with, i. 7, 22, 189, ii. 146.

Ovek, *adv.* withal, at the same time, i. 242.

Overer (*lat.* operari), to work, to proceed at law, i. 245, 342, 411.

Owel, ouwel, equal, ii. 75, 79; **en owele meyn**, in an impartial hand, i. 251.

Oyer (*lat.* audire, *m. fr.* ouir), to hear.

Oyl (*m. fr.* œil), eye, i. 123.

Oyl (*m. fr.* oui), yes, i. 174, *note.*

Panel, panel, list of jurors, i. 91.

Pannage, pannage, mast, ii. 69.

Par quei, par quei qe, provided that, i. 256, ii. 238.

Par si qe, provided that, ii. 282.

Parcelerie, fractional division, ii. 250.

Paremplir, parempler, to fill up (a ditch), i. 401, 409.

Parfournir, to perform, ii. 89. *See* **fornir.**

Parfundesce, depth, i. 17.

Parjuri, parjurie, perjury, ii. 213, 214.

Parler vers eus, to take proceedings against them, i. 121.

Paroche (*m. fr.* paroisse), parish, i. 333.

Paroge, parouge, *subj. from* **parler** (*med. lat.* parobolare), to speak, i. 31, 350.

Parole, plea, legal proceeding, i. 5, 141, ii. 204.

Parount, par ount, whereby, i. 5.

Parout (*from* **parler**), speaks, i. 334.

Parpayer, to pay, i. 270.

Partable, subject to partition, ii. 77.

Partir, to share, divide, ii. 70.

Passage; general passage = general pelrinage, a crusade, i. 295, ii. 349.

Payer (*lat.* pacare), to appease, satisfy, pay; **se payer**, to be satisfied, ii. 240, 249.

Pece (*m. fr.* pièce); **vendre par peces**, to retail, i. 83; **graunt pece**, a long space (of time), i. 228.

Penance, punishment, i. 74; the penalty for standing mute, *since called* peine forte et dure, i. 26.

Perge, *subj.* may appear, ii. 172.

Perice, peresce, peerage, equality, i. 281.

Perigalté, equality, ii. 141.

Perne, pernent (*from* **prendre**), takes, take, i. 180, ii. 52, 59.

Pernour (*from* **prendre**), taker, i. 92, 180.

Personage, parsonage, ii. 179.

Persone (*med. lat.* persona), parson, ii. 179.

Pesson, mast, pannage, i. 371, ii. 69. *See Duc. Gloss. s.v.* paisso.

Pessoun (*m. fr.* poisson), fish, i. 96, 358.

Pestour (*lat.* pistor), baker, i. 190.

Pestre (*m. fr.* paître), to feed, graze, i. 264.

Peus=puis, then, i. 10, 11.

Pier, peer (*m. fr.* pair), peer, equal, i. 92, 355, ii. 58.

Piert, peert, it appears, i. 127, ii. 101.

Pledable, pleadable, adapted for pleading, i. 177; **tens pledable**, time proper for legal proceedings, i. 6, 45,

Plee, plé, play, *pl.* **plez, pletz** (*med. lat.* placitum), a plea, or action, i. 59; **en plé pledaunt**, in the course of pleading, i. 307.

Plegage, pledging, i. 104.

Plege (*med. lat.* plegius), a pledge, one who answers for another; **lesser par plege**, to bail, i. 14.

Plevine, plevin, pledging, i. 129; **plevine de fey**, promise, ii. 56.

Plevir, to pledge, to be pledge for a person, i. 129; to promise, ii. 347.

Plevisable, bailable, subject to be released upon pledge or bail, i. 87, 112.

Poi (*m. fr.* peu), little, ii. 220.

Point, *adv.* at all, in any way, i. 103.

Pontage, a kind of toll, i. 75, *note.*

Pountbreche, breach of pound, the illegal taking of cattle out of pound, i. 180.

Pour, poour (*m. fr.* peur), fear, i. 47.

Pouz (*m. fr.* pouce), inch, i. 189.

Prendre; se prendre a soen heritage, to come to, acquire, or take possession of, his inheritance, ii. 52.

Prenge, prengent, *subj. from* prendre, to take, ii. 52, 55, 56.

Prenotarie (prothonotarius, *Bracton, f.* 185 *b*, prænotarius, *Fleta*, p. 230, § 2), prothonotary, *an officer of the Court of Common Pleas*, i. 349.

Prentiz (*med. lat.* apprenticius), apprentice, learner, ii. 323.

Prerogaunce, privilege, prerogative, ii. 171.

Preyser (*m. fr.* priser), to appraise, i. 35.

Primes=en primes, first, i. 50, ii. 115.

Prisoun (*med. lat.* priso), prisoner, i. 43.

Prisouner, to imprison, i. 46.

Procurer, to procure, suborn, i. 14.

Prode homme; *see* **prudehomme.**

Profrer (*m. fr.* proférer), to offer, proffer, ii. 262.

Proscher, to approach, ii. 159.

Proscheineté, proscheynté, proximity, i. 273, ii. 310.

Prosme (*lat.* proximus), neighbour, ii. 213.

Provable, probable, 145 a.

Provende (*m. fr.* prébende), prebend, i. 317.

Provost (*lat.* præpositus), **provost; provost de vile**, i. 19; *as to this officer, see Fleta, p.* 164.

Provour, pruvour, a prover or approver, a felon who becomes a witness for the Crown, i. 17, 180.

Prudehomme, *pl.* **prudeshommes, prodeshommes**, a freeholder or householder, i. 191, 385, *note*, ii. 295.

***Puralé**, *pl.* **puralez**, perambulation, i. 319, 331.

Purceu (*lat.* porcellus, *m. fr.* pourceau), little pig, i. 91.

Purceynte, precinct, ii. 340.

Purchace, purchaz, *s.* (*lat.* perquisitum), purchase, acquisition, i. 215, 249; purchase of writ, ii. 208; perquisite, ii. 69, 253.

Purchacer, to acquire, i. 212; **purchacer un bref**, to purchase or obtain a writ, i. 315; *hence* **purchacer**, to take legal proceedings, ii. 293.

Purgiser, to ravish, violate, i. 41, 98, 105.

Purloigner, to prolong, i. 121.

Purparlance, proposition, i. 338.

Purparler, to propose, contrive, i. 100, 106.

Purpartie, proportion, ii. 67, 75.

Purpensé, prepensed, contrived beforehand, i. 15.

Purpos (*lat.* propositum), purpose, i. 97.

Purposer, to propose, i. 314.

Purprendre, to encroach, i. 76.

Purprestour, a purprestor, one who usurps or encroaches, i. 72.

Purpresture, a purpresture, or encroachment, i. 72.

Pust, *pret. from* **pestre**, to feed, i. 366.

Pusz, puyz (*m. fr.* puits), well, i. 15, 365.

Quarenteine, the period of forty days, during which a widow was allowed to remain in her husband's house, ii. 247, 251.

Quatuor temple (*lat.* Quatuor tempora), Ember-days, i. 346.

Quere (*lat.* quærere), to seek, i. 306, ii. 31; *fut.* **querra**, i. 342; *subj.* **querge**, ii. 31.

Queu, keu (*lat.* coquus), cook, i. 192.

Qi, ky, who, whose, i. 325, ii. 115.

Quider (*lat.* cogitare), to think, i. 265, 355, ii. 115.

Quiete (*lat.* quies), quiet, release, ii. 13.

Quir (*m. fr.* cuir), skin, leather, i. 179.

Quisent (*m. fr.* cuisent), cook, i. 83.

Quiteclamaunce, quiteclemaunce, quit-claim, discharge, i. 230, 251.

Quiteclamer (*med. lat.* quietum clamare), to quitclaim, release, i. 207.

Rap, raap (*lat.* raptus), rape, i. 55.

Rasture, rasure (*from* **rere**, to erase), erasure in writing, i. 14, 314.

Raunceun, rancoun, raunsoun (*lat.* redemptio), redemption, ransom, fine at the king's pleasure, i. 14, 46, 48, 322.

Reaver (*m. fr.* ravoir), to have back, ii. 331.

Rebaut, 3*rd pers. sing. pres. indic. from* **rebailler**, to redeliver, i. 176.

Rebotable, subject to be rejected, ii. 313.

Receptour, receiver, i. 48.

Record (*med. lat.* recordum), record, authentic testimony, oral or written, of the proceedings of a court of justice, i. 4, 5, 6, 136. *See Coustumier de Normandie, c.* 101, *ad fin.* Record est racontement de chose qui ad esté faicte.

Recrese (se), *qu. subj. from* **recroire** (*med. lat.* recredere), to yield, to be recreant, i. 319; *but perhaps the true reading is* **retret**, *or* **retree**.

Reddesseisine, re-disseisine, repeated disseisine, i. 183.

Reddour, rigour, i. 167.

Refetir, *qu.* to repair with a new roof or coping, i. 409, *var. read. See Duc. Gloss. s. v.* festissare.

Refute (*m. fr.* refuite), resource, refuge, means of escape, ii. 211, 307.

Regard, reward or recompense, i. 393, ii. 69. *See Duc. Gloss. s. v.* regardum.

Regehir (*lat.* refiteri), to confess, i. 261.

Rehercer, to recite, rehearse, i. 349, ii. 198.

Reints, reynts, *part. from* **reyndre** (*lat.* redimere), to ransom, i. 94, 95, 335, ii. 24.

Relef, relief (*med. lat.* relevium), relief (*a law term*). *See* ii. 49.

Releiver, relevier, to relieve, to take up a feudal estate upon payment of relief, ii. 50.

Remenaunt, remanaunt (*lat.* remanens); **a remanaunt**, in future, i. 78.

Remeyndre (*lat.* remanere), to remain, i. 166, 318; to follow as a consequence, i. 380, ii. 141; to stand over, be stayed (*of an action or writ*), i. 305, 330, ii. 129.

Remist, remistrent, *pret. from* **remeyndre**, to remain, i. 24, ii. 185.

***Remuable**, subject to removal, *a term used of the inferior officers of monasteries, who could not make contracts, sue, or be sued, without their superiors*, i. 159, ii. 302, 340; *Bracton, f.* 12, 336 *b*; *Year Book,* 31 *Edw. I. p.* 454.

Remuer, to replace, remove, i. 12, 321.

Ren, rien, anything, nothing, i. 7, 71; **en nule rien accessorie**, in any accessory thing, ii. 175. *See s. v.* **nul**.

Renable, reasonable, i. 73, ii. 80.

Reparillier, reperiler, to repair, i. 78, 364.

Repeler, repeller (*m. fr.* rappeler), to recall, repeal, i. 2, 223.

Replevir, replever (*med. lat.* replegiare), to replevy, regain possession by giving pledge, i. 68, 80.

Replevisable, subject to be replevied, bailable, i. 14. *See* **plevisable**.

Reprises, outgoings, ii. 67.

Rere, to erase, i. 6.

Rescous (*med. lat.* excussus, *Leg. Hen. I. c.* 51.), rescued, i. 276.

Reseaunt, resident, i. 389, ii. 224.

Resomouns, resummoned, ii. 91.

Resomounse, repeated summons, ii. 88.

***Resorte**, *pl.* **resortz**, resort (*a technical term used of tracing the descent of an inheritance in the collateral line*), ii. 166, 328. *In i.* 204, *where it is written* **resource**, *we should probably read* **resorte**. *See ii.*164, *note; Year Book,* 32 *Edw.I.p.*17.

Resoun, reason, i. 352; sentence, proposition, i. 317, 352, ii. 52, 134; plan, mode of proceeding, case, i. 141, ii. 304.

Resource; *see* **resorte**.

Respit, delay, adjournment, ii. 261.

Respiter, to adjourn, i. 319, ii. 159.

Responable, responsible, i. 322.

Ret (*span.* reto, *old span.* riepto, *Fuero Real, p.* 163.), accusation or suspicion of crime; **de mauveis ret**, of bad character, i. 61. *See Duc. Gloss. s. v.* reatus; *Stat. Marl. c.* 28; *Stat. Westm. I. c.* 2; *Year Book,* 30 *Edw. I. p.* 505; *Bracton, f.* 124 (§ 3), 126 (§ 8), 133; *Coke, Inst. pt. ii.* 150.

Retree, *pl.* **retreent,** *subj. from* **retrere,** to withdraw, i. 13, 118, 306.

Retret de la meer, ebb of the sea, ii. 350.

Retter (*span.* retar), to accuse, impute, i. 208, ii. 224.

Revers; la reverse, the contrary proposition, ii. 269.

Reverser, to reverse (a judgment), ii. 269.

Ribaud, ribald, rogue, i. 32, 124, 125.

Rien; *see* **ren.**

Riffiure, a scratch, i. 122. *See Duc. Gloss. s. v.* **riffiura.**

Roudle, roule, roulle (*lat.* **rotulus**), a roll, a record preserved upon parchment, i. 6, 18, 23.

Rout (*lat.* **ruptus**), broken or torn, i. 314.

Roveysouns, Rogation days, i. 346.

Rule de ley, rule of law, ii. 542.

Saintz, Saintz, Seyntz. *In the expressions,* **Jurer sur Sainctz,** i. 9, **Si mei ayde Deus et les Saintz,** i. 64, 106, &c. *the word denotes the Holy Evangelists. See* i. 346, 347.

Sakebere, the prosecutor in a suit of felony, where the thief was caught in the act, i. 56, *note*, i. 182. *The meaning of this word was already obscure in the beginning of the fourteenth century. In the following example it is transferred, in a slightly altered form, from the prosecutor to the thief, and is evidently used in the sense of carrying in a bag.* Et habent libertatem suam in eadem villa, et de infangenethef et utfangenethef, et debent facere judicium latronum et malefactorum captorum in prædictam libertatem cum manu opere, videlicet, sakberande bacberande et handhabbend. (Extenta manerii de Hadleghe, *printed in the Proceedings of the Suffolk Archæological Institute, vol. iii. p.* 244.)

Saner, to heal; **saner sa defaute** (*law lat.* sanare defaltam), to clear his contempt, ii. 106; i. 20, *var. read.* 3.

Saunt, sauntz (*m. fr.* sans), without, i. 138, ii. 11, 171.

Sauvageyne, sauvagine, wildness, wild animals, i. 122, 215.

Saver moun; *see* **a saver moun.**

Scotalles (*an English word*), scot-ales. *See* i. 91, *note.*

Scrit, writing, i. 387.

Sei, sey, se, himself, herself, themselves, i. 105, 115, 325, ii. 164.

Seignurages, lordships, *frequently used for* **seignurs,** i. 36, ii. 38. *So in Stat. Exon.; Madox, Formulare Anglicanum, p.* 192.

Seler (*m. fr.* sceller), to seal, i. 25.

Semblaunt; par semblaunt, presumptively, prima facie, ii. 100.

Sen, sense, intellect, ii. 135, 166; meaning, i. 102.

Sengle (*lat.* singulus), single,

Serjaunt (*med. lat.* serviens), 1. a servant, i. 89; 2. a serjeant or baillif, i. 5, 12; 3. an esquire, i. 222, ii. 5, *note;* 4. a serjeant at law, i. 93.

Serjauntie, serjeanty, a species of tenure. *See* ii. 10.

Servage, 1. servitude, slavery, i. 194; 2. servile or villain tenement, i. 196; 3. servitude, easement, i. 253.

Sete (*lat.* sagitta), arrow, i. 354.

Seute; *see* **sute.**

Severalté, separation, ii. 264.

Seyns (*m. fr.* céans), within, at home, i. 362.

Si la qe; *see* **ci la qe.**

Sicum, as, i. 2.

Sigler (*m. fr.* cingler), to sail, i. 16.

Socage, socage, *a species of tenure,* ii. 143.

Soefferté = soeffraunce, permission, sufferance, i. 369.

Soen, *fem.* **sa, sue,** his, her, i. 12, 67.

Sokeman, sokeman, tenant in ancient demesne, ii. 13, 143.

Sokemanerie, the estate of a sokeman, ii. 11.

Soleit (*lat.* solet *or* solebat), is, or was, used, i. 36, ii. 291, 300.

Solempne (*m. fr.* solemnel), solemn, ii. 339.

Solom, solum (*lat.* secundum, *m. fr.* selon), according, ii. 333.

Somilleus, light-headed, i. 165. *See Roq. Gloss., s. v.* semilleus.

Somounable, liable to be summoned, ii. 13.

Somouns (*lat.* summonitus), summoned, i. 9.

Somounse, sommouns (*lat.* summonitio, *m. fr.* semonce), a summons, i. 21, ii. 328.

Sot nastre, an idiot from birth, ii. 20. *See* **fol nastre.**

Sotiveté, subtlety, ii. 166.

Soute (*lat.* solutio), payment, i. 163, ii. 125.

South, *pl.* (*lat.* solidi), shillings, i. 344; (*as a measure of weight*), i. 186.

Southe (*var. lect.* **soudeez,** *med. lat.* solidatæ); **xx. southe de terre,** twenty shillings a year of land, i. 91.

Sovereyn, superior, supreme, ii. 213; **seignur sovereyn**, lord paramount, i. 256.

***Sucein** (*var. read.* **susané, sursané**; *qu. med. lat.* superannatus; *see Duc. Gloss. s. v.*); **chars suceines**, stale meat, i. 83. *In the Latin* Judicium Pillorii *and* Statutum de Pistoribus (Statuta temporis incerti), *the words are* carnes susceinatas, *and* carnes supersennuatas.

Sue (*lat.* sua, *fem. sing.*), his, her, i. 67, 414.

Supposer, *qu.* to suppress (*med. lat.* supponere, *Leg. Hen. I. c.* 1.), ii. 152, 351, *var. read.* 4–4.

Suppris, suspris, *part. from* supprendre (*m. fr.* surprendre), to supprise, i. 26, ii. 345.

Sure, suyr (*m. fr.* suivre), to follow, sue, prosecute, i. 108, 112.

Surgien (*m. fr.* chirurgien), surgeon, i. 34.

Sursané; *see* **sucein.**

Sursece, i. 131, ii. 330; **sursete** (*qu.*), i. 71, *subj. from* **surseoir**, to neglect.

Sursise, soursise, neglect, default, i. 21, ii. 328.

Suspecioun (*m. fr.* soupçon), suspicion, i. 10, 314.

Susteinaunce (*m. fr.* sustentation), sustenance, provision, ii. 247.

Sute, seute, suite (*med. lat.* secta), 1. suit, prosecution, legal proceeding, i. 52, 59, 97; 2. suit, testimony of one or more witnesses or compurgators, i, 135, 162, 205; 3. suit, duty of appearing at courts, grinding corn at the lord's mill, &c., i. 73, 177, 255.

Suth, de suth, de south (*lat.* subtus, *m. fr.* sous), below, under, i. 8, ii. 324.

Sutier, suytour, suiter, seutour (*med. lat.* sectator), suitor, one who performs suit at a court or elsewhere, i. 7, 134, 135, ii. 357.

Syer, seyer (*lat.* secare, *m. fr.* scier), to reap or mow, i. 346, 392, 402; *qu.* to lop wood, i. 395.

Symenel, a fine kind of bread, i. 186.

Taillage, talliage, *a tax paid by a peasant to his lord*, ii. 70.

Talent, wish, i. 236, *note*, ii. 235.

Tard ou tempre, late or early, i. 246.

Targer, to put off, delay, i. 333. **Targer**, *verb. neut.* to delay, *is found in the Statute of Exeter.*

Tast, touch, feeling with the hands, ii. 15.

Tauntsoulement (*lat.* tantum, solum), only, ii. 84.

Tayler, to shape, cut down; **fee taylé**, fee tail, i. 225.

Tenour, *sm.* **tenure**, *sf.* tenor, purport, ii. 331, 337.

Termer, a termor or farmer, one that has a term of years, i. 418.

Terrien (*lat.* terrenus), earthly, ii. 39.

Thefbote, *an English word; see* i. 83, *note*, 180.

Tierz, tierce, terce (*lat.* tertius), third, ii. 128, 129.

Tiphanie (*lat.* Theophania), the Epiphany, i. 346.

Toil, toyl, trouble, dispute, i. 129, 283; **toil de court**, litigation, ii. 264.

Toiller, to dispute, ii. 284, 285.

Tolet; *see* **toulle.**

Toloun, tolun, toluen, tolune (*med. lat.* thelonium), toll, i. 59, 75, 92, ii. 69.

Tor (*lat.* taurus), a bull, i. 176.

Torcenous, tortious, wrongful, i. 92.

Toulle, *v. subj.* (*lat.* tollat), take away, i. 35; **tollet, tolet, tolu**, *part.* taken away, i. 123, 249, 358; **toust**, takes away, i. 243; **tolirent**, took away.

Tourn, tour (*m. fr.* tour), turn, rotation, ii. 174; **tourn de viscounte**, sheriff's tourn, i. 7, 177.

Toust (*m. fr.* tôt), soon, ii. 156.

Toust, *v.*, *see* **toulle.**

Transsailler, to leap over, ii. 320.

Travers, a kind of toll, i. 75, *note*, ii. 69.

Traversel, collateral, oblique, ii. 166.

Traverser, 1. to traffick, i. 193; 2. to traverse or deny (*a term of pleading*), i. 380, ii. 156.

Trayer (*m. fr.* trahir), to betray, i. 99.

Trayner, traygner, to draw, or drag on the ground to the place of execution (*part of the punishment of treason*), i. 33, 40, 108. *A wrong interpretation is given in Duc. Gloss. s. v.* trahere.

Trayt; **payn de trayt**, a kind of bread, i. 186.

Trespassaunt, a passenger, or passer-by, i. 403.

Trespasser, to trespass, offend, i. 123.

Trestourner, transtourner, to divert, i. 81, 364.

Trestut, *pl.* **trestous**, all, i. 19, ii. 63.

Tresun, tresoun, treysoun (*m. fr.* trahison), treason, i. 40.

Tret (*m. fr.* trait), draught of fishes, ii. 78.

Treve, troeve, troeffe, *subj. from* **trover,** to find, i. 13, ii. 56.

***Treve;** *see* **vileyn de eve et de treve,** i. 196.

Trier, to draw, ii. 182, *where in the last line* **triez** *should be read for* **tirez;** to choose, i. 385; to try, i. 30.

Triplicant, *part.* rejoining (*in pleading*), ii. 116.

Triplicacioun, rejoinder, ii. 121.

Troeffe; *see* **treve.**

Troveure (*m. fr.* trouvaille), something found, i. 66.

Trovez, *part.* provided, i. 44.

Truisse, truyse, let him find, i. 109, 159, 160, 185.

Tumberel, tumbrell (*instrument of punishment*), i. 61, 75.

Turberie, turbary, right of digging turf, i. 397.

Tuycioun (*lat.* tuitio), protection.

***Udif,** *fem.* **udive** (*lat.* otiosus); **udives bestes,** animals not used for labour, i. 344.

Un *is used in the plural number to signify identity, as* **unes mesmes persones, uns mesmes jurours,** ii. 233, 234; *also in the expression* **uns esporouns, uns gauntz,** *qu.* a pair of spurs, a pair of gloves, ii. 11. *The expression,* uns esperons d'or u dorés, *occurs in L'Ordene de Chevalerie, Fabliaux, &c. publiés par Barbazan, vol. i. p.* 81.

Uncore (*m. fr.* encore), still, yet, again, i. 417, ii. 173.

Uncouth (*an English word*), unknown, i. 49.

Uniement, equally, i. 287, 305.

Universeté, a general body or community, i. 331, ii. 339.

Unkes, unques (*lat.* unquam), ever, i. 11, ii. 121; **ou qe unques,** wheresoever, ii. 52; **qi qe unques,** whosoever, ii. 54.

Us, oes (*lat.* usus), use, i. 18, 214, 260.

Us, uihs (*lat.* ostium), door, i. 261, ii. 236.

Utaves, the Octaves, or week following a feast, as the Octaves of Easter, i. 345.

Vedue (*lat.* vidua), a widow, i. 71.

Veduetê, widowhood, ii. 79.

Vee, vé, refusal, i. 136, 141; **vee de naam** (*law lat.* vetitum namium, *or* vetitum namii, *Bracton,* f. 155 *b*), refusal to deliver up a distress upon offer of security, i. 75; **plees de vee,** i. 133, ii. 252 (*lat.* placita de vetito namio), actions of replevin, *so called because the plaintiff alleged a refusal by the defendant to deliver up the distress. See* i. 140.

Veftee = veduetê, widowhood, ii. 287.

Veie, voie (*lat.* via), way (or method), i. 376, ii. 154.

Veier, veyer (*m. fr.* envoyer), to send, i. 368, ii. 268.

Veirs, veyrs, *fem.* **veyre,** true, i. 119, ii. 152.

***Ventresce; molyn ventresce,** wind-mill, i. 279. *Compare* **eweresce.**

Verge (*lat.* virga, virgata), rod, verge; **verge del hostel,** the limits of the jurisdiction of the steward of the king's household, ii. 3, 4. Virgata regia, idem quod potestas marescalli virgam portantis, *Fleta, p.* 66.

Vergee (*lat.* virgata terræ), a virgate, yard-land, ii. 144.

Verray, verrei, true, i. 30, ii. 130.

Vertie, turned, diverted, i. 409.

Vesqui (*m. fr.* vécu), *part.* lived, ii. 135.

Vestuz, *part.* clothed, invested of a feudal estate, i. 36.

Veyer; *see* **veier.**

Veynt (*lat.* vincit, *m. fr.* vainc), ii. 239.

Vicarie (*m. fr.* vicairie, vicariat), vicarage, ii. 179.

Vicarie (*m. fr.* vicaire), vicar, ii. 179.

Vier, vyer, veer (*lat.* vetare), to refuse, i. 140, 142, 150.

***Vileyn de eve et de treve** (*lat.* villanus ab avo et tritavo), a villain by ancestry, i. 196, *note.*

Villee (*lat.* villata), township, vill, i. 9.

Vitayle, victuals, i. 23.

Voider (*m. fr.* vider), to empty, ii. 201; to become vacant, ii. 185.

Voise, voist (*lat.* vadat), let him go, i. 189, 300; **se voise, s'en voise,** i. 33, 415.

Voucher (*lat.* vocare), to vouch or call in defence, ii. 272.

Voucheresce (*lat.* vocatrix), a woman who vouches, ii. 272.

Vousist (*lat.* voluisset), had wished, i. 149.

Vout (*lat.* voluit), wished, i. 145.

***Wakerours** (*var. read.* **waucreours**), vagrants, i. 181; *from* vaucrer, to wander: *see Duc. Gloss. s. v.* vaxare; *and see* **waucrue.**

*__Waucrue__ (*used with* __viaunde__), diseased or tainted, *perhaps* overdriven, i. 192. *The verb* vaucrer *is used by Froissart in the sense of* to wander, (*see* __wakerour__, *above*); *also*, to move, *va.* vaucrer la barge amont e aval, *Froissart, vol. ii. c.* 76. *The English* walk *is derived by Skinner from the A. S.* wealcan, to roll.

__Wayour__ (*A. S.* wær), a weir or pool made for fish in a river, i. 279. *This word appears to be wrongly interpreted in Duc. Gloss. s. v.* wayeria.

__Weyf, weif__, a waif, or thing abandoned, i. 66; the right of a lord to appropriate such things found upon his manor, ii. 252.

__Weyver__, to waive, abandon, i. 200, 326, ii. 49; *used of the outlawry of a woman*, i. 50.

__Wrek, wrek de meer__, wreck, shipwreck, the right to appropriate goods wrecked, i. 18, ii. 252.

__Wythernam__ (*A.S.* wiðername), withernam, counter-distress, i. 138.

__Yse__, *subj. from* __issir__ (*lat.* exire), go forth.

__Yvronke__ (*m. fr.* ivrogne), drunkard, i. 165.

INDEX.

☞ The Roman numerals preceded by the letter *p.* refer to the Introduction; the other references are to volume and page.

ERRATA.

VOL. I.

p. 178, *translation, line* 6. *For* summoned, ought in general to appear *read* summoned by general summons ought to appear.

p. 222, *last reference in margin.* *For* li. 3 *read* li. 2.

p. 297, *last reference in margin.* *For* c. 16 *read* c. 17.

p. 344, *translation, line* 16. *For* beasts of pleasure *read* beasts not used for labour.

p. 393, *translation, line* 1. *For* digging *read* mowing.

„ „ *line* 2. *For* recompense *read* compliment.

p. 395, *translation, line* 6. *For* mowing *read* digging.

VOL. II.

p. 10, *marginal reference.* *For* Brac. 356 *read* Brac. 35 *b*.

„ *note, second column, line* 1. *For* s. 3 *read* s. 31.

p. 23, *last reference in margin.* *For* Stat. West. 2. (13 Edw. I.) *read* Stat. West. 1. (3 Edw. I.)

p. 59, *text,* s. 10. *Add reference to* Stat. Glouc. (6 Edw. I.) c. 6.

p. 73, *first reference in margin.* *For* s. 11 *read* s. 9.

p. 182, *last line of text.* *For* tirez *read* triez.

REPRINTS OF LEGAL CLASSICS & OTHER SIGNIFICANT WORKS PUBLISHED BY THE LAWBOOK EXCHANGE, LTD.

ENGLISH LEGAL HISTORY

Adams, W.H. Davenport. *Learned in the Law; or Examples and Encouragements from the Lives of Eminent Lawyers.* London: S.W. Partridge & Co., [1882?]. vi, 392 pp. Reprinted 2002 by The Lawbook Exchange, Ltd. ISBN 1-58477-238-7. Cloth. $80.

* A set of biographical sketches of eminent jurists from the 17th through 19th centuries, including Lord Bacon, John Selden, the Earl of Mansfield, Sir William Jones, and Lord Brougham. Conceived for young readers, Adams offers a series of "Great Man" portraits in the manner of Carlyle in the hope that their lives will encourage emulation. Adams [1828-1891] therefore emphasizes the outstanding moral character, determination, and diligence of his subjects and their crucial contributions to Britain. Like many Victorians, Adams feared that the need for professional specialization created by the growth of science and industry would eliminate the type of well-rounded personality dear to the English. This concern is evident in his choice of representative figures. He demonstrates in each case that these were men of many parts, and that their breadth of interests contributed to their greatness in the annals of the law.

[American Association of Law Schools]. *Select Essays in Anglo-American Legal History. By Maitland, Pollock, Holmes, Beale, Holdsworth and Others.* Boston: Little, Brown, and Company, 1907. Three volumes. 847; 823; 862 pp. Reprinted 1992 by The Lawbook Exchange, Ltd. LCCN 91-77977. ISBN 0-9630106-1-1. Cloth. $195.

* Originally conceived as a companion volume to Pollock and Maitland's *History of English Law*, this valuable work of legal scholarship, long out-of-print, has become increasingly difficult to obtain. Its 76 essays fill some 2,500 pages. At the time of its original publication the Harvard Law Review stated: "No one can fail to be impressed with the deep research, the deliberate construction, and the substantial worth of these essays."

Bacon, Sir Francis. *The Elements of the Common Lawes of England, Branched into a Double Tract: The One Contayning A Collection of Some Principall Rules and Maximes of the Common Law, With Their Latitude and Extent. Explicated for the More Facile Introduction of Such as are Studiously Addicted to That Noble Profession.* **[with]** *The Other: The Use of the Common Law, for the Preservation of our Persons, Goods, and Good Names. According to*

the Lawes and Customes of this Land. London: Printed by the assignes of I. More Esq., 1630. xix, 104, vii, 84 pp. Reprint available 2003 by The Lawbook Exchange, Ltd. LCCN 2002025942. ISBN 1-58477-248-4. Cloth. $85.

* Bacon [1561-1626], one of the great intellectuals of the age, held the posts of Solicitor General, Attorney General and Lord Chancellor during the reign of James I. *The Elements of the Common Laws of England* is the general title for a work that is comprised of two different treatises: *A Collection of Some Principall Rules and Maximes of the Common Lawes of England* and *The Use of the Law, Provided for the Preservation of Our Persons, Goods and Good Names.* The first contains twenty-five maxims, or *regulae.* They are remarkable for their stylistic vigor, intellectual rigor, meticulousness and clarity. It was the first part of *De Regulis Juris*, a codification of English law that Bacon never completed. This is quite unfortunate, observes Holdsworth, because "he alone had the philosophical capacity, the historical knowledge and the literary taste needed to select the subject matter and shape the form of the books. (...) [Had he completed the book] there would be many who would question whether, as a lawyer, he was not Coke's superior." The second treatise is a review of the history and practical application of criminal law, estate law, personal property law and the law of slander (i.e. "the preservation of our good names from shame and infamy"). Holdsworth, *A History of English Law* V:498-499. Marvin, *Legal Bibliography* (1847) 83-84.

Beard, Charles Austin. *The Office of the Justice of the Peace in England, in its Origin and Development.* New York: Columbia University Press, 1904. 184, [1] pp. Reprinted 2001 by The Lawbook Exchange, Ltd. ISBN 1-58477-102-X. Cloth. $60.

* Beard's first book, in which he points out that the office of the justice of the peace was originally a creation of the Crown, traces the struggle of the office to establish its independence. "It was the King's Peace that after many ages swallowed up every other 'peace,' and it is as a phase of the prolonged struggle for mastery between the principle of centralized administration and the principle of local independence that we must view the evolution of the office of Justice of the Peace. This is well brought out by Dr. Beard, and he is especially clear in tracing the long series of tentative steps and experiments that led up to the final establishment of the office by the statute of 1360." H.J.R., Law Quarterly Review 21:186-188 as cited in Marke, *A Catalogue of the Law Collection at New York University* (1953) 198.

Brown, Basil. *Law Sports at Gray's Inn (1594) Including Shakespeare's connection with the Inns of Court, the origin of the Capias Utlegatum re Coke and Bacon, Francis Bacon's connection with Warwickshire, together with a reprint of the Gesta Grayorum.* New York: [Privately Printed by the Author], 1921. xciv, 188, 88, [9] pp. LCCN 99-049829. ISBN 1-58477-056-2. Reprinted 2002 by The Lawbook Exchange, Ltd. Cloth. $85.

* In this interesting volume Brown examines the law in the writings of Shakespeare and Bacon. Includes the text of the hard-to-find *Gesta Grayorum*, of which Bacon was thought to be one of the authors. Brown also describes the origin of the *Capias Utlegatum* insult offered to Bacon by Queen Elizabeth's attorney general, Sir Edward Coke.

Coke, Sir Edward. *The First Part of the Institute of the Laws of England, or, A commentary upon Littleton. Not the name of the Author only, but of the Law Itself. Revised and Corrected With Additions of Notes, References, and Proper Tables, by Francis Hargrave and Charles Butler, Esqrs. Of Lincoln's Inn, Including also The Notes of Lord Chief Justice Hale and Lord Chancellor Nottingham; and An Analysis of Littleton, written by an unknown Hand in 1658-9.* By Charles Butler, Esq. The Eighteenth Edition, Corrected. London, J. & W.T. Clarke, 1823. Two volumes. ccxvi,[606]; iv, [772] pp. Reprinted 2000 by The Lawbook Exchange, Ltd. LCCN 99-41675. ISBN 1-58477-033-3. Cloth. $195.

* Coke's *Institutes* are thought to be the first textbooks on the modern common law. This reprint of the eighteenth edition is among the editions that Marvin claims are "preferred to the elder editions, both on account of the convenient reference to notes and for the excellent index." Marvin 205. "If Bracton first began the codification of the common law, it was Coke who completed it.... In the *Institutes*,... the tradition of the common law from Bracton to Littleton, whose name Coke's *Commentary* made famous, firmly established itself as the basis of the constitution of the Realm." *Printing and the Mind of Man* 126.

Coke, Sir Edward. *The Second Part of the Institutes of the Laws of England; Containing the Exposition of Many Ancient and Other Statutes.* London: Printed for W. Clarke and Sons, 1817. Star-paged. [18], 746, [49] pp. Reprinted 2002 by The Lawbook Exchange, Ltd. ISBN 1-58477-200-X. Cloth. $125.

* Reprint of the last and best edition with Butler and Hargrave's notes, with mistakes corrected from the folio edition. "[Coke's] Commentary upon the Magna Charta, and particularly on the celebrated 29th Chapter [on *habeas corpus*], is deeply interesting to the lawyers of the present age, as well from the value and dignity of the text, as the spirit of justice and of civil liberty which pervades and animates the work." Marvin, *Legal Bibliography* (1847) 208.

Coke, Sir Edward. *The Third Part of the Institutes of the Laws of England; Concerning High Treason, and Other Pleas of the Crown and Criminal Causes.* London: Printed for W. Clarke and Sons, 1817. Star-paged. [10], [244], [20] pp. Reprinted 2002 by The Lawbook Exchange, Ltd. ISBN 1-58477-201-8. Cloth. $75.

* Reprint of the last and best edition with Butler and Hargrave's notes, and with mistakes corrected from the folio edition. "Coke's *Third Institutes* gives us

a Treatise of great learning, and not unworthy the hand that produced it;... Having run over all criminal matters, and their legal punishments, he concludes with the nature of pardons and restitutions; showing how far, in each of these, our Kings can process alone, and where they want the assistance and joint power of the Parliaments." Marvin, *Legal Bibliography* (1847) 208.

(32406)

Coke, Sir Edward. *The Fourth Part of the Institutes of the Laws of England; Concerning The Jurisdiction of the Courts.* London: Printed for W. Clarke and Sons, 1817. Star-paged. [12], 364, [49] pp. Reprinted 2002 by The Lawbook Exchange, Ltd. ISBN 1-58477-202-6. Cloth. $85.

* Reprint of the last and best edition with Butler and Hargrave's notes, and with mistakes corrected from the folio edition. For this *Institute* Coke gathered miscellaneous materials that were not in the first three *Institutes*, and included translations of ancient statutes that appeared in the earlier *Institutes* in the original Latin or Law French, with notes and references to later authorities cited by Butler and Hargrave. *The Fourth Part* outlines the authority and jurisdictions of the Court of Star-Chamber, Kings Court, Chancery, the Court of Common Pleas, Ecclesiastical Courts, Courts of Exchequer, Augmentations, Admiralty, the Justices Assise, Courts in Universities of Cambridge and Oxford, Court of the Commissioners Upon the Statute of Bankrupts, the Marshalsea, the Stannaries, the Eighteen Courts of the City of London, the Court of Pipowders (concerning Markets and Fairs), the Courts of the Forest Countries, various ecclesiastical courts and many more.

(32407)

Coke, Sir Edward. *The Reports of Sir Edward Coke, Knt. In Thirteen Parts. A New Edition, with Additional Notes and References, and with Abstracts of the Principal Points: The First Three Parts and the Fourth to Fol. 38a. by John Henry Thomas, Esq. The Rest of the Fourth and the Remaining Nine Parts by John Farquhar Fraser, Esq.* London: Joseph Butterworth and Son, 1826. Six volumes. With a new introduction by Stephen M. Sheppard. Reprint available 2002 by The Lawbook Exchange, Ltd. ISBN 1-58477-239-5. Cloth. $595.

* "The best and last [edition], which has superceded all older ones, is in English; the whole thirteen Parts in 6 vols. 8vo. London, 1826." Wallace 194-195. This edition is also noteworthy for the inclusion of Coke's complete prefaces. Coke [1552-1643] was considered to be the greatest legal practitioner of his day. Written between 1572 and 1616, *The Reports* are not reports in the conventional sense but highly detailed anthologies of precedents organized according to the cases they consider. In each instance Coke assembled a large body of cases, outlined their arguments, and explained the reasons for the judgment, using it as a basis for a statement of general principles. They are, in effect, a series of treatises on the points of law adjudged. Taken together, *The Reports* form the most extensive and detailed treatment of Common Law pleading that had yet appeared. A work of immense authority, it was often cited as *The Reports*, there being no need to

mention the author's name. His accounts, especially of pleadings, were applauded for both their clarity and usefulness as stylistic models for students. And his selection of cases, cited frequently in subsequent years, has served as the starting point for numerous decisions. He also attracted some powerful enemies, however, principally James I, who was angered by some of his opinions concerning royal prerogative. Coke's refusal to retract them and apologize to the King cost him his seat on the Bench. See Marvin, *Legal Bibliography* (1847) 209-211, Wallace, *The Reporters* (1882) 165-196.
(33687)

Fortescue, Sir John. *DeLaudibus Legum Angliae. A Treatise in Commendation of the Laws of England.* With Translation by Francis Gregor. Notes by Andrew Amos and a Life of the Author by Thomas (Fortescue) Lord Clermont. Cincinnati: Robert Clarke & Co., 1874. lxiv, 302 pp. Reprinted 1999 by The Lawbook Exchange, Ltd. LCCN 99-16485. ISBN 1-58477-019-8. Cloth. $65.

* Written in 1470, *De Laudibus* was intended for the instruction of Edward, Prince of Wales. Written in the form of a dialogue, this book contains one of the earliest sketches of the English legal system.

This is the first appearance of the modern edition, based on the 1825 Amos edition, which includes for the first time the life of the author by Lord Clermont, a direct descendant, as well as his corrected version of both the text and translation, these having appeared only in an 1869 privately published edition of Fortescue's works limited to 120 family copies.
(26071)

Fortescue, Sir John. *The Governance of England: Otherwise Called The Difference between an Absolute and a Limited Monarchy. A Revised Text edited with Introduction, Notes, and Appendices by Charles Plummer.* London: Oxford University Press, 1885. xxiii, 387pp. Reprinted 1999 by The Lawbook Exchange, Ltd. ISBN 1-886363-79-X. Cloth. $65.

* "This work cannot be described as the first law book written in English, but it has the distinction of being the first book about law in that language..." Winfield, *The Chief Sources of English Legal History* 317-318. Examines and compares the value of absolute and limited monarchy in the governments of France and England. First published in 1714, this edition, which was edited by Christopher Plummer, was published in 1885. Winfield also describes this edition as "The best edition." Marke, *A Catalogue of the Law Collection at New York University (1953)* 365.
(24080)

Foss, Edward. *The Judges of England; with Sketches of Their Lives, and Miscellaneous Notices Connected with the Courts of Westminster, from the Time of the Conquest.* London: Longman, Brown, Green, and Longmans, 1848-1864. Nine volumes. Reprint available May 2003 by The Lawbook Exchange, Ltd. LCCN 2002040730. ISBN 1-58477-304-9. Cloth. $895.

* Authoritative biographies of chancellors, masters of the rolls, and judges of the courts are provided for each reign, from the time of the Norman Conquest

through the reign of Queen Victoria. Based on original sources, it is an important reference work for legal historians.
Frequently cited by Holdsworth in *A History of English Law*.
- Volume I covers the years 1066-1199 and the reigns of William I, William II, Henry I, Stephen Henry II and Richard I.
- Volume II covers the years 1199-1272 and the reigns of John and Henry III.
- Volume III covers the years 1272-1377 and the reigns of Edward I, Edward II and Edward III.
- Volume IV covers the years 1377-1485 and the reigns of Richard II, Henry Iv, Henry V, Henry VI, Edward IV, Edward V and Richard III.
- Volume V covers the years 1485-1603 and the reigns of Henry VII, Henry VIII, Edward VI, Mary and Elizabeth.
- Volume VI covers the years 1603-1660 and the reigns of James I, Charles I and the Interregnum.
- Volume VII covers the years 1660-1714 and the reigns of Charles II, James II, William III and Anne.
- Volume VIII covers the years 1714-1820 and the reigns of George I, George II and George III.
- Volume IX covers the years 1820-1864 and the reigns of George IV, William IV and Victoria.

Foss [1787-1870] was a founder and later president of the Incorporated Law Society. A prolific magazine contributor during his professional practice, upon retirement he dedicated himself to a study of the history of the legal profession, and lent various materials from his collection to Lord Campbell for *Lives of the Chancellors.* In 1843 he published *The Grandeur of the Law* and then went on to write his nine volume master work, *The Judges of England,* published over a sixteen year period; "the standard authority" in its field according to J.C. Robertson in the Law Times of Sept. 24, 1870, quoted in *Dictionary of National Biography* VII:491-492. Sweet and Maxwell, *A Legal Bibliography of the British Commonwealth of Nations* II:127. *Catalogue of the Library of the Law School of Harvard University* (1909) I:715. "A" rated American Association of Law Schools, *Law Books Recommended for Librarians.*

Hale, Matthew. *The History and Analysis of the Common Law of England.* Stafford: J. Nutt, 1713. [x], 264, [28], 176 pp. Reprinted 2000 by The Lawbook Exchange, Ltd. LCCN 99-33739. ISBN 1-58477-024-4. Cloth. $85.

* The highly respected first history of the common law ever written is reprinted here in its first edition. A series of chronological essays that were not intended for publication comprise a sketch of the history of legal doctrine. "...it does give us a clear statement of the history of some of the important external features of the common law...Sketch as it is his history is living history because its author had a clear view of its whole course." Holdsworth, *Sources and Literature of English Law* 151-152. Hale [1609-1676] was a Judge of the Common Pleas, well-known for his *History of the Pleas of the Crown.* Plucknett, *A Concise History of the Common Law* 252-253.

Hale, Sir Matthew. *Historia Placitorum Coronae. The History of the Pleas of the Crown. Now First Published from his Lordship's Original Manuscript, and the Several References to the Records Examined by the Originals, with Large Notes.* By Sollem Emlyn of Lincoln's Inn, Esq. To which is added a Table of the Principle Matters. [London]: Printed by E. and R. Nutt and R. Gosling, 1736. Two volumes. Reprint available 2003 by The Lawbook Exchange, Ltd. LCCN 2002034063. mISBN 1-58477-282-4. Cloth. $295.

*Reprint of the first edition. Widely acclaimed for its skillful, comprehensive and masterful discourse, this is the first history of English criminal law. Although Hale [1609-76] had planned to write this work in three books, only the first book was completed before his death. It covers the capital offenses - treasons and felonies. "This book, so far as it extends, gives a complete presentment of this branch of the law, both in its development and in its condition at Hale's own time...Ever since its first publication it has been regarded as a book of the highest authority." Holdsworth, *Sources and Literature of English Law* 152-153. See Winfield, *The Chief Sources of English Legal History* 327-8.

Holdsworth, Sir William. *An Historical Introduction to the Land Law.* London: Oxford University Press, 1927. xxiv, 339 pp. Reprint available 2003 by The Lawbook Exchange, Ltd. LCCN 2002025949. ISBN 1-58477-262-X. Cloth. $95.

* Sir William Holdsworth [1871-1944] was one of the most distinguished historians of English common law. He wrote this book to provide students of Real Property with a concise history of the field. This knowledge was necessary, he believed, because contemporary land law was difficult to understand without an understanding of its roots. Fortunately Holdsworth took on the task. Fifoot commends this book in his English Law and its Background for its history of the rules against perpetuities (121). The Law Quarterly Review noted that "every beginner will certainly have to read [this] book before he reads anything else" (44:105). Both sources cited in Marke, *A Catalogue of the Law Collection at New York University* (1953) 773.

Hutchinson, John. *A Catalogue of Notable Middle Templars, with Brief Biographical Notices.* [London]: The Honourable Society of the Middle Temple, 1902. xiv, 284 pp. Reprint available 2003 by The Lawbook Exchange, Ltd. LCCN 2002041361. ISBN 1-58477-323-5. Cloth. $80.

* Brief biographies of nearly one thousand distinguished Templars admitted between 1501 to 1901, such as Sir William Blackstone, Joseph Chitty, Henry Fielding, Sir William Jones, Lord Kenyon and Sir John Skene. A handy volume for the scholar of English law.

James I. *The Political Works of James I.* Reprinted from the Edition of 1616. With an Introduction by Charles Howard McIlwain. Cambridge: Harvard University Press, 1918. cxi, 354 pp. Reprinted 2002 by The

Lawbook Exchange, Ltd. LCCN 2001053981. ISBN 1-58477-222-0. Cloth. $95.

* The Collected works of James I [1566-1625], the first Stuart King of England, with an extensive introduction and appendices. Includes the "Basilikon Doron," "The Trew Law of Free Monarchies," "An Apologie for the Oath of Allegiance," "A Premonition to all Christian Monarchies, Free Princes and States," "A Defence of the Right of Kings, against Cardinall Perron," and "Speech in the Star Chamber, 1616."

Jenks, Edward. *The Constitutional Experiments of the Commonwealth: A Study of the Years 1649-1660.* Cambridge: The University Press, 1890. iv, 154 pp. Reprinted 2002 by The Lawbook Exchange, Ltd. LCCN 00-067823. ISBN 1-58477-141-0. Cloth. $60.

* A detailed account of the various changes in governmental administration between the death of Charles I and the Restoration. A member of the Middle Temple, a Fellow of King's College, Cambridge, and dean of the Faculty of Law at the University of Melbourne, Jenks argues that the Commonwealth era was not an aberration, but an important and natural step in the development of English political ideas.

Kames, Henry Home, Lord. *Historical Law-Tracts. The Second Edition.* Edinburgh: A. Kincaid, 1761. xv, 463 pp. LCCN 99-43133. ISBN 1-58477-038-4. Reprinted 2000 by The Lawbook Exchange, Ltd. Cloth. $95.

* In this celebrated treatise Lord Kames [1696-1782] proposes the concept of a historical treatment of law as a "rational science" (Preface p. xv) and sets forth the methodology and order of such. He holds that "law in particular becomes then only a rational study, when it is traced historically, from its first rudiments among savages, through successive changes, to its highest improvements in a civilized society." (Preface p. v) From this perspective the fourteen tracts cover the history of criminal law, promises and covenants, property, creditor and debtor, courts, etc. First published during the "Scottish enlightenment" in 1758, this is the second edition as published in 1761. This popular and influential work reached a fourth edition by 1792, and was read widely by European and American thinkers such as Hume, Bentham, Adams, Jefferson, Madison, Franklin and Adam Smith. Kames was a prolific author whose many works appeared in numerous editions. Marke, *A Catalogue of the Law Collection of New York University* (1953) 140. Walker, *Oxford Companion to Law* 578.

Lambard, William. *Eirenarcha: Or, of the Office of the Justices of Peace in Two Bookes, Gathered 1579 and Now Revised and Firste Published in the 24. Yeare of the Peaceable Reigne of our Gratious Queene Elizabeth.* London: Newbery, 1581.[viii], 511, [xv] pp. Reprint available 2003 by The Lawbook Exchange, Ltd. LCCN 2002025944. ISBN 1-58477-246-8. Cloth. $95.

* First published in 1581, this treatise is esteemed for its comprehensive and systematic account of the organization of local government under the justices of the peace at the end of the sixteenth century. It was the standard authority for several decades and often reprinted. Like many books of its kind, *Eirenarcha* offers a unique perspective on the society that produced it. This is evident in the descriptions of detailed indictments for such offenses as killing a man through witchcraft, raping a child or maid (the age of distinction was ten), hearing a Catholic Mass, practicing usary and operating a bowling alley. Lambard [1536-1601], a barrister and legal historian, was the keeper of records at the Rolls Chapel and the Tower of London.

[Macaulay, Thomas Babington]. *A Penal Code Prepared by the Indian Law Commissioners, and published by Command of the Governor General of India in Council.* London: Pelham Richardson, Cornhill, 1838. viii, 138 pp. Reprinted 2002 by The Lawbook Exchange, Ltd. LCCN 99-16486. ISBN 1-58477-018-X. Cloth. $65.

* Considered to be one of the greatest codes of law ever written, this important code shows the practical influence of Bentham. At the time of its drafting, the dominant East India Company's regulations conflicted with Muslim and Hindu law, and the common law itself, providing a chaotic landscape ripe for Macaulay's order and clarity. Macaulay [1800-1859], a British colonialist, member of Parliament and author of many renowned works including the *History of England,* was president of the Indian Law Commission and composed most of the code himself. This volume is a reprint of the London edition that was reprinted from the Calcutta edition of the original text of the Penal Code as issued by the Indian Law Commission, October 14, 1837.

Maitland, Frederick W., Montague, Francis C., *A Sketch of English Legal History.* Edited with Notes and Appendices by James F. Colby. New York: G.P. Putnam's Sons, 1915. x, 234pp. Reprinted 1998 by The Lawbook Exchange, Ltd. LCCN 98-11337. ISBN 1-886363-50-1. Cloth. $50.

* In this work Professor Colby has gathered, annotated and arranged into a sequential history of English law numerous essays by Maitland and Montague. Marke, *A Catalogue of the Law Collection of New York University* (1953) 142.

Maitland, Frederick William. *English Law and the Renaissance (The Rede Lecture for 1901) with Some Notes.* Cambridge: at the University Press, 1901. 98 pp. Reprinted 2000 by The Lawbook Exchange, Ltd. LCCN 99-41654. ISBN 1-58477-034-1. Cloth. $60.

* "Professor Maitland's Rede Lecture is exactly what an exoteric lecture addressed by a specialist to a mixed audience ought to be- an interesting discourse with plenty of illustration and anecdote, and not too much pressing of any definite argument. The general thesis, however, is clear enough to

students of legal history." The notes are full of curious and amusing matters, and almost as good reading as the text." *Law Quarterly Review* 18:98.

Maitland, F.W. *The Constitutional History of England. A Course of Lectures Delivered.* Cambridge: Cambridge University Press, 1908. xxviii, 547 pp. Reprinted 2001 by The Lawbook Exchange, Ltd. LCCN 00-068895. ISBN 1-58477-148-8. Cloth. $95.

* Although Maitland reportedly never desired these lectures to be published, they have long been regarded by scholars as among the best of introductions to the subject. They cover the period from 1066 to the end of the nineteenth century, but rather than a narrative historical format, focus on describing the work of the constitution during five distinct periods in English history (1307, 1509, 1625, 1702, 1887). The lectures were delivered in the winter of 1887 and spring of 1888, and provide an entry to some of the major concepts he later expounded on in his seminal work written with Sir Frederick Pollock, *The History of English Law.* This volume was compiled and edited two years after Maitland's death by one of his students, Herbert A.L. Fisher. Marke, *A Catalogue of the Law Collection at New York University* (1953) 367.

McKechnie, William Sharp. *Magna Carta. A Commentary on the Great Charter of King John. With an Historical Introduction. Second Edition, Revised and in part Re-written.* Glasgow: James Maclehose and Sons, 1914. xvii,530, [2] pp. Reprinted 2000 by The Lawbook Exchange, Ltd. LCCN 99-38731. ISBN 1-58477-031-7. Cloth. $95.

* "Dr. McKechnie's work is an elaborate commentary upon the Charter - clause by clause -containing everything that any ordinary student is likely to require, with very full and exact references, but it is something much more than this... It is a most admirable piece of work distinguished alike by felicity of language, deep historical insight, and varied and exact learning." H.J.R. Lawyer's Quarterly Review 32:117-118. "Strikes me as an excellent book, not so much for novelty as for careful lucid exposition." Holmes to Pollock-July 15, 1906. *Holmes-Pollock Letters* I:128.

Merriam, C.E., Jr. *History of the Theory of Sovereignty Since Rousseau.* New York: Columbia University Press, [1900]. x, [11]-233 pp. Reprinted 1999 by The Lawbook Exchange, Ltd. LCCN 98-32385. ISBN 1-886363-76-5. Cloth. $65.

* Reprint of the Columbia University Press edition of 1900, from the Studies in History, Economics and Public Law series published by Columbia University. "... a full and useful account of the chief doctrines put forward on the subject, not stating a theory of his own, but adding pertinent criticisms on the views which he summarizes." Marke, *A Catalogue of the Law Collection of New York University* (1953) 948. Chapters include The Kantian Theory, The Patrimonial Theory, Sovereignty and the American Union, Federalism and Continental Theory, Popular and State Sovereignty. With bibliographical notes.

Nichols, Francis Morgan. *Britton: The French Text Carefully Revised with an English Translation, Introduction and Notes.* Oxford: Clarendon Press, 1865. Two volumes. Reprint available 2003 by The Lawbook Exchange, Ltd. LCCN 2002024326. ISBN 1-58477-258-1. Cloth. $165.

* Probably originally compiled by John le Breton around 1290, it is the oldest English law book in French. Consisting of French text with parallel English translation and a glossary of French terms, this edition edited and translated by Nichols is considered to be the "standard edition." Walker, *The Oxford Companion to Law* 154. Along with Fleta, Britton is one of two significant law books produced during the reign of Edward I [1272-1307]. The origins of Britton may be traced to a project of Edward I to produce a digest of the English law in the spirit of Justinian's *Institutes.*

Book One outlines the authority of justices and officers and defines the nature of various personal pleas (including pleas of the crown). Book Two describes disseisins and their remedies. Book Three treats intrusions and their remedies. Book Four describes pleas relating to advowsons and the property of churches (and of attaints). Book Five outlines pleas of dower and entry. Book Six defines different kinds of proprietary actions. In all, this treatise offers an incomparable overview of British law during the medieval era. See Holdsworth, *A History of English Law* II: 319-321.

Oakley, Thomas Pollack. *English Penitential Discipline and Anglo-Saxon Law in Their Joint Influence.* New York: Columbia University Press, 1923. 226 pp. Reprint available 2003 by The Lawbook Exchange, Ltd. LCCN 2002042753. ISBN 1-58477-302-2. Cloth. $65.

* Penitentials are manuals for confessors that outline penances and their fines. They originated in the Celtic church and their use spread throughout the British Isles during the early middle ages. Though restricted to church discipline, they often influenced secular law. Beginning with a history and discussion of the penitentials, Oakley examines the legal traditions that influenced their development and their reciprocal influence on the development of the common law.

Originally published as Volume CVII, Number 2 in Columbia's series, Studies in History, Economics and Public Law.

Parnell, Henry. *A History of the Penal Laws Against the Irish Catholics, from the Treaty of Limerick to the Union.* Dublin: Printed by H. Fitzpatrick, 1808. 226, xxii pp. Reprint available 2003 by The Lawbook Exchange, Ltd. LCCN 2002044357. ISBN 1-58477-313-8. Cloth $80.

* Reprint of first edition. Sir Henry Parnell [1776-1842], later Lord Congleton, was an Anglo-Irish parliamentarian and treasury official sympathetic to the plight of Irish Catholics. Enhanced by its extensive quotation of source records, this book traces the history of laws against "religious non-conformists" between 1689 and 1801. Though certainly partisan, it is valuable for Parnell's perspective and first-hand knowledge of several crucial events of the 1780s and `90s.

Perry, Ross R. *Common-law Pleading: Its History and Principles. Including Dicey's Rules Concerning Parties to Action and Stephen's Rules of Pleading.* Boston, Little, Brown and Company, 1897. xxvi, 494 pp. Reprinted 2001 by The Lawbook Exchange, Ltd. ISBN 1-58477-105-4. Cloth. $95.
* This treatise, intended for the student and scholar of the late nineteenth-century, examines the fundamentals of common-law pleading as originally outlined by Pollock and Maitland, Chitty, Stephen and Dicey.

Plucknett, Theodore F.T. *A Concise History of the Common Law. Fifth Edition.* Boston: Little, Brown and Company, 1956. Reprinted 2001 by The Lawbook Exchange, Ltd. LCCN 00-067821. ISBN 1-58477-137-2. Cloth. $125.
* "Professor Plucknett has such a solid reputation on both sides of the Atlantic that one expects from his pen only what is scholarly and accurate...Nor is the expectation likely to be disappointed in this book. Plucknett's book is not...a mere epitome of what is to be found elsewhere. He has explored on his own account many regions of legal history and, even where the ground has been already quartered, he has fresh methods of mapping it. The title which he has chosen is, in view of the contents of the volume, rather a narrow one. It might equally well have been *A Concise History of English Law*...In conjunction with *Readings on the History and System of the Common Law* by Dean Pound...this book will give an excellent grounding to the student of English legal history." Percy H. Winfield. Harv. L. Rev. 43:339-340.

Pollock, Frederick and Frederic William Maitland. *The History of English Law before the Time of Edward I.* Cambridge: Cambridge University Press, 1898. Two volumes. xxxviii, 688; xiv, 691 pp. Reprinted 1996 by The Lawbook Exchange, Ltd. LCCN 96-16003. ISBN 1-886363-22-6. Cloth. $165.
* Second edition. A landmark work on English legal history. Professors Maitland of Cambridge and Pollock of Oxford joined forces (although Maitland is credited with the lion's share) to write what has been termed an epoch-making work. The authors elucidate the origins of English law, providing for the first time a systematic presentation of the early stages of its evolution. The first volume gives an historical overview, beginning with ecclesiastical law and proceeding to cover Anglo-Saxon law, Norman law, Roman and Canon law, and law in the time of Glanvill and Bracton. The second treats the doctrines of English law, including all aspects of tenure, the law of personal condition, status, and estate, and the jurisdiction and the communities of the land. Clear exposition and countless references make this an essential book for anyone interested in early English law.

Powell, Chilton Latham. *English Domestic Relations 1487-1653. A Study of Matrimony and Family Life in Theory and Practice as Revealed by the Literature, Law, and History of the Period.* New York: Columbia University

Press, 1917. xii, 274 pp. Reprinted 2001 by The Lawbook Exchange, Ltd. ISBN 1-58477-096-1. Cloth. $75.

* From its first appearance in English writing in 1487, the marriage contract, its making and breaking, and its subsequent effect on English family life, is examined here through the lens of the law, literature and events of the period. Powell includes discussions of contemporary attitudes toward women, and domestic conduct books, with selections from several conduct books included in the appendix. This unique treatise also offers the only existing account of English writings on the subject of the divorce of Henry VIII at the time of original publication.

Stock, Leo Francis. *Proceedings and Debates of the British Parliaments Respecting North America.* Five volumes. Washington, D.C.: The Carnegie Institution of Washington, 1924. Reprint available 2003 by The Lawbook Exchange, Ltd. LCCN 2002025966. ISBN 1-58477-254-9. Cloth. $495.

* This set collects all references to North America in the proceedings and debates of the parliaments of England, Scotland and Ireland recorded between 1542 and 1783. The "proceedings" are taken from the officially published Journals; the "debates" are taken from several sources, such as the transcripts of Parliamentary sessions published in the Gentlemen's Magazine. The scope of the work is not confined to North America. It includes all items relating directly or by implication to Canada, Central America, South America, the Caribbean, the Philippines and Africa. It also includes items relating to the navigation acts, the Royal African Company and the Asientos, and all that concerns enactments, repeals or alterations of duties and other acts concerning tobacco, sugar, coffee, furs, indigo, whale products and other colonial products. A useful source for the admiralty, maritime or commercial law historian.

Thomson, Richard. *An Historical Essay on the Magna Charta of King John: to which are added, the Great Charter in Latin and English, the charters of liberties and confirmations, granted by Henry III and Edward I, the original Charter of the forests, and various authentic instruments connected with them: Explanatory Notes on their Several Privileges; A Descriptive Account of the Principal Originals and Editions Extant, Both in Print and Manuscript; and Other Illustrations, Derived from the Most Interesting and Authentic Sources.* London: John Major and Robert Jennings, 1829. xxxii, 612 pp. Reprinted 2000 by The Lawbook Exchange, Ltd. LCCN 99-40987. ISBN 1-58477-030-9. Cloth. $95.

* "Contains the text of John's charter, with a translation; also translations of the articles of the barons, the forest charter, and the confirmations of Henry III. And Edward I.; with elaborate notes, based largely on Coke's Second Institute. This is one of the 'standard' works on the Great Charter." Gross, *The Sources and Literature of English History from the Earliest Times to about 1485* 2019. Each page is bordered with an elaborate embellishment.

[Thorpe, B., editor]. *Ancient Laws and Institutes of England; Comprising Laws Enacted under the Anglo-Saxon Kings from Æthelbirtht to Cnut, With an English Translation of the Saxon; The Laws called Edward the Confessor's; The Laws of William the Conqueror, and those Ascribef to Henry the First: Also, Monumenta Ecclesiastica Anglicana, From the Seventh to the Tenth Century; and the Ancient Latin Version of the Anglo-Saxon Laws. With a Compendious Glossary, &c.* [London: Printed by George E. Eyre and Andrew Spottiswoode, Printers to the Queen's most Excellent Majesty, 1840]. x, [iv], 548, [79] pp. (9" X 12"). Reprint available 2003 by The Lawbook Exchange, Ltd. LCCN 2002024242. ISBN 1-58477-264-6. Cloth. $195.

* A critical edition of laws issued before 1066 based on original manuscript sources, with most in their original languages. With thorough notes, extensive commentary, a concordance of sources, an index to the Anglo-Saxon laws and an index to the *Monumenta Ecclesiastica.* Benjamin Thorpe [1782-1870] was a well-known Anglo-Saxon scholar and translator who published a number of principal works in this field, including the important *Analecta Anglo-Saxonica.* This edition remains a standard source for scholars of this period. *Dictionary of National Biography* XIX: 795-796.

Thorpe, W.[illiam] G.[eorge]. *Middle Temple Table Talk: With Some Talk about the Table Itself.* London: Hutchinson & Co., 1894. xxiv, 376 pp. Reprint available 2003 by The Lawbook Exchange, Ltd. ISBN 1-58477-341-3. Cloth $80.

* Reprint of first edition. Thorpe [d.1902], a barrister and literary historian, was admitted to the Middle Temple in 1875. His book is a delightful miscellany of Middle Temple anecdotes, discussions of its official and unofficial customs, legal lore, literary history and other topics discussed socially among Templars. Interesting in itself, this book is equally valuable as a document of the Middle Temple's institutional character at the turn of the century.

Willis, John. *The Parliamentary Powers of English Government Departments.* Cambridge: Harvard University Press, 1933. 214 pp. Reprint available 2003 by The Lawbook Exchange, Ltd. LCCN 2002025940. ISBN 1-58477-271-9. Cloth. $95.

* A thorough study of issues relating to legislation enacted by persons or bodies to whom Parliament has delegated specific powers. "This is the best book that has yet been published on delegated legislation in England. It has learning, it is well written, and it possesses what is still rare in books of law-a graceful power of wit." Harold Laski, Harvard Law Review 47:1452-1453 cited in Marke, *A Catalogue of the Law Collection at New York University* (1953) 263. Originally published as Volume IV in the Harvard Studies in Administrative Law series.